THE INNOVATIVE ENTREPRENEUR

Innovative entrepreneurs are the prime movers of the economy. The innovative entrepreneur helps overcome two types of institutional frictions. First, existing firms may not innovate efficiently because of incumbent inertia resulting from adjustment costs, diversification costs, the replacement effect, and imperfect adjustment of expectations. The innovative entrepreneur compensates for incumbent inertia by embodying innovations in new firms that compete with incumbents. Second, markets for inventions may not operate efficiently because of transaction costs, imperfect intellectual property protections, costs of transferring tacit knowledge, and imperfect information about discoveries. The innovative entrepreneur addresses inefficiencies in markets for inventions through own-use of discoveries and adoption of innovative ideas. *The Innovative Entrepreneur* presents an economic framework that addresses the motivation of the innovative entrepreneur, the innovative advantage of entrepreneurs versus incumbent firms, the effects of competitive pressures on incentives to innovate, the consequences of creative destruction, and the contributions of the innovative entrepreneur to the wealth of nations.

Daniel F. Spulber is the Elinor Hobbs Distinguished Professor of International Business and Professor of Management Strategy at the Kellogg School of Management, Northwestern University, where he has taught since 1990. He is also Professor of Law at the Northwestern University Law School (Courtesy). Professor Spulber is the Research Director for the Searle Center on Law, Regulation and Economic Growth. He served as the founding director of Kellogg's International Business and Markets Program. He is also the author of numerous books, including *The Theory of the Firm: Microeconomics with Endogenous Entrepreneurs, Firms, Markets, and Organizations* (Cambridge University Press, 2009); *Economics and Management of Competitive Strategy* (2009); *Networks in Telecommunications: Economics and Law* (with Christopher Yoo, Cambridge University Press, 2009); and *Global Competitive Strategy* (Cambridge University Press, 2007). He received his Ph.D. in economics from Northwestern University.

The Innovative Entrepreneur

Daniel F. Spulber
Northwestern University

CAMBRIDGE
UNIVERSITY PRESS

University Printing House, Cambridge CB2 8BS, United Kingdom

One Liberty Plaza, 20th Floor, New York, NY 10006, USA

477 Williamstown Road, Port Melbourne, VIC 3207, Australia

314-321, 3rd Floor, Plot 3, Splendor Forum, Jasola District Centre, New Delhi - 110025, India

79 Anson Road, #06-04/06, Singapore 079906

Cambridge University Press is part of the University of Cambridge.

It furthers the University's mission by disseminating knowledge in the pursuit of education, learning and research at the highest international levels of excellence.

www.cambridge.org
Information on this title: www.cambridge.org/9781107047259

First published 2014

A catalogue record for this publication is available from the British Library

Library of Congress Cataloging in Publication data
Spulber, Daniel F.
The innovative entrepreneur / Daniel F. Spulber, Northwestern University.
pages cm
Includes bibliographical references and index.
ISBN 978-1-107-04725-9 (hardback) – ISBN 978-1-107-66811-9 (paperback)
1. Entrepreneurship. 2. Creative ability in business. I. Title.
HB615.S696 2014
338′04–dc23 2013044708

ISBN 978-1-107-04725-9 Hardback
ISBN 978-1-107-66811-9 Paperback

Contents

Preface

Managers of existing firms already innovate – why is there any need for entrepreneurs to start new firms? The answer comes from the individuality of entrepreneurs, whether acting alone or as members of a team of founders. The economic contributions of the innovative entrepreneur result from individual initiative and creativity. Entrepreneurs can be innovative in ways that may be difficult or impossible for managers of existing institutions. This basic insight helps address the major questions in the economics of innovation and entrepreneurship.

The *innovative entrepreneur* is defined as someone who introduces commercial, scientific, and technological discoveries to the marketplace by embodying them in new firms. Innovative entrepreneurs not only provide new products and production processes but also create new transaction methods, business institutions, and industries that fundamentally change how the economy operates. Their impact on economic growth and development is extensive and evident.

The innovative entrepreneur differs from the *replicative entrepreneur* who establishes a firm by imitating or acquiring existing business models. Understanding the contributions of the innovative entrepreneur does not imply any criticism of the replicative entrepreneur. Both types of entrepreneurs establish firms that implement and diffuse inventions. Both types of entrepreneurs take risks, exercise judgment, and contribute time, effort, and personal funds. Both types of entrepreneurs provide useful products and services, invest in productive capacity, increase employment, and stimulate economic activity.

This book presents an economic theory of the innovative entrepreneur. The theory helps answer the major questions that continue to challenge researchers in economics, law, and management. The theory considers the motivation of individuals to become innovative entrepreneurs. The theory shows how individual initiative can give entrepreneurs an innovative advantage over incumbent firms. The theory examines how competitive pressures impact entrepreneurial incentives to innovate. The theory shows how market frictions affect the choice between entrepreneurship and technology transfer to existing firms. Finally, the theory considers the contributions of innovative entrepreneurs to economic prosperity in an international context.

Innovative entrepreneurs are essential to the economy because they establish the firms that form new industries, foster economic development, and stimulate aggregate growth. Improvements in the quality of life require new products and productive efficiencies. Economic growth depends on technological change because of the limits imposed by resource scarcity and diminishing returns to factors of production. Economic development is based on the creation of new institutions, organizations, and markets. The measure of the economic contribution made by innovative entrepreneurs is the economic value generated by the firms that they establish.

The study of the entrepreneur is particularly challenging because it is located at the intersection of the *individual* and the *firm*. The entrepreneur's life-cycle consumption decisions are interconnected with the start-up's strategic business decisions. The economic theory of the entrepreneur examines the individual's decision whether or not to become an entrepreneur, the business decisions he makes during the period of entrepreneurship, and the decision to launch the firm. The book addresses entrepreneurial finance in the context of the motivation and decision making of the innovative entrepreneur although a detailed consideration of finance is beyond the current discussion.

This book continues the work I began in *The Theory of the Firm* (Spulber, 2009a) that introduces the entrepreneur into the economic theory of the firm. There, I emphasize that entrepreneurs arise endogenously as individuals choose whether or not to become entrepreneurs and engage in establishing firms. The key step is the definition of what is a firm. The definition extends Irving Fisher's Separation Theorem, which is fundamental to neoclassical economics and finance. A *firm* is defined as a transaction institution whose objectives are *financially* separable from the consumption objectives of its owners. Through the actions of entrepreneurs, firms arise endogenously in the economy. In turn, firms establish markets and generate organizations, making these important economic institutions endogenous as well. The activities of individual entrepreneurs thus are fundamental for market economies.

This book encompasses important developments in the economics of entrepreneurship. The topic of entrepreneurship has been addressed throughout the history of economic thought.[1] The dynamic theory of the entrepreneur presented

1 A major exception has been in the development of neoclassical economics. William Baumol (2006, p. 2) observed that the entrepreneur is mentioned virtually never in the modern theory of the firm: "The more critical explanation of the absence of the entrepreneur is that in mainstream economics the theory is generally composed of equilibrium models in which, structurally, nothing is changing. But, this excludes the entrepreneur by definition"; see also Baumol (1993). The economic theory of entrepreneurship draws on other behavioral views of the entrepreneur including psychological, sociological, and managerial approaches.

here includes and extends many important developments in the study of entrepreneurs. At the dawn of classical economics, Richard Cantillon (1755) introduced the entrepreneur in his pathbreaking economic treatise. Jean-Baptiste Say (1841, 1852) provided the first comprehensive discussion of the entrepreneur in economic analysis, emphasizing how the entrepreneur's earnings depend on his personal reputation, judgment, and attitude toward risk. Entrepreneurs are central to Frank Knight's (1921) discussion of risk, uncertainty, and profit, which emphasizes both the supply of and demand for entrepreneurship.

The major works of Joseph Schumpeter lay the foundations of the theory of innovative entrepreneurship. Schumpeter (1934) in the *Theory of Economic Development* defines entrepreneurs as individuals who start firms. Later, in *Business Cycles*, Schumpeter (1939, p. 103) states that entrepreneurs are individuals who start firms in the time of competitive capitalism but suggests that innovators may be firm owners, corporate managers, or salaried employees in "the times of giant concerns" or "trust capitalism."[2]

In the present work, I restrict the definition of entrepreneurs to *individuals who establish firms*, whether they act alone or in teams of founders. Entrepreneurs can create start-ups and establish firms from scratch, as appears to be most common. Entrepreneurs also can be firm owners, corporate managers, or salaried employees who start new firms through spin-offs, split-offs, and spin-outs. I distinguish innovative entrepreneurs from managers whose innovations remain within existing firms.

An explosion of economic research has generated significant insights into the economic activities of entrepreneurs. Entrepreneurs play a role in developing management strategy and fostering the growth of firms (Penrose, 1959). Entrepreneurs address transaction costs by establishing firms that are market makers and specialized intermediaries (Casson, 1982, 2003). The new firms that entrepreneurs establish then create and manage markets and organizations that handle most of the economy's transactions (Spulber, 1999, 2009). Entrepreneurs are important in labor markets through both the occupational choice of entrepreneurs themselves (Lazear, 2005; Parker, 2009) and employment by new firms (Thurik et al., 2008). Entrepreneurs are key drivers of economic growth and the macroeconomy (Audretsch et al., 2006; Schramm, 2006b; Baumol et al., 2007). Entrepreneurship and innovation have made inroads in macroeconomic growth models (Aghion and Howitt, 1992, 1997, 2009). Baumol's (1993, 2002, 2010) work contributes prominently to the discussion of innovation and entrepreneurship. Entrepreneurs raise critical issues for public policy makers affecting antitrust, regulation, and fiscal policy (Holtz-Eakin, 2000; Lundstrom and Stevenson, 2005; Lerner, 2009).

2 For an illuminating biography of Schumpeter, see McCraw (2007). Brouwer (1991) identifies and clarifies many "Schumpeterian puzzles" within the context of Schumpeter's work; see also Brouwer (2002).

Simon Parker (2009) provides a valuable comprehensive discussion of the economics of entrepreneurship. Parker (2009) offers an integrative survey of the empirical and theoretical aspects of entrepreneurship that gives an in-depth analysis of the field. His discussion addresses the determinants of entrepreneurship, financing of new ventures, performance of entrepreneurial firms, and public policy toward entrepreneurs. His wide-ranging and penetrating discussion illustrates the vast set of issues in labor economics, financial economics, and industrial organization that are important parts of the study of entrepreneurship.

Innovation and entrepreneurship are becoming a field of study in economics because of the fundamental issues raised by innovation and the establishment of firms. The American Economic Association's *Journal of Economic Literature* classification system lists "Entrepreneurship" as L26, a third-level subject in which L denotes the subject category "Industrial Organization" and L2 denotes "Firm Objectives, Organization, and Behavior." Perhaps a better location might be a major topic within the subject category: O, "Economic Development, Technological Change, and Growth." The discussion in this book suggests that combining the study of innovation with the study of entrepreneurship helps form a substantial field in economics.

This book is directed at researchers and advanced students in economics, law, technology, and management strategy. Entrepreneurs' significant contributions to the economy call for increased attention in economics teaching and research. The entrepreneur also tends to be absent from undergraduate and graduate economics courses. Johansson (2004) studies PhD programs and textbooks in economics and finds that required PhD courses in microeconomics, macroeconomics, and industrial organization and the textbooks in these fields completely exclude the concept of the entrepreneur. Johansson (2004, p. 533) concludes that "there is a need for economics Ph.D. training based on theories that incorporate entrepreneurship and institutions."

The book is organized as follows. Chapter 1 introduces a dynamic economic framework consisting of three stages: invention, entrepreneurship, and competitive entry. The process begins with an *inventor* who makes commercial, scientific, and technological discoveries. Next, an *innovative entrepreneur* applies these discoveries, creates a start-up enterprise, and attempts to establish a firm. The entrepreneur is innovative by being the first to introduce inventions to the marketplace. An entrepreneur who is successful in establishing a firm ceases to be an entrepreneur, becoming instead an *owner* of the new firm or selling the firm to outside investors. The final stage in which the role of the individual changes from entrepreneur to owner is referred to as the *foundational shift*. The framework considers the innovative entrepreneur in the context of the theory of the firm (Spulber, 2009a, 2009b).

Chapter 2 examines the Question of Entrepreneurial Motivation and presents a life-cycle theory of entrepreneurship. The inventor and the innovative entrepreneur maximize utility of consumption over their life cycle, taking into account various market opportunities. The chapter shows, based on life-cycle theory, that inventors and entrepreneurs make consumption-saving decisions that are interdependent with their business decisions. As a result, the inventor's research and development (R&D) and commercialization decisions are interdependent with the inventor's preferences, endowment, and other characteristics. Also, the innovative entrepreneur's business decisions are interdependent with the entrepreneur's preferences, endowment, and other individual characteristics.

Chapter 3 addresses the Question of Innovative Advantage. Entrepreneurs can gain an innovative advantage over incumbent firms through individual initiative. Innovative entrepreneurs have incentives to enter the market when the profits from introducing new technologies exceed entry costs. In contrast, existing firms are subject to incumbent inertia as a result of the replacement effect of existing business and other factors. When an independent inventor can license the new technology to either an incumbent firm or an independent entrepreneur, the inventor will license to both so that the market equilibrium always generates entrepreneurial entry. With sufficiently differentiated products, the inventor licensing to both the incumbent and an independent entrepreneur has greater incentives to invent than an incumbent monopolist. The chapter also considers the importance of commercial inventions and business strategies for innovative entrepreneurship.

Chapter 4 addresses the Question of Competitive Pressures. It has often been suggested that competitive pressures discourage innovative entrepreneurship by dissipating economic rents from innovation. The chapter shows that innovative entrepreneurs generate more creative projects than a multi-project monopoly incumbent. This occurs because the average expected returns to innovation for competing entrepreneurs are greater than the incremental expected returns for the multi-project monopoly incumbent. The chapter also considers competition among innovative entrepreneurs when there are capacity constraints so that multiple entrepreneurs remain active in equilibrium. Postentry competition among entrepreneurs selects the best technologies and adjusts capacity to market demand. The chapter emphasizes that competitive entry and exit of entrepreneurs are consistent with profit maximization rather than irrational exuberance.

Chapters 5 to 8 address the Question of Creative Destruction and show how innovative entrepreneurs overcome frictions in the market for inventions. These chapters consider a strategic innovation game in which an inventor and an established firm choose whether to cooperate or to compete. If the inventor and the existing firm choose to compete, the inventor becomes an entrepreneur. The entrepreneur establishes a firm that enters the market with a more efficient production technology and displaces the incumbent firm. If the inventor and the existing firm choose to cooperate, the inventor transfers the new technology to the existing firm.

Chapter 5 examines the effect of intellectual property (IP) and transaction costs on creative destruction. The option of entrepreneurship increases incentives to invent by reducing the impact of imperfect IP protections and transaction costs.

This need not imply that reducing IP protections is a means of increasing innovative entrepreneurship. The discussion emphasizes that commercial inventions are an important foundation for entrepreneurship and a channel for the introduction of scientific and technological inventions. IP protections for commercial discoveries are essential for efficiency in the market for inventions and contribute to innovative entrepreneurship.

Chapter 6 extends the strategic innovation game to study innovative entrepreneurs who make "new combinations." The model examines the innovative entrepreneur when multidimensional innovation consists of a new production process and a new product. Entrepreneurship can occur in equilibrium as a result of imperfect transferability of multidimensional technologies. By mitigating creative destruction, product differentiation increases the returns to entrepreneurship relative to the returns from technology transfer to incumbents.

Chapter 7 examines how the problem of tacit knowledge affects the trade-off between technology transfer and innovative entrepreneurship. The inventor's tacit knowledge generates returns from own-use of inventions. This contrasts with the standard view that the complementary assets of established firms generate an advantage for technology transfer over entrepreneurship. The inventor's tacit knowledge affects the inventor's R&D investment and the existing firm's investment in absorptive capacity. Higher-quality inventions result in entrepreneurship, and lower-quality inventions result in technology transfer.

Chapter 8 considers how asymmetric information about the features of the invention affects the outcome of the strategic innovation game. Imperfect adoption decisions by existing firms because of organizational architecture can create frictions that favor entrepreneurship over technology transfer. Adverse selection in the market for inventions can create transaction costs that result in own-use of inventions by innovative entrepreneurs. The need for investment in costly signaling in the market for inventions can increase returns to innovative entrepreneurship in comparison to technology transfer. Agency costs associated with technology transfer further generate gains from own-use of technology by inventors who choose to become innovative entrepreneurs.

Chapter 9 examines issues relevant to the Question of the Wealth of Nations. The chapter addresses the globalization of entrepreneurship by examining the effects of international trade and foreign direct investment (FDI) on innovative entrepreneurship. Many countries have become more open to international trade and relaxed economic regulations on their domestic markets, generating extensive diffusion of entrepreneurship. Cross-country differences in labor supply and potential entrepreneurs cause differences in the extensive margins of technology utilization. International trade increases product variety but is not sufficient to address technological differences and labor immobility. Many new firms choose to internationalize their operations by operating or outsourcing abroad. By transferring innovative technology embodied in new firms, entrepreneurial FDI equalizes the extensive margins of technology adoption across countries and harmonizes the intensive margin of technology utilization. The combination of international trade and entrepreneurship increases total benefits in comparison to both autarky and international trade without FDI.

Chapter 10 concludes the discussion by considering how innovative entrepreneurs contribute to economic growth and development. The motivation of innovative entrepreneurs suggests that public policy makers should consider the decisions of individuals contemplating innovative entrepreneurship. Policy makers should remove disincentives for individual asset accumulation and reduce legal and regulatory barriers to market entry of new firms. These policy changes should help unleash the creativity and initiative of innovative entrepreneurs.

Acknowledgments

I am particularly grateful to the Ewing Marion Kauffman Foundation for their support that made it possible for me to carry out and complete this research study. I thank Carl Schramm, Bob Litan, and Bob Strom of the Ewing Marion Kauffman Foundation for their interest in this work, their very helpful comments, and their encouragement of entrepreneurship research. Without their understanding and insights, this work would not have been realized.

I am very grateful to the Kellogg School of Management and the Strategy Department for providing the opportunity and environment to conduct this research. I am also very pleased to acknowledge the research support of the Kellogg School of Management and the Office of the Dean.

I also am highly grateful to the Northwestern University Law School's Searle Center on Law, Regulation and Economic Growth, where I serve as research director. I particularly thank Max Schanzenbach, former director of the Searle Center, and Matt Spitzer, current director of the Searle Center, for their support and great collegiality. I also thank authors, discussants, and other participants in the Searle Center Annual Conference on Innovation and Entrepreneurship for the intellectual stimulation that helped this project move along.

I thank the following people for their very valuable and detailed suggestions that improved the manuscript: Andrei Hagiu, F. Scott Kieff, Jin Li, Inés Macho-Stadler, Simon Parker, Jesús David Pérez-Castrillo, David Sappington, Dane Stangler, and Rosemarie Ziedonis. I thank participants in a Seale Center Research Roundtable for their helpful comments and suggestions that improved the book: Esther Barron, Ola Bengtsson, Bernie Black, Shane Greenstein, David Haddock, Lynne Kiesling, Pierre Larouche, Kate Litvak, Joaquin Poblete, Stephen F. Reed, E. J. Reedy, and Arvids Ziedonis.

I thank my wife Sue and my children, Rachelle, Aaron, and Benjamin, for their support and encouragement. They are the inspiration that motivates my work.

I have drawn on the following publications in preparing the book:

Daniel F. Spulber, "Innovation and International Trade in Technology," *Journal of Economic Theory*, 138, January, 2008, pp. 1–20, Amsterdam: Elsevier.

Daniel F. Spulber, "Discovering the Role of the Firm: The Separation Criterion and Corporate Law," *Berkeley Business Law Journal*, 6, 2, Spring, 2009, pp. 298–347.

Daniel F. Spulber, "The Quality of Innovation and the Extent of the Market," *Journal of International Economics*, 80, 2010, pp. 260–270. http://dx.doi.org/10.1016/j.jinteco.2009.11.008f, Amsterdam: Elsevier.

Daniel F. Spulber, "Competition among Entrepreneurs," *Industrial and Corporate Change*, 19, 1, February, 2010, pp. 25–50. doi:10.1093/icc/dtp038, Oxford: Oxford University Press.

Daniel F. Spulber, 2011, "The Innovator's Decision: Entrepreneurship versus Technology Transfer," in David Audretsch, O. Falck, Stephan Heblich, and Adam Lederer, eds., *Handbook of Research on Innovation and Entrepreneurship*, Northampton, MA: Edward Elgar, pp. 315–336.

Daniel F. Spulber, 2011, "Intellectual Property and the Theory of the Firm," in F. Scott Kieff and Troy Paredes, eds., *Perspectives on Commercializing Innovation*, Cambridge: Cambridge University Press, pp. 9–46.

Daniel F. Spulber, "Should Business Method Inventions Be Patentable?," *Journal of Legal Analysis*, 3, 1, Spring, 2011, pp. 265–340, Oxford: Oxford University Press.

Daniel F. Spulber, 2011, "The Role of the Entrepreneur in Economic Growth," in Robert Litan, ed., *Handbook of Law, Innovation, and Growth*, Northampton, MA: Edward Elgar, pp. 11–44.

Daniel F. Spulber, 2012, "How Entrepreneurs Affect the Rate and Direction of Inventive Activity," in Josh Lerner and Scott Stern, eds., *The Rate and Direction of Inventive Activity Revisited*, National Bureau of Economic Research Conference, Chicago: University of Chicago Press, pp. 277–315, © 2012 by the University of Chicago. All rights reserved.

Daniel F. Spulber, "Tacit Knowledge and Innovative Entrepreneurship," *International Journal of Industrial Organization*, 3, 6, November, 2012, pp. 641–653.

Daniel F. Spulber, "Competing Inventors and the Incentive to Invent," *Industrial and Corporate Change*, 22, 1, February, 2013, pp. 33–72, doi:10.1093/icc/dts013, Oxford: Oxford University Press.

Daniel F. Spulber, "How Do Competitive Pressures Affect Incentives to Innovate When There is a Market for Inventions," *Journal of Political Economy*, 121, 6, December, 2013, pp. 1007–1054, Chicago: University of Chicago Press, © 2013 by the University of Chicago. All rights reserved.

1

Introduction

Much like the popular myth that a bumblebee's flight is aerodynamically impossible, experts often suggest that innovative entrepreneurship is economically impossible. Entrepreneurs must be irrationally optimistic because there are few economic returns to innovative entry. Entrepreneurs cannot innovate effectively because incumbent firms have better complementary assets. Entrepreneurs cannot possibly innovate because only incumbent firms have the necessary size and market power to support innovation. And yet, they fly!

Innovative entrepreneurs add value to the economy through individual initiative, creativity, and flexibility. Innovative entrepreneurs help overcome two types of institutional frictions. First, existing firms may not innovate efficiently because of incumbent inertia resulting from various organizational rigidities. The innovative entrepreneur compensates for incumbent inertia by embodying innovations in new firms.

Second, markets for inventions may not operate efficiently because of transaction costs (search, bargaining, contracting, monitoring), imperfect IP protections, costs of transferring tacit knowledge, and imperfect information about discoveries. The innovative entrepreneur addresses frictions in markets for inventions through own-use of discoveries and adoption of innovative ideas.

This chapter presents a dynamic economic framework that will be applied to study the innovative entrepreneur. The entrepreneurial process has three stages: invention, entrepreneurship, and competitive entry. The dynamic framework emphasizes the interaction between the personal consumption-saving decisions and the business decisions of the individual inventor and entrepreneur. As economic functions change, the individual's role shifts from inventor to entrepreneur to owner, although there may be different individuals at each stage. The time line of the three-stage entrepreneurial process appears in Figure 1.1.

At the *invention stage*, an independent inventor expends effort and investment in commercial, scientific, and technological R&D. The independent inventor implements discoveries either by becoming an entrepreneur or by contracting to transfer technology to potential entrepreneurs, established firms, or market intermediaries.

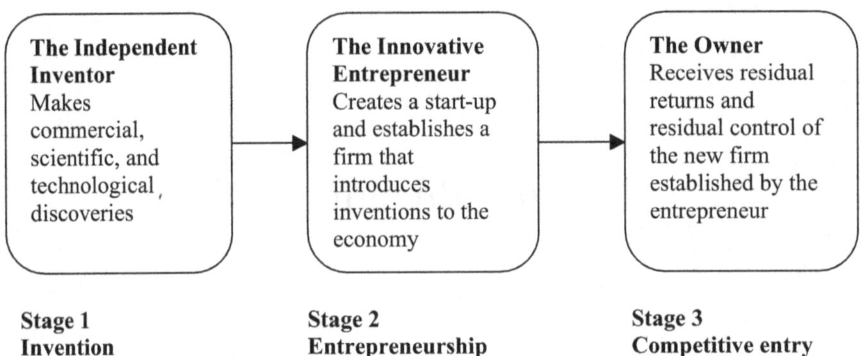

Figure 1.1. The dynamic economic theory of the innovative entrepreneur has three stages: invention, entrepreneurship, and competitive entry. The individual's role shifts from independent inventor to innovative entrepreneur to owner. The same individual or different individuals or teams of individuals can act in each stage and the process can terminate at any stage.

At the *entrepreneurship stage*, an entrepreneur creates a start-up to implement inventions and to form the basis of a new firm. The innovative entrepreneur who creates the start-up can be the initial inventor, a specialist entrepreneur, or a member of a team of entrepreneurs. The entrepreneur decides whether to be innovative or replicative. Innovative entrepreneurs differ from replicative entrepreneurs who imitate or purchase existing business models. The innovative entrepreneur combines inventions, initiative, and investment to create the start-up.

Finally, at the *competitive entry stage*, the entrepreneurial process ends successfully when the *foundational shift* occurs, that is, when the innovative entrepreneur converts the start-up to a firm that enters the marketplace. The start-up becomes a firm when it is financially separable from the entrepreneur and other owners in the sense of Irving Fisher's Separation Theorem (see Spulber, 2009a, 2009b). Sufficient investment and earnings are necessary to generate financial separation. An entrepreneur who founds the firm then becomes an owner of the firm, receiving residual returns and residual rights of control. Ownership of the firm is shared among members of the entrepreneurial team and with investors.

Understanding the decisions and characteristics of innovative entrepreneurs helps answer the major questions in the field of Innovation and Entrepreneurship:

1. The Question of Entrepreneurial Motivation: Why do individuals choose to become innovative entrepreneurs?
2. The Question of Innovative Advantage: When do entrepreneurs innovate more efficiently than do incumbent firms?
3. The Question of Competitive Pressures: How does competition affect incentives to innovate?
4. The Question of Creative Destruction: When do markets choose innovative entrepreneurship over technology transfer to incumbents?

5. The Question of the Wealth of Nations: How do innovative entrepreneurs affect international trade and economic prosperity?

1.1 The Independent Inventor and the Market for Inventions

Invention and entrepreneurship are different functions and involve different capabilities. Specialization of function and division of labor among inventors and innovative entrepreneurs can generate economic efficiencies. These efficiencies are realized through market transactions between independent inventors and innovative entrepreneurs, leading to gains from trade in the commercialization of inventions. Conversely, individuals may realize complementarities between inventive and entrepreneurial capabilities, leading some inventors to become innovative entrepreneurs. Also, inventors may become innovative entrepreneurs to avoid frictions in the market for inventions.

The Independent Inventor

Independent inventors are individuals who engage in R&D and obtain rewards from their discoveries. Independent inventors include freelancers, academics, consultants, employees, and managers of existing firms. The inventor's capabilities can include those of a researcher in the sciences, mathematics, computer science, engineering, social sciences, and business, including finance, marketing, accounting, operations, and management strategy. Independent inventors are distinct from companies that engage in R&D, including specialized research firms and laboratories, consulting companies, and firms that vertically integrate R&D and production. Firms also engage in R&D through research consortia and joint ventures.

Inventors maximize their life cycle utility of consumption. The independent inventor may anticipate financial rewards from the commercialization of inventions through licensing or sales. The independent inventor also may expect rewards from becoming an innovative entrepreneur and implementing the inventions. The independent inventor may receive grants for ongoing research and may expect future grants if current research is successful. The independent inventor also may receive compensation from future employment and consulting. The independent inventor may obtain indirect rewards, including enjoyment of research, satisfying scientific curiosity, and recognition of achievement by peers and society at large. University researchers benefit from salary increases, promotions, and a share of royalties.

Independent inventors are likely to design inventions that address particular needs of consumers and firms. For example, Andrew R. Hicks (2008) designed a curved automobile mirror with a 45-degree field of view that eliminates the driver's blind spot with minimal distortion. Improving the driver's view of traffic has the potential to reduce accidents and save lives. The inventor, a mathematics professor at Drexel University, introduced a mathematical algorithm that solved the mirror design problem.[1]

An independent inventor differs from an employee whose inventions are owned by the company that employs him. However, some independent inventors are employees of universities, research laboratories, and companies. Some employees keep their inventions secret and leave the company to become independent inventors and possibly innovative entrepreneurs (Bhide, 1994). Some companies create spin-offs that allow employees to implement their inventions (Anton and Yao, 1995). Inventors who are researchers at universities and laboratories can commercialize their inventions through their organizations, or they may be able to commercialize their inventions independently.[2]

The Market for Inventions

The market for inventions has transaction costs as in most markets: search, bargaining, pricing (royalties and transfer fees), and contingent contracting. Imperfect protections for IP rights also create frictions in markets for inventions, because inventors may need to reveal the details of their inventions to potential buyers, raising the risks of imitation or expropriation. The imperfect transferability of complex multidimensional innovations also can create market inefficiencies because of the transaction costs of coordinating the transfer of interrelated inventions. The problem of inventors' tacit knowledge generates market frictions because of the costs of codifying, communicating, and absorbing that knowledge. Asymmetric information about the features of inventions results in transaction costs associated with adverse selection and moral hazard.

Despite these frictions, the market for inventions is a major contributor to technological change.[3] The market for inventions includes many types of disembodied technology, such as patents, licenses, blueprints, chemical formulas, biological molecular structures, industrial designs, business plans, training, and consulting. The market for inventions also includes embodied technology, such as software,

1 Robert A. Hicks received United States Patent 8180606, "Wide Angle Substantially Non-Distorting Mirror," assigned to Drexel University on May 15, 2012. http://www.uspto.gov/web/patents/patog/week20/OG/html/1378-3/US08180606-20120515.html.

2 For studies of university researchers and specialized research firms, see Prevezer (1997), Galambos and Sturchio (1998), Zucker, Darby, and Armstrong (1998), Zucker, Darby, and Brewer (1998), Audretsch (2001), Jensen and Thursby (2001), and Lowe and Ziedonis (2006).

3 For empirical studies, see Machlup (1962), Cohen and Levinthal (1990), Mowery and Rosenberg (1991), Malerba and Orsenigo (2002), Ziedonis (2004), Laursen et al. (2010), and Clausen (2011). For useful surveys, see Arora et al. (2001), Malerba (2007), and Arora and Gambardella (2010). Markets for inventions are also international; Anand and Khanna (2000) study licensing agreements in chemicals, electronics, and computers; Tilton (1971) and Grindley and Teece (1997) examine licensing in the international diffusion of semiconductors and electronics; and Arora et al. (2001a, 2001b) consider international markets for technology in the chemical industry.

information and communications technology (ICT), laboratory equipment, and capital equipment. The market for inventions further includes commercial inventions in the form of franchise contracts that require up-front payments, royalties, and purchases of complementary resources. Inventions also can be embodied in start-ups and firms so that some mergers and acquisitions (M&A) involve technology transfers.[4]

The demand side of the market for inventions includes entrepreneurs and established firms who implement inventions. The supply side of the market for inventions consists of independent inventors and companies engaged in R&D. The market for inventions also includes specialized intermediaries that buy and sell inventions. The activities required to obtain an invention include: licensing or buying the invention from the inventor; subcontracting R&D to an independent inventor or to another firm; forming a partnership with an inventor to conduct research and to develop to the invention; and establishing internal R&D facilities.

Private ordering addresses the problem of transaction costs in the market for inventions. First, firms may internalize R&D by vertically integrating invention and production. Choosing whether to vertically integrate R&D and production or to purchase inventions is a form of the Coasian "make-or-buy" choice. Firms will internalize R&D when the costs of managing transactions within the firm are less than transaction costs in the market for inventions. Firms may both make and buy inventions. Furman and MacGarvie (2009), for example, find that the growth of in-house R&D capabilities in large pharmaceutical firms depends heavily on technology transfer through firm-university collaborations and contract research.

Second, intermediaries can improve efficiency of the market for inventions. These types of intermediaries perform a variety of important economic functions that increase allocative efficiency and reduce transaction costs. Intermediaries in the market for inventions engage in pricing, market making, matching buyers and sellers, reducing moral hazard, providing information to reduce adverse selection, and providing contracting services. Specialized intermediaries in markets for IP invest in legal protections for patents, pool patents to reduce costs of coordination, and provide market information to buyers and sellers. Companies such as Intellectual Ventures buy and sell patents and finance invention.

Finally, and most importantly for our discussion, inventors may bypass the market for inventions entirely through own-use of their inventions as innovative entrepreneurs. The "use-or-sell" choice is affected by the trade-off between the transaction costs of innovative entrepreneurship and transaction costs in the market for inventions. Various studies of individual academic scientists and engineers illustrate the basic choice between innovative entrepreneurship and technology transfer. Many entrepreneurial firms are spin-offs from universities.[5] Lowe and

4 Blonigen and Taylor (2000) consider acquisition of start-ups by established firms in the U.S. electronics industry.

5 See O'Shea et al. (2005) and the references therein.

Ziedonis (2006) consider a sample of 732 inventions at the University of California that were licensed exclusively to a firm. They distinguish between licensing to entrepreneurial start-ups and licensing to existing firms, and find that start-up firms licensed 36 percent of the inventions and existing firms licensed the remainder. The study implicitly provides evidence of the choice between licensing to a start-up and licensing to an incumbent because more than 75 percent of inventions licensed to start-ups "were reviewed by established firms either sponsoring the research or through nondisclosure agreements with the opportunity to license" (Lowe and Ziedonis, 2006, pp. 176–177).

In practice, vertically integrated producers that undertake internal R&D also purchase technologies in the market for inventions. The commercialization of inventions depends on the relative performance of independent inventors and vertically integrated research labs within major corporations (Chandler, 1977; Audretsch, 1995a). Veugelers and Cassiman (1999) find that small firms either conduct their own R&D or purchase inventions, and large firms combine R&D activities with external purchases of inventions.[6] Pellegrino et al. (2011) show that for "young innovative companies," innovation intensity mainly depends on embodied technical change from external sources rather than in-house R&D, while in-house R&D plays a more important role for mature innovative firms.

Biotech inventors who are associated with universities establish new firms or attract firms seeking technology transfers (see Prevezer, 1997; Audretsch, 2001). Zucker, Darby and Armstrong (1998) distinguish between biotech firms that are entrepreneurial entrants and those that are incumbents and consider both ownership and contractual technology transfers:

> Our telephone survey of California star scientists found that academic stars may simultaneously be linked to specific firms in a number of different ways: exclusive direct employment (often as CEO or other principal), full or part ownership, exclusive and nonexclusive consulting contracts (effectively part-time employment), and chairmanship of or membership on scientific advisory boards. (p. 69)

Zucker, Darby and Brewer (1998) provide indirect evidence of the choice between technology transfer and entrepreneurship, and find

> strong evidence that the timing and location of initial usage by both new dedicated biotechnology firms ("entrants") and new biotech subunits of existing firms ("incumbents") are primarily explained by the presence at a particular time and place of scientists who are actively contributing to the basic science as represented by publications reporting genetic-sequence discoveries in academic journals. (p. 290)

6 See Cassiman and Veuglers (2002, 2006) on complementarity between the firm's knowledge sourcing and innovation. See also Ropera et al. (2008), Laursen et al. (2010), and Clausen et al. (2011).

The presence of both types of firms in the sample is suggestive of the choice between entrepreneurship and technology transfer (511 entrants, 150 incumbents, 90 unclassified), although their study does not identify whether the star scientists commercialized their technology by establishing new firms or by transferring technology to existing firms (Zucker, Darby, and Brewer, 1998).

Academic inventors and universities choose among various commercialization options, essentially choosing between entrepreneurship and technology transfer to existing firms. Vohora et al. (2004) study nine entrepreneurial start-ups in the United Kingdom that were university spinouts (USOs). The academic entrepreneur that established the company Stem Cell attempted to transfer his technology to existing firms that had sponsored his research. He observed: "Commercial partners and industry were not interested. It was so early stage they thought it was a bit wacky. They all had first option to acquire the patents that had been filed from the sponsored research but did not take any of them up which left the university in an interesting position with a huge patent portfolio to exploit commercially" (Vohora et al., 2004, p. 156). They observe that for those academic entrepreneurs who were not able to transfer their technology to others,

> the opportunity was re-framed in order to take account of what the academic had learnt: industry's lack of desire to license or co-develop early stage technologies in this field and a preference instead to market later stage technologies that showed a high probability of generating commercial returns. Instead of selecting licensing or co-development as route to market, the academic entrepreneur had learnt that the best route to market was to assemble the necessary resources and develop the capabilities required to exploit the IP himself through a USO venture. (p. 156)

University inventors tend to receive greater royalties from entrepreneurial entrants (Lowe and Ziedonis, 2006). Commercialization tends to occur through agreements between inventors and existing firms in industries such as biotech (Lerner and Merges, 1998). Gans and Stern (2000, p. 486) find that in biotech, "nearly all successful firms have either licensed their key innovations, joined in downstream alliances, or been acquired outright by product-market incumbents."[7]

Inventors also can be specialized firms that develop products and processes that are inputs to other firms. These specialized firms face the problem of choosing between entrepreneurial entry downstream and technology transfer to downstream firms. In biotech, for example, many innovators were new firms. These start-ups carried out most of the initial stages of applied research in recombinant DNA technology and molecular genetics (Galambos and Sturchio, 1998). In U.S. biotech, about 5,000 small and start-up firms provided technology inputs to health care, food and agriculture, industrial processes, and environmental cleanup industries (Audretsch, 2001). These biotech firms were themselves innovators that needed to decide how best to commercialize their discoveries. Small biotech firms and major

7 See also Orsenigo (1991) and Stern (1995).

pharmaceutical companies chose between cooperation and competition. Small biotech firms tended to engage in technology transfer to larger pharmaceutical companies rather than entering the market to produce and sell products based on their discoveries: "The large companies exchanged financial support and established organizational capabilities in clinical research, regulatory affairs, manufacturing, and marketing for the smaller firms' technical expertise and/or patents" (Galambos and Sturchio, 1998, p. 252).

Similar patterns of technology transfers occurred in other industries. For example, in the chemical industry, specialized engineering firms (SEFs) chose entrepreneurial entry in R&D rather than transferring technologies to incumbent chemical companies. However, once they were established, these entrepreneurial entrants marketed process technology to large oil companies and chemical companies (Arora and Gambardella, 1998). In the photolithographic alignment equipment industry between 1960 and 1985, innovative entrants sold equipment to major semiconductor manufacturers (Henderson, 1993). Initially single-product start-ups entered the industry, but as incumbent firms became large and diversified, later entrants were firms with experience in related technologies (Henderson, 1993). Incumbents were displaced by later entrants who introduced innovations in photolithography rather than transferring their technology (Kato, 2007).

Increased invention by university researchers has resulted in the emergence of commercialization efforts by universities themselves. The university technology transfer office (TTO) acts as an intermediary that commercializes the inventions of university faculty. The TTO invests in expertise needed to evaluate and certify the quality of inventions. The TTO also handles the transactions involved with licensing inventions to potential adopters.[8] The university generally takes ownership of inventions produced by faculty based on employment contracts. Additionally, the Bayh-Dole Act permits universities, nonprofit organizations, and small businesses to own inventions that result from federal government funding rather than transferring ownership to the government.[9] Just prior to the Act, the government owned 28,000 patents, of which only about 5 percent were commercialized.[10] A study found that university patent licensing in the first 25 years of the Act resulted in 4,350 new products and the establishment of 6,000 new firms, with a rate approaching 700 new firms per year.[11] The costs of commercializing and developing university inventions is estimated to exceed invention costs by a factor of 10, with a new drug having

8 See Heidrun and Ozdenoren (2005), Jensen and Thursby (2001a, 2001b, 2003), and Siegel et al. (2000).

9 University and Small Business Patent Procedures Act, 1980, 35 U.S.C. § 200–212, 37 C.F.R. 401.

10 Council on Governmental Relations, The Bayh-Dole Act: A Guide to the Law and Implementing Regulations 1–2 (1999), http://www.cogr.edu/docs/Bayh_Dole.pdf, cited by McDonough (2006, p. 199).

11 See Bayh, Allen, and Bremer (2009, p. 3). They also cite a study by the Biotechnology Industry Organization (BIO) of university patent licensing between 1996 and 2007, which found that half of those reporting said their companies were based on university licenses while three-quarters of companies report that they had university licensing agreements.

development costs of $800 million to $1.3 billion and requiring 10 years for development and regulatory approval.[12] An alternative to IP ownership and intermediation by universities would allow faculty to seek intermediation by competitive independent licensing agents that play important roles in IP markets.[13]

The development of large-scale corporate laboratories may reflect economies of scale in R&D and economies of scope between innovation and manufacturing.[14] Larger existing firms' incentives to innovate are different from those of smaller firms, including entrepreneurial entrants, and larger firms pursue different types of inventive activity.[15] Acs and Audretsch (1987) find that large firms tend to have a competitive advantage in industries that are capital intensive, concentrated, highly unionized, and produce differentiated goods, whereas small firms tend to have a competitive advantage in industries that are highly innovative, rely on skilled labor, and innovate earlier in the industry life cycle. Mowery (1983) found that in the period between 1900 and 1940, there was a complementarity between in-house research and contract research projects so that contract research was not an effective substitute for in-house research, and firms without in-house facilities experienced a disadvantage in R&D and innovation.[16]

Competition among inventors offering substitute technologies can occur with the diffusion of new categories of technologies (Baptista, 1999). Karlson (1986) studies the adoption of competing inventions by U.S. steel producers. Stoneman and Toivanen (1997) consider the simultaneous diffusion of five different technologies (computer numerical controlled machines, numerically controlled machines, coated carbide tools, computers, and microprocessors) and discuss whether technologies are complements or substitutes. Huckman (2003) examines hospital adoption decisions for substitute cardiac procedures. Legal decisions involving a wide variety of inventions in different industries have considered the effects of competition among substitute inventions.[17]

1.2 The Innovative Entrepreneur and the Start-Up

An *innovative entrepreneur* is an entrepreneur who creates a start-up and establishes a firm that is the first to apply an invention. An *invention* is a commercial, scientific,

12 See Bayh, Allen, and Bremer (2009, p. 3).

13 See Schramm et al. (2009).

14 See Schumpeter (1942).

15 See Winter (1984), Acs and Audretsch (1988), and Audretsch (1995b).

16 See Mowery and Rosenberg (1991) on the commercialization of invention.

17 For example, Schlicher (2000) examines *Grain Processing Corp. v. American Maize-Products Co.*, 185 F.3d 1341, 51 U.S.P.Q.2d 1556 (Fed. Cit. 1999) and related decisions. Schlicher (2000, p. 504) observes: "For purposes of determining a reasonable royalty, the market value of any invention is the difference between the profits available from use of that invention by the patent owner or, if more efficient, by the infringer, and the profits available to persons other than the patent owner from use of the next best available substitute technology that would not infringe any patent of that patent owner."

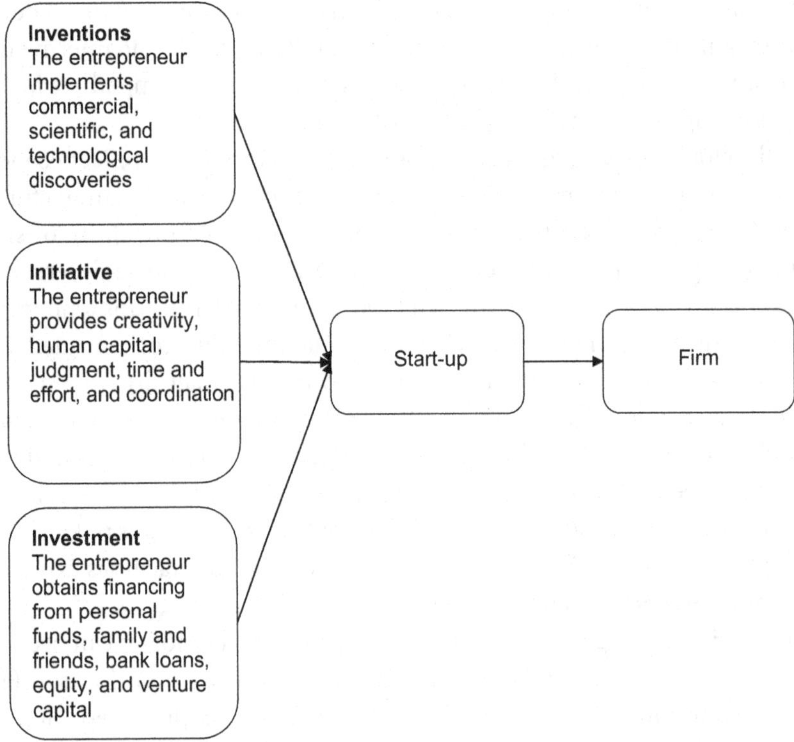

Figure 1.2. An entrepreneur creates a start-up and establishes a firm by combining inventions, initiative, and investment.

or technological discovery, but an *innovation* is something new that is introduced to the marketplace. An innovative entrepreneur can begin as an inventor who then applies commercial, scientific, and technological discoveries by becoming an entrepreneur. An innovative entrepreneur also can be a specialist who purchases or licenses discoveries from inventors and intermediaries.

The Entrepreneur

Innovative entrepreneurship is endogenous to the economy and depends on the decisions of individual inventors and entrepreneurs, among other economic actors. Entrepreneurs maximize their expected life cycle utility of consumption. Because of financial and liquidity constraints, their personal consumption and savings decisions are interconnected with their business decisions.

Innovative entrepreneurs provide a combination of inventions, initiative, and investment to the economy (see Figure 1.2). The innovative entrepreneur implements his own inventions or obtains those of independent inventors. The innovative entrepreneur applies personal initiative to create the start-up, providing creativity, human capital, judgment, time and effort, and coordination. The innovative entrepreneur's investment in the start-up is funded by personal income and wealth, contributions from friends and family, and outside financing including bank loans, equity, and venture capital.

The entrepreneur has expertise in the market transactions required to create a start-up and to establish a firm. Entrepreneurs require judgment and knowledge to identify combinations of market opportunities and the inventions and resources needed to achieve them. Entrepreneurs contract with investors, managers, employees, customers, suppliers, and partners. Entrepreneurs put together financial capital, human capital, and inventions, navigating financial markets, labor markets, and markets for inventions. Entrepreneurs often must address the legal requirements and regulatory barriers involved in establishing and operating a business.

The entrepreneur's capabilities are those needed to create a start-up and establish a firm. The entrepreneur is a specialist in the identification of market opportunities and the establishment of a firm to address those opportunities. This contrasts somewhat with Lazear's (2005) suggestion that the entrepreneur is a jack-of-all-trades who earns greater returns as a generalist than he would earn applying his skills in more specialized occupations. Because of initial financial and liquidity constraints, the entrepreneur may initially perform many of the tasks needed to operate the business, including management, marketing, finance, and production. However, as these constraints are relaxed, the entrepreneur can hire managers and employees and contract with firms to obtain these services.

A critical determinant of innovative entrepreneurship is whether new firms are needed to implement inventions. If existing firms can implement inventions more efficiently, independent inventors have an incentive to transfer their technology to those firms. Conversely, if entrepreneurs can implement inventions more efficiently, independent inventors have an incentive to become innovative entrepreneurs or to transfer their inventions to specialist entrepreneurs.

The independent inventor may become an innovative entrepreneur as a way to avoid transaction costs in the market for inventions; see Chapters 5 to 8. The independent inventor may happen to have the capabilities of both an inventor and an entrepreneur. The inventor's discoveries may be rudimentary and therefore difficult to transfer, requiring the individual to become an entrepreneur as a means of developing these inventions. The inventor's ability to apply inventions as an innovative entrepreneur may be enhanced by familiarity with the technology. The inventor may have tacit knowledge that is needed to apply the invention so that the individual becomes an entrepreneur as a means to transferring tacit knowledge to the start-up enterprise.

The Start-up

The *start-up* is defined as a new business enterprise that is subject to the entrepreneur's financial and liquidity constraints. The start-up becomes a firm when it no longer is subject to the entrepreneur's financial and liquidity constraints.

Because of these financial and liquidity constraints, the start-up's business decisions reflect the consumption preferences and endowments of the entrepreneur.

The individual's role shifts from entrepreneur to owner on establishment of the firm. The time that this transition occurs reflects the preferences and endowments of the entrepreneur as well as the market opportunities associated with competitive entry of the new firm. The entrepreneur can remain as owner and participate in managing the enterprise. Entrepreneurs need not become owners of new firms and owners of new firms need not begin as entrepreneurs; a specialist entrepreneur can transfer ownership of the start-up to a specialist investor such as a venture capitalist who completes the establishment of the firm. Entrepreneurs can sell control to others through a buyout or an initial public offering (IPO), stepping away from corporate control and management.

The entrepreneur creates a start-up as an instrument to establish a firm. The start-up is neither a small firm nor a new firm, but rather an institution that is used to generate a firm. The start-up exists until the new firm is established. What makes the start-up distinct from the firm is that it is closely tied to the entrepreneur's human capital and financial capital. Entrepreneurship can begin before the start-up is created, but entrepreneurship ends if and when the start-up is converted to a firm.[18] The firm is financially distinct from the entrepreneur in the sense of Irving Fisher's Separation Theorem, as will be discussed in the next section. This framework provides a formal way to define the time period during which entrepreneurship takes place.

The innovative entrepreneur embodies *inventions* in the start-up and the new firm. Commercial discoveries are the foundation for economic innovation. For entrepreneurs to access those ideas, the inventors must be outside incumbent firms, either working independently, being employed by universities, or operating specialized firms. Alternatively, inventors can be inside existing firms that work with entrepreneurs to create spin-offs. Innovative entrepreneurs depend on the supply of talented inventors who produce high-quality commercial, scientific, and technological inventions.

The innovative entrepreneur provides *initiative* that introduces discoveries to the economy. Economic growth and development benefit from an abundant supply of talented entrepreneurs who choose to be innovative rather than choosing to pursue replicative opportunities. Individuals must choose not only to bear the costs and risks of entrepreneurship but also to take on the additional challenges of

18 In the management literature, the term "start-up" is sometimes used to designate the new firm rather than the enterprise that exists before the new firm. For example, van Gelderen et al. (2005, p. 366) suggest that there are four phases in the "pre-start-up" period: "the development of an intention to start an enterprise," "an entrepreneurial opportunity is recognized and a business concept is developed," "resources are assembled and the organization is created," and "the organization starts to exchange with the market."

innovation. Innovative entrepreneurs translate commercial discoveries into market innovations by establishing new firms. They help move scientific and technological discoveries from the laboratory to the market. Innovation is likely to involve greater costs and risks than purchasing or copying existing business models.

The innovative entrepreneur must secure *investment* by obtaining financial capital. The entrepreneur needs financing to cover the initial costs of human resources, capital equipment, and other inputs needed by the new enterprise. The entrepreneur must also cover the transaction costs of creating the start-up and establishing the firm. Innovative entrepreneurs encounter financing and liquidity constraints in creating start-ups and establishing firms. The entrepreneur's personal income and wealth constrain his ability to finance the start-up. The innovative entrepreneur can encounter tighter financing constraints than the replicative entrepreneur because of the inherent uncertainty of innovation. As a consequence of financial constraints, the entrepreneur's business decisions and personal consumption and savings decisions are interdependent, as will be discussed in the next chapter.

The entrepreneurial process can end at any stage. The entrepreneurship stage does not occur if the independent inventor chooses to transfer his discoveries to existing firms. Existing firms can implement inventions by modifying their current businesses or diversifying their activities. The entrepreneurial process terminates and the competitive entry stage does not occur if the entrepreneur is unable to convert the start-up to a new firm. The competitive entry stage also does not occur if the entrepreneur transfers ownership of the start-up to an existing firm. Transferring inventions and start-ups to existing firms avoids costly competition between incumbents and entrants.

Imperfections in capital markets generate transaction costs of obtaining credit that are likely to weigh more heavily on new enterprises than on established firms. Entrepreneurial start-ups tend to have limited earnings, few assets, and little if any track record of performance. Innovative entrepreneurs must attract investors on the basis of the quality of the commercial, scientific, and technological inventions they will introduce to the market. Innovative entrepreneurs need to interest investors in purchasing shares of the start-up and the new firm. Additionally, innovative entrepreneurs must persuade inventors, employees, managers, partners, and customers to bear the risks of transacting with a speculative enterprise and to trust the entrepreneur's judgment.

Innovative versus Replicative Entrepreneurs

Individual innovators and entrepreneurs constitute different but overlapping categories. Innovative entrepreneurs are those individuals in the intersection of the set of entrepreneurs and the set of innovators in the economy as illustrated by the Venn diagram in Figure 1.3. Not all entrepreneurs are innovative; an entrepreneur

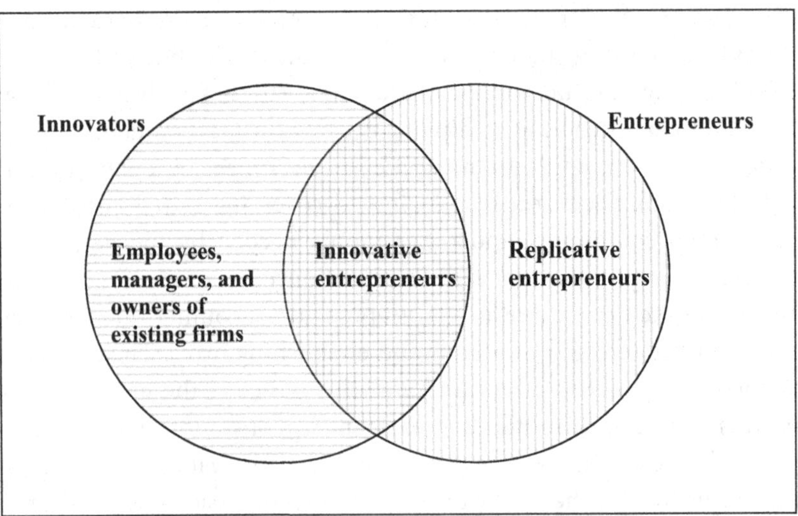

Figure 1.3. Innovative entrepreneurs are the individuals at the intersection of the set of innovators and the set of entrepreneurs.

who is *not* innovative is referred to as a *replicative entrepreneur*.[19] Not all innovators are entrepreneurs; innovators include employees, owners, and managers of existing firms. Innovative entrepreneurs are distinct from these innovators because innovative entrepreneurs implement commercial, scientific, and technological discoveries by embodying them in new firms. Innovative entrepreneurship is endogenous because the entrepreneur chooses whether to be innovative or replicative.

The entrepreneur is an individual who creates a start-up and establishes a firm. The entrepreneur can act alone or as part of a team of entrepreneurs. The innovative entrepreneur introduces commercial, scientific, and technological inventions to the economy. Innovative entrepreneurs can be independent inventors who become entrepreneurs to implement their inventions. Alternatively, innovative entrepreneurs can be specialists who obtain strategies and discoveries from independent inventors and then adapt, develop, and implement those strategies by establishing a firm.

Innovative entrepreneurs embody inventions in start-ups and eventually in new firms, generating new products and manufacturing processes, transaction methods,

19 Leibenstein (1968, p. 72) distinguishes between the innovative entrepreneur described by Schumpeter and "routine entrepreneurship, which is really a type of management." Leibenstein (1968, pp. 72–72) states that "By routine entrepreneurship we mean the activities involved in coordinating and carrying on a well-established, going concern in which the parts of the production function in use (and likely alternatives to current use) are well known and which operates in well-established and clearly defined markets. By N-entrepreneurship [Schumpeterian or 'new type' entrepreneurship] we mean the activities necessary to create or carry on an enterprise where not all the markets are well established or clearly defined and/or in which the relevant parts of the production function are not completely known."

and organizational structures. For example, Thomas Edison established the Edison Electric Light Company in 1878 "to own, manufacture, operate, and license the use of various apparatus used in producing light, heat, and power by electricity" (Sobel and Sicilia, 1986, p. 12). Table 1.1 provides a list of some innovative entrepreneurs and the firms they established.

Replicative Entrepreneurs

Replicative entrepreneurs enter the market by establishing a firm that provides, produces, and delivers a standard product in a standard way. Replicative entrepreneurs may apply commercial, scientific, and technological inventions – but they are not the first to introduce them to the market place.[20] Replicative entrepreneurs establish firms that implement existing business models. Replicative entrepreneurs obtain generic strategies from incumbent firms and intermediaries, or they imitate and expropriate the strategies of existing firms.

The distinction between innovative and replicative entrepreneurs helps address the familiar question of whether establishing a company that operates a hot dog stand represents entrepreneurship. The answer is clearly yes because such companies are firms even when no innovation is involved. Someone who establishes a generic hot dog stand or acquires a hot dog stand franchise is a replicative entrepreneur. Someone who establishes a hot dog stand firm that introduces a new type of hot dog, new ingredients, a new cooking technique, or a new delivery method is an innovative entrepreneur.

Both innovative and replicative entrepreneurs provide the new firms and productive capacity that expand existing industries and develop new industries. Entrepreneurs, whether they are innovative or replicative, play an important role in the economy by helping discover the size of the market. They face risk because they establish firms in the face of uncertainty about market demand. Even though their business models are the same as incumbents, specialist entrepreneurs continue to establish new firms until the industry discovers the size of the market. Creane (1996) finds that when entrants learn about the size of the market on the basis of the existing market price, an information externality exists that may lead to excessive entry.[21]

Entry by both innovative and replicative entrepreneurs provides information about the size of the market. Over time, the entry and exit of new firms adjusts

20 Baumol (1968, p. 65) describes the entrepreneur as follows: "It is his job to locate new ideas and to put them into effect. He must lead, perhaps even inspire; he cannot allow things to get into a rut and for him today's practice is never good enough for tomorrow. In short, he is the Schumpeterian innovator and some more." In the economic model of the firm without entrepreneurs, "the firm is taken to replicate precisely its previous decisions, day after day, year after year" (p. 67).

21 See also Alpern and Snower (1988) and Zeira (1994).

Table 1.1. *Some innovative entrepreneurs, the firms they established, and the year that the firms were founded*

Name(s)	Company	Year Founded
Paul Revere	Revere Copper Co.	1801
Francis Cabot Lowell	Boston Manufacturing Co.	1813
John Deere	Deere & Co.	1837
Isaac M. Singer	Singer Sewing Machines	1851
Elisha Otis	E. G. Otis Co.	1853
Gail Borden	New York Condensed Milk Co.	1858
Henry J. Heinz	Heinz & Noble Co.	1869
Joseph A. Campbell	Campbell Preserve Co.	1869
Eli Lilly	Eli Lilly	1876
Alexander Graham Bell, Gardiner Hubbard, Thomas Watson, Thomas Sanders	Bell Telephone Co.	1877
Thomas Edison	Edison Electric Light Co.	1878
Henry Solomon Wellcome Silas Burroughs	Burroughs Wellcome	1880
Gustavus Swift	Swift & Co.	1885
Robert Wood Johnson, James Wood Johnson, Edward Mead Johnson	Johnson & Johnson	1886
George Westinghouse	Westinghouse Electric Co.	1886
Andrew Carnegie	Carnegie Steel Co.	1892
Asa Griggs Candler	Coca-Cola Co.	1892
Milton Hershey	Hershey Chocolate Co.	1894
King Gillette	Gillette Safety Razor Co.	1901
Henry Leland	Cadillac Automobile Co.	1902
Adolph Zukor	Famous Players Film Co.	1912
Clarence Saunders	Piggly Wiggly	1916
Walter Elias Disney	Walt Disney Co.	1923
Paul Galvin	Galvin Manufacturing (Motorola)	1928
Howard Hughes	Hughes Aircraft	1935
William Redington Hewlett, Dave Packard	Hewlett-Packard	1939
John H. Johnson	Johnson Publishing Co.	1942
Masaru Ibuka Akio Morita	Tokyo Tsushin Kogyo (Sony)	1947
Berry Gordy, Jr.	Motown Records	1960
Malcolm McLean	Sea-Land Service	1960
Sam Walton	Wal-Mart	1962
Mary Kay Ash	Mary Kay Cosmetics	1963
Robert Noyce Gordon Moore	Intel	1968
Fred Smith	Federal Express	1971
Bill Gates, Paul Allen	Microsoft	1975

Name(s)	Company	Year Founded
Larry Ellison Bob Miner, Ed Oates	Software Development Laboratories (Oracle)	1977
Steve Jobs, Steve Wozniak	Apple Computer	1977
Lakshmi Mittal	Ispat International (Mittal Steel)	1978
Mitchell Kapor	Lotus Development	1982
Charles Geschke, John Warnock	Adobe	1982
Michael Dell	Dell Computer Corporation	1984
Jeff Bezos	Amazon.com	1994
Pierre Omidyar	eBay	1995
Bill Gross	Idealab	1996
Marc Randolph, Reed Hastings	Netflix	1997
Larry Page, Sergey Brin	Google	1998
Jack Ma	Alibaba.com	1999
Mark Zuckerberg	Facebook	2004
Chad Hurley, Steve Chen, Jawed Karim	YouTube	2005
David Karp	Tumblr	2007

Sources: Jackson (1997), Schweikart and Doti (2010), Sobel and Sicilia (1986), and company websites.

aggregate capacity to fluctuations in market demand. Replicative entrepreneurs help replace firms that exit the market as a result of failure, mismanagement, natural disaster, or malfeasance. Also, replicative entrepreneurs establish firms that enter the market when market demand grows, supplementing existing firms that are capacity constrained.

Evidence suggests that there is substantial specialization by inventors and by entrepreneurs. An indication of the ubiquity of specialist inventors and entrepreneurs is the wide availability of standard business strategies in practically any industry. Specialist entrepreneurs can purchase standard business strategies in the market for IP. Potential specialist entrepreneurs can obtain generic strategies from managers, consultants, publications, websites, and business courses. For example, Entrepreneur.com provides a large number of off-the-shelf "business ideas" for most industry categories.[22] In retail, suggested business ideas include antique

22 These categories include advertising, arts and crafts, autos/transportation, beauty/personal care, business services, children's businesses, computers, education/instruction, entertainment and events, financial, food, health care/medical, home products/services, import/export, maintenance, manufacturing, media/publishing, online businesses, pet businesses, plants/agriculture,

furniture sales, candy stores, carts and kiosks, consignment clothing, convenience stores, dollar stores, glass shops, gun shops, inventory liquidation, lighting shops, musical instrument sales, network marketing, pawnbroker, and used furniture dealer. In each category, Entrepreneur.com provides guidance and an estimate of start-up costs. For instance, the estimated start-up costs of a convenience store are $10,000 to $50,000.

Franchisees are an important example of replicative entrepreneurs because they start firms that apply a franchiser's business model. Michael (2003, p. 63) states: "Franchising engages in simple replication of a business concept across time and space, and this replication overcomes managerial limits to growth. Can other entrepreneurs replicate the firm's business model at lower cost than the firm itself – and should the entrepreneur then focus on the terms of transfer rather than expanding the firm?" Franchising is a major source of entrepreneurship, providing a significant share of new firms to the economy.[23]

Franchise firms are specialist enterprises that sell strategies to franchisees who are replicative entrepreneurs. Franchise operators establish firms using business strategies, brand names, product designs, production processes, and services provided by the franchiser.[24] The founder of the franchiser firm must be an innovative entrepreneur to be competitive with other franchisers and standard business models that are freely available. The franchise contract developed from the principal-agent relationship.[25] Early franchisers include the McCormick Harvesting Machine Co., the Singer Sewing Machine Co., the Ford Motor Co., and soft-drink companies.[26] There are about 3,000 franchise brands in the United States with approximately 900,000 establishments.[27] The top 10 franchisers in 2010 were Subway,

real estate, recreation, retail businesses, security, sports, technology, and travel. See Entrepreneur .com.

23 See Blair and Lafontaine (2005), Lafontaine and Shaw (1999, 2005), Kalnins and Lafontaine (2004), and Lafontaine (2009).

24 The FTC defines a franchise on the basis of three criteria: "(1) The franchisee will obtain the right to operate a business that is identified or associated with the franchisor's trademark, or to offer, sell, or distribute goods, services, or commodities that are identified or associated with the franchisor's trademark; (2) The franchisor will exert or has authority to exert a significant degree of control over the franchisee's method of operation, or provide significant assistance in the franchisee's method of operation; and (3) As a condition of obtaining or commencing operation of the franchise, the franchisee makes a required payment or commits to make a required payment to the franchisor or its affiliate." FTC, 16 CFR Parts 436 and 437, Disclosure Requirements and Prohibitions Concerning Franchising and Business Opportunities; Final Rule, Federal Register, Vol. 72, No. 61, March 30, 2007, Rules and Regulations, p. 15544.

25 See Gurnick and Vieux (1999, p. 42).

26 See Gurnick and Vieux (1999).

27 As of 2005, franchising accounted for more than 11 million jobs; see International Franchise Association Educational Foundation, 2005, Economic Impact of Franchised Businesses, Volume 2, Washington, DC, http://www.franchise.org/uploadedFiles/Franchisors/Other_Content/economic_impact_documents/EconomicImpactVolIIpart1.pdf, accessed January 4, 2010.

MacDonald's, 7-Eleven, Hampton Inn, Supercuts, H&R Block, Dunkin' Donuts, Jani-King, Servpro, and ampm Mini Market.[28] Franchises also include automobile dealers and other specialized dealers that contract with manufacturers.[29] Franchisers should be distinguished from companies that provide "direct sales" to individuals rather than to entrepreneurs who establish firms.[30] Franchisers also differ from companies that offer "business opportunities" to individuals.[31]

1.3 Innovative Entrepreneurs and the Theory of the Firm

The theory of the innovative entrepreneur builds on the general theory of the firm. An *entrepreneur* is an individual who creates a start-up enterprise and then establishes a firm. The *start-up* is not a firm because it is subject to the entrepreneur's financial and liquidity constraints. These constraints limit the start-up's ability to maximize profits. Once the start-up is free of the entrepreneur's financial constraints, either through growth or external financing, the start-up becomes a firm. If and when the entrepreneur is successful in establishing a firm, he ceases to be an entrepreneur, becoming instead an *owner* of the new firm or selling the firm to outside investors.

Archimedes is said to have observed "Give me a place to stand on, and I will move the Earth." The innovative entrepreneur creates the firm as a lever with which to change the economy. The new firm multiplies the effects of the entrepreneur's innovative effort just as a mechanical lever multiplies input force. The entrepreneur devotes effort to creating new products, production processes, and transaction methods and embodies these innovations in a new firm. The new firm multiplies

28 *Entrepreneur* magazine lists the largest 500 franchisers in 2010; see http://www.entrepreneur.com/franchise500/index.html, accessed January 2, 2010.

29 On automobile dealers, see Marx (1985).

30 These companies include Avon Products, Amway Corporation, Mary Kay Cosmetics, Herbalife, and Tupperware. The US Direct Selling Association has 200 member companies that offer direct marketing and estimates that there more than 15.9 million people in the United States who are direct sellers and more than 92 million worldwide; see http://www.dsa.org/about/, http://www.dsa.org/research/industry-statistics/and http://www.dsa.org/about/faq/, accessed December 18, 2013.

31 A critical difference between a franchise and a "business opportunity" is that the latter is a one-time transaction that does not involve ongoing control by the seller. The seller of a "business opportunity" is an intermediary that provides a buyer of the "business opportunity" both access to suppliers of goods and services and access to retail outlets, locations, and customers. The FTC definition of "business opportunity" excludes: franchises, relationships between an employer and an employee or among business partners, memberships in a cooperative, or agreements to purchase or license a "trademark, service mark, trade name, seal, advertising, or other commercial symbol." See FTC, 16 CFR Parts 436 and 437, p. 15569. There is an extensive market for "business opportunities," many of which are fraudulent work-at-home and pyramid marketing (Ponzi) schemes. See Pareja (2008) for a discussion of the law applying to "business opportunities."

the effects of these innovations through the volume of its sales, production, and transactions.

Innovative entrepreneurs transform the economy because creating new firms sets in motion significant economic change, far beyond what an individual might otherwise achieve. The firm employs, trains, and develops a group of managers and employees. The firm forms an organization with communication channels, delegation of authority, specialization of functions, and division of labor. The firm builds brands and a market reputation. The firm expands through investment, mergers, and acquisition of other firms. The firm conducts R&D, acquires inventions, and introduces further innovations. The growth of the firm thus magnifies the initial contribution of the innovative entrepreneur who established it.

Innovative entrepreneurs help generate what Hayek (1991) terms "spontaneous order": the order that grows through voluntary interaction among individuals in society. They introduce new types of organizations and market transactions that respond to changes in the needs of individual consumers. Innovative entrepreneurs create market institutions that are more effective than government agencies for which "order in human affairs requires that some should give orders and others obey" (Hayek, 1960, p. 160).

The definition of the firm used here is based on the Fisher Separation Theorem, which is fundamental to finance and neoclassical economics.[32] According to the "separation criterion" (Spulber, 2009a, 2009b), what distinguishes the firm from other types of transaction institutions is that the firm's *business objectives* are *financially separable* from the *consumption objectives* of its owners. Therefore, corporations and similar institutions are firms, whereas clubs, worker cooperatives, and related institutions are not firms.

Understanding the firm as a social institution brings the economic role of the entrepreneur into sharper focus. Entrepreneurs engage in the transactions needed to create the start-up enterprise and to convert the start-up into a new firm. The entrepreneurial function is distinct from that of an owner, manager, innovator, or investor. An entrepreneur's economic contributions are the incremental benefits generated by the newly established firm net of the costs of establishing the firm.

Entrepreneurship – the establishment of new firms – is critical for the economy. There is considerable evidence that the level of firm formation in the U.S. economy does not vary much from year to year over long periods of time, as Stangler and Kedrosky (2010a) show.[33] This means that entrepreneurship helps generate a

32 The Fisher Separation Theorem shows that with price taking by consumers and firms, the firm's owners operate the firm to maximize its profits. In finance, the Fisher Separation Theorem explains present value maximization and capital budgeting.

33 Stangler and Kedrosky (2010a, p. 4) find that the number of new firms does not vary much from year to year over long periods using various measurements: "New establishments (which includes not only unique firms but also new locations established [by] existing firms, such as Walmart or McDonald's) and tracked by both the Census Bureau and the Bureau of Labor Statistics (BLS);

continual turnover of firms across the economy.[34] Most job creation comes from new and young firms (five years old or less) but a substantial portion of job creation comes from a small number of large firms, many of which are young and highly susceptible to failure (Stangler, 2010). The new firms established by entrepreneurs make an important contribution to employment.

The many economic contributions of firms are apparent. Firms are responsible for most of the economy's gross domestic product (GDP), employment, innovation, international trade, and economic growth. The U.S. Census counts more than 27.7 million firms, 6 million of which have paid employees with total receipts exceeding $29.7 trillion and total employment of more than 120 million people.[35] There are millions more firms in other developed economies and a growing number of firms in developing countries.[36] There are more than 82,000 multinational firms that operate across national boundaries with 810,000 foreign affiliates (UNCTAD, 2009, p. 8).

Firms take various legal forms including corporations, close corporations, sole proprietorships, limited-liability partnerships (LLPs), and limited-liability corporations (LLCs). Some nonprofit corporations are firms when they have clearly defined objectives that are distinct from the consumption objectives of their owners, whereas others function more like social clubs. Defining firms is a question of determining the economic functions of the institution rather than the many legal labels that describe business enterprises. An operational definition of the firm should distinguish between what is or is not a firm in practice. Various transaction institutions that are not firms include groups of contracting individuals, social clubs, buyers' cooperatives, workers' cooperatives, merchants' associations, and some basic partnerships. Government enterprises typically are not firms because they pursue public policy objectives.

At issue are the special characteristics that define firms. A firm can be owned and managed by one or more individuals, but the firm is an institution that is distinct from the individual or individuals who own it. A sole proprietorship can

Employer firms as tracked by Census and the Small Business Administration (SBA); Firm births in a dataset tabulated by the Census Bureau using OECD methodology; and, Startups (in data collection parlance, 'age zero' firms)." They examine the period from 1977 to 2005. Additionally, data from Census Statistical Abstracts also show constancy in the number of new firms in the 1940s and 1950s, with the exception of 1946, although additional work would be needed to compare these two periods. See also Stangler and Kedrosky (2010b).

34 Stangler (2010, p. 5) observes that in 2007 "the U.S. economy contained 5.5 million firms. About half a million of these were brand new (age zero, that is); another two million, or just over one-third, were five years old or younger."

35 U.S. Census data for 2008, http://www.census.gov/epcd/www/smallbus.html, accessed December 18, 2013.

36 Cross-country studies examine firms in developed economies; see Scarpetta et al. (2002) and Bartelsman and Doms (2000). There are also studies of firms in developing economies; see, for example, Tybout (2000).

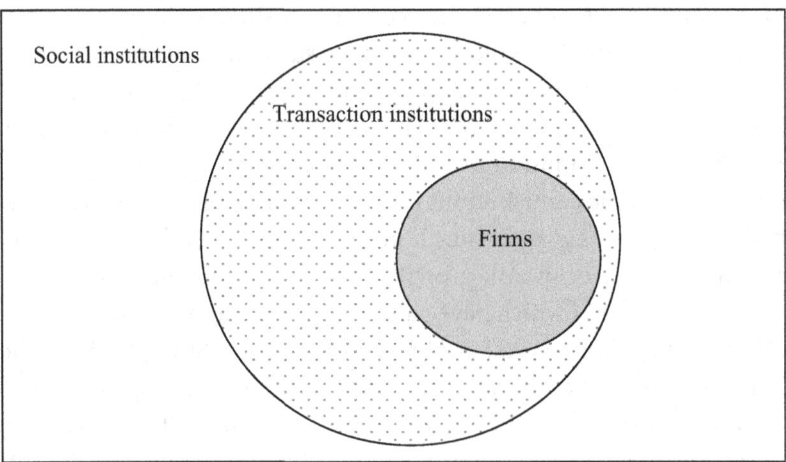

Figure 1.4. Firms are a subset of transaction institutions, which, in turn, are a subset of social institutions.

still be a firm, even if the owner carries out all of the tasks including production and management. Entrepreneurs are individuals who establish firms such as corporations and some types of nonprofit corporations. Although they may be extremely creative and innovative, individuals who establish other forms of social institutions that are not firms are not classified here as entrepreneurs. For example, individuals who establish social clubs, cooperatives, or government enterprises are not entrepreneurs.

We begin with the universe of social institutions (see Figure 1.4). Social institutions involve relationships among individual members of the society. Economic transactions are themselves social relationships, but not all social relationships are economic transactions. Indeed, economic transactions are embedded in other distinct social relationships. Karl Polanyi (1944, p. 44) argues that "man's economy, as a rule, is submerged in his social relationships," through reciprocity, redistribution, and the household. John R. Commons (1931, p. 648) emphasizes the context of law and social traditions: "Transactions are the means, under operation of law and custom, of acquiring and alienating legal control of commodities, or legal control of the labor and management that will produce and deliver or exchange the commodities and services, forward to the ultimate consumers."

Ian R. Macneil also stresses that economic transactions are within the context of a variety of distinct social institutions. He observes (1980, p. 1): "Contract without the common needs and tastes created by society is inconceivable; contract between totally isolated, utility-maximizing individuals is not contract, but war; contract without language is impossible; and contract without social structure and stability is – quite literally – rationally unthinkable. The fundamental root, the base, of contract is society." Macneil (1980, p. 10) defines a "discrete contract" as "one in which no relation exists between the parties apart from the simple exchange of goods. Its paradigm is the transaction of neoclassical microeconomics." However,

Macneil argues that such a contract is rarely observed because "every contract is necessarily partially a relational contract, that is, one involving relations other than a discrete exchange." For Macneil (1974), a relational contract has many characteristics including significant duration, close personal relations as in employment, social reputation and norms, anticipation of future cooperative behavior, and a view that the relationship will evolve over time rather than being fully specified at the outset.

The members of a society form social institutions either deliberately through explicitly cooperative agreements, implicitly through competition, or even informally through "spontaneous order" in the sense of Friedrich Hayek (1977). Institutions include political mechanisms and other forms of social order. Institutions also include evolving social conventions such as language, rules, customs, kinship, community traditions, cultural values, and behavioral norms. Institutions also include the common law, governments, social and ethnic groups, political parties, and religious organizations. Institutions also include families (Ben-Porath, 1980), affinity groups, associations, and other social relationships. Early institutions that presage the contemporary firm but are distinct social institutions include feudal estates (Ekelund et al., 1996), merchant associations (Greif, 1989, 1993), armies (Weber, 1968), and government bureaucracies (Schumpeter, 1934, pp. 163–164). Many of these social institutions are not concerned with economic transactions and thus should not be considered as transaction institutions or as firms.

Economic institutions, referred to here as transaction institutions, are a subset of the universe of social institutions. Firms constitute a subset of transaction institutions (see Figure 1.4). In the absence of firms, individuals can engage in a variety of transactions, including barter, spot transactions with fiat money, and contracts. In addition, individuals can form many types of "consumer organizations" including clubs, buyers' cooperatives, workers' cooperatives, nonprofits, merchants' associations, and basic partnerships.

I refer to economic transactions without the social contrivance of firms as "direct exchange." A society composed of two individuals who transact voluntarily with each other also does not constitute a firm. The individuals necessarily structure their transactions for mutual benefit. For example, a group of two or more individuals who engage in barter or who form contracts does not constitute a firm, even though their cooperative agreements are transaction institutions. If all economic relationships were to be considered firms, then the concept of the firm would not be useful; it would simply be synonymous with any and all economic transactions. A workable definition of the firm must be distinct from the general concept of an economic transaction.

The family and the household are social institutions that also provide ways to organize exchange but are not firms. Ben-Porath (1980, p. 1) points out that through implicit contracts, the "family plays a major role in the allocation and distribution of resources." Ben-Porath notes that between the two extremes of the family transaction and the market transaction are a range of transaction modes and institutions including transactions between friends, business partners, and employers and employees. Families usually are characterized by altruism and close ties and seek to maximize the well-being of their members. Traditional merchant families did not separate their personal finances from those of their business. Family members managed the business and generally served as its representatives: "the business being in the family and the family being in the business" (Reynolds, 1952, p. 352).

Firms intermediate transactions through incentives such as prices, wages, and contracts that generate "spontaneous order." Market transactions are the result of voluntary agreements between buyers and sellers who receive gains from trade. Organizational transactions also are the result of voluntary agreements between the firm and its employees, who each receive gains from trade. Alchian and Demsetz (1972) emphasize the voluntary nature of employment: "managing, directing, or assigning workers to various tasks" is just a form of continual contract renegotiation within organizations.

Firms address transaction costs by forming and managing markets and organizations. The major role that firms play in the contemporary economy suggests that firms possess substantial transaction cost advantages over direct exchange (Spulber, 1999, 2009a). Firms provide markets with various intermediation and coordination mechanisms including price adjustment, marketing, sales, media, and other types of mass communication. Firms create and operate physical and virtual market places that allocate all kinds of goods and services. Firms design and manage organizations that transact in markets and govern internal operations.

Understanding the role of the firm as a transaction institution implies a more general view of the firm's activities. Seen in this light, the firm is more than a set of activities occurring within the boundaries of an organization. The *scope of the firm* is the combination of the firm's market making and organizational activities. The firm improves transactional efficiency in the economy both through internal governance of transactions and external management of transactions. A firm is a nexus of transactions, as Jensen and Meckling (1976) correctly observe, but a nexus of transactions need not constitute a firm.

The role of the firm in improving transactional efficiency suggests an "intermediation hypothesis" (Spulber, 2009a). This is an empirical proposition stating that increases in the costs of transactions among individuals as compared to transactions intermediated by firms lead to growth in the scope of the firm. The intermediation hypothesis examines what determines the economy's reliance on firms as intermediaries. The hypothesis suggests that as a result of transaction costs, the extent of the market explains the establishment of firms to replace other types of organizations and direct exchange among individuals. The general theory of the firm presented in Spulber (2009a) yields useful insights that can be tested empirically. The great diversity of firms provides substantial data that can be applied to study their activities and structure.

Firms intermediate transactions using a variety of mechanisms including the creation and management of markets. Transaction costs addressed by firms include costs that result from communication and information processing, search and matching, bargaining, adverse selection, moral hazard, free riding, and contracting. Advances in transaction techniques improve the efficiency of firms' intermediation activities. Firms establish organizations as a means of implementing market transactions and as a way of managing organizational transactions. Firms can be complex organizations with many members and many trading partners. They allocate resources within their organizations, including labor services, capital financing, parts and components, and IP. Firms coordinate the activities of their employees through many types of management procedures and organizational relationships.

Much of the standard discussion of firms in economics focuses on a very different question: the "internalization hypothesis" based on the "make-or-buy" choice first identified by Coase (1937). The "internalization hypothesis" considers those activities that are contained within a particular firm. The "internalization hypothesis" posits that firms are able to avoid some types of market transaction costs by vertical integration – that is, by substituting organizational governance for market transactions when it is efficient to do so. Coase argued that firms add activities when the marginal costs of increasing the boundaries of the organization are less than the marginal costs of delegating the activity to others through market transactions.

The "intermediation hypothesis" in contrast views firms as market makers rather than market takers. Firms intermediate transactions by creating a combination of markets and organizations. The general theory of the firm thus provides a theory of endogenous institutions (Spulber, 2009a).

Entrepreneurs are the foundation of this general theory because they are the prime movers. Individuals begin the process of creating institutions by forming start-ups and establishing firms. Firms continue the process of institutional development by creating and operating markets so that markets also are endogenous. Firms also create and manage organizations that transact internally and in the market place, making organizations endogenous. Finally, interactions of buyers and sellers through markets and organizations generate economic outcomes. Entrepreneurship, firms, markets, and organizations, as well as economic outcomes, are therefore endogenous. This framework is summarized in Figure 1.5.

1.4 The Question of Entrepreneurial Motivation

Why do individuals choose to become innovative entrepreneurs? The Question of Entrepreneurial Motivation is fundamental because of the major economic contributions of innovative entrepreneurs. The answer to this question is straightforward:

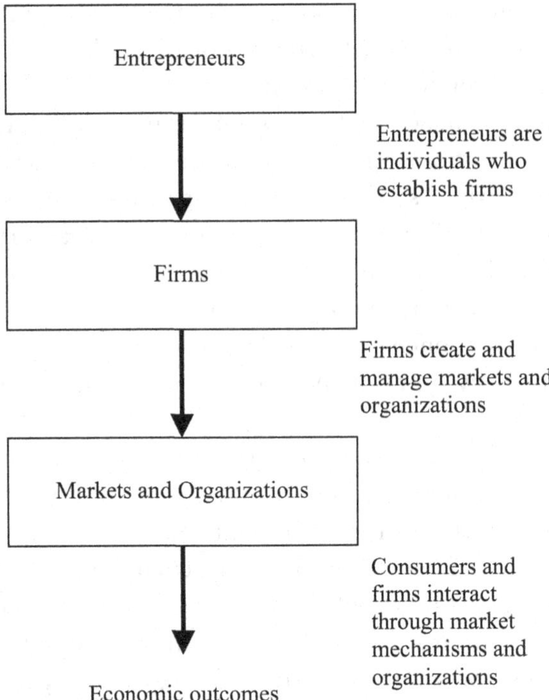

Figure 1.5. Microeconomics with endogenous entrepreneurs, firms, markets, and organizations.

like other individuals in the economy, *innovative entrepreneurs are motivated by the benefits of final consumption.*

Economic analysis of the entrepreneur must combine the tools of consumer choice and firm optimization. Entrepreneurs' personal consumption decisions are interconnected with their business decisions as they struggle to establish a firm. Entrepreneurs must cope with personal budget constraints and business financing constraints. Having created a start-up, the entrepreneur's ability to establish a firm is limited by asymmetric information about the firm's prospects and by the availability of financial capital and human capital. An entrepreneur's decisions about when to convert the start-up to a firm depend on the success of the start-up, the prospects of the new firm, and the interaction of financial and liquidity constraints.

Innovative entrepreneurship is *endogenous* – that is, it is the result of individual decisions in response to market incentives. The basic framework in this book shows that innovative entrepreneurship involves clearing three significant hurdles. First, an inventor must make commercial, scientific, or technical discoveries that will form the basis of the economic innovation. Second, the inventor must choose to become an entrepreneur and create a start-up enterprise or to transfer the necessary discoveries to an entrepreneur who in turn must choose to adopt the discovery and create a start-up. Third, the innovative entrepreneur must successfully transform the start-up enterprise into a new firm that embodies the discoveries.

In the *invention* stage, an inventor makes a *commercial discovery* that identifies a market need and a new way to address that need. The inventor may make related scientific and technological discoveries, or the inventor may identify scientific or technological discoveries made by others. The inventor's commercial discovery can be expressed as a business strategy, which consists of a plan of action for achieving a goal in the market place and identification of necessary capabilities, resources, and technologies.

In the *entrepreneurship* stage, the inventor chooses to become an innovative entrepreneur and implement the discovery, or the inventor may contract with an innovative entrepreneur who will in turn implement the discovery. The innovative entrepreneur applies inventions, creates and develops a start-up enterprise, and prepares to launch a new firm. The start-up is the mechanism that the entrepreneur uses to establish a new firm. Start-ups are closely connected with the individuals who launch them. The entrepreneur's initiative and judgment form the objectives and strategy of the start-up. The entrepreneur's human capital shapes the capabilities of the start-up. The entrepreneur's financial capital is connected to the financing of the start-up. Perhaps most importantly, the entrepreneur's creativity and discoveries affect the innovativeness of the start-up.

In the *competitive entry* stage, the entrepreneur establishes a new firm and becomes an owner. The new firm enters the market and competes with other entering firms, existing firms, and non-firm institutions. The change in the individual's role from entrepreneur to owner is referred to as the *foundational shift* (Spulber, 2009a). When the entrepreneur's consumption objectives and the start-up's business objectives are *financially separable* – even though the entrepreneur may continue on as owner, manager, and innovator – the new firm is established. This refers to financial separation in the sense of Irving Fisher (1906, 1907, 1930).

Individuals tend to maximize the utility of their *life-cycle consumption* subject to various budget constraints that depend on income, wealth, and liquidity.[37] Individuals make choices regarding consumption, saving, and investment within the context of their personal life-cycle consumption plans. For this reason, an individual's consumption choices depend on his personal preferences over goods, occupational activities, and leisure as well as age and other personal characteristics. Individuals respond to market incentives including the prices of goods, wages and

37 The literature on life-cycle consumption has tended to emphasize consumption and savings decisions and generally does not consider activities such as entrepreneurship. On life-cycle consumption, see, for example, Fisher (1930), Modigliani and Brumberg (1954), Tobin (1967), Heckman (1974), Artle and Varaiya (1978), Mariger (1987), Carroll (1994), Hubbard et al. (1994), Attanasio and Browning (1995), Gourinchas and Parker (2002), Cocco et al. (2005), and Bullard and Feigenbaum (2007). In their survey, Browning and Crossley (2001, p. 20) observe that "Our belief is that relatively parsimonious models drawn from the life-cycle framework have had more successes than failures. But the economics profession is just at the start of a systematic application of theoretical models to micro data." See Evans and Jovanovic (1989) on liquidity constraints and entrepreneurship.

salaries, employment opportunities, and availability of credit. Individuals further respond to public policy incentives resulting from taxation, laws, and regulations.

Because they are individuals, innovative entrepreneurs make *business decisions* within the context of their life-cycle consumption plans. Entrepreneurs face the problem of imperfect financial separation of their consumption decisions from their business decisions. This means that the Fisher Separation Theorem does not apply to the entrepreneur – instead the entrepreneur's consumption and business decisions are interconnected. The entrepreneur's personal preferences and endowments affect his business decisions. In turn, the technological and financial features of the entrepreneur's start-up affect his consumption decisions. These interconnections are described at some length in Spulber (2009a).

1.5 The Question of Innovative Advantage

Max Levchin, cofounder of PayPal, observed that the company was not founded as a payments intermediary.[38] Focusing on software for handheld devices, Levchin and PayPal set out in a completely different direction from the company's eventual orientation. As with many innovative entrepreneurs, Levchin worked from a basic conception of the new strategy and continued to invent during the start-up phase: "What I wanted to do was capitalize on that emergence of technology. And then, of course, enterprise requires security; security requires these scarce skills, I have the skills; start a company."[39] The new strategy focused on handheld devices in the belief that "[e]very corporate dog in America will hang around with a Palm Pilot or some kind of a device."[40] Although mobile devices eventually would emerge as a dominant force in personal and corporate communications, Levchin's approach was far too early.

Levchin's strategy began to narrow, and the company focused on storing money securely on Palm Pilots. Even after receiving the first round of venture capital funding, the innovative strategy was still not fully formed. Levchin and his associates built an application for the Palm Pilot and posted a demonstration version on a website. The response of users was surprising: "we realized that all of these people were trying to use the website for transactions, and the growth of that was actually more impressive than the growth of the handheld device one, which was inexplicable because the handheld device one was cool and the website was just a demo."[41]

Market pressures began to change the company's strategy. The company kept hearing from people using a new website named eBay, asking for permission to provide payment services for their auction. Because these requests were inconsistent

38 Livingston (2007, p. 1).
39 Livingston (2007, p. 3).
40 Livingston (2007, p. 3).
41 Livingston (2007, pp. 5–6).

with the company's initial direction, they resisted: "So for a while we were fighting, tooth and nail, crazy eBay people: 'Go away, we don't want you.'"[42] The innovative idea began to take shape as the company realized that there was growing demand for the website version of their service.[43] Finally, the start-up changed its strategy when the website had about 1.5 million users and the handheld version of the product only had about 12,000 users.[44]

PayPal became the first online payment intermediary. PayPal implemented the commercial discovery of online payment intermediation as well as introducing associated technological developments in computer software and Internet applications. According to the company, "PayPal is re-imagining money. We're creating a better shopping experience, from start to finish, no matter what's being bought, how it's being paid for, or where it's being sold."[45] Within 15 years of its being founded in 1998, the company had more than 100 million accounts in 190 countries and offered transactions in 25 currencies.

Levchin and PayPal's other founders acted both as inventors and innovative entrepreneurs. Combining invention and entrepreneurship offers advantages that stem from uncertainty and learning in the innovative process. There are complementarities between invention and implementation of inventions. PayPal, the online payments intermediary, evolved through a combination of invention and innovative entrepreneurship. What began as software for handheld devices became a new transaction technique: payment intermediation in online commerce. A commercial discovery – an online payment system, a "moment of epiphany," a new strategy – generated PayPal. Online intermediaries such as PayPal would transform economic transactions.

Like PayPal, many entrepreneurial entrants created innovations that successfully competed with existing firms. This raises the Question of Innovative Advantage: When do entrepreneurs innovate more efficiently than do incumbent firms? There are plenty of established financial intermediaries in the economy including banks and credit card companies that could have developed online payment systems. There also are many online retailers, auctioneers, and other intermediaries that could have conceived of online payment systems. However, the flexibility and creativity of an innovative entrepreneur helped a start-up create the leading online payment system.

Incumbent firms have many advantages including assets that are complementary to obtaining, generating, and implementing inventions. However, existing firms are subject to *incumbent inertia* that can reduce their incentives to innovate. Existing firms may have bureaucratic rigidities that reduce their ability to evaluate, obtain, and implement innovations. Existing firms may lack the skills needed to

42 Livingston (2007, pp. 5–6).

43 Livingston (2007, p. 3).

44 Livingston (2007, p. 3).

45 https://www.paypal-media.com/payments/vision#.

develop inventions in comparison to specialized independent inventors. Managers of existing firms focus on running the business, leaving them less time to innovative. Arrow's (1962b) replacement effect also causes incumbent inertia because an existing firm's opportunity costs of innovation include the returns to operating using its existing products and production technologies.

In contrast, the innovative entrepreneur can exercise *individual initiative.* This gives the innovative entrepreneur the flexibility and creativity that may not be feasible for an organization. The innovative entrepreneur obtains the full returns to innovation because the start-up and the new firm do not have to overcome the hurdle of displacing an ongoing business. The combination of incumbent inertia and the entrepreneur's individual initiative can give the entrepreneur an innovative advantage.

1.6 The Question of Competitive Pressures

How does competition affect incentives to innovate? The Question of Competitive Pressures is part of a debate that has been raging for more than a century. Schumpeter (1912, 1934) argues that competition increases innovation; entrepreneurs initiate "gales of creative destruction" as they establish new firms that compete with and displace incumbent firms. Schumpeter (1942, p. 132) later suggests that competition decreases innovation because incumbents with market power innovate so that "[t]echnological progress is increasingly becoming the business of teams of trained specialists who turn out what is required and make it work in predictable ways."

The debate over competitive pressures has generated a vast empirical and theoretical literature in economics. Understanding the effects of competition on innovation has implications for practically every area of public policy, including patents, education, taxes, regulation, finance, and antitrust. Chapter 4 shows that entrepreneurial competition increases incentives to innovate. Entry of entrepreneurs generates more R&D projects than a multi-project incumbent firm. This is because the average incentive to innovate of competing entrepreneurs is greater than the marginal incentive to innovate of the multi-project monopoly incumbent. The result is that competition among entrepreneurs generates better innovations than the multi-project monopoly incumbent. Also, when entrepreneurial entrants compete with a multi-project monopoly incumbent, the equilibrium number of R&D projects is the same as what would be generated by entry of entrepreneurs without an incumbent firm and therefore greater than the projects chosen by a monopoly incumbent in the absence of entrepreneurial competition.

Entrepreneurs face three types of competition: Type-I competition is among entrepreneurs themselves, which includes competition among innovative entrepreneurs and competition with replicative entrepreneurs that expropriate or imitate innovations; Type-II competition is between entrepreneurs and informal and traditional organizations; and Type-III competition is between entrepreneurs and existing firms (Spulber, 2009a). Chapter 4 examines both competition among entrepreneurs and competition between entrepreneurs and a monopoly incumbent. Chapters 5 to 8 consider innovation when potential entrepreneurs and incumbent firms choose whether to compete or to cooperate. Chapter 10 discusses competition between entrepreneurs and informal institutions.

1.7 The Question of Creative Destruction

When do markets choose innovative entrepreneurship over technology transfer to incumbents? The Question of Creative Destruction is based on the observation that existing firms should be more efficient than entrants in providing economic innovations. Existing firms can internally develop inventions and introduce those inventions to the market. Even if independent inventors make significant discoveries, they can contract with established firms to introduce their innovations without the cost of establishing new firms. Existing firms may obtain greater returns from implementing inventions because they already have formed market relationships and own complementary resources.

Creative destruction is costly because competition between innovative entrants and existing firms dissipates economic returns to innovation. Entrants and existing firms expend resources on competition. Entering firms can duplicate existing facilities and capital equipment that have economic value. It is efficient to replace existing facilities and capital equipment only if they are obsolete or if the adjustment costs of modernization exceed the costs of new facilities and capital equipment. The exit of existing firms also involves transaction costs including bankruptcy liquidation and reorganization.[46]

Creative destruction is costly because innovative entrepreneurs must create a start-up and establish a firm. Innovative entrepreneurship involves substantial transaction costs because acquiring or developing commercial, scientific, and technological inventions can involve purchase costs and innovative effort. Innovative entrepreneurs also incur transaction costs by acquiring resources that are complementary to the inventions they introduce.

To avoid the costs of creative destruction, inventors can transfer their technologies to established firms. Inventors are more likely to rely on cooperation with existing firms when they have greater IP protections, when attorneys and venture capitalists act as intermediaries, and when existing firms have substantial complementary assets (Gans, Hsu, and Stern, 2002). Gans and Stern (2000, p. 487)

46 Bris et al. (2006, p. 1253) find that "Chapter 7 liquidations are not cheaper than Chapter 11 reorganizations, particularly after we control for endogenous self-selection of firms into bankruptcy procedure. Bankruptcy professionals (attorneys, accountants, trustees) regularly end up with most of the post-bankruptcy firm's value in Chapter 7."

suggest that because cooperation yields greater profits than competition, "under the traditional assumptions of the literature on technological competition, and in the absence of non-contractible information asymmetries between the incumbent and entrant, observations of entry by the startup into the product market represent something of an economic puzzle."

Various frictions in the market for inventions help explain creative destruction. Entrepreneurship acts as a remedy for market failure in the market for inventions. Transaction costs in the market for inventions generate inefficiencies in technology transfers. As a result, inventors can obtain greater returns from own-use of their discoveries through entrepreneurship than from technology transfers. Also, inventors who disclose their inventions to existing firms face risks of imitation or expropriation by existing firms, as Arrow (1962b) explained. To overcome appropriability problems in the market for inventions, inventors become entrepreneurs as a means of embodying inventions in new firms. This is discussed in Chapter 5.

The complexity of multidimensional innovation also provides incentives for inventors to become entrepreneurs. The various elements of an innovation may have different transaction costs of technology transfer, so that even if a product or process technology is readily transferable, the overall costs of technology transfer are high. Kline and Rosenberg (1986, p. 279) point out: "There is no single, simple dimensionality to innovation. There are, rather, many sorts of dimensions covering a variety of activities." The OECD (2002, p. 18) defines "technological innovation activities" as "all of the scientific, technological, organizational, financial and commercial steps, including investments in new knowledge, which actually, or are intended to, lead to the implementation of technologically new or improved products and processes." Schumpeter (1912) refers to the entrepreneur as making "new combinations." The inventor has an incentive to become an innovative entrepreneur when the costs of implementing combinations of innovations are less than the costs of transferring such combinations. This is considered further in Chapter 6.

The inventor often has tacit knowledge about the innovation and complementary knowledge that is necessary to implement the invention. The inventor must codify and transmit the knowledge to the existing firm and also faces the possibility that some knowledge is only partially transferable. The existing firm must invest in absorption to understand and apply the invention. Tacit knowledge generates benefits from own-use so that the inventor has an incentive to become an innovative entrepreneur. This is examined further in Chapter 7.

Even if the individual's knowledge is explicit and transferable, it can be difficult to communicate to others because of asymmetric information. Inventors often have the best understanding of their invention and its potential applications but may not be able to demonstrate the value of the invention to existing firms. Because inventors have an incentive to overstate the quality of their inventions, asymmetric information creates problems of adverse selection. Inventors engage in entrepreneurship because asymmetric information reduces the returns from technology transfer. This is examined further in Chapter 8.

1.8 The Question of the Wealth of Nations

How do innovative entrepreneurs affect international trade and economic prosperity? The Question of the Wealth of Nations has challenged economists at least since 1776 when Adam Smith (1998) emphasized the benefits of the specialization of function that result from the division of labor across countries.[47] Traditional economic analyses of the gains from trade generally are based on principles of static general equilibrium without innovation or entrepreneurship. However, inventors, entrepreneurs, and firms increasingly compete in a global marketplace of ideas. On the supply side of the marketplace, R&D has become global with the spread of inventive effort across a wide range of industrialized countries and expansion of invention in leading developing countries. On the demand side of the marketplace, many companies have abandoned "not-invented-here" policies and purchase innovations produced in other countries, either through arms-length license sales or by internal transfers from foreign subsidiaries.

The benefits of a larger market are not just economies of scale in production but also improvements in the quality of inventions. I show elsewhere that the quality of invention is limited by the extent of the market. There is increasing international trade in both disembodied and embodied technology. The international market for inventions increases returns to invention because there is greater demand for inventions by producers in a larger market. The international market also increases the quality of inventions because it draws from a larger supply of inventions. Therefore, the international market for inventions increases the quality of invention and generates gains from trade in inventions (Spulber, 2008c, 2010b).[48]

Innovative entrepreneurs generate gains from trade, and their economic contributions also depend on the extent of the market. A larger market as a result of international trade increases the demand for innovative entrepreneurship leading to greater innovation. Also, a larger market increases the supply of innovative entrepreneurs as individuals in many countries establish innovative firms. This implies that innovative entrepreneurs contribute to the wealth of nations. Countries that participate in the world trade system will benefit from a combination of domestic and foreign entrepreneurship. Countries may have differences in endowments of labor, capital, and technology. Innovative entrepreneurs can establish

47 Adam Smith identifies the division of labor within the economy and across countries as the source of the wealth of nations: "It is the great multiplication of the productions of all the different arts, in consequence of the division of labour, which occasions, in a well-governed society, that universal opulence which extends itself to the lowest ranks of the people" (Smith, 1998, I 1.8).

48 See also Schmookler (1962, 1966) and Vives (2008).

firms that take advantage of differences across countries and help achieve factor price equalization.

Adam Smith (1998) considered specialist inventors who make discoveries that improve capital equipment. In addition, Smith considered specialist entrepreneurs ("philosophers") who innovate by introducing these inventions to the economy.

> All the improvements in machinery, however, have by no means been the inventions of those who had occasion to use the machines. Many improvements have been made by the ingenuity of the makers of the machines, when to make them became the business of a peculiar trade; and some by that of those who are called philosophers or men of speculation, whose trade it is not to do any thing, but to observe every thing; and who, upon that account, are often capable of combining together the powers of the most distant and dissimilar objects. In the progress of society, philosophy or speculation becomes, like every other employment, the principal or sole trade and occupation of a particular class of citizens. Like every other employment too, it is subdivided into a great number of different branches, each of which affords occupation to a peculiar tribe or class of philosophers; and this subdivision of employment in philosophy, as well as in every other business, improves dexterity, and saves time. Each individual becomes more expert in his own peculiar branch, more work is done upon the whole, and the quantity of science is considerably increased by it. (Smith, 1998, I 1.8)

Although the traditional sources of gains from trade exist in a world without technological change, they result from technological differences among countries. Ricardian comparative advantage, for example, is based on differences in relative productivities of activities across countries. Countries gain from trade by specializing in those activities in which they have a comparative advantage and exchanging the additional production. Clearly, innovation impacts trade and economic prosperity by continually changing the set of activities in which particular countries have a comparative advantage.

International trade includes technology transfers embodied in goods and services and in disembodied form. Spulber (2008c) presents a general equilibrium model of international trade in which inventors auction their technology in both domestic and foreign markets. International trade in technology bridges the technology gap between countries by directly transferring knowledge rather than by transferring goods. When countries share knowledge through technology trade, they benefit from employing the best technology. International trade in technology has a number of significant economic effects. Technology trade improves the quality of innovation by widening the pool of R&D experiments from which the best technology is chosen. Technology trade increases the efficiency of invention because inventions are applied in multiple countries and may require fewer inventors than without technology trade. Technology trade increases the volume of trade in goods, and it increases product variety at the market equilibrium. Technology trade also increases national income in each country and increases total gains from trade. International markets for inventions therefore generate gains from trade directly through international technology transfers and indirectly by increasing product trade. The market for inventions is of increasing importance as a source of the wealth of nations.

Entrepreneurs are essential to international trade because they establish the firms that engage in international business. Practically all international trade is carried out by firms.[49] International business firms handle importing and exporting of most goods and services. Firms establish and operate divisions in multiple countries through foreign direct investment (FDI). Firms and trade associations establish and manage international financial and commodity markets. Firms manage the transactions that connect national economies.

As we have emphasized, entrepreneurs are important contributors to economic innovation. This also applies in the international context; innovative entrepreneurs establish firms that realize new import and export opportunities. Innovative entrepreneurs increase the participation of countries in the international economy by creating new industries. New firms help developing countries provide goods and services to international markets and provide import-export services that increase a country's participation in international trade. Conversely, as a country opens to international markets, entrepreneurs establish firms that benefit from serving larger markets.

Writing more than forty years before Adam Smith, Richard Cantillon (1755, p. 187) connects entrepreneurship with international trade,

> [We] can see that the 100,000 ounces paid by the ladies of Paris for lace comes into the hands of the merchants who send Champagne wine to Brussels, and that the 100,000 ounces consumers paid for Champagne wine in Brussels comes into the hands of lace merchants. The entrepreneurs on each side distribute this money to those who work for them, either in the wine or the lace business.

Cantillon recognized that entrepreneurs establish firms to address new trade opportunities.

The opening of more national economies to international trade has been accompanied by greater entrepreneurship. Klapper et al. (2010) analyze *The World Bank Group Entrepreneurship Survey* and find that entrepreneurship is growing in many countries as a result of economic and financial development and improvements in the legal and regulatory environment.[50] Box (2009), summarizing studies by

49 Although, almost all national governments regulate, tax, and subsidize international trade and participate in negotiations concerning trade regulations. However, governments generally do not participate directly in international transactions with the exception of state-owned enterprises, government procurement, and sovereign wealth funds.

50 The *World Bank Group Entrepreneurship Survey* measures entrepreneurial activity and provides "cross-country, time-series data on the number of total and newly registered businesses for 84

the Organization for Economic Cooperation and Development (OECD), observes that "globalization and the ongoing shift to knowledge economies highlights the importance of innovation and thus of entrepreneurship and firm creation." The *Global Entrepreneurship Monitor* survey extensively documents entrepreneurship in fifty-four countries (Bosman and Levie, 2009; Levie and Autio, 2008). Glaeser and Kerr (2009) find that the availability of workers and their human capital provides an important explanation for variations in entrepreneurship across cities in the United States. This suggests that availability of labor relative to technology could potentially explain variations in entrepreneurship across countries.

Chapter 9 suggests that variations in consumer preferences, technology endowments, labor forces, and the costs of doing business help explain differences in entrepreneurship across countries. In addition, variations in international trade in goods and openness to FDI will affect entrepreneurship across countries. Controlling for differences in labor forces, variations in technology help explain FDI that flows from the high-technology country to the low-technology country. Emerging markets with large populations experience the reinforcing effects of a smaller technology endowment and a greater work force, increasing their extensive margins of technology utilization. As countries open to international trade, economic efficiency improves with handicrafts and small shops in the informal economy being replaced by more productive service and manufacturing enterprises.

This suggests the need for additional study of new and young firms in the international context. Small- and medium-sized enterprises (SMEs) contribute significantly to international trade (Lu and Beamish, 2001) although additional research is needed to identify new firms among SMEs. There is extensive evidence of entrepreneurial FDI in the form of new ventures with an international presence. Coeurderoy and Murray (2008) study British and German international new ventures that employ new technologies. They find evidence that entrepreneurs enter country markets that offer better production for intellectual property (IP) although industry and firm characteristics matter more for internationalization than the foreign regulatory regime. Oviatt and McDougall (2005, p. 31) define an international new venture as "a business organization that, from inception, seeks to derive significant competitive advantage from the use of resources and the sale of outputs in multiple countries." Entrepreneurial start-ups have incentives to internationalize their operations including bringing their technology and capabilities into new markets (Brush, 1995; Zahra et al., 2000). Reynolds (1997a) finds that SMEs tend to expand abroad not only through exports but also through FDI. A study of Japanese SMEs by Lu and Beamish (2001) finds that although FDI initially reduces profits, greater levels of FDI are associated with higher performance. A study of Swedish

countries" (Klapper et al., 2010). Although these indicators are pooled into an index, they include openness of a country to international trade. There are variations in entrepreneurship across countries with similar levels of economic development; see van Stel et al. (2005) and Klapper et al. (2010).

SMEs by George et al. (2005) examines internationalization decisions including internationalization of operations.

Entrepreneurial FDI can be implemented not only by establishing a firm abroad but also by outsourcing offshore, franchising contracts, and licensing agreements. Entrepreneurial FDI benefits from lower costs of labor and greater extensive margins of technology utilization in the host country as compared to the home country. The framework has a north-south interpretation in which the north indicates industrialized countries and the south designates emerging markets with large populations. Even with the same technology endowment, the higher population south operates inefficiently at the margin. This corresponds to widespread entrepreneurship with less efficient technologies in emerging markets, with traditional handicrafts, small-scale artisanal manufacturing, and mom-and-pop retailers. FDI by entrepreneurs from the north takes advantage of additional labor in the south and improves efficiency at the extensive margin, displacing inefficient traditional businesses. This corresponds to observed improvements through FDI. In many countries, FDI contributes more to economic growth than domestic investment by transferring technology when the host country has sufficient human capital (Borensztein et al., 1998) although empirical evidence on spillovers is mixed (Keller and Yeaple, 2005). Technology transfer through FDI has a stronger impact on per capita GDP growth than domestic technology (Schneider, 2005; Chowdhury and Mavrotas, 2006). Chapter 9 shows that entrepreneurial FDI can reduce entrepreneurship in the country having the relatively larger per capita technology endowment, which is consistent with Grossman's (1984) result that FDI crowds out entrepreneurs in an open economy.

Entrepreneurs contribute to the wealth of nations by establishing the firms that carry out international trade. Countries benefit when domestic entrepreneurs launch industries that enter into international transactions and when foreign entrepreneurs launch new ventures that trade with and invest in their economies. Innovative entrepreneurs discover new customers and suppliers in international markets and develop new international transaction methods. Innovative entrepreneurs promote the international diffusion of technology through the trade and investment activities of new firms, as will be shown in Chapter 9. Chapter 10 considers some of the implications of the preceding discussion for economic growth and development.

1.9 Conclusion

There is general agreement among economic researchers about what the entrepreneur accomplishes – the establishment of a firm. The economic theory of the innovative entrepreneur builds on this consensus about its central character. Beyond creating start-ups and firms, the innovative entrepreneur generates economic development by introducing new types of transactions, markets, and organizations. This book develops an economic theory of the innovative entrepreneur.

The economic theory of the innovative entrepreneur emphasizes the individual initiative and creativity of entrepreneurs. Understanding the innovative entrepreneur is critical for inventors, investors, managers, and potential entrepreneurs themselves. The public policy implications extend widely, including IP protections, antitrust, taxation, market entry regulations, corporate law, and regulation of financial markets.

Innovative entrepreneurs establish firms that embody commercial, scientific, and technological inventions and introduce these discoveries to the economy. Innovative entrepreneurs implement new strategies by founding firms that offer new products, production processes, and transaction techniques. Firms launched by innovative entrepreneurs form new types of organizations and construct new types of markets. In this way, entry by innovative firms generates competition that fundamentally transforms the economy.

Independent inventors and innovative entrepreneurs make important economic contributions because they overcome the inertia of incumbent firms. The process of innovative entrepreneurship involves decision making by individuals who perform the functions of inventors, entrepreneurs, and owners. The individuality of inventors and entrepreneurs distinguishes them from firms and other social institutions. The inertia of existing firms derives from their potential earnings from existing technologies, even though many managers of existing firms provide leadership and creativity. In the absence of this source of inertia, independent inventors and entrepreneurs have different opportunity costs of invention and innovation.

Economic analysis of entrepreneurship is challenging because it examines the nexus of the individual and the institution. Entrepreneurs are individuals with other economic roles, as consumers, investors, workers, managers, and inventors. Entrepreneurs create economic institutions, both start-up enterprises and the wide variety of new firms. Their personal and business decisions are closely interconnected in the transition from invention to entrepreneurship, during the period of entrepreneurship, and in the transition from entrepreneurship to ownership. The individual's personal characteristics, preferences, and endowments tend to play an important role in the decision to become an entrepreneur, to create a start-up, and to establish a firm.

Although the major questions regarding the innovative entrepreneur are inspired by the classic work of Schumpeter, the proposed answers in this book are new. The analysis reflects historical developments in the century since Schumpeter first began work in this area. The analysis also reflects advances in the economic analysis of invention and innovation. The following chapters develop a theory of innovative entrepreneurship that addresses these major questions.

2

Entrepreneurial Motivation

Maximizing Life-Cycle Utility

Why do individuals choose to become innovative entrepreneurs? The life-cycle theory of entrepreneurship presented here shows that entrepreneurs create start-ups and establish firms as a form of *asset accumulation*. Entrepreneurship is integral to the individual's life-cycle planning because of the close connection between saving and investment decisions. Entrepreneurs make consumption and savings decisions at the same time that they provide effort, IP, and investment to create and develop the start-up. The entrepreneur's ownership shares in the start-up and the firm are among the assets accumulated over the individual's lifetime. The entrepreneur may divest ownership of the firm after it is established or later during retirement. The entrepreneur may transfer ownership of the firm and other assets to younger generations. This approach draws on Modigliani and Brumberg's life-cycle theory of consumption, which argues that individuals accumulate assets over their lifetime and begin to sell off assets during retirement, resulting in a transfer of assets to younger generations.[1]

The innovative entrepreneur maximizes life-cycle utility subject to budget constraints that include the costs and returns associated with entrepreneurship. The entrepreneur both contributes personal assets and builds personal assets. The entrepreneur often faces financing and liquidity constraints in creating the start-up and establishing the new firm. The entrepreneur's personal contributions to the start-up and the new firm include IP, human capital, and investment capital. As a consequence, the entrepreneur's business decisions and personal consumption and saving decisions tend to be financially interdependent.[2]

The life-cycle theory of entrepreneurship has many important implications. First, it implies that the individual's decision regarding whether or not to become an entrepreneur reflects *rational planning*. The entrepreneurship decision is made

1 See Modigliani and Brumberg (1954, 1990), Modigliani (1976, 1998), and the discussion in Deaton (2005). Tobin (1967, 1972) distinguishes liquidity constraints from wealth constraints.

2 The life-cycle theory of entrepreneurship presented here extends work begun in Spulber (2009a). See also Vereshchagina and Hopenhayn (2009) and Buera (2009).

in the context of the individual's many other life-cycle choices regarding occupation, education, housing, insurance, and saving. The interdependence between the entrepreneur's consumption and saving decisions, occupational choices, and business decisions helps explain various empirical puzzles. Some research suggests that entrepreneurs earn less than they could earn from alternative occupations. Also, some other research suggests that entrepreneurs earn less from investment in private equity than a market portfolio. Interdependence implies that the entrepreneur's returns to various activities appear to be less attractive than market alternatives when these returns are considered in isolation rather than as part of life-cycle utility maximization. Entrepreneurship provides a means of asset accumulation and portfolio diversification.[3]

Second, the life-cycle theory of entrepreneurship implies that *the entrepreneur's personal characteristics affect the start-up's business decisions.* The entrepreneur's age, as well as consumption preferences, income, wealth, and human capital, help explain decisions regarding development of the start-up and establishment of the firm. Because of financing and liquidity constraints during entrepreneurship, the conditions of the Fisher Separation Theorem (Fisher, 1906, 1907, 1930) do not hold. The entrepreneur's business decisions reflect life-cycle planning so that the start-up's activities need not maximize the present value of profits. Financial separation – the foundational shift – and profit maximization begin when the start-up is converted to a firm.

Third, the life-cycle theory of entrepreneurship implies that *the start-up's characteristics affect the entrepreneur's consumption and saving decisions.* The start-up's technology, IP, market demand, financing, costs, and earnings help explain the entrepreneur's consumption and saving decisions. Because of the imperfect financial separation between the individual's consumption and saving decisions and business decisions, the time pattern of the start-up's costs and returns, rather than the net present value of the start-up's income, will affect the time pattern of consumption and asset accumulation. For example, the business opportunities of the start-up will affect the entrepreneur's personal expenditures for education or housing. After the foundational shift takes place, the entrepreneur's consumption and saving decisions depend only on the market value of his equity in the firm.

This chapter examines the transition from invention to entrepreneurship and the transition from entrepreneurship to ownership of the firm. The discussion examines the inventor's R&D and commercialization decisions. The discussion then considers the decisions of the innovative entrepreneur in creating and developing the start-up and establishing the firm. Finally, the discussion turns to the foundational shift in which the entrepreneur establishes a new firm and becomes an owner.

3 Yao and Zhang (2005) show that in comparison with renters, homeowners use home equity as a buffer to labor-market and financial-market risks, leading them to diversify by holding a greater proportion of stock and a smaller proportion of bonds in their financial portfolio.

The chapter presents three "interdependence theorems." The inventor's commercialization decisions are interdependent with his consumption and saving decisions. The entrepreneur's start-up decisions are interdependent with his consumption and saving decisions. Also, the entrepreneur's decisions regarding establishment of a new firm are interdependent with his consumption and saving decisions. Interdependence implies that the innovative entrepreneur's preferences and endowments affect his business decisions. In turn, the innovative entrepreneur's business opportunities affect his consumption and savings decisions in ways that extend beyond standard wealth effects.

The entrepreneurial process also creates tradable financial assets. The inventor's discoveries can take the form of IP such as patents, trademarks, copyrights, and trade secrets. Inventions are transferable assets that provide a means of securing financing for R&D and commercialization. The entrepreneur's start-up may be converted to a transferable asset that is separable from the entrepreneur, providing a means of sharing the returns with investors. Start-ups provide a means for founders to make investments and to obtain financing from family, friends, partners, banks, and venture capitalists. Finally, the new firm is an asset that is financially separable and distinct from the individual entrepreneurs who developed the start-up. The owners of the new firm receive residual returns and residual rights of control.

2.1 The Inventor's Life Cycle: R&D and Commercialization

The independent inventor maximizes life-cycle utility subject to budget constraints in making R&D and commercialization decisions. Because of the speculative nature of R&D and commercialization of inventions, the independent inventor is likely to face financing and liquidity constraints. Accordingly, the inventor's consumption and saving decisions will be interdependent with the inventor's R&D and commercialization decisions.

Discrete-time dynamic programming is useful for modeling life-cycle decision making. The dynamic programming framework can be applied to study discrete decisions, such as commercialization of discoveries and occupational choice, as well as choices of continuous variables such as consumption, saving, and investment. The utility of consumption x_t in each period t is given by the function $u(x_t)$, which is differentiable, increasing, and concave. The individual has a lifetime of length T and a positive discount factor $\delta = \frac{1}{1+\rho}$, where ρ is a subjective rate of time preference. The individual maximizes life-cycle utility $\sum_{t=0}^{T} \delta^t u(x_t)$ subject to budget constraints in each time period and $x_t \geq 0$. Let ω_t represent the entrepreneur's wealth in each period t, with given initial wealth ω_0. Let $\psi(\omega_{T+1})$ be an increasing and concave function denoting the terminal value from bequests.

The individual's budget constraints depend on sequential consumption and saving decisions in response to market opportunities for consumption and saving.

Letting s_t denote savings in period t, consumption equals

$$x_t = \omega_t - s_t. \tag{1}$$

Consider first the life-cycle maximization problem of an individual who cannot borrow. The individual can save $s_t \geq 0$ in period t and earns interest r on savings. The individual's wealth depends on returns to saving,

$$\omega_{t+1} = (1 + r)s_t. \tag{2}$$

The present value of life-cycle utility of an individual of age $t \leq T$ who has wealth ω solves the recursive equation

$$V_t(\omega) = \max_s u(\omega - s) + \delta\, V_{t+1}(s(1 + r)), \tag{3}$$

subject to $\omega \geq s \geq 0$ and $V_{T+1}(\omega_{T+1}) = \psi(\omega_{T+1})$. The individual's savings $s_t^* = s_t^*(\omega)$ depends on the individual's wealth, age, rate of time preference, and the market interest rate. The first order condition for savings s^* is

$$u'(\omega - s^*) = (1 + r)\delta\, V'_{t+1}(s^*(1 + r)). \tag{4}$$

By the envelope theorem, the marginal value of wealth in period t equals the marginal utility of consumption in that period, $V'_t(\omega) = u'(\omega - s^*)$, so that the individual's benefit function is increasing in wealth.[4]

The individual inventor's budget constraints and wealth can be modified to reflect investment and asset accumulation decisions such as developing an invention, commercializing IP, creating a start-up, and establishing a firm. These types of discrete decisions generate stopping rules familiar from search models. Consider, for example, the life-cycle problem of an inventor who must decide when to stop research and commercialize the technology through licensing. I adapt the endogenous growth model of R&D and resource usage in Spulber (1977, 1980). In that model, capital investment and resource exhaustion affect the planner's decision to terminate R&D and introduce an innovation.

An inventor conducts R&D by making an observation θ_t in each period at a cost of k per observation that is incurred in the previous period. The inventor must choose between continuing to conduct R&D and commercializing the invention, so that R&D involves sequential search. The results of R&D, θ_t, are independent and identical draws from the cumulative probability distribution, $F(\theta)$, on the unit interval. The inventor who commercializes the invention can obtain a lump-sum royalty that depends on the quality of the invention, $R(\theta)$, which is increasing in the quality of the invention.

The inventor's wealth is reduced by expenditures on R&D so that the inventor's R&D process can be viewed as a form of asset accumulation. The inventor cannot sell the R&D process and cannot obtain financing for R&D expenditures.

4 Yaari (1964) shows that consumption increases, is constant, or decreases depending on whether the market interest rate, r, is greater than, equal to, or less than the subjective discount rate, ρ.

To continue conducting R&D, the inventor must have sufficient wealth to cover R&D costs in each period, $\omega_t \geq k$. Otherwise, the inventor must commercialize the existing invention without continuing to engage in R&D. Once the inventor has commercialized the invention, the R&D process ceases, so that the decision to commercialize the invention only occurs once.

Consider profit-maximizing R&D as a benchmark. Suppose that investment in the R&D process is not constrained by the inventor's budget constraints and is not embedded in the inventor's life-cycle decision making. A profit-maximizing inventor compares the returns to commercialization, $R(\theta)$, with the returns to continuing R&D. The expected value of the R&D project would then be determined by

$$v = E \max \left\{ R(\theta), -k + \frac{1}{1+r} v \right\}. \tag{5}$$

Because the lump-sum royalty is increasing in the quality of the invention, this determines a unique stopping rule θ^0 that solves

$$R(\theta^0) = -k + \frac{1}{1+r} v, \tag{6}$$

for any given value of the R&D project. The inventor ceases R&D and commercializes high-quality inventions, $\theta \geq \theta^0$, and continues R&D after observing low-quality inventions, $\theta < \theta^0$.

The profit-maximizing stopping rule does not depend on the inventor's personal characteristics such as the inventor's age, discount factor, or wealth. Using the stopping rule, the expected value of the R&D project is

$$v = \left(-k + \frac{1}{1+r} v \right) F(\theta^0) + \int_{\theta^0}^{1} R(\theta) dF(\theta). \tag{7}$$

The expected value of the R&D project that solves the stopping rule is

$$v = (1+r)(R(\theta^0) + k). \tag{8}$$

The profit-maximizing stopping rule is obtained by combing equations (7) and (8),

$$R(\theta^0) = \frac{-k(1+r) + \int_{\theta^0}^{1} R(\theta) dF(\theta)}{1 + r - F(\theta^0)}. \tag{9}$$

The critical value θ^0 is decreasing in the cost of R&D, k, and decreasing in the interest rate, r.

Now, consider the inventor's life-cycle R&D and commercialization decisions. The life-cycle returns to commercializing the invention are obtained by adding the lump-sum royalty to the individual's wealth in the period that commercialization occurs, $V_t(\omega_t + R(\theta_t))$. To simplify notation, we drop the subscripts indicating the current period for wealth and the quality of the invention. The inventor chooses between commercialization and continuing R&D after the outcome is observed. Let $V_t^I(\omega, \theta)$ represent the inventor's expected returns in period t and let $V_t^R(\omega)$ represent the inventor's returns from continuing R&D:

$$V_t^I(\omega, \theta) = \max \left\{ V_t(\omega + R(\theta)), V_t^R(\omega) \right\}. \tag{10}$$

The returns from continuing R&D $V_t^R(\omega)$ are given by

$$V_t^R(\omega) = \max_s u(\omega - k - s) + \delta E V_{t+1}^I(s(1 + r), \theta), \tag{11}$$

subject to $\omega - k \geq s \geq 0$.

The life-cycle framework generates a stopping rule for R&D that depends on the inventor's personal characteristics, including age t, wealth in the current period ω_t, the discount factor δ, and the form of the utility function $u(x)$. This contrasts with the profit-maximizing stopping rule, which does not depend on the inventor's personal characteristics. The inventor's stopping rule equates the benefits from commercializing the invention to the benefits from continuing R&D:

$$V_t(\omega + R(\theta^*)) = V_t^R(\omega). \tag{12}$$

Because the benefit function $V_t(\omega + R(\theta^*))$ is strictly increasing in wealth and the lump-sum royalty is increasing in the quality of the invention, this determines a unique stopping rule, θ^*. The inventor commercializes the invention when the quality of the invention exceeds the threshold so that for $\theta \geq \theta^*$ the inventor receives benefits from the lump-sum royalty, $V_t^I(\omega, \theta) = V_t(\omega + R(\theta))$. The inventor continues R&D when the quality of the invention is less than the threshold so that for $\theta < \theta^*$, the inventor's return equals the value of continuing R&D, $V_t^I(\omega, \theta) = V_t^R(\omega)$. It follows from the stopping rule in equation (12) that for all $\theta < \theta^*$ the inventor receives the benefits of the lump-sum royalty evaluated at the threshold quality level, $V_t^I(\omega, \theta) = V_t(\omega + R(\theta^*))$.

The effect of the inventor's wealth on the stopping rule is

$$\frac{\partial \theta^*}{\partial \omega} = \frac{V_t^{R\prime}(\omega) - V_t^{\prime}(\omega + R(\theta^*))}{V_t^{\prime}(\omega + R(\theta^*)) R^{\prime}(\theta^*)}. \tag{13}$$

The critical value θ^* is increasing (decreasing) in the inventor's wealth if the marginal effect of wealth on the value of continuing R&D is greater than (less than) the marginal effect of wealth on the value of commercializing the current invention.

We can rewrite the value of continuing R&D using the life-cycle benefit function (3) and the stopping rule θ^*,

$$V_t^R(\omega) = \max_s u(\omega - k - s) + \delta \Bigg[V_{t+1}^R((1 + r)s) F(\theta^*) + \int_{\theta^*}^1 V_{t+1}((1 + r)s + R(\theta)) dF(\theta) \Bigg], \tag{14}$$

subject to $\omega - k \geq s \geq 0$. The first-order condition for savings s^{**} when the inventor continues R&D is

$$u'(\omega - k - s^{**}) = (1+r)\delta\left[V_t^{R\prime}((1+r)s^{**})F(\theta^*) + \int_{\theta^*}^{1} V_{t+1}'((1+r)s^{**} + R(\theta))dF(\theta)\right],$$

when the constraints $\omega - k \geq s \geq 0$ are not binding.

The inventor's wealth increases the value of continuing R&D, $V_t^{R\prime}(\omega) = u'(\omega - k - s^{**}) > 0$, by the envelope theorem. The inventor's wealth also increases the value of commercialization, $V_t'(\omega + R(\theta^*)) = u'(\omega + R(\theta^*) - s^*)$, where the individual with wealth $\omega + R(\theta^*)$ saves s^*. The effect of wealth on the inventor's stopping rule can be written as

$$\frac{\partial \theta^*}{\partial \omega} = \frac{u'(\omega - k - s^{**}) - u'(\omega + R(\theta^*) - s^*)}{u'(\omega + R(\theta^*) - s^*)R'(\theta^*)}. \tag{15}$$

The critical value θ^* is increasing (decreasing) in the inventor's wealth ω if the cost of R&D plus savings when continuing R&D, $k + s^{**}$, is greater than (less than) savings net of the royalty received from commercializing the invention, $s^* - R(\theta^*)$.

The individual inventor's R&D and commercialization decisions maximize his expected discounted utility of consumption over his life cycle subject to financing and liquidity constraints. The life-cycle analysis of the inventor's R&D and commercialization decisions suggests the following general interdependence theorem.

Interdependence Theorem 1. If the inventor faces financing and liquidity constraints, the inventor's consumption and saving decisions and the inventor's R&D and commercialization decisions are financially interdependent.

The main implication of interdependence is that the inventor's commercialization decisions are affected by personal characteristics such as age, wealth, risk aversion, and rate of time preference. In turn, the inventor's asset accumulation decisions are affected by the success of R&D and the effect of the quality of the invention on market returns to commercialization. The inventor could achieve financial separation if the project could be sold to a profit-maximizing firm. Because the project is interdependent with the inventor's life-cycle utility maximization, the quality threshold generally will differ from the profit-maximizing threshold.

2.2 The Life-Cycle Theory of Entrepreneurship: Creating the Start-Up

The innovative entrepreneur creates a start-up and establishes a new firm as part of overall life-cycle asset accumulation decisions. Financing and liquidity constraints are particularly challenging for innovative entrepreneurs because they offer new products, technologies, and business methods. As a consequence of these financing and liquidity constraints, the entrepreneur's consumption-savings decisions will be interdependent with business decisions associated with launching the start-up and establishing the firm. Considering the innovative entrepreneur's life-cycle decision making helps answer the Question of Entrepreneurial Motivation.

Building the Start-up

In the first stage of the entrepreneurship process, the inventor chooses whether or not to become an entrepreneur or to transfer inventions to an independent entrepreneur. In the second, stage, the innovative entrepreneur creates and develops a *start-up*, an emergent enterprise that begins to apply inventions and implement the new strategy. The entrepreneur contributes directly to the start-up, providing IP, human capital, business strategy, effort, and financial capital. The start-up is an institutional vehicle for the entrepreneur to identify market opportunities, form an organization, obtain and develop IP, raise financial capital, and attract human capital.

In addition to being a mechanism for establishing the firm, the start-up is also a financial asset. The start-up embodies the invention, initiative, and investment contributed by the innovative entrepreneur but is not yet separate from the entrepreneur. Myers (1999, p. 134) observes: "The company starts up with human capital. As and if it succeeds, an intangible real asset is created: the technology is embodied in product design; the production process used, and in the product's reputation with customers." Then, as Myers (1999, p. 134) points out: "This real asset separates from the people who created it and can in due course be appropriated by financial investors. The venture could not raise outside money otherwise." Myers expresses concern that once the asset exists separately, the entrepreneur will lose bargaining power to outside investors. Myers (1999, 2000) also notes out that for innovative start-ups, the information costs and potential for adverse selection require concentrated ownership. Going public provides incentives to the innovative entrepreneur because dispersed ownership dilutes the bargaining power of outside equity investors (Myers, 1999, 2000). Innovative firms in high tech may go public early to reduce the ex post bargaining power of outside investors (Myers, 1999).

The entrepreneur owns the start-up and has rights of residual control and rights to residual returns. The start-up's decisions will depend on the entrepreneur's age, income, wealth, preferences (risk aversion, discount rate), expectations, human capital, and IP rights. The entrepreneur's consumption decisions will be affected not only by the pattern of income from the start-up but also by the start-up's technology, assets, transaction costs, investment requirements, sales, reputation, and business relationships.

The entrepreneur's decision to create a start-up is affected by wealth and access to financing. Evans and Jovanovic (1989) find that entrepreneurs face liquidity constraints and a potential entrepreneur's wealth positively affects the likelihood of starting a business. They observe that entrepreneurs with less wealth devote a greater proportion of their assets to their business, although as firms grow the importance of initial wealth constraints tends to diminish. Kerr and Nanda (2011) find that if the entrepreneur is liquidity constrained, then the propensity for entrepreneurship depends on an individual's wealth. However, they raise concerns about spurious correlations because accumulation of wealth by individuals is endogenous. An individual's wealth accumulation might depend, for example, on effort, risk taking, career choices, and business judgments. Kerr and Nanda (2011) also point out that entrepreneurial abilities, preferences for entrepreneurship, or social connections may be correlated with wealth. For example, if entrepreneurship involves enjoyable activities that are consumption goods, analogous to leisure or luxuries, wealth effects on consumption can generate a positive correlation between wealth and entrepreneurship that are not related to financing constraints (see Hurst and Lusardi, 2004).

It is reasonable to suppose that newly established family businesses of all kinds encounter financing constraints, whether in developed or developing economies. Even without entering into business, households need credit. Households make many financial decisions related to their consumption objectives, including borrowing in the form of mortgages, auto loans, bank loans, and credit cards.[5] In addition to consumption-related financing, households engage in business-related financing. Samphantharak and Townsend's (2010) analysis of household finance in developing countries suggests that households function as firms because they engage in farm and nonfarm production and manage a collection of assets.[6] Farms are an important example of family businesses in developed as well as developing economies. In North America, Allen and Lueck (2002, p. 24) find that "farm numbers have declined, farm size has increased, and technological changes have converted farms into capital-intensive enterprises, yet family farming still dominates in most farming sectors." Their study implicitly assumes that the Fisher Separation Theorem applies because they posit profit maximization by family farms (Allen and Lueck, 2002, p. 171).

The entrepreneur often contributes personal resources to the start-up including financial capital, human capital, IP, and managerial effort. The entrepreneur must pass through the start-up phase when he faces market limitations in securing financing, human capital, IP, suppliers, and customers. The start-up is not a firm

5 See Campbell (2006) and the references therein.

6 Samphantharak and Townsend (2010) argue that the household in a developing country is analogous to a corporation because its net income is the household's disposable income and because it pays dividends to its owners in the form of consumption. Although the analogy is useful for purposes of illustration, it is unlikely that households in developing countries satisfy the Fisher Separation Theorem and operate as corporations. It is likely that for households in developing countries, market constraints and income limits prevent the separation of the consumption objectives of the owners and the profit objectives of the corporation.

by definition because the start-up's objectives are not financially separable from the entrepreneur's personal consumption objectives. As a result of the trade-offs between business development and personal consumption, the start-up generally is not a profit-maximizing enterprise.

The Start-up and the Fisher Separation Theorem

Consider a model of an innovative entrepreneur who develops a start-up enterprise. It is well known that a firm will immediately choose the present-value maximizing level of investment. The firm will only approach the optimal investment level gradually in the presence of adjustment costs, uncertainty, or financing constraints.[7] An entrepreneur investing in a start-up enterprise who faces financing constraints will invest gradually because of imperfect financial separation of consumption and saving decisions from investment decisions. The interdependence of the entrepreneur's consumption decisions and the business decisions of the start-up enterprise is the converse of the Fisher Separation Theorem (Fisher, 1906, 1907, 1930).[8]

It is helpful to review the basic Fisher Separation Theorem. The Fisher Separation Theorem shows that a firm's consumer-owners prefer that the firm maximize profits. The firm is owned by consumers who have preferences over current and future consumption bundles. The consumer-owners consume and save through product markets and financial markets and do not use the firm to allocate resources over time. The profit-maximizing firm sells its products in competitive product markets and finances its investments in competitive financial markets. The Fisher Separation Theorem demonstrates that the firm's optimal investment decisions are independent of the preferences of its owners and independent of how the investment is financed.

Consider a profit-maximizing neoclassical firm that makes financing and investment decisions in a two-period setting. The firm has a commonly known technology $q = H(k)$ that produces a good, q, in the second period given durable capital investment, k, in the first period. Assume that the firm has no initial endowment and that it can fully finance its investment by borrowing money at interest rate r. The firm purchases k units of the consumption good to invest in production. The firm's investment decision will be the same regardless of whether or not it has an initial endowment of the consumption good. The firm's profit in present-value terms is

7 Adjustment cost studies suggest that the costs of integrating new investment in production processes depend on the speed at which the investment is introduced; see Eisner and Strotz (1963) and Spulber and Becker (1983). Zeira (1987) shows that uncertainty about a threshold investment results in gradual investment.

8 The Fisher Separation Theorem assumes price-taking behavior by firms and consumers and the presence of neoclassical markets for consumer goods, investment goods, and financial capital. The Fisher Separation Theorem also assumes that there are no transaction costs and that there exists a complete set of competitive markets. The Fisher Separation Theorem can be extended to more general environments with price-setting firms and transaction costs; see Spulber (2009a).

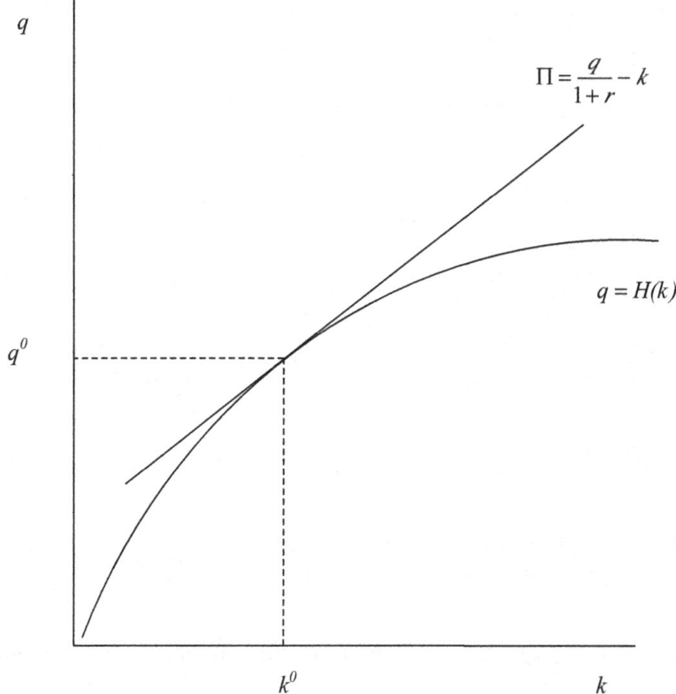

Figure 2.1. Profit-maximizing investment by a price-taking firm with access to capital markets.

$\Pi = \frac{H(k)}{1+r} - k$. The firm's optimal investment decision equates the marginal revenue product of investment to the per-unit cost of investment,

$$H'(k^0) = 1 + r. \tag{16}$$

The per-unit cost of investment is the purchase price of the consumption good times the cost of borrowing. The profit-maximizing investment is shown in Figure 2.1.

Now consider a consumer who lives for two periods and consumes the same good in each period. Let x and X represent the amounts of the good consumed in the two periods. Suppose that the consumer does not derive benefits from bequests. In the standard Robinson Crusoe economy, the consumer does not have access to product markets and owns and operates the technology $q = H(k)$. Suppose further that there is no capital market so that there is no possibility of borrowing or lending money. Suppose further that there is no possibility of buying or selling the consumption good. The production technology and the consumer's initial endowment, ω, generate a production possibilities frontier, $X = H(\omega - x)$. Then, the consumer will manage production using the technology to maximize the consumer's benefit subject to the production function. Under autarky, the consumer solves

$$\max_{x,X}\ u(x) + \delta u(X)$$

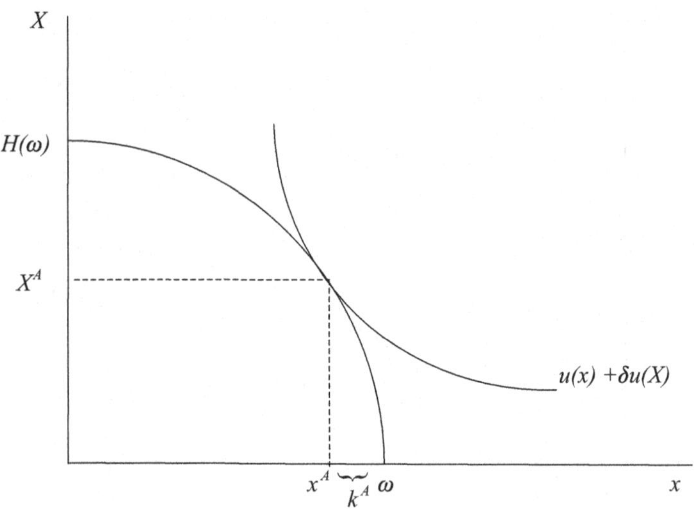

Figure 2.2. The Robinson Crusoe equilibrium with consumption and investment by a consumer who owns the technology.

subject to $X = H(\omega - x)$ and $x \leq \omega$. The optimal consumption x^A solves

$$u'(x^A) = H'(\omega - x^A)\delta u'(X^A).$$

When there is an interior solution, $x^A < \omega$, second period consumption is $X^A = H(\omega - x^A)$, and investment equals $k^A = \omega - x^A$. The solution for the Robinson Crusoe economy is represented in Figure 2.2 with first-period consumption on the x axis and second-period consumption on the y axis.

Consider now the situation in which the individual is an entrepreneur who owns the firm. Assume that both the consumer and the firm have access to product and capital markets. Then, the Fisher Separation Theorem shows that the firm's investment decision is independent of the preferences of its consumer-owner. The consumer-owner wishes to obtain the greatest present value of profit so the firm chooses the profit-maximizing investment. Then, taking the firm's profit as given, the consumer maximizes utility subject to the consumer's endowment plus the firm's profit. The consumer problem is

$$\max_{x, X} u(x) + \delta U(X)$$

subject to

$$x + \frac{1}{1+r}X = \omega + \Pi.$$

The consumer's first-order condition is

$$u'(x^*) = (1+r)\delta u'(X^*),$$

where the consumer's second-period consumption is equal to $X^* = (1 + r)(\omega - x^*) + (1 + r)\Pi$.

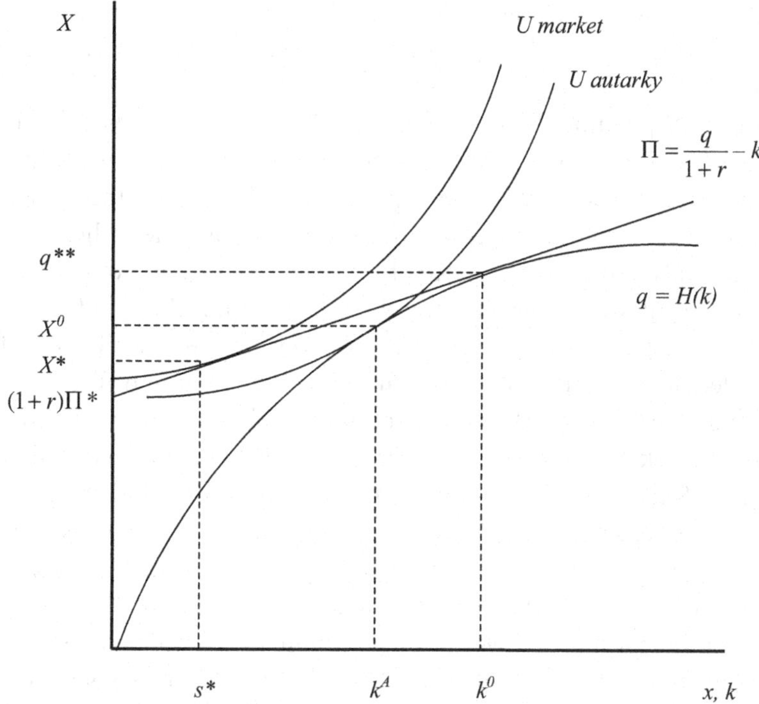

Figure 2.3. The Fisher Separation Theorem shows that the firm's optimal investment decision is independent of the preferences of a consumer-owner.

The Fisher Separation Theorem demonstrates that the consumer is better off letting the firm choose the profit-maximizing investment instead of the utility-maximizing investment. This is depicted in Figure 2.3. The consumer has a different consumption profile in the Robinson Crusoe economy from that in the market economy. With initial endowment ω, the consumer invests k^A and consumes $x^A = \omega - k^A$ and $X^A = H(\omega - k^A)$ in the Robinson Crusoe economy. The consumer in the market economy consumes $x^* = \omega - s^*$ and $X^* = (1 + r)s^* + (1 + r)\Pi^*$, where s^* is savings. The consumer in the case depicted in Figure 2.3 has a higher amount of consumption in the first period in the market economy as compared to the Robinson Crusoe economy, because the consumer uses less of the initial endowment, $k^0 > k^A$.

In the case shown, the consumer consumes less in the second period in the market economy as compared to the Robinson Crusoe economy but is still better off. The benefits of additional consumption in the first period outweigh the benefits of less consumption in the second period. The additional consumption in the first period occurs because the firm purchases more of the investment good in the market than the consumer supplies to the market $s^* < k^A < k^0$. The firm invests more in the market economy than in the Robinson Crusoe economy in the case shown in Figure 2.3. Also in this case, the consumer supplies less of the endowment of the investment good in the market economy than in the Robinson Crusoe economy.

This illustrates how the market for goods and the market for capital investment allow the decoupling of the firm's investment decision and the consumer's saving and consumption decisions.

The Fisher Separation Theorem depends critically on the existence of three types of markets: investment goods, consumption goods, and financial capital. This dependence is obscured by the triple nature of the good that can be used for investment, consumption, and financial transactions. The Fisher Separation Theorem depends also on the absence of transaction costs. Not only are markets established exogenously but also neither the consumer nor the firm face a bid-ask spread in their market transactions. Again, the consumer is made better off when consumer decisions and firm decisions are separated because of the presence of outside opportunities. Both the consumer and the firm realize gains from trade through their market transactions with other unobserved consumers and firms.

The Fisher Separation Theorem explains why consumption and firm investment decisions can be separated. The consumer and the firm achieve gains from trade because they do not encounter transaction costs. Both the consumer-owner and the firm are price takers. The firm chooses an investment and output plan taking prices as given, and the consumer solves a consumption-saving problem. The decision of the consumer and the firm are separable because both the consumer and the firm realize gains from trade with other trading partners. The consumer wants the firm to maximize its profit because the consumer is only interested in the firm as a source of income. The consumer makes consumption and saving transactions, and the firm makes sales and investment transactions in established markets.

Now consider the situation in which the consumer also is an innovative entrepreneur who creates a start-up. Suppose that the entrepreneur's technology $q = h(k, \theta)$ includes IP θ that is not observable to potential investors. The entrepreneur then has imperfect access to the capital market because he cannot secure credit on the basis of future production. As a consequence, the entrepreneur faces an asymmetric credit constraint. The consumer-entrepreneur can lend to the capital market at interest rate r but cannot borrow from the capital market to finance the start-up's investment. The consumer-entrepreneur, or equivalently the start-up, cannot borrow because the loan cannot be secured by the start-up's future earnings. Accordingly, the start-up's investment is restricted by the consumer-entrepreneur's initial endowment, ω.

As a result, the entrepreneur's consumption objectives are closely connected with the business objectives of the start-up. The entrepreneur's credit-constrained problem is thus

$$V(\omega) = \max_{k,x,X} u(x) + \delta U(X),$$

subject to $s \geq 0$, $x + s + k = \omega$, and $X = (1 + r)s + h(k, \theta)$. If the entrepreneur's savings constraint is nonbinding, $s \geq 0$, the Fisher Separation Theorem holds (see Figure 2.4). Investment equals the profit-maximizing investment level, k^0. The start-up becomes a firm because its objectives are separate from those of its owner.

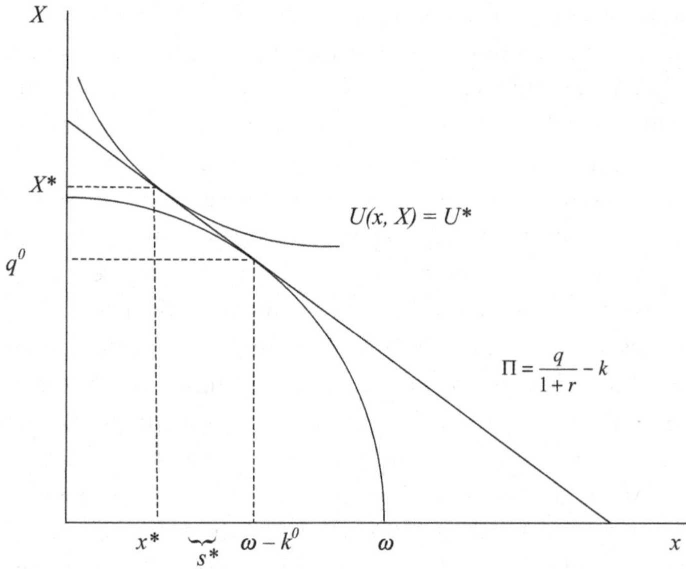

Figure 2.4. The savings constraint is nonbinding, and the start-up's business objectives are separable from the consumption objectives of the entrepreneur.

The foundational shift occurs immediately, and the entrepreneur becomes an owner of the firm.

Conversely, the entrepreneur's savings constraint may be binding, $s = 0$. Then, the Fisher Separation Theorem does not hold, and the consumer is forced back to the autarky outcome, U^0. This situation is shown in Figure 2.5. The start-up is not

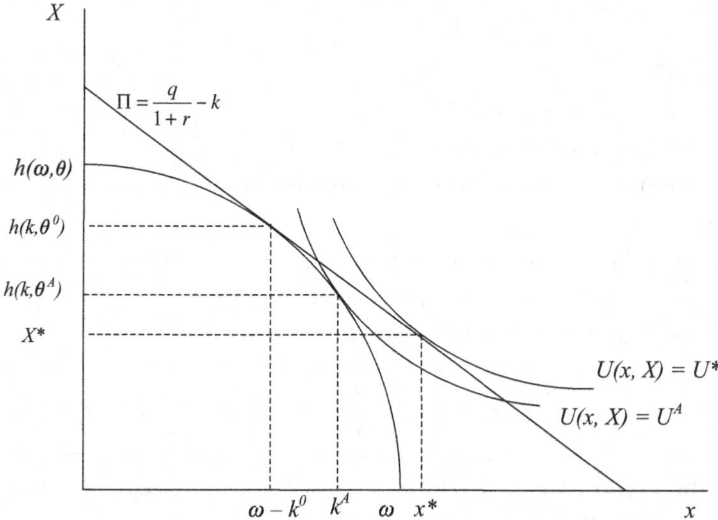

Figure 2.5. The savings constraint is binding, and the start-up's business objectives are not separable from the consumption objectives of the entrepreneur.

a firm because its business objectives are not separable from those of its owner. The start-up's investment depends on the consumer's preferences and wealth.

The entrepreneur's preferences $U(x, X)$, endowment ω, and technology $q = h(k, \theta)$, determine whether or not the entrepreneur's savings constraint is binding. When the entrepreneur is sufficiently patient, the entrepreneur does not need as much endowment to self finance the start-up and cover first-period consumption. When the new technology is sufficiently productive, the entrepreneur can trade off a reduction in first-period consumption in return for an increase in second-period consumption resulting from the additional income from the firm.

All this suggests that the entrepreneur faces a *continuum* of possibilities depending on the size of the initial endowment, all other things equal. As the endowment increases, the financial constraint is relaxed. For small initial endowments, the entrepreneur's investment and consumption-saving decisions are far from their optimal levels. As the initial endowment increases, the entrepreneur's investment and consumption-saving decisions approach their optimal levels. Finally, with a sufficient large initial endowment, the entrepreneur's investment and consumption-saving decisions reach their optimal levels, and the Fisher Separation Theorem is satisfied.

Thus, when the entrepreneur's initial endowment is sufficiently large, the entrepreneur can self-finance the start-up and establish a firm. When the entrepreneur's initial endowment is not sufficiently large, the entrepreneur must work for some time on the start-up subject to financial constraints before establishing a new firm. If the entrepreneur builds up investment through the start-up's earnings and external financing, the entrepreneur can travel down the continuum from a financially constrained start-up to financial separation and establishment of the new firm.

The Entrepreneur's Investment Decisions

Consider the effects of financial constraints on the entrepreneur's investment decisions in the life-cycle model. Production involves a one-period lag after the initial investment. The production function $h(k, \theta)$ is differentiable, increasing, and concave in k, and $h(0, \theta) = 0$. The production function is increasing in the technology parameter θ.

In the absence of frictions, a profit-maximizing firm will immediately reach the optimal capital stock. The optimal capital stock maximizes the net present value of profits from production in all future periods,

$$k^0 = \arg\max_k \frac{1}{r} h(k, \theta) - k. \tag{17}$$

Therefore, the present-value maximizing investment level equates the marginal product of capital to the interest rate,

$$h_k(k^0, \theta) = r. \tag{18}$$

The optimal investment level depends on the rate of interest and the technological parameter. The present value of profits equals $\pi = \frac{1}{r}h(k^0, \theta) - k^0$.

Suppose that the entrepreneur establishes a start-up by investing capital and begins producing and selling output. Suppose that the start-up becomes a firm when capital investment reaches the optimal investment level, k^0. The entrepreneur cannot obtain financing for investment because the value of the new technology θ is difficult to observe.[9] Also, suppose that the entrepreneur cannot sell the start-up to investors because the new technology is not fully transferable.

The entrepreneur's budget constraints depend on sequential consumption and saving decisions in response to market opportunities for consumption and saving. The entrepreneur can save $s_t \geq 0$ in period t and earns interest r on savings. The entrepreneur invests $k_{t+1} - k_t \geq 0$ in period t. Consumption in period t equals the entrepreneur's initial wealth plus output produced in period t minus savings and investment,

$$x_t = \omega_t + h(k_t, \theta) - s_t - (k_{t+1} - k_t). \tag{19}$$

The entrepreneur's wealth depends on returns to savings,

$$\omega_{t+1} = (1 + r)s_t. \tag{20}$$

The present value of life-cycle utility of an entrepreneur of age $t \leq T$ who has wealth ω solves the recursive equation

$$V_t(\omega_t, k_t) = \max_{s,k} u(\omega_t + h(k_t, \theta) - s - (k - k_t)) + \delta V_{t+1}(s(1 + r), k), \tag{21}$$

subject to $x_t \geq 0$, $s_t \geq 0$, and $k \geq k_t$. Also, ω_0 is given, $k_0 = 0$, and $V_{T+1}(\omega_{T+1}, k_{T+1}) = \psi(\omega_{T+1}, k_{T+1})$.

Let $\lambda_t \geq 0$ be the multiplier on the savings constraint, $s_t \geq 0$. The first-order conditions for savings s^* and capital k^* are

$$\begin{aligned} &u'(\omega_t + h(k_t, \theta) - s_{t+1}{}^* - (k_{t+1}{}^* - k_t)) - \lambda_t \\ &= (1 + r)\delta \frac{\partial V_{t+1}(s_{t+1}{}^*(1 + r), k_{t+1}{}^*)}{\partial \omega}, \end{aligned} \tag{22}$$

$$u'(\omega_t + h(k_t, \theta) - s_{t+1}{}^* - (k_{t+1}{}^* - k_t)) = \delta \frac{\partial V_{t+1}(s_{t+1}{}^*(1 + r), k_{t+1}{}^*)}{\partial k}. \tag{23}$$

By the envelope theorem, the marginal value of wealth in period t equals the marginal utility of consumption in that period,

$$\frac{\partial V_t(\omega_t, k_t)}{\partial \omega} = u'(\omega_t + h(k_t, \theta) - s_{t+1}{}^* - (k_{t+1}{}^* - k_t)). \tag{24}$$

9 Alternatively, we could assume that the entrepreneur has access to external capital but must pay a premium that reflects the absence of collateral and asymmetric information about the start-up. The premium can be an increasing function of non-collateralized debt (Gentry and Hubbard, 2004). The interest cost of external debt is $\rho > r$, which is an increasing function of external financing, $\rho = \rho(k)$.

Also, by the envelope theorem, if the entrepreneur invests in period t, the marginal value of the capital stock in period t equals the marginal utility of consumption times the marginal product of capital,[10]

$$\text{(25)} \qquad \frac{\partial V_t(\omega_t, k_t)}{\partial k} = u'(\omega_t + h(k_t, \theta) - s_{t+1}{}^* - (k_{t+1}{}^* - k_t))(h_k(k_t, \theta) + 1).$$

The entrepreneur's investment gradually approaches the optimum when the entrepreneur would prefer to borrow money to fund investment. Using the first-order conditions (22) and (23), a binding savings constraint implies that

$$(1 + r)\frac{\partial V_{t+1}(0, k_{t+1}{}^*)}{\partial \omega} < \frac{\partial V_{t+1}(0, k_{t+1}{}^*)}{\partial k}.$$

Simplifying this expression using equations (24) and (25) implies that the marginal product of capital is greater than the rate of interest,

$$r < h_k(k_{t+1}{}^*, \theta).$$

This implies that the capital stock is less than the unconstrained optimum, $k_{t+1}{}^* < k^0$.

The result that $k_{t+1}{}^* < k^0$ implies that the entrepreneur faced with borrowing constraints gradually approaches the optimum investment level. The start-up gradually approaches the critical level of investment needed to establish a firm. Because of the entrepreneur's borrowing constraint, investment depends on the individual's age, wealth, and consumption preferences. In turn, the entrepreneur's consumption and saving decisions depend on the start-up's returns. This implies the following interdependence theorem.

Interdependence Theorem 2. If the entrepreneur faces financing and liquidity constraints, the entrepreneur's consumption and saving decisions and the start-up's investment decisions are financially interdependent.

2.3 The Life-Cycle Theory of Entrepreneurship: Investment and Occupational Choice

Answering the Question of Entrepreneurial Motivation requires understanding the individual entrepreneur's life-cycle decisions regarding investment and occupational choice. The entrepreneur faces a complex bundle of personal decisions that interact with the business decisions required to create a start-up and establish

10 If the entrepreneur does not invest in period t, $k_{t+1} = k_t$, the marginal value of the capital stock in period t equals the marginal utility of consumption times the marginal product of capital plus the discounted marginal value of capital in the next period,

$$\frac{\partial V_t(\omega_t, k_t)}{\partial k} = u'(\omega_t + h(k_t, \theta) - s^*)h_k(k_t, \theta) + \delta\frac{\partial V_{t+1}(s(1 + r), k_t)}{\partial k}.$$

a firm.[11] In turn, the entrepreneur's business decisions affect his investment and occupational choices.

Entrepreneurship and Investment

The life-cycle theory of entrepreneurship suggests that creating the start-up and establishing the firm are forms of asset accumulation. This implies that the entrepreneur must consider the returns to alternative assets, including human capital, real estate, and financial assets such as stocks, bonds, and mutual funds. In creating the start-up and building the firm, the entrepreneur turns to self-financing and seeks help from friends and family. Bhidé (1999) interviewed entrepreneur-owners of 100 of the fastest growing, privately held entrants and found that they had median start-up capital of $10,000. Bhidé (1999) observed that 80 percent financed their ventures from their personal savings and by borrowing, with only about 5 percent relying on venture capitalists. In addition, the entrepreneur supplies ideas, IP, effort, judgment, and management to the start-up.

Some researchers have questioned whether entrepreneurs are motivated by financial rewards by comparing the returns to private equity in the start-up and the new firm to the returns for other types of financial investments. According to the "private equity premium puzzle," entrepreneurs may not be sufficiently diversified because they hold an inefficiently large share of their financial portfolio in their own business.[12] Because private equity does not offer greater returns than publicly traded equity, lack of portfolio diversification would seem to imply that business owners bear excessive risk given the returns to investment in private equity. Some small business owners are entrepreneurs, so that the private equity premium puzzle suggests that entrepreneurs bear excessive risk because of a lack of diversification.

Schumpeter emphasizes the importance of financing. Schumpeter (1934, p. 102) notes that the entrepreneur "in principle and as a rule – does need credit, in the sense of a temporary transfer to him of purchasing power, in order to produce at all, to be able to carry out his new combinations, to *become* an entrepreneur."[13] The entrepreneur "is the typical debtor in capitalist society" and indeed "no one else is a debtor by the nature of his economic function."[14] The entrepreneur is different from a capitalist, although an individual with sufficient income and wealth may perform both functions.

Adverse selection in entrepreneurial finance likely results in imperfect separation of the business and consumption-saving decisions of entrepreneurs. The

11 See Evans and Jovanovic (1989), Hubbard and Kashyap (1992), King and Levine (1993), Gentry and Hubbard (2004), Buera (2009), and Vereshchagina and Hopenhayn (2009).

12 See Gentry and Hubbard (2001), Moskowitz and Vissing-Jorgensen (2002), and Heaton and Lucas (2000).

13 Schumpeter (1934, p. 102), emphasis in original.

14 Schumpeter (1934, pp. 102–103).

first-time entrepreneur is likely to have no track record in contrast to established firms. The entrepreneur may have better information about his abilities and other personal characteristics than creditors do. Also, because innovative start-ups offer new products, production processes, and business methods, the entrepreneur is likely to be better informed about the innovation than creditors are. The "pecking order" rule of Myers and Majluf (1984) states that with asymmetric information, insiders who are better informed invest their own funds before turning to outside financing. This general rule applies with particular force to innovative start-ups and helps explain why entrepreneurs invest their own funds before turning to outside financing.

The problem of moral hazard also leads to a "pecking order" for investment. When owners provide unobservable management effort, they have better information about the performance of the firm than outside investors. Because these owners are better informed, they must invest their own funds before turning to outside financing. Entrepreneurs typically provide management effort in building the start-up so that they have an incentive to provide their own investment funds. Because of limited liability, the entrepreneur's income and wealth affect the form of loan contract when there is moral hazard.[15]

The market for corporate control implies that owners who provide management effort will concentrate their holdings to maintain management control. Turning to outside investors for equity financing will expose the enterprise to takeovers aimed at replacing management. Owners who believe that their management of the enterprise will provide greater returns than divestiture will concentrate their holdings.

The entrepreneur's equity need not be generated by an investment portfolio choice. Instead, the entrepreneur builds equity through innovation, productive effort, and business judgment rather than through financial investment. Equity is the entrepreneur's return rather than an indicator of the entrepreneur's investment. Gentry and Hubbard (2004) show that entrepreneurship is an important means of building wealth in comparison with other sources of earnings.[16] Entrepreneurs have greater wealth per capita than non-entrepreneurs. Gentry and Hubbard (2004, p. 7) conclude that "differences in how households decide on investing in active business assets and other assets may provide important modifications for life-cycle models that focus on saving through financial assets." Their results suggest that "some portion of the pattern that wealth-income ratios rise with income may be related to entrepreneurial selection and investment decisions." Campanale (2009)

15 See Poblete and Spulber (2012).

16 Gentry and Hubbard define an entrepreneur as a household that owns one or more businesses with a total market value of at least $5,000. They classify 8.7 percent of households as entrepreneurs on the basis of the 1989 Survey of Consumer Finances: "Overall, the 8.7 percent of households defined as entrepreneurs own 37.7 percent of assets and 39.0 percent of net worth" Gentry and Hubbard (2004, p. 5).

finds that entrepreneurial investment is optimal even with small negative excess returns in comparison to a diversified portfolio by taking into account the returns to establishing a business, including the returns to human capital.

The accumulation of wealth by entrepreneurs then raises the question of why entrepreneurs would continue to hold equity in their own enterprises rather than liquidating the equity so as to diversify their portfolios.[17] Gentry and Hubbard (2004, p. 26) suggest that this is consistent with imperfect access to capital markets combined with a preference for control that increases as the entrepreneur grows older. As the business grows, the entrepreneur cannot diversify because of asymmetric information in comparison to investors. The business then becomes a larger part of the entrepreneur's portfolio. Diversification means not only sharing returns with investors but also ceding control. As the entrepreneur builds the start-up and establishes the firm, he may wish to bear greater portfolio risk in return for maintaining control over the business.

Mondragón-Vélez (2009) considers the effects of age and education on the transition to entrepreneurship, noting that wealth is correlated with age and education. Emphasizing life-cycle choices, Mondragón-Vélez shows that the levels of wealth matter because changes in wealth have different effects on the likelihood of transition to entrepreneurship depending on the age and education of individuals. These results extend the analysis of Hurst and Lusardi (2004) who find aggregate wealth effects only at the top of the wealth distribution. An individual's liquidity constraints in establishing a firm affect the likelihood of becoming an entrepreneur (Mondragón-Vélez, 2010). The precautionary demand for savings by those consumers who are liquidity-constrained modifies the predictions of the traditional life-cycle consumption theory and helps explain patterns of saving behavior (Deaton, 1991; Gourinchas and Parker, 2002).

Life-cycle consumption models tend to perform less well in predicting saving patterns among the wealthy. This may be because these models generally do not consider entrepreneurial investment. Entrepreneurs own a substantial share of total wealth and income, and their share increases throughout the wealth and income distributions, so that entrepreneurship affects the pattern of saving in the economy, according to Gentry and Hubbard (2004). Entrepreneurs' wealth-income ratios and saving rates are higher than other households after controlling for age and other demographic factors (Gentry and Hubbard, 2004). They emphasize that "interdependence between entrepreneurs' investment and saving decisions... would affect the consumption choices and the portfolio allocation of both current and potential entrepreneurs" (Gentry and Hubbard, 2004, p. 1).

Financial market constraints affect the creation of start-ups and the launch of new firms. Kerr and Nanda (2011) suggest that start-ups can be classified along two dimensions: innovative technology and capital investment. Kerr and Nanda

17 Holmes and Schmitz (1990, 1995, 1996) consider the role of the entrepreneur in business turnovers.

(2009) find that improved access to credit from U.S. branch banking deregulation contributed to creative destruction, increasing both rates of entrepreneurship and exit rates of incumbent firms, although productivity effects are difficult to identify. Kerr and Nanda (2010) further show that U.S. branch banking deregulation resulted in greater entry rates of small firms, and among firms that survived at least four years a greater proportion of firms entered the market at or near their maximum size.

Because entrepreneurs differ from corporate borrowers, entrepreneurial finance should be distinguished from corporate finance. Entrepreneurs employ their personal funds and personal credit to finance their business. They obtain credit from family and friends as personal loans. They also finance the business through bank loans and venture capital. One indicator of entrepreneurial finance is small business credit. Small businesses often obtain credit on the basis of the endowments and personal credit histories of their owners (Mach and Wolken, 2006). Lopez (1986) finds: "[T]he financial resources of the small firm are arguably intertwined with those of the household. This interdependence of resources suggests a theoretical model, where the small business activity is integrated into the household utility maximization model."[18] The effects of income on entrepreneurship also appear in studies of taxation. Gentry and Hubbard (2000) find that a progressive income tax schedule with imperfect offsets for losses can discourage individuals from entering entrepreneurship.[19]

Statistics about small businesses can provide information about entrepreneurship because new businesses tend to be small.[20] This indicator is necessarily imperfect because the set of small businesses includes not only new entrants but also existing firms that have remained small and larger existing firms that have gotten smaller.[21] According to the U.S. Small Business Administration (SBA, 2009, p. 1), small businesses "employ about half of the nation's private sector work force, and provide half of the nation's nonfarm, private real gross domestic product (GDP)." Since the mid-1990s, "small businesses have generally created 60 to 80 percent of the net new employment" with similar shares of job losses in economic downturns.[22] The total number of private firms is divided between those without employees,

18 See also López (1985) on the economic decisions of self-employed producers.

19 See also Meh (2005).

20 The 2003 Survey of Small Business Finances (SSBF) survey of U.S. small businesses conducted by the Board of Governors of the Federal Reserve covers firms with less than 500 employees; http://www.federalreserve.gov.

21 Empirical studies tend to employ very different definitions of the entrepreneurial firms. Some studies define entrepreneurial firms as new entrants, which is consistent with the definition emphasized here. Other studies simply define entrepreneurial firms as small businesses that have some number of employees below a threshold, regardless of the age of the business. Still other studies define entrepreneurial firms as young firms regardless of size, for example, firms that are less than seven years old. See van Praag and Versloot (2007) for an overview.

22 SBA (2009, p. 9).

more than 23 million, and those with employees, more than 6 million.[23] It is estimated that about 600,000 firms with employees enter and exit the economy each year, with a net entry of 30,000 firms with employees.[24]

The complexities of portfolio optimization suggest the need for further consideration of entrepreneurial investment. Studies of consumption and saving behavior offer some indirect insights into entrepreneurship. The entrepreneur's private equity holdings, which are concentrated in his own business, interact with other portfolio investments. Cocco et al. (2005) show that if risky labor income substitutes for riskless asset holdings, the share invested in equities increases early in life and decreases later in life. Although entrepreneurial income is risky, it may substitute for other types of assets.

Occupational Choice

There are millions of entrepreneurs in the U.S. economy. The U.S. Small Business Administration estimates that there were more than 612,000 new firms with employees in the year 2000 (SBA, 2001). Reynolds (1997a, 2000) estimates that about 4 percent of the U.S. labor force participates in the entrepreneurial process (with the labor force exceeding 110 million people). Reynolds et al. (2004) estimate that in the year 2000 there were more than 11.8 million "nascent entrepreneurs" and about 6.5 million start-up efforts in progress. Reynolds (1997b, p. 460) finds that more than 80 percent of those trying to establish a firm are self-employed in an existing business or are part-time or full-time employees.

Becoming an entrepreneur involves an occupational choice. Because entrepreneurship is time-consuming, the potential entrepreneur often must choose between entrepreneurship and employment. Potential entrepreneurs who are employed also need to choose between entrepreneurship and employment as a result of contractual restrictions that limit outside activities. The opportunity cost of entrepreneurship reflects the value of pursuing or continuing an alternative occupation. The opportunity cost of time devoted to entrepreneurship also includes the value of education, training, and leisure.

An entrepreneur obtains returns to a bundle of inputs that are imperfectly substitutable. The entrepreneur makes various contributions to the start-up, including his effort, judgment, knowledge, IP, and investment. The entrepreneur's returns from operating the start-up and establishing the firm often cannot be identified as distinct returns to labor, capital, and IP. The entrepreneur obtains returns that include salary, investment returns, wealth accumulation, and returns to IP. The entrepreneur obtains some nonpecuniary benefits from building a business, which include enjoyment from creating a business, serving customer needs, and working independently. The entrepreneur may earn profits from operating the start-up

23 SBA (2009, p. 8), data are for 2008 and based on 2006 counts.

24 SBA (2009, p. 8), data are for 2008 and based on 2006 counts.

enterprise. Finally, the entrepreneur earns returns from ownership of the firm, which can be realized through residual returns once the firm is established or through divesting equity.

The various costs and returns to entrepreneurship should be evaluated as part of the entrepreneur's life-cycle decisions so as to obtain a more complete picture of the incentives for entrepreneurship. This helps solve the various empirical puzzles that just look at the returns obtained by entrepreneurs from specific inputs to the new venture. Because of financial constraints and other market-based constraints, the entrepreneur and the start-up are not separated financially so that the entrepreneur's financial endowment and preferences affect entrepreneurial motivation. This has led to suggestions that entrepreneurs are primarily motivated by enjoyment of entrepreneurship rather than economic returns, entrepreneurs behave irrationally in choosing among alternatives, or entrepreneurs are overly optimistic about their prospects. It is more reasonable to suppose that entrepreneurs maximize life-cycle utility subject to budget constraints that include the returns to entrepreneurship.

The choice between employment and entrepreneurship can vary over time depending on the individual's wealth. Buera (2009) examines the occupation choice decision in a life-cycle model that allows individuals to move back and forth between employment and entrepreneurship within each period. The occupational choice decision is static and depends on a comparison of wages and returns to entrepreneurship. The entrepreneur's wealth affects his borrowing constraints. Buera (2009) finds that individuals with low initial wealth converge to a zero-wealth worker steady state, and individuals with high initial wealth follow a path to a high-wealth entrepreneurial steady state. For individuals with high ability, it is optimal to have high savings rates and to converge to a high-wealth and high-consumption steady state for all levels of initial wealth. Buera (2009) finds that for high-wealth levels, entry into entrepreneurship and wealth become negatively related. He attributes this to individuals with high entrepreneurial skills being selected out of the pool of workers and suggests that this selection effect increases with wealth. Buera (2009) observes that in the United States, wealth has greater effects on the capitalization of business than on the number of business start-ups.

Vereshchagina and Hopenhayn (2009) also consider a life-cycle model in which individuals can move back and forth between employment and entrepreneurship within each period. The discrete choice between occupations in each period generates non-concavity of preferences – that is, the individual prefers to take on some risk. Because employment at a fixed wage provides an outside option and because the entrepreneur faces financing constraints, the individual has a desire for risk at low-wealth levels and takes on less risk at higher wealth levels. They assume that entrepreneurs can invest in risky projects with only two outcomes so that entrepreneurs can eliminate non-concavities in their continuation value by a suitable choice of projects. This result derives risk-taking behavior by entrepreneurs on the basis of wealth rather than attitudes toward risk.

The life-cycle theory of entrepreneurship applies to the individual's occupational choice decision. The occupational choice decision may involve long-term commitments. There may be switching costs associated with moving between employment and entrepreneurship. To represent this possibility, suppose that the individual must choose whether or not to stop working and become an entrepreneur. The individual has the option of employment at a wage W in each period until period T. If the individual chooses to become an entrepreneur, he develops the firm until period T.

While working, the potential entrepreneur observes technological opportunities. Suppose that the potential entrepreneur's technology is subject to a non-negative random shock, θ, with distribution function $F(\theta)$ on the unit interval. The technology does not change once it is embodied in the start-up. The potential entrepreneur's occupational choice decision is given by

$$V_t^L(\omega, \theta) = \max\left\{V_t^W(\omega), V_t^E(\omega, 0, \theta)\right\}, \tag{26}$$

where V^L is the expected value of the individual with wealth ω and technology θ.

The value of continuing to work is given by

$$V_t^W(\omega) = \max_s u(\omega + W - s) + \delta E\, V_{t+1}^L(s(1+r), \theta), \tag{27}$$

subject to $\omega + W \geq s \geq 0$ and $V_{T+1}(\omega_{T+1}) = \psi(\omega_{T+1})$. The value of becoming an entrepreneur is given by the return to investing in developing a firm that was studied earlier in the chapter:

$$V_t^E(\omega_t, k_t, \theta) = \max_{s,k} u(\omega_t + h(k_t, \theta) - s - (k - k_t)) + \delta V_{t+1}(s(1+r), k, \theta). \tag{28}$$

The initial capital stock is zero in the first period of entrepreneurship.

This framework generates a "starting rule" for entrepreneurship similar to the stopping rule for the inventor choosing whether or not to continue R&D:

$$V_t^W(\omega) = V_t^E(\omega, 0, \theta^*). \tag{29}$$

The individual chooses to become an entrepreneur when he observes a higher-quality technology, $\theta > \theta^*$. The individual chooses to continue to work when he observes a lower-quality technology, $\theta \leq \theta^*$. The threshold technology level is increasing in the wage.

The "starting rule" decision to become an entrepreneur depends on the individual's age, wealth, and preferences. We can rewrite the value of continuing to work as follows:

$$V_t^W(\omega) = u(\omega + W - s^W) + \delta V_{t+1}^W((1+r)s^W)F(\theta^*) + \delta \int_{\theta^*}^1 V_{t+1}^E((1+r)s^W, 0, \theta))dF(\theta), \tag{30}$$

where s^W solves the optimization problem in equation (27). By the envelope theorem, the marginal return to wealth is positive, $V_t^{W\prime}(\omega) = u'(\omega + W - s^W)$.[25]

The life-cycle theory of entrepreneurship as a form of asset accumulation is related to the optimal life-cycle housing decisions examined by Artle and Varaiya (1978). In their setting, the life-cycle consumption pattern of an individual has three segments. In the first segment, the individual rents to save for a down payment on a house; in the second segment, the individual becomes a homeowner; and in the final segment, the individual sells the house and obtains the equity. The consumer faces a financing constraint because the down payment must be a fixed share of the purchase price of a house. The consumer prefers to own rather than to rent because the rental cost is greater than the interest cost of the home loan.

The occupational choice decision is comparable to the three stages of home ownership. Initially, the individual may pursue education and employment to accumulate human capital and savings. Then, the entrepreneur creates the start-up and eventually establishes a firm. When the firm is established, the individual obtains returns from his equity through residual returns or through divestiture.

The "occupational choice puzzle" is based on the empirical observation that entrepreneurs may earn less than their best alternative as an employee of an existing firm. An individual's potential earnings in the labor market depend on his capabilities, experience, education, and training. Individuals select among job opportunities on the basis of wages, salaries, and benefits as well as preferences over nonpecuniary factors such as location, working conditions, opportunities for advancement, effort required, and types of workplace activities. The potential entrepreneur compares entrepreneurship with self-employment, employment by others, leisure, and education. Because of occupational choice decisions, entrepreneurs' creation of start-ups and efforts to establish firms depend on entrepreneurs' human capital, preferences, income, and wealth. Also, job market conditions such as wages, the rate of unemployment, and demand for various skills affect entry into entrepreneurship.

Parker (2009) emphasizes the role of pecuniary incentives for entrepreneurship. He points out that empirical variables affecting the individual's (unobserved) preference to become an entrepreneur can include alternative employment opportunities, human capital, social capital, risk and risk aversion, psychological characteristics, demographic characteristics, industry-specific factors, macroeconomic factors, and employer characteristics (Parker, 2009, pp. 106–107). Parker provides a careful overview and valuable synthesis of the empirical literature. He suggests that multivariate analysis is often necessary because there tend to be correlations among these explanatory variables. He argues that there are conceptual and data problems associated with some studies that attempt to cast doubt on pecuniary motivations for entrepreneurship. He concludes (2009, p. 110) that "more

25 Given $h(0, \theta) = 0$, it follows that $\frac{\partial V_t^E(\omega_t, 0, \theta)}{\partial \theta} = \delta \frac{\partial E V_{t+1}(s(1+r), k, \theta)}{\partial \theta} > 0$, where s and k solve (28).

careful research is needed to shed further light on entrepreneurs' responsiveness to pecuniary incentives."

Labor economists sometimes identify entrepreneurship as a form of self-employment.[26] This approach can be useful for studying labor market data, although becoming an entrepreneur involves more than basic self-employment. The category of self-employed individuals includes independent contractors and workers for hire but excludes some individuals who establish firms. As Lazear (2004, 2005) points out, self-employment is quite different from someone who "responds affirmatively to the question, 'I am among those who initially established the business.'"

The potential entrepreneur's occupation choice decision cannot be separated from other consumption and saving decisions. Greater wealth increases the likelihood of a switch to self-employment, which includes entrepreneurship.[27] Holtz-Eakin et al. (1994a, 1994b) show that the entrepreneurs' endowments matter for occupational choice decisions.[28]

Adachi (2008) considers occupational choice in the context of a life-cycle model in which human capital in the form of education and job-market experience affect the occupational choice decision. He tests a life-cycle model in which an individual maximizes the expected discounted value of utility. The individual chooses between entrepreneurship and alternative occupations while making consumption decisions on the basis of the returns to employment income and income derived from asset accumulation.

Reynolds (2000) reviews the National Panel Study of U.S. Business Startups, which provides an extensive and detailed statistical overview of new businesses and the personal characteristics of entrepreneurs. The personal information that is studied includes all of the usual demographic data such as age, sex, ethnic background, education, and household income. In addition, interviews and questionnaires are used to obtain information about the entrepreneur's motivation, expectations, knowledge, career experiences, competitive strategy, decision-making style, and risk preferences.

Asymmetric information affects occupational choice. Individuals have private information about their personal characteristics including their capabilities and opportunity costs. The potential entrepreneur considers how his private information about his capabilities will affect returns in the different occupations. Asymmetric information affects the allocation of individuals between the labor market, self-employment, and entrepreneurship. The different categories of occupations have different types of contractual arrangements, which result in different

26 Empirical studies are highly inconsistent in differentiating between self-employment and the establishment of firms; see van Praag and Versloot (2007) for an overview.

27 See Evans and Leighton (1989), Díaz-Giménez et al. (1997), Quadrini (1999, 2000), and Åstebro and Bernhardt (2003, 2004).

28 See also Evans and Jovanovic (1989), and Blachflower and Oswald (1998).

incentives to reveal private information. For example, employment in the labor market can involve agency relationships with the employer as principal and the employee as agent. Entrepreneurship allows the individual to take advantage of private information about his capabilities, judgment, and preferences.

The most successful entrepreneurs, such as Bill Gates or Steve Jobs, establish well-known firms and obtain high rewards. Rosen (1981) suggests that rewards for talent in some types of markets can be highly skewed, leading to the phenomenon of "superstars." His model of labor-market matching generates convexity of returns, which implies that small increments in talent at the high end of the distribution result in large increases in rewards. If the rewards to entrepreneurial skills are convex, small increases in talent among the most talented entrepreneurs will yield large increases in rewards.

The rewards to entrepreneurship reflect self-selection by individuals choosing between employment, self-employment, and entrepreneurship. MacDonald (1988) considers a dynamic model of a labor market with uncertain rewards in which individuals have different abilities. In equilibrium, individuals enter the market when they are young and only remain when they are successful. He shows that young entrants earn incomes less than current alternative offers and only a few obtain the high rewards that come with success. Self-selection effects are likely to be present in the market for entrepreneurs.

According to some studies, entrepreneurs appear to earn less over their lifetime on average than individuals with similar skills earn in the labor market.[29] For example, Hamilton (2000) compares paid employment with self-employment and concludes that the self-employed earn less in terms of salary and equity in the business, attributing the difference to the benefits of "being your own boss."[30] However, van der Sluis et al. (2006) show that introducing the proper controls eliminates differences between entrepreneur and employee earnings. With the same data, Hartog et al. (2007) show that ability is an important explanation for differences in earnings between entrepreneurs and employees, and controlling for ability eliminates these differences. In a survey of empirical studies on entrepreneurship and education, van der Sluis et al. (2008) find that although education does not significantly affect occupational choice of potential entrepreneurs, it does improve performance. They also find that education has a greater effect on entrepreneurial earnings in the United States than in Europe. Additional study is needed that captures the long-run returns to entrepreneurship and distinguishes entrepreneurship from self-employment; see van Praag and Versloot (2007).

29 See Hamilton (2000) and the references therein.

30 Hamilton (2000, p. 606) observes: "After 10 years in business, median entrepreneurial earnings are 35 percent less than the predicted alternative wage on a paid job of the same duration, regardless of the self-employment earnings measure used. Moreover, median entrepreneurial earnings are always less than the predicted starting wage (for zero job tenure) available from an employer, regardless of the length of time in business."

Some researchers argue that entrepreneurs have preferences and behavioral characteristics that differ from the general population. Consistent with Schumpeter (1934), some suggest that entrepreneurs are less averse to risk than other investors.[31] Other researchers suggest that entrepreneurs choose to earn low risk-adjusted returns because they are motivated by nonpecuniary returns. Entrepreneurs enjoy establishing new firms, they take pleasure from being creative, or they value independence and self-employment.[32] Using survey data, Puri and Robinson (2013) find that entrepreneurs derive greater non-pecuniary benefits from work, are more likely to say that they never intend to retire, are more tolerant of risk, and tend to have longer planning horizons than wage earners. Puri and Robinson (2013) also find that entrepreneurs are more optimistic than wage earners, controlling for wealth, education, and other personal characteristics (see also Puri and Robinson, 2007). They suggest that more optimistic entrepreneurs work harder but have greater marginal returns to effort, so that firms run by optimists perform better.

The various types of irrationality often attributed to entrepreneurs may result from imperfect measurement of returns to entrepreneurship and distortions associated with self-reporting of goals and motivation in surveys. Sarada (2013) suggests that consumption expenditures may provide a more accurate measure of entrepreneurial earnings. As in other occupations, however, entrepreneurship can involve nonpecuniary benefits that may be associated with market-based compensating differentials in returns.

2.4 The Life-Cycle Theory of Entrepreneurship: Establishing the Firm

In the third stage of entrepreneurship, the entrepreneur makes the transition from developing the start-up to establishing the firm. When the entrepreneur establishes a firm, a foundational shift occurs – the individual's role changes from entrepreneur to owner. The entrepreneur can continue as an owner of the new firm or transfer his equity to others. The life-cycle theory of entrepreneurship suggests that the timing of the establishment of the firm depends on the age, wealth, preferences, and other characteristics of the entrepreneur. When the entrepreneur establishes the firm, its objectives are financially separable from the personal consumption objectives of its owners. As a result of separation, the firm generally is a profit-maximizing enterprise (Fisher, 1906, 1907, 1930). Schumpeter (1934, p. 78) observes that being an entrepreneur is "not a lasting condition;" "Everyone is an entrepreneur when he actually carries out new combinations, and loses that character as soon as he has built up his business, when he settles down to running it as other people run their businesses."

31 See Kanbur (1982), Moskowitz and Vissing-Jorgensen (2002), Bitler et al. (2005), Puri and Robinson (2007, 2013), and the references therein.

32 See Evans and Leighton (1989) and Blanchflower and Oswald (1998).

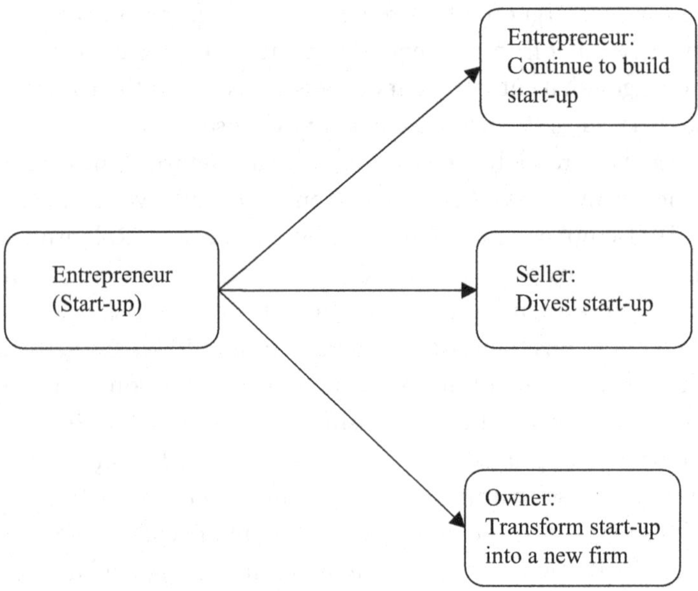

Figure 2.6. The entrepreneur's decision: continue building the start-up, divest the start-up, or transform the start-up into a new firm.

From Start-up to Firm

The life-cycle theory of entrepreneurship predicts that the entrepreneur's age, preferences, and endowments affect the rate of development of the start-up and the timing of the establishment of the firm. As a consequence, the timing of the launch of the new firm may be inefficient. Financing and liquidity constraints may delay the launch of the firm by slowing the development of the start-up. Conversely, financing and liquidity constraints may accelerate the launch of the firm because external financing may be necessary to realize market opportunities, and the entrepreneur may wish to divest his equity for consumption purposes.

The entrepreneur's decision to establish the firm is similar to exercising a real option. The entrepreneur decides when to exercise the option depending on a comparison of the value of continuing to develop the start-up and the market value of the firm. Market conditions include customer demand and competition from entrepreneurial entrants, existing institutions, and established firms. The development of the start-up reflects conditions in markets for IP, human capital, and financial capital. The start-up may fail as a result of the entrepreneur's personal financial constraints rather than the start-up's market potential. The entrepreneur can continue to develop the start-up, divest the start-up, or transform the start-up into a new firm on the basis of market conditions and life-cycle considerations (see Figure 2.6).

The time required to establish a firm may be substantial. Kaplan et al. (2005) study forty-nine venture-capital-financed companies and find that the average time elapsed from early business plan to public company is almost six years. The relative importance of human capital, especially the entrepreneur's expertise, appears to decline over time, whereas there is an increase in the importance of IP and physical assets. The entrepreneur achieves a separation of objectives when converting the start-up to a firm, either through organic growth and development, a sale of securities in an initial public offering (IPO), or acquisition by outside investors. The entrepreneur can continue his association with the firm as an owner and can keep working to develop, expand, and diversify the firm. After becoming an owner, the entrepreneur can choose whether or not to continue to exercise control and obtain returns from the firm. He can divest his ownership share without necessarily affecting the survival of the firm. The new firm has an independent identity and its own objectives.

The speed at which the firm is established is likely to depend on the entrepreneur's level of investment. The transaction costs associated with assembling the resources needed to establish a firm are likely to be increasing in the speed of the transactions. For example, there may be premiums associated with faster approval of financing or faster procurement of equipment, parts, and materials. The speed at which the start-up implements inventions and develops innovations depends on the level of investment. The date at which the firm is established also depends on investment in hiring and training employees and other costs of building an organization.

When the start date depends on the stream of expenditures made to establish the firm but is subject to uncertainty, the innovative entrepreneur's decision problem resembles an R&D investment problem.[33] Suppose that the entrepreneur learns about the technology and market opportunities in the process of developing the start-up. Greater investment in the start-up allows the entrepreneur to develop business plans, prototypes, and market experiments that can be used to launch the new firm. The entrepreneur's investment helps develop the start-up into an asset that can attract financing.

To illustrate the effects of investment in the start-up on the duration of entrepreneurship, let the time required to establish a firm be a decreasing function of the entrepreneur's level of investment, $\tau = \tau(k)$. The value of establishing a firm depends on an innovation, $\pi(\theta)$. The discount rate is r so that the net present value of establishing the firm equals

$$v(\theta) = \max_k \frac{\pi(\theta)}{(1+r)^{\tau(k)}} - k. \tag{31}$$

Suppose that there are two levels of investment, $k_L < k_H$. A higher level of investment reduces the time required to establish a firm, $\tau(k_L) > \tau(k_H)$. Suppose further that a more rapid launch of the firm is efficient:

$$v(\theta) = \frac{\pi(\theta)}{(1+r)^{\tau(k_H)}} - k_H > \frac{\pi(\theta)}{(1+r)^{\tau(k_L)}} - k_L.$$

33 The patent race literature based the duration of invention on the level of R&D investment; see Reinganum (1981, 1982) and see Reinganum (1989) for a survey.

Suppose also that the entrepreneur can afford the cost of slowly establishing the firm but cannot afford the costs of rapidly establishing the firm, $k_L \leq \omega < k_H$. Then, the entrepreneur will establish the firm later than is efficient. Even if the entrepreneur can afford the costs of rapidly establishing the firm, life-cycle consumption and saving decisions may result in a later launch of the firm.

Alternatively, financing and liquidity constraints may cause the entrepreneur to establish the firm more rapidly than is efficient. The entrepreneur lacks the funds to "stick it out" (Holtz-Eakin et al. 1994a, 1994b). To illustrate this possibility, suppose that the entrepreneur incurs investment costs k for each period devoted to developing the start-up. The start-up operates for τ periods and the value of the firm when it is established $\pi(\theta, \tau)$ is increasing in the life of the start-up. The net present value of establishing a firm equals

$$v(\theta) = \max_\tau \frac{\pi(\theta, \tau)}{(1+r)^\tau} - k\sum\nolimits_{t=0}^{\tau} \frac{1}{(1+r)^t}. \tag{32}$$

For purposes of illustration, suppose that there are two possible dates at which the firm can be established, $\tau_L < \tau_H$. Suppose that a longer gestation period sufficiently improves the value of the firm so that a later launch of the firm is efficient:

$$\frac{\pi(\theta, \tau_H)}{(1+r)^{\tau_H}} - k\sum\nolimits_{t=0}^{\tau_H} \frac{1}{(1+r)^t} > \frac{\pi(\theta, \tau_L)}{(1+r)^{\tau_L}} - k\sum\nolimits_{t=0}^{\tau_L} \frac{1}{(1+r)^t}.$$

Suppose that the entrepreneur can afford the cost of an earlier launch of the firm but cannot afford the cost of a later launch, $\tau_L k \leq \omega < \tau_H k$. Then, the entrepreneur will establish the firm earlier than is efficient. Even if the entrepreneur can afford the costs of establishing the firm more slowly, life-cycle consumption and saving decisions may result in an earlier launch of the firm.

Risk also plays a role in the entrepreneur's decisions about when to launch the firm. The entrepreneur may launch the firm earlier or later than is efficient to mitigate risks associated with developing the start-up. Suppose, for example, that a longer start-up phase increases the value of the firm when it is established. However, the growth in the value of the firm is subject to random shocks, $\theta \geq 0$,

$$\pi_{t+1} = \pi_t + \theta, \tag{33}$$

where the mean of the random shocks is $\hat{\theta}$. The entrepreneur must decide whether or not to continue developing the start-up before observing θ. Then, the entrepreneur should continue developing the start-up as long as the expected present value of the return to continuing to develop the start-up for an additional period $\frac{\pi_t+\hat{\theta}}{1+r}$ is greater than the return to establishing the firm π_t. It follows that the optimal stopping rule for the start-up is

$$\pi^0 = \frac{\hat{\theta}}{r}. \tag{34}$$

The profit-maximizing entrepreneur will establish the firm as soon as its value is greater than or equal to the threshold π^0.

When faced with financing and liquidity constraints, the entrepreneur maximizing life-cycle utility will choose a different threshold that is based on his age, wealth, and preferences, including risk aversion and rate of time preference. To illustrate the basic issues, consider a two-period setting in which the entrepreneur chooses whether to launch the firm in the first or in the second period. If the entrepreneur launches the firm in the first period, the entrepreneur earns profit π and obtains benefits equal to

$$V^1(\omega + \pi) = \max_{s^1} u(\omega + \pi - s^1) + \delta u((1+r)s^1), \tag{35}$$

subject to $x \geq 0$, $s^1 \geq 0$, and ω given. If the entrepreneur chooses to wait until the second period to launch the firm, the entrepreneur earns profit $\pi + \theta$ in the second period and obtains benefits equal to

$$V^2(\omega, \pi) = \max_{s^2} u(\omega - s^2) + \delta E u((1+r)s^2 + \pi + \theta), \tag{36}$$

subject to $x \geq 0$, $s^2 \geq 0$, and ω given. Let s^{1*} and s^{2*} be the optimal savings in the two cases.

The entrepreneur that maximizes life-cycle utility chooses a stopping rule π^* that satisfies

$$V^1(\omega + \pi^*) = V^2(\omega, \pi^*). \tag{37}$$

If profits are greater than the threshold π^* the entrepreneur will establish the firm in the first period. Otherwise, the entrepreneur will wait until the second period to establish the firm.

Because of financing constraints, the entrepreneur will tend to establish the firm earlier than the profit-maximizing optimum, $\pi^* \leq \pi^0$. Suppose instead that $\pi^* > \pi^0$. Define the savings rate $s^{1\prime} = s^{2*} + \pi^*$. By optimization it follows that

$$V^1(\omega + \pi^*) \geq u(\omega - s^{2*}) + \delta u((1+r)(s^{2*} + \pi^*)).$$

From $\pi^* > \pi^0$, it follows that

$$u(\omega - s^{2*}) + \delta u((1+r)(s^{2*} + \pi^*)) > u(\omega - s^{2*}) + \delta u((1+r)s^{2*} + \pi^* + r\pi^0).$$

Noting that $r\pi^0 = \hat{\theta}$, Jensen's inequality implies that

$$u(\omega - s^{2*}) + \delta u((1+r)s^{2*} + \pi^* + r\pi^0) \geq u(\omega - s^{2*}) + \delta E u((1+r)s^{2*} + \pi^* + \theta) = V^2(\omega, \pi^*).$$

Therefore, $V^1(\omega + \pi^*) > V^2(\omega, \pi^*)$, which is a contradiction, so that $\pi^* \leq \pi^0$. This implies that the entrepreneur launches the firm at a lower profit and thus earlier than the profit-maximizing optimum. In a different setting, however, if the entrepreneur's investment were to decrease the risk of launching the new firm, the entrepreneur might have an incentive to launch the firm later than is optimal as a means of reducing risk.

The entrepreneur's consumption objectives are connected to his objectives as the owner of the start-up. This affects the start-up's growth plans, products and prices, financing and hiring, and competitive strategy. The innovation often is difficult to observe, technically complex, or impossible to verify. The entrepreneur's idea often is not fully developed and requires additional experimentation, production runs, product prototypes, and market trials. As a consequence, the entrepreneur faces asymmetric information, contracting costs, and other transaction costs when raising financial capital or when obtaining commitments from managers and skilled workers. The entrepreneur encounters further difficulties in contracting with customers, suppliers, and partners. The entrepreneur may not be able to avoid financing and liquidity constraints by selling the start-up to others because the innovation is not sufficiently developed and may be difficult to observe by potential acquirers.

As a consequence, the entrepreneur cannot fully rely on market transactions to separate from the start-up's business activities. The entrepreneur must commit his personal wealth, labor, and IP to operate the start-up and establish the firm. The entrepreneur often manages the start-up and provides specialized services such as engineering, marketing, and sales. The entrepreneur sometimes enters into agreements with customers, suppliers, partners, and investors that entail personal liability. This implies that the entrepreneur's personal characteristics affect the start-up's business activities including invention, innovation, investment, employment, products, processes, expansion, and conversion to a firm. Because of imperfect information and market transaction costs, the start-up faces constraints that depend on the entrepreneur's age, wealth, and consumption preferences.

Interdependence Theorem 3. If the entrepreneur faces financing and liquidity constraints, his consumption-saving decisions and the decision to establish a firm are financially interdependent.

The interdependence theorems emphasize that the start-up's decisions depend on the personal characteristics of the entrepreneur. The start-up cannot obtain gains from trade by using the market to obtain capital investment and management. The entrepreneur is affected by the start-up not only through the income of the start-up but also through the pattern of earnings over time and through his inputs to the start-up. The entrepreneur's consumption and saving decisions in turn depend on the characteristics of the start-up.

The start-up is a transaction institution that does not satisfy the conditions for the Fisher Separation Theorem to hold. Because its business objectives cannot be financially separated from the consumption objectives of its entrepreneur-owner, *the start-up is not a firm.* The start-up need not maximize profits or even operate profitably. The start-up may not invest efficiently in either management, technology, operations, procurement, or sales.

The Foundational Shift

Extending the Fisher Separation Theorem, Spulber (2009a) introduces the *separation criterion* for determining whether an institution is a firm. According to this criterion, a transaction institution is a firm when its objectives can be financially separated from the consumption objectives of its owners. Publicly traded corporations certainly pass the separation criterion, as do most closely held corporations and limited-liability partnerships. Companies such as Microsoft, Google, News Corporation, or Berkshire Hathaway certainly are firms, whether or not their owners are active in running the business or own substantial shares.[34] These corporations necessarily pass the Fisher Separation test because investors insist on corporations maximizing shareholder value.

Owner involvement in business decisions is a natural reflection of the residual returns and residual control that comes with ownership. However, the corporation's investors only derive benefits from the company through the contribution that owning shares makes to their personal income. The owners' *consumption decisions* are financially separate from the business decisions of the corporation. Corporations such as Exxon Mobil, Walmart Stores, Chevron, ConocoPhillips, General Electric, Ford Motor, AT&T, and Hewlett-Packard are also firms. Banks, insurance companies, brokerages, and other financial enterprises are firms.

Firms also include privately held companies such as Cargill, Koch Industries, Dell, Bechtel, Mars, PricewaterhouseCoopers, Pilot Flying J, Publix Super Markets, Love's Travel Shops and Country Stores, Ernst & Young, Reyes Holdings, C&S Wholesale Grocers, US Foods, HE Butt Grocery, and Enterprise Holdings.[35] Family-controlled firms account for more than one-third of companies in the Fortune 500, including Ford and Walmart. (Anderson and Reeb, 2003). Firms with high family involvement represent more than half of all businesses with employees (Astrachan and Shanker, 2003, p. 216).

The Fisher Separation Theorem provides a foundation for the study of the firm's investment and financing decisions and individual investors' saving decisions. Consumer-owners receive a share of the present value of the firm's profits. The firm's owners are affected by the firm's decisions only through their budget constraint. Accordingly, consumer-owners unanimously agree that the firm should maximize the present value of profits. The Fisher Separation Theorem further shows that the firm's investment decisions are independent of how the firm finances its

34 Although Bill Gates is involved with Microsoft as an owner, manager, or director, the company's investment decisions are financed through the capital markets and certainly do not involve Bill Gates personally financing Microsoft's activities, as occurs with entrepreneurial start-ups. In turn, Bill Gates' personal consumption and savings decisions are only affected by Microsoft through his ownership of corporate securities.

35 Andrea Murphy, 2013, "America's Largest Private Companies 2013," http://www.forbes.com/sites/andreamurphy/2013/12/18/americas-largest-private-companies-2013/ (accessed December 22, 2013).

investment. Investment might be financed from an initial endowment of funds or through borrowing, or in some other manner such as issuance of securities. The level of investment maximizes the present value of profits, so that the efficient investment level equates the marginal return to investment to the marginal cost of investment.

Individuals in the economy form all sorts of non-firm institutions. Individuals enter into economic transactions and contractual agreements. These arrangements cannot be financially separated from the consumption objectives of their owners. The benefits of a transaction or a contract are those of its participants and, thus, are not financially separable from their consumption and saving decisions. Bilateral or multilateral contract models thus do not provide a model of the firm consistent with the separation criterion. For example, Hart and Moore (1990) consider a situation in which a group of economic agents form coalitions and each agent chooses an action that maximizes his share of the value of the coalition. Such coalitions are not firms because they maximize the net benefits of their members in contrast to a firm whose objective is financially separate from its owners.

Generally, consumer organizations maximize the benefits of their members, so that the organization's objectives are not financially separate from the consumption interests of its members. Such organizations include clubs, buyer cooperatives, worker cooperatives, merchants' associations, nonprofits, and basic partnerships. These institutions may perform some functions that are similar to those carried out by firms, including intermediation of transactions. These consumer organizations may be precursors to firms and may evolve into firms. However, many such organizations often have objectives that are not financially separable from the interests of those consumers who establish, own, manage, or are members of the organization.

Typically, the start-up is a sole proprietorship, consisting initially of the entrepreneur himself, although it can also be a partnership or a newly formed corporation. The separation criterion is satisfied by corporations with outside investors, more complex partnerships, and some types of sole proprietorships. The foundational shift occurs when the entrepreneur's consumption objectives become separate from the institution's objectives.

The separation of objectives makes the firm a valuable economic actor. Because firms maximize profits, they can select different allocations and contracts than consumer organizations that maximize the average benefits of their members. The foundational shift allows the firm to provide limited liability for its owners. Establishing a firm provides an additional actor to the economy that augments the variety of potential transactions. The firm plays various economic roles as a seller of outputs, a buyer of resources, a borrower of finance capital, an employer of workers, and a party to contracts. The firm is an intermediary that matches buyers and sellers and makes markets. The firm's managers choose goals, strategies to achieve the goals, and means to implement strategies. Although it acts under the owner's delegated authority, the newly established firm is an additional decision maker in the economy.

The entrepreneur's costs of establishing the firm should be distinguished from the costs of the firm itself, which start to be incurred once the firm begins its operation. The entrepreneur incurs transaction costs during the period that he is establishing the firm. The entrepreneur necessarily bears risk because of the delay between the time that he begins to establish the firm and the time the firm begins to operate. This time lag introduces uncertainty about the firm's profit. The dynamic nature of the entrepreneur's activity implies that starting a firm is a type of investment.

The theory of the firm is crucial to the economic theory of the entrepreneur. In contrast to the relationship between a firm and its owners, the start-up and the entrepreneur are connected by much more than the start-up's income. The entrepreneur's age, wealth, and consumption preferences affect the start-up's business decisions. The start-up's risk, pattern of earnings over time, financial capital, and labor requirements affect the entrepreneur's consumption decisions.

The life-cycle theory of entrepreneurship predicts that the entrepreneur acts in pursuit of profit. The reward of the entrepreneur is a share of the economic value of the firm. In turn, the firm's economic value depends on its provision of transaction efficiencies that the economy cannot attain otherwise. Accordingly, entrepreneurs choose to establish firms if and only if doing so increases transaction benefits net of transaction costs in comparison with the best institutional alternative. The transaction costs of establishing a firm limit entry and reduce the erosion of profit by competitive entry. Moreover, costly transactions mean that competitors will encounter difficulties discerning and imitating entrepreneurial innovations. Economic frictions reduce the prospect of perfect competitive challenges.

The firm generally becomes a financial asset at the date that it is established. The entrepreneur becomes an owner with rights of residual control over the firm's activities and a share of residual returns. The owner wishes the firm to maximize profit so as to increase the owner's income rather than making decisions to benefit the owner as a consumer. By the Fisher Separation Theorem, the entrepreneur receives the rewards of ownership after the firm is established. After the foundational shift, the individual no longer acts in the economic capacity of an entrepreneur, having completed the task of establishing the firm. The owners of the firm can divest their shares of the firm or direct the firm's activities using rights of residual control. The firm's managers act under the authority delegated to it by its owners.

Although an owner may exercise considerable control over the firm, the firm is distinguished from the owner's personal budget and personal activities. After the foundational shift occurs, there is a separation of the owner's consumption decisions from the firm's decisions. The entrepreneur can maintain a connection to the firm after the foundational shift by remaining as an owner and also by performing such functions as manager, consultant, supplier, or customer. The entrepreneur can still be creative and innovative as an owner and manager, or the entrepreneur can delegate these duties to managers and employees. After the foundational shift, the entrepreneur can choose to end all economic ties to the firm by divesting the ownership share. Even after divesting his ownership share, the entrepreneur-turned-owner can maintain other economic relationships with the firm.

The entrepreneur often does not earn returns until he establishes the firm. As in other professions such as the sciences or the arts, the entrepreneur earns money indirectly by creating something new. This indirect payment may explain why entrepreneurs sometimes say that they do not do it for the money. Of course, entrepreneurs also may enjoy the creative process involved in designing the firm and seeing it take shape. The return to being an entrepreneur is a share of the value of the firm at the time it is established. The value of the firm is affected by market demand and supply conditions and by transaction benefits and transaction costs. Competition with other firms is a major determinant of the firm's value. The motivation of the entrepreneur is to obtain the value of the firm. The value of the firm depends on the entrepreneur's market knowledge, IP, judgment, and creativity.

The entrepreneur's returns are equal to the value of his equity in the firm, discounted to account for the time it takes to establish the firm, less the costs that the entrepreneur incurs in establishing the firm. The former entrepreneur receives a share of the firm's profit by remaining an owner of the firm over time and thereby receiving the residual returns from the firm's operation. Alternatively, the entrepreneur can realize a share of the value of the firm by selling the firm to others after it is established. The entrepreneur also can form contracts with investors that allow the start-up to be sold before the firm is established.

2.5 Conclusion

The life-cycle theory of entrepreneurship helps address the long-standing debate over whether the entrepreneur maximizes profit or primarily pursues some other objective such as the enjoyment, creativity, or independence from authority. The innovative entrepreneur's life-cycle decisions affect the transitions between invention, entrepreneurship, and competition. One of the main implications of the analysis is that entrepreneurial decision making is related to life-cycle asset accumulation and consumption decisions. The analysis suggests that the entrepreneur seeks to maximize expected discounted utility of consumption subject to his budget constraints. This framework provides a basis for better understanding the Question of Entrepreneurial Motivation.

The life-cycle theory of entrepreneurship highlights the interdependence between the entrepreneur's personal consumption activities and business activities. Because of financing and liquidity constraints, the entrepreneur's business decisions affect consumption and saving decisions and labor and leisure decisions. The inventor becomes an entrepreneur when his discoveries and complementary resources are intrinsic and therefore difficult to transfer to existing firms. The innovator's preferences, endowment, and IP affect the choice between entrepreneurship and alternative occupations. There is also interdependence between the entrepreneur's consumption and saving decisions and his management and development of the start-up. Because of the absence of financial separation, financial and liquidity constraints may prevent the start-up from maximizing profits. These constraints also affect the entrepreneur's choice of when to establish the firm.

The life-cycle theory of the entrepreneur provides a consistent conceptual framework for addressing the entrepreneur's decisions concerning adopting inventions, creating and developing the start-up, and launching the new firm. The innovative entrepreneur succeeds in establishing a firm by addressing these three financial interdependence problems. The entrepreneur does not experience financial separation until the firm is established, at which point the entrepreneur becomes an owner of the firm. As an owner, the entrepreneur can continue to provide ideas and leadership. However, after the foundational shift occurs, the new firm maximizes profit so that its business objectives become financially separate from the preferences and endowments of the entrepreneur.

3

Innovative Advantage

Entrepreneurial Initiative and Incumbent Inertia

When do entrepreneurs innovate more efficiently than do incumbent firms? Entrepreneurs encounter *entrepreneurial inertia* as a result of the costs of establishing new firms, the costs of obtaining complementary assets, and the opportunity costs of innovation. Entrepreneurs, however, can benefit from individual initiative and creativity that may not be feasible for managers of established organizations. Existing firms suffer from *incumbent inertia* as a result of adjustment costs, diversification costs, the replacement effect, and imperfect adjustment of expectations. This chapter examines the *innovative advantage* of entrepreneurs in comparison to existing firms.

Incumbents often appear to have insurmountable advantages over entrepreneurial entrants. Most significantly, existing firms have *complementary assets* that enhance the returns to new technologies, including human capital, business reputations, market knowledge, customer and supplier relationships, and sources of finance. Existing firms have the necessary expertise to develop new technologies when they already engage in extensive internal R&D and participate in R&D joint ventures and consortia. Existing firms have the ability to obtain new technologies because of their experience in licensing and purchasing inventions, commissioning research by specialized contractors, and working with technical consultants and university researchers. Additionally, existing firms have trained scientific and technical personnel with experience in applying existing technologies that can be used to obtain, develop, and apply new technologies. Entrepreneurial entrants in contrast face various barriers to innovation including the transaction costs of obtaining assets that are complementary to innovation.

The successful entry of innovative entrepreneurs and the resulting exit of incumbent firms in many industries provide evidence that entrepreneurial initiative can overcome incumbent advantages. Innovative entrepreneurs are not subject to incumbent inertia because they do not operate an existing business. They are not subject to the effects of adjustment costs, diversification costs, business replacement, and imperfect adjustment of expectations. Innovative entrepreneurs, however, do face various types of entrepreneurial inertia: the costs of obtaining complementary assets, the incremental costs of establishing an innovative firm, and the opportunity costs of forgoing replicative entry. Through individual initiative, innovative entrepreneurs often seize opportunities that are missed by existing firms.

The innovative entrepreneur implements inventions in formulating a business strategy, creating the start-up, and establishing the new firm. Doing something new in the economy necessarily begins with *commercial* inventions. Traditional scientific and technological inventions are neither necessary nor sufficient for innovation. The chapter introduces a formal definition of commercial inventions based on the economics of transaction costs. Commercial inventions include what are known as "business method inventions." The chapter also introduces a formal definition of business strategy that is based on economic transactions and examines how innovative entrepreneurs formulate new business strategies.

3.1 Entrepreneurial Initiative

The economic functions of innovative entrepreneurs derive from a simple fact: they are *individuals*. This endows innovative entrepreneurs with capabilities that are fundamentally different from institutions such as firms and other organizations. Working alone or in teams, individual entrepreneurs bring their unique perspectives to innovation based on their personal capabilities, experiences, judgment, and knowledge. Innovative entrepreneurs are creative in developing new types of firms rather than copying existing ones, just as some individuals are creative in art, science, or invention.

As individuals, innovative entrepreneurs have the best knowledge of their personal needs and the needs of individuals with whom they are closely acquainted. This allows innovative entrepreneurs to introduce new products, technologies, and transaction methods that meet those needs. As Friedrich Hayek observes, the demand side of a market contains "dispersed bits of incomplete and frequently contradictory knowledge which all the separate individuals possess."[1] Large-scale companies and government agencies cannot make decisions as well as the "man on the spot" (Hayek, 1945, p. 524). When it comes to launching new businesses, the innovative entrepreneur is the "man on the spot."

As individuals, innovative entrepreneurs can experiment in ways that may not be feasible for existing firms. Through small-scale start-ups, innovative entrepreneurs can set up ventures that are uncertain and unconventional and, therefore, pose problems for large-scale enterprises that avoid risk and emphasize conformity. Entrepreneurs can be fast, flexible, and responsive to market opportunities in contrast to existing firms with bureaucratic hierarchies, organizational rules and routines, and the distraction of ongoing business activities. Innovative entrepreneurs respond to personal rewards derived from market incentives that differ from salaries and bonuses for managers of existing firms.

1 Hayek (1945, pp. 521–522). See also Hayek (1973).

Despite their limitations, it is evident that innovative entrepreneurs continually establish new firms that change the economy. Using the *leverage* of these new firms, entrepreneurs generate new industries and change the direction of existing industries. Innovative entrepreneurs introduce commercial, scientific, and technological inventions into the economy by embodying these inventions in new types of firms. Entrepreneurial entrants form industries from scratch, such as railroads, automobiles, aircraft, telecommunications, or computers. Entrepreneurial entrants fundamentally transform industries, forcing existing firms to innovate or exit the market. New firms introduce product designs, production processes, and transaction procedures that bring forth commercial innovations in such industries as retail, wholesale, information and communications, electronics, pharmaceuticals, medical equipment, and aerospace.

Established firms can be subject to the inflexibility of bureaucracy, the inconsistencies of collective decision making, the myopia of managed institutions, and the insularity and conformity of social groups. Because they are *purpose-built*, firms have specialized organizations, personnel, capital equipment, and facilities that are correspondingly not applicable to innovative alternatives. Firms face *adjustment costs* of changing products, production methods, suppliers, customers, and organizational structures. Successful firms are subject to *inertia*, as Arrow (1962b) discovered, because implementing innovations must generate sufficient returns to justify abandoning current technologies.

Conversely, as individuals, entrepreneurs often encounter constraints on innovation that only existing firms can overcome. Firms manage organizations that can overcome the human capital limitations and bounded rationality of individuals. Existing firms can be proficient in carrying out innovation that requires teams of specialized personnel, including scientists, engineers, designers, and marketers. Existing firms can achieve economies of scale and scope not just in transactions and production but also in R&D and product design. Firms have reputations that are helpful in developing customer and supplier relationships, thus facilitating sales of new products. Firms have assets, financial reputations, and records of past performance needed to attract financing for capital investment in new technologies. In short, individuals are better suited for some types of creativity and firms are better suited for others.

Introducing economic innovations is inherently difficult; it requires individuals who identify market opportunities and the means to achieve them. Say (1852, I, p. 97) emphasizes the individuality of the entrepreneur, whose "main quality is judgment." Say (1852) distinguishes the innovative entrepreneur from the scientist, who studies nature, and from the worker, who takes directions from the scientist and the entrepreneur.[2] Say (1852, I, p. 94) asserts that the entrepreneur innovates

2 The entrepreneur's role as an innovator is evident in Say's (1852, I, pp. 97–98) discussion: "Personally, he can do without science, by making a judicious application of that of others; he can avoid manual labor by employing the services of others; but he would not know how to do without judgment; because he could incur high costs in making something without any value."

by applying scientific inventions: "This art of application, which constitutes such an essential component of production, is the occupation of a class of men that we call industrial entrepreneurs."[3] For Say (1841, pp. 579–582), "the entrepreneur applies acquired knowledge, the services of capital and those of natural agents to produce goods that people value."

Knight (1921, p. 285) also emphasizes that the innovative entrepreneur is an individual, arguing that the entrepreneur receives profit in return for his private knowledge of the quality of his own judgment. Entrepreneurial innovation is not only a matter of risk but also a problem of Knightian uncertainty. Commercial innovations are necessarily untried and their benefits are unknown. The leap into the unknown is more than a philosophical problem. The innovative entrepreneur must put at risk his own time, effort, capabilities, IP, income, and wealth. The innovative entrepreneur exercises judgment regarding market opportunities and the resources needed to address them. In addition, the innovative entrepreneur requires personal knowledge to evaluate the quality of his own judgment.

Schumpeter recognizes the importance of the entrepreneur as an individual. "The entrepreneur, Schumpeter repeatedly states, is fundamentally a '*man of action*' and always ready to leap into '*energetic action*' ('*Man der Tat*'; 1911: 128, 133, emphasis added). It is consequently in his 'spiritual constitution' that the entrepreneur differs from the ordinary person ('*Geistesverfassung*'; 1911: 163, cf. 142–3)."[4] Swedberg (2002, p. 234) points out:

> In the 1911 version of his theory of entrepreneurship, Schumpeter emphasizes very strongly that what is most remarkable about the entrepreneur is not that he has figured out some new combination – good ideas are plentiful and cheap, we are told – but that it is extremely difficult to transform these ideas into reality. "New combinations are easy to come by, but what is necessary and decisive is the action and the force to act" (1911: 163).

Schumpeter (1934, p. 93) speculates about the psychology of the entrepreneur, suggesting that "there is the dream and the will to found a private kingdom, usually, though not necessarily, also a dynasty" through industrial or commercial success. Also, Schumpeter (1934, p. 93) identifies the personal aspects of competition: "the will to conquer: the impulse to fight, to prove oneself superior to others, to succeed for the sake, not of the fruits of success, but of success itself." Finally, Schumpeter (1934, p. 93) points to the personal rewards of entrepreneurship: "the joy of creating, of getting things done, or simply of exercising one's energy and ingenuity."

Building on the insights of Say, Schumpeter, and Knight, other economists also emphasize that entrepreneurs are individuals. Liebenstein (1968, p. 75) defines the entrepreneur as "an individual or group of individuals with four major characteristics: he connects different markets, he is capable of making up for market

3 Emphasis removed.

4 Swedberg (2002, p. 234).

deficiencies (gap-filling), he is an 'input-completer,' and he creates or expands time-binding, input-transforming entities (i.e., firms)." Kirzner (1973, p. 81) argues that "it is entrepreneurial alertness to unnoticed opportunities which creates the tendency toward the even circular flow of equilibrium."[5] Schultz (1975, p. 827) considers "how education and experience influence the efficiency of human beings to perceive, to interpret correctly, and to undertake action that will appropriately reallocate their resources."

Emphasizing the entrepreneur's individual initiative, Schumpeter points out that entrepreneurs' ideas may come from others – the entrepreneur innovates by introducing these discoveries into the market. Schumpeter (1939, pp. 85–86) distinguishes between the personal features of the inventor and the innovator, emphasizing that even when innovation consists of commercializing a particular invention, "the making of the invention and the carrying out of the innovation are completely different things . . . Personal aptitudes – primarily intellectual in the case of the inventor, primarily volitional in the case of the businessman who turns the invention into an innovation – and the methods by which the one and the other work, belong to different spheres."[6] Schumpeter distinguishes between the scientist and the innovator who is either an entrepreneur or a manager of an existing firm.

Schumpeter considers the profit of the entrepreneur who brings a power loom to a textile industry that had previously relied on manual labor:

> Now to whom does it fall? Obviously to the individuals who introduced the looms into the circular flow, not to the mere inventors, but also not to the mere producers or users of them. Those who produce them to order will only receive their cost price, those who employ them according to instructions will buy them so dearly at first that they will hardly receive any profit. The profit will fall to those individuals whose achievement it is to introduce the looms, whether they produce and use them or whether they only produce or only use them. . . . The introduction is achieved by founding new businesses, whether for production or for employment or for both. (Schumpeter, 1934, p. 132)

The entrepreneur earns a return to introducing the innovation by acting as an intermediary. The entrepreneur obtains the invention from the inventor and capital equipment from the producers of the equipment. Then, the entrepreneur supplies the invention and the equipment to the manufacturer that will use them. The entrepreneur need not be a manufacturer, either of the capital equipment or of the final product.

Mises (1998, p. 255) observes: "Entrepreneur means acting man in regard to the changes occurring in the data of the market." For Mises (1998, p. 259), "[t]he market process is entirely a resultant of human action." He (1998, p. 312) argues:

5 Kirzner (1973, p. 83) notes the "active, alert, searching role of entrepreneurial activity." See also Kirzner (1979).

6 Schumpeter (1939, pp. 85–86).

"The market is a social body; it is the foremost social body. The market phenomena are social phenomena." Mises (1998, p. 255) distinguishes the usage of the term entrepreneur as establishing firms from the more commonplace usage by economists and others as "those who are especially eager to profit from adjusting production to the expected changes in conditions, those who have more initiative, more venturesomeness, and a quicker eye than the crowd, the pushing and promoting pioneers of economic improvement."[7]

Because of the individuality of entrepreneurs, many have speculated on their motivation. Are innovative entrepreneurs' judgments the carefully considered choices of experts who simply know what they are doing and are good at making such decisions? For Knight, the entrepreneur receives profit in return for his private knowledge of the quality of his own judgment: "[T]rue profit, therefore, depends on an absolute uncertainty in the estimation of the value of judgment" (Knight, 1921, p. 285). Or, are innovative entrepreneurs driven by the "thrill of the unknown," "irrational exuberance," or Keynesian "animal spirits – a spontaneous urge to action?"[8]

The individuality of the entrepreneur explains the extensive economic analysis of their personal characteristics. The determinants of entrepreneurship include wealth, income, age, experience, education, risk preferences, location, marital status, ethnicity, and gender (Parker, 2009). According to survey studies, the desire for independence is the most reported factor in determining entrepreneurship (Parker, 2009). Although many have questioned whether entrepreneurs are primarily motivated by financial incentives, Parker (2009, p. 110) observes that because individuals are known to be responsive to price incentives, "it would be puzzling if the same calculus ceased to apply entirely in the realm of entrepreneurship as an occupational choice."

I apply the term *entrepreneur* only to individuals who establish firms. This distinguishes the term from its expanding popular usage. Entrepreneurs are fashionable; they are seen as successful, energetic, creative, independent, ambitious, and even rebellious. For this reason, many people wish to describe themselves or those who they admire as "entrepreneurial." Managers of existing firms who innovate and grow the business often are referred to as entrepreneurs, or perhaps more accurately as "intrapreneurs." People with initiative, artistic talent or scientific insights also claim the entrepreneur label. Entrepreneurs are sometimes viewed as adventurers,

7 Mises (1998, p. 255) suggests that the notion of the entrepreneur as a highly eager person is actually the narrower one and should perhaps be called "promoter." See Kirzner (1997) for an overview of the Austrian approach to the entrepreneur, which emphasizes individual discovery of market opportunities.

8 As John Maynard Keynes famously put it: "Most, probably, of our decisions to do something positive, the full consequences of which will be drawn out over many days to come, can only be taken as the result of animal spirits – a spontaneous urge to action rather than inaction, and not as the outcome of a weighted average of quantitative benefits multiplied by quantitative probabilities" (1936, pp. 161–162).

taking risks through gambling, smuggling, exploration, or fortune hunting. Going further, the term entrepreneur has come to mean someone who establishes practically any type of social institution. Pozen (2008, p. 283) ironically observes that "we are all entrepreneurs now" and notes the increasingly frequent use of the term to designate all kinds of activities.[9]

Entrepreneurial initiative overcomes existing firms' failure to innovate efficiently. Not only do innovative entrepreneurs grow the economy, but also the firms that they establish transform the economy's technology, markets, and organizations. The entry of innovative firms causes creative destruction: selecting the best innovations, supplanting inefficient institutions, and motivating or replacing existing firms. Entrepreneurs help lift the economy out of crises by creating new investment projects and employment opportunities.

3.2 Innovative Advantage

Innovative entrepreneurs make economic contributions when they have an innovative advantage over incumbent firms. This is the heart of the matter; new firms are needed for innovation only if they generate incremental benefits relative to existing firms. This section considers individual initiative and sources of entrepreneurial inertia. The discussion also identifies sources of incumbent inertia: adjustment costs, diversification costs, the replacement effect, and imperfect adjustment of expectations.

The Entrepreneur's Decision to Be Innovative

Entrepreneurs face the key decision of whether to innovate or to replicate. An entrepreneur is *innovative* if the firm that they establish is the first firm to implement particular commercial, scientific, and technological discoveries. Replicative entrepreneurs in contrast implement already applied commercial, scientific, and technological discoveries. Innovative entrepreneurship is *endogenous* – that is, entrepreneurs decide whether or not to be innovative by matching their ideas and capabilities with market opportunities. This is illustrated in Figure 3.1.

Innovative entrepreneurship offers various benefits. Being the first to implement discoveries gives first-mover advantages to the newly established firm.

9 Pozen (2008, p. 316) suggests that terms such as *social entrepreneurship* and *policy entrepreneurship* have become trendy "in part because no one knows precisely what they mean." He observes that "[e]veryone, it seems, is an entrepreneur these days. People who tackle civic problems through innovative methods are 'social entrepreneurs.' Those who promote new forms of legislation or government action are 'policy entrepreneurs.' Those who seek to change the way society thinks or feels about an issue are 'norm entrepreneurs.' Those who try to alter the boundaries of altruism or deviance are 'moral entrepreneurs'" (2008, p. 283).

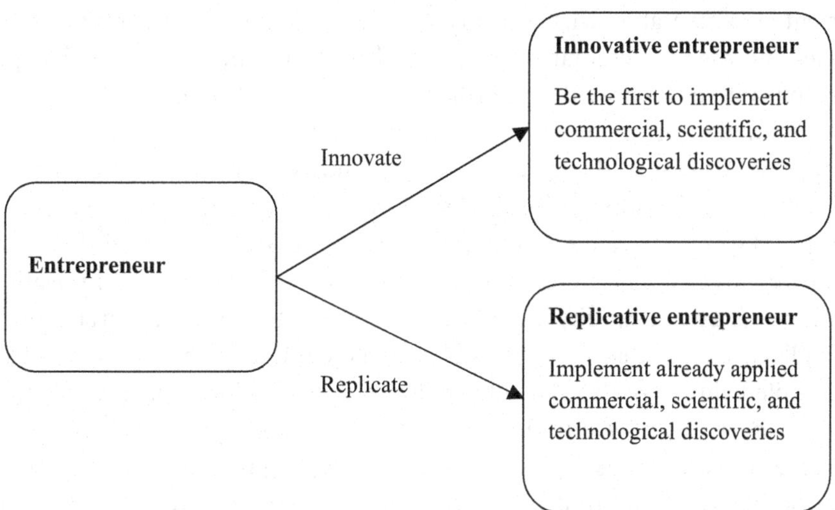

Figure 3.1. The entrepreneur's key decision: to innovative or to replicate.

Innovative entrepreneurship provides incremental revenues from product differentiation, cost reductions from more efficient technologies, and competitive advantages from new types of transactions. Innovation allows the entrepreneurial entrant to compete with incumbent firms that have complementary assets.

Conversely, innovative entrepreneurship also requires various costs. First, the innovative entrepreneur incurs the costs of acquiring or developing new technologies. Innovative entrepreneurs discover economic opportunities and find new ways to address those opportunities. Although economic innovations need not involve scientific and technical discoveries, innovative entrepreneurship at least requires commercial discoveries – these are the innovative ideas that are essential for innovation. The innovative entrepreneur can directly incur the costs of R&D to make the necessary discoveries. Alternatively, the innovative entrepreneur can obtain inventions in the market place through licensing or acquisition.

Second, the innovative entrepreneur incurs the incremental costs of establishing an innovative firm in comparison to those of establishing a replicative firm. It can be difficult to obtain financing for projects with new products, production processes, or transaction methods. There are also costs of implementing untried technologies including learning through trial and error. The innovative entrepreneur faces the costs of legally defending the new firm's IP, searching for prior art, and obtaining licenses to use related inventions. The innovative entrepreneur also must acquire complementary assets necessary to implement new technologies, which can exceed the costs of implementing existing technologies.

Third, the innovative entrepreneur faces the opportunity costs of forgoing replicative entry. This is analogous to Arrow's (1962b) replacement effect for incumbent firms. Entry costs aside, the innovative entrepreneur compares profit from innovative entry with profit from replicative entry. Innovative entry must generate sufficient incremental returns to justify the additional costs of obtaining new technologies and the incremental costs of establishing an innovative firm. The profit from replicative entry provides a hurdle that is comparable to the existing business of the incumbent firm. For example, the potential entrepreneur contemplating a new type of business evaluates the potential returns from franchising an existing business model. Let Π^I be the profit from innovative entrepreneurship and let Π^R be the profit from replicative entrepreneurship. The entrepreneur will choose to be innovative only if the net returns to innovation exceed the costs of innovation k, $\Pi^I - \Pi^R > k$. The possibility of replicative entry creates entrepreneurial inertia.

Replicative entry may not be feasible when incumbent firms own or control IP and complementary assets needed to operate existing business models. Incumbent firms may have first mover advantages in offering existing products and operating existing technologies. Existing business models may be protected from imitation or expropriation by patents, trademarks, copyrights, and trade secrets. Also, replicative entry can be restricted by government regulations that raise the costs of entering the market to operate traditional businesses. These barriers to replicative entry affect the profits from replicative entry, thus reducing or removing the opportunity costs of innovative entry. Innovative entrepreneurs then do not face entrepreneurial inertia, having instead incentives to invent around barriers to entry.

Sources of Incumbent Inertia

Entrepreneurs can have an innovative advantage over existing firms because they are not subject to various types of incumbent inertia. First, firms encounter incumbent inertia in the form of *adjustment costs* that limit adaptation to new technologies and changing markets. Capital adjustment costs are widely studied by economists. For example, Cooper and Haltiwanger (2006) observe capital adjustment costs at the plant level. Firms experience human capital adjustment costs; innovation requires retraining or firing existing personnel and hiring, training, and absorbing new personnel. Existing firms that innovate incur incremental costs of changing operations, marketing, sales, and procurement. Applying new technologies can require fundamental changes in the firm's organizational structure. These adjustment costs conceivably could be greater than the set-up costs of establishing a new firm. There is evidence that larger existing firms have different incentives to innovate than smaller firms including entrepreneurial entrants (see Winter, 1984; Acs and Audretsch, 1988; and Audretsch, 1995b).

Second, firms face incumbent inertia as a result of *diversification costs* when innovation involves new products or entry into new markets. A critical determinant of the costs of diversification is what distinguishes the existing product from the new product. The differences between the existing product and the new product may be fundamental differences in features. The incumbent's products may be differentiated horizontally, such as Coke and Sprite, or vertically, such as the Toyota Avalon and the Lexus ES.

Diversification costs include the costs of organizational changes. Offering new products, even those that are substitutes for the incumbent's initial product, can require establishing new divisions to handle the different sales channels and marketing required for the new product. This entails costs of establishing the new division and costs of coordination across divisions. In some industries, such diversification is feasible and incumbents tend to absorb multiple innovations by adding new products. In other industries, incumbent firms may face limitations on managerial attention that constrain the number of products they produce. Using illustrations from the history of Microsoft and IBM, Bresnahan et al. (2011) suggest that firms experience diseconomies of scope because their complementary organizational assets need not be suited for multiple markets. The firm's costs of producing multiple products then would be greater than the total costs of single-product firms supplying those products. Therefore, specialized assets and diseconomies of scope imply that diversification by existing firms can be inefficient.

Existing firms may experience difficulties in extending their brand or launching new brands. A firm offering multiple brands must adjust its marketing and sales efforts to coordinate its brand portfolio. In some cases, an existing firm diversifies its offerings by extending its brand to a variety of products. An entrepreneurial entrant may create a new brand that is difficult to transfer to an existing firm because its identity is distinct from that of the incumbent. For example, whether the sales channel is online versus bricks-and-mortar affects consumer brand loyalty for retail products (Danaher et al., 2003). This suggests that a brand identified with the online retailer itself, such as Amazon.com, could be difficult to transfer to a brand identified with a bricks-and-mortar retailer.

Third, firms encounter incumbent inertia as a result of the *replacement effect.* Arrow (1962b) identified inertia in R&D as the replacement effect for incumbent monopolists. Economic analyses that find "persistence of monopoly" or the "efficiency condition" suggest that incumbent firms have competitive advantages over entrants. Some of these studies assume that incumbent firms can diversify without cost and make the corresponding implicit assumption that an entrant cannot diversify. Then, an incumbent monopolist can coordinate its prices across multiple differentiated products. Such diversification would generate greater profits than a competitive industry for the obvious reason that competition dissipates rents. Rather than establishing a firm, an inventor would always transfer the technology to an incumbent firm who could then diversify and obtain monopoly rents with multiple goods.[10]

The economic lifetime of a firm need not end the moment an innovation appears. Rather than incurring costs of adjustment and diversification, incumbent firms may choose to continue earning returns to existing assets. Incumbent firms

10 The persistence of monopoly is related to models of increasing dominance in which a leading firm obtains increasing advantage over other firms; see Gilbert and Newberry (1982), Budd et al. (1993), Bagwell et al. (1997), and Cabral (2003).

continue to obtain returns even in declining industries, staying in business as long as revenues cover operating costs. They must weigh the returns to operating without changing their business practices against the returns to innovating. Here sunk costs are important; entrants must cover both operating costs and the costs of entry.

Finally, firms encounter incumbent inertia as a result of *imperfect adjustment of expectations.* Existing firms face uncertainty regarding technological change and the returns to innovation. Because economic agents have different information, their expectations can differ. In particular, entrepreneurs may have expectations that differ from those of existing firms. Firms and other economic agents face limitations on information processing that generates expectations inertia.[11] Firms must choose their actions in the face of residual uncertainty because they cannot fully extract signals (see Phelps, 1970, and Lucas, 1973). Firms face delays in obtaining information that leads to sticky expectations (Mankiw and Reis, 2002). Expectations inertia provides an explanation for sticky prices without menu costs and other price-adjustment costs (see Mankiw and Reis, 2002). These types of expectations inertia not only explain sticky prices and sticky investment but also can explain sticky innovation.

A new firm may be needed for innovation if existing firms do not correctly judge the economic value of the invention. Managers of existing firms sometimes appear to underestimate the competitive threat posed by technological change. This management problem commonly is referred to as "management myopia."[12] The managers of existing firms may follow such a narrow definition of their market that they fail to identify technological changes that create products that are substitutes in demand. Thus, managers of companies that manufacture fax machines may not see the value of e-mail if they believe that they are in the fax machine business rather than in the communication business. Similarly, managers may not understand the impact of technologies that create substitute production processes or improved transactions. For example, Levitt (1960) notes that neighborhood grocery store chains once believed that supermarkets did not pose a competitive threat. Sears failed to understand that Walmart would become a direct competitor because Walmart began by serving rural areas. American automobile manufacturers did not initially perceive competitive threats from foreign automakers such as Toyota, Nissan, or Mercedes-Benz.

Entrepreneurs also may be more innovative than larger existing firms because start-up enterprises are not subject to inertia generated by bureaucratic decision making. Baumol et al. (2007) distinguish between entrepreneurial capitalism and state-guided, oligarchic, and big firm capitalism. They suggest that large firms focus on incremental improvements rather than drastic breakthrough innovations. The manager of an established firm is part of an existing hierarchy, often with

11 See Sims (2003), Morris and Shin (2002, 2006), and Amato and Shin (2006).

12 The term comes from Theodore Levitt (1960) who wrote about "marketing myopia" in which managers do not understand the implications of inventions for their business.

bureaucratic routines, risk aversion, and procedural inefficiencies that are observed in some large business organizations (Schramm, 2006b).

Incumbent inertia does not imply that the economy is subject to "technology lock-in" because entrepreneurial initiative provides an impetus for technological change. Some economists argue that "technology lock-in" can occur because the social benefits of using common technologies generate *network effects* from adoption that favor early inventions over later ones. *Customer switching costs* and brand loyalties make it difficult for new or existing firms to offer new products (Klemperer, 1995). However, these concerns about "technology lock-in" are inconsistent with observed technological change throughout the economic and the continual replacement of obsolete products and processes with new ones. There are many private ordering mechanisms that address coordination problems, allowing buyers and sellers to cooperate in obtaining the benefits of technological change. Economy-wide "technology lock-in" therefore is unlikely to occur because of the significant returns to technological change.[13] Rather than locking in technology, incumbent inertia creates opportunities for innovative entrepreneurs to drive aggregate technological change.

Innovative Advantage: Entrepreneurs versus Incumbents

Incumbent inertia aside, incumbent firms have various innovative advantages over entrepreneurs. Existing firms are *organizations* that benefit from the combined human capital of their managers and employees. The organizational capital of incumbent firms yields competitive advantages in identifying, obtaining, absorbing, and applying new technologies. Entrepreneurs in contrast are *individuals* and therefore are subject to bounded rationality, personal budget constraints, and human capital limitations. These can limit the innovative capability of entrepreneurs in comparison to incumbent firms.

Incumbent firms benefit from having already sunk costs of entry. The incumbents' costs of innovation are the incremental costs of R&D and technology transfer. Entrepreneurs in contrast must incur the set-up costs of creating a start-up and establishing a new firm. The incumbent firm already has complementary assets that increase the incremental returns to innovation (see particularly Teece, 1986, 1988, 2006). Entrepreneurial entrants may encounter substantial transaction costs in developing or acquiring complementary assets.

Innovation poses a particular challenge for entrepreneurial finance. By their very nature, innovative projects are untested and difficult to evaluate. Innovative uncertainty compounds the financing problems of entrepreneurs who must obtaining financing for a new venture. Incumbent firms are likely to have better access to finance than potential entrants. Existing firms can finance their operations, investment, and innovation from earnings. They can raise funds through securities,

13 Spulber (2008d).

bonds, and bank loans. Existing firms have reputations with investors that can be applied to fund new products, production methods, and diversification – even new technologies are speculative. Existing firms have assets that can serve as collateral and can provide creditors with information about the past performance of the business. This suggests that existing firms have competitive advantages in obtaining financing for innovative projects.

The entrepreneur, however, can gain an innovation advantage over incumbents by exercising individual initiative. The innovative entrepreneur benefits from the ability to design a new firm "from scratch," thus avoiding adjustment costs. Firms are purpose-built institutions; a railroad is not the same as an airline. The firm that runs a railroad cannot be adapted easily to operate an airline. It is likely to be far less costly to launch an airline firm than to turn a railroad firm into an airline firm. In many situations, an existing firm attempting to introduce innovative products or production processes would need to change practically all of its marketing, sales, manufacturing, and procurement activities. Innovative entrepreneurs can build new firms for the purpose of implementing the innovation they introduce to the market place. The new firm's start-up costs may be less than the existing firm's adjustment costs.

The innovative entrepreneur need not incur diversification costs. A new firm may be best suited to produce new products, to apply new production processes, to serve new customers, and to seek new sources of supply. A new firm's human capital, sales, marketing, organizational structure, operations, and technology are adapted to the innovation. The human capital requirements for new technologies may be entirely different, so that it might be less costly to start over, hiring new managers and new employees. The organizational structure of existing firms may be less efficient than innovative structures, but because of the complexities of communication, incentives, and delegation of authority, it may be more costly to change organizations than to create a new one.

New firms that focus on a particular innovation obtain the benefits of specialization and division of labor. For example, online retailers and other e-commerce intermediaries develop expertise in Internet transactions. Economic efficiencies may result from existing firms and new firms concentrating their efforts on different types of products, even if the eventual result is creative destruction. New transaction methods may open additional sales channels. It may be difficult for an existing firm to manage multiple sales channels, thus providing returns to specialized organizations. For example, Amazon focused on building an online book store, whereas Borders and Barnes & Noble focused on operating a traditional retail bookstore. Netflix focused on building an online movie rental service with delivery by mail and over the Internet, whereas Blockbuster focused on operating a video rental chain. Such divisions of labor within industries may have been efficient despite the difficulties encountered by Borders, Barnes & Noble, or Blockbuster. It is may be more efficient for new firms to operate new sales channels rather than for existing firms to simultaneously operate multiple sales channels.

New firms are relatively low-cost experiments compared to the costs of restructuring and repositioning large existing firms. There are many alternative innovations to choose from and considerable uncertainty about which ones will succeed in the market place. Entrepreneurial entry provides a way for the economy to make many small bets on a variety of innovations. This provides economic benefits that are similar to portfolio diversification. Additionally, multiple experiments allow winners to emerge through market competition.

Larger existing firms standardize their offerings to benefit from economies of scale, so that switching to a new product or production process can be very costly because it requires change on a large scale. Larger firms also bear costs of offering many diverse goods as a means of experimentation because that would cause them to lose economies of scale. Some large existing firms find ways to experiment internally with isolated projects. For example, aircraft maker Lockheed Martin established an Advanced Development Projects unit referred to as the Skunk Works that produced such advanced designs as the U-2 and SR-71 Blackbird surveillance aircraft (Rich and Janos, 1994). The Skunk Works also introduced stealth technology and developed a number of stealth fighter planes such as the F-117 Nighthawk and the F-22 Raptor.

Performance incentives may differ in start-ups and existing firms. Because of their smaller size, entrepreneurial start-ups have different incentive structures than do larger existing firms. As a result, the entrepreneur may have better incentives to apply an innovation than a manager of an existing firm. It should be emphasized that large-scale existing firms can be innovative. Prior to encountering serious difficulties in adapting to challenges from foreign automakers and other market changes, leading U.S. automakers Ford and GM innovated for nearly a century. Sears offered innovations in mass marketing even if they missed opportunities discovered by new entrants Walmart, Target, and Costco.

Entrepreneurs can apply creative entry strategies and innovations to surmount potential advantages of incumbent firms. Growing market demand or changes in consumer tastes generate opportunities for entry. Technological change allows entrants to introduce new products, lower production costs, or arrange novel transactions. Generally, with technological change, the need to sink cost is not an insurmountable barrier to the entry of new competitors. If an entrant employs new technologies to reduce its operating costs, it can enjoy a cost advantage over an incumbent operating outdated technology. Even if the incumbent and entrant compete on price, an entrant with differentiated products or an operating cost advantage will obtain earnings that are sufficient to cover entry costs.

Sunk costs need not be an entry barrier because the entrant's investment is a matter of strategic choice. The entrepreneur makes various decisions about how much to spend on manufacturing, planning, marketing, sales, or R&D. The entrant can serve different sets of customers than the incumbent, thus changing the entrant's need for distribution facilities and marketing expenditures. The entrepreneur can adopt different production or distribution technologies than incumbent firms, often drastically changing the mix of investment and operating costs. Even with similar products and technology, an entrepreneur can reduce the risk associated with making investment commitments by forming contracts with customers before irreversible investments are made. The entrant can compete with the incumbent for customers before deciding to enter the market and then only incur entry costs if customer contracts generate sufficient revenues.

3.3 Incumbent Inertia and Innovative Advantage

This section presents some basic models of incumbent inertia and innovative entrepreneurship. The discussion explores the effects of the incumbent's replacement effect on incentives to innovate by the incumbent firm and the entrepreneurial entrant.

Effects of Incumbent Inertia

Consider an incumbent monopolist with initial process technology represented by unit costs c_0. The firm can obtain a new technology c_1 that improves on the initial technology, $c_1 < c_0$. Market demand for the final product, $D(p)$, is a twice continuously differentiable and strictly decreasing function of the final product price, p. The monopolist's profit function is

$$\Pi(p, c) = (p - c)D(p), \tag{1}$$

and $p^M(c)$ is the profit-maximizing monopoly price. Monopoly profits at the profit-maximizing price are given by $\Pi^M(c) = \Pi(p^M(c), c)$.

The incumbent firm faces innovative inertia because of the *replacement effect.* Suppose that the cost of developing or acquiring the new technology is k. As Arrow (1962b) showed, the monopolist will innovate only if the incremental returns cover the costs of obtaining the new technology,

$$\Pi^M(c_1) - \Pi^M(c_0) \geq k.$$

This results from the opportunity cost of losing profits it would earn from continuing to operate its initial technology $\Pi^M(c_0)$. The better is the initial technology – that is, the lower c_0, the greater is the replacement effect.

Unlike the existing firm, an entrepreneur does not have the initial technology. The entrepreneur incurs a fixed cost K to establish a firm and also incurs the cost k of developing or acquiring the new technology. Then, the entrepreneur innovates only if the incremental returns to entry cover the cost of obtaining the new technology,

$$\Pi^M(c_1) - K \geq k.$$

The entrepreneur has an innovative advantage over the existing firm if the cost of establishing a firm is less than the profit of an existing firm using the initial technology,

$$K < \Pi^M(c_0).$$

When entry costs are not too high, an entrepreneur innovates more than an existing firm.

Consider incentives to innovate when the entrepreneurial entrant competes with the existing firm. Suppose first that the existing firm does not innovate and operates with the initial technology, c_0. The entrepreneurial entrant and the incumbent firm engage in Bertrand-Nash price competition. With constant unit costs and homogeneous products, an innovative entrepreneur competes with and displaces an incumbent firm.

There are two important possibilities that were identified by Arrow's (1962b) classic discussion.[14] The innovation is said to be *drastic* if the monopoly price at the new technology is less than or equal to the initial unit cost, $p^M(c_1) \leq c_0$. If the invention is drastic, the entrant can offer a monopoly price that is less than the incumbent's unit cost and displace the incumbent. The innovation is said to be *non-drastic* if the monopoly price at the new technology is greater than the initial unit cost, $p^M(c_1) > c_0$. If the invention is non-drastic, the entrant will be constrained by competing with the incumbent and will price at the incumbent's unit cost c_0. Therefore, the entrepreneurial entrant's price is

$$p^*(c_0, c_1) = \min\{p^M(c_1), c_0\}. \tag{2}$$

Compare the entrepreneur's incentive to innovate with that of the incumbent monopolist. The entrepreneur innovates when the incremental returns to entry cover the cost of developing or acquiring the new technology,

$$\Pi(p^*(c_0, c_1), c_1) - K \geq k.$$

If the invention is drastic, the entrepreneur obtains the full monopoly profit, $\Pi(p^*(c_0, c_1), c_1) = \Pi^M(c_1)$. The entrepreneur has a greater incentive to innovate than would a monopoly incumbent if and only if the cost of entry is less than monopoly profits at the initial technology, $K < \Pi^M(c_0)$.

If the invention is non-drastic, $p^M(c_1) > c_0$, the entrepreneur's profit,

$$\Pi(p^*(c_0, c_1), c_1) = (c_0 - c_1)D(c_0),$$

14 In the R&D literature, the term *drastic* is sometimes applied to inventions and at other times to innovations. What did Arrow (1962b) actually say? He uses the term drastic exactly once – it appears in the phrase "the cost reduction is sufficiently drastic" – and does not use the term non-drastic. Arrow refers to major and minor inventions and refers to an invention that is "sufficiently cost reducing." We consider an innovation to be the application of the invention to reduce costs. Accordingly, because the cost reduction is the innovation, we apply the term drastic to innovations.

is less than monopoly profit, $\Pi^M(c_1)$. The entrepreneur has a greater incentive to innovate than a monopoly incumbent if $(c_0 - c_1)D(c_0) - K > \Pi^M(c_1) - \Pi^M(c_0)$. In comparison to the situation with a drastic invention, a tighter bound on entry costs is needed for the entrepreneur to have a greater incentive to innovate than a monopoly incumbent,

$$K < \Pi^M(c_0) + (c_0 - c_1)D(c_0) - \Pi^M(c_1) < \Pi^M(c_0).$$

Define the critical cost value for a drastic innovation by $p^M(c_1{}^*) = c_0$. Innovations with unit cost less than or equal to the critical value $c_1{}^* = c_1{}^*(c_0)$ are drastic. The derivative $p^{M\prime}(c)$ is the familiar cost pass-through. So, the effect of the initial technology on the critical value is equal to the reciprocal of the cost pass-through,

$$\frac{dc_1{}^*(c_0)}{dc_0} = \frac{1}{p^{M\prime}(c)}.$$

When the first-order condition holds for the monopolist's profit maximization problem, the cost pass-through effect is

$$p^{M\prime}(c) = \frac{-\Pi_{pc}(p^M(c), c)}{\Pi_{pp}(p^M(c), c)} = \frac{D'(p^M(c))}{(p^M(c) - c)D''(p^M(c)) + 2D'(p^M(c))}.$$

For the monopolist with a constant unit cost, price and cost are strict complements, $\Pi_{pc}(p, c) = -D'(p) > 0$.[15] Concavity of profit in price implies that the monopoly price is strictly increasing in costs, so that the cost pass-through is positive, $p^{M\prime}(c) > 0$.[16] The critical value for a drastic innovation $c_1{}^*(c_0)$ is increasing in the initial technology.[17]

Efficiency Effects of Incumbent Inertia

Innovation provides private benefits to innovative entrepreneurs and innovative firms and their customers, suppliers, and investors. Entrepreneurial entrants

15 Without assuming concavity of profits, this implies that the monopoly price $p^M(c)$ is nondecreasing in costs by standard monotone comparative statics arguments.

16 Also, notice that cost pass-through can be written as

$$p^{M\prime}(c) = \frac{1}{2 - [D(p^M(c))D''(p^M(c))]/[(D'(p^M(c))]^2}.$$

Demand is log-concave (log-convex) as $d^2(\log D(p))/dp^2 < (>)\ 0$. Cost pass-through is less than (greater than) one for one, $p^{M\prime}(c) > (<)\ 1$, as demand is log-concave (log-convex). See Weyl and Fabinger (2012) for an overview of cost pass-through.

17 A positive cost pass-through also implies that the monopolist's profit at the profit-maximizing price is convex in costs. With a positive cost pass-through, maximum profit is convex in cost, $\Pi^{M\prime\prime}(c) = -D'(p^M(c)p^{M\prime}(c) > 0$. This implies that the monopolist is risk-loving when cost is subject to random shocks, as occurs with risky R&D. By Jensen's inequality, the monopolist prefers expected profit to profit evaluated at expected cost.

increase competition, which can generate losses for inefficient entrants and incumbents. The firms established by innovative entrepreneurs displace other entrants and incumbent firms with less attractive products or less productive technologies. The costs of entrepreneurial entry are the costs of developing a start-up and establishing a new firm. The costs of creative destruction include the foregone value of the existing firm, based on its facilities, capital equipment, organizational capital, brand name, and reputation. Economic decisions depend only on the prospective costs and benefits affected. The costs of creative destruction do not include the sunk costs of the existing firm, which have no bearing on economic decisions. As a result of creative destruction, the incumbent monopoly does not obtain profits $\Pi^M(c_0)$ that would have been earned from continuing to operate the initial technology. The social welfare effects of innovative entrepreneurship are equal to the sum of the price effects on consumers and the difference between the profits of the entrant and the incumbent firm evaluated at the initial technology,

$$(3) \qquad B^{ME} = \int_{p^*(c_1,c_0)}^{p^M(c_0)} D(x)dx + \Pi(p^*(c_1, c_0), c_1) - K - \Pi^M(c_0).$$

Entrepreneurial entry only occurs if the entering firm's profits cover the costs of entry, $\Pi(p^*(c_1, c_0), c_1) \geq K$. This implies that the social welfare effects of innovative entrepreneurship are greater than or equal to consumer surplus gains net of the lost profits of the incumbent,

$$B^{ME} \geq \int_{p^*(c_1,c_0)}^{p^M(c_0)} D(x)dx - \Pi^M(c_0).$$

The price after entry is bounded above by the initial costs of the incumbent firm, $p^*(c_1, c_0) \leq c_0$, so that

$$\int_{p^*(c_1,c_0)}^{p^M(c_0)} D(x)dx - \Pi^M(c_0) \geq \int_{c_0}^{p^M(c_0)} (D(x) - D(p^M(c_0)))dx > 0.$$

The last term is positive because the monopoly price of the incumbent is greater than his unit costs, and demand is downward sloping. This implies that innovative entrepreneurship has positive social welfare effects, $B^{ME} > 0$.

Some discussions of innovation argue that creative destruction causes a "negative externality."[18] Entrepreneurial entrants do not take into account the lost profits of incumbent firms, which are said to be a social cost. This results in a difference

18 In a model of economic growth, Aghion and Howitt (1998, p. 53), for example, state: "On the *normative* side, although current innovations have positive externalities for future research and development, they also exert a negative externality on incumbent producers. This *business-stealing effect* in turn introduces the possibility that growth be excessive under laissez-faire." Additionally, they state: "The private research firm does not internalize the loss to the previous monopolist caused by an innovation. In contrast, the social planner takes into account that an innovation destroys the social return from the previous innovation. This effect will tend to generate *too much* research under laissez-faire" (1998, p. 62).

between the private benefits and the social benefits of innovation. The result is excessive innovation, which leads researchers to call for government regulation to correct the outcome by deterring innovation, limiting entry and competition, or protecting incumbent firms.

Creative destruction does not create a "negative externality" because the effects of innovation are entirely mediated by markets. Benefits and costs are internalized by market participants. Entry by innovative entrepreneurs generates profits for the new firms as well as benefits for consumers from lower prices or improved products. The profits or losses of entrants and incumbents are determined by the firms' competitive strategies. Consumers' choices are the result of purchasing decisions based on product features and market prices. Unlike externalities that result from pollution or depletion of natural resources, there is no failure of property rights. The entering and incumbent firms are privately owned enterprises.

Comparing creative destruction to an externality is related to Pigou's "pecuniary externality." Pigou posits an industry that is subject to diminishing marginal returns – that is, increasing marginal costs. Pigou suggests that competitive entry results in a negative externality because rising prices of productive factors caused a divergence between social and private costs, not taking into account that economic rents are part of the costs of increasing output.[19] This argument is shown to be false by many economists including Frank Knight (1924, p. 584): "The fallacy to be exposed is a misinterpretation of the relation between social cost and entrepreneur's cost."[20] A similar error appears in the notion that externalities are caused by "indirect network effects," which also involves market mediated price effects.[21] The "negative externality" attributed to creative destruction is simply foregone profits of incumbent firms and not an externality.

Entry need not maximize social welfare because equilibrium market structure can differ from the social optimum. For example, racing in R&D games can lead to excessive entry.[22] Entry of Cournot firms leads to excessive entry and entry of Bertrand competitors offering differentiated products can lead to excessive product

19 See Pigou (1912, 1924, 1932).

20 Ellis and Fellner (1943, p. 493) observe that "one may find difficulty in understanding how theorists such as Marshall, Pigou, Viner, Graham, Hicks, and Lange could be ranged squarely against Allyn Young, Knight, and Stigler."

21 Liebowitz and Margolis (1994, 2002) demonstrate that "indirect network effects" are handled by the market for complementary goods and therefore should not be considered as "externalities," pointing out the connection to Pigou's notion of a "pecuniary externality." As they point out "The impact of one firm's actions on competing firms is just another externality that distorts market outcomes away from the ideal. This of course is false, since the additional payments going to inframarginal inputs as industry output increases (assuming upward sloping supply) are rents, which are not part of the social cost of providing additional output" (Liebowitz and Margolis, 1994, p. 136).

22 See Salant (1984), Katz and Shapiro (1987), and Reinganum (1981, 1982, 1989).

Table 3.1. *The R&D game with payoffs (Existing firm, Entrepreneur)*

	Entrepreneur Engage in R&D	Entrepreneur Do not engage in R&D
Existing firm Engage in R&D	v_{11}, V_{11}	v_{10}, 0
Existing firm Do not engage in R&D	v_{01}, V_{01}	$\Pi^M(c_0)$, 0

variety.[23] The socially optimal number of firms maximizes the sum of consumers' surplus and total industry profits. Assuming for convenience that the number of firms is a continuous variable, entry continues until rents are dissipated – that is, until profits are zero. This implies that the market equilibrium with entry need not correspond to the social-welfare maximizing market structure.[24]

Incumbent Inertia and Endogenous R&D

The existing firm faces inertia even if both the incumbent firm and the entrepreneurial entrant have a chance of operating after entry takes place. To illustrate this, suppose that the existing firm and the potential entrepreneur each must decide whether or not to invest k in R&D. The initial technology is c_0 and the new technology is c_1, where $c_1 < c_0$. Investing in R&D yields the new technology with probability β. The entrepreneur incurs an entry cost of K. Assume that an incumbent monopolist would choose to engage in R&D, $\beta(\Pi^M(c_1) - \Pi^M(c_0)) > k$. Table 3.1 shows the expected payoffs of the R&D game.

If neither the entrepreneur nor the incumbent engage in R&D, the incumbent continues to operate with the initial technology and earns profits $\Pi^M(c_0)$, and the entrepreneur does not receive any profits. If only the incumbent engages in R&D, the incumbent operates with the initial technology if R&D is unsuccessful and operates with the new technology if R&D is successful, obtaining a expected payoff

$$v_{10} = \beta\Pi^M(c_1) + (1 - \beta)\Pi^M(c_0) - k. \tag{4}$$

Again, the entrepreneur does not receive any profits. If only the potential entrant engages in R&D, then the entrepreneur only enters the market if the project is successful. For ease of presentation, assume that the innovation is drastic so that

23 See Spulber (1989, pp. 505–526) for a survey of some of these results.

24 Social welfare in a reduced-form model equals the sum of consumers' surplus and total per-firm profits net of entry costs, $CS(n) + n\pi(n)$. When the number of firms n is a continuous variable, entry occurs until profits are zero, $\pi(n) = 0$, with profits per firm decreasing in the number of firms. Social welfare is maximized when $CS'(n^0) + n^0\pi'(n^0) + n^0\pi(n^0) = 0$. If $CS'(n^0) + n^0\pi'(n^0) < 0$, then $\pi(n^0) > 0$ so that the market equilibrium industry structure with free entry has more firms than at the social optimum.

entry by an innovative entrepreneur displaces the existing firm operating the initial technology. Then, the incumbent's expected payoff is $v_{01} = (1 - \beta)\Pi^M(c_0)$, and the entrepreneur's expected payoff is $V_{01} = \beta(\Pi^M(c_1) - K) - k$.

Finally, if both the incumbent and the potential entrepreneur invest in R&D, they enter a race to develop the new technology.[25] There are four possible outcomes of the R&D race. If neither the existing firm nor the entrepreneur is successful, then the existing firm continues to operate using the initial technology. If only the existing firm is successful, the existing firm operates using the new technology. If only the entrepreneur is successful, then the entrepreneur enters with the new technology and displaces the existing firm. Finally, if both the existing firm and the entrepreneur are successful, they compete for the market using the new technology with each having an equal chance at emerging as the winner. In the R&D race, the incumbent's expected payoff is

$$(5) \quad v_{11} = (1 - \beta)(1 - \beta)\Pi^M(c_0) + \beta(1 - \beta)\Pi^M(c_1) + \frac{1}{2}\beta^2\Pi^M(c_1) - k.$$

In the R&D race, the entrepreneur's expected payoff is

$$(6) \quad V_{11} = \beta\left[(1 - \beta) + \frac{1}{2}\beta\right]\Pi^M(c_1) - \beta K - k.$$

Consider the conditions such that both firms conduct R&D at a dominant-strategy equilibrium. The entrepreneur's expected return from R&D is reduced when the incumbent engages in R&D, $V_{01} > V_{11}$. So, R&D is a dominant strategy for the entrepreneur if $V_{11} > 0$.

When the entrepreneur does not engage in R&D, there is no threat of entrepreneurial entry so that the incumbent firm will engage in R&D because by assumption $v_{10} > \Pi^M(c_0)$, which is equivalent to

$$\beta(\Pi^M(c_1) - \Pi^M(c_0)) > k.$$

This illustrates the replacement effect with uncertain R&D. When the entrepreneur does engage in R&D, the incumbent firm also will engage in R&D if $v_{11} > v_{01}$, which is equivalent to

$$\frac{1}{2}\beta^2\Pi^M(c_1) + \beta(1 - \beta)[\Pi^M(c_1) - \Pi^M(c_0)] > k.$$

This illustrates the replacement effect with both uncertain R&D and the threat of entry by an innovative entrepreneur. R&D is a dominant strategy for the incumbent firm when both of these conditions hold.

Because a monopolist would engage in R&D by assumption, the incumbent firm would engage in R&D without the threat of entry. Using this assumption, it also follows that a sufficient but not necessary condition for R&D to be a dominant

25 See Gans and Stern (2000, p. 487) for a model of racing to invent with technological spillovers and technology licensing.

strategy for the incumbent firm is for its profits using the new technology to be sufficiently large, $\beta\Pi^M(c_1) > 2k$. When this condition holds and $V_{11} > 0$, both the incumbent firm and the entrepreneur engage in R&D at the dominant strategy equilibrium.[26]

Now consider the conditions for there to be a Nash equilibrium such that the entrepreneur engages in R&D and the incumbent does not. The incumbent chooses not to engage in R&D as best response to entrepreneurial R&D when $v_{11} \leq v_{01}$. The entrepreneur chooses R&D as a best response to the incumbent not engaging in R&D when $V_{01} > 0$. These conditions imply that there is a Nash equilibrium at which only the entrepreneur engages in R&D. Together, these conditions give an upper bound on entry costs,

$$\frac{1}{2}\beta\Pi^M(c_1) + (1-\beta)\Pi^M(c_0) > K.$$

Because of the replacement effect, the upper bound is increasing in the profits of the incumbent using the initial technology $\Pi^M(c_0)$.

The Nash equilibrium in which only the entrepreneur engages in R&D is unique if we also have $V_{11} > 0$. This implies that $V_{01} > 0$ because $V_{01} > V_{11}$. So, engaging in R&D is a dominant strategy for the entrepreneur. Recall that the incumbent firm will not engage in R&D as a best response to the entrepreneur engaging in R&D if $v_{11} \leq v_{01}$. Then, combining $V_{11} > 0$ and $v_{11} \leq v_{01}$ implies that there is a unique Nash equilibrium with an innovative entrepreneur and incumbent inertia. Combining these two conditions gives an upper bound on entry costs,

$$(1-\beta)\Pi^M(c_0) > K.$$

This condition illustrates incumbent inertia. The existing firm chooses to risk being replaced by creative destruction so as to avoid the costs of obtaining the new technology. This occurs when the profit from the initial technology times the probability that the entrepreneur's R&D is not successful exceeds entry costs.

3.4 Incumbent Inertia and Technology Transfer

This section considers a basic model in which an independent inventor licenses a general purpose technology. The inventor's commercialization options include technology transfer to an existing firm, an innovative entrepreneur, or both (see Figure 3.2). The innovative entrepreneur uses the technology to produce a new product that is different from that of the existing firm. If the innovative entrepreneur

26 Note that $(1/2)\beta^2\Pi^M(c_1) + \beta(1-\beta)[\Pi^M(c_1) - \Pi^M(c_0)] > (1/2)\beta^2\Pi^M(c_1) + (1-\beta)k > k$. The first inequality follows from $\beta(\Pi^M(c_1) - \Pi^M(c_0)) > k$, and the second inequality follows from $\beta\Pi^M(c_1) > 2k$.

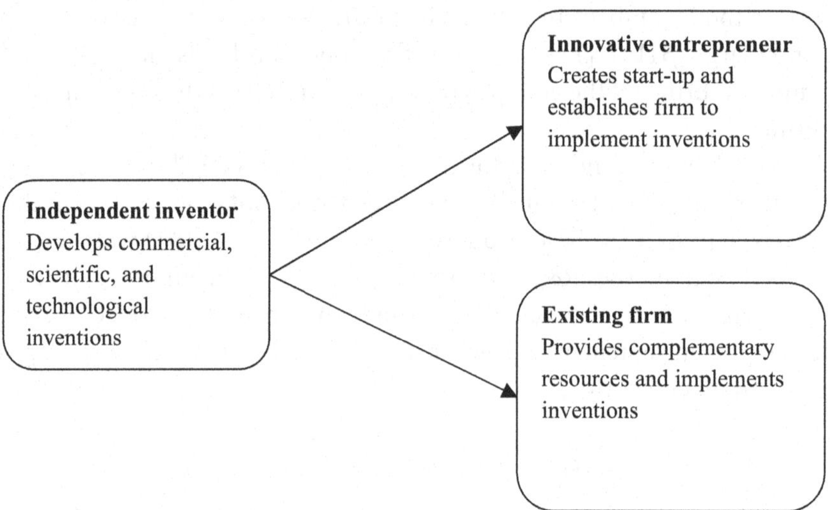

Figure 3.2. The independent inventor can transfer inventions to an innovative entrepreneur, an existing firm, or both.

enters the market, the existing firm and the entrepreneurial entrant engage in differentiated products competition. Because of incumbent inertia, independent inventors have an incentive to license inventions to both incumbents and entrepreneurial entrants.

The strategic innovation game in this section involves an incumbent monopolist and an inventor. The model is related to that of Anton and Yao (1995), who compare the effects of transferring an invention to a start-up, an internal venture, or a a spin-off. When the incumbent firm's property rights are weak, an employee inventor can leave the firm and become an innovative entrepreneur by creating a start-up that uses the new technology. Alternatively, the employee inventor can reveal the discovery to the firm, which then employs the invention in an internal venture. Finally, the firm and the employee inventor can form a contract that transfers the technology to a spin-off. If the employee establishes a start-up, it competes with the existing firm if the existing firm also develops the invention. The advantage of a spin-off is that it avoids creative destruction and has a monopoly over the invention.[27]

The strategic innovation game also is related to the analysis of Gans and Stern (2000) who consider the trade-off between the threat of product market entry and the threat of expropriation of the technology by the incumbent.[28] They observe

27 See also Anton and Yao (1994).

28 Gans and Stern (2000) consider a three-stage model in which there is an R&D race between an incumbent and a potential entrant in the first stage. If the incumbent wins the race, the incumbent remains a monopolist, and if the entrant wins the race, the incumbent and entrant engage in bargaining in the second stage, with either technology licensing or entry occurring in the third stage. The third stage is a reduced-form representation of competition. Gans and

that "under the traditional assumptions of the literature on technological competition, and in the absence of noncontractible information asymmetries between the incumbent and entrant, observations of entry by the startup into the product market represent something of an economic puzzle" (p. 487).

Technology Transfer when the Entrepreneur Cannot Obtain the Initial Technology

Consider a strategic innovation game in which an independent inventor seeks to commercialize an invention. The industry consists of a monopoly firm that operates with an existing technology. An innovative entrepreneur cannot obtain the initial technology and can only enter the industry by licensing the new technology from the independent inventor. Then, the innovative entrepreneur establishes a firm that implements the invention and provides a new product. To highlight the effects of incumbent inertia, suppose that the innovative entrepreneur's entry costs are zero except for the costs of the technology license.

The inventor must decide whether to license the technology to the entrepreneurial entrant, the incumbent firm, or both. Suppose that the inventor must offer a non-exclusive license and cannot engage in price discrimination. In the first stage, the inventor offers the invention to the existing firm and to the potential entrepreneur. In the second stage, the incumbent firm and the potential entrepreneur play an adoption-and-entry game. The existing firm chooses whether or not to adopt the new process technology. The potential entrepreneur chooses whether or not to adopt the new process technology and enter the market. If the entrepreneur enters the market, the entrant and the incumbent firm compete in the product market with differentiated products.

The two-stage innovation game is solved by backward induction. We begin by characterizing the outcome of the adoption-and-entry subgame that takes place in the second stage. Then, we consider the equilibrium royalty chosen by the monopoly inventor in the first stage. For ease of discussion, suppose that the inventor chooses an up-front lump-sum royalty, R.[29] This is sometimes called a

Stern (2000, p. 487) introduce a property rights or spillover parameter and allow the incumbent to continue to invest in R&D during the bargaining stage that may be used to "expropriate the entrant's rents from successful innovation." Therefore, the incumbent considers the start-up's R&D a strategic substitute for the incumbent's in-house research. See also Gans et al. (2002) and Gans and Stern (2003).

29 Spulber (2013b) shows that with differentiated products, an independent inventor should choose a combination of a per-unit royalty and a lump-sum royalty. There is vast literature on royalties and technology licensing; see Fauli-Oller and Sandonis (2002) and the references therein. Katz and Shapiro (1986) find that a monopoly inventor earns greater profits licensing using a lump-sum royalty than with a per-unit royalty for a non-drastic innovation; see also Salant (1984) and Katz and Shapiro (1987). Muto (1993) shows that with product differentiation and quadratic utility in the downstream product market, a monopoly inventor prefers a per-unit royalty to a

"fixed fee" in economic models. In practice, licenses can involve a combination of lump-sum royalty payments and per-unit royalties.[30]

The existing firm's initial production process is represented by unit cost c_0, and the invention is a new production process represented by unit cost c_1. Assume that the new technology is superior to the existing technology, $c_1 < c_0$. Suppose first that the entrepreneur can only enter the market by adopting the new process technology so that the entrepreneur chooses between entry with adoption and not entering. This assumption will be relaxed later in this section by allowing the entrepreneur access to the initial process technology.

Let firm 1 be the existing firm and let firm 2 be the entrepreneurial entrant. Suppose that the firms engage in differentiated-products Bertrand competition if the entrepreneur enters the market. The reduced form profits of the existing firm and the entrepreneurial entrant are given by $\Pi_1(x_1, x_2)$ and $\Pi_2(x_1, x_2)$ respectively, where x_1 is the unit cost of firm 1 and x_2 is the unit cost of firm 2. The profit functions of the two firms are otherwise the same.

Assume that cost differences between the initial technology and the new technology are not so drastic that the low-cost firm could eliminate the high-cost firm by either monopoly pricing or profit-maximizing limit pricing. Assume that profits are decreasing in the firm's own costs,

$$\frac{\partial \Pi_1(x_1, x_2)}{\partial x_1} < 0, \qquad \frac{\partial \Pi_2(x_1, x_2)}{\partial x_2} < 0.$$

Assume further that profits are increasing in rival firm's costs,

$$\frac{\partial \Pi_1(x_1, x_2)}{\partial x_2} > 0, \qquad \frac{\partial \Pi_2(x_1, x_2)}{\partial x_1} > 0.$$

Also, assume that the marginal effect of the firm's own costs on its profits is decreasing in the costs of the competing firm,

$$\frac{\partial^2 \Pi_1(x_1, x_2)}{\partial x_1 \partial x_2} < 0, \qquad \frac{\partial^2 \Pi_2(x_1, x_2)}{\partial x_1 \partial x_2} < 0.$$

If the product market is monopolistic, profits equal $\Pi^M(c)$ as before. When the difference between the firms' costs is sufficiently large, the low-cost firm displaces

lump-sum royalty but does not consider combining the two. Erutku and Richelle (2007) show that a monopoly inventor will choose to combine a per-unit royalty and a lump-sum royalty when downstream products engage in Cournot competition. Fauli-Oller and Sandonis (2002) show a downstream producer licensing to another downstream producer using a combination of a per-unit royalty and a lump-sum royalty. Hernandez-Murillo and Llobet (2006) obtain nonlinear royalty contracts when the inventor has asymmetric information about downstream producers.

30 Per-unit royalties also are known as "running royalties." For a discussion of licensing royalties, see Epstein and Malherbe (2011).

Table 3.2. *The technology adoption-and-entry game with payoffs (Existing firm 1, Entrepreneurial firm 2)*

	Entrepreneurial firm 2 Enter	**Entrepreneurial firm 2 Do not enter**
Existing firm 1 Adopt	$\Pi_1(c_1, c_1) - R, \Pi_2(c_1, c_1) - R$	$\Pi^M(c_1) - R, 0$
Existing firm 1 Do not adopt	$\Pi_1(c_0, c_1), \Pi_2(c_0, c_1) - R$	$\Pi^M(c_0), 0$

the high-cost firm and earns monopoly profit – that is, if firm 1 has costs sufficiently lower than those of firm 2, $\Pi_1(x_1, x_2) = \Pi^M(x_1)$, or if firm 2 has costs sufficiently lower than those of firm 1, $\Pi_2(x_1, x_2) = \Pi^M(x_2)$.

The adoption-and-entry game has four possible outcomes. The existing firm chooses between continuing with the initial technology and adopting the new technology. The potential entrepreneur chooses whether or not to enter the market. If both the incumbent and the entrepreneur adopt the new technology, the payoffs are symmetric, $\Pi_1(c_1, c_1) - R$ and $\Pi_2(c_1, c_1) - R$. If only the entrepreneur adopts the new technology, the payoffs are asymmetric, with the incumbent firm earning profits $\Pi_1(c_0, c_1)$ and the entrepreneur earning net returns $\Pi_2(c_0, c_1) - R$. If only the incumbent firm adopts the new technology, the incumbent earns $\Pi^M(c_1) - R$ and the entrepreneur's payoff is zero. If neither firm adopts the new technology, the incumbent firm earns $\Pi^M(c_0)$ and the entrepreneur's payoff is again zero. Table 3.2 shows the adoption-and-entry game.

The royalty chosen by the inventor affects the outcome of the adoption-and-entry game between the incumbent firm and the entrepreneur. Suppose first that the inventor chooses royalties that are less than or equal to the incumbent's incremental returns from adoption when there is entrepreneurial entry,

$$R \leq \Pi_1(c_1, c_1) - \Pi_1(c_0, c_1).$$

Then, (Adopt, Enter) is the unique dominant strategy equilibrium.

First, notice that Adopt is a dominant strategy for the incumbent firm. The incumbent firm will prefer to adopt the new technology as a best response to entry by the entrepreneur because $R \leq \Pi_1(c_1, c_1) - \Pi_1(c_0, c_1)$ implies that

$$\Pi_1(c_1, c_1) - R \geq \Pi_1(c_0, c_1).$$

The incumbent firm also will prefer to adopt the technology even if there is no entrepreneurial entry. To see why, notice that because $c_1 < c_0$ and each firm's profits are decreasing in own costs, it follows that $\Pi_1(c_1, c_1) > \Pi_1(c_0, c_1)$ and $\Pi^M(c_1) > \Pi^M(c_0)$.

Also, because $\partial^2\Pi_1(c_0, c_1)/\partial c_0 \partial c_1 < 0$ and $c_1 < c_0$, it follows that the incremental returns to adopting the new technology are less for a firm facing competition from an entrant with the new technology than for a monopolist,

$$\Pi_1(c_1, c_1) - \Pi_1(c_0, c_1) \leq \Pi^M(c_1) - \Pi^M(c_0).$$[31]

This implies that the royalty is less than the incremental returns to adoption by a monopolist,

$$R \leq \Pi_1(c_1, c_1) - \Pi_1(c_0, c_1) \leq \Pi^M(c_1) - \Pi^M(c_0).$$

Therefore, the incumbent firm will adopt the new technology even without the threat of entry,

$$\Pi^M(c_1) - R \geq \Pi^M(c_0).$$

So, adoption is a dominant strategy for the incumbent firm.

Next, notice that entry with the new technology is a dominant strategy for the entrepreneur. The entrepreneur will adopt the technology and enter the market when the incumbent firm also adopts the technology. If the incumbent firm adopts the technology and $R \leq \Pi_1(c_1, c_1) - \Pi_1(c_0, c_1)$, it follows by symmetry that $R \leq \Pi_1(c_1, c_1) = \Pi_2(c_1, c_1)$. Because the entrepreneur earns greater profits when the incumbent does not adopt the technology, it follows that $R \leq \Pi_2(c_1, c_1) \leq \Pi_2(c_0, c_1)$. This implies that the entrepreneur also will choose to enter the market when the incumbent does not adopt the new technology. So, entry is a dominant strategy for the entrepreneur. This implies that when $R \leq \Pi_1(c_1, c_1) - \Pi_1(c_0, c_1)$, (Adopt, Enter) is the dominant strategy equilibrium of the adoption-and-entry game.

Now consider the outcome of the adoption-and-entry game when the royalty is greater than the incremental returns to adoption when faced with entry. Suppose also that the royalty is less than the entrant's return when the incumbent sticks with the initial technology. We have

$$\Pi_1(c_1, c_1) - \Pi_1(c_0, c_1) < R \leq \Pi_2(c_0, c_1).$$

This implies that the entrepreneur would enter as a best response to the incumbent firm using the initial technology. It also implies that the entrepreneur would enter as a best response to the incumbent firm using the new technology because $R \leq \Pi_2(c_0, c_1) < \Pi_2(c_1, c_1)$. Then, entry is a dominant strategy for the potential entrepreneur. The incumbent firm's best response to entry is to stick with the initial technology because $\Pi_1(c_1, c_1) - R < \Pi_1(c_0, c_1)$. Therefore, (Do Not Adopt, Enter) is a Nash equilibrium of the strategic game.

We are now ready to examine the profit-maximizing royalty chosen by the independent inventor in the first stage of the innovation game. The inventor who licenses to both the incumbent and entrant increases royalties until they equal incremental returns to adoption for the incumbent firm facing entry,

$$R^* = \Pi_1(c_1, c_1) - \Pi_1(c_0, c_1). \tag{7}$$

31 This holds because for all $x \geq c_1$, $\Pi_1(c_1, c_1) - \Pi_1(c_0, c_1) \leq \Pi_1(c_1, x) - \Pi_1(c_0, x)$. For sufficiently large values of x, note that $\Pi_1(c_1, x) - \Pi_1(c_0, x) = \Pi^M(c_1) - \Pi^M(c_0)$.

The inventor who licenses to induce entry by the entrepreneur without adoption by the incumbent firm increases royalties until they equal the returns from entry,

(8) $$R^{**} = \Pi_2(c_0, c_1).$$

The independent inventor's profit, therefore, equals

(9) $$V^*(c_0, c_1) = \max\{2R^*, R^{**}\}.$$

If $2R^* \geq R^{**}$, the independent inventor chooses royalty R^*, and the outcome of the adoption-and-entry game is for both the incumbent firm and the entrepreneurial entrant to license the technology. Otherwise, if $2R^* < R^{**}$, the independent inventor chooses royalty R^{**}, and the outcome of the adoption-and-entry game is exclusive licensing to the entrepreneur. The entrepreneurial entrant competes with the incumbent firm, which retains the existing technology. This outcome corresponds to that of a strategic game in which the inventor must choose between transferring the technology to an existing firm or a start-up.

The incumbent firm has less incentive to adopt the new process technology than the innovative entrepreneur because of the *inertia* generated by the initial technology. The royalty that induces only the entrepreneur to adopt the technology is greater than the royalty that induces both the incumbent and the entrepreneur to adopt the technology, $R^{**} > R^*$. This is because $\partial^2\Pi_1(c_0, c_1)/\partial c_0 \partial c_1 < 0$ and $c_1 < c_0$ imply that

$$\begin{aligned} R^* &= \Pi_1(c_1, c_1) - \Pi_1(c_0, c_1) \\ &< \Pi_1(c_1, c_0) - \Pi_1(c_0, c_0) \\ &< \Pi_1(c_1, c_0) = \Pi_2(c_0, c_1) = R^{**}. \end{aligned}$$

This also implies that the incumbent firm's profit when both firms adopt the technology is less than industry profits when only the entrant adopts the technology, $\Pi_1(c_1, c_1) < \Pi_1(c_0, c_1) + \Pi_2(c_0, c_1)$. The inventor chooses the lower royalty when he earns more from both firms adopting the innovation, $2R^*$, than from adoption by the entrepreneur, R^{**}.

Incumbent inertia has two interesting effects on royalties. Improving the initial technology – that is, lowering c_0 – lowers the royalty that attracts both the incumbent and the entrepreneur by improving the incumbent's efficiency and, hence, improving the incumbent's postentry profits using the initial technology,

$$\frac{\partial R^*}{\partial c_0} = -\frac{\partial \Pi_1(c_0, c_1)}{\partial x_1} > 0.$$

Also, improving the initial technology – that is, lowering c_0 – lowers the royalty that attracts only the entrepreneur because it lowers the returns to entry by improving the incumbent's efficiency, thus lowering the entrant's returns from creative destruction,

$$\frac{\partial R^{**}}{\partial c_0} = \frac{\partial \Pi_2(c_0, c_1)}{\partial x_1} > 0.$$

The technology transfer decision of an independent inventor has the following interesting implication: *innovative entrepreneurship always takes place in equilibrium.* Royalties that allow technology transfer to the incumbent firm always involve also selling to the entrepreneur. Royalties that exclude the incumbent firm still attract the innovative entrepreneur because of the incumbent's inertia, $R^* < R^{**}$. When the inventor only transfers the technology to the entrepreneur, the innovative entrepreneur competes with an inefficient incumbent.

The innovation game helps answer the Question of Creative Destruction. Because innovative entrepreneurship always occurs in equilibrium, the outcome supports Schumpeter's observation that entrepreneurial entrants operate beside incumbent firms.[32] The innovation game further shows that there is a market equilibrium at which only the entrepreneurial entrant adopts the new technology. Then, an innovative entrepreneur competes with a less efficient incumbent firm, even though the incumbent firm could have adopted the new technology.

We now compare the independent inventor's incentive to invent with that of a vertically integrated monopolist, which again is subject to Arrow's (1962b) replacement effect. Suppose that products are sufficiently differentiated such that industry profits after entry exceed monopoly profits using the new technology, $\Pi_1(c_0, c_1) + \Pi_2(c_0, c_1) \geq \Pi^M(c_1)$.[33] From the definition of V^*, it follows that the independent inventor has a greater incentive to invent than a vertically integrated monopolist,

$$\begin{aligned} V^*(c_0, c_1) &\geq \Pi_2(c_0, c_1) \\ &\geq \Pi^M(c_1) - \Pi_1(c_0, c_1) \\ &> \Pi^M(c_1) - \Pi^M(c_0). \end{aligned}$$

This is because competition lowers the opportunity cost of adoption of the technology for the incumbent firm, $\Pi_1(c_0, c_1) < \Pi^M(c_0)$. The independent inventor would have a greater incentive to invent just by licensing to the innovative entrepreneur. The independent inventor could obtain additional returns by licensing to both the incumbent and the entrant, so that the independent inventor always has a greater incentive to invent than the vertically integrated monopolist.

Now suppose that industry profits after entry do not exceed monopoly profits using the new technology, $\Pi_1(c_0, c_1) + \Pi_2(c_0, c_1) < \Pi^M(c_1)$. The independent inventor still would have a greater incentive to invent than the vertically integrated monopolist if

$$2(\Pi_1(c_1, c_1) - \Pi_1(c_0, c_1)) \geq \Pi^M(c_1) - \Pi^M(c_0).$$

32 Schumpeter (1934, p. 66) states: "new combinations are, as a rule, embodied, as it were, in new firms which generally do not arise out of the old ones but start producing beside them."

33 As shown in Chapter 6, this holds in the quadratic utility setting when the substitution parameter is less than a critical value, b^*. This outcome with differentiated products shows that it is restrictive to make the standard assumption that an "efficiency effect" holds such that competition always reduces industry profits.

The independent inventor can do better than the vertically integrated monopolist even with less product differentiation when the inventor obtains sufficient returns by licensing to both the incumbent and the potential entrepreneur. This can hold even though competition lowers the returns to technology adoption for the incumbent firm, $\Pi_1(c_1, c_1) - \Pi_1(c_0, c_1) \le \Pi^M(c_1) - \Pi^M(c_0)$. The independent inventor also would have a greater incentive to invent than the vertically integrated monopolist if the returns to selling exclusively to the innovative entrepreneur exceed the inertia effect on the incumbent's profits,

$$\Pi_2(c_0, c_1) \ge \Pi^M(c_1) - \Pi^M(c_0).$$

With a high-quality invention, the returns to entry by an entrepreneur approach monopoly profits and can therefore exceed the monopolist's net returns from adopting the new technology.

The incumbent monopolist who develops an invention also has the option of licensing to an entrant or spinning off a new firm with the new technology. The monopolist licensing to such a competitor would choose a royalty $R = \Pi_2(c_1, c_1)$. The monopolist will license to a competitor with differentiation products if and only if the total returns exceed the returns to monopoly, $\Pi_1(c_1, c_1) + \Pi_2(c_1, c_1) \ge \Pi^M(c_1)$. The returns to invention for an incumbent monopolist licensing within the industry thus equal

$$V^L(c_0, c_1) = \Pi_1(c_1, c_1) + \Pi_2(c_1, c_1) - \Pi^M(c_0). \tag{10}$$

Compare with the independent inventor's incentive to invent. If the independent inventor were to license to both firms, then $V^*(c_0, c_1) = 2(\Pi_1(c_1, c_1) - \Pi_1(c_0, c_1))$. By symmetry, $\Pi_1(c_1, c_1) = \Pi_2(c_1, c_1)$, so that

$$V^*(c_0, c_1) - V^L(c_0, c_1) = \Pi^M(c_0) - 2\Pi_1(c_0, c_1). \tag{11}$$

This is positive if the returns from competition for the high-cost firm are sufficiently small compared to monopoly profits at the initial technology. Then, an independent inventor would have a greater incentive to invent than an incumbent monopolist who licenses to other firms within the industry.

Technology Transfer when the Entrepreneur Can Obtain the Initial Technology

Consider the strategic licensing game with an independent inventor when the initial technology is available to the innovative entrepreneur. The innovative entrepreneur introduces a new product whether or not the inventor licenses the production technology to the new firm.

Suppose that the entrepreneur can obtain the initial technology from a third party or by independent research at a cost k. This is an entry cost for the entrepreneur. Then, both the incumbent and the entrant are subject to inertia effects from the initial technology. Suppose that entry using the initial technology is profitable even if the incumbent firm adopts the new technology, $\Pi_2(c_1, c_0) \ge k$, so that the

Table 3.3. *The technology adoption game with payoffs (Existing firm 1, Entrepreneurial firm 2) when the initial technology is available to the entrepreneurial entrant at cost k*

	Entrepreneurial firm 2 Adopt	Entrepreneurial firm 2 Do not adopt
Existing firm 1 Adopt	$\Pi_1(c_1, c_1) - R, \Pi_2(c_1, c_1) - R$	$\Pi_1(c_1, c_0) - R, \Pi_2(c_1, c_0) - k$
Existing firm 1 Do not adopt	$\Pi_1(c_0, c_1), \Pi_2(c_0, c_1) - R$	$\Pi_1(c_0, c_0), \Pi_2(c_0, c_0) - k$

entrepreneur can establish a firm without adopting the new technology. After the independent inventor makes a licensing offer, the entrepreneur and the incumbent firm make adoption decisions. Other than the cost of obtaining the initial technology, the payoffs for the technology adoption game are symmetric (see Table 3.3).

The cost of obtaining the initial technology reduces the entrepreneur's opportunity cost of adopting the new technology. This implies that the entrepreneur values the new technology more than the incumbent firm does. Because profits are symmetric, the independent inventor can attract both firms by offering royalties equal to the benefits of the incumbent firm,

$$R^* = \Pi_1(c_1, c_1) - \Pi_1(c_0, c_1) < \Pi_2(c_1, c_1) - (\Pi_2(c_1, c_0) - k).$$

The independent inventor can attract only the entrepreneur by offering a higher royalty that is equal to the net benefit of the entrepreneur,

$$R^{**} = \Pi_2(c_0, c_1) - (\Pi_2(c_0, c_0) - k).$$

The royalty that only attracts the entrepreneurial entrant is greater than the royalty that attracts both firms because

$$R^{**} - R^* = [\Pi_2(c_0, c_1) - \Pi_2(c_0, c_0)] - [\Pi_2(c_1, c_1) - \Pi_2(c_1, c_0)] + k > k.$$

This follows because the marginal effect of the firm's own costs on its profits is decreasing in the costs of the competing firm. The independent inventor's profit equals $V^*(c_0, c_1) = \max\{2R^*, R^{**}\}$. As before, if $2R^* \geq R^{**}$, the independent inventor chooses royalty R^* and both the incumbent firm and the entrepreneurial entrant license the technology. Otherwise, if $2R^* < R^{**}$, the independent inventor chooses royalty R^{**} and only the entrepreneur licenses the new technology.

The equilibrium outcome of the innovation game is very similar to that in the previous innovation game in which the entrepreneurial entrant could not obtain the initial technology. As before, the entrepreneur always adopts the new technology in equilibrium, whether or not the incumbent firm adopts the technology. This is because inertia reduces the returns from adoption for the existing firm, $\Pi_1(c_1, c_1) - \Pi_1(c_0, c_1)$. The entrepreneur also experiences inertia, whether the incumbent adopts the new technology, $\Pi_2(c_1, c_1) - (\Pi_2(c_1, c_0) - k)$, or does not adopt the new technology, $\Pi_2(c_0, c_1) - (\Pi_2(c_0, c_0) - k)$. However, the entrepreneur's inertia is offset by the cost of obtaining the initial technology.

As before, innovative entrepreneurship and creative destruction always occur in equilibrium. Again, there is a market equilibrium at which only the entrepreneurial entrant adopts the new technology and competes with a less efficient incumbent firm.

3.5 Innovative Entrepreneurs and Commercial Inventions

The experience of innovative entrepreneurs who founded companies such as Amazon.com, eBay, or PayPal illustrates how innovative entrepreneurship is based on the introduction of commercial inventions to the market place. The innovative entrepreneur implements commercial inventions in the process of creating a new type of start-up enterprise, establishing a new type of firm, and launching new industries. The start-up and the new firm *embody* the inventor's commercial discoveries and any associated scientific and technology discoveries. An economic innovation is doing something new in the market place and thus requires commercial inventions. Traditionally defined scientific and technological inventions are neither necessary nor sufficient for economic innovation.

Commercial Inventions and Economic Innovation

A *commercial invention* is a discovery of a new type of economic transaction or a new type of process for producing economic transactions. New types of transactions include contractual forms, financial instruments, pricing strategies, auction procedures, market microstructure designs, management systems, and organizational structures.[34] New types of processes for producing transactions include information and communications technologies (ICT) such as computers or other hardware used in transactions, software applications used in transactions, and communications devices used in transactions. Commercial inventions are based on discoveries in economics, finance, accounting, marketing, operations research, management, communication, informatics, and computer science. Commercial inventions are not restricted to the firm's operations; they can apply to all functional areas, including marketing, sales, procurement, inventory management, R&D, customer service, accounting, and finance.

Such a formal definition of a commercial invention is important for understanding economic innovation by entrepreneurs and incumbent firms. Commercial inventions include what the U.S. Patent and Trademark Office (USPTO) refers to as *business method inventions*.[35] The absence of a clear definition of business method

34 *Market microstructure* refers to the rules, procedures, and institutions in a market; see Spulber (1999) on the economic theory of market microstructure.

35 The USPTO awards three types of patents: "Utility patents may be granted to anyone who invents or discovers any new and useful process, machine, article of manufacture, or composition of matter, or any new and useful improvement thereof. . . . Design patents may be granted to anyone

inventions has posed a problem for researchers, inventors, judges, and public policy makers.[36] Commercial discoveries gained attention in the heated debate over IP protections for business method inventions. This debate has crucial implications not only for the economic study of entrepreneurs but also for public policy toward invention, innovation, and entrepreneurship.

Commercial inventions such as business method inventions are critical for a wide range of innovations that I refer to as the Business Revolution. Elsewhere, I define the Business Revolution as the augmentation and replacement of human effort in business transactions by computers, communications systems, and the Internet (Spulber, 2011b). The Business Revolution is changing the office, the store, and the market, just as the Industrial Revolution earlier changed the factory. As a consequence, limiting IP protections for business method inventions would constrain the Business Revolution itself. Scientific and technological advances in ICT have generated changes in commerce on a scale that rivals or surpasses the Industrial Revolution. ICT advances automate practically all business transactions, thereby increasing productivity in retail, wholesale, finance, and many other industries. This explains the large number of business method patent applications and awards. Removing or weakening patent protections for business method inventions potentially jeopardizes advances in e-commerce, ICT, and the Internet.

Business method patents extend IP protections to commercial discoveries, which are the foundation of Schumpeterian innovation. Business method patents are helpful to entrepreneurs who often transfer their IP to the start-ups and new firms that they establish. Business method patents not only are useful to innovative entrepreneurs but are crucial for commercializing scientific and technological discoveries. Often, scientific and technological discoveries are developed in conjunction with business methods.

Business method inventions increase the market value of complementary scientific and technological discoveries. Business method inventions are a growing class

who invents a new, original, and ornamental design for an article of manufacture. Plant patents may be granted to anyone who invents or discovers and asexually reproduces any distinct and new variety of plant." http://www.uspto.gov/patents/ (accessed January 5, 2014).

36 Bronwyn Hall (2009, p. 445) asserts: "There is no precise definition of business method patents" and "many scholars make little distinction between business method patents, internet patents, and software patents more broadly, at least when making policy recommendations. This is inevitable in the present day, because many business method patents are in fact patents on the transfer of a known business method to a software and/or web-based implementation, so the distinction is hard to maintain." Stefan Wagner (2008, p. 4) states: "The concept of business methods is notoriously difficult to define. From an economic perspective, the term 'business method' is very broad and comprises various economic activities such as selling and buying items, marketing or finance methods, schemes and techniques. From a legal perspective, it is hard to find an abstract definition of what exactly constitutes a business method and what makes it different from other 'methods'. Currently, neither European nor US (patent) laws contain a legal definition of the term business method while actually using it frequently." See also Hart et al. (2000).

of discoveries because they often involve advances in ICT technologies. Commercial discoveries augment and replace human effort in business transactions, increasing the efficiency of transactions and improving the performance of firms.

The concept of a commercial invention also helps define an innovation. An *economic innovation* is the first introduction of a commercial invention to the market, possibly accompanied by scientific and technological inventions, either by incumbent firms or by entrepreneurial entrants. Innovation often involves inherently uncertain creative processes, highly technical scientific advances, and complex business decisions.[37] A consistent definition of innovation has presented major challenges for economists and management scholars.[38] The definition of innovation must be tractable for ease of use in theoretical and empirical studies, yet it must be sufficiently general that it can be applied in most sectors of the economy. Consequently, many economic and management studies are guided more by the application of scientific or technological inventions than by commercial inventions.[39]

Commercial inventions are fundamental for innovation because actions require ideas. Commercial inventions are necessary for innovation even if the entrepreneur discovers or refines the idea in the process of creating the start-up. Commercial inventions are the innovative ideas that generate new products, new production processes, new transaction techniques, new market designs, and new forms of organization. Even if a new product design is the result of a scientific or technological invention, a commercial invention is needed to translate the basic science into a marketable product.

Schumpeter (1939, p. 84) defines innovation as "'doing things differently' in the realm of economic life."[40] Schumpeter's (1934, pp. 65–66) "innovations in the

37 Innovation is examined most notably by Jean-Baptiste Say (1841, 1852) and Schumpeter (1934). For Kline and Rosenberg (1986, p. 275): "Successful outcomes in innovation thus require the running of two gauntlets: the commercial and the technological."

38 Garcia and Calantone (2002) find more than fifteen definitions in a set of empirical studies that use various concepts from engineering, marketing, management, and economics. They (2002, p. 112) point out that even the word "new" presents difficulties; is the innovation new to the world, the scientific community, the innovating firm, the adopting firm, the industry, the market, or the consumer? A Schumpeterian innovation is one that is new to the market.

39 See Griliches (1957) for an early empirical treatment of commercialization that focuses on the geographic diffusion on a single invention: hybrid corn.

40 The *Oxford English Dictionary* (*OED*) presents a multipart definition of innovation that recognizes the Schumpeterian description of innovation: "5. *Comm.* The action of introducing a new product into the market; a product newly brought on to the market." *Oxford English Dictionary*, s.v. "innovation" http://dictionary.oed.com/ (accessed June 30, 2010). The initial definition is generic: "1. a. The action of innovating; the introduction of novelties; the alteration of what is established by the introduction of new elements or forms," and "2. a. A change made in the nature or fashion of anything; something newly introduced; a novel practice, method, etc." The *OED* definition of innovation in commerce also cites John Jewkes et al. (1958, p. 249): "It seems impossible to establish scientifically any final conclusion concerning the relation between monopoly

economic system" include the "introduction of a new good," "introduction of a new method of production," "opening of a new market," "conquest of a new source of supply of raw materials or half-manufactured goods," and "carrying out of the new organization of any industry."[41]

Because Schumpeter is concerned with economic innovation, he argues that "[i]nnovation is possible without anything we should identify as invention, and invention does not necessarily induce innovation."[42] Schumpeter observes that "[a]lthough most innovations can be traced to some conquest in the realm of either theoretical or practical knowledge, there are many which cannot." Schumpeter finds no economic distinction between the two situations because the economic effects of the innovation need not depend on its "scientific novelty."[43] The market value of an innovation depends on the extent to which consumers are willing to pay for the goods and services of firms who "do things differently." Emphasizing the distinction between economic innovation and invention, Schumpeter argued that attention to invention was misplaced.[44]

However, inventions are central to innovation in the marketplace. Broadening the concept of invention to include commercial discoveries implies that such inventions are necessary preconditions for innovation. The innovative entrepreneur need not be the individual who develops commercial inventions. Yet, the innovative entrepreneur acts on the basis of commercial inventions.

Commercial inventions can involve the development of complementary scientific and technological discoveries or new ways of applying existing scientific and technological inventions. This might suggest that traditionally defined scientific and technological inventions that generate new products and production techniques are both necessary and sufficient for economic innovation. However, scientific and technological inventions are not necessary for economic innovation because commercial inventions need not involve machines or transformation of materials. Also, scientific and technological inventions are not sufficient for

and innovation"; Rogers (1962, p. 124), who suggests: "It matters little whether or not an innovation has a great degree of advantage over the idea it is replacing. What does matter is whether the individual perceives the relative advantage of the innovation"; and Allen (1967, p. 8), who states: "Innovation is the bringing of an invention into widespread, practical use.... Invention may thus be construed as the first stage of the much more extensive and complex total process of innovation."

41 Among "changes in the methods of supplying commodities," Schumpeter (1939, p. 84) lists "[t]echnological change in the production of commodities already in use, the opening up of new markets or of new sources of supply, Taylorization of work, improved handling of material, the setting up of new business organizations, such as department stores."

42 Schumpeter (1939, p. 84), also cited by the OED. See also Schumpeter (1934, 1942).

43 Schumpeter (1939, p. 84).

44 Schumpeter (1934, p. 89) cautions: "It is, therefore, not advisable, and it may be downright misleading, to stress the element of invention as much as many writers do."

economic innovation because there must be a commercial invention that describes how the scientific and technological inventions will be implemented.

Commercial Inventions and Economic Transactions

Because commercial inventions are new types of transactions and new methods of producing transactions, they can serve to reduce transaction costs. Such inventions are highly valuable because the production of transactions represent a major share of the economy. The retail, wholesale, and financial sectors generate more than a quarter of GDP.[45] Small improvements in transaction efficiency can generate large economic rewards because reductions in transaction costs increase the volume of economic transactions and allow the opening of new types of markets. The returns to improvements in transaction costs are the gains from trade that result from new transactions.

In addition, transaction costs are important determinants of economic activity. As Coase (1937) first observed, firms will organize their activities on the basis of a comparison of market transaction costs and management costs within the firm. Financial innovations increase entrepreneurship and economic growth by increasing the availability of financial capital and the efficiency of financial markets.[46] Lerner (2006, p. 224) points out that "financial innovations enable firms of all industries to raise capital in larger amounts and at a lower cost than they could otherwise." Lerner finds that in the period from 1990 to 2002, smaller firms accounted for a disproportionate share of financial innovations, and financial firms obtained limited patent protections for financial innovations.[47]

Commercial Inventions and Patents for Business Method Inventions

A package of Wrigley's chewing gum crossed a bar code scanner at Marsh's Supermarket in June 1974 in Troy, Ohio. Thus began a major transformation of retail and wholesale transactions. The Universal Product Code (UPC) and bar code scanners are important business method inventions because they automate transactions. They replace workers' efforts with capital equipment in the supply of commercial transactions. In only two years after the first product with the UPC symbol appeared, more than three-quarters of supermarket products carried the symbol.[48] The use of UPC codes spread quickly to other consumer goods industries such as clothing, household products, and toys and also to commercial and industrial products.

45 Spulber (1996b).

46 See Miller (1986) and Merton (1992).

47 *See* Lerner (2006). *See also* Peter Tufano (2003) and Bronwyn Hall et al. (2009).

48 *See* Dunlop and Rivkin (1997, p. 5).

Joseph Woodland and Bernard Silver obtained the first patent for a bar code on October 7, 1952. Their early conception of a bar code was a drawing of a bull's-eye pattern with the thickness of the rings conveying product information.[49] The patent is for a "classifying apparatus and method," so it involved both a machine and a business method.[50] The bar code patent states that "it is the object of the invention to provide an automatic apparatus that will execute with precision and dispatch classifying orders which are given to it and will yield up the results of the classifying process in an intelligible manner."[51] The patent specifically mentions supermarkets although it is not limited to that application. The patent also includes a description of equipment to read the bar code, allowing the processing and utilization of the information it conveys.

The combination of bar coding and scanner technology provides a useful illustration of a commercial invention. The invention is much more than a combination of an information storage process (the bar code itself) and a reader (the scanner). In itself, the storage-reader technology would constitute an ICT invention. However, the discovery is a commercial invention because it changes the way business is conducted. The invention identifies a market opportunity and provides a commercial technique that greatly improves economic efficiency for practically any retail or wholesale transaction.

Bar codes speed customers through the checkout counter, providing convenience for consumers and increasing the productivity of cashiers. Customers receive detailed receipts that identify the products that are purchased. Product data from bar codes is used to provide marketing promotions and targeted discounts. Bar codes also reduce the cost to merchants of generating information used to track sales and to update inventories. Better inventory control reduces the costs of carrying inventory and improves the match between inventories and customer demands, thus enhancing immediacy. Bar codes also lower the costs of price adjustment for retailers and wholesalers, because prices can be posted on store shelves and adjusted on the firm's cash registers and in their databases. Moreover, the information generated at the checkout counter changes the relationship with wholesalers and manufacturers, allowing them to exchange sales data electronically. Bar coding underlies automated ordering and billing systems that are used in Internet transactions.

By the end of the 1990s, more than eighty countries had organizations that issued product codes.[52] UPC codes and scanner technology, together with related advances in information technology, are used at small retailers, supermarket chains, and large discount retailers, such as Walmart, Costco, and Target. UPC codes and scanner technology are used by shipping firms for packages, such as UPS and Federal

49 U.S. Patent 2,612,994.
50 U.S. Patent 2,612,994.
51 U.S. Patent 2,612,994.
52 See Dunlop and Rivkin (1997, p. 9).

Express, and by manufacturing companies for identifying parts, components, and materials. UPC codes and scanners also facilitate information exchange between companies.

The bar code patent illustrates how some business method inventions commercialize scientific or technological discoveries. The bar code invention includes both a business process discovery and an ICT discovery. The business process discovery is a way to utilize digital codes to identify objects. The ICT discovery is a way to represent information that can be read by a machine and the design of a machine that can read the digital code. The bar code invention is much more than either a way to index objects or an ICT discovery of a process for information storage and retrieval. It is the combination of the indexing of objects and the information storage and retrieval process that makes this particular invention so significant. Taken together, these ideas revolutionize all manner of transactions because they allow the automation of handling of almost any type of object, whether it is a retail or wholesale product being exchanged, a product being inventoried, a product being shipped, or an input or an output produced or used in a factory.

Commercial inventions include *business method inventions.* To administer the system of awarding patents, the USPTO necessarily defines business method inventions through extensive categorization. The USPTO mainly identifies business method inventions through its class 705 Data Processing: Financial, Business Practice, Management, or Cost/Price Determination.[53] The USPTO's 705 class definition suggests both computer hardware and software (apparatus and method) that are used to "change" data. The definition emphasizes applications of data processing to business management or financial data.[54] The USPTO's definition under this

53 "This is the generic class for apparatus and corresponding methods for performing *data processing* operations, in which there is a significant change in the data or for performing *calculation operations* wherein the apparatus or method is uniquely designed for or utilized in the *practice*, administration, or management of an *enterprise*, or in the processing of financial data. This class also provides for apparatus and corresponding methods for performing *data processing* or *calculating operations* in which a charge for goods or services is determined" (emphasis in original). http://www.uspto.gov/web/patents/classification/uspc705/defs705.htm, accessed January 25, 2011. The USPTO class 705 also includes the preceding "in combination with cryptographic apparatus or method."

54 The USPTO "scope of the class" for class 705 identifies the importance of patent claims that relate to business management and transactions involving commodities and finance. According to the USPTO "scope of the class: 1. The *arrangements* in this class are generally used for problems relating to administration of an organization, commodities or financial transactions. 2. Mere designation of an arrangement as a 'business machine' or a document as a 'business form' or 'business chart' without any particular business function will not cause classification in this class or its subclasses. 3. For classification herein, there must be significant claim recitation of the data processing system or calculating computer and only nominal claim recitation of any external art environment. Significantly claimed apparatus external to this class, claimed in combination with apparatus under the class definition, which perform data processing or calculation operations are classified in the class appropriate to the external device unless specifically excluded therefrom.

class is by no means exhaustive because the USPTO further references twenty-eight other classes of related inventions, such as electronic funds transfer.[55]

The courts have struggled to address business method inventions in part because many of these discoveries are intertwined with other scientific or technological breakthroughs. When that is the case, a patent could presumably be awarded for the complementary scientific or technological invention directly, with commercial applications being covered in the patent claim. If the courts or the USPTO were to rule out patenting of business method inventions, the impact would be mitigated because of these scientific and technological connections.

As Allison and Hunter (2006) point out, skilled patent attorneys can draft patents strategically to opt out of, or in to, particular categories, as occurred with software patents. Patents applications for business method inventions would similarly include descriptions of production technologies and applications. This is implicitly recognized by the USPTO's 705 class. Many business method inventions could be patented as ICT inventions but doing so would affect the disclosure function of patents.

The critical question is whether stand-alone commercial inventions should be accorded the same patent protections as scientific and technological inventions. This question arose in the Supreme Court's contentious *Bilski* decision that addressed

4. Nominally claimed apparatus external to this class in combination with apparatus under the class definition is classified in this class unless provided for in the appropriate external class.
5. In view of the nature of the subject matter included herein, consideration of the classification schedule for the diverse art or environment is necessary for proper search." http://www.uspto.gov/web/patents/classification/uspc705/defs705.htm, accessed January 25, 2011.

55 Id. See also USPTO (2009) (referencing other classes that may apply to business methods). For example, other related sections include 186, Merchandising, various subclasses for customer service methods and apparatus in a variety of areas including banking, restaurant and stores; 235, Registers (e.g., cash registers, voting machines); 283, Printed Matter, various subclasses for business forms and methods of using such forms; 307, Electrical Transmission or Interconnection Systems; 340, Communications: Electrical; 341, Coded Data Generation or Conversion; 345, Computer Graphics Processing and Selective Visual Display Systems; 359, Optics: Systems and Elements; 360, Dynamic Magnetic Information Storage or Retrieval; 365, Static Information Storage and Retrieval; 369, Dynamic Information Storage or Retrieval; 370, Multiplex Communications; 371, Error Detection/Correction and Fault Detection/Recovery; 375, Pulse or Digital Communications; 377, Electrical Pulse Counters, Pulse Dividers, or Shift Registers: Circuits and Systems; 379, Telephonic Communications; 380, Cryptography; 382, Image Analysis; 434, Education and Demonstration; 463, Amusement Devices: Games (a method or apparatus for moving or processing information specified as game or contest information); 700, Data Processing: Generic Control Systems; 704, Data Processing: Speech Signal Processing, Linguistics, Language Translation, and Audio Compression/Decompression; 708, Electrical Computers: Arithmetic Processing and Calculating; 709, Electrical Computers and Digital Processing Systems: Multicomputer Data Transferring or Plural Process Synchronization; 713, Electrical Computers and Digital Processing Systems: Support; 714, Error Detection/Correction and Fault Detection/Recovery; 902, Electronic Funds Transfer.

whether business method inventions should be patentable: "The question in this case turns on whether a patent can be issued for a claimed invention designed for the business world."[56]

Questioning the patentability of business methods is a lot like trying to close the barn door after the horse has bolted. The United States has awarded business method patents practically since the establishment of the patent system in 1790.[57] In its first fifty years, the U.S. Patent Office granted forty-one financial patents covering arts of bank notes, bills of credit, bills of exchange, check blanks, detecting and preventing counterfeiting, coin counting, interest calculation tables, and lotteries.[58] The USPTO has awarded many business method patents in a wide variety of categories, including more than 100,000 patents since 1976 in Patent Class 705, Data Processing: Financial, Business Practice, Management, or Cost/Price Determination.[59]

At issue is whether stand-alone commercial inventions should be distinguished from traditionally defined scientific and technological discoveries involving advances in chemistry, physics, biology, engineering, and medicine. The question of whether commercial discoveries are valuable inventions stems from a long-standing debate over the relative economic value added by distribution versus production. In *The Wealth of Nations*, Adam Smith argued that both production and distribution are important: "The capital of the merchant exchanges the surplus produce of one place for that of another, and thus encourages the industry and increases the enjoyments of both."[60] Public policies that distinguish transaction technologies from production technologies are likely to generate biases that adversely affect invention and commercialization. The main implication of a more precise understanding of business method inventions is that public policies should treat them in the same way as other types of inventions.

The argument that industrial processes should be patentable while business methods should not recalls unfortunate but long-standing social biases. Contempt for professional merchants dates back at least to ancient Greece and Rome, reflecting the fear of the newly rich on the part of those who inherited their wealth.[61] Schumpeter (1934) observes that social resentment of entrepreneurs occurs because

56 *Bernard L. Bilski and Rand A. Warsaw v. David J. Kappos, Undersecretary of Commerce for Intellectual Property and Director, Patent and Trademark Office*, U.S. Supreme Court Slip Opinion No. 08–964 (June 28, 2010), 561 U.S. ____ (2010), hereafter *Bilski*.

57 USPTO (2010, p. 2) ("The first financial patent was granted on March 19, 1799, to Jacob Perkins of Massachusetts for an invention for 'Detecting Counterfeit Notes.'").

58 Ibid., citing Edmund Burke, Commissioner of Patents, List of Patents for Inventions and Designs, Issued by the United States from 1790 to 1847 (1847).

59 A search conducted by author on July 8, 2010, of the USPTO database for Patent Class 705 yielded 1,143 hits before 1976 and 105,811 hits from 1976 to the present. See http://patft.uspto.gov/.

60 See Smith (1998, II, 5.6 at).

61 See Veyne (1987, p. 129).

some are successful despite the rarity and temporary nature of their success.[62] Veyne (1987) also finds that resentment of success explains why commerce was "almost universally devalued until the industrial revolution."[63] The notion that manufacturing is somehow superior to commerce and entrepreneurship also resembles Marxian criticisms of merchants, intermediaries, and business in general.[64]

Countering this bias, McCloskey (2006) provides an extended defense of "bourgeois virtues," arguing that commerce helps promote ethical behavior: "But the assaults on the alleged vices of the bourgeoisie after 1848 made an impossible Best into the enemy of the actual Good."[65] Sowell (2009, p. 62) observes that "[t]he organizations, large and small, which produce and distribute most of the goods and services that make up a modern standard of living – businesses – have long been targets of the intelligentsia."

The distinction between commerce and production has little practical basis. Public policies that draw artificial distinctions between commercial and industrial inventions either to support or oppose business method inventions will generate economic distortions. Courts seeking to identify differences between transactions and production would face an impossible task. As Coase demonstrated, firms determine whether to carry out a particular task by comparing market transaction costs with internal governance costs.[66] Transaction costs affect whether a task is part of a firm's production process or part of its market transactions, thus determining the boundaries of the firm. As compared with internal governance costs, relatively high market transaction costs favor vertical integration, and relatively low market transaction costs favor outsourcing.

Because firms solve Coase's "make-or-buy" problem, what might appear to be a production task in one context could appear to be a market transaction in another context. This makes the distinction between manufacturing inventions and business method inventions impractical for the patent office and for the courts. Even knowing how the firm resolves the "make-or-buy" choice, it remains difficult to distinguish in-house production from market purchases because both activities

62 Schumpeter (1934, p. 165): "Because there are always entrepreneurs and relatives and heirs of entrepreneurs, public opinion and also the phraseology of the social struggle readily overlook these facts."

63 See Veyne (1987, p. 129): "They key to the mystery lies in the fact that commercial wealth belonged to the newly rich, while the old wealth was based on land. Inherited wealth defended itself against upstart merchants by imputing to them every conceivable vice: merchants are rootless, greedy, the source of all evil; they promote luxury and weakness; they distort nature by travelling to far-off lands, violating the natural barrier of the seas and bringing back what nature will not permit to grow at home."

64 This is typical of Marxist writings. See, for example, van Zanden (1993, p. 7): "[M]erchant capitalism often employed the systems of exploitation that already existed in the pre-capitalist modes of production."

65 McCloskey (2006, p. 2). In the year 1848, a major revolutionary wave swept across Europe, see Mike Rapport (2009).

66 See Coase (1937, 1960, 1988).

involve market transactions and internal management.[67] As Demsetz (1991, p. 162) observes, the tasks are highly similar:

> Hence, in-house production does not constitute a clear elimination of transaction costs. Similarly, purchasing goods from another firm, rather than producing these in house, involves an implicit purchase of the management services undertaken by the other firm, so management cost is not eliminated by purchasing more nearly complete goods across markets.

Demsetz concludes that the correct question is not whether the transaction cost of purchase is less than the management cost of production, but rather whether the sum of management and transaction cost incurred through in-house production is more or less than the sum of management and transaction cost incurred through purchase across markets, because either option entails expenditures on both cost categories.[68]

Firms create and manage both market and organizational transactions (Spulber, 2009a). The scope of the firm can be viewed as the combination of its market making and organizational activities. Therefore, the absence of an operational distinction between commerce and production suggests that business method exceptions to patents cannot be justified by economic analysis. Business method inventions should be accorded the same IP protections as other inventions. A business method patent formalizes and codifies various aspects of the commercial discovery.[69] Patent protections for commercial inventions allow inventors to sell or license such inventions to innovative entrepreneurs, to incumbents, or to market intermediaries.

3.6 Innovative Entrepreneurs and Business Strategy

Some commercial inventions are new types of business models. A *business model* is the overall strategy and structure of the firm rather than a particular technology that can be used by many types of firms, such as a bar code scanner. Casadesus-Masanell and Ricart (2010, p. 196) refer to a business model as "the logic of the firm, how it operates and creates value" and refer to business strategy as "the choice of business model through which the firm will compete in the marketplace." Teece (2010, p. 173) argues: "To profit from innovation, business pioneers need to excel not only at product innovation but also at business model design."

67 Demsetz (1991, p. 162) states: "It is not so easy to distinguish purchase across a market from in-house production because in-house production involves the use of inputs that are *purchased.* Purchasing inputs (across markets) is substituted for purchasing goods that are more nearly complete (across markets)."

68 Ibid., Demsetz.

69 This is discussed at greater length in Spulber (2011b).

In economic terms, a *business strategy* can be defined as the design of a system of organizational and market transactions to be implemented by a firm. A novel business model specifies how the firm will provide a new type of economic transaction or apply a new type of process for producing economic transactions. The innovative entrepreneur introduces a business strategy to the market that differs substantially from strategies pursued by incumbent firms. The new strategy identifies new combinations of market opportunities and the resources needed to achieve them. Innovative entrepreneurs implement new business strategies by creating start-ups and establishing firms. Ray Kroc, who established MacDonald's, introduced standardization and assembly-line techniques to food preparation and service. In establishing Amazon.com, Jeff Bezos developed a variety of new online retail and wholesale transaction techniques. Pierre Omidyar, who established eBay, developed an online auction sales platform and various ways of organizing an online community.

A business strategy constitutes a system of transactions because a firm's activities are interconnected by profit maximization. A system is greater than the sum of its parts, which interact in complex ways. A business strategy forms a system because the manager coordinates the firm's many transactions that generate the firm's profits. The manager chooses transactions to maximize profits subject to market demand and supply characteristics, technological constraints, organizational limitations, competitive conditions, and legal and regulatory limitations. The firm's transactions are interconnected because of interactions among financing, capital investment, purchasing, inventory, production, and sales. The manager must plan the firm's transactions with customers, suppliers, partners, investors, inventors, employees, and managers. Firms obtain the resources needed to implement the strategy and to address market opportunities.

Viewing innovation in the context of economic transactions allows for a multidimensional description of technological change. The basic elements of the innovation are similar things – economic transactions. An innovator engages in the purposeful design and creation of the new system of transactions to obtain the greatest economic return. The innovative bundle of transactions includes purchasing and selling IP, applying new production methods, offering new products, developing new business methods, introducing new distribution methods, obtaining finance, and employing human capital.

The transaction approach to business strategy lends itself to economic modeling and empirical analysis. Evaluating the effectiveness of alternative business strategies depends on a comparison of the costs and benefits of different mixtures of transactions, including market interactions and organizational processes. The transaction approach to strategy also allows the application of industrial organization models of competition. A business strategy generates a competitive advantage for a firm when it offers a more efficient system of transactions than the strategies of rival firms.

The entrepreneur realizes economic returns when the start-up becomes a firm that implements the new strategy. The entrepreneur's business plan can take the form of a written statement that identifies the goal of the business, describes the prospective business, and provides an analysis of the market and regulatory environment. The business strategy sets out the manager's broad plan of action and the types of transactions that a firm needs to achieve business goals.

The strategy identifies resources necessary to implement the strategy successfully, including scientific and technological inventions. The business plan often is a prospectus for raising financial capital. The business plan for a new venture identifies the resources that the entrepreneur will contribute including financial capital, human capital, and IP. The business plan usually includes specific arrangements for marketing, manufacturing and operations, financing, and hiring. The business plan looks at prospective customers, suppliers, and partners and examines the challenges posed by prospective competitors. The business plan also considers the management and organizational structure of the new business.

In formulating strategy, an entrepreneur or the manager of an existing business begins by selecting the goals of the business. Next, the entrepreneur or manager gathers information by performing a comprehensive external analysis of market conditions and a careful internal analysis of the company's organizational resources. The decision maker adjusts the company's goals to make the best match between market opportunities and available resources. The entrepreneur or manager identifies critical factors that distinguish the firm from its competitors and allow the firm to attain a competitive advantage. The entrepreneur or manager formulates a competitive strategy that anticipates the strategies of competitors and chooses market actions to outperform competitors. Finally, the entrepreneur or manager turns to implementation of the strategy through organizational and market transactions. Figure 3.3 illustrates the elements of business strategy formulation.

3.7 Conclusion

Existing firms have various innovative advantages over entrants resulting from organizational efficiencies and complementary assets. In contrast to incumbents, innovative entrepreneurs encounter the costs of creating a start-up and establishing a firm. Innovative entrepreneurs must obtain complementary assets needed to implement inventions and new business models. The profits of innovative entrants are reduced by competition with incumbent firms and other entrants.

Innovative entrepreneurs can achieve innovative advantages over incumbent firms because they can exercise individual initiative and are not subject to the inertia of operating existing businesses. Entrepreneurs gain an innovative advantage over incumbent firms when the costs of entry are relatively low compared to incumbents' opportunity costs of innovation. Because competition tends to increase output, the

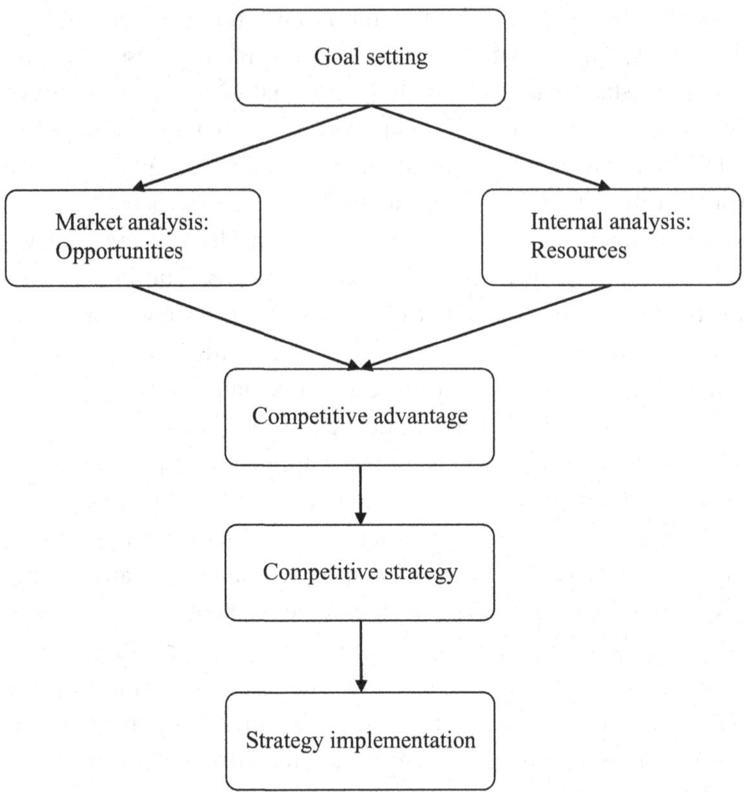

Figure 3.3. The elements of business strategy formulation.

innovative entrepreneur generally has a greater marginal incentive to invent than would an incumbent monopolist without the threat of entry.

Innovative entrepreneurship is founded on commercial discoveries such as business method inventions. Commercial inventions are the basis for new types of products, manufacturing processes, and transactions. Innovative entrepreneurship generally involves new business strategies, which are systems of organizational and market transactions. The innovative entrepreneur implements commercial discoveries by creating a start-up and establishing a new firm.

4

Competitive Pressures and Entrepreneurial Incentives to Innovate

How does competition affect incentives to innovate? The significant economic contributions made by innovative entrepreneurs strongly suggest that competition *increases* incentives to innovate. The discussion in this chapter explains why entrepreneurs generate more innovative projects than an incumbent monopoly with multiple projects. Additionally, competition between entrepreneurs and a monopoly incumbent with multiple projects generates more innovative projects than would the incumbent firm without competition.

At first glance, however, it might seem that competitive pressures would decrease entrepreneurial incentives to innovate. Creative destruction dissipates economic rents thereby reducing incentives to enter the market with new products, manufacturing processes, or transaction methods. Innovative entrepreneurs face many types of vigorous competition: from other entrepreneurs both present and future; from traditional and informal institutions; and from incumbent firms. Entrepreneurial entrants face the risk that the new firms will expand industry capacity above the level that is needed to serve the market. Then, entry will generate vigorous competition, leading to rapid exit or protracted shakeouts of new and existing firms. Entrepreneurial entrants face the risk of unsuccessful entry because other entrants or existing firms will offer better innovations. Entrepreneurial entrants also face the risk that their innovations will fail to perform well: new products may prove unpopular with customers, new manufacturing processes may not function efficiently, and new transaction methods may not be widely adopted. Finally, entrepreneurial entrants face the risk that their innovations will be imitated or expropriated by other entrants and incumbent firms.

Although competition challenges entrepreneurs, competitive pressures create incentives to innovate. The chapter is organized as follows. Section 4.1 discusses whether innovative entrepreneurship is based on incentives to innovate or on irrational exuberance. Section 4.2 presents a model of creative destruction in which there is a winning innovative entrepreneur that serves the market. Section 4.3 considers the effects of imperfect IP protections on incentives to innovate. Sections 4.4 and 4.5 present a three-stage model of competition among entrepreneurs with capacity constraints. In the initial entry stage, entrepreneurs invest in innovation and establish firms. In the next stage, entrepreneurs choose prices strategically, make irreversible investments, and compete to serve consumers, while faced with asymmetric information about each others' innovations. In the final creative destruction stage, firms with better technologies remain in the market, whereas firms with inferior technologies exit the market.

4.1 Incentives to Innovate versus Irrational Exuberance

When examining the effects of competitive pressures on innovation, it is necessary to consider innovation both by entrants and by incumbents. Newly established firms that embody entrepreneurial innovations are initially small and without market power, even though they may eventually grow in size and market share. Incumbent firms may be monopolists protected from competitive entry, or they may face competition from entrants and other incumbents. In isolation, greater competition may diminish entrepreneurial incentives to innovate by reducing the rewards to innovation. However, to evaluate the effects of competitive pressures on innovation, it is useful to compare innovation by entrepreneurs with innovation by monopoly incumbents. Also, it is useful to evaluate how competition between entrepreneurs and a monopoly incumbent with multiple projects affects innovation in comparison with a monopoly incumbent without entrepreneurial entry.

Competitive Pressures and Incentives to Innovate

Entrepreneurs are rewarded by ownership of newly established firms, giving them residual returns and residual rights of control. These rewards must be sufficient to induce entrepreneurs to choose innovation over replication and thus incur the incremental costs and risks of providing new products, new production technologies, and new transaction methods. Answering the Question of Competitive Pressures requires an examination of how competition affects the rewards to innovation. Entrepreneurs face competitive pressures from other innovators, firms with traditional technologies, and firms that imitate entrepreneurial innovations. By dissipating economic rents, more intense competition reduces rewards for entrepreneurial innovation. However, competitive entry of entrepreneurs can increase innovation in comparison to a monopoly incumbent.[1]

Schumpeter (1912, 1934), an ardent advocate of entrepreneurial entry in his early writings, argues that entrepreneurs stimulate innovation by establishing new firms and competing with existing firms. Schumpeter (1942, p. 102)points out that "entrepreneurial profits... are the prizes offered by capitalist society to the successful innovator." Schumpeter (1942, p. 132), however, worries that the social

1 The discussion of the literature in this chapter draws upon the overview in Spulber (2013b).

function of entrepreneurship is "already losing importance" as innovation becomes routine and technological progress is "the business of teams of trained specialists who turn out what is required and make it work in predictable ways."

Schumpeter (1942) advances the hypothesis that a firm's innovativeness increases with its size and market power, so that competition *discourages* innovation. In emphasizing the advantages of large incumbents with market power, Schumpeter likely was influenced by the rise of corporate R&D. In the first half of the twentieth century, practically all funded research in the United States and Europe took place in corporate R&D labs or in government labs (Carlsson et al., 2009).

The Schumpeterian hypothesis influences a large number of empirical studies although these studies offer mixed results on the relationship between market concentration and incentives for innovation.[2] Sidak and Teece (2009, p. 588) observe: "Despite 50 years of research, economists do not appear to have found much evidence that market concentration has a statistically significant impact on innovation."[3] Sutton (1998, p. 4) points out that "there appears to be no consensus as to the form of relationship, if any, between R&D intensity and concentration." Earlier tests of the Schumpeterian hypothesis were based on the traditional Industrial Organization structure-conduct-performance paradigm that took market structure as a cause of competitive conduct and performance. As Sutton (1996, p. 512) points out, the dispute over the direction of causation from market concentration to R&D intensity "faded out in the late 1970s with the widespread acceptance of the view that these were both endogenous variables and they should be seen as being simultaneously determined within an equilibrium system." Later more sophisticated empirical studies recognize the joint determination of market structure and innovation and test the effects of market demand and entry costs on innovation.[4] Additional tests of the Schumpeterian hypothesis consider the effects of a firm's size on its propensity to innovative.[5]

2 For critical overviews, see Cohen and Levin (1989), Blundell et al. (1999), Yoo (2002), and Cohen (2010).

3 Various empirical studies of the effects of competition on invention assume that firms carry out both R&D and goods production, so that the two activities are vertically integrated. Blundell et al. (1999) point out such studies are subject to several problems: there is reverse causality because firms that innovate will have higher market shares because of growth; there is unobservable heterogeneity because firms have different technological and market opportunities; and measures of R&D such as Solow residuals, R&D expenditures, and patents present difficulties. Blundell et al. (1999, p. 530) observe that "[t]he results from applied work on market structure and innovation have been disturbingly sensitive to data source and estimation technique" (see also Cohen and Levin, 1989).

4 See Link (1980), Acs and Audretsch (1988), Angelmar (1985), Nickell (1996), Sutton (1996, 1998), Blundell et al. (1999), Shelanski (2000), Marin and Siotis (2001), and Aghion et al. (2005).

5 Brouwer and Kleinknecht (1996), for example, find that larger established firms tend to have greater sales from innovative products.

Empirical tests of the Schumpeterian hypothesis generally examine the effects of competition on innovation with the implicit assumption that firms vertically integrate R&D and goods production.[6] Therefore, measures of competition pressures are based on product market competition among innovative firms. For example, some empirical studies measure the relative markup in the downstream product market to infer the elasticity of product demand which serves as a proxy for product market competition. Empirical studies by Nickell (1996) and Aghion et al. (2005) measure competition on the basis of the reciprocal of the elasticity of demand in the product market (the Lerner index) as indicated by the relative markup. Aghion et al. (2005) find that invention (citation-weighted patents) is initially increasing and then decreasing in the Lerner index. Blundell et al. (1999) examine the relationship between product market share and innovation together with the impact of product market share on the relationship between innovations and corporate stock market value. Shelanski (2000) finds that faster deployment times of innovations in telecommunications are correlated with more competitive product market structures. Angelmar (1985) finds that with low R&D costs, low uncertainty, and barriers to imitation, product market concentration has a positive impact on R&D intensity but otherwise can reduce R&D intensity. Acs and Audretsch (1988) distinguish innovative output from inventive inputs and suggest that R&D expenditures and industry structure in the product market affect innovation by firms rather than the size of the firm, with lower downstream industry concentration increasing innovation by firms.

A large theoretical literature tends to support the Schumpeterian hypothesis by showing that competitive pressures reduce incentives for innovation. These studies often assume that R&D and production are vertically integrated. Competing firms each undertake internal R&D to lower their own costs of production (Dasgupta and Stiglitz, 1980a, 1980b; Gilbert and Newbery, 1982; Spence, 1984; Bester and Petrakis, 1993; Qiu, 1997; Cabral, 2003; Vives, 2008). Dasgupta and Stiglitz (1980a), for example, examine a Cournot oligopoly model in which each firm undertakes R&D to lower its costs (see also Dasgupta and Stiglitz, 1980b). In their model, the effect of product-demand elasticity on per-firm and total R&D is unclear, although total R&D expenditures can exceed the socially optimal level under some conditions. Gilbert and Newbery (1982) find that vertically integrated

6 Fisher and Temin (1973) criticize empirical tests of the Schumpeterian hypothesis, pointing out that tests of economies of scale in R&D – suggesting advantages for larger firms – are problematic. They reference among others Villard (1958), Schmookler (1959), Worley (1961), Mansfield (1964), Hamberg (1964), Scherer (1965a, 1965b), and Comanor (1965, 1967) and critiques by Markham (1965), and Grabowski and Mueller (1970). Rosenberg (1976) finds a negative relationship between internal R&D, as measured by the percentage of total employment allocated to R&D, and the firm's market share. The Schumpeterian hypothesis also is related to studies of the "differential productivity growth question" (see, for example, Nelson and Winter, 1977, and the references therein).

incumbent monopolists have greater incentives for R&D than potential entrants because competition reduces industry profits.

Vives (2008) presents a highly useful model of vertically integrated R&D and production. Competing firms engage in cost-reducing R&D and offer differentiated products. Vives examines how different measures of competitive pressures affect R&D. He shows that competitive pressures as a result of more producers or lower entry costs tend to decrease incentives to innovate as the Schumpeterian hypothesis suggests. Vives also shows that higher product substitutability and greater market size increase incentives to innovate.[7]

The Schumpeterian hypothesis does not hold when there is a market for inventions in contrast to vertically integrated R&D and production.[8] Competitive pressures consist of both competition among inventors – the supply side of the market for discoveries – and competition among producers who will use the discoveries – the demand side of the market for discoveries.

Greater competition among inventors, although it dissipates economic rents, leads to more invention and more innovation among producers who adopt the inventions, in comparison to a multi-project monopoly incumbent. Greater competition among producers generates more rents for inventors leading to greater entry of inventors. Greater competition among producers increases incentives for inventors, which generalizes Arrow's (1962b) result that a competitive product market generates greater incentives to invent than does a monopolistic product market.

Consider incentives to innovate when there is competition among vertically integrated producers of differentiated products. Suppose that there are m producers j that have identical costs after innovation. Suppose also that the market equilibrium is symmetric, so that each producer has an equilibrium price equal to $p^*(c, m)$, which depends on costs and the number of producers. Define the demand per producer with symmetric equilibrium prices as $q(p, m)$, which corresponds to the Chamberlain DD demand curve (Vives, 2008). A producer's incentive to invest in R&D is the effect on profit of a reduction in unit costs, which is equal to the producer's output. Therefore, the effects of competition on incentives for internal R&D depend on how competition affects output per producer,

$$\frac{dq(p^*(c, m), m)}{dm} = \frac{\partial q(p^*(c, m), m)}{\partial p}\frac{\partial p^*(c, m)}{\partial m} + \frac{\partial q(p^*(c, m), m)}{\partial m}.$$

Vives (2008) points out that the first term, the *price-pressure effect*, is positive, whereas the second term, the *demand effect*, generally is negative and dominates the price-pressure effect, so that competitive pressures reduce internal R&D expenditures. Vives (2008) also observes that increases in product substitutability tend to

7 Vives's (2008) reduced-form model of product market competition is useful for the development of a model of the market for inventions in Spulber (2013b).

8 See Spulber (2013a, 2013b).

have reinforcing price-pressure and demand effects on output per producer and, hence, increase internal R&D expenditures.

Now consider incentives to innovate when there is a market for inventions in which inventors compete to sell their discoveries to downstream producers. Producers do not engage in R&D but obtain their technology in the market for inventions. Suppose that the winning inventor sells to all of the downstream producers. Then, the incentive to invent depends on supply-side competition among inventors and demand-side competition among producers. The number of producers increases industry output,

$$\frac{dmq(p^*(c, m), m)}{dm} = m\left[\frac{\partial q(p^*(c, m), m)}{\partial p}\frac{\partial p^*(c, m)}{\partial m} + \frac{\partial q(p^*(c, m), m)}{\partial m}\right] + q(p^*(c, m), m) > 0.$$

The bracketed term is likely to be negative because the demand effect outweighs the price pressure effect of competition, as was just noted. However, the last term, $q(p^*(c, m), m)$, is an *industry growth effect* from increased competition – that is, the equilibrium output of the additional firm. The entry of an additional producer results in an increase in total output that will add to the total industry benefits of cost reduction. The industry growth effect reinforces the total price pressure effect. When the industry growth effect and the total price pressure effect are sufficient to overwhelm the total demand effects of competition, competitive pressures increase incentives to innovate. Therefore, when there is a market for inventions, greater competition will increase incentives to innovate.

In the next section, we compare innovation with competition among innovative entrepreneurs with innovation by a multi-project monopoly incumbent. Even though the entrepreneurs and the incumbent have vertically integrated R&D and production, competition among entrepreneurs increases incentives to innovate in comparison with the monopoly incumbent. The reason is that the expected incentives to innovate depend on industry output whether there is competition among entrepreneurs or a monopoly incumbent. When entrepreneurs compete to serve the market, the expected return to entrepreneurship depends on industry output contingent on winning the market. The incumbent monopolist's incentive to innovate also depends on industry output. Competition among entrepreneurs decreases the product price and increases equilibrium market demand. Therefore, for any given level of costs, market demand will be greater with competing entrepreneurs than with a monopoly firm.

Innovation and Irrational Exuberance

Are competitive pressures from entrepreneurial entry beneficial to the economy? Competition among innovative entrepreneurs and between entrepreneurs and incumbents can result in entry and exit: as the most successful firms remain in the industry, less successful firms exit. This may correspond to industry expansion and contraction, as initial entry is followed by exit. This pattern of industry expansion and contraction is sometimes said to accompany boom-and-bust cycles in the economy.

Some economic observers have associated economic boom-and-bust cycles with major innovations such as the development of the steam locomotive, the power loom, petroleum for lighting, the sewing machine, and electric current (Schumpeter, 1939). More recently, some have suggested that the rise of the Internet dot-com companies led to an economic boom-and-bust cycle. Public policy makers may seek to dampen boom-and-bust cycles so as to protect existing firms from innovative entrepreneurs entering the market. Such industrial policies are designed not only to pick winners but also to rescue losers. This type of industrial policy reduces incentives to innovate and often provides incentives for firms to engage in unproductive rent seeking in return for government subsidies and protections.

Some economists attribute boom-and-bust cycles to irrational exuberance of entrepreneurs who are said to overestimate the rewards to entry thereby wasting capital investment and disrupting the economy. For example, Kindleberger (1996, p. 13) states: "Overestimation of profits comes from euphoria, affects firms engaged in the productive and distributive processes, and requires no explanation." According to Irving Fisher (1933, p. 348), events start with "*new opportunities to invest at a big prospective profit* as compared with ordinary profits and interest, such as through new inventions, new industries, development of new resources, opening of new lands or new markets."[9] Fisher (1933, p. 349) emphasizes the "public psychology of going into debt for gain" as a cause of boom-and-bust cycles, including "the lure of big prospective dividends or gains in *income* in the remote future," the hope of "a *capital* gain in the immediate future," "the vogue of reckless promotions, taking advantage of the habituation of the public to great expectations," and "downright fraud" (emphasis in original).

Schumpeter (1939, p. 140) criticizes this pessimistic view, arguing that "most people will link up recessions with errors of judgment, excesses (overdoing), and misconduct." Schumpeter emphasizes that "it is understandable that mistakes of all sorts should be more frequent than usual (i.e. when untried things are being put into practice and adaptation to a state of things becomes necessary the contours of which have not yet appeared)." Far from being irrational or wasteful, however, boom-and-bust cycles serve important economic functions. Often, a boom-and-bust cycle is the outcome of rational competitive decisions: profit-maximizing entrepreneurs enter the industry, engage in innovation, establish firms, and make investments. Creative destruction often occurs after significant technological innovation and also in newly established industries. Creative destruction serves to select the most efficient new technologies and to reduce excess productive capacity to the level of market demand.

9 Emphasis in original, quoted in Schumpeter's discussion of business cycles (1939, p. 146). Irving Fisher is discussing debt problems leading to the Great Depression.

Schumpeter (1939, p. 138) emphasizes that many types of innovation create opportunities for entrepreneurs who then move the economic system away from an equilibrium position in the upturn of the cycle and toward another equilibrium position in the downturn of the cycle. After significant innovations, entry and expansion tend to create industry capacity that substantially outruns market demand. Creative destruction denotes much more than the effects of random fluctuations in demand or the occasional exit of badly managed firms. Firms enter the market to develop innovative technologies. The entry and investment of new firms combined with the facilities of existing firms expand industry capacity above the level that is needed to serve the market efficiently. Technological uncertainty followed by innovative entry shapes industry structure.[10]

It has long been debated whether entrepreneurs are rational profit maximizers taking a calculated risk or irrationally exuberant gamblers who overestimate the chance of success or who simply enjoy creating a new business. The models of competitive entry presented in this chapter establish conditions under which the productive capacity of firms that enter the industry exceeds the size of the market. Excess entry occurs even though firms anticipate vigorous price competition that will result in creative destruction. Because firms in these models are expected profit maximizers, the analysis shows how creative destruction and shakeouts are consistent with rational behavior.

When entrepreneurs simultaneously create related innovations, more capacity enters the market than is needed to satisfy demand because each entrant correctly believes that their variant of the production technology has a chance of being among the best. The driving forces of the model are uncertainty about the outcome of innovation before entry and differences in technology across firms after entry. By investing in innovation and capacity, firms purchase an option that allows them to remain in the industry if it is profitable to do so. Costs of entry and investment are the price of the option. The firm's profit depends on its relative performance, with efficient firms exercising their option to operate in the market.

During the boom, there can be a wide variety of technologies and business models, so that a rising tide appears to lift all boats. Depending on the length of the boom period, entrepreneurs can succeed even without competitive advantage. If market demand outruns industry capacity, inframarginal firms can operate profitably with diverse products and a variety of production technologies, just as inframarginal land is brought into production in the Ricardian framework. However, if industry capacity outruns market demand, high-cost firms are shaken out at the margin. Firms must have some competitive advantages to survive the shakeout. The need for competitive advantage depends on the relative size of the market in comparison with industry capacity and the capacity of individual firms. When individual firms

10 See Nelson and Winter (1982), Flaherty (1980), Dasgupta and Stiglitz (1980a, 1980b), and Spulber (2010a).

are not capacity constrained or equivalently when capacity constraints are large relative to the size of the market, competitive advantage becomes essential and few technologies survive. When individual firms have capacity constraints that are small relative to the size of the market, there is less need for competitive advantage and diverse technologies survive shakeouts.

The process of boom-and-bust that accompanies innovation is costly but need not be wasteful. Entrepreneurs often enter an industry concurrently. Because of technological uncertainty and complexity, each entrant will try out a different discovery or business model. The innovative process requires market experiments, with firms putting product, process, and transaction innovations into practice. The entry of more capacity than is required to serve the market stimulates both investment and price competition. Creative destruction adjusts industry capacity to the size of the market and selects the most efficient technologies.

Creative Destruction

The entrepreneur must launch a firm that provides more effective organizations, better market transactions, more efficient technologies, or differentiated goods and services in comparison with the competing alternatives. Through creative destruction, more innovative and efficient firms displace their rivals.

Competition among entrepreneurs is an economically important phenomenon because it generates information about the comparative performance of innovations. At the start of the twentieth century, hundreds of entrepreneurs entered automobile manufacturing, and many subsequently exited the industry.[11] At the end of the twentieth century, hundreds of entrepreneurs entered into business-to-business electronic commerce, and again many subsequently exited the market place in the wake of the dot-com boom.[12] Entrepreneurial competition in these industries revealed what innovations were best suited to meet the needs of consumers.

The process of creative destruction can involve multiple entrepreneurs entering the market followed by intense competition that results in exit of firms and consolidation of capacity. Schumpeter (1939, p. 100) observes "that innovations do not remain isolated events, and are not evenly distributed in time, but that on the contrary, they tend to cluster, to come about in bunches, simply because first some, and then most firms follow in the wake of successful innovation." Additionally, "innovations tend to concentrate in certain sectors and their surroundings" (1939, pp. 100–101). Feldman (1996) examines geographic clustering of innovations, which she explains by knowledge spillovers, while controlling for geographic concentration of production. The resulting creative destruction induces much more than the effects of random fluctuations in demand or the occasional exit of badly

11 See Seltzer (1928), Pound (1934), and Bresnahan and Raff (1991).

12 See Lucking-Reiley and Spulber (2001).

managed firms. The clustering of entrepreneurs at a particular time or place implies that entrepreneurs compete among themselves as well as with existing firms.

By creating start-ups and establishing firms, innovative entrepreneurs discover the benefits and costs of operating new technologies. Incomplete information about demand requires that entrepreneurs experiment by offering different types of products and transactions. Uncertainty about the performance of alternative technologies requires entrepreneurs to experiment by applying the new technology in production. Competition among entrepreneurs sorts through these experiments, allowing those firms with the best products and the most efficient technologies to survive while eliminating excess productive capacity.

Hayek (2002, p. 18) states that "competition is important primarily as a discovery procedure whereby entrepreneurs constantly search for unexploited opportunities that can also be taken advantage of by others." The market yields knowledge that "consists to a great extent of the ability to detect certain conditions – an ability that individuals can use effectively only when the market tells them what kinds of goods and services are demanded, and how urgently" (2002, p. 13).[13] Rosenberg (1992) observes that the freedom of companies to conduct experiments is the central feature of market economies, with industries that are "characterized by a truly extraordinary pattern of organizational diversity." The technological heterogeneity of firms within industries has been studied extensively.[14]

Innovative entrepreneurs offering diverse products have competed for the market in industries such as retail, wholesale, airlines, Internet companies, media, computer software, and computer hardware manufacturing.[15] Shakeouts have been observed in a wide variety of industries including supermarkets, motor vehicle manufacturers, pharmaceutical wholesalers, computer manufacturers, television producers, airlines, media companies, Internet companies, online publishers, beer brewers, law firms, and clothing designers.[16]

Fein (1998) finds shakeouts in wholesaling in more than a dozen industries including flowers, woodworking machinery, locksmiths, specialty tools and

13 Like Schumpeter, Hayek distinguishes market discoveries, which are made by competing entrepreneurs, from scientific and technological discoveries.

14 See, for example, Klein (1977), Audretsch (1991), and Malerba and Orsenigo (1997).

15 A number of studies consider entry and exit of innovative producers in the computer industry (McClellan, 1984), airlines (Peterson and Glab, 1994; Morrison and Winston, 1995), and media companies (Maney, 1995). Management studies have examined competition between innovative start-ups and established firms; see Henderson and Clark (1990) and Christensen (1997). Innovative entrepreneurs entered markets for software (Torrisi, 1998), including encryption software (Giarratana, 2004).

16 Studies documenting significant exit of firms include supermarkets (Craswell and Fratrick, 1985–1986), the computer industry (McClellan, 1984), airlines (Peterson and Glab, 1994; Morrison and Winston, 1995), and media companies (Maney, 1995). Press reports include Internet companies (Tedeshi, 2000), online publishing (Schiesel, 1997), beer brewing (Moriwaki, 1996; Horvath et al., 2001), law firms (Deutsch, 1995), and clothing designers (King, 1998).

fasteners, sporting goods, wholesale grocers, air conditioning and refrigeration, electronic components, wine and spirits, waste equipment, and periodicals. Fein (1998, p. 234) points out that in the pharmaceutical wholesaling industry, "a combination of new technologies set off a chain-reaction within the entire business model of drug wholesaling." Fein emphasizes the effects of multiple new practices and technologies being adopted at approximately the same time and creating productive complementarities, including electronic ordering systems, warehouse automation, and application of information technology to inventory management. Fein suggests that such complementarities explain why the design and selection of a single dominant business model was so difficult for individual firms. Because of the complexity of the wholesale technology, only a process of competition could identify the more efficient systems.

There were many innovative entrepreneurs in early automobile manufacturing, and early cars had many different features and designs.[17] Entrepreneurial automobile companies also differed in terms of manufacturing technologies. Bresnahan and Raff (1991) demonstrate that the motor vehicle industry before its Depression-era shakeout exhibited considerable intra-industry heterogeneity that they attribute to the partial diffusion of mass production technology. They show that those plants and organizations that benefited from mass production economies had a competitive advantage so that low-average-cost firms survived market downturns. Lieberman (1990) considers exit from thirty market segments of the chemical industry and shows that small plants had higher rates of closure, but, holding plant size effects constant, large multiplant firms were more likely to close individual plants. Deily's (1991) study of the steel industry suggests that plant closings resulted from plant-specific characteristics that affect long-run profitability, such as size of the plant or competition from minimills.

Empirical analysis of entry suggests that entrepreneurs act as innovators. In a study of the computer industry, Bayus and Agarwal (2007) find that technology strategies employed after entry are critical for firm survival. Entry often can be relatively easy, but survival is difficult (Geroski, 1995). However, entry is a valuable mechanism for introducing product and process innovations, with the best products and processes selected through competition between firms once they are established and operating within the industry.

Competition among innovative entrepreneurs generally differs from patent races. Innovation involves competition for customers rather than a race for exclusive legal protections for IP. Entrepreneurial competition involves discovering the best match between innovations and customer needs. The innovative entrepreneur engages in multidimensional innovation consisting of new products, production processes, transaction techniques, and organizational structures.

17 The *Standard Catalog of American Cars 1805 to 1942* (Kimes and Clark, 1996) lists a vast array of automobile manufacturers, each offering different product features and designs.

Through competition among entrepreneurial firms, the market discovers the best "new combinations." There may be multiple winners of the competition among entrepreneurs because entering firms may serve different segments of the market. Entrepreneurs in the same industry may commercialize the same invention in different ways, or they may commercialize different types of inventions. Competing entrepreneurs can obtain inventions in different ways: creating their own inventions, licensing inventions from independent inventors, applying publicly available knowledge, or adapting existing business models. Entrepreneurial success depends not only on technological differences but also on the personal attributes of entrepreneurs such as preferences, income, wealth, judgment, knowledge, ability, ideas, and opportunity costs.

Competition for the market among diverse innovative entrepreneurs differs from industry attrition that is a result of demand-side shocks and falling demand.[18] With demand shocks, firms may be uncertain about whether the market equilibrium price will cover costs and choose to exit if their costs turn out to be too high.[19] Competition among diverse entrepreneurs also differs from entry and exit in R&D races. In models of R&D races, inventions are identical and a patent goes to the firm that wins the race.[20] Competition among diverse entrepreneurs also differs from R&D tournaments. In the literature on R&D tournaments, a sponsor designs the prize for the best technology, and inventors devote effort to producing inventions.[21] In contrast to tournaments, innovative entrepreneurs provide diverse inventions. Also, incentives to innovate depend on market rewards rather than prizes chosen by the contest designer.

Studies of shakeouts based on the industry life-cycle approach consider long-term industry adjustments and the emergence of a "dominant design." Following a technological innovation, firms introduce products with different designs although over time a particular design may emerge as a set of technological standards. For example, software firms offered a variety of operating systems for desktop computers with a graphical user interface, with the eventual dominance of Microsoft's

18 Harrigan (1980) provides case studies of declining industries. Ghemawat and Nalebuff (1985) consider a model of declining demand in a duopoly with different market shares and show that the largest firm is the first to leave. Reynolds (1988) shows that when firms have the same number of plants, high-cost plants close first, and that a firm with more plants closes plants first as long as cost differences are not too large.

19 See Mansfield (1962) and Jovanovic (1982a). Jovanovic and MacDonald (1994) present a life-cycle model of industry evolution.

20 See the survey by Reinganum (1989). See also Cabral (2003) and the references therein. In Cabral (2003), the returns obtained by competing inventors depend on the quality differences in inventions. Gans and Stern (2000) model the choice between technology transfer and entrepreneurship when there is R&D racing; see also Gans et al. (2002). Spulber (2008c, 2010b) considers the market for inventions in an international trade setting. Spulber (2010a) considers competition among entrepreneurs with differentiated technologies.

21 See Baye and Hoppe (2003).

Windows over Apple's Mac OS and IBM's OS2. According to Suarez and Utterback (1995, pp. 416–417), "the emergence of a dominant design is the result of a fortunate combination of technological, economic, and organizational factors."[22] Teece (1986) points out that the dominant design concept is well suited for mass-market consumer goods. Abernathy and Utterback (1978) consider the product life cycle in the auto industry and consider the possibility of uncertainty on the part of consumers and firms about consumer preferences with respect to product features. With learning, a dominant design emerges, and those firms that cannot produce the dominant design efficiently are shaken out of the market. Suarez and Utterback (1995) show empirically that firms entering before a dominant design emerges have a higher probability of success, which increases the greater is the number of years before the dominant design emerges.[23]

4.2 A Model of Competition among Innovative Entrepreneurs

This section presents a model of competition among innovative entrepreneurs. Products are homogeneous, and there are no capacity constraints. Through Bertrand competition, a single innovative entrepreneur serves the entire market. The analysis shows that competition increases incentives to innovate. Competing entrepreneurs generate more innovative projects than a multi-project monopoly incumbent. This is because *average* expected returns to innovation with competition among entrepreneurs are greater than *incremental* expected returns to innovation with a multi-project monopoly incumbent.

Entrepreneurial Competition

Consider a two-stage model of innovation and competition. In the first stage, innovative entrepreneurs obtain inventions and establish new firms that embody innovative process technologies. Innovative entrepreneurs obtain technologies by engaging in uncertain R&D or by arranging exclusive contracts with inventors. Innovative entrepreneurs embody the inventions in the new firms and do not observe the quality of their innovations until they have entered the market. Let $k > 0$ denote the costs of obtaining inventions and establishing an innovative firm. The equilibrium number of innovative entrepreneurs n^* is a positive integer and is determined endogenously. Innovation is modeled as an independent draw c_i from a cumulative distribution function $F(c)$ defined on the interval $[0, 1]$ with $F(0) = 0$ and $F(1) = 1$. The distribution has a continuous density function $f(c)$.

In the second stage, the innovative entrepreneurs' process technologies c_i are revealed and become common knowledge. We can list unit costs in increasing

22 See Utterback and Abernathy (1975).

23 See also Utterback and Suarez (1993).

order, $c_1 < c_2 < \ldots < c_n$, so that c_1 denotes the best innovation and c_2 denotes the second-best innovation. Innovative entrepreneurs engage in full-information Bertrand-Nash competition in the product market.

Market demand $D(p)$ is a twice continuously differentiable and decreasing function of the final product price, p. Assume that the profit function is concave in price, where profits equal

$$\pi(p, c) = (p - c)D(p). \tag{1}$$

Let $p^M(c)$ be the profit-maximizing monopoly price, which is unique and increasing in cost c, and denote monopoly profits by $\pi^M(c) = \pi(p^M(c), c)$.

The Bertrand-Nash equilibrium corresponds to the Arrow (1962b) outcome with an important difference – the second-best innovation takes the place of the initial technology as the outside option. Competitive differences between the best and the second-best innovation are drastic if the entrepreneur with the best innovation can offer the monopoly price to customers without being constrained by the entrepreneur with the second-best innovation, $p^M(c_1) < c_2$. The innovation is non-drastic if the entrepreneur with the best innovation is constrained by the entrepreneur with the second-best innovation, $p^M(c_1) \geq c_2$. When competitive differences between the best and the second-best innovation are non-drastic, the entrepreneur with the best innovation chooses a product price equal to the unit cost given by the second-best innovation. The final product price is

$$p^*(c_1, c_2) = \min\{p^M(c_1), c_2\}.$$

All entrepreneurs other than the one with the best innovation price at unit cost and so have profits equal to zero. The incentive to innovate equals the expected profit of the entrepreneur with the best innovation.

The expected profit of an innovative entrepreneur is the expectation of a successful entrepreneur's profits $\pi(p^*(c_1, c_2), c_1)$ times the likelihood of having the best invention, $1/n$. From the theory of order statistics, the joint density of the best innovation and the second-best innovation is given by

$$f(c_1, c_2, n) = n(n-1)(1 - F(c_2))^{n-1} f(c_1) f(c_2),$$

for $c_1 \leq c_2 < 1$ and equals $f(c_1, c_2, n) = 0$ otherwise. The expected return of an entrepreneur when more than one entrepreneur enters the market equals

$$\Pi(n) = \int_0^1 \int_{c_1}^1 \pi(p^*(c_1, c_2), c_1)(1/n) f(c_1, c_2, n) dc_2 dc_1. \tag{2}$$

The equilibrium market structure n^* is the largest number of entrepreneurs such that $\Pi(n) \geq k$. To focus attention on competition among entrepreneurs, suppose that at least two will enter the market, $\Pi(2) \geq k$.

If competitive differences are drastic, $p^*(c_1, c_2) = p^M(c_1)$ so that the cost of the second-best innovation does not affect the profits of the winning entrepreneur,

$$\frac{d\pi(p^*(c_1, c_2), c_1)}{dc_2} = 0.$$

If competitive differences are non-drastic, $p^*(c_1, c_2) = c_2 < p^M(c_1)$ so that the profits of the winning entrepreneur are constrained by the quality of the second-best innovation. This implies that the profits of the winning entrepreneur are increasing in the second-best innovation,

$$\frac{d\pi(p^*(c_1, c_2), c_1)}{dc_2} > 0.$$

Integrating the second integral in equation (2) by parts gives

$$\text{(3)} \quad \Pi(n) = \int_0^1 \left\{ \int_{c_1}^{p^*(c_1,1)} [(c_2 - c_1)D'(c_2) + D(c_2)](1 - F(c_2))^{n-1} dc_2 \right\} \times f(c_1)dc_1.$$

When competition constrains the profit function of the winning entrepreneur, profit is increasing in the second-best innovation. The expected profit function $\Pi(n)$ in equation (3) is decreasing in the number of entrepreneurs, so the competitive equilibrium with entry is well defined. The equilibrium market structure is non-increasing in entry costs k.

The size of the market is one measure of competitive pressures. The number of innovative entrepreneurs is increasing in the size of the market. Suppose that demand has a shift parameter S, so that $D(p) = SD^*(p)$. This is equivalent to the situation in which the demand function is $D^*(p)$ and entry costs equal k/S. Therefore, an increase in the size of the market increases innovation.

Consider the effects elasticity of demand on innovation by entrepreneurs. Let demand be given by $D(p, \eta)$, where η is a parameter that increases the absolute value of demand elasticity. Differentiate expected profit with respect to the elasticity of demand and apply the envelope theorem using $p^*(c_1, c_2) = \min\{p^M(c_1), c_2\}$:

$$\frac{d\Pi(n)}{d\eta} = \int_0^1 \int_{c_1}^1 (p^*(c_1, c_2) - c_1) \frac{\partial D(p^*(c_1, c_2), \eta)}{\partial \eta} (1/n) f(c_1, c_2, n) dc_2 dc_1.$$

Therefore, increasing the elasticity of demand increases or decreases entry depending on whether it increases or decreases demand at a given price. For example, suppose that demand has a constant elasticity, $D(p) = p^{-\eta}$ where $\eta > 1$. Then,

$$\frac{d\Pi(n)}{d\eta} = \int_0^1 \int_{c_1}^1 \pi(p^*(c_1, c_2), c_1)[-\ln(p^*(c_1, c_2))](1/n) f(c_1, c_2, n) dc_2 dc_1 > 0.$$

This is positive because $0 < p^*(c_1, c_2) \leq c_2 \leq 1$, so that $\ln(p^*(c_1, c_2))$ is less than or equal to zero and strictly negative for $p^*(c_1, c_2) < 1$. A greater expected profit increases equilibrium entry of entrepreneurs so that an increase in the elasticity of product market demand increases innovation, $dn^* / d\eta \geq 0$. An increase in demand elasticity increases competition among entrepreneurs.

In equilibrium, the relative markup and entry are jointly determined. When competitive differences are large, the relative markup equals the Lerner index, $(p^M(c_1) - c_1)/c_1 = 1/\eta$. Then, the relative markup is unaffected by the quality of the best or the second-best innovation and an increase in the elasticity of demand lowers the relative markup with competitive entry. However, when the best innovation is not drastically different from the second-best innovation, the relative markup equals $(c_2 - c_1)/c_2$, which depends on the quality of the best and the second-best innovation and not on the elasticity of demand. Also, the entry of more entrepreneurs lowers the expected value of both the best and the second-best innovation. So, competition makes it more likely that the second-best innovation will constrain prices. Then, entry may increase or decrease the relative markup.

Comparison with a Multi-Project Monopoly Incumbent

To evaluate the effects of competition on incentives to innovate, compare the outcome with competing entrepreneurs with a multi-project monopoly incumbent. The multi-project monopoly firm chooses the best realization from m parallel uncertain R&D projects. The number of R&D projects m is integer valued, and the cost per R&D project is k. The probability distribution of the best invention is that of the lowest order statistic with a sample of size m, $F_1(c, m) = 1 - (1 - F(c))^m$, with density $f_1(c, m)$. The incumbent firm has an initial technology $c_0 \geq 1$.

The incumbent obtains benefits from adopting the new technology c equal to the change in profits. The expected return of the multi-project monopoly incumbent equals

$$Y(m) = \int_0^1 (\pi^M(c) - \pi^M(c_0)) f_1(c, m) dc. \tag{4}$$

The monopoly inventor chooses the number of projects m^* to maximize expected benefits net of the costs of R&D, $Y(m) - km$. The optimal number of projects with a monopoly inventor m^* is the largest number of projects m such that incremental returns to invention are greater than or equal to the cost per project, $Y(m) - Y(m-1) \geq k > Y(m+1) - Y(m)$.

The multi-project monopolist's incremental expected return equals

$$Y(m+1) - Y(m) = \int_0^1 \pi^M(c)[f_1(c, m+1) - f_1(c, m)] dc. \tag{5}$$

Therefore, incremental returns do not depend on profits from using the initial technology $\pi^M(c_0)$. There is no inertia effect if the monopolist chooses to conduct more than one project. Integrating by parts and noting that $d\pi^M(c)/dc = -D(p^M(c))$, the monopolist's incremental expected return depends on demand at the monopoly price evaluated at the new technology,

$$(6) \qquad Y(m+1) - Y(m) = \int_0^1 D(p^M(c))(1 - F(c))^m F(c)dc.$$

The monopolist's problem is well defined because the incremental expected return $Y(m+1) - Y(m)$ is decreasing in m.

A comparison of competing entrepreneurs with the multi-project monopoly incumbent depends on the difference between the *average incentive to innovate* for competing entrepreneurs and the *incremental incentive to innovate* for the multi-project incumbent monopoly. Entry of entrepreneurs continues until an additional entrepreneur would cause expected profits per entrepreneur to be less than entry costs. In contrast, the multi-project monopolist increases the number of projects until the incremental returns from an additional project would be less than the cost of a project.

With competition among entrepreneurs, the market price at the new technology is less than or equal to the monopoly level even if the second-best invention is at the lowest quality level, $p^*(c, 1) \leq p^M(c)$. This implies that the quantity demanded with competing entrepreneurs is greater than or equal to the monopoly level,

$$D(p^*(c, 1)) \geq D(p^M(c)).$$

Integrating the first integral in equation (3) by parts implies that

$$(7) \qquad \Pi(n) = \int_0^1 \left[D(c) + \int_c^{p^*(c,1)} D'(c_2) \frac{(1 - F(c_2))^{n-1}}{(1 - F(c))^{n-1}} dc_2 \right] \times (1 - F(c))^{n-1} F(c)dc.$$

The expected profit of an entrepreneur evaluated at $n + 1$ satisfies the following inequality,

$$\Pi(n+1) > \int_0^1 D(p^M(c))(1 - F(c))^n F(c)dc.$$

This implies that the average expected return for an entrepreneur evaluated at $n + 1$ is greater than the incremental expected return for the multi-project monopoly incumbent,

$$\Pi(n+1) > Y(n+1) - Y(n).$$

Competing entrepreneurs thus generate more innovations than the multi-project monopoly incumbent firm, $n^* \geq m^*$. So, competition among entrepreneurs increases incentives to innovate.

Competition among entrepreneurs increases the quality of innovation in comparison to the multi-project incumbent. This is because increasing the number of projects lowers the expected unit cost by order statistics arguments. With competing entrepreneurs, the equilibrium price depends on both the best and the second-best innovations. So, competition among innovative entrepreneurs lowers prices:

$$E[p^*(c_1, c_2) \mid n^*] \leq E[p^M(c_1) \mid n^*] \leq E[p^M(c_1) \mid m^*].$$

The entry of entrepreneurs therefore has two benefits: it improves the quality of the best innovation, and competition among the new entrants reduces prices. Competition among entrepreneurs thus increases output in comparison to the multi-project monopoly firm, which increases the economic benefits of lowering production costs.

Competition between Entrepreneurs and a Monopoly Incumbent

This section compares innovation when an incumbent faces competition from entrepreneurial entry with innovation when the incumbent has a protected monopoly. Suppose that a multi-project monopoly incumbent faces competition from a "fringe" consisting of single-project entrepreneurs. The entry of innovative entrepreneurs decreases the monopoly incumbent's incentives to innovate. However, innovation by the industry rises to the competitive level. The competitive outcome generates the same amount of innovation as in a market with only competing entrepreneurs so that entry of entrepreneurs increases innovation in comparison with a protected multi-project monopoly.

The multi-project incumbent decides on the number of projects at the same time that entrepreneurs make their entry decisions. At a Nash equilibrium, the multi-project incumbent chooses m^C projects, and n^C single-project entrepreneurs enter the market. If the multi-project incumbent has the best innovation, it must compete against the best entrepreneurial innovation. The multi-project incumbent applies the best innovation resulting from the m^C projects, c_1, which is the lowest order statistic from a sample of size m^C. The best invention among the fringe, c_2, is the lowest order statistic from a sample of size n^C. The entrepreneur with the best invention, c_1, competes against the second-best innovation, c_2, regardless of whether the second-best innovation is provided by a multi-project incumbent or another entrepreneur.

The profit of an entrepreneur therefore depends on the total number of projects, $m + n$. The expected return of each entrepreneur equals

$$(8) \quad \Pi(m+n) = \int_0^1 \int_{c_1}^1 \pi(p^*(c_1, c_2), c_1)[1/(m+n)] f(c_1, c_2, m+n) dc_2 dc_1.$$

The expected return of the multi-project incumbent equals

$$(9) \quad Y(m, n) = \int_0^1 \left[\int_{c_1}^1 \pi(p^*(c_1, c_2), c_1) f_1(c_2, n) dc_2 \right] f_1(c_1, m) dc_1.$$

The Nash equilibrium number of entrepreneurs entering the market, n^C, is the largest n such that

$$\Pi(m^C + n) \geq k.$$

The Nash equilibrium number of projects chosen by the multi-project inventor, m^C, maximizes profits, $Y(m, n^C) - km$, as a best response to the number of entrepreneurs entering the market. The Nash equilibrium (n^C, m^C) need not be unique. However, the total number of projects with heterogeneous competition is unique and equals the equilibrium number of competing entrepreneurs who enter the market when there is no incumbent firm,

$$m^C + n^C = n^*. \tag{10}$$

Therefore, the entry of innovative entrepreneurs increases innovation in comparison to a market with only a multi-project monopoly incumbent.

To see why this is the case, notice that the incremental return for the multi-project incumbent equals

$$Y(m+1, n) - Y(m, n) = \int_0^1 \left[\int_{c_1}^1 \pi(p^*(c_1, c_2), c_1) f_1(c_2, n) dc_2\right] \times [f_1(c_1, m+1) - f_1(c_1, m)] dc_1. \tag{11}$$

Because $p^*(c, c_2) \leq p^*(c, c_0)$ and strictly for some values of c and c_2, it follows that for $n \geq 1$,

$$Y(m+1, n) - Y(m, n) < \int_0^1 \pi(p^*(c, c_0), c)(1 - F_1(c, n))[f_1(c_1, m+1) - f_1(c_1, m)] dc_1.$$

The right-hand side is the same as the incremental return for a monopoly incumbent with $m + n + 1$ number of projects. The expected profit of the entrepreneur also depends on the total number of projects, $\Pi(m + n)$. This implies that $m^C + n^C = n^*$.[24] It follows that competitive pressures from entrepreneurial entrants increase incentives for innovation. The incumbent firm decreases innovation to accommodate the entrants, but overall innovation increases relative to a multi-project monopoly incumbent that is protected from entry.

24 Suppose to the contrary that $n^* < m^C + n^C$. Then, $\Pi(m^C + n^C) < k$, and because $n^C \geq m^C$, $Y(m^C, n^C) - Y(m^C - 1, n^C) < k$, so that (m^C, n^C) is not an equilibrium, which is a contradiction. Also, suppose to the contrary that $m^C + n^C < n^*$. Then, there are incentives for additional entry, $\Pi(m^C + n^C + 1) > k$, so that (m^C, n^C) is not an equilibrium, which is a contradiction. Therefore, $m^C + n^C = n^*$.

4.3 Competitive Pressures and IP

The problem of appropriating IP is of critical importance for entrepreneurial incentives to innovate. The analysis thus far assumes that innovators are able to fully appropriate the market returns to their innovations. However, incumbents and replicative entrepreneurs may imitate or expropriate innovations when there are imperfect protections for IP. Inventors also face regulatory and legal costs associated with establishing and protecting their IP from infringement, which also reduces appropriability of the returns to invention. Competition from existing firms and new entrants that copy or expropriate innovations reduces the returns to innovative entrepreneurship.

To formalize the risks and frictions faced by innovators, let a be the probability that innovators are able to appropriate the returns to their inventions, where $0 < a < 1$. Entrepreneurs enter only when the expected return exceeds the cost of entry,

$$aV(n) \geq k.$$

Therefore, imperfect appropriability of innovations corresponds to a market with higher costs of entry, $V(n) \geq k/a$. Because the average returns to innovation $V(n)$ are decreasing in the number of entrepreneurs, entry of competing entrepreneurs n^* is increasing in the likelihood of appropriability a.

For the multi-project monopoly incumbent, imperfect appropriability also reduces the net returns to innovation, $aY(n, m) - k$, which corresponds to higher marginal costs of invention, $Y(n, m) - k/a$. Because the marginal returns to R&D are decreasing in the number of projects, the number of R&D projects for the multi-project monopoly N^* is increasing in the likelihood of appropriability a.

This suggests an extension of the Schumpeterian hypothesis: larger incumbent firms have a greater incentive to innovate than entrepreneurial entrants if they have a sufficiently higher degree of appropriability. Then, the multi-project monopoly inventor would develop more projects than competing entrepreneurs. Larger firms may benefit from economies of scale in protecting IP as a result of administrative and legal costs associated with patents, trademarks, copyrights, and trade secrets. The higher earnings of the multi-project monopoly inventor in comparison with competing entrepreneurs can be invested in filing patents, challenging patent infringement and marketing patent licenses. However, specialized intermediaries in the market for inventions can supply independent inventors and innovative entrepreneurs with IP services that have economies of scale.

4.4 Competition among Innovative Entrepreneurs with Capacity Constraints

This section extends the basic model of competition among innovative entrepreneurs to include capacity constraints and investment. The model has three stages:

entry, competition, and creative destruction. In the initial entry stage, entrepreneurs decide whether or not to invest in innovation and in the establishment of firms. In the intermediate competition stage, entrants strategically choose prices and make cost-reducing investments after observing their own technology but without observing the technology of rival firms. In the final creative destruction stage, consumers search across firms, and market conditions can result in exit of newly established firms. Firms with higher-quality innovations remain in the market, whereas firms with lower-quality innovations exit the market. The innovations are sufficiently drastic so that no incumbent firms remain in the market.

The analysis shows that both entry and exit can result from entrepreneurial innovation. Profit-maximizing entrepreneurs enter the industry, engage in innovation, establish firms, and make investments. Entrepreneurs continue to invest even after learning about their own technology because they face uncertainty about the technology of other firms, further increasing excess capacity. The exit of firms serves to select the most efficient innovations, and it also adjusts productive capacity to the level of market demand.

The analysis characterizes entrepreneurs' business strategies in the competition stage. Entrepreneurs' levels of investment are increasing in the likelihood of being active in the creative destruction stage. Entrepreneurs with higher-quality innovations offer lower prices and higher investment levels. The analysis shows the critical importance of the size of the market, with a larger market lowering competitive pressures and allowing entrepreneurs to increase prices in the competition stage.

The analysis provides a necessary and sufficient condition for creative destruction. There is a critical level of entry costs such that when entry costs are below that level, competitive entry will surpass the size of the market, leading to the exit of new firms. The critical value of the entry cost is increasing in the size of the market and in the entrepreneurs' discount factor. Entrepreneurial entry can involve heterogeneous technologies, and firms that remain after the exit of entrepreneurial start-ups also can have heterogeneous technologies. This suggests that entrants and survivors have diverse costs, prices, investment levels, and technologies.

The model in this chapter differs from models of industry evolution under uncertainty. Hopenhayn (1992) considers a perfect competition model of industry evolution in which firms experience independently distributed productivity shocks in each period (see also Hopenhayn, 1993). Hopenhayn's exit decision resembles a search rule in which firms exit when they experience a particularly high-cost realization. A process innovation shared by a proportion of firms expands productive capacity by shifting out the supply curve of the firms that have innovated, thus decreasing the number of firms that can operate profitably. Jovanovic and MacDonald (1994) consider industry evolution when firms in the industry can observe a low-tech innovation and a high-tech refinement. All low-tech firms have the same technology, and all high-tech firms have the same technology. Jovanovic and MacDonald (1994) consider a standard Walrasian equilibrium in each period.

The present model differs from these analyses by specifying invention as a random draw and innovation as establishing a firm, with all established firms having a unique technology. The model of competition in this section also differs from those of Hopenhayn (1992, 1993) and Jovanovic and MacDonald (1994) because it allows both strategic competition in price and investment as strategic exit decisions. The present model does not yield multiperiod patterns of exit, but instead demonstrates the connection between innovation, prices, and market structure.

The model of competition with diverse technologies presented here is related to patent races.[25] In a patent race, the winning firm receives the patent, and other firms are partially or completely excluded from the industry by inventing too late. Thus, later innovators are shaken out of the industry as a result of property rights to an invention conferred by a patent. In the present model, entrepreneurs must innovate by establishing firms, so that success depends on market performance of innovations rather than achieving a specific patent for an invention. Moreover, the present model only features a winner-take-all outcome only if firms do not face capacity constraints.

Consumers

Aggregate demand is common knowledge so that exit decisions are not a result of any demand uncertainty. There is a continuum of identical consumers. Each consumer has a demand function $D(p)$ that is differentiable and decreasing in the price p. Let L be a measure representing the total density of consumers, also referred to as the size of the market. For ease of presentation and without loss of generality, let L be an integer. Denote the measure of customers that is served by an individual firm by s in the competition stage and by S in the creative destruction stage. Demand $D(p)$ represents the quantity of output or the level of product quality provided to each customer.

Search is costly for consumers. To represent search costs, assume that consumers are able to observe historical prices rather than current prices.[26] Consumers are randomly matched with firms in the competition stage because all firms are operating in the market for the first time. Then, in the creative destruction stage, consumers know the prices that firms charged in the previous stage and can seek out those firms that had the lowest prices. In equilibrium, consumers search by visiting firms in ascending order of prices that were observed in the previous stage. The analysis shows that the consumer search rule must be an equilibrium strategy

25 See Reinganum's (1989) survey of the literature on patent races. Various theories link technological change and market structure (Nelson and Winter, 1982; Flaherty, 1980; Dasgupta and Stiglitz, 1980a, 1980b).

26 Bagwell et al. (1997) employ a similar search rule.

for consumers because the prices offered by firms in the creative destruction stage are ordered the same way as in the competition stage.

Innovative Entrepreneurs

Entrepreneurs have a common discount factor, δ, which is positive and less than one. Entrepreneurs decide whether or not to enter the market in the initial entry stage. The number of entrepreneurs that choose to enter the market and establish firms is denoted by an integer n, which is common knowledge. To enter the market, an entrepreneur must incur an irreversible cost k that represents R&D costs.

All of the firms that are established by entrepreneurs operate in the competition stage. Exit, if any takes place, occurs in the subsequent creative destruction stage. Let the integer m represent the number of firms that operate in the creative destruction stage. Because there may be exit and no additional entry occurs, it follows that $m \leq n$. Exit occurs if the number of start-ups in the creative destruction stage is strictly less than the number that initially entered, $m < n$.

Innovative entrepreneurs engage in R&D that results in a process invention. After incurring k, each firm observes a realization of the cost parameter θ^i, $i = 1, \ldots, n$, which represents a technological invention such as a new production process or distribution technique. The cost parameters are independent draws from the cumulative distribution function $F(\theta)$, which is common knowledge and has a positive continuous density $f(\theta)$. The cost parameters θ^i take values in $[0, 1]$. The cost parameters are the firm's private information during the competition stage. The differences in cost parameters across firms represent fundamental differences in technology and business methods. Because each firm's invention is a different draw from the distribution, each firm creates a different technology.

Innovative entrepreneurs have asymmetric information about each other's costs. Because technology is the entrepreneur's private information, the only way of selecting the best technology is through competition and exit. This leads to the possibility of excess entry followed by a process of creative destruction in which less efficient firms exit the industry. The model allows for heterogeneous technologies to survive the process of creative destruction. When firms do not have capacity constraints, only one firm is active in the creative destruction stage, as in the previous model in this chapter. However, when firms encounter capacity constraints, multiple firms with diverse technologies are active in the creative destruction stage. Firms have different technologies and pursue pure strategies in a Bayes-Nash equilibrium, thus allowing for the study of innovation.[27]

27 The model of price competition under asymmetric information in this section is related to Spulber (1995), who examines a static model of Bertrand price competition when rivals' costs are unknown. The three-stage model in this section extends the static approach to allow multiple firms with different technological innovations to survive by employing the probability

In the intermediate competition stage, each firm that has entered the market chooses both a price p and an irreversible cost-reducing investment z. The firm invests after having observed its technology parameter θ^i. This investment is not recoverable if the firm does not survive. If investment is greater than it would be in a one-period setting, it follows that firms commit resources to a particular technology even with the possibility of exit. The firm's pricing decision in the competition stage trades off current profit against potential earnings in the final creative destruction stage if the firm survives. The firm will choose a price less than what it would choose in a one-period setting so as to attract customers in the creative destruction stage.

The cost-reducing investment z reduces operating costs in both the competition and creative destruction stages. Assume that the firm's unit operating cost $c(z)$ is twice differentiable, decreasing, and convex in investment. The cost parameter θ^i denotes the production, distribution, and transaction costs of dealing with an individual customer. Define π as the profit per customer for an active firm in either the competition or creative destruction stage:

$$\pi(p, z, \theta) = (p - c(z))D(p) - \theta. \tag{12}$$

Define $v(\theta, s)$ as the profit that a firm would obtain if it were to operate for only one period:

$$v(\theta, s) = \max_{r,z} \pi(r, z, \theta)s - z. \tag{13}$$

The one-period profit is decreasing in θ and is increasing in s.[28]

In the final creative destruction stage, consumers visit firms on the basis of their information about prices in the preceding competition stage. At the beginning of the creative destruction stage, firms decide whether to exit or to remain in the market on the basis of anticipated consumer decisions. The firms that are active in the creative destruction stage then choose the one-period monopoly price $r = r^*(z)$ to maximize profit per customer $\pi(r, z, \theta)$. The price $r^*(z)$ is strictly increasing in cost-reducing investment z.[29]

distribution for order statistics. The present analysis differs from Bagwell et al. (1997) who consider a three-stage model of investment and exit in a mixed-strategy setting with identical firms. The model of competition in this section considers competition under asymmetric information with competing firms choosing pure strategies. In the present model, firms have different technologies and multiple types of firms survive in equilibrium.

28 The solution to the one-period problem r^0, z^0 need not be unique. Assume that there exists at least one price p such that a high-cost firm is profitable without cost-reducing investment, $\pi(p, 0, 1) = (p - c(0))D(p) - 1 \geq 0$. It follows that a firm can operate profitably for a single period, $v(\theta, s) \geq 0$ for all θ and $s > 0$. This does not guarantee profitable entry because single-period profit may not be sufficient to cover the entry cost k.

29 Note that the price and cost-reducing investment are substitutes, $\pi_{rz}(r, z, \theta) = -c'(z)D'(p) < 0$, because c is decreasing in z and demand is decreasing in r. This implies that the price $r^*(z)$ in the creative destruction stage is strictly decreasing in investment z by standard monotone comparative statics arguments; see Topkis (1978, 1998) and Milgrom and Roberts (1994).

Consider the basic model both with and without a capacity constraint on the number of customers that can be served by individual firms. The capacity constraint does not limit the firm's product quality or quantity of output per customer $D(p)$. If there is no capacity constraint, the creative destruction stage will resemble Bertrand competition, and all firms but the lowest-cost firm will be shown to exit the market. If there is a capacity constraint for individual firms, then the creative destruction stage will resemble Edgeworth competition.

A set of low-cost firms serves the market, and the remaining higher-cost firms exit the market. The interesting aspect of the Edgeworth competition case is that there exists a pure-strategy equilibrium with capacity constraints, unlike the standard static Edgeworth setting. The market outcome in which a set of profitable firms with diverse technologies survives is similar to the Ricardian concept of infra-marginal types of land earning positive rents. All results hold both with and without capacity constraints unless explicitly indicated otherwise.

Definition of the Equilibrium

In the entry stage, firms are identical because they have not yet engaged in invention. Entry occurs until all firms in the industry have nonnegative expected discounted profits and entry of an additional firm would cause each firm's profit to be negative.

In the competitive stage, firms act as Bayes-Nash players choosing price and investment strategies, p^i and z^i, on the basis of expectations of the other firm's equilibrium strategies. Let G be the (endogenous) likelihood that the firm is active in the final stage. Each firm in the competition stage chooses price and investment to maximize the net present value of profit in the competition and creative destruction stages, denoted by V,

$$V(p, z, s, S, G, \theta) = \pi(p, z, \theta)s - z + \delta\pi(r^*(z), z, \theta)SG. \tag{14}$$

The Bertrand-Nash equilibrium is a vector of prices and investments, p^{i*}, z^{i*}, $i = 1, \ldots, n$. Each firm's strategy depends on its own cost parameter. Given that firms are otherwise identical, consider equilibria in which the probability of being active in the final stage is symmetric and firms follow symmetric pricing and investment strategies, $p^*(\theta)$ and $z^*(\theta)$.

The pricing strategy can be shown to be increasing in the cost parameter. Bertrand price competition requires that a higher price cannot raise firm i's chance of being active. Recall that customers in the creative destruction stage visit firms in order of increasing price. Thus, using the properties of the Binomial distribution, the likelihood that a firm of type θ is active in the final creative destruction stage for $m < n$ equals

$$G(\theta; n, m) = 1 - \sum_{j=m}^{n-1} \binom{n-1}{j} F(\theta)^j (1 - F(\theta))^{n-1-j}, \tag{15}$$

and for $m = n$, let $G(\theta; n, m) = 1$. For $m < n$, $G(\theta; n, m)$ is strictly decreasing in θ. Also, $G(\theta; n, m)$ is decreasing in n and increasing in m. For convenience, we will sometimes write $G(\theta)$.[30]

In the initial entry stage, firms choose whether or not to enter the industry. Let expected profits in the competition stage equal $\Pi(n) = EV(p, z, s, S, G, \theta)$. A firm enters if and only if the discounted value of expected profit covers the cost of entry,

$$\delta\Pi(n) \geq k.$$

Thus, the equilibrium is described by initial entry n^*, competition-stage price and investment strategies p^* and z^*, creative-destruction-stage prices r^*, and survivors of creative destruction m^*.

4.5 Market Equilibrium with Capacity Constraints

The equilibrium of the three-stage competition model is characterized by backward induction beginning with the final creative destruction stage, then the intermediate competition stage, and then the initial entry stage. The outcome of the creative destruction stage depends on whether or not there is a capacity constraint on the number of consumers that each firm can serve.

The Creative Destruction Stage

In the creative destruction stage, consumers purchase from those firms that had the lowest prices in the previous competition stage. Consumers attempt to purchase first from the firm with the lowest price and then the firm with the next lowest price and so on. The profit per customer in the final creative destruction stage equals

$$\pi(r^*(z), z, \theta) = (r^*(z) - c(z))D(r^*(z)) - \theta. \tag{16}$$

An active firm's profit per customer in the creative destruction stage is strictly increasing in investment z by the envelope theorem,

$$\frac{d\pi(r^*(z), z, \theta)}{dz} = -c'(z)D(r^*(z)) > 0.$$

As a benchmark, consider the equilibrium if firms do not face any capacity constraint on the number of customers that they can serve. Then, because consumers visit firms in order of increasing prices in the previous competition period, all consumers L will be served by the firm that offered the lowest price in the preceding period. If $n \geq 2$, firms exit, and it can be shown that only the lowest-cost firm

30 The marginal likelihood of being active in the creative destruction stage is $g(\theta; n, m) = -m\binom{n-1}{m}F(\theta)^{m-1}(1 - F(\theta))^{n-1-m}f(\theta) < 0$. The properties of the function $G(\theta; n, m)$ can be derived using arguments from stochastic orders; see Shaked and Shanthikumar (2007).

survives and serves the entire market. The size of the exit is $n - 1$. If firm i is the lowest-cost firm, then the market price offered by the firm is $r^*(z(\theta^i))$. This case corresponds to Bertrand-style price competition.

Competition to stay in the market in the previous competition stage resembles a first-price sealed-bid auction. Thus, if there are no capacity constraints, and n firms have entered the market, the creative destruction stage is a winner-take-all competition, and the likelihood of being active is $G(\theta; n, 1) = (1- F(\theta))^{n-1}$. This exactly corresponds to the likelihood of winning in a standard first-price auction of a single unit. The number of consumers can take any integer value in the situation where there is a capacity constraint.[31]

Now suppose that firms face capacity constraints equal to one. Each active firm has a different technology θ^i, and each offers a different price, $r^*(z(\theta^i))$. Because consumers search on the basis of prices offered by firms, and the number of consumers and the number of firms are integers, all active firms operate at full capacity – that is, each firm serves a measure of consumers equal to one. If $n > L$, then there will be an exit of size $n - m$ and only $m = L$ active firms remain. If $n \leq L$, then no exit occurs and all firms operate at full capacity. Competition between firms to remain in the industry in the competition stage resembles a multi-unit auction. In multi-unit auctions with independent private values equilibrium bids depend on the distribution of order statistics.[32] This case corresponds to Edgeworth-style competition. The present model with technological uncertainty avoids the existence problems that arise in the classic Edgeworth model.

Without capacity constraints, only one firm is active in the creative destruction stage, $m^* = 1$, and serves all customers, $S = L$. With unit capacity constraints, multiple firms are active in the creative destruction stage, $m^* = L$, and operate at full capacity, $S = 1$. This demonstrates that with capacity constraints, diverse technologies can be operated profitably at the same time. Capacity constraints allow for multiple technologies to be viable after creative destruction occurs. The subsequent results all hold without or with capacity constraints – that is, whether there is only one firm that survives or whether multiple firms survive.

The Competition Stage

In the intermediate competition stage, consumers are randomly assigned to firms, so that all firms are visited by the same number of consumers. So, sales equal

31 Note also that if m is not an integer, the results would be similar to the case in which m is the next highest integer. In particular, if m were strictly less than one, the results would be similar to the case in which m exactly equals one. The analysis can be generalized as follows. Let $[m]$ be the smallest integer greater than or equal to m; there can be $[m] - 1$ firms at full capacity, $s = 1$, and an additional firm at less than full capacity, $s = [m] - m$, and the rest of the firms shaken out. When m is not an integer, then a shakeout occurs if and only if $[m] < n$.

32 See Vickrey (1962) and Myerson (1981).

$s = L/n$ if there are no capacity constraints or if the unit capacity constraints are nonbinding – that is, $L \leq n$. If there are unit capacity constraints and they are binding, $L > n$, then $s = 1$.

Firms simultaneously choose their investment and pricing strategies p and z to maximize the net present value of profits $V(p, z, s, G, \theta)$. It is useful to consider the optimal level of investment for a given price and then to derive the firm's optimal pricing strategy. Given the firm's price in the competition stage, the firm chooses the cost-reducing investment z to maximize the net present value of profit in the competition and creative destruction stages. The firm's optimal investment strategy is based on the marginal return to investment in the competition and creative destruction stages. Let $V_z(p, z, s, S, G, \theta) = 0$ and apply the definitions of the cost and profit functions to obtain the firm's investment strategy,

$$(17) \qquad -c'(z)D(p)s - \delta c'(z)D(r^*(z))SG = 1.$$

The firm's investment strategy $z(p, \theta)$ is used to characterize the firm's pricing strategy.

Investment and the competition-stage price are substitutes because demand is downward sloping and investment reduces costs,

$$V_{zp} = -c'(z)D'(p)s < 0,$$

so that investment $z(p, \theta)$ is decreasing in p. Investment and technology are substitutes $V_{z\theta} = -\delta c'(z)D(r^*(z))Sg(\theta) < 0$ so that investment $z(p, \theta)$ is decreasing in θ. Investment and the probability of remaining active in the creative destruction stage are complements,

$$V_{zG} = -\delta c'(z)D(r^*(z))S > 0,$$

so that investment $z(p, \theta)$ is increasing G. Because G is decreasing in n, investment is also decreasing in n. A firm will invest more if it is more likely to be active after the creative destruction stage.

Investment and the number of customers in the competition and in the creative destruction stages are complements:

$$V_{zs} = -c'(z)D(p) > 0,$$
$$V_{zS} = -\delta c'(z)D(r^*(z))G > 0.$$

So, investment $z(p, \theta)$ is increasing in s and S if there are no capacity constraints or if there are capacity constraints that are nonbinding. Finally, investment and the discount factor are complements,

$$V_{z\delta} = -c'(z)D(r^*(z))SG > 0,$$

so that investment $z(p, \theta)$ is increasing in δ. A higher discount factor increases investment because it raises the present value of the marginal return to investment to be obtained in the creative destruction stage.

Firms play a Bayes-Nash game in prices in the competition stage. By the revelation principle, the equilibrium strategy for each firm in the Bayes-Nash game can be represented as a direct mechanism that is incentive compatible and individually rational. Let $p(\theta)$ represent the firm's pricing strategy and let $z(\theta) = z(p(\theta), \theta)$ represent the type-θ firm's investment strategy. Let $\Pi(y, \theta)$ represent the expected profits of a type-θ firm that acts as a type-y firm,

$$\Pi(y, \theta) = V(p(y), z(y), s, S, G(y), \theta). \tag{18}$$

Incentive compatibility requires $\Pi(\theta, \theta) - \Pi(y, \theta) \geq 0$ for all y and θ in $[0, 1]$. Individual rationality requires that $\Pi(\theta, \theta) \geq 0$.

By incentive compatibility, a truthful report maximizes the expected profits of the type-θ firm. The investment strategy is optimal for any given price, so the envelope theorem can be applied to simplify the first-order condition. Maximizing the expected profit of the type-θ firm in equation (18) with respect to y and letting $y = \theta$ implies that the equilibrium pricing strategy solves

$$\begin{aligned} &V_p(p^*(\theta), z^*(\theta), s, S, G(\theta), \theta)p^{*\prime}(\theta) \\ &\quad + V_G(p^*(\theta), z^*(\theta), s, S, G(\theta), \theta)g(\theta) = 0. \end{aligned} \tag{19}$$

The pricing strategy thus solves a differential equation,

$$p^{*\prime}(\theta) = \frac{-\delta\pi(r^*(z^*(\theta)), z^*(\theta), \theta)Sg(\theta)}{\pi_p(p^*(\theta), z^*(\theta), \theta)s}. \tag{20}$$

The pricing strategy $p^*(\theta)$ is increasing and differentiable in the technology parameter θ.

Because more efficient firms have lower prices, they also have higher demand per customer, which signifies higher quality or better service for each customer. The least-efficient firm chooses the price and investment that maximize one-period profit. The least-efficient firm's price and investment determine the boundary conditions for the pricing problem, $p^*(1) = r^0$, $z^*(1) = z^0$, and $\pi(p^*(1), z^*(1), 1)s - z^*(1) = v(1, s)$. Even if the highest-cost firm is shaken out in the creative destruction stage, it still earns positive profit in the competition stage, $\Pi(1) = v(1, s)$.

Let equilibrium profit be defined by $\Pi(\theta) = \Pi(\theta, \theta)$. By the envelope theorem, profit is decreasing in the technology parameter,

$$\Pi'(\theta) = -s - \delta SG(\theta). \tag{21}$$

Because the highest-cost firm is profitable, $\Pi(\theta)$ is positive for all θ and individual rationality is satisfied. By integration $\Pi(\theta)$ is defined by

$$\Pi(\theta) = \Pi(1) + \int_\theta^1 (s + \delta SG(x))dx. \tag{22}$$

This can be written as follows:

$$\pi(p^*(\theta), z^*(\theta), \theta)s - z^*(\theta) + \delta\pi(r^*(z^*(\theta)), z^*(\theta), \theta)SG(\theta) = v(1, s) + \int_\theta^1 (s + \delta SG(x))dx. \tag{23}$$

Recall that the equilibrium investment strategy $z(p, \theta)$ is decreasing in p and θ. Because the pricing strategy $p^*(\theta)$ is increasing in θ, the firm's investment strategy $z^*(\theta)$ is decreasing in θ. Lower-cost firms have lower prices and higher investment levels.[33]

The profit of a type-θ firm is increasing in the size of the market L and decreasing in the number of entrants n. Without capacity constraints, recall that $s = L/n$ and that only one firm is active in the creative destruction stage, $m = 1$, and serves all customers, $S = L$. Also, recall that $v(1, s)$ is increasing in s so that, from equation (22), $\Pi(\theta)$ is increasing in L and decreasing in n. With unit capacity constraints, $s = \min\{1, L/n\}$ and multiple firms are active in the creative destruction stage, $m = L$, and operate at full capacity, $S = 1$. It follows from the properties of G and equation (22) that $\Pi(\theta)$ is increasing in L and decreasing in n.

Prices in the competition stage are increasing in the size of the market L:

$$\frac{\partial p^*(\theta)}{\partial L} = \frac{v_s(1, s)}{\pi_p(p^*, z^*, \theta)s}.$$

Prices in the competition stage are decreasing in the discount factor because greater returns in the creative destruction stage intensify competition:

$$\frac{\partial p^*(\theta)}{\partial \delta} = \frac{-\pi(r^*, z^*, \theta)SG(\theta) + S\int_\theta^1 G(x)dx}{\pi_p(p^*, z^*, \theta)s}.$$

It can be shown that the numerator is negative so that $p^*(\theta)$ is decreasing in δ.

33 Conversely, suppose that incentive compatibility and individual rationality are satisfied. Suppose that $\Pi'(\theta) = -s - \delta SG(\theta)$ and that $\Pi(\theta)$ is defined by equation (22). Then, there exists an equilibrium strategy $p^*(\theta)$ defined by

$$V(p^*(\theta), z^*(\theta), s, S, G(\theta), \theta) = \Pi(1) + \int_\theta^1 (s + \delta SG(x))dx,$$

where $\Pi(\theta, \theta) = V(p^*(\theta), z^*(\theta), s, S, G(\theta), \theta)$ is the global maximum profit. Because any equilibrium strategy must be incentive compatible, $\Pi(\theta, \theta) \geq \Pi(y, \theta)$ for all y and θ,

$$(y - \theta)(s + \delta SG(\theta)) \geq \Pi(\theta, \theta) - \Pi(y, y) \geq (y - \theta)(s + \delta SG(y))$$

so that $y \geq \theta$ implies that $G(\theta) \geq G(y)$, which in turn implies that $p^*(\theta)$ is nondecreasing and differentiable in θ. By standard arguments, it can be shown that the pricing function must be strictly increasing in θ because a slightly lower price will increase the likelihood of being active in the search period without significantly lowering profits. Divide through the inequalities in the preceding equation by $(y - \theta)$ and take limits as y approaches θ. This implies that $\Pi(\theta)$ is differentiable and satisfies equation (21) for all θ. Therefore, because $p^*(\theta)$ is defined by $\Pi(\theta) = V(p(\theta), z(\theta), s, S, G(\theta), \theta)$ and V is differentiable in p, z, G, and θ, and $G(\theta)$ is differentiable in θ, it follows that $p^*(\theta)$ is differentiable as well.

The Entry Stage

We now can consider how competitive pressures affect incentives to innovate. Because $\Pi(\theta)$ is increasing in L, decreasing in n, and increasing in δ, the same holds for the expected profit for a potential entrant,

$$\Pi(n) = E\Pi(\theta). \tag{24}$$

The number of entrepreneurs that enter the market is such that $\delta\Pi(n^*) \geq k$. A larger market size L generates more innovative entrepreneurs. Also, higher entry costs decrease entry of entrepreneurs and a higher discount factor increases entry of entrepreneurs. The size of the exit is $n^* - 1$ without capacity constraints and $n^* - L$ with capacity constraints.

Necessary and Sufficient Condition for Exits

Exits always occur for entry costs less than or equal to a critical value. Exit of entrepreneurs is thus consistent with profit maximization. Before observing their technology, entrepreneurs are willing to incur entry costs in the expectation that they will survive. Even after observing their technology, entrepreneurs are willing to make cost-reducing investments in the expectation that they will survive. In the competition stage, firms choose a greater cost-reducing investment z than if they were to operate for only a single period.

Consider under what conditions equilibrium market structure n^* is strictly greater than the number of firms in the creative destruction stage, m. Integrating by parts, expected profit equals

$$\Pi(n) = v(1, s) + \int_0^1 (s + \delta S G(\theta)) F(\theta) d\theta. \tag{25}$$

First, suppose that there are no capacity constraints, so that $s = L/n$, $S = L$, $m^* = 1$, and $G(\theta) = (1 - F(\theta))^{n-1}$. Then, at least one firm too many will enter the market if and only if k is less than or equal to the critical value $k^* = \delta\Pi(2)$. Suppose that there are unit capacity constraints, so that $s = \min\{1, L/n\}$, $S = 1$, and $m^* = L$. Then, at least one firm too many will enter the market if and only if k is less than or equal to the critical value $k^* = \delta\Pi(L+1)$. The critical value k^* is increasing in the size of the market and in the discount factor.

To see why this condition holds, suppose that there are no capacity constraints. Then, $k^* = \delta\Pi(2)$ is positive because $v(1, L/2)$ is nonnegative and the second term in equation (20) is positive for $S = L$ and $G(\theta) = 1 - F(\theta)$. Suppose that there are unit capacity constraints. Then, $k^* = \delta\Pi(L+1)$ is positive because $v(1, L/(L+1))$ is nonnegative and the second term in equation (20) is positive for $S = 1$, and $G(\theta, L+1, L) = 1 - (F(\theta))^L$.

As the market gets larger, the value of entry rises so that more companies are attracted for any given entry cost. This means that larger markets are likely to experience more exits as well. In addition, a higher discount factor raises the return to entry, which also leads to more exits. Therefore, given $k \leq k^*$, the number of firms n is strictly greater than the size of the market L. This means that these firms will compete after entry, and firms will exit the market in the creative destruction stage. The firms are aware both during the entry stage and during the competition stage of the impending exits in the creative destruction stage. However, firms continue to make cost-reducing investments in the competition stage at a higher level than if they expected to operate for a single period. In the competition stage, all firms other than the highest-cost firm select an investment level above the single-period investment level, $z^*(\theta) > z^0$, and select a price less than the single-period price, $p^*(\theta) < r^0$. All firms other than the highest-cost firm have expected profits strictly greater than the single-period profit, $\Pi(\theta) > v(1, s)$.

Recall that the firm's equilibrium pricing strategy $p^*(\theta)$ is increasing in θ, and the firm's equilibrium investment strategy, $z^*(\theta)$ is decreasing in θ. Expected profit exceeds the single-period profit of the highest-cost firm by an amount equal to information rent:

$$\Pi(\theta) - v(1, s) = s(1 - \theta) + \delta S \int_{\theta}^{1} G(x)dx. \tag{26}$$

Firms invest in cost reduction in the face of impending exits because of asymmetric information about the costs of the other firms. The lower are their own costs, the more they invest. Also, the lower are their own costs, the greater are the firms' likelihood of survival and expected profits in the creative destruction stage. This is because $G(\theta)$ and $\Pi(\theta)$ are strictly decreasing in θ for θ in $[0, 1)$ and $n^* > m^*$.

Total industry profit is greater in the creative destruction stage than in the competition stage. This occurs because exits cause market shares to rise for those firms with relatively higher profit. In addition, firms that survive have greater profits in the creative destruction stage than they did in the competition stage. This may be counterintuitive because it differs from exits that are a result of other factors such as declining demand. Observing an increase or a decrease in industry profits after exits may provide a way to determine whether exits were caused by a demand contraction or by technology differences.

Profits increase in the creative destruction stage:

$$\pi(p^*(\theta), z, \theta) \leq \pi(r^*(z), z, \theta).$$

Note that $\pi(r^*(z), z, \theta)$ is strictly increasing in z and strictly decreasing in θ. Because $z^*(\theta)$ is strictly decreasing in θ, $\pi(r^*(z^*(\theta)), z^*(\theta), \theta)$ is strictly decreasing in θ.

Industry profits are increased by the shift of customers to lower-cost firms after the exit of higher-cost firms. Therefore, putting the θ^i parameters in increasing order:

$$\sum_{i=1}^{n^*} \pi(p^*(\theta^i), z^*(\theta^i), \theta^i)(m^*/n^*) \leq \sum_{i=1}^{n^*} \pi(r^*(z^*(\theta^i)), z^*(\theta^i), \theta^i)(m^*/n^*)$$
$$< \sum_{i=1}^{m^*} \pi(r^*(z^*(\theta^i)), z^*(\theta^i), \theta^i).$$

Efficiencies that result from consolidation of demand among the most efficient firms increase industry profit. In the competition stage, all entrants operate. In the creative destruction stage without capacity constraints, the lowest-cost firm serves the market. In the creative destruction stage with capacity constraints, the exit of high-cost firms allows the remaining lower-cost firms to operate at full capacity.

Increasing Dominance

In the creative destruction stage, customers purchase from the firms that offered the lowest prices in the competition stage. Consumers correctly identify the firms that will have the lowest prices in the creative destruction stage for several reasons. First, firms with low prices in the competition stage are those with a low cost per customer because those firms have greater returns from price competition. Second, firms with a low cost per customer invest more in the competition stage. A higher level of investment in the competition stage lowers the firm's price in the creative destruction stage. Also, a lower price in the competition stage, by being associated with a lower θ, means that the low-price firm has a higher likelihood of being active in the creative destruction stage, which further reinforces the incentive to engage in cost-reducing investment.

If only one firm were to survive creative destruction, the consumer search rule in this case would be to visit only the firm that was the low-price leader in the competition stage. In equilibrium, the consumer search strategy would be optimal because that firm also would be the low-price leader in the creative destruction stage. Prices in the creative destruction stage $r^*(\theta) = r^*(z^*(\theta))$ are increasing in θ. This is because the firm's investment strategy $z^*(\theta)$ is decreasing in the cost parameter θ, and the pricing strategy $r^*(z)$ is decreasing in cost-reducing investment z. Because the pricing strategy $p^*(\theta)$ is increasing in θ in the competition stage, the search strategy of consumers is justified in equilibrium.

The equilibrium is an example of increasing dominance; the better is the firm's technology, the greater is its likelihood of surviving the creative destruction stage. Also, the better is the firm's technology, the lower is its price in the competition stage and the greater is its cost-reducing investment. Greater cost-reducing investment means that among firms active after the exit, the better is the firm's technology, the lower are its prices and the greater its sales per customer. Thus, for $\theta^1 < \theta^2$,

$$D(r^*(z^*(\theta^1))) > D(r^*(z^*(\theta^2))).$$

Market shares calculated in terms of customers served increase from $1/n$ to 1 for the winning firm when there are no capacity constraints and from $1/n$ to $1/L$ when there are capacity constraints.

Prices are greater in the creative destruction stage than in the competition stage, $p^*(\theta) < r^*(\theta)$ for all θ in $[0, 1)$ if $\pi(p, z, \theta)$ is concave in p. To see why prices rise, recall that $r^*(z) = \text{argmax}_r\, \pi(r, z, \theta)$. Because the price $p^*(\theta)$ is increasing in θ, $\pi_p(p^*(\theta), z^*(\theta), \theta) > 0$. Therefore,

$$p^*(\theta) < r^*(z^*(\theta)) = r^*(\theta).$$

Prices are lower in the competition stage because they affect consumer purchasing decisions in the subsequent creative destruction stage. Prices are lower in the competition stage because firms seek to establish a reputation for having a low price. Firms lower prices below the monopoly level to increase the probability that the firm will remain active in the creative destruction stage. The reputation effect of low prices is no longer present in the creative destruction stage so that prices rise.

Without capacity constraints, competition is followed by monopoly in the creative destruction stage. Prices rise after exits because the lower prices in the initial stage are the result of competition. Moreover, the surviving firm has the lowest cost per customer and the highest level of cost-reducing investment. Moreover, by operating at full capacity the surviving firm serves more customers than in the competition stage.[34]

In the capacity-constrained case, multiple firms survive the creative destruction stage. Although prices increase, there is still price dispersion across firms, and no single firm dominates the market. Instead, prices reflect investment decisions in the competition stage and the distribution of cost parameters across surviving firms. Moreover, prices in the final stage depend on the size of the market, the discount factor, and the amount of entry because these factors influence cost-reducing investment decisions in the competition stage.

By affecting the level of entry, the set-up cost k determines how many firms operate in the competition stage, which also affects the level of investment and ultimately the price level in the creative destruction stage. Moreover, the firms that operate in the market depend on pricing decisions in the previous period through the consumer search rule. Accordingly, even though firms do not compete directly on price in the creative destruction stage, prices reflect earlier price and investment competition. In the creative destruction stage, consumers are served by the firms with the lowest costs operating at full capacity. Thus, exits help create an efficient match between the number of consumers in the market and the productive capacity of the industry.

The equilibrium of the model yields some interesting implications about the effects of the number of consumers and of the discount factor on the equilibrium of the model. For ease of presentation, consider only the case without capacity constraints. Because there is a winner-take-all competition in the creative destruction stage when there are no capacity constraints, it is possible to consider the technology, price, and investment of the winning firm. By the properties of order statistics, the cumulative distribution of the lowest sample value for a sample of size n is $F_1(\theta, n) = 1 - (1 - F(\theta))^n$.[35] By the form of the distribution, it follows that $F_1(\theta, n') > F_1(\theta, n'')$ for $n' > n''$ for all θ in (0, 1) so that $F_1(\theta, n'')$ (first degree)

34 This argument supports related discussions in Craswell and Fratrick (1985–1986), Bagwell et al. (1997) and Cabral and Riordan (1994).

35 The density is density $f_1(\theta, n) = nf(\theta)(1 - F(\theta))^{n-1} = nf(\theta)G(\theta, n, 1)$.

stochastically dominates $F_1(\theta, n')$ for $n' > n''$. Applying the theory of stochastic orders, if $f_1(\theta, n)$ is the density of the lowest order statistic for a sample of size n, then for any decreasing real-valued function h defined on $[0, 1]$, the expression $\int_0^1 h(\theta) f_1(\theta, n) d\theta$ is strictly increasing in n.[36]

The size of the market improves the quality of innovation. The statistical sample of firms is greater in a larger market, which improves the expected technology that will survive. Recall that the equilibrium market structure $n^* = n^*(k, L, \delta)$ is nondecreasing in the size of the market L and nondecreasing in the discount factor δ. Consider the model in which firms do not have capacity constraints. Then, the expected value of the technology parameter, $E\theta$, and of the price offered by the winning firm in the creative destruction stage, Er^*, are nonincreasing in the size of the market L and nondecreasing in the discount factor δ. Also, the expected value of the cost-reducing investment, Ez^*, is increasing in n^*. The winning firm's profit in the creative destruction stage is nondecreasing in the size of the market L and in the discount factor δ.

The size of the market lowers expected costs and prices and increases investment. The expected value of the winning firm's technology parameter is $E\theta = \int_0^1 \theta f_1(\theta, n^*) d\theta$, which is decreasing in n^* by the properties of the probability density $f_1(\theta, n)$. Also, because the firm's price in the creative destruction stage, $r^*(\theta) = r^*(z^*(\theta))$, is increasing in θ, the properties of $f_1(\theta, n)$ imply that the expected value of the price $Er^* = \int_0^1 r^*(\theta) f_1(\theta, n^*) d\theta$ is decreasing in n^*. The firm's investment, $z^*(\theta)$, is decreasing in the cost parameter θ, so that the expected value of investment Ez^* is increasing in n^*.

Because the optimal investment strategy is increasing in the number of customers served in the competition stage, s, and in the creative destruction stage, S, without capacity constraints, it is strictly increasing in L. Also, it is strictly increasing in δ. The firm's profit is decreasing in θ because it is increasing in z and $z^*(\theta)$ is decreasing in the cost parameter θ. The properties of $f_1(\theta, n)$ imply that the expected value of profit is increasing in n^* and therefore nondecreasing in the size of the market L and in the discount factor δ.

This suggests that population growth improves technology by stimulating entry and intensifying competition to serve the market. Economic integration of countries through trade agreements and common markets will improve the technology of the combined economies. By increasing the population of consumers, economic integration will increase the number of entrants and improve the technology of the combined economies, while at the same time reducing expected prices and increasing expected investment and profit. More entrants increase the total costs of entry and investment and also lead to greater exit of firms. If the improvements in technology offset these costs, then there will be gains from trade from economic integration.

36 See Shaked and Shanthikumar (2007) on stochastic orders.

4.6 Some Implications for Economic Growth

A major challenge that remains in understanding economic growth is to make innovative entrepreneurship endogenous. Although endogenous growth models examine how new and existing firms engage in invention, the establishment of firms themselves should be an important consideration. Firms appear exogenously in the neoclassical general equilibrium setting or in partial-equilibrium industrial organization entry models. The entrepreneur often is not present because the models do not address the decision to establish a firm to carry out innovation.

For Schumpeter (1939, 86), "innovation is the outstanding fact in the economic history of capitalist society." Schumpeter (1934, p. 75) identifies entrepreneurship as "the fundamental phenomenon of economic development," emphasizing that entrepreneurs provide a large share of the technological innovations that stimulate growth in capitalist economies. Schumpeter states: "Development in our sense is then defined by the carrying out of new combinations" (1934, p. 66). Schumpeter (1934, p. 63) contrasts his view of development with more standard notions of economic growth: "Nor will the mere growth of the economy, as shown by the growth of population and wealth, be designated here as a process of development. For it calls forth no qualitatively new phenomena, but only processes of adaptation of the same kind as changes in the natural data."

GDP measures the value added by the economy and can be constructed by summing the value added by each industry.[37] The standard measure of economic growth as the change in GDP over time reflects changes in the firms and industries that generate value added, including value added by innovative entrepreneurship. The growth of GDP per capita provides additional information about productivity and innovation. These indispensible measures of aggregate performance must be

37 Consider the measurement of GDP by industry that is prepared by the Bureau of Economic Analysis (BEA) based on the National Income and Product Accounts (NIPAs) (Lindberg and Monaldo, 2008). According to the BEA: "Current-dollar value added in the annual industry accounts is measured as the sum of industry distributions of compensation of employees, gross operating surplus, and "taxes on production and imports less subsidies." The BEA prepares current-dollar statistics on value added by industry "by extrapolating industry statistics on compensation of employees, gross operating surplus, and 'taxes on production and imports less subsidies' with published and unpublished industry data from the NIPAs." According to the BEA, "Compensation of employees by industry is extrapolated using the sum of industry wage and salary accruals and supplements to wages and salaries. Gross operating surplus by industry is extrapolated using the sum of industry corporate profits, proprietors' income, capital consumption allowances, net interest, and net business current transfer payments." Additionally, the BEA obtains value added for farms and government from the NIPAs (Lindberg and Monaldo, 2008, p. 42). GDP industry components could be decomposed into firm-level value added. Some of the firm-level contributions to economic growth are a result of expansion of incumbent firms. Other firm-level contributions are because of the value added by the entry of new firms. Competition between entrants and incumbents leads to the contraction and exit of less efficient incumbents.

supplemented by additional measures of structural change in the economy to better understand economic growth and development.

The critical question is, what drives economic growth and development? The traditional answer has been accumulation of capital rather than technological change. Growth with constant technology is observed both in the Keynesian growth analysis of Harrod (1939) and Domar (1946, 1957) and in the neoclassical growth analysis of Solow (1956, 1957, 1970), Cass (1965), and Koopmans (1965). Economies face a trade-off between current and future consumption. By foregoing current consumption, economies can invest in productive capital that yields benefits in terms of future consumption. However, with a stationary population and technology, diminishing marginal returns to capital suggest that the economy reaches a steady-state capital and output level.

With a stationary technology, exogenous population expansion is the key driver of economic growth.[38] In the Harrod-Domar growth model, the growth rate of population is the natural rate of economic growth. In Solow's (1956) growth model, total output grows at the rate of population growth so that GDP per capita remains constant. Population growth alone cannot drive increases in GDP per capita; consider the disparities in GDP per capita between India, China, the United States, and European economies.

Technological change is needed to explain economic growth, as Solow (1957, 1960, 1962) recognized. Economic growth models initially introduce technological change as an exogenous source of benefits that is achieved without costs. With a continued focus on capital accumulation, technological change is embodied in vintages of capital.[39] Growth theory next introduces endogenous technological change in the aggregate production function (see Uzawa, 1965; Phelps, 1966; and Shell, 1967). Spulber (1977, 1980) considers endogenous R&D in a model of economic growth and identifies a trade-off between investment in the uncertain accumulation of knowledge and investment in productive capital.

38 Economic growth models without innovation consider continual expansion of GDP toward the steady state. Population growth results in continual expansion of GDP per capita toward the steady state, therefore leading to unlimited and continual expansion of GDP. The introduction of technological change further stimulates economic growth, resulting again in unlimited and continual expansion of GDP. Even with the addition of some forms of creative destruction, basic growth models feature unlimited growth of GDP. The economy experiences uncertainty in the timing of the next innovation, but growth is inexorable. The effects of innovation on continual expansion of GDP are further enhanced by intertemporal spillover effects. For example, in the aggregate production function, $Y = A_0 \gamma^t F(X)$, the economy's technology parameter, γ^t, grows proportionately with each generation of technology, t. Each innovation results in a jump in productivity because the technology parameter, γ, is greater than one. GDP grows continually as innovations introduce new generations of technology.

39 See Johansen (1959), Solow (1960), Kaldor and Mirrlees (1962), and Nelson (1964). Hahn and Matthews (1964) and Kennedy and Thirlwall (1972) are early surveys of growth and technological change.

A comprehensive study by Fritz Machlup (1962) examines the production and distribution of knowledge in the economy. Zvi Griliches (1979) emphasizes the external benefits that result from knowledge. In this tradition, Romer (1986) introduces a growth model in which endogenous technological change yields external benefits from accumulation of knowledge. Individual firms engage in R&D that creates a positive externality for other firms because of imitation and imperfect IP rights. Each firm has an invention production function in which inventions are a stock of knowledge that enters into the production of future inventions. Each firm also has an output production function that depends on that firm's stock of knowledge as well as the stock of knowledge of other firms. Lucas (1988) extends this reasoning to economic development by considering the trade-off between investment in physical capital and in human capital, with human capital having external effects.

Based on Romer (1986, 1990) and Lucas (1988), the endogenous growth literature examines how firms conduct R&D and also features external benefits from the accumulation of knowledge (see Aghion and Howitt, 1997, for an overview). Firms create new technology in the form of new products or processes. Aghion and Howitt (1992) model the economy's output production function, $Y(t) = A_0 \gamma^t F(X)$, where t is the current generation of technology, $Y(t)$ is GDP, A_0 is the initial technology parameter, $\gamma > 1$ is the proportional increase in the initial technology as a result of an innovation, and X is an intermediate good produced by the innovating firm. Innovating firms earn returns to innovation by selling intermediate goods to the downstream final-output industry.[40]

In Aghion and Howitt (1992), technology improves exogenously. A succession of monopolists produces intermediate goods that embody new technology. The innovating firm invests in R&D that allows it to enter the market by adopting the next generation technology, t. This introduces an external benefit from past research as in Romer (1986) because the new technology is a proportional increase in current productivity, which depends on all past innovations.[41] The innovating firm has an invention production function that yields a new invention with Poisson arrival rate. The Poisson arrival rate depends on the amount of labor chosen by the

40 The economy's final product is the numeraire good, and the downstream industry purchases the intermediate good X from the innovating firm at a price p. The downstream industry equates the marginal revenue product to the marginal cost of the intermediate good, $A_0 \gamma^t F'(X) = p$. The innovating firm produces the intermediate good with a simple linear technology, $X = L$, where L is labor. The innovating firm chooses X units of the intermediate good to maximize profits $(A_0 \gamma^t F'(X) - w)X$, where w is the wage rate. Because the downstream output demand is perfectly elastic, this framework differs from a monopoly inventor who sells to a perfectly competitive downstream industry. Compensating the innovating firm through the intermediate good introduces additional inefficiency in comparison with a monopoly royalty on the downstream industry output.

41 Knowledge externalities in growth models are either contemporaneous, among existing firms, or dynamic, transmitted from firms at one date to firms at another date.

innovating firm. An existing firm has no incentive to develop the next generation technology as a result of Arrow's replacement effect, so that new firms continually replace existing firms. The economy is stationary between innovative jumps and grows with proportion γ at each jump. To represent patent races, innovating firms appear exogenously. Aghion and Howitt (1992) extend their analysis by considering competition between producers of differentiated intermediate goods. The adoption of new technologies by a succession of monopolists is related to earlier models of capital vintages (see Benhabib and Rustichini, 1991). Aggregate output in vintage capital models is the sum of production by firms using capital of different vintages, with newer vintages having a greater productivity.

Models of industry evolution extend the endogenous growth approach. Klette and Kortom (2004) investigate the connection between the R&D of individual firms and aggregate R&D. In their framework, product variety is fixed, and innovating firms replace individual products with higher-quality versions. Individual firms have an invention production function that determines the Poisson arrival rate of inventions. The firm's arrival rate for a new invention λ depends on the firm's capital investment in R&D and the firm's stock of knowledge, n. The stock of knowledge is the number of products produced by the firm that have not yet been replaced by better products. The firm adds a new product with Poisson hazard rate λ and the firm loses a product with Poisson hazard rate μn. With a continuum of firms, aggregate innovation by existing firms is also λ. Letting the rate of innovation by new entrants equal η, the rate of obsolescence is, therefore, $\mu = \eta + \lambda$. Innovating firms appear exogenously as in Aghion and Howitt (1992).[42]

Audretsch (1995a) emphasizes the contribution of entrepreneurs and suggests that individuals rather than firms should be the unit of observation. A country's growth then depends on its "entrepreneurship capital," that is, on its endowment of entrepreneurs.[43] Audretsch et al. (2006) introduce the entrepreneur's decision in a model of economic growth. They formulate the "Knowledge Spillover Theory of Entrepreneurship" that posits that entrepreneurial opportunities result from efforts to produce knowledge by firms, universities, and research institutes. In their framework, existing firms do not take full advantage of available knowledge so that "entrepreneurship makes an important contribution to economic growth by providing a conduit for the spillover of knowledge that might otherwise have remained uncommercialized" (Audretsch et al., 2006, p. 5).[44] Entrepreneurial

42 Aghion and Howitt (1992) builds on the quality ladders approach of Grossman and Helpman (1991a, 1991b). In an endogenous growth setting, Aghion et al. (2001) examine step-by-step innovation with imitation, and Acemoglu (2008) considers innovation by entrants and established firms. The heterogeneity of firms also is observed in Thompson (2001).

43 See Acs and Audretsch (2003a) and Audretsch and Keilbach (2004).

44 Audretsch et al. (2006) modify the Romer (1986) and Lucas (1988) models to include endogenous entrepreneurship. Entrepreneurial activity, measured by E, depends on individuals' occupational choices based on the difference between the returns to starting a firm, π, and the employment wage, w, $E = g(\pi - w)$.

activity reflects barriers to entrepreneurship, and entrepreneurial profit depends on economic growth and knowledge externalities. Entrepreneurial activity enhances economic growth as a capital input to the aggregate production function.

Clemens (2008) explicitly introduces entrepreneurs in an overlapping-generations growth model.[45] In Clemens (2008), each individual makes an occupational choice between being a worker and being an entrepreneur. Because entrepreneurs encounter uncertainty and workers earn a certain wage, less risk-averse individuals become entrepreneurs. Entrepreneurs establish firms in the intermediate goods industry so that entrepreneurial entry determines the number of firms that produce intermediate goods. Entrepreneurs engage in monopolistic competition by offering differentiated intermediate goods to final goods producers. Greater risk tolerance by entrepreneurs results in more innovation, which then increases the economy's rate of growth.

The microeconomic building blocks of entrepreneurship are useful in identifying the contribution of innovative entrepreneurs to economic growth. Wennekers and Thurik (1999) point out the importance of identifying the relationships between individual entrepreneurs, individual firms, and macroeconomic aggregates. Theoretical models of economic growth have begun to examine the microeconomic foundations of innovation. Klette and Kortom (2004, p. 987) observe: "Endogenous growth theory has sketched the bare bones of an aggregate model of technological change. Firm-level studies of research and development, productivity, patenting, and firm growth could add flesh to these bones. So far they have not."

4.7 Conclusion

Competition among innovative entrepreneurs is important because more entry increases the expected quality of the best innovation. Competition among innovative entrepreneurs also limits the returns to the winning entrepreneur and reduces prices. Competition among entrepreneurs results in more innovation than a multi-project monopoly incumbent.

When clusters of entrepreneurs create related innovations, entry provides greater capacity than is needed to satisfy demand. Uncertainty about the outcome of innovation before entry and differences in technology across firms after entry lead to exit of some innovative firms. Firms with the best technologies survive, offering lower prices, higher product quality or service, and greater investment than those firms that end up exiting the market.

Market entry by entrepreneurs generates a variety of technologies and business models. If market demand is greater than industry capacity, inframarginal firms

45 Clemens (2008) applies Romer's (1986) knowledge externalities framework by assuming that the capital stock of each final good producer enhances the productivity of all other final good producers. See also Clemens and Heinemann (2006) and Martin (2008).

can operate profitably with diverse products and technologies. Creative destruction implies that firms must have some competitive advantages to survive. The need for competitive advantage depends on the relative size of the market in comparison with industry capacity and the capacity of individual firms.

Where there is technological uncertainty, both entry and exit of entrepreneurial start-ups are consistent with profit-maximizing behavior. The number of firms that enter the industry can exceed the size of the market, even though entrepreneurs anticipate competition. Competition among entrepreneurs matches industry capacity with the size of the market and identifies the most efficient technologies.

5

Creative Destruction

Transaction Costs and Intellectual Property Rights

When do markets choose innovative entrepreneurship over technology transfer to incumbents? To address the Question of Creative Destruction, this chapter and Chapters 6, 7, and 8 consider a strategic innovation game with endogenous entrepreneurship. An inventor and an existing firm choose between cooperation and competition. When the inventor and the existing firm cooperate, the inventor transfers technology to the existing firm. When the inventor and the existing firm choose competition, the inventor becomes an entrepreneur and establishes a firm that competes with the existing firm. The strategic innovation game illustrates the trade-offs between entrepreneurship and technology transfer.

Creative destruction is an efficient form of innovation if there are net benefits from entry and growth of new firms and displacement of existing firms. Creative destruction can be inefficient if there are greater benefits from growing and restructuring existing firms than from establishing new firms. Entrepreneurs innovate by establishing new firms that embody new products, manufacturing processes, transaction patterns, and business methods. Existing firms can innovate by commercializing products and processes developed through their internal R&D laboratories and collaboration with R&D partners. Existing firms also can innovate by acquiring or licensing new technologies from independent inventors and other firms and by acquiring start-ups. This chapter shows that transaction costs and imperfect protections for IP rights generate market frictions that favor creative destruction over cooperation.

Entrepreneurship generally dissipates economic rents through creative destruction, often lowering prices and increasing industry investment. Competition between innovative entrants and incumbents can cause the exit of inefficient entrants, or it can cause the decline or even the demise of existing firms, particularly those that are subject to innovative inertia. The costs of creative destruction suggest that all innovation should be carried out by incumbent firms either through internal innovation or acquisition of technologies from independent inventors. However, frictions in the market for inventions can induce inventors to become innovative entrepreneurs.

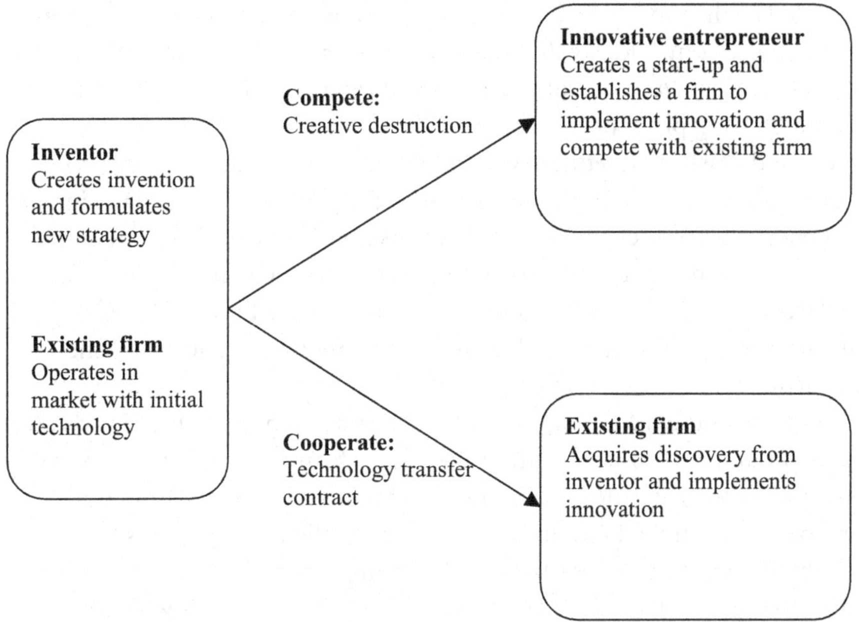

Figure 5.1. The strategic innovation game: innovative entrepreneurship versus technology transfer.

5.1 The Innovation Game with Homogeneous Products

Consider a strategic innovation game involving an independent inventor and an existing monopoly firm. The innovation game illustrates how inventors commercialize their discoveries. The inventor and the existing firm can *cooperate* by agreeing to a contract in which the inventor sells or licenses an invention to the existing firm. Alternatively, the inventor and the existing firm can *compete*, with the inventor becoming an entrepreneur and establishing a firm that competes with the existing firm. The inventor also can sell or license the discovery to an independent entrepreneur who then sets up a firm that competes with the existing firm. The strategic innovation game is illustrated in Figure 5.1.

The inventor owns the new technology and can transfer the technology to an existing firm. Suppose initially that the inventor can transfer the discovery and any accompanying technology without incurring any transaction costs. Suppose further that the inventor has IP protections so that he can commercialize the new strategy without the risk of imitation or expropriation. See Gans and Stern (2000) for a related reduced-form model of a strategic innovation game with IP protections and technology licensing. Later sections of the chapter will consider the effects of weakening IP protections. The chapter also considers the effects of transaction costs in the market for inventions.

The invention consists of a cost-reducing process technology. Products are homogeneous so that the invention does not involve creating a new product. The initial technology is represented by the unit cost c_1 and the new technology is represented by the unit cost c_2, where $c_2 < c_1$. Market demand for the final product, $D(p)$, is a twice continuously differentiable and strictly decreasing function of the final product price, p. The profit-maximizing monopoly price is $p^M(c)$, and at the profit maximizing price, profits equal $\Pi^M(c) = \Pi(p^M(c), c)$.

Bertrand-Nash competition with homogeneous products results in *creative destruction*, with the entrant displacing the incumbent firm. The innovative entrepreneur incurs a set-up cost, $K > 0$, to establish a firm. The competitive price is $p^*(c_1, c_2) = \min\{p^M(c_2), c_1\}$. So, with competition, the innovative entrepreneur earns $\Pi(p^*(c_1, c_2), c_2) - K$. Because of creative destruction, the incumbent firm earns zero profits if the inventor becomes an entrepreneur and establishes a competing firm.

Transferring the technology to the incumbent monopoly firm avoids creative destruction and the costs of setting up a new firm. The incumbent firm earns monopoly profits evaluated at the new technology if the inventor transfers the technology to the incumbent firm. The incumbent firm's willingness to pay for the new technology includes the returns to deterring entry. This eliminates any inertia for the monopoly incumbent. Therefore, the incumbent firm's willingness to pay for the new technology equals monopoly profits at the new technology.

Because $\Pi^M(c_2) \geq \Pi(p^*(c_1, c_2), c_2)$, the inventor always obtains returns from technology transfer that are greater than the returns from entrepreneurship, $\Pi^M(c_2) > \Pi(p^*(c_1, c_2), c_2) - K$. This implies that the outcome of the strategic innovation game between the inventor and the incumbent firm with homogeneous products is always technology transfer rather than entrepreneurship. This is the case whether the innovation is drastic or non-drastic. With market frictions or imperfect IP protections, however, entrepreneurship can occur in equilibrium.

Entrepreneurship provides a threat point in bargaining with the existing firm. Even if entrepreneurship does not occur at the market equilibrium, the possibility of entrepreneurship affects the incentives to invent for both the independent inventor and the existing firm.[1] To represent bargaining between the inventor and the existing firm, consider the generalized Nash bargaining game. Let α be the inventor's bargaining power, $0 \leq \alpha \leq 1$.[2] Let R denote the lump-sum royalty that the existing firm pays to the inventor.[3] The outcome of Nash bargaining solves the maximization problem

$$\max_R [R - (\Pi(p^*(c_1, c_2), c_2) - K)]^\alpha [\Pi^M(c_2) - R]^{1-\alpha}.$$

1 When entrepreneurial entrants offer differentiated products, competition between the entrant and existing firms are mitigated, which can lead inventors to choose entrepreneurship over technology transfer (Spulber, 2012b).

2 The bargaining game between the inventor and the existing firm can be recast as an alternating offer bargaining game in which there is a unique subgame perfect equilibrium that depends on the discount factors of the two parties (Rubinstein, 1982).

3 In practice, licenses can involve a combination of lump-sum royalty payments and per-unit royalties (recall the discussion in Chapter 3). The lump-sum royalty also can refer to a licensing fee or a technology transfer fee.

The lump-sum royalty is a weighted average of the existing firm's monopoly profits with the new technology and the inventor's profit if he were to become an entrepreneur,

$$(1) \qquad R(c_2; c_1) = \alpha\Pi^M(c_2) + (1-\alpha)(\Pi(p^*(c_1, c_2), c_2) - K).$$

A lump-sum royalty avoids the efficiency distortion from double marginalization that would occur with a per-unit royalty when transferring the technology to the incumbent monopolist.

Comparison with a Competitive Downstream Market

To examine the effects of existing market structure, consider also the inventor's decision when the downstream product market is perfectly competitive. Suppose that the inventor is a monopolist dealing with many downstream firms so that the inventor is able to extract all rents from the downstream industry. The initial price before the invention is introduced equals unit cost under the old technology, c_1. The inventor transferring the technology to a perfectly competitive downstream industry would set a royalty per-unit of output r. When the downstream market is perfectly competitive, the post-royalty price is $p = r + c_2$. A monopoly inventor chooses the per-unit royalty to maximize profit $rD(r)$ subject to the maximum royalty constraint,

$$r \leq c_1 - c_2.$$

At the profit-maximizing royalty, the product price equals $p^*(c_1, c_2)$. This is because the new product price equals the monopoly price $p^M(c_2)$ if the innovation is drastic, and the new product price equals initial costs c_1 if the innovation is non-drastic. With technology transfer, the inventor who transfers the technology to a competitive industry will earn profits $\Pi(p^*(c_1, c_2), c_2)$.[4]

If the inventor becomes an innovative entrepreneur, the new firm competes with and displaces the competitive industry. As a consequence, the final product price for the entrepreneurial entrant is exactly the same as with technology transfer, $p^*(c_1, c_2)$. This implies that the innovative entrepreneur will earn the same return that he would obtain from transferring the technology, $\Pi(p^*(c_1, c_2), c_2)$ and, yet, will need to incur set-up costs K. Again, the inventor would strictly prefer technology transfer to entrepreneurship whether the innovation is drastic or non-drastic. The inventor is constrained by the initial technology in either case, when selling to a competitive market or when entering a competitive market. Therefore, with a competitive downstream industry the outcome of the innovation game is always technology transfer.

4 This outcome also could be achieved by setting a lump-sum royalty such that all producers but one would exit the downstream market. Selling to one producer downstream would save on possible technology transfer costs although there also could be costs resulting from the expansion of the producer that adopted the technology and the displacement of the other producers.

Now, compare incentives to invent. In the strategic innovation game, the inventor obtains a royalty equal to $R(c_2; c_1) = \alpha\Pi^M(c_2) + (1-\alpha)(\Pi(p^*(c_1, c_2), c_2) - K)$ from technology transfer when the downstream market is monopolistic and royalty revenues equal to $\Pi(p^*(c_1, c_2), c_2)$ from technology transfer when the downstream market is perfectly competitive. If the innovation is drastic, the inventor's incentives to invent are greater when faced with a competitive downstream market,

$$(2) \qquad R(c_2; c_1) = \Pi^M(c_2) - (1-\alpha)K \leq \Pi^M(c_2) = \Pi(p^*(c_1, c_2), c_2).$$

When the existing firm is a monopolist, the royalty takes into account the inventor's opportunity costs. This inequality is strict unless the inventor can extract all rents from the existing firm, $\alpha = 1$, in which case incentives to invent are equal with a monopolistic or a competitive downstream market. Therefore, when the innovation is drastic and the inventor does not have full bargaining power, the innovation game with a competitive downstream market generates greater incentives to invent than the innovation game with a monopolistic downstream market.

Suppose now that the innovation is non-drastic, $\Pi(p^*(c_1, c_2), c_2) < \Pi^M(c_2)$. Then, the comparison of incentives to invent depends on the inventor's bargaining power. Let α^* equate the royalty with a monopolist downstream with the returns to selling to a competitive industry,

$$(3) \qquad \begin{aligned} R(c_2; c_1) &= \alpha^*\Pi^M(c_2) + (1-\alpha^*)(\Pi(p^*(c_1, c_2), c_2) - K) \\ &= \Pi(p^*(c_1, c_2), c_2). \end{aligned}$$

Rearranging terms implies

$$(4) \qquad \alpha^* = \frac{K}{\Pi^M(c_2) - (\Pi(p^*(c_1, c_2), c_2) - K)}.$$

The incentives to invent are greater when selling to a downstream monopolist than to a competitive downstream market when the inventor's bargaining power is greater than α^*. This includes the case in which the inventor has all of the bargaining power, $\alpha = 1$. Otherwise, the incentives to invent are greater when selling to a competitive downstream market, $\alpha \leq \alpha^*$.

Comparison with Arrow's Incentives to Invent

The effect of downstream competition on incentives to invent in the strategic innovation game differs from Arrow's (1962b) analysis. The option of entrepreneurship in the innovation game changes the effect of competition on incentives to invent. Arrow shows that incentives to invent are always strictly greater when an inventor sells to a competitive downstream market rather than to a monopolistic downstream market. In the innovation game with a drastic invention, incentives to invent when the inventor sells to a monopolistic downstream market are greater than or equal to those when the inventor sells to a competitive downstream market. This is also the case in the innovation game with a non-drastic invention when the inventor has sufficient bargaining power.

In Arrow's analysis, the incumbent monopolist's willingness to pay for the new technology equals the incremental returns $\Pi^M(c_2) - \Pi^M(c_1)$, which creates an inertia effect for the monopolist, so that $\Pi^M(c_2) - \Pi^M(c_1) < \Pi(p^*(c_1, c_2), c_2)$. If the invention is drastic, the monopolist's willingness to pay is less than that of a competitive industry as a result of the inertia effect, $\Pi^M(c_2) - \Pi^M(c_1) < \Pi^M(c_2)$. If the invention is non-drastic, the monopolist's willingness to pay is less than a competitive industry because of the inertia effect and because demand is downward sloping and the monopoly price is increasing in costs:

$$\Pi^M(c_2) - \Pi^M(c_1) = \int_{c_2}^{c_1} D(p^M(c))dc < (c_1 - c_2)D(p^M(c_2)).$$

Compare incentives to invent in the innovation game with those in Arrow's analysis when the downstream market is competitive. The inventor has full bargaining power in either setting. The option of entrepreneurship has no effect on incentives to invest in the innovation. The inventor obtains revenues $R(c_2; c_1) = \Pi(p^*(c_1, c_2), c_2)$ in either setting so incentives to invent in the innovation game are the same as in Arrow's analysis.

Compare incentives to invent in the innovation game with those in Arrow's analysis when the downstream market is monopolistic. Suppose first that the inventor in the innovation game has all the bargaining power, $\alpha = 1$ so the inventor obtains $R(c_2; c_1) = \Pi^M(c_2)$ when selling to a downstream monopolist. This is strictly greater than incentives to invent for an existing monopolist $\Pi^M(c_2) - \Pi^M(c_1)$ because the threat of entrepreneurial entry eliminates the existing monopolist's inertia effect. In the innovation game, the incumbent monopolist transfers all monopoly profits to the inventor rather than just the incremental benefits of the new technology because the alternative is entrepreneurial entry and creative destruction.

Now suppose that the inventor selling to a downstream monopolist in the innovation game does not necessarily have all of the bargaining power. If the inventor's bargaining power is sufficiently large, then the inventor's incentive to invent in the innovation game is greater than an existing monopolist. The critical bargaining power equates royalties to the incremental benefits of the new technology,

$$\begin{aligned} R(c_2; c_1) &= \alpha^{**}\Pi^M(c_2) + (1 - \alpha^{**})(\Pi(p^*(c_1, c_2), c_2) - K) \\ &= \Pi^M(c_2) - \Pi^M(c_1). \end{aligned} \tag{5}$$

Rearranging terms implies

$$\alpha^{**} = 1 - \frac{\Pi^M(c_1)}{\Pi^M(c_2) - (\Pi(p^*(c_1, c_2), c_2) - K)}. \tag{6}$$

Incentives to invent in the innovation game when the inventor's bargaining power exceeds α^{**} are greater than those for an existing monopolist.

5.2 Innovation, Creative Destruction, and Economic Efficiency

The strategic innovation game illustrates two alternative transaction methods associated with commercializing inventions. The inventor who becomes an innovative entrepreneur vertically integrates R&D and establishment of a firm. The value of embodying the invention in a firm reflects the returns to the entrepreneur's capabilities and creative efforts in establishing a firm. In contrast, the inventor who enters the market for inventions relies on others to realize the gains from implementation. The market value of the invention reflects demand by existing firms or innovative entrepreneurs.

Innovation and Economic Efficiency

When there are no transaction costs and when IP rights are well defined, the entrepreneur and the existing firm always agree to transfer technology rather than engaging in competition. Cooperative technology transfer yields the benefits of lower production costs while avoiding the costs of setting up a new firm.

With a monopoly product market, the social benefits of technology transfer equal the sum of the increase in consumers' surplus as a result of the price reduction and the increase in the incumbent's profit as a result of lower unit costs,

$$B^{MT} = \int_{p^M(c_2)}^{p^M(c_1)} D(x)dx + \Pi^M(c_2) - \Pi^M(c_1). \tag{7}$$

Innovation through technology transfer always increases social benefits. Recall from Chapter 3 that the social welfare effects of innovative entrepreneurship are equal to

$$B^{ME} = \int_{p^*(c_1,c_2)}^{p^M(c_1)} D(x)dx + \Pi(p^*(c_1, c_2), c_2) - K - \Pi^M(c_1). \tag{8}$$

The difference between the social benefits of technology transfer and entrepreneurship equals

$$\begin{aligned} B^{MT} - B^{ME} = & \int_{p^M(c_2)}^{p^M(c_1)} D(x)dx + \Pi^M(c_2) \\ & - \int_{p^*(c_1,c_2)}^{p^M(c_1)} D(x)dx - \Pi(p^*(c_1, c_2), c_2) + K. \end{aligned} \tag{9}$$

With a drastic innovation, $p^*(c_1, c_2) = p^M(c_2)$, the social benefits of technology transfer exceed those of entrepreneurship by exactly the set-up costs of the new firm,

$$B^{MT} - B^{ME} = K. \tag{10}$$

This implies that when the innovation is drastic, technology transfer is efficient because it avoids the costs of setting up a new firm. Because technology transfer always occurs with homogenous products and without transaction costs, the outcome of the innovation game is always socially efficient when the innovation is drastic.

With a non-drastic innovation, competition between the existing firm and the entrepreneurial entrant generates benefits for consumers by lowering prices.[5] The entrant's price is constrained by the existing firm's initial technology, $p^*(c_1, c_2) = c_1$, so the difference in benefits equals

$$(11) \qquad B^{MT} - B^{ME} = \int_{c_1}^{p^M(c_2)} (x - c_2)D'(x)dx + K.$$

Technology transfer is socially efficient if and only if set-up costs exceed the gain in consumer's surplus from entrepreneurial entry in comparison to technology transfer,

$$K \geq -\int_{c_1}^{p^M(c_2)} (x - c_2)D'(x)dx.$$

The strategic innovation game results in a socially efficient outcome only when this condition holds. Technology transfer occurs at the expense of consumers when the innovation is non-drastic because some of the benefits of competitive entry are lost.

Consider now the efficiency of the innovation game when the downstream market is perfectly competitive. With a competitive product market, the social benefits of technology transfer equal the gain in consumers' surplus plus the inventor's profits net of the incumbent's initial profits,

$$(12) \qquad B^{CT} = \int_{p^*(c_1,c_2)}^{c_1} D(x)dx + \Pi(p^*(c_1, c_2), c_2) - \Pi^M(c_1).$$

With a competitive product market, the social benefits of entrepreneurship equal the gain in consumers' surplus plus the inventor's profits net of the incumbent's initial profits,

$$(13) \qquad B^{CE} = \int_{p^*(c_1,c_2)}^{c_1} D(x)dx + \Pi(p^*(c_1, c_2), c_2) - K - \Pi^M(c_1).$$

The difference between the social benefits of technology transfer and entrepreneurship equals entry costs, $B^{CT} - B^{CE} = K$. Therefore, whether the innovation is drastic or non-drastic, technology transfer is efficient because it avoids the costs of setting up a new firm. Technology transfer always occurs when the

5 With a non-drastic innovation, the difference in profits with technology transfer and with entrepreneurship can be expressed as

$$\Pi^M(c_2) - \Pi(p^*(c_1, c_2), c_2) = \int_{c_1}^{p^M(c_2)} [D(x) + (x - c_2)D'(x)]dx.$$

downstream market is perfectly competitive. This implies that when the downstream market is perfectly competitive, the innovation game with homogenous products and without transaction costs always has an efficient outcome.

The strategic innovation game suggests a Coasian theorem.[6] The property rights associated with establishing a new firm and engaging in competition generally are well defined. Entrepreneurs usually have the right to establish new firms and enter markets, although many types of government regulations act as barriers to entry. The ability to enter the market therefore provides a basis for efficient negotiation between an inventor and an existing firm because the existing firm then can pay the inventor not to enter the market. The agreement by the inventor not to establish a firm that competes with the existing firm can accompany an agreement to transfer the technology to the existing firm.

Innovation and Transaction Costs

Creative destruction generates productive efficiencies when new firms displace existing firms with obsolete technologies. However, the outcome of the strategic innovation game is altered by transaction costs in the market for discoveries. The transaction costs of technology transfer include the costs of interaction between the inventor and the technology adopter, whether the adopter is an existing firm or a specialized entrepreneur. Existing firms who apply inventions incur transaction costs, including adjustment costs from changing production methods and capital equipment and the costs of organizational restructuring. By becoming an entrepreneur, the inventor avoids transaction costs in the market for inventions. The inventor turned entrepreneur embodies the invention in a new firm, which can provide additional protections for IP.

Entrepreneurs also encounter substantial transaction costs. The entrepreneur expends effort and incurs the costs needed to create a start-up and to establish a firm. The entrepreneur incurs transaction costs in dealing with investors who

6 Creative destruction should not be viewed as an externality as already noted in Chapter 3. However, it is useful to consider Coase's (1960) classic article "The Problem of Social Cost," which points out the efficiency of private bargaining and the importance of property rights in mitigating externalities. The Coase theorem asserts that when property rights are well defined and when there are no transaction costs, the creators of a nuisance externality and the parties harmed by the nuisance will negotiate an efficient allocation. If the creators of a nuisance have property rights, the parties harmed by the nuisance will pay the creators of the nuisance to abate. If the parties harmed by the nuisance have property rights, the creators of the nuisance will need to pay them compensation and choose to abate. In either situation, the marginal private costs of the nuisance will equal the marginal private costs of abatement, thus yielding an efficient outcome regardless of the assignment of property rights. This means that in the absence of transaction costs, policy makers should be indifferent between assigning rights to the parties generating or harmed by the nuisance. In the absence of property rights, there is no basis for negotiation over abatement of the nuisance and damage payments.

supply investment capital to the new enterprise. In addition, the entrepreneur contracts with employees and managers who provide skills and human capital. The entrepreneur encounters governance costs because he must hire employees and managers and create an organization to implement the new strategy.

Coase (1937, 1988, 1994b) found that firms combine activities when internal governance costs are less than market transaction costs. The boundaries of the firm are determined by a comparison of governance costs and market transaction costs. For Coase, the firm expands its activities until the point where further expansion would raise governance costs above market transaction costs. The firm outsources activities when market transactions are more efficient.

The inventor who becomes an innovative entrepreneur vertically integrates the functions of invention and entrepreneurship. This combines the formulation, commercialization, and implementation of the new strategy. The inventor compares transaction costs of transferring knowledge with transaction costs of creating a start-up and establishing a firm and the governance costs associated with operating the firm. By becoming an innovative entrepreneur, the inventor avoids transaction costs in the market for inventions. Therefore, Coase's analysis suggests that relatively higher transaction costs in the market for inventions may encourage innovative entrepreneurship.[7] Relatively higher transaction costs in the market for inventions also reduce incentives for some types of innovative entrepreneurship by discouraging the entry of specialized firms that develop and market inventions.

High transaction costs in markets for inventions encourage vertical integration by existing firms. When contracting costs in markets for inventions exceed governance costs of in-house R&D, existing firms also have an incentive to establish R&D departments. As a consequence, firms will not outsource invention to independent inventors but rather will rely on corporate R&D. Company managers and strategy departments formulate new strategies and commercialize them by implementing them within the organization. To implement new strategies, companies can reposition their existing businesses or restructure their organizations through diversification and divestiture, giving them an alternative to contracting with independent inventors.

There is some evidence that transaction costs affect internalization of R&D by existing firms. Pisano (1990) identifies transaction costs of small-numbers bargaining in the market for inventions. He examines data on ninety-two biotechnology R&D projects that major pharmaceutical companies have conducted in-house or through market contracts and finds that bargaining costs increase internalization of R&D. Teece (1986, 1988) shows that IP problems induce firms to internalize R&D. These effects reduce entrepreneurship because existing firms rely less on contracts with innovative entrants for new technologies. Shan (1990) finds in contrast that entrepreneurial entrants in biotechnology commercialize technologies through cooperative relationships with existing firms, with larger firms less likely to seek

7 See also Teece (1988), Mowery (1983, 1995), and Zeckhauser (1996).

cooperative relationships and start-ups operating in foreign markets more likely to seek cooperative relationships.

Transaction costs in the market for inventions include the full range of transaction costs observed in product markets. Inventors seeking to sell or license their discoveries to existing firms or to specialized entrepreneurs can expect to encounter some or all of these transaction costs.

1. There are costs of communication and information processing that may be significant for complex scientific and technological discoveries. The inventor must communicate information about the invention and its application to potential adopters. The inventor's knowledge may be tacit in nature requiring investment in codification and investment in absorption capacity by the potential adopter. This is discussed further in Chapter 7.
2. There are costs of search and matching, with inventors seeking firms that are interested in applying their discoveries and firms seeking to acquire IP. Inventors and producers incur costs of searching among patents to determine what technology has already been invented.[8] The costs of searching in the market for inventions may exceed the costs of searching the well-documented patent database.
3. There are costs of bargaining between inventors and potential adopters. This reflects inherent difficulties in identifying the properties of new technologies and evaluating how such technologies will perform in the market place, whether they modify product designs, production processes, or transaction techniques. The process of evaluating new technologies and strategies by existing firms is comparable to costly due diligence that accompanies mergers and acquisitions. Additionally, licensing contracts involve royalty payments that depend on returns from applying the invention, so that the parties encounter the costs of designing and monitoring contingent contracts.
4. The contract between the inventor and potential adopter may be subject to moral hazard if the inventor must expend effort to help the adopter understand and implement the invention. Then, the adopter must provide incentives to induce the inventor to devote effort to this task. Moral hazard problems are present because the inventor's efforts are highly specialized and can be difficult to monitor. The form of the technology transfer contract itself can lead to inefficient production and investment decisions.
5. The contract to license or to transfer technology is likely to be subject to adverse selection problems because aspects of the invention may be unobservable or unverifiable. This can lead to a breakdown in negotiations even when there would be gains from trade under full information. So even though technology transfer would be more efficient under full information, bargaining under asymmetric information can result in the inventor choosing to become an

8 Bessen and Meurer (2008).

innovative entrepreneur. Asymmetric information in the market for discoveries is discussed further in Chapter 8.

Transaction costs affect the outcome of the innovation game. Suppose that per-unit transaction costs in the market for inventions depends linearly on the extent of the innovation, $t(c_1 - c_2)$. More significant inventions are assumed to increase transaction costs. The returns to technology transfer equal $\Pi^M(c_2) - t(c_1 - c_2)$, and the returns to entrepreneurship equal $\Pi(p^*(c_1, c_2), c_2) - K$. So, technology transfer occurs if and only if

$$\Pi^M(c_2) - t(c_1 - c_2) \geq \Pi(p^*(c_1, c_2), c_2) - K.$$

This determines a critical value of per-transaction costs equal to the net benefits of technology transfer divided by the extent of the innovation,

$$t^* = \frac{\Pi^M(c_2) - (\Pi(p^*(c_1, c_2), c_2) - K)}{c_1 - c_2}. \tag{14}$$

The numerator is positive because competition lowers profits and entry is costly. Entrepreneurship occurs when transaction costs are greater than the critical value t^*.

When the innovation is drastic, $p^M(c_2) \leq c_1$, the critical value of the transaction cost parameter is simply the ratio of entry costs to the extent of the innovation,

$$t^* = \frac{K}{c_1 - c_2}. \tag{15}$$

For drastic innovations, the social benefits of technology transfer equal the difference between the set-up costs of the new firm and transaction costs,

$$B^{MT} - B^{ME} = K - t(c_1 - c_2). \tag{16}$$

Then, technology transfer is efficient if and only if the costs of setting up a new firm are greater than or equal to the transaction costs of technology transfer. Therefore, if the innovation is drastic, technology transfer occurs in the strategic innovation game if and only if it is cost efficient.

When the innovation is non-drastic, $p^M(c_2) > c_1$, the critical value of the transaction cost parameter equals

$$t^* = \frac{\int_{c_1}^{p^M(c_2)} [D(x) + (x - c_2)D'(x)]dx + K}{c_1 - c_2}, \tag{17}$$

which is greater than the parameter value for non-drastic innovations. Technology transfer is efficient only when set-up costs of the new firm minus the transaction costs of technology transfer exceed the benefits of creative destruction,

$$B^{MT} - B^{ME} = \int_{c_1}^{p^M(c_2)} (x - c_2)D'(x)dx + K - t(c_1 - c_2). \tag{18}$$

Transaction costs in the market for discoveries make entrepreneurship more likely, so that with non-drastic innovations, transaction costs can improve the efficiency of the innovation game. With a non-drastic innovation, technology transfer occurs if and only if

$$\int_{c_1}^{p^M(c_2)} (x - c_2)D'(x)dx + K - t(c_1 - c_2) \geq - \int_{c_1}^{p^M(c_2)} D(x)dx.$$

If technology transfer is efficient, then the outcome of the innovation game always will be technology transfer. However, there is a range of discoveries for which entrepreneurship is efficient but the outcome of the innovation game is still technology transfer. Therefore, with non-drastic innovations, the innovation game does not generate sufficient entrepreneurship.

Innovation with Complementary Resources

The choice between contracting and entrepreneurship also depends on the potential adopter's ownership of complementary resources. Contracting is more efficient when the adopter has complementary resources that help implement the new strategy. Both the inventor and the potential adopter can have complementary resources that are useful in implementing the new strategy. Entrepreneurship is more efficient when the inventor has complementary resources that are difficult to transfer to others.

Inventors may provide IP resources that are complementary to their new strategy. It has long been recognized that scientific and technological inventions are particularly important complementary resources for innovative entrepreneurs. For example, Say (1852, I, chapter 29) discusses how machines for spinning cotton changed the cotton industry. He observes that around the year 1769 the English barber Richard Arkwright asks whether one could spin hundreds of threads of cotton simultaneously on large spinning wheels.[9] Arkwright not only improved the spinning machine but also built a water-powered cotton-spinning mill in 1771, which was perhaps the first factory and signaled the start of the Industrial Revolution. Arkwright was an innovative entrepreneur whose inventions of the improved spinning machine and the water-powered mill were complementary to his business strategy in the spinning industry.

Teece (1986, 2006) argues that the market value of knowledge depends on buyers' complementary assets, such as IP, human capital, marketing channels, and necessary manufacturing and design technologies. The returns to innovation reflect the returns to both knowledge and complementary assets. Teece (1986) asks who profits most from innovation: the new entrant that applies the innovation, follower firms that imitate the first-mover, or firms that have assets and capabilities that

9 Say's mention of Arkwright and his discussion of cotton spinning bring to mind Schumpeter's (1934) discussion of the introduction of the power loom.

the innovator needs? Teece (1986) provides a number of examples to illustrate this question. The British firm Electrical Musical Instruments (EMI) developed computerized axial tomography (CAT) technology and was the first to market CAT scan medical equipment. Within eight years, other companies entered the market for CAT scan equipment, and EMI exited the market. RC Cola introduced canned soft drinks but was eclipsed by Coca-Cola and Pepsi-Cola. Bowmar pioneered the pocket calculator but was driven out of business by Texas Instruments, Hewlett Packard, and other entrants. Xerox developed office computer products based on the mouse and on-screen icons but could not compete with Apple's innovations. MITS introduced the Altair, the first personal computer, but was displaced rapidly by competition from Apple, IBM, and others (Teece, 1986).

Teece (1986) points out that the firms with complementary assets profit from innovation. Existing firms that would adopt the new strategy may already have the necessary complementary assets. The innovative entrepreneur would need to obtain complementary assets either by developing and purchasing them or obtaining them through outsourcing contracts for services, manufacturing, and distribution. Teece (1986) emphasizes that the inventor must take into account transaction costs in the market for complementary assets. This suggests that the inventor choosing between entrepreneurship and technology transfer should compare the transaction costs of obtaining complementary assets needed to implement the invention with transaction costs in the market for inventions.

Gans and Stern (2003) suggest that the risk of expropriation reduces incentives for cooperation between inventors and existing firms. They argue that existing firms that own complementary assets are the firms that have greater incentives to expropriate the innovator's technology. The start-up considers the trade-off between the risk of expropriation and the benefits of transferring technology to existing firms with complementary assets. They note, for example, that Netscape considered licensing their technology to Microsoft before choosing to offer a browser that would compete with Microsoft's product. They conclude that stronger IP rights and incumbent ownership of key complementary resources will favor cooperation between inventors and incumbents. The inventor and the existing firm may face different transaction costs of obtaining complementary assets. Because of transaction costs in the market for complementary assets, the existing firm may have an advantage in implementing the invention. This would increase the likelihood that the strategic innovation game would result in technology transfer because the incumbent firm's complementary assets would augment the returns from technology transfer in addition to avoiding rent dissipation from creative destruction. However, frictions in the market for inventions may be sufficient to overcome the effects of the incumbent's complementary asset advantage.

Differences in the complementary assets of an incumbent firm and an entrant need not result in technology transfer. Both the existing firm and the entrant may survive creative destruction because of the trade-off between the new technology and complementary assets. Both firms may compete profitably even if the invention were to give the entrant a production-cost advantage. The existing firm continues to operate profitably using its initial technology or because it has valuable assets. The entrepreneur benefits from the new technology even without the assets of the existing firm. For example, the existing firm may have a valuable asset such as a chain of retail stores. The entrant lacks such valuable assets but develops e-commerce techniques for selling products online. The incumbent and the entrant are differentiated both by technology and access to complementary assets.

5.3 The Innovation Game with Invention

With homogeneous products the returns to technology transfer to an incumbent monopolist exceed the returns to innovative entrepreneurship, as the preceding section shows. The innovative entrepreneur's marginal incentive to innovate is greater than that of a monopolistic incumbent firm whether the innovation is drastic or not.

Consider the innovation game when the inventor engages in R&D. The inventor generates a process invention by engaging in costly R&D. The inventor chooses the extent of the process invention,

$$\theta = c_1 - c_2, \tag{19}$$

where $0 \leq \theta \leq c_1$. R&D costs depend on the initial technology,

$$k(\theta) = \frac{1}{c_1 - \theta}. \tag{20}$$

The R&D cost function is increasing and convex in the level of R&D, θ. R&D lowers the unit costs of production, but it is not feasible to reduce those costs to zero, $\lim_{\theta \to c_1} k'(\theta) = \infty$. Suppose that $D(p^M(0))$ is finite. To make sure that some R&D is desirable, assume that $D(p^M(c_1)) > 1/(c_1)^2$.

Consider the incentive to invent for an inventor who expects to transfer his invention to the existing firm and captures all of the rents. This is equivalent to the monopolist's incentive to invent. The monopolist chooses the extent of the invention θ^M to maximize the net benefit of the invention,

$$V^M(\theta) = \Pi^M(c_1 - \theta) - k(\theta), \tag{21}$$

so that $-\Pi^{M\prime}(c_1 - \theta^M) = k'(\theta^M)$. The monopolist's marginal return to R&D equals

$$V^{M\prime}(\theta) = D(p^M(c_1 - \theta)) - k'(\theta). \tag{22}$$

The monopolist's profit, $\Pi^M(c_1 - \theta)$, is increasing and convex in θ, so that the profit-maximizing level of R&D, θ^M, need not be unique. Solutions to the monopolist's problem exist and are interior because $D(p^M(c_1)) > 1/(c_1)^2$ and $D(p^M(0))$ is finite.

An inventor who anticipates becoming an entrepreneur would choose the extent of the invention θ^E to maximize the net benefit of the invention,

$$V^E(\theta) = \Pi(p^*(c_1, c_1 - \theta), c_1 - \theta) - K - k(\theta). \tag{23}$$

From the definition of $p^*(c_2, c_1)$, the entrepreneur's postentry marginal return equals

$$V^{E\prime}(\theta) = D(p^*(c_1, c_1 - \theta)) - k'(\theta). \tag{24}$$

There exists a solution to the inventor's optimization problem although there need not be a unique profit-maximizing effort level θ^E. The solutions to the inventor's problem θ^E are interior.

Postentry competition implies that prices with entrepreneurial entry for a given new technology are less than or equal to the monopoly price at that technology, $p^*(c_1, c_1 - \theta) \leq p^M(c_1 - \theta)$, and strictly less for a non-drastic innovation because of postentry competition – that is, when $p^M(c_1 - \theta) > c_1$. Because demand is downward sloping, the amount demanded is greater with entrepreneurial entry and a given new technology, $D(p^*(c_1, c_1 - \theta)) \geq D(p^M(c_1 - \theta))$, and strictly greater for a non-drastic innovation. By the envelope theorem, for any R&D cost function, it follows that the marginal returns to R&D for an entrepreneurial entrant are greater than or equal to the marginal returns to R&D for an incumbent monopolist,

$$V^{E\prime}(\theta)) \geq V^{M\prime}(\theta).$$

The marginal returns to R&D for an entrepreneurial entrant are strictly greater for non-drastic innovations.

Therefore, an inventor who anticipates becoming an entrepreneur devotes more effort to R&D than does an inventor who anticipates technology transfer to an existing monopolist, $\theta^E \geq \theta^M$.[10] Although the returns to technology transfer to an incumbent monopolist are greater than the returns to innovative entrepreneurship, the returns to R&D depend on marginal returns to invention. Competition between the entrant and the incumbent causes the marginal returns to reducing production costs to be greater for the entrant than for the incumbent firm.

Consider now the innovation game between the inventor and the existing firm. When products are homogeneous and there are no transaction costs in the market for discoveries, the preceding analysis showed that the outcome of the innovation game is always technology transfer. The inventor and the existing firm bargain over the royalties to be paid for the invention. The inventor's threat point is the return he would obtain from entrepreneurial entry. The existing firm's threat point is the existing firm's return if the inventor becomes an entrepreneur and enters the market. Because of creative destruction with homogeneous products, the existing

10 This applies to both the highest and the lowest equilibrium values and follows from monotone comparative statics arguments; see Topkis (1998, ch. 3).

firm is driven out of the market and earns a zero return if entrepreneurial entry occurs. The existing firm's threat point therefore equals zero.

Suppose that the innovation game takes place after the inventor obtains an invention of type θ. Ex post bargaining between the inventor and the existing firm is equivalent to assuming that R&D effort θ is non-contractible. Recall that the inventor's royalty equals $R(c_2; c_1) = \alpha\Pi^M(c_2) + (1 - \alpha)(\Pi(p^*(c_1, c_2), c_2) - K)$. The inventor chooses the level of R&D θ^* that maximizes the royalty net of R&D costs,

$$V^I(\theta) = R(c_1 - \theta; c_1) - k(\theta). \tag{25}$$

The inventor's marginal returns to R&D equal

$$V^{I\prime}(\theta) = R'(c_1 - \theta; c_1) - k'(\theta). \tag{26}$$

This implies that for a given new technology, the inventor's marginal returns to R&D are in between the marginal returns of the existing monopolist and the marginal returns form entrepreneurial entry,

$$V^{E\prime}(\theta) \geq V^{I\prime}(\theta) \geq V^{M\prime}(\theta).$$

This implies that an inventor who anticipates technology transfer with ex post bargaining devotes less effort than an inventor who anticipates becoming an entrepreneur and more effort to R&D than would an existing monopolist, $\theta^E \geq \theta^* \geq \theta^M$.[11]

The inventor's incentive to engage in R&D is greater than or equal to that for a monopolist because competition increases the marginal returns to invention. Even though a monopolist has a greater return than an entrepreneurial entrant, the incentive to invent of the independent inventor reflects the returns to technology transfer. The royalties earned from technology transfer depend on both the marginal returns to innovation from the transfer and the marginal returns to innovation by an entrant as a result of the bargaining threat point. Because the marginal returns to innovation are greater for the competitive entrant, this raises the marginal royalty above the marginal incentive to invent for the monopolist.

Suppose now that R&D is contractible. The inventor and the existing firm bargain over the level of the inventor's R&D and the royalty for transferring the technology. Because bargaining takes place before R&D, the inventor's threat point is the return to inventing and then becoming an entrepreneur to apply that invention, $V^E(\theta^E)$. The outcome of Nash bargaining solves the maximization problem

$$\max_{R,\theta}[R - k(\theta) - V^E(\theta^E)]^\alpha[\Pi^M(c_1 - \theta) - R]^{1-\alpha}.$$

Because R&D is contractible, the level of R&D that solves the Nash bargaining problem equals the level that would be chosen by a monopolist, θ^M. The royalty is a weighted average of the existing firm's monopoly profits with the new technology

11 As before, this applies to both the highest and the lowest equilibrium values.

and the inventor's profit if he were to become an entrepreneur plus the costs of R&D,

$$R = \alpha\Pi^M(c_1 - \theta^M) + (1 - \alpha)[k(\theta^M) + V^E(\theta^E)]. \tag{27}$$

Ex ante contracting lowers investment in R&D in comparison to an inventor who anticipates technology transfer or in comparison with an inventor who anticipates becoming an entrepreneur.

5.4 The Innovation Game with Competitive Invention

Consider the innovation game in which the inventor and the existing firm engage in an R&D race.[12] The new technology is given by c_2. The first to discover the new technology obtains property rights to the invention. If the existing firm is the first to discover the new technology, then the inventor becomes inactive. If the inventor is the first to discover the new technology, the strategic innovation game begins, and the inventor transfers the technology to the existing firm as shown in the previous sections. The royalty is given by the Nash bargaining solution evaluated at the new technology, $R = \alpha\Pi^M(c_2) + (1 - \alpha)[\Pi(p^*(c_1, c_2), c_2) - K]$. The royalty is increasing in the inventor's bargaining power, decreasing in unit costs under the new technology, and decreasing in entry costs.

The probability of being the first to discover the new technology depends on relative levels of investment in R&D by the existing firm and the inventor, k_1 and k_2, respectively. The probability that the existing firm is first equals $\frac{k_1}{k_1+k_2}$, and the probability that the inventor is first equals $\frac{k_2}{k_1+k_2}$. Let $k_1{}^*$ and $k_2{}^*$ denote the Nash noncooperative equilibrium investment levels.[13]

The existing firm always obtains the new technology because it either wins the race or it contracts with the winner to obtain the new technology. This implies that the existing firm chooses investment to maximize monopoly profit $\Pi^M(c_2)$ net of the expected royalty payment and the cost of investment,

$$V^M = \max_{k_1} \Pi^M(c_2) - \frac{k_2{}^*}{k_1 + k_2{}^*} R - k_1. \tag{28}$$

The independent inventor only obtains a benefit by being the first discoverer so that the inventor's investment solves

$$V^I = \max_{k_2} \frac{k_2}{k_1{}^* + k_2} R - k_2. \tag{29}$$

12 Gans and Stern (2000) examine a strategic innovation game with R&D racing and entry, see also Gans et al. (2002). Baye and Hoppe (2003) show the strategic equivalence of rent seeking, innovation tournaments, and patent-race games.

13 This uses the functional form of the Tullock all-pay auction; see Baye et al. (1994, 1996).

The equilibrium investment levels solve

$$\frac{k_2^*}{(k_1^* + k_2^*)^2} R = 1, \qquad \frac{k_1^*}{(k_1^* + k_2^*)^2} R = 1. \tag{30}$$

Despite the asymmetry of the innovation game, the existing firm and the inventor who are racing to invent always choose the same R&D investment levels,

$$k_1^* = k_2^* = \frac{R}{4}.$$

This result holds regardless of bargaining power in the determination of the royalty. The incumbent monopolist engages in R&D to avoid paying a royalty to the inventor, and the inventor engages in R&D to receive the royalty. The existing firm's expected net benefit equals the monopoly profit at the new technology minus three-quarters of the royalty, and the inventor's expected net benefit equals one-quarter of the royalty,

$$V^M = \Pi^M(c_2) - \frac{3R}{4}, \qquad V^I = \frac{R}{4}.$$

If the inventor has all of the bargaining power, $R = \Pi^M(c_2)$ so that the inventor and the existing firm receive the same expected net benefits, $V^M = V^I = \frac{\Pi^M(c_2)}{4}$.

5.5 Innovation and Intellectual Property

Arrow (1962b) points out that selling information requires revealing it to potential buyers who then may expropriate the information. Arrow (1962b, p. 151) observes that without IP rights "the only effective monopoly would be the use of the information by the original possessor." Inventors take into account the risks of imitation and expropriation when considering whether or not to enter the market for inventions (see Anton and Yao, 1994).[14] Weak protections for IP rights can favor innovative entrepreneurship when establishing a firm offers better legal protections than technology transfer contracts. However, IP rights also help protect the returns to implementation of inventions, so that innovative entrepreneurs benefit from stronger IP rights.

14 Anton and Yao (1994) consider the possibility of expropriation and show that the inventor's wealth affects his decision to reveal his invention to a potential buyer. Anton and Yao (1995) look at entrepreneurs who initially are employees of firms, discover a significant invention, and then leave to start a new firm. The employee has three options: keep silent and leave to start a new firm, reveal the invention to the employer in hopes of a reward, or negotiate a reward with the employer before revealing the invention. Dealing with the employer also can result in a new firm through a spin-off. Anton and Yao (2004) find that large inventions are protected by secrecy when property rights are weak. Anton and Yao (2002) find that partial disclosure, even when it can be expropriated, can act as a signaling device; see also Anton and Yao (2003).

The Innovation Game and IP

The extent of legal protections for IP affects the outcome of the innovation game. Stronger IP protections for inventions make technology transfer contracts more likely and, therefore, make some types of entrepreneurship less likely. With weaker IP protections, the inventor and the existing firm are less likely to cooperate and more likely to compete. Innovative entrepreneurship provides an alternative means of IP protection for the inventor. By establishing a firm, an inventor can conceal a new technology in the form of trade secrets during the start-up period. After the firm is established, the new strategy is embodied not only in the new firm but also in the products, production processes, and transaction techniques offered by the new firm. It may be difficult to obtain IP protections for disembodied knowledge. Various legal protections such as patents exist for business method inventions, production processes, and product designs.

The risk of expropriation modifies the innovation game with homogeneous products. When IP rights are not well defined, creative destruction can occur even when it is inefficient. Suppose that to offer the innovation for sale, the inventor must reveal the discovery to the existing firm. Then, the risk of expropriation by the existing firm favors entrepreneurship and leads to creative destruction. Let β be the probability that the existing firm can expropriate the idea after observing it. If the existing firm expropriates the inventor's discovery, the inventor will not be able to establish a firm using that discovery because of the costs of market entry and the need to compete with the existing firm. The expected return from revealing the discovery to the existing firm reflects the likelihood of retaining the inventor's IP, $1 - \beta$, which also can be interpreted as the strength of the inventor's patents.

An inventor who offers to sell his discovery expects to receive $(1 - \beta)R$. The royalty equals $R(c_2; c_1) = \alpha\Pi^M(c_2) + (1 - \alpha)(\Pi(p^*(c_1, c_2), c_2) - K)$. Facing the possibility of expropriation, the inventor will choose to establish a firm if the returns to entrepreneurship are greater than or equal to the expected royalty,

$$\Pi(p^*(c_1, c_2), c_2) - K \geq (1 - \beta)R.$$

This yields a critical value of the probability of expropriation equal to the inventor's bargaining power times returns from technology transfer divided by the royalty,

$$\beta^* = \alpha \frac{\Pi^M(c_2) - (\Pi(p^*(c_1, c_2), c_2) - K)}{R(c_2; c_1)}.$$

The inventor will choose entrepreneurship if the risk of expropriation is sufficiently high, $\beta \geq \beta^*$. If the existing firm has substantial bargaining power, the inventor gains little from licensing and faces the risk of expropriation, so that the inventor will choose to become an entrepreneur. When the probability of expropriation is sufficiently high, creative destruction can result even if it is inefficient.

The better the innovation – that is, the lower the value of the unit cost c_2 – the lower is the critical cutoff for the probability of expropriation, $d\beta^*/dc_2 > 0$. The returns from technology transfer $\Pi^M(c_2) - (\Pi(p^*(c_1, c_2), c_2) - K)$ are increasing in c_2. The royalty is decreasing in c_2. Therefore, the critical probability of expropriation is increasing in c_2. When the likelihood of expropriation differs across inventions, inventors with low-quality innovations will choose to transfer their technology to existing firms, and those with higher-quality innovations will protect their IP by establishing firms.

The better the initial technology – that is, the lower the value of the unit cost c_1 – the higher is the critical cutoff for the probability of expropriation, $d\beta^* / dc_1 \leq 0$. If the innovation is drastic, the critical value of the probability of expropriation reduces to $\beta^* = \frac{\alpha K}{\Pi^M(c_2) - (1-\alpha)K}$, which does not depend on the initial technology. In the innovation is non-drastic, the numerator is decreasing in c_1 and the denominator is increasing in c_1 so that $d\beta^* / dc_1 < 0$. The better the initial technology c_1, the more an entrepreneur will be constrained by competition and the lower the royalty. The inventor is willing to take on greater risk of expropriation because a better initial technology increases the critical cutoff, making technology transfer more likely. Therefore, a better initial technology increases the likelihood of innovation by the incumbent from technology transfer. This contrasts with incumbent inertia in which a better initial technology makes the incumbent less likely to invent as a result of the replacement effect.

The greater the cost of entry K, the higher is the critical cutoff for the probability of expropriation, $d\beta^* / dK > 0$. When entrepreneurship is costly, the inventor is willing to take greater risks of expropriation in the market for inventions. The greater the inventor's bargaining power α, the higher is the critical cutoff for the probability of expropriation, $d\beta^* / d\alpha > 0$. When technology transfer contracts yield greater returns, the inventor is willing to take greater risks of expropriation.

Entrepreneurship and IP

Although inventors may become innovative entrepreneurs as a means of protecting their IP, this should not suggest that weakening IP rights is a way to encourage entrepreneurship. Patents and other IP are important for both application and transfer of inventions. Patents not only provide incentives to invent *before* the patent award but also facilitate innovation that implements the invention *after* the patent award. Patents increase dynamic, allocative, and transaction efficiencies in the market for discoveries because they facilitate the use of inventions. Weak IP protections will distort the mix of innovative entrepreneurship and technology transfer.

Innovative entrepreneurs implement commercial, scientific, and technological inventions by establishing new firms that use the inventions. Entrepreneurship provides an important market outlet for independent inventors who can either transfer their inventions to specialized entrepreneurs or become entrepreneurs themselves and embody their inventions in new firms. Entrepreneurship thus gives independent inventors an alternative to transferring technology to existing firms or market intermediaries. IP rules affect entrepreneurship in fundamental ways because they impact the inventor's choice between technology transfer and entrepreneurship. IP rules that penalize or reward one of these options will bias market outcomes and lead to economic inefficiency. The result may be too much or too little entrepreneurship, with too much entrepreneurship resulting in costly creative destruction and too little entrepreneurship reducing competition and favoring incumbent firms.[15]

Entrepreneurs tend to benefit from patents, which confer competitive advantage, protect technology from copying by rivals, assist in obtaining financing, and enhance the start-up's reputation. A major study conducted by Graham et al. (2009) analyzes the results of the Berkeley Patent Survey of 2008 that examines 1,332 early-stage technology companies founded since 1998. To focus on innovation, they target their survey to chief executive officers (CEOs), presidents, and chief technology officers (CTOs). They discover a highly interesting connection between invention and entrepreneurship: "[I]t is common for start-ups' patents to originate with founders prior to the company's founding date. Such patents may first issue to founders (as individuals, with no initial corporate assignee) and only later be assigned to the company."[16] Graham et al. find that patent ownership is more widespread among new firms than previously reported, although many start-ups do not hold patents. When start-ups patent, "they are often seeking competitive advantage, and the associated goals of preventing technology copying, securing financing, and enhancing reputation."[17]

Graham et al. find that the main factors explaining patenting by start-ups include

> "preventing others from copying products or services; improving the chances of securing investment; obtaining licensing revenues; improving the chances/quality of liquidity (e.g., acquisition/IPO); preventing patent infringement actions against the company; improving the company's negotiating position with other companies (e.g., cross-licensing); and enhancing the company's reputation/product image."[18]

Graham et al. find substantial differences in the effects of patents across the economy with patents more common in the health-related sector (biotechnology and medical devices) and less common in software and Internet. However, start-ups

15 Merges (1994) argues that transaction costs in markets for inventions prevent the application of the Coase theorem to the allocation of IP rights. There are difficulties in detecting infringement of IP and complexities in evaluating inventions. Although inventors are harmed by expropriation of their IP, infringement should not be viewed as a form of externality. Expropriation of IP more closely resembles the taking of property than damages from a nuisance.

16 Graham et al. (2009, 1275).

17 Graham et al. (2009, 1297).

18 Graham et al. (2009, 1297).

with venture capital financing tend to hold more patents than start-ups with other types of funding. Start-ups primarily forego patenting because of the legal costs of obtaining and defending patents, suggesting that improvements in the effectiveness of the patent system would be beneficial to entrepreneurs. Graham et al. also find that start-ups license technology from others to gain knowledge and settle IP disputes, highlighting the role of entrepreneurs in the commercialization and implementation of inventions.

In creating start-ups and establishing firms, entrepreneurs commercialize both business method inventions and other types of scientific and technological inventions. Simcoe et al. (2009, 776) find that "[e]ntrepreneurs often develop innovations that are only valuable as part of a larger platform, such as the Internet, the personal computer or the cellular phone network." Their study shows that entrepreneurial entrants' IP strategies differ from those of large established firms. Entrepreneurs may have an interest in protecting platform standards to earn rents, whereas larger existing firms may prefer more open standards that yield returns to their complementary assets. Their empirical results suggest that patents are important to entrepreneurs and to the division of innovative labor in markets.[19]

Casadesus-Masanell and Zhu (2012) study strategic interactions between an innovative entrant and an incumbent when the entrant needs to strategically choose whether to reveal an innovation by competing through a new business model or to conceal it by adopting a traditional business model. They find that when the innovative business model offers substantial benefits, the incumbent monopolist will copy the entrant's model even though the incumbent must then compete directly with the entrant.

The relationship between IP and entrepreneurship is complex. Improvements in legal protections for IP in the market for technology transfer can reduce entrepreneurship that would occur as a means of realizing the value of IP. Better IP protections increase the expected returns to contracting, making technology transfer relatively more attractive in comparison with entrepreneurship, which reduces the supply of entrepreneurs. Own use of inventions through entrepreneurship provide the inventor with some IP protection because the inventor can protect the discovery from business rivals through secrecy. However, the innovative entrepreneur encounters costs of keeping the secret and faces the risk of independent invention.[20] IP protections also reduce the need for existing firms to rely on corporate R&D, allowing them to outsource innovation to new firms. By decreasing the transaction costs of cooperation between existing firms and new firms, IP protections increase incentives for innovative entrepreneurs to establish firms that develop, sell, and license technology.

19 Simcoe et al. (2009, p. 807).

20 See Horstmann et al. (1985) on the choice between patenting and secrecy when there is asymmetric information. See also Gallini (1992) and Cugno and Ottoz (2006).

5.6 Conclusion

The strategic innovation game helps explain innovative entrepreneurship and addresses the question of why an inventor would become an innovative entrepreneur. Without market frictions and with homogeneous products, the strategic innovation game always results in technology transfer rather than entrepreneurship. The inventor and the existing firm prefer to cooperate in transferring the invention to the existing firm. Technology transfer avoids both rent dissipation from creative destruction and the costs of setting up a new firm. When the performance of the invention depends on the use of complementary assets, which are difficult to obtain through markets for assets, there may be incentives for the inventor and the existing firm to choose competition over cooperation.

Frictions in the market for inventions can induce innovative entrepreneurship in the strategic innovation game. Sufficient transaction costs in the market for inventions generate incentives for the inventor to become an entrepreneur and compete with the existing firm. Also, inventors may become innovative entrepreneurs to protect IP that may be subject to expropriation in the market for inventions. However, IP protections also can increase incentives for innovative entrepreneurs by protecting new products, production processes, and transaction techniques from infringement by competitors.

6

Creative Destruction

Making New Combinations

Jeff Bezos's establishment of Amazon.com involved launching a new brand, introducing new business methods, and developing novel e-commerce technologies. Amazon.com provided a product that was differentiated from those of other book retailers. Amazon's business methods as an online retailer differed from traditional bricks-and-mortar retailers such as Borders or Barnes & Noble. Amazon.com also introduced new transaction techniques, such as its patented invention of the "1-click" checkout system ("Method and system for placing a purchase order via a communications network").[1] Amazon.com subsequently licensed its ordering system to Apple for use in its iTunes online store.[2] Innovation is typically multifaceted. Inventors rarely confine their activities to new products, new production techniques, or new business methods, because they often change many things at once.

This chapter shows how multidimensional innovation helps explain innovative entrepreneurship. Imperfect transferability of product and process innovations affects the mix of entrepreneurship and contracting. Inventors affect the rate and direction of inventive activity by either transferring technology to existing firms or by becoming entrepreneurs who embody new technology in new firms. The resulting market outcomes determine what types of firms innovate and how product and process inventions are commercialized.

In practice, innovations often involve simultaneous improvements in product features, production costs, and transaction techniques. Multidimensional innovations are what Schumpeter termed "new combinations."[3] Alfred Chandler (1990, p. 597) observes:

> The first movers – those entrepreneurs that established the first modern industrial enterprises in the new industries of the Second Industrial Revolution – had to innovate in all of these activities. They had to be aware of the potential of

1 U.S. Patent 5,960,411, Inventors: P. Hartman, J. P. Bezos, S. Kaphan, and J. Spiegel, Assignee: Amazon.com Inc., Awarded September 28, 1999.

2 Kienle et al. (2004).

3 See Schumpeter (1934, p. 66) and Schumpeter (1942, p. 82).

> new technologies and then get the funds and make investments large enough to exploit fully the economies of scale and scope existing in the new technologies. They had to obtain the facilities and personnel essential to distribute and market new or improved products on a national scale and to obtain extensive sources of supply. Finally, they had to recruit and organize the managerial teams essential to maintain and integrate the investment made in the processes of production and distribution.

The entrepreneur may combine commercial, scientific, and technological inventions in developing new products, production processes, and transaction methods.

This chapter introduces a multidimensional invention consisting of a new product design and a new production process. The key insight of the analysis is that *product differentiation* offsets the creative destruction that results from more efficient production. When inventors encounter difficulties in either partial or full transfers of technology, innovative entrepreneurs enter the market with both a differentiated product and lower production costs.

The innovation game with new combinations generates the following outcomes. First, when only process innovations are transferable, greater product differentiation tends to generate entrepreneurship, helping address the challenge of entrepreneurship. Incremental innovations tend to favor entrepreneurship, and significant innovations favor technology transfer. Greater product differentiation gives inventors greater incentives to invent than existing firms because of the incremental returns that inventors can obtain from entrepreneurship. Second, when only product design innovations are transferable, entrepreneurial entry occurs if products are sufficiently differentiated or the production process innovation is significant. In that situation, the inventor's incentive to invent is again greater than that of an incumbent monopolist.

6.1 The Innovation Game with Product Differentiation

Consider the strategic innovation game with product differentiation. An existing firm and an inventor choose between cooperation and competition. If they choose to cooperate, the inventor transfers technology to the existing firm. If they choose to compete, the inventor becomes an entrepreneur and establishes a firm that competes with the existing firm.

Multidimensional Invention

Different types of inventions may not be equally transferable. For example, the transaction costs of transferring manufacturing process technologies can differ from the transaction costs of transferring new product designs. In a frictionless world, an inventor could perfectly and costlessly transfer any technology to an incumbent firm. Also, in a frictionless world, an incumbent could absorb any type of technology and expand its operations to include new products, manufacturing processes, inputs, and transaction methods.

Suppose that an inventor makes a two-dimensional discovery that consists of a new product design and a new production process. Also, suppose that there is an incumbent firm that cannot diversify without obtaining a new product design, either through R&D or from an inventor. The inventor can become an innovative entrepreneur who can only enter the market by offering a single product, which is the newly discovered product.[4] The discussion examines conditions under which inventors who choose between entrepreneurship and technology transfer have greater incentives to develop new products and new processes than incumbent monopolists.

The strategic innovation game has two stages as in the previous chapter. In stage one, the inventor and the incumbent monopolist choose between cooperation and competition. If the inventor and the existing firm choose to cooperate, we assume that the inventor can transfer some aspect of the invention to an existing firm: the new product design, the new production process, or both. Also, as a means of deterring entry, the existing firm can pay the inventor to license the discovery without necessarily adopting the new technology. If the inventor and the incumbent monopolist choose to compete, the inventor can enter the market by becoming an entrepreneur and establishing a new firm to implement the innovation.

Firms implement the innovation, engage in production, and supply products in stage two. If the inventor and the existing firm choose to cooperate in the first stage, the existing firm operates as a monopolist in the second stage. If the inventor and the existing firm do not choose to cooperate in the first stage, then in the second stage, the new firm established by the entrepreneur and the incumbent firm engage in differentiated-products Bertrand-Nash competition, with each firm supplying one good. The new firm established by the entrepreneur employs the new discovery, introducing both the new product design and the new production process. Sufficient product differentiation implies that industry profits can be greater than the profits of the incumbent monopolist.[5]

4 Klette and Kortum (2004) consider costly diversification in a model with exogenous entry of single-product firms. After entry, existing firms invest in innovation that leads to product diversification. Their discussion focuses on incumbent firm innovation without a market for technology transfer. The discussion in this chapter could be generalized by allowing entrants to offer multiple products.

5 This contrasts with related work by Gans and Stern (2000, 2003) and Gans et al. (2002). For example, Gans and Stern (2000) assume that industry profits after entrepreneurial entry are less than the profits of the incumbent monopolist with the new technology, and as a result, entrepreneurial entry does not occur in equilibrium. With homogeneous products, a monopolist has a greater incentive to invent than does an entrant; see Gilbert and Newbery (1982) and Gilbert (2006). The standard assumption of homogeneous products implies that an incumbent monopolist has profits that are greater than those of the entire industry after entry. This condition is referred to as the "persistence of monopoly" and the "efficiency condition." Chen and Schwartz

The inventor's discovery consists of a new production process and a new product design. The existing firm's initial production process is represented by unit cost c_1, and the new production process is represented by unit cost c_2. Assume that the new technology is superior to the existing technology, $c_2 < c_1$. The analysis can be extended to allow for the new technology to be inferior in which case the existing firm would acquire the new production technology to deter entry without applying the new technology.

The existing firm initially is a single-product monopolist. The new product is horizontally differentiated from the existing product. If the existing firm adopts the new product design, the existing firm becomes a two-product firm. If the inventor becomes an entrepreneur and establishes a firm, the entrant is a single-product firm that produces the new product. Let q_1 be the output of the good initially produced by firm 1. Let q_2 be the new good, which can be the supplied by the existing firm through diversification or by the new entrant.

Market demand is derived from the preferences of a representative consumer, $U(q_1, q_2; b)$, where b represents a substitution parameter such that $0 \leq b < 1$. The consumer's utility is quadratic and symmetric in its arguments, so that products are differentiated horizontally,

$$U(q_1, q_2; b) = 2q_1 + 2q_2 - \frac{1}{2}(q_1)^2 - \frac{1}{2}(q_2)^2 - bq_1q_2. \tag{1}$$

The representative consumer chooses consumption q_1 and q_2 to maximize surplus, $U(q_1, q_2; b) - p_1q_1 - p_2q_2$.[6] The consumer's demand functions are

$$q_i = D_i(p_1, p_2; b) = \frac{2 - 2b + bp_j - p_i}{1 - b^2}, \quad i \neq j, i, j = 1, 2.$$

The demand for a good is decreasing in the good's own price and, for $b > 0$, increasing in the price of the substitute good, $\partial D_i(p_1, p_2; b)/\partial p_i < 0$ and $\partial D_i(p_1, p_2; b)/\partial p_j > 0$, $i \neq j$, $i, j = 1, 2$.

The incumbent monopolist is assumed to be viable with the initial technology, $c_1 < 2$, so that the monopolist also is viable with the new technology.[7] The existing monopolist's profit equals

$$\Pi^M(c_1) = (p^M(c_1) - c_1)D_1(p^M(c_1)) = \frac{(2 - c_1)^2}{4}. \tag{2}$$

(2009) consider vertical product differentiation in which the dominant firm produces multiple goods and find that competition can yield greater returns than monopoly (see also Greenstein and Ramey, 1998). This differs from my analysis in which the incumbent firm and the entrant compete on equal terms. They do not consider the question of innovation and entrepreneurship. Also, in Anton and Yao's (2003) study of imitation and technology transfer, the imitative firm and the inventor are Cournot duopolists with homogeneous products.

6 The consumer's demand functions solve the first order conditions, $U_1(q_1, q_2; b) = p_1$ and $U_2(q_1, q_2; b) = p_2$.

7 To derive the existing firm's monopoly profit, let $q_2 = 0$. The representative consumer's utility function implies that $U(q_1, 0) = 2q_1 - (1/2)(q_1)^2$. The consumer's demand for the incumbent's product is $D_1(p_1) = 2 - p_1$. The monopoly price is $p^M(c_1) = (2 + c_1)/2$.

If the inventor transfers the new product design to the existing firm, the incumbent becomes a two-product monopolist. The profit of a two-product monopolist is given by

(3) $\Pi^M(c_1, c_2, b) = \max_{p_1, p_2}(p_1 - c_1)D_1(p_1, p_2; b) + (p_2 - c_2)D_2(p_1, p_2; b).$

The first-order conditions for the two-product monopolist are as follows:

$$-(p_1 - c_1) + b(p_2 - c_2) + 2 - 2b + bp_2 - p_1 = 0,$$
$$-(p_2 - c_2) + b(p_1 - c_1) + 2 - 2b + bp_1 - p_2 = 0.$$

Solving these conditions gives the two-product monopolist's profit-maximizing prices, $p_1 = 1 + c_1/2$ and $p_2 = 1 + c_2/2$. Using the envelope theorem and evaluating at the profit-maximizing prices, the two-product monopolist's profit is decreasing in the substitution parameter,

$$\frac{\partial \Pi^M(c_1, c_2, b)}{\partial b} = \sum_{i=1}^{2} (p_i - c_i)\frac{\partial D_i(p_1, p_2; b)}{\partial b} < 0.$$

This is because at $p_1 = 1 + c_1/2$ and $p_2 = 1 + c_2/2$,

$$\frac{\partial D_i(p_1, p_2; b)}{\partial b} = (1 + b^2)\left(\frac{c_2}{2} - 1\right) + 2b\left(1 - \frac{c_1}{2}\right) < 0,$$

where $c_2 < c_1 < 2$. With symmetric costs, the monopolist's profits from producing both goods are greater than the profits from producing only one good for all $b < 1$,

$$\Pi^M(c, c, b) = \frac{2}{1 + b}\frac{(2 - c)^2}{4} > \Pi^M(c).$$

Entrepreneurial Entry and Competition

If the inventor and the existing firm choose to compete, the inventor becomes an entrepreneur by establishing a new firm that embodies the new product design and the new production technology. The existing firm continues to produce a single product with the existing technology. Designate the existing firm as firm 1 and the market entrant as firm 2. The incumbent firm and the entrepreneurial entrant engage in Bertrand-Nash price competition with differentiated products. The Bertrand-Nash equilibrium prices $p_1{}^*$ and $p_2{}^*$ solve

(4) $\Pi_1(c_1, c_2, b) = \max_{p_1}(p_1 - c_1)D_1(p_1, p_2{}^*; b),$

(5) $\Pi_2(c_1, c_2, b) = \max_{p_2}(p_2 - c_2)D_2(p_1{}^*, p_2; b).$

The equilibrium prices depend on the costs of the two firms and the product differentiation parameter, $p_1{}^*(c_1, c_2, b)$ and $p_2{}^*(c_1, c_2, b)$. We restrict attention to cost values such that outputs and profits are nonnegative for both firms. For $b = 0$, each of the firms is a monopolist.

The intensity of product-market competition depends positively on the substitution parameter b and on the difference between costs. With duopoly competition, the price functions are

$$(6) \qquad p_i^*(c_1, c_2, b) = \frac{2c_i + bc_j + 2(2+b)(1-b)}{4-b^2}, \quad i \neq j,\ i, j = 1, 2.$$

When duopoly output levels are positive, they equal

$$(7) \qquad q_i^*(c_1, c_2) = \frac{(2-b^2)(2-c_i) - b(2-c_j)}{(1-b^2)(4-b^2)}, \quad i \neq j,\ i, j = 1, 2.$$

The profits of the firms equal:

$$(8) \quad \Pi_i(c_i, c_j, b) = \frac{[(2-b^2)(2-c_i) - b(2-c_j)]^2}{(1-b^2)(4-b^2)^2}, \quad i \neq j,\ i, j = 1, 2.$$

Both firms operate profitably in equilibrium when the new technology is close to the existing technology because positive profits follow from $2 > b^2 + b$. Profits are decreasing in the firm's own cost, $\partial \Pi_i(c_i, c_j, b)/\partial c_i < 0$ and increasing in the competitor's cost, $\partial \Pi_i(c_i, c_j, b)/\partial c_j < 0$, $i \neq j$, $i = 1, 2$. For $b > 0$, the firms' costs are substitutes in the profit functions, $\partial^2 \Pi_i(c_i, c_j, b)/\partial c_i \partial c_j < 0$, $i \neq j$, $i = 1, 2$.

Because the new technology is superior to the existing technology, both firms operate when the incumbent firm operates profitably. If the entrepreneurial entrant is sufficiently efficient, it drives out the incumbent firm. From equation (7), $q_1 = 0$ defines the cost threshold $c_2{}^0(b, c_1)$ for firm 2,

$$(9) \qquad c_2{}^0(b, c_1) = \frac{2b - (2-b^2)(2-c_1)}{b}.$$

Zanchettin (2006) shows that only the entrant operates when costs are less than or equal to the threshold, $c_2 \leq c_2{}^0(b, c_1)$, and both firms operate when the entrant's costs are above the threshold, $c_2 > c_2{}^0(b, c_1)$. The cost threshold for the new technology is less than the initial technology, $c_2{}^0(b, c_1) < c_1$, and is increasing in the substitution parameter, b. If the innovation is sufficiently drastic, then the entrepreneurial entrant can drive out the incumbent by offering a monopoly price, $p^m(c_2) = (2 + c_2)/2$. Driving out the incumbent with monopoly pricing occurs when the invention is sufficiently drastic. This occurs when the entrant's costs are below a lower threshold, $c_2 \leq c_2{}^{00}(b, c_1)$, which exists only if $c_1 + b < 2$,

$$(10) \qquad c_2{}^{00}(b, c_1) = \frac{2(c_1 + b - 2)}{b} < c_2(b, c_1).$$

When the innovation is below the threshold $c_2{}^0(b, c_1)$ but not sufficiently drastic, $2(c_1 + b - 2)/b < c_2 \leq c_2{}^0(b, c_1)$, the more efficient firm engages in limit pricing to deter the higher-cost firm from operating. The entrepreneurial entrant, firm 2, is the limit-pricing firm, and firm 1's output is

$$q_1 = 2(1-b) - p_1 + bp_2 \leq 0.$$

Then, firm 2's reaction function becomes $p_2 = (1/b)[p_1 - 2(1-b)]$. The incumbent firm 1 has a zero output and chooses $p_1 = c_1$. The limit-pricing entrant, firm 2, produces output greater than the monopoly output,

$$q_2^L(c_1, c_2) = 2 - p_2 = \frac{2 - c_2}{b} > q^M(c_2) = \frac{2 - c_2}{2}.$$

The limit-pricing entrant sets a price less than the monopoly price,

$$p_2^L(c_1, c_2, b) = \frac{c_1 - 2(1-b)}{b} < p^M(c_2) = 1 + \frac{c_2}{2}.$$

The limit-pricing firm earns profits less than monopoly profits,

$$\Pi_2^L(c_1, c_2, b) = \frac{(2 - c_1)[b(2 - c_2) - (2 - c_1)]}{b^2} < \Pi^M(c_2) = \frac{(2 - c_2)^2}{4}.$$

The properties of the profit and price functions hold more generally.[8]

Cooperation versus Competition

If the inventor and the incumbent firm choose to cooperate, the incumbent firm is a monopolist with profits Π^M that will depend on what technology is transferred. If the inventor and the incumbent firm choose to compete, the incumbent firm earns duopoly profits $\Pi_1(c_1, c_2, b)$, and the entrepreneurial entrant earns the duopoly profits $\Pi_2(c_1, c_2, b)$. The incumbent firm's net benefit from adopting the new technology offered by the inventor equals the difference between monopoly profits at the new technology and duopoly profits when the incumbent has the old technology and the entrant has the new technology. Therefore, the incumbent firm's net benefit from adopting the new technology equals the incremental returns from remaining a monopolist, $\Pi^M - \Pi_1$. This is the maximum amount that the inventor can obtain from transferring the technology to the incumbent firm.

The outcome of the strategic innovation game depends on the total returns to cooperation and competition for the inventor and the incumbent firm. The inventor prefers entrepreneurship to technology transfer if and only if the returns to entry are greater than the incremental returns to the incumbent firm from technology transfer,

$$\Pi_2 > \Pi^M - \Pi_1.$$

8 For additional discussion of the class of utility functions that yield similar properties for comparative statics analysis of a duopoly equilibrium, see Milgrom and Roberts (1990b). For differentiated duopoly with symmetric costs, see Singh and Vives (1984), and for differentiated duopoly with asymmetric costs and qualities, see Zanchettin (2006). The analysis can be extended to other differentiated product settings such as Hotelling-type (1929) price competition. The results of the following analysis do not require price competition. They could be examined with the two firms engaging in Cournot quantity competition with differentiated products.

This is equivalent to the condition that total industry profits when the incumbent firm has the initial technology and the entrepreneurial firm has the new technology are greater than monopoly profit at the new technology,

$$\Pi_1 + \Pi_2 > \Pi^M.$$

If this condition holds, the inventor with a superior technology will become an entrepreneur and enter the market. If this condition does not hold, full information bargaining will result in the inventor transferring his technology to the incumbent.

For the inventor and the incumbent firm to choose competition over cooperation, the incumbent firm using the new technology must earn lower profits than the competitive industry after entrepreneurial entry, $\Pi_1 + \Pi_2 > \Pi^M$. This outcome may seem counterintuitive because it may appear that with technology transfer the monopolist will always earn greater profits than the competitive industry. As we will see, competitive industry profits can be greater than the incumbent's profits when technology transfer is imperfect. Imperfect technology transfer lowers the profits of the incumbent monopolist using the new technology. If only the process innovation is transferred, the incumbent has lower costs but only produces one good. If only the product innovation is transferred, the incumbent diversifies but produces both goods at a high cost.

Conversely, industry profits with competitive entry are increased by product differentiation and cost differences. The incumbent firm produces one good at the high initial cost, and the entrant produces one good using the more efficient new technology. Product differentiation mitigates the effects of price competition between the incumbent and the entrant, thus, increasing industry profits. Also, industry profits are increased by the cost differences between the low-cost entrant and the high-cost incumbent.

If the inventor and the established firm choose cooperation, they bargain over the royalty, R. Let the relative bargaining power of the inventor in the bargaining game be represented by the parameter, α, where $0 \leq \alpha \leq 1$. This represents the reduced form of a bargaining game between the inventor and the incumbent firm. Because there is a lump-sum royalty, bargaining is efficient, and relative bargaining power does not affect the outcome of the strategic innovation game. With full information, the outcome of the strategic innovation game is efficient for the inventor and the incumbent firm. They decide whether to cooperate or to compete, and if cooperation is efficient, they bargain over the division of the surplus. The inventor receives a royalty from transferring the technology equal to $R = \alpha(\Pi^M - \Pi_1) + (1 - \alpha)\Pi_2$.

Imperfect Transferability of the Invention

Because of various transaction costs, the invention may be imperfectly transferable. The transferability of the invention will affect the outcome of the strategic interaction between the existing firm and the inventor. Transferability will affect

Table 6.1. *Four scenarios based on the transferability of a two-dimensional invention*

	Production process Transferable	**Production process Not transferable**
Product design Transferable	Incumbent profits: $\Pi^M(c_2, c_2, b)$ Outcome is cooperation with monopoly diversification and cost efficiency	Incumbent profits: $\Pi^M(c_1, c_1, b)$ Monopoly diversification at initial costs versus entrepreneurial competition
Product design Not transferable	Incumbent profits: $\Pi^M(c_2)$ Monopoly cost efficiency versus entrepreneurial competition	Incumbent profits: $\Pi^M(c_1)$ Single-product monopoly at initial costs versus entrepreneurial competition

the returns to licensing the invention, and it will affect whether the existing firm and the inventor choose to compete or to cooperate. Because the innovation is two-dimensional, there are four possibilities.

(1) The new technology is fully transferable – that is, both the new product design and the new production process are transferable, and the new production process is applicable to producing both goods.
(2) The new technology is nontransferable – that is, neither the new product design nor the production process are transferable, although the existing firm still can license the new technology as a means of deterring entry, without using the new technology.
(3) The new product design is not transferable, and the new production process is transferable, so the existing firm can apply the production process to the initial good.
(4) If the new product design is transferable but the new production process is not transferable, then the existing firm produces both the initial product and the new product and applies the initial production process to both products.

These possibilities are shown in Table 6.1.

6.2 The Innovation Game with a Fully Transferable Invention

With a fully transferable invention, the existing firm obtains profit from producing both goods using the new production technology, $\Pi^M(c_2, c_2, b)$. If the inventor and the incumbent firm choose to compete, the incumbent firm earns duopoly profits, $\Pi_1(c_1, c_2, b)$, and the entrepreneurial entrant earns duopoly profits, $\Pi_2(c_1, c_2, b)$. Total industry profits are continuous in the new process technology c_2, and the curve representing total profits has up to three segments. If the innovation is sufficiently drastic, $c_2 \leq c_2^{00}(c_1, b)$, then a monopoly-pricing entrant eliminates the incumbent, and industry profits equal single-product monopoly profits with the new process technology:

$$\Pi_1(c_1, c_2, b) + \Pi_2(c_1, c_2, b) = \Pi^M(c_2).$$

For an intermediate value of the new process technology, ${c_2}^{00}(c_1, b) < c_2 \leq {c_2}^0(c_1, b)$, the entrepreneurial entrant engages in limit pricing so that industry profits equals

$$\Pi_1(c_1, c_2, b) + \Pi_2(c_1, c_2, b) = \Pi_2^L(c_1, c_2, b) < \Pi^M(c_2).$$

These two situations correspond to creative destruction. Finally, for incremental innovations, ${c_2}^0(c_1, b) < c_2 < c_1$, both firms operate and total industry profits are calculated by adding the two firms' profits using equation (8). With both firms operating, industry profits are decreasing and convex in c_2. As c_2 approaches c_1, total industry profits approaches its minimum for $c_2 \leq c_1$,

(11) $$\Pi_1(c_1, c_1, b) + \Pi_2(c_1, c_1, b) = (2 - c_1)^2 \frac{2(1-b)}{(1+b)(2-b)^2}.$$

This is the minimum for the three segments, as shown in Figure 6.1.

With fully transferable technology, the returns to cooperation exceed the returns to competition. The monopolist with the new product design and the new production process earns more than industry profits with entrepreneurial entry for all $b > 0$,

$$\Pi^M(c_2, c_2, b) > \Pi_1(c_1, c_2, b) + \Pi_2(c_1, c_2, b).$$

This holds because of the rent-dissipating effects of competition and because the incumbent uses the old production process when there is entrepreneurial entry. The net returns to technology transfer, $\Pi^M(c_2, c_2, b) - \Pi_1(c_1, c_2, b)$, are greater than the returns to entrepreneurship, $\Pi_2(c_1, c_2, b)$. This immediately implies that when technology is fully transferable, the inventor and the existing firm always choose to cooperate. *With fully transferable technology, entrepreneurial entry does not occur, and the inventor transfers the technology to the existing firm.*

Compare this result with Arrow's (1962b) original investigation of the incentive to invent. The incumbent monopolist's incentive to invent equals the returns to producing both goods and applying the new process technology,

(12) $$V^M = \Pi^M(c_2, c_2, b) - \Pi^M(c_1).$$

Although generalized to include diversification, the monopolist's incentive to invent reflects the inertia identified by Arrow. The firm that expects to continue to be a monopolist is concerned only about incremental profits.

Now, compare the monopolist's incentive to invent with that of the inventor. With fully transferable technology, the inventor's incentive to invent equals the royalties from technology transfer,

(13) $$V^I = R = \alpha[\Pi^M(c_2, c_2, b) - \Pi_1(c_1, c_2, b)] + (1-\alpha)\Pi_2(c_1, c_2, b).$$

The inventor's incentive to invent derives from transferring the technology or from competing with the incumbent firm. If the inventor licenses the technology to the incumbent monopolist, the incumbent monopolist's willingness to pay is the difference between the incumbent's monopoly profit and the incumbent's profit after competitive entry. Because of the effects of competition, the incumbent's initial profit is greater than the incumbent's profit after entry, $\Pi^M(c_1) > \Pi_1(c_1, c_2, b)$. So, the monopolist's incentive to invent is less than the benefit of adopting the new technology,

$$V^M = \Pi^M(c_2, c_2, b) - \Pi^M(c_1) < \Pi^M(c_2, c_2, b) - \Pi_1(c_1, c_2, b).$$

The inventor's incentive to invent is greater than or equal to the returns to entrepreneurial entry and less than or equal to the incumbent's benefit from technology adoption. Define the critical value of the inventor's bargaining power by

$$\alpha^* = \frac{\Pi^M(c_1, c_2, b) - \Pi^M(c_1) - \Pi_2(c_1, c_2, b)}{\Pi^M(c_1, c_2, b) - \Pi_1(c_1, c_2, b) - \Pi_2(c_1, c_2, b)}. \tag{14}$$

With fully transferable technology, the inventor's incentive to invent is greater than that of the incumbent monopolist if and only if the inventor has sufficient bargaining power, $\alpha \geq \alpha^*$. Even though the inventor transfers the technology to the incumbent firm, the possibility of entrepreneurship overcomes the incumbent firm's inertia. The threat of creative destruction provides a competitive benchmark that increases the incumbent's incentive to adopt in comparison to the monopoly benchmark.

6.3 The Innovation Game with a Nontransferable Invention

Suppose that neither the new product design nor the new production process is transferable. The inventor can still contract with the existing firm to receive a payment for not entering the market, with the incumbent licensing the technology without actually using the new product design or the new production process.[9] The existing firm that buys out the inventor would continue to operate as a single-product monopoly with profits, $\Pi^M(c_1)$. The lowest value of industry profits, $\Pi_1(c_1, c_1, b) + \Pi_2(c_1, c_1, b)$, is greater than, equal to, or less than the incumbent's profits, $\Pi^M(c_1)$ depending on the substitution parameter. Entrepreneurial entry need not always occur because the inventor and the existing firm still have incentives to avoid competition.

For a given degree of product differentiation, entrepreneurial entry occurs if the process innovation is sufficiently large. With nontransferable technology, the

9 Rasmusen (1988) considers an entrant that seeks a buyout after entry in a homogeneous-products Cournot game with capacity constraints, although he does not consider technological change.

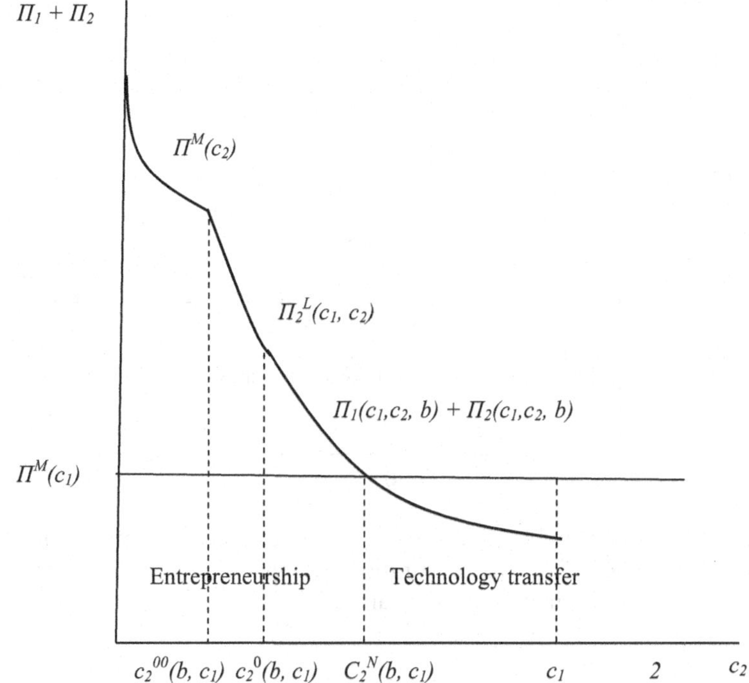

Figure 6.1. With a nontransferable invention, the outcome of the innovation game is entrepreneurship only if the process innovation, c_2, is sufficiently less than the initial cost – that is, if the new costs are less than a critical value, $C_2^N(b, c_1)$, where $C_2^N(b, c_1) \leq c_1$.

incumbent and the entrant have greater incentives to cooperate to avoid creative destruction only when the innovation is incremental, as shown in Figure 6.1. With nontransferable technology, a significant innovation increases the returns to entry for the entrepreneur who drives out the incumbent. The pure creative destruction effect means that the entrepreneur's returns to entry exceed the benefits to the incumbent from buying out the inventor.

With a nontransferable invention, entry occurs if and only if the substitution parameter is either greater than or less than an intermediate range, as shown in Figure 6.2. With vigorous competition resulting from less product differentiation, the inventor and the existing firm have less incentive to cooperate because the entrepreneurial entrant will displace the incumbent firm. With less competition resulting from more product differentiation, the inventor and the existing firm also have less incentive to cooperate because they earn sufficient profits after entrepreneurial entry.

This discussion suggests the following results. With a nontransferable invention, entrepreneurial entry occurs if and only if the substitution parameter is less than the critical value $b^N = b^N(c_1, c_2)$ or greater than the critical value $b^{NN} = b^{NN}(c_1, c_2)$, where $b^N(c_1, c_2) < b^{NN}(c_1, c_2)$. Also, with a nontransferable invention, entrepreneurial entry occurs if and only if costs are less than the critical

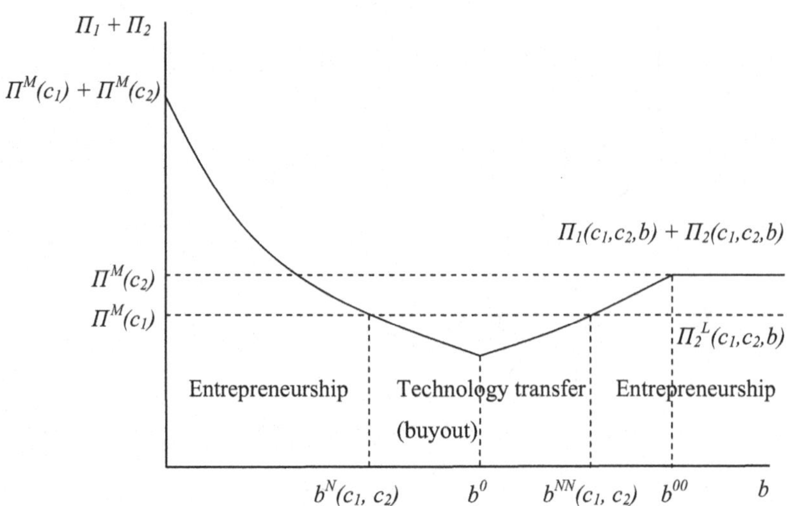

Figure 6.2. With a nontransferable invention, the outcome of the innovation game is entrepreneurship if and only if the substitution parameter is less than the critical value $b^N = b^N(c_1, c_2)$ or greater than the critical value $b^{NN} = b^{NN}(c_1, c_2)$.

value, ${C_2}^N(b, c_1)$, where ${C_2}^N(b, c_1) \leq c_1$, so that significant process innovations result in entrepreneurship.

To establish this result, we first show that the industry profits function is continuous in b with three segments. Using the quadratic formula, the critical value $0 < b^0 < 1$ that solves $c_2 = {c_2}^0(b^0, c_1)$ is given by

$$b^0 = \frac{-(2 - c_2) + [(2 - c_2)^2 + 8(2 - c_1)^2]^{1/2}}{2(2 - c_1)}.$$

The critical value b^{00} that solves $c_2 = {c_2}^{00}(b_0, c_1) = 2(c_1 + b^{00} - 2)/b^{00}$ is given by

$$b^{00} = \frac{2(2 - c_1)}{2 - c_2}.$$

For $0 \leq b < b^0$, both firms operate profitably so that industry profits equal

$$\text{(15)} \quad \Pi_1(c_1, c_2, b) + \Pi_2(c_1, c_2, b) = \frac{(4 - 5b^2 + b^4)A - (4b - 2b^3)B}{(1 - b^2)(4 - b^2)^2},$$

where $A = (2 - c_1)^2 + (2 - c_2)^2$ and $B = 2(2 - c_1)(2 - c_2)$. For $b^0 \leq b < b^{00}$, limit pricing occurs so that only firm 2 operates profitably, and industry profits equal

$$\text{(16)} \quad \Pi_1(c_1, c_2, b) + \Pi_2(c_1, c_2, b) = \Pi_2^L(c_1, c_2, b) = \frac{(2 - c_1)[b(2 - c_2) - (2 - c_1)]}{b^2}.$$

There is a third region only if the invention is sufficiently drastic, $2(2 - c_1) < (2 - c_2)$. Then, for $b^{00} \leq b < 1$, the entrant deters the incumbent with monopoly pricing and industry profits equal the entrant's profits, $\Pi^M(c_2)$. The industry profits function is continuous at b^0, because $c_2 = c_2(b^0, c_1)$ so that from equation (16),

$$(17) \quad \Pi_1(c_1, c_2, b^0) + \Pi_2(c_1, c_2, b^0) = \frac{(2 - c_2)^2[1 - (b^0)^2]}{[2 - (b^0)^2]^2} = \Pi_2^L(c_1, c_2, b^0).$$

The industry profits function is continuous at b^{00}, because $c_2 = 2(c_1 + b^{00} - 2)/b^{00}$ so that industry profits equal

$$(18) \quad \Pi_2^L(c_1, c_2, b^{00}) = \frac{(2 - c_2)^2}{4} = \Pi^M(c_2).$$

For $0 \leq b < b^0$, the industry profits function in equation (15) is strictly decreasing in b.[10] For $b^0 \leq b \leq b^{00}$, $\Pi_2^L(c_1, c_2, b)$ is strictly increasing in b because $b < b^{00}$. The analysis shows that there exists a unique critical value of the substitution parameter $b^N(c_1, c_2) < b^0 < 1$ that solves

$$(19) \quad \Pi_1(c_1, c_2, b^N) + \Pi_2(c_1, c_2, b^N) = \Pi^M(c_1).$$

Also, there is a critical value $b^0 < b^{NN}(c_1, c_2) < 1$ that equates industry profits with the incumbent's profits at the initial technology. So, industry profits are greater than the monopolist's profits at the new technology if and only if either $0 \leq b < b^N(c_1, c_2)$ or $b^{NN}(c_1, c_2) \leq b < 1$. Because the industry profits curve is downward sloping in the new process technology, and minimum industry profits are greater than, equal to, or less than $\Pi^M(c_1)$ depending on the substitution parameter, it follows that entrepreneurial entry occurs if and only if costs c_2 are less than the critical value, $C_2^N(b, c_1) \leq c_1$. This establishes the result.

With a nontransferable invention, entrepreneurship takes place only if the innovation is significant. The critical cost value $C_2^N(b, c_1)$ is less than c_1 only if industry profits in equation (11) are less than $\Pi^M(c_1)$. When the substitution parameter b is sufficiently low, competition is mitigated so that entrepreneurial entry takes place for any cost level, so that the critical value $C_2^N(b, c_1)$ equals c_1.

The incumbent monopolist can have greater incentives to invent than the inventor because nontransferable technology reduces the returns from licensing.

10 Differentiating with respect to b gives

$$\frac{\partial(\Pi_1(c_1, c_2, b) + \Pi_2(c_1, c_2, b))}{\partial b} = \frac{2[b(4 - 9b^2 + 2b^4 - b^6)A - (8 + 2b^2 - 5b^4 + 3b^6)B]}{(1 - b^2)^2(4 - b^2)^3}.$$

Note that $(8 + 2b^2 - 5b^4 + 3b^6) > 0$ for $0 \leq b < 1$. If $(4 - 9b^2 + 2b^4 - b^6) \leq 0$, it follows that $\partial(\Pi_1(c_1, c_2; b) + \Pi_2(c_1, c_2; b))/\partial b < 0$. Conversely, suppose that $(4 - 9b^2 + 2b^4 - b^6) > 0$. Note that when c_2 is above the threshold, it follows that $(2 - b^2)B > bA$, so that again $\partial(\Pi_1(c_1, c_2; b) + \Pi_2(c_1, c_2; b))/\partial b < 0$.

With nontransferable technology, the incumbent monopolist has a greater incentive to invent than the inventor when products are sufficiently differentiated,

$$b \leq \frac{\Pi^M(c_2) - \Pi^M(c_1)}{\Pi^M(c_2) + \Pi^M(c_1)}.$$

To see why the incumbent monopolist's incentive to invent is larger, recall that the profits of the two-product monopolist with the initial technology equal $\Pi^M(c, c; b) = \frac{2}{1+b}\frac{(2-c)^2}{4}$. If the outcome of the innovation game is entrepreneurship, the inventor obtains $V^I = \Pi_2(c_1, c_2; b)$. Then,

$$\begin{aligned} V^M - V^I &= \Pi^M(c_2, c_2, b^N) - \Pi^M(c_1) - \Pi_2(c_1, c_2, b) \\ &= [\Pi^M(c_2) - \Pi_2(c_1, c_2, b)] + \left[\frac{1-b}{1+b}\Pi^M(c_2) - \Pi^M(c_1)\right] > 0. \end{aligned}$$

The first term is positive because of the effects of competition, and the second term is positive from the upper limit on b. If the outcome of the innovation game is licensing, the inventor obtains

$$V^I = R = \alpha[\Pi^M(c_1) - \Pi_1(c_1, c_2, b)] + (1-\alpha)\Pi_2(c_1, c_2, b)$$

so that $V^I \leq \Pi^M(c_1) - \Pi_1(c_1, c_2, b)$. Then,

$$V^M - V^I \geq \Pi_1(c_1, c_2, b) + 2\left[\frac{1}{1+b}\Pi^M(c_2) - \Pi^M(c_1)\right].$$

The second term is positive for $b \leq \frac{\Pi^M(c_2) - \Pi^M(c_1)}{\Pi^M(c_1)}$, which holds from the upper limit on b, so that again $V^M > V^I$.

A nontransferable technology reduces incentives to invent because the inventor obtains returns from entrepreneurial entry or from a buyout to prevent entry. Greater product differentiation is sufficient for the monopolist's incentive to invent to exceed the returns from entry or from a buyout.

6.4 The Innovation Game When Only the New Production Process Is Transferable

If the new product design is not transferable and the new production process is transferable, then with technology transfer the existing firm remains a single-product monopolist and obtains profit using the new production technology, $\Pi^M(c_2)$. Therefore, the incumbent firm's net benefit from adopting the new technology equals the incremental returns from remaining a monopolist, $\Pi^M(c_2) - \Pi_1(c_1, c_2, b)$. This is the maximum amount that the inventor can obtain from transferring the technology to the incumbent firm.

The outcome of the strategic innovation game depends on the total returns to cooperation and competition for the inventor and the incumbent firm. The inventor prefers entrepreneurship to technology transfer if and only if the returns to entry are greater than the incremental returns to the incumbent firm from technology transfer, $\Pi_2(c_1, c_2, b) > \Pi^M(c_2) - \Pi_1(c_1, c_2, b)$. This is equivalent to the condition that total industry profits when the incumbent firm has the initial technology and the entrepreneurial firm has the new technology are greater than monopoly profit at the new technology,

$$\Pi_1(c_1, c_2, b) + \Pi_2(c_1, c_2, b) > \Pi^M(c_2).$$

Product differentiation makes entrepreneurial entry possible even when the inventor can transfer only the new production process. When products are not close substitutes, the total profits of the incumbent firm and the entrant are greater than the profits of the existing firm with the new production technology. Without competition ($b = 0$), industry profits exceed the incumbent's profits evaluated at the new technology,

$$\Pi_1(c_1, c_2, b = 0) + \Pi_2(c_1, c_2, b = 0) = \Pi^M(c_1) + \Pi^M(c_2) > \Pi^M(c_2).$$

For b near zero, the threshold $c_2{}^0(b, c_1)$ is less than or equal to 0, so that limit pricing is ruled out for b near zero and both firms operate profitably. The threshold $c_2{}^0(b, c_1)$ is increasing in b and approaches c_1 as b goes to 1. When products are not close substitutes, both firms operate and the industry earns greater profits than a single-product monopolist using the new production process. As the degree of product substitution increases, industry profits decrease, and eventually the lower-cost firm is able to displace the incumbent firm through limit pricing. This reduces industry profits to the profits of the entrepreneurial entrant, which are less than the profits of a single-product monopolist using the new production process. With limit pricing, the lower-cost firm's profits are increasing in the degree of product substitution. When products are very close substitutes, and the invention is sufficiently drastic, the more efficient entrant with monopoly pricing can displace the incumbent using the initial technology. Then, transferring the technology generates the same profits as entrepreneurial entry.

Because the industry profits curve is downward sloping in the new process technology, there exists a unique cost threshold $C_2{}^*$, where $c_2{}^0(c_1, b) < C_2{}^*(c_1, b) \leq c_1$, such that

$$\Pi_1(c_1, C_2{}^*, b) + \Pi_2(c_1, C_2{}^*, b) = \Pi^M(C_2{}^*). \qquad (20)$$

The cost threshold is illustrated in Figure 6.3. When the process innovation is significant, industry profits with competition are less than or equal to the profits of a single-product monopoly, thus leading to cooperation and technology transfer. The result establishes a critical threshold for technology transfer that is greater than the critical threshold for limit pricing. Below that threshold, technology transfer is preferable to entrepreneurship for the inventor and the existing firm. If $c_2 \leq c_2(c_1, b)$, the returns to technology transfer outweigh the profit of the entrepreneurial entrant that drives out the incumbent, either through limit pricing or, when the invention is drastic, with a monopoly price. This implies that there is

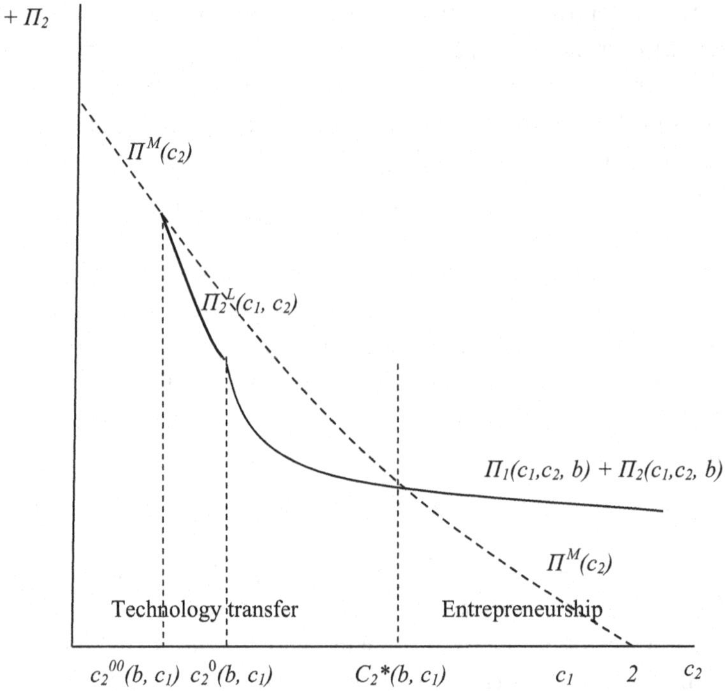

Figure 6.3. When only the new production process is transferable, the outcome of the innovation game is entrepreneurship if and only if the new process technology is incremental, $c_2 > C_2^*(c_1, b)$.

an additional range of costs, $c_2(c_1, b) < c_2 \leq C_2^*(c_1, b)$, such that the returns to technology transfer outweigh industry profits even when both firms operate after entry.

Sufficiently differentiated products or incremental innovations generate entrepreneurship when only the production process is transferable. *When only the production process is transferable, entrepreneurial entry occurs when products are differentiated sufficiently,* $0 \leq b < b^*(c_1, c_2)$, *where the threshold* $b^*(c_1, c_2)$ *is unique, positive, and less than one. Also, there exists a positive critical value of the new technology,* $C_2^*(c_1, b)$, *such that entrepreneurship occurs in equilibrium when the process innovation is incremental,* $c_2 > C_2^*(c_1, b)$. *The cost threshold is greater than that for limit pricing and less than or equal to the initial technology,* $c_2^0(c_1, b) < C_2^*(c_1, b) \leq c_1$.

This result illustrates Schumpeter's observation that the entrepreneur will enter beside the existing firm. Sufficient product differentiation attenuates competition so that industry profits are greater than monopoly profits using the new production technology, and the inventor obtains greater returns from entrepreneurship than from technology transfer. Because product differentiation limits product market competition, entrepreneurship also can occur when the new production technology is inferior to the incumbent's production technology.

Additionally, entrepreneurship is associated with incremental process inventions, whereas technology transfer is associated with significant process inventions.

With significant improvements in production technology, cost savings and monopoly profits outweigh the returns to product differentiation and entry so that the incumbent firm and the inventor choose cooperation over competition. With incremental improvements in technology, inventors embody their discoveries in new firms offering new products, and creative destruction occurs at the margin. When entrepreneurial entry occurs in waves as Schumpeter suggested, each new entrant will introduce new products and incremental process innovations.

The industry profits function is decreasing in the substitution parameter when both firms operate profitably so that the cost threshold is increasing in the substitution parameter, $\partial C_2{}^*(b, c_1)/\partial b \geq 0$. This implies that with greater product differentiation – that is, with lower values of b – the cost threshold falls and the range of innovations that results in entrepreneurship widens. *With a transferable production process, greater product differentiation (lower b) implies an increase in the range of innovations for which entrepreneurship occurs, with the marginal process innovation at which entrepreneurship occurs becoming more significant.*

The effects of product differentiation suggest potential industry dynamics. Suppose that the substitution parameter initially takes a high value. Then, a series of inventors with superior process technologies will choose to sell their idea to the incumbent firm, which experiences technological improvements. Then, suppose that the substitution parameter declines over time. For a particular process innovation, the outcome of the innovation game would switch from technology transfer to entrepreneurial entry. In contrast, with a rising substitution parameter, the outcome of the innovation game would switch from entrepreneurial entry to technology transfer.

When only the production process is transferable, the inventor's incentive to invent both a new product and a new process technology reflects the returns from commercializing the process invention through licensing or through entrepreneurship. The inventor's incentive to invent equals

$$\begin{aligned} V^I = \max\{&\alpha[\Pi^M(c_2) - \Pi_1(c_1, c_2, b)] \\ &+ (1-\alpha)\Pi_2(c_1, c_2, b), \Pi_2(c_1, c_2, b)\}. \end{aligned} \tag{21}$$

For purposes of comparison, consider the incumbent monopolist's incentive to invent only a new process technology, $V^M = \Pi^M(c_2) - \Pi^M(c_1)$. The incumbent firm using its initial technology earns more as a monopolist than with competitive entry, $\Pi^M(c_1) > \Pi_1(c_1, c_2, b)$. This implies that the monopolist's incentive to invent is less than the benefit of adopting the new technology,

$$V^M = \Pi^M(c_2) - \Pi^M(c_1) < \Pi^M(c_2) - \Pi_1(c_1, c_2, b).$$

If entrepreneurial entry is more profitable than the monopolist's returns to technology transfer – that is, $\Pi^M(c_2) - \Pi_1(c_1, c_2, b) \leq \Pi_2(c_1, c_2, b)$ – the entrepreneur's incentive to invent a new product and process is greater than the monopolist's incentive to invent a new production process.

Consider incentives to invent when only the new production process is transferable. When products are sufficiently differentiated, $0 \leq b \leq b^*(c_1, c_2)$, or when the process innovation is incremental, $c_2 > C_2{}^*(c_1, b)$, the inventor's incentive to invent is greater than that of an incumbent monopolist, $V^I > V^M$. This holds for all values of the bargaining power parameter. When technology transfer is the equilibrium outcome, the inventor's incentive to invent may be lower than that of the monopolist when bargaining power is low.

For any given level of product differentiation, the inventor's incentive to invent depends on the relative bargaining power of the inventor and incumbent firm. We can then define a critical value of the product differentiation parameter, $\alpha^* = \max\{0, \alpha'\}$, where

$$(22) \qquad \alpha' = \frac{\Pi^M(c_2) - \Pi^M(c_1) - \Pi_2(c_1, c_2, b)}{\Pi^M(c_2) - \Pi_1(c_1, c_2, b) - \Pi_2(c_1, c_2, b)}.$$

When the inventor has sufficient bargaining power – that is, $\alpha^* \leq \alpha \leq 1$ – the inventor's incentive to invent, V^I, is greater than that of an incumbent monopolist, V^M, whether or not the new technology improves on the existing technology.[11]

The innovative monopolist experiences inertia because of initial monopoly profit. When an inventor provides an invention to the incumbent firm, the threat of entry provides a benchmark that is less than monopoly profits, which reduces the monopolist's inertia. The incumbent monopolist compares the profits from technology adoption to profit after entry of the entrepreneur. The inventor's incentive to invent reflects the returns to technology transfer and entrepreneurial entry. If the inventor becomes an entrepreneur, the return from entry must be greater than what could be obtained from transferring the technology to the incumbent. The inventor's return from being an entrepreneur is obtained by competing with the incumbent firm. Therefore, the inventor's total rents derive from the returns to differentiated products competition.

6.5 The Innovation Game When Only the New Product Design Is Transferable

If the new product design is transferable but the new production process is not transferable, then with technology transfer the existing firm obtains profit from

11 The inventor's incentive to invent when the new technology is equivalent or inferior to that of the incumbent firm, $c_2 \geq c_1$, equals

$$V^I = \max\{\alpha(\Pi^M(c_1) - \Pi_1(c_1, c_2, b)) + (1 - \alpha)\Pi_2(c_1, c_2, b), \Pi_2(c_1, c_2, b)\}.$$

The inventor's incentive to invent is positive even with an equivalent or inferior technology. The incumbent monopolist would have an incentive to invent equal to zero if the new technology were equivalent or inferior to the existing technology, $V^M = 0$. Then, $V^I > 0 = V^M$, so the inventor's incentive to invent is always greater than that of an incumbent monopolist. This holds for all values of the substitution parameter.

producing both goods using the initial technology, $\Pi^M(c_1, c_1, b)$. The inventor prefers entrepreneurship to technology transfer if and only if the returns to entry are greater than the incremental returns to the incumbent firm from technology transfer,

$$\Pi_2(c_1, c_2, b) > \Pi^M(c_1, c_1, b) - \Pi_1(c_1, c_2, b).$$

This is equivalent to the condition that total industry profits when the incumbent firm has the initial technology and the entrepreneurial firm has the new technology are greater than monopoly profits with the new product design and the initial production process,

$$\Pi_1(c_1, c_2, b) + \Pi_2(c_1, c_2, b) > \Pi^M(c_1, c_1, b).$$

When the substitution parameter equals zero, industry profits exceed the incumbent's profits evaluated at the initial production technology as a result of a pure efficiency effect,

$$\begin{aligned}\Pi_1(c_1, c_2, b = 0) + \Pi_2(c_1, c_2, b = 0) &= \Pi^M(c_1) + \Pi^M(c_2) > 2\Pi^M(c_1)\\ &= \Pi^M(c_1, c_1, b = 0).\end{aligned}$$

However, when products are closer substitutes, competition between the entrant and the incumbent firm diminishes the benefits of entrepreneurial entry in comparison with technology transfer. Industry profits are decreasing in the substitution parameter, although the monopolist's profits also are decreasing in the substitution parameter.

The lowest value of industry profits is less than the profit of the incumbent monopolist that produces two products with the initial process technology, for all positive b,

$$\Pi_1(c_1, c_1, b) + \Pi_2(c_1, c_1, b) = \frac{4 - 4b}{4 - 4b + b^2}\Pi^M(c_1, c_1, b) < \Pi^M(c_1, c_1, b).$$

This implies that entrepreneurship occurs if and only if the substitution parameter is outside an intermediate range.

The transferability of the new product design reverses the previous result with a transferable process technology. There is a critical cost threshold that solves

$$\Pi_1(c_1, c_2^D, b) + \Pi_2(c_1, c_2^D, b) = \Pi^M(c_1, c_1, b).$$

The lowest value of industry profits is greater than the profits of the two-product monopolist at $b = 0$. Then, the cost threshold c_2^D goes to c_1, so that all inventors choose to become entrepreneurs. For sufficiently differentiated products, the lowest value of industry profits is greater than the profits of the two-product monopolist so that the cost threshold c_2^D is strictly less than c_1. Incremental process innovations result in technology transfer, and significant innovations generate entrepreneurship.

When only the new product design is transferable, entrepreneurial entry occurs if and only if the substitution parameter is less than the critical value

$b^D = b^D(c_1, c_2)$ or greater than the critical value $b^{DD} = b^{DD}(c_1, c_2)$. Also, entrepreneurial entry occurs if and only if $c_2 < C_2^D(c_1, b)$, so that significant process innovations result in entrepreneurship.

Compare the inventor's incentive to invent to that of the incumbent monopolist when the invention consists of a new product design. The monopolist develops or adopts a new product design to diversify. With the initial process technology, the monopolists' incentive to develop a new product design is less than the benefit from adopting a new product design,

$$V^M = \Pi^M(c_1, c_1, b) - \Pi^M(c_1) < \Pi^M(c_1, c_1, b) - \Pi_1(c_1, c_2, b).$$

The inventor's incentive to invent the combination of a new product and a new process technology equals

$$\text{(23)} \qquad V^I = \max\{\alpha[\Pi^M(c_1, c_1, b) - \Pi_1(c_1, c_2, b)] + (1-\alpha)\Pi_2(c_1, c_2, b), \Pi_2(c_1, c_2, b)\}.$$

When either the substitution parameter is less than the critical value $b^D = b^D(c_1, c_2)$ or greater than the critical value $b^{DD} = b^{DD}(c_1, c_2)$, the process innovation is significant, $c_2 < C_2^D(c_1, b)$, and the inventor's incentive to invent is greater than that of an incumbent monopolist, $V^I > V^M$.

6.6 Conclusion

Multidimensional innovation, with new product designs and new production processes, illustrates Schumpeter's assertion that entrepreneurs make "new combinations." The discussion extends Arrow (1962b), which classifies a process innovation as being drastic or non-drastic depending on whether the monopoly price with the new production technology is less than or greater than the unit costs under the old technology. Multidimensional innovation implies that the extent of an innovation depends both on the degree of product differentiation and on changes in production costs. The new product design and the new production process interact in an interesting way. The degree of product differentiation between the new and the existing product helps determine the critical threshold that defines a significant process innovation. The extent of multidimensional innovation is important because it affects both the returns to technology transfer and the returns to entrepreneurial entry.

Multidimensional innovation provides a compelling explanation for why entrepreneurship occurs in established industries. By mitigating competition, product differentiation generates rents for entrepreneurial entrants. These rents allow inventors to pursue entrepreneurship as a profitable alternative to transferring technology to incumbent firms. By making entrepreneurship a viable option for inventors, product differentiation also means that the incumbent firm must consider how entrepreneurial entry will affect its profits. With sufficient product differentiation, industry profits with entrepreneurial entry are greater than monopoly profits for an incumbent firm. Equivalently, the returns to technology transfer from the inventor to the incumbent firm will then be less than the returns to entrepreneurial entry. When this occurs, entrepreneurship is the equilibrium outcome of the innovation game. Product differentiation sheds light on Schumpeter's concept of "creative destruction," with innovative entrepreneurs operating beside existing firms.

Transaction costs and other impediments to the transfer of discoveries make entrepreneurship a potential outcome of the innovation game. When product and process are fully transferable to the existing firm, entrepreneurship will not take place. However, imperfect transferability generates incentives for inventors to become entrepreneurs. When the incumbent firm can buy out the inventor but neither the product nor the production technology is transferable, entrepreneurship occurs when process innovations are significant. This effect is reversed when only the process innovation is transferable; incremental process innovations lead the inventor to choose entrepreneurship, and significant innovations lead the inventor to transfer the technology to the incumbent firm. When only the product innovation is transferable, significant process innovations lead the inventor to choose entrepreneurship, and incremental process innovations lead the inventor to transfer the technology to the incumbent firm. The outcome of the strategic innovation game and the transferability of technology affect the mix of new products and new production processes. By embodying innovations in new firms, entrepreneurs influence the rate and direction of inventive activity.

7

Creative Destruction

Tacit Knowledge

An inventor's tacit knowledge is a fundamental aspect of both the process of discovery and subsequent diffusion of the innovation. In a classic example, Collins (1974) examined the transfer of knowledge about the Transversely Excited Atmospheric Pressure CO_2 (TEA) Laser. Collins (1974, p. 183) found that "the unit of knowledge cannot be abstracted from the 'carrier.' The scientist, his culture and skill are an integral part of what is known" (see also Ravetz, 1971). Collins (1974, p. 167) observed that "[a]ll types of knowledge, however pure, consist, in part, of tacit rules which may be impossible to formulate in principle." Researchers in various laboratories experienced difficulties in developing their own working versions of the TEA laser from technical specifications and research articles. Their success in developing prototypes depended on the extent of their interaction with scientists who had tacit knowledge of the invention.

Inventors' *tacit knowledge* can make it difficult to separate discoveries from the individuals who make them. Although both inventors and adopters may *know that* a discovery has particular features, some inventors may *know how* to apply their discoveries better than do potential adopters. Inventors can benefit from their tacit knowledge by becoming innovative entrepreneurs who establish firms to implement their discoveries. However, entrepreneurship entails costs of setting up new firms and rent dissipation from competing with existing firms. Alternatively, inventors can transfer their discoveries to existing firms, but this entails costs of codifying, transferring, and absorbing tacit knowledge and imperfect implementation of discoveries.

Tacit knowledge thus creates a fundamental trade-off between own-use of discoveries by their inventors and adoption of discoveries by others. To address this trade-off, this chapter examines how inventors' tacit knowledge influences the choice between innovative entrepreneurship and technology transfer. The option of innovative entrepreneurship changes the market for discoveries and affects both inventors' investment in R&D and potential adopters' investment in absorption of discoveries.

The economic analysis of tacit knowledge highlights the important role of the individual inventor. The individual inventor's tacit knowledge is essential for implementing technology. Tacit knowledge gives an *own-use advantage* to inventors who become innovative entrepreneurs in comparison with technology transfer to existing firms. This contrasts with the standard view that complementary assets give existing firms an advantage in implementing technology.[1] Tacit knowledge creates problems for technology transfer that differ from the effects of adverse selection, moral hazard, and imperfect IP protections. Tacit knowledge affects incentives for endogenous investments in knowledge production and absorption and provides incentives for innovative entrepreneurship.

An inventor's own-use of tacit knowledge through entrepreneurship generates greater *marginal* returns than technology transfer to a monopolist even though the *total* returns to entrepreneurship can be either greater than or less than the total returns to technology transfer. The first reason for this is creative destruction; after entering the market, the new firm competes with the existing firm. By lowering costs, and thus lowering prices and raising output demanded by consumers, the new technology generates greater benefits for a competitive entrant than for a monopolist. The second reason is the problem of tacit knowledge; transferring the technology to an existing monopolist has a lower marginal return than own-use because the existing firm may not be fully successful in applying the new technology. Therefore, the marginal effects of creative destruction and transferring tacit knowledge reinforce each other. An inventor who anticipates entrepreneurship invests more in R&D than an inventor who anticipates technology transfer.

The analysis shows that tacit knowledge implies that higher-quality inventions result in entrepreneurship and lower-quality inventions result in technology transfer. Also, even though investments in R&D and absorptive capacity are complements in technology transfer, they can be strategic substitutes in the innovation game. An inventor who anticipates greater absorptive capacity reduces R&D effort, and an existing firm that anticipates more R&D investment reduces its absorption investment. Additionally, introducing the option of innovative entrepreneurship increases R&D investment and lowers absorption investment. Finally, the equilibrium probability of entrepreneurship is decreasing in the costs of R&D, increasing in the costs of technology transfer, and decreasing in the set-up costs of new firms. Also, because the inventor and the existing firm choose between cooperation and competition, the likelihood of technology transfer is correspondingly increasing in the costs of R&D, decreasing in the costs of technology transfer, and increasing in the set-up costs of new firms.

1 Teece (1986, 1988) shows that IP problems induce firms to internalize R&D and emphasizes the importance for technology transfer of the complementary assets of established firms, such as IP, human capital, marketing channels; see also Teece (2006). Gans and Stern (2003) provide a highly interesting and useful discussion of the market for ideas and the competitive interaction between start-up innovators and established firms. Their discussion does not address tacit knowledge.

The chapter is organized as follows. Section 7.1 presents a basic model of tacit knowledge in an innovation game with entrepreneurship and technology transfer. Section 7.2 characterizes the equilibrium of the innovation game with tacit knowledge. Section 7.3 extends the basic model of tacit knowledge to a market with differentiated produces. Section 7.4 considers some limitations and extensions of the present model.

7.1 An Innovation Game with Tacit Knowledge

By its very nature, tacit knowledge may not be transferable to others unless it is converted to explicit knowledge. Generating explicit knowledge on the basis of tacit knowledge entails various economic costs. An inventor seeking to transfer tacit knowledge must first attempt to codify the knowledge in explicit form, including written documents, technical descriptions, mathematics, diagrams, blueprints, computer code, and prototypes. Next, the individual seeking to transfer tacit knowledge must communicate with the receiver through messages, discussions, teaching, training, and other means. Finally, the receiver must devote time, effort, and resources to absorb the transferred knowledge, including R&D, management, and specialized equipment. Receiving tacit knowledge also entails explicit costs of education, training, consulting, scholarly publications, and information services. Taken together these costs represent *absorption investment.*

This section examines a three-stage model of strategic interaction between an inventor and an existing firm. In the first stage, the inventor chooses R&D investment, and an existing firm chooses investment in absorptive capacity. In the second stage, the inventor's discovery is realized and observed by both the inventor and the existing firm. The inventor and the existing firm choose whether to cooperate or to compete. If the inventor and the existing firm choose to cooperate, they form a contract to transfer the new technology from the inventor to the existing firm. If the inventor and the existing firm choose to compete, the inventor becomes an entrepreneur and establishes a firm. In the third stage, the market reaches equilibrium. If the inventor and the existing firm contracted to transfer technology, the existing firm operates as a monopolist using the new technology and observes its absorptive capacity. If the inventor and the existing firm did not choose to cooperate, the new firm established by the innovative entrepreneur enters the market and displaces the existing firm through competition.

The Inventor

Let $c_1 > 1$ represent the existing firm's initial production cost with the existing technology. An inventor invests z in uncertain R&D at a cost of kz. The new technology, c_2, is given by the knowledge production function,

$$c_2 = t(z, x), \tag{1}$$

which depends on R&D investment and a random variable, x.[2] The random variable x is an input to the knowledge production function that represents scientific and technological uncertainty. The random variable has a cumulative probability distribution $F(x)$ on the nonnegative real line, with nonnegative continuous density $f(x)$. The inventor's investment in R&D is chosen before the random variable is realized. Let $\partial t(z, x)/\partial z = t_z(z, x)$ and $\partial t(z, x)/\partial x = t_x(z, x)$.

The knowledge production function, $t(z, x)$, is normalized so that it takes values in $[0, 1]$ and is differentiable and decreasing in z and x. Let $t(z, 0) = 1$ for all z, and let unit costs approach zero as the R&D shock, x, becomes large, $\lim_{x\to\infty} t(z, x) = 0$. The ratio $\frac{t_z(z,x)}{t_x(z,x)}$ is the marginal rate of technical substitution (MRTS) of R&D investment, z, for the shock, x. This is the amount that R&D investment must be reduced given an increase in the shock for the resulting new technology, c_2, to be kept constant. The MRTS is increasing in the shock x if and only if R&D investment z is a normal input. Assume that R&D investment z is a normal input so that MRTS is increasing in the shock x.

We also assume that the product of the MRTS and the density function, $\frac{t_z(z,x)}{t_x(z,x)} f(x)$, is nondecreasing in x.[3] This assumption will be used to characterize the equilibrium. The assumption is satisfied if the density function $f(x)$ is increasing in x, constant in x, or otherwise does not decrease too rapidly for a given z – that is, $\frac{d \ln f(x)}{dx} \geq -\frac{\partial}{\partial x} \ln\left(\frac{t_z(z,x)}{t_x(z,x)}\right)$. This holds for commonly used probability distributions. For example, the density function is constant for the uniform distribution and increasing for the Pareto (or Power Law) distribution. The exponential distribution has a decreasing probability density, $f(x) = \lambda e^{-\lambda x}$, where $\lambda > 0$. Suppose for example that the production function has a normalized Cobb-Douglas form, $t(z, x) = (1 + z^{\gamma} x^{1-\gamma})^{-1}$, so that

$$\frac{\partial}{\partial x} \ln\left(\frac{t_z(z, x)}{t_x(z, x)}\right) = \frac{\partial}{\partial x} \ln\left(\frac{\gamma}{1-\gamma}\frac{x}{z}\right) = \frac{1}{x}.$$

Then, when the production function has the normalized Cobb-Douglas form, the exponential density function is well behaved if the parameter is not too large, $\lambda \geq 1/x$.[4]

Market demand for the final product, $D(p)$, is a twice continuously differentiable and decreasing function of the final product price, p. The profit of a monopoly firm with price p and costs c equals $\Pi(p, c) = (p - c)D(p)$. Assume that the profit function is concave in price. The profit-maximizing monopoly price, $p^M(c)$, is

2 On the knowledge production function, see Griliches (1979).

3 This property is related to the critical ratio, introduced by Poblete and Spulber (2012) in an agency setting, which is the product of the MRTS and the hazard rate of the shock.

4 Distributions that are not monotonic also satisfy the definition when they do not decrease too rapidly. For example, consider the truncated normal distribution defined for $x \geq 0$ with parameters μ and σ, and let the production be Cobb-Douglas. Then, the distribution is well behaved for x such that $(x - \mu)/\sigma^2 \leq 1/x$.

unique and increasing in cost c, and initial profits equal $\Pi^M(c) = \Pi(p^M(c), c)$. Monopoly profit is decreasing and convex in cost c, $\Pi^{M\prime}(c) = -D(p^M) < 0$ and $\Pi^{M\prime\prime}(c) = -D'(p^M)p^{M\prime}(c) > 0$.

The inventor can transfer the new technology to the existing firm or become an entrepreneur and apply the technology. If the inventor chooses to become an entrepreneur, the inventor has the tacit knowledge to successfully apply the new technology, c_2. To enter the product market, the inventor incurs entry costs, $K > 0$. The new firm enters the market and competes with the existing firm. The entrant and the incumbent offer homogeneous products and engage in Bertrand-Nash price competition. Entrepreneurship results in creative destruction – that is, the entrant displaces the incumbent, because $c_2 \leq 1 < c_1$.[5]

The invention is drastic if $p^M(c_2) \leq c_1$ and non-drastic if $p^M(c_2) > c_1$. The entrant's price equals $p^*(c_2, c_1) = \min\{p^M(c_2), c_1\}$. The entrepreneur's profits are written as $\Pi^E(c_2) = \Pi(p^*(c_2, c_1), c_2)$, suppressing the initial cost c_1. This represents dissipation of economic rents because of creative destruction.[6] The profits of the newly established firm equal the costs of a competitive entrant net of set-up costs, $\Pi^E(c_2) - K$.

Assume that very high realizations of the R&D shock generate drastic inventions, $p^M(0) < c_1$. Also, assume that very low realizations of the R&D shock generate non-drastic inventions, $p^M(1) > c_1$. This implies that the entrant earns lower profits than a monopolist using the new technology as a result of both entry costs and competition with the incumbent, $\Pi^E(1) - K < \Pi^M(1)$. To simplify the discussion, assume that entry is profitable with a non-drastic invention, $\Pi^E(1) - K > 0$. This allows the discussion to focus on the trade-off between entrepreneurship and technology transfer. Then, profit from innovative entrepreneurship equals

$$\pi^E(c_2) = \Pi^E(c_2) - K. \tag{2}$$

The entrepreneur's profit with a non-drastic invention, $\Pi^E(1) - K$, may be greater than or less than monopoly profits at the existing technology, $\Pi^M(c_1)$.

The Existing Firm

The inventor's *tacit knowledge* is the *know-how* needed to apply the new technology, c_2. This means that after R&D takes place, the new technology, c_2, is commonly observable but imperfectly transferable. The inventor and the existing firm are symmetrically informed about the quality of the new technology.

5 The results extend to Bertrand competition with differentiated products, where the entry of new firms reduces the profits of existing firms, but incumbent firms may survive.

6 If the invention is drastic, the entrant earns monopoly profits, $\Pi(p^*(c_2, c_1), c_2) = \Pi^M(c_2)$. If the invention is non-drastic, the entrant's profits are constrained by competition with the incumbent, $\Pi(p^*(c_2, c_1), c_2) < \Pi^M(c_2)$.

Although both the inventor and the existing firm *know that* the new technology is c_2, the existing firm does not have the *know-how* to apply the invention, so that technology transfer between the inventor and the existing firm is imperfect. The representation of tacit knowledge can be embedded in many different types of R&D models.

The existing firm invests b in building its *know-how* to improve the quality of technology transfer at a cost of hb. The existing firm's absorption rate is given by the production function

$$a = a(b, y), \tag{3}$$

where y is a random variable with cumulative probability distribution $G(y)$ on the nonnegative real line, with nonnegative and finite continuous density $g(y)$. The absorption rate $a(b, y)$ is nonnegative, differentiable and increasing in b and y, and $\int_0^\infty a(b, y)dG(y) < 1$. Some investment is necessary for absorption, $a(0, y) = 0$ for all y.

If the inventor transfers the technology to the existing firm, the transfer is imperfect because of tacit knowledge. The absorption rate determines the existing firm's costs after adopting the new technology,

$$c = a(b, y)c_2 + (1 - a(b, y))c_1. \tag{4}$$

The imperfect transfer of knowledge to the existing firm, $c > c_2$, is an *implicit* cost of transferring technology. The outcome of the game would not be affected by explicit costs, so such costs are normalized to zero without affecting the discussion.

The representation of imperfect knowledge transfers is very general. The knowledge transfer formulation is sufficiently general to include situations in which there is no uncertainty about the absorption rate and the transferred technology is simply of lower-quality than the discovery, $a(b, y) = a(b) < 1$ for all y.[7] Then, the existing firm can be viewed as choosing the quality of the technology that will be implemented. The formulation also includes situations in which the new technology is implemented by the existing firm with some probability of success, so that $a(b, y) = 1$ for $y \geq y(b)$ and $a(b, y) = 0$ otherwise. Then, the existing firm can be viewed as choosing the probability of successful technology transfer, $1 - F(y(b))$.[8]

7 The imperfect transmission of knowledge can be interpreted as an implicit cost in which only a fraction of tacit knowledge reaches its destination – that is, knowledge is lost in transmission. This corresponds to the representation of transportation costs in international trade as a reduction in the quantity or quality of the good being shipped. Transporting ice is costly because it melts away so that only a fraction of ice reaches its destination ("only a fraction of ice exported reaches its destination as unmelted ice," Samuelson (1954b, p. 268).

8 The analysis of tacit knowledge is related to some problems of imperfect knowledge transmission in organizations (Dewatripont, 2006; Dessein and Santos, 2006). A question in models of organization is whether tasks should be centralized or decentralized depending on the trade-off between imperfect coordination between two agents and the advantages of division of labor. This

The existing firm's absorption investment, b, is chosen before the new technology, c_2, is observed and before the shock, y, is realized. The existing firm does not observe the shock y until after the new technology is implemented. So, for any new technology, c_2, the existing firm's expected profits equal

$$\text{(5)} \qquad \pi^M(b, c_2) = \int_0^\infty \Pi^M[a(b, y)c_2 + (1 - a(b, y))c_1]dG(y).$$

Assume that at the best invention, $c_2 = 0$, monopoly profits net of entry costs exceed monopoly profits with technology transfer, $\Pi^M(0) - K > \pi^M(b, 0)$. Therefore, because $p^M(0) < c_1$ implies that $\Pi^E(0) = \Pi^M(0)$, the profits from innovative entry for sufficiently high realizations of x exceed monopoly profits at the existing technology, $\pi^E(0) > \pi^M(b, 0)$.

The Three-Stage Game

The time line for the three-stage game is as follows. At the start of stage one, the inventor chooses R&D investment, z, and the existing firm chooses absorption investment, b. Then, the new technology, $c_2 = t(z, x)$, is commonly observed at the end of the first stage. In the second stage, the inventor and the existing firm choose whether to compete or to cooperate through technology transfer. In the third stage of the game, if technology transfer occurs, the existing firm observes the absorption rate, $a(b, y)$, and engages in production. If entrepreneurship occurs, the new firm enters the market and competes with the existing firm.

Define the net return from the inventor's own-use of tacit knowledge through entrepreneurship,

$$\text{(6)} \qquad \Gamma(b, c_2) = \pi^E(c_2) - \pi^M(b, c_2).$$

This is the return to entrepreneurship using the new technology net of the return from technology transfer to the existing firm. The benefits of own-use of tacit knowledge are reduced by the costs of setting up a new firm and the rent dissipation from creative destruction. The returns to technology transfer are the opportunity cost of own-use of tacit knowledge. Increased investment in absorption by the existing firm increases the benefits of technology transfer and thus reduces the net return from own-use of tacit knowledge.

The inventor and the existing firm will choose to compete if and only if the net return from own-use of tacit knowledge is nonnegative, $\Gamma(b, c_2) \geq 0$. If the inventor

is related to our analysis in which the inventor and the existing firm choose whether to cooperate or to compete, depending on the trade-offs between knowledge transfer and own-use of knowledge. This allows the endogenous formation of organizations through the choice between contracts for technology transfer to the existing firm and the establishment of a new firm that competes with the existing firm. In the economics of organizations, for example, Dessein and Santos (2006) assume that an organization chooses the probability that a worker successfully learns a task from another worker, which they interpret as the quality of communication.

and the existing firm choose to compete, then (in the third stage) the inventor earns $\pi^E(c_2)$. The existing firm exits the market when products are homogeneous. The existing firm may continue to operate when products are differentiated as will be seen in a later section. If the inventor and the existing firm choose to cooperate, then in the third stage the inventor earns a royalty, R, and does not enter the market, and the existing firm applies the new technology and earns expected profits, $\pi^M(b, c_2) - R$. Any explicit technology transfer cost paid by the inventor would be equivalent to a reduction in the cost of establishing a firm. Suppose that T is an explicit transfer cost. Then, the inventor's net return is $R - T - (\Pi^E(c_2) - K) = R - [\Pi^E(c_2) - (K - T)]$. Therefore, T can be normalized to zero without any loss of generality.

The inventor and the existing firm bargain over the royalty payment for the new technology in the second stage.[9] R&D costs and knowledge transfer costs are sunk costs when bargaining occurs. Without loss of generality, suppose that the outcome of bargaining is given by Nash bargaining. The royalty, R, is contingent on the quality of the technology transfer. The inventor's threat point in bargaining equals postentry profits from entrepreneurship net of the costs of setting up a new firm. The existing firm's threat point equals zero because if the firm and the inventor do not cooperate, the inventor becomes an entrepreneur and establishes a new firm that displaces the existing firm. When products are differentiated, the postentry profits of the existing firm affect the royalty as will be shown in a later section. The investment costs of R&D and absorption do not affect the outcome of bargaining because investment decisions are made before bargaining takes place; hence, these costs are sunk. Therefore, for any new technology, c_2, the expected royalty is

$$R(b, c_2) = (1/2)\pi^M(b, c_2) + (1/2)\pi^E(c_2). \tag{7}$$

After technology transfer takes place, the existing firm's absorption rate $a(b, y)$ is realized, which determines the existing firm's costs and the royalty payment to the inventor.

In the first stage of the game, the inventor and the existing firm choose investment levels. The inventor and the existing firm play a noncooperative game because investments in R&D and in absorptive capacity are not contractible.[10] Denote the Nash equilibrium by (z^*, b^*). The inventor chooses R&D investment, z, to maximize expected profit,

$$\begin{aligned} z^* = \arg\max_z\{&E[\pi^E(c_2) \mid \pi^M(b^*, c_2) \leq \pi^E(c_2)] \\ &+ E[R(b^*, c_2) \mid \pi^M(b^*, c_2) > \pi^E(c_2)] - kz\}, \end{aligned} \tag{8}$$

9 The bargaining game between the inventor and the existing firm can be recast as an alternating offer bargaining game in which there is a unique subgame perfect equilibrium that depends on the discount factors of the two parties (Rubinstein, 1982).

10 Contracting problems have been widely studied in general settings. See Spulber (2002a, 2009a) for an overview and discussion, and see Grout (1984) and Grossman and Hart (1986) on incomplete contracting.

where $c_2 = t(z, x)$. The existing firm chooses absorption investment, b, to maximize expected profit,

$$(9)\quad b^* = \arg\max_b \left\{ E[\pi^M(b, c_2) - R(b, c_2) \mid \pi^M(b, c_2) > \pi^E(c_2)] - hb \right\},$$

where $c_2 = t(z^*, x)$ and expectations are taken over the R&D shock x.

7.2 Equilibrium of the Innovation Game with Tacit Knowledge

This section examines the equilibrium of the strategic innovation game. The equilibrium is fully described by R&D investment, z, and the absorption investment, b, which are determined in the first stage, and the choice between technology transfer and entrepreneurship in the second stage. The three-stage game is solved by backward induction. The third stage has already been fully described by the reduced-form profit and royalty functions.

The Choice between Competition and Cooperation

After the inventor chooses R&D investment, z, and the existing firm chooses absorption investment, b, the choice between cooperation and competition in the second stage depends on the realization of the shock, x. Recall that entrepreneurship occurs if and only if $\Gamma(b, c_2) \geq 0$. We now show that the marginal return to R&D is greater for an entrepreneurial firm than it is for an existing firm receiving a technology transfer. This means that regardless of whether applying tacit knowledge through entrepreneurship generates a net benefit or loss, the marginal net return to R&D investment, $(\partial / \partial z)\Gamma(b, c_2)$, is always positive.

We now establish a single-crossing condition that is useful for analyzing the equilibrium of the innovation game. *An increase in R&D investment increases the net return from own-use of tacit knowledge,*

$$(10)\quad \frac{\partial \Gamma(b, c_2)}{\partial z} = \Gamma_c(b, c_2) t_z(z, x) > 0.$$

For $\pi^E(c_2) > 0$,

$$(11)\quad \Gamma_c(b, c_2) = \left\{ \Pi^{E\prime}(c_2) - \int_0^{\infty} \Pi^{M\prime}[a(b, y)c_2 + (1 - a(b, y))c_1] a(b, y) dG(y) \right\}.$$

By the envelope theorem, $\Pi^{E\prime}(c_2) = -D(p^*(c_2, c_1))$ and $\Pi^{M\prime}(c) = -D(p^M(c))$. Because of imperfect transmission of tacit knowledge, it follows that $c \geq c_2$, where the inequality is strict for some values of y. Therefore, because the monopoly price is increasing in unit cost, $p^M(c) \geq p^M(c_2)$, and because of competition between the entrant and the incumbent, $p^M(c_2) \geq p^*(c_2, c_1)$. Downward-sloping demand implies that

$$D(p^M(c)) \leq D(p^*(c_2, c_1)).$$

It follows that $-\Pi^{M\prime}(c) \leq -\Pi^{E\prime}(c_2)$ and with a strict inequality for some values of y. Therefore,

$$\Gamma_c(b, c_2) \leq \Pi^{E\prime}(c_2)\left[1 - \int_0^\infty a(b, y)dG(y)\right] < 0,$$

so that $t_z(z, x) < 0$ implies $\Gamma_c(b, c_2)\, t_z\,(z, x) > 0$. Because the new technology, $t(z, x)$, is decreasing in the shock, x, it follows that an increase in the R&D shock x also increases the net returns from own-use of tacit knowledge, $(\partial / \partial x)\Gamma(b, c_2) = \Gamma_c(b, c_2)t_x(z, x) > 0$.

Competition and tacit knowledge both increase incentives for R&D investment. Competition increases R&D investment because the marginal benefit from R&D that reduces unit cost is proportional to market demand. This is because the firm's marginal profit from a cost reduction equals demand for the firm's output. Demand is greater under entrepreneurship than it is for an incumbent with technology transfer because the new firm competes with the incumbent firm, which strictly lowers prices when the invention is drastic in comparison to the incumbent's cost.

Tacit knowledge increases R&D investment because imperfect transfer of knowledge to the incumbent firm increases the costs of the existing firm in comparison with unit costs with own-use of new technology. This in turn increases the monopoly price charged by the existing firm in comparison with the monopoly price at the cost corresponding to own-use of the new technology. The higher price lowers the demand for the output of the existing firm in comparison with a monopolist with own-use of the new technology. With homogeneous products, competition increases the marginal return to cost reductions because of the price reduction effect.[11]

11 This contrasts with Vives' (2008) model in which the demand-reducing effect of entry outweighs the price-reducing effect of competition on output per firm. This means that competition reduces the marginal return to cost reduction. The result that an increase in R&D investment increases the net return from own-use of tacit knowledge does not depend on Bertrand competition with homogeneous products, as will be seen in the subsequent discussion of differentiated products competition. It is shown that even with differentiated products, and even if the entrant does not displace the incumbent, the price-reducing effect of competition on output per firm can outweigh the demand-reducing effect of entry. The option of entrepreneurship further distinguishes the present model from the R&D literature with differentiated products, as will be seen in a later section.

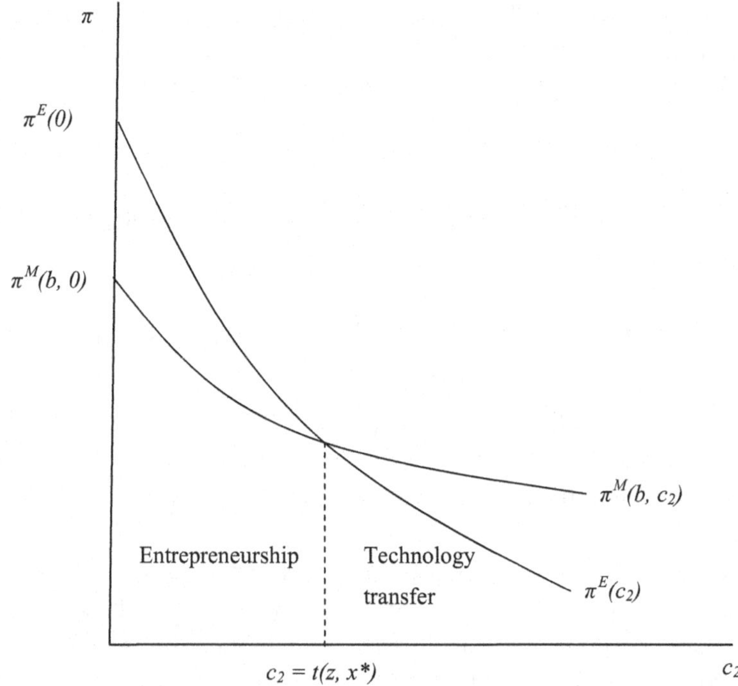

Figure 7.1. The critical value of the new technology determines whether the outcome of the innovation game is entrepreneurship or technology transfer.

The marginal returns to innovation are greater for the innovative entrepreneur than for the incumbent firm because the better is the entrant's technology, the less that competition with the incumbent firm dissipates economic rents.[12] This implies that the inventor's own-use of tacit knowledge generates greater marginal returns than a transfer of knowledge to the incumbent firm. Therefore, imperfect transfers of knowledge increase the difference in the marginal returns to innovation for the entrepreneur and the monopolist.

The single-crossing property is important for our analysis (see Figure 7.1). The derivative of the return to entrepreneurship, $\pi^E(c_2)$, with respect to the R&D shock, x, is greater than that of the return to technology transfer, $\pi^M(b, c_2)$, where both functions are increasing in the R&D shock. If $\pi^E(t(z, 0)) < \pi^M(b, t(z, 0))$, the curve representing $\pi^E(c_2)$ crosses the curve representing $\pi^M(b, c_2)$ at most once from above. By assumption, $\pi^E(0) > \pi^M(b, 0)$, so that the two curves cross at some x^*. At this critical value, the net return to own-use of tacit knowledge equals zero,

$$\Gamma(b, t(z, x^*)) = 0. \tag{12}$$

12 This extends Arrow's (1962b) result that downstream competition in the product market increases incentives to invent relative to those for monopolist – that is, $\Pi^M(c_2) - \Pi^M(c_1) \leq \Pi(p^*(c_2, c_1), c_2)$. The present result is at the margin rather than being a result of the monopolist's inertia.

The net return to own-use of tacit knowledge is such that $\Gamma(b, t(z, x)) > 0$ for $x > x^*$ and $\Gamma(b, t(z, x)) < 0$ for $x < x^*$. If, on the other hand, $\pi^E(t(z, 0)) \geq \pi^M(b, t(z, 0))$, let $x^*(b, z) = 0$. In this case, note that $\pi^E(c_2) \geq \pi^M(b, c_2)$ for all x.

There exists a unique critical value of the R&D shock, $x^*(b, z)$, that is finite and nonnegative for any b and z.[13] *The net return to own-use of tacit knowledge, $\Gamma(b, t(z, x^*))$, equals zero if $x^*(b, z)$ is positive and is positive if $x^*(b, z) = 0$. Entrepreneurship occurs if and only if $x \geq x^*(b, z)$.*

The single-crossing property has the following implication. With tacit knowledge, inventors with higher-quality inventions, $x \geq x^*(b, z)$, become entrepreneurs and inventors with lower-quality inventions, $x < x^*(b, a)$, transfer their technology to the existing firm. We can characterize the properties of the critical value of the R&D shock. When the critical value of the shock has an interior solution, equations (10) and (11) imply the following. The critical value is decreasing in R&D investment, and the change in the critical value is -1 times the MRTS,

$$\frac{\partial x^*(b, z)}{\partial z} = -\frac{t_z(z, x^*)}{t_x(z, x^*)} < 0.$$

The critical value is increasing in absorption investment,

$$\frac{\partial x^*(b, z)}{\partial b} = \frac{\pi_b^M(b, c_2)}{\Gamma_c(b, c_2)t_x(z, x^*)} > 0.^{14}$$

Also, the critical value is increasing in the entrepreneur's set-up costs, K,

$$\frac{\partial x^*(b, z)}{\partial K} = \frac{1}{\Gamma_c(b, c_2)t_x(z, x^*)} > 0.$$

Strategic Investment in R&D and in Absorption

This section characterizes the first stage of the strategic innovation game. To establish some benchmarks, define the R&D investment of an inventor who expects with certainty to become an entrepreneur,

$$z^E = \arg\max_z \mathrm{E}\Pi^E(c_2) - kz.$$

If the existing firm expects entrepreneurship with certainty, the firm will not invest in absorption, $b^E = 0$. Also, define the R&D investment of an innovative monopoly firm,

$$z^M = \arg\max_z \mathrm{E}\Pi^M(c_2) - kz.$$

13 This follows by continuity and the intermediate value theorem.

14 From equation (5), the marginal expected profit of absorption investment for the monopolist receiving the transfer is positive,

$$\pi_b^M(b, c_2) = \int_0^\infty \Pi^{M\prime}[a(b, y)c_2 + (1 - a(b, y))c_1]a_b(b, y)dG(y)(c_2 - c_1) > 0.$$

Finally, define the Nash equilibrium R&D investment and absorption investment when the inventor and the existing firm expect technology transfer with certainty,

$$z^T = \arg\max_z \mathrm{E}R(b^T, t(z, x)) - kz,$$
$$b^T = \arg\max_b \mathrm{E}[\pi^M(b, t(z^T, x)) - R(b, t(z^T, x))] - hb.$$

When technology transfer occurs with certainty, R&D investment, z, and absorption investment, b, are *strategic complements*,

$$\frac{\partial^2}{\partial b \partial z}\left[\int_0^\infty R(b, c_2) dF(x) - kz\right] > 0,$$

$$\frac{\partial^2}{\partial b \partial z}\left[-(1/2)\int_0^\infty \Gamma(b, c_2) dF(x) - hb\right] > 0.$$

R&D investment induces more investment in absorptive capacity and vice versa. This is because R&D investment and absorption investment are complements in technology transfer, $\pi_{bc}^M(b, c_2) t_z(z, x) > 0$.[15]

The expected marginal return to R&D effort is greater for the innovative entrepreneur than that for either the inventor expecting to transfer the technology or the innovative monopolist. *An innovative entrepreneur chooses more R&D investment than an inventor expecting technology transfer, $z^E \geq z^T$, and more R&D investment than a monopoly firm, $z^E \geq z^M$.*

This holds because

$$\frac{d}{dz}[\pi^E(c_2) - R(b, c_2)] = \frac{1}{2}\frac{d\Gamma(b, c_2)}{dz} > 0,$$

so that $z^E \geq z^T$, for all b. By similar arguments,

$$\frac{d}{dz}[\pi^E(c_2) - \Pi^M(c_2)] > 0,$$

so that $z^E \geq z^M$.

Given the critical value of the shock $x^*(b, z)$ and the form of the royalty, we can characterize the objective functions for the inventor and the existing firm. The expected net benefits of the inventor and the existing firm are

$$U(b, z) = \int_0^{x^*(b,z)} R(b, c_2) dF(x) + \int_{x^*(b,z)}^\infty \pi^E(c_2) dF(x) - kz, \tag{13}$$

$$V(b, z) = \int_0^{x^*(b,z)} [\pi^M(b, c_2) - R(b, c_2)] dF(x) - hb, \tag{14}$$

15 Absorption investment and unit costs are substitutes for the existing firm, $\pi_{bc}^M(b, c_2) = \int_0^\infty \{\Pi^M[a(b, y)c_2 + (1 - a(b, y))c_1] a(b, y) a_b(b, y) dG(y)(c_2 - c_1) + \frac{\pi_b^M(b, c_2)}{(c_2 - c_1)} < 0$. This expression is less than zero because profit is convex in costs and $c_2 < c_1$.

where $c_2 = t(z, x)$. Substituting for the royalty function, the expected net benefits of the inventor and the existing firm can be written using the net return from own-use of tacit knowledge,

$$U(b, z) = -(1/2)\int_0^{x^*(b,z)} \Gamma(b, c_2)dF(x) + \int_0^{\infty} \pi^E(c_2)dF(x) - kz, \tag{15}$$

$$V(b, z) = -(1/2)\int_0^{x^*(b,z)} \Gamma(b, c_2)dF(x) - hb, \tag{16}$$

where $c_2 = t(z, x)$.

Using the form of the critical value of the shock, the marginal returns to R&D investment and to absorption investment are

$$\begin{aligned} U_z(b, z) = &\int_0^{\infty} \pi^{E\prime}(c_2)t_z(z, x)dF(x) \\ &- (1/2)\int_0^{x^*(b,z)} \Gamma_c(b, c_2)t_z(z, x)dF(x) - k, \end{aligned} \tag{17}$$

$$V_b(b, z) = (1/2)\int_0^{x^*(b,z)} \pi_b^M(b, c_2)dF(x) - h. \tag{18}$$

The inventor chooses R&D effort in equilibrium that is less than or equal to the effort chosen by an inventor who anticipates entrepreneurship with certainty. Clearly, if technology transfer cannot occur in equilibrium, the incumbent firm does not invest in absorption, $b^* = 0$, and the inventor invests in R&D in anticipation of becoming an entrepreneur, $z^* = z^E$. Entrepreneurship always occurs in equilibrium, $x^* = 0$, if and only if $\Pi^M(c_1) \leq \Pi^E(1) - K$.

Conversely, the necessary and sufficient condition for both entrepreneurship and technology transfer to be possible in equilibrium, $x^* > 0$, is that monopoly profit at the existing technology is greater than to the return to entrepreneurship at the lowest realization of the shock, $\Pi^M(c_1) > \Pi^E(1) - K$. Then, *the Nash equilibrium R&D investment and absorption investment are such that* $z^* \leq z^E$ *and* $b^* >$ 0. We now restrict attention to the situation in which both entrepreneurship and technology transfer can occur in equilibrium.

When the inventor has the option of applying tacit knowledge through entrepreneurship, R&D investment and absorption investment can be *strategic substitutes.* The intuition for this result is that in the innovative game with tacit knowledge, R&D investment and absorption investment affect the relative likelihood of technology transfer versus entrepreneurship. Therefore, the option of entrepreneurship changes the technology transfer game, so that the inventor invests *less* in R&D when expecting a higher absorption investment, and the existing firm invests *less* in absorption when expecting a higher R&D investment.

If $f(x)$ is well behaved on $[0, x^*(b, z)]$ for all z and b, then R&D investment, z, and absorption investment, b, are strategic substitutes, $U_{zb}(b, z) = V_{zb}(b, z) < 0$

for all z and b.[16] First, consider the inventor's net benefit. From equation (13) and the royalty function, we have

$$U(b, z) = \int_0^\infty R(b, c_2)dF(x) + (1/2)\int_{x^*(b,z)}^\infty \Gamma(b, c_2)dF(x) - kz.$$

The marginal returns to R&D investment are

$$U_z(b, z) = \frac{\partial}{\partial z}\int_0^\infty R(b, c_2)dF(x) + (1/2)\int_{x^*(b,z)}^\infty \Gamma_c(b, c_2)t_z(z, x)dF(x) - k.$$

Because the marginal net benefits of R&D investment for own-use of tacit knowledge by the innovative entrepreneur are positive for $x > x^*$, it follows that $U_z(b, z) > \frac{\partial}{\partial z}\int_0^\infty R(b, c_2)dF(x) - k$. This implies that the reaction function is greater than that with certain technology transfer, $z^*(b) > z^T(b)$, for any b.

The analysis of the incumbent firm's net benefit is similar. From equation (14),

$$V(b, z) = \int_0^\infty [\pi^M(b, c_2) - R(b, c_2)]dF(x) - \int_{x^*(b,z)}^\infty [\pi^M(b, c_2) - R(b, c_2)]dF(x) - hb.$$

The marginal returns to absorption investment are

$$V_b(b, z) = \frac{\partial}{\partial b}\int_0^\infty [\pi^M(b, c_2) - R(b, c_2)]dF(x) - (1/2)\int_{x^*(b,z)}^\infty \pi_b^M(b, c_2)dF(x) - h.$$

Because $\pi_b^M b, c_2) > 0$, it follows that $V_b(b, z) < \frac{\partial}{\partial b}\int_0^\infty [\pi^M(b, c_2) - R(b, c_2)] dF(x) - h$. This implies that the reaction function is less than that with certain technology transfer, $b^*(z) < b^T(z)$, for any z. With strategic complements (substitutes), the reaction functions are increasing (decreasing).

16 Find the cross-partial derivatives and note that $U_{zb}(b, z) = V_{zb}(b, z)$, so that it is sufficient to consider only $U_{zb}(b, z)$. Substituting for $\partial x^*/\partial z$ and $\partial x^*/\partial b$ and rearranging terms, the expression for $U_{zb}(b, z)$ can be written as follows:

$$U_{zb}(b, z) = (1/2)\left[\int_0^{x^*(b,z)} \pi_{bc}^M(b, t(z, x))t_x(z, x)\frac{t_z(z, x)}{t_x(z, x)} f(x)dx - \pi_b^M(b, t(z, x^*))\frac{t_z(z, x^*)}{t_x(z, x^*)} f(x^*)\right].$$

If the product of the MRTS of the knowledge production function and the density function are constant in x for x in $[0, x^*]$, then $U_{zb}(b, z) = -(1/2)\frac{t_z(z,x^*)}{t_x(z,x^*)} f(x^*)\pi_b^M(b, t(\theta, 0)) < 0$. If the product of the MRTS of the knowledge production function and the density function are increasing in x for x in $[0, x^*]$, then $U_{zb}(b, \theta) < -(1/2)\frac{t_z(z,x^*)}{t_x(z,x^*)} f(x^*)\pi_b^M(b, t(\theta, 0)) < 0$. Therefore, $U_{zb}(b, z) < 0$ when $\frac{t_z(z,x)}{t_x(z,x)} f(x)$ is increasing in x.

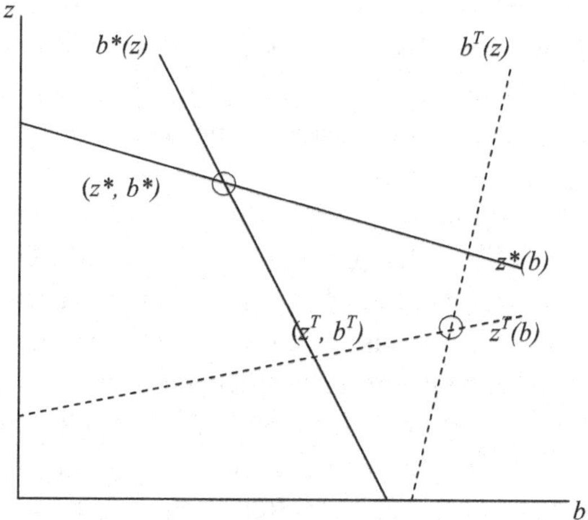

Figure 7.2. Comparison of the Nash equilibrium of the investment game when the inventor has the option of entrepreneurship, (z*, b*), with the Nash equilibrium of the investment game with certain technology transfer, (z^T, b^T).

Therefore, comparing the reaction functions when there is the option of entrepreneurship with the reaction functions when technology transfer is certain implies that R&D investment is greater than with certain technology transfer, $z^* > z^T$, and absorption investment is lower than with certain technology transfer, $b^* < b^T$. See Figure 7.2. The intuition for this result is as follows. The inventor invests more in R&D in anticipation of possibly using that knowledge as an entrepreneur because of higher marginal returns to invention under competition and because own-use avoids imperfect knowledge transfers. The existing firm invests less in absorption than with certain technology transfer because of the substitution effect of higher R&D investment by the inventor if the technology is transferred and the possibility that the technology will not be transferred.

We now characterize the Nash equilibrium of the innovation game. There may be multiple Nash equilibria, and there exist smallest and largest pure Nash equilibria.[17] In what follows, a Nash equilibrium (z^*, b^*) refers to both the smallest and the largest Nash equilibria, $(z_L{}^*, b_L{}^*)$ and $(z_H{}^*, b_H{}^*)$, where $z_L{}^* \geq z_H{}^*$ and $b_L{}^* \leq b_H{}^*$.

The costs of R&D investment and absorptive investment have opposite effects on equilibrium strategies. Equilibrium R&D investment, z^*, is decreasing in

17 The game in investment strategies satisfies the conditions for a smooth supermodular game (Milgrom and Roberts, 1990, 1994; Topkis, 1998). Letting $Z = -z$, we can define the objective functions $u(b, Z) = U(b, -Z)$ and $v(b, Z) = V(b, -Z)$. The strategies Z and b take values in compact intervals on the real line $[-z^E, 0]$ and $[0, b^T]$, respectively. The objective functions $u(b, Z)$ and $v(b, Z)$ are twice continuously differentiable. The strategies Z and b are complements, $u_{Zb}(b, Z) = v_{zb}(b, Z) > 0$, for all Z and b. Then, using Milgrom and Roberts (1990b, Theorem 5), there exist smallest and largest pure Nash equilibria, $(Z_L{}^*, b_L{}^*)$ and $(Z_H{}^*, b_H{}^*)$. Letting $Z_L{}^* = -z_L{}^*$ and $Z_H{}^* = -z_H{}^*$, note that $z_L{}^* \geq z_H{}^*$ and $b_L{}^* \leq b_H{}^*$.

the costs of R&D, k, and increasing in the costs of absorption investment, h. Equilibrium absorption investment, b^*, is increasing in the costs of R&D, k, and decreasing in the costs of technology transfer, h. Also, the probability of entrepreneurship, $1 - F(x^*)$, is decreasing in the costs of R&D, k, and increasing in the costs of absorption investment, h.[18]

The costs of R&D and the costs of absorptive effort affect the critical value of the shock only indirectly through equilibrium strategies. More costly R&D, which directly affects the production of knowledge, makes entrepreneurship less likely by reducing the net returns to own-use as well as technology transfer. More costly absorptive effort, which directly affects knowledge transfers, makes entrepreneurship more likely. When investments in R&D and absorption are strategic substitutes, the costs of setting up a new firm affect R&D investment and absorption investment in opposite ways. Equilibrium R&D investment, z^*, is decreasing in the set-up costs of a new firm, K, and the equilibrium absorption investment, b^*, is increasing in the set-up costs of a new firm, K. Also, when x^* is interior, the probability of entrepreneurship, $1 - F(x^*)$, is decreasing in the set-up costs of a new firm, K.[19]

The costs of setting up a firm increase R&D investment because of the returns to own-use of tacit knowledge but decrease absorption investment, in part because R&D investment and absorption investment are strategic substitutes. Set-up costs increase the critical level of the shock both directly and indirectly by affecting equilibrium strategies, thus reducing the likelihood of entrepreneurship. The set-up

18 From the objective functions $u(b, Z)$ and $v(b, Z)$, we obtain $u_{Zk}(b, Z) = 1$ and $v_{bk}(b, Z) = 0$. Then, applying Milgrom and Roberts (1990b, Theorem 6) implies the strategies (b, Z) at the smallest, and the largest Nash equilibria are increasing in k. This implies that $b_L{}^*$ and $b_H{}^*$ are increasing in k, and $z_L{}^*$ and $z_H{}^*$ are decreasing in k. Also, note that $u_{Zh}(b, Z) = 0$ and $v_{bh}(b, Z) = -1$. Then, $b_L{}^*$ and $b_H{}^*$ are decreasing in h, and $z_L{}^*$ and $z_H{}^*$ are increasing in k. Recall that $\partial x^*/\partial z < 0$ and $\partial x^*/\partial b > 0$. These results further imply that

$$\frac{dx^*}{dk} = \frac{\partial x^*}{\partial z}\frac{\partial z^*}{\partial k} + \frac{\partial x^*}{\partial b}\frac{\partial b^*}{\partial k} > 0, \qquad \frac{dx^*}{dh} = \frac{\partial x^*}{\partial z}\frac{\partial z^*}{\partial h} + \frac{\partial x^*}{\partial b}\frac{\partial b^*}{\partial h} < 0.$$

The results on the probability of entrepreneurship follow because $1 - F(x^*)$ is decreasing in x^*.

19 Differentiate equations (17) and (18) with respect to K,

$$U_{zK}(b, z) = -(1/2)\Gamma_c(b, c_2)t_z(z, x^*)\, f(x^*)\frac{\partial x^*(b, z)}{\partial K},$$

$$V_{bK}(b, z) = (1/2)\pi_b^M(b, c_2)\, f(x^*)\frac{\partial x^*(b, z)}{\partial K},$$

where $c_2 = t(z, x^*)$. Recall that $\partial x^*/\partial K > 0$, so that $U_{zK}(b, z) < 0$ and $V_{bK}(b, z) > 0$. Therefore, $u_{ZK}(b, Z) > 0$ and $v_{bK}(b, Z) > 0$. Using Milgrom and Roberts (1990b, Theorem 6), this implies that $b_L{}^*$ and $b_H{}^*$ are increasing in K, and $z_L{}^*$ and $z_H{}^*$ are decreasing in K. Recalling $\partial x^*/\partial z < 0$ and $\partial x^*/\partial b > 0$, this implies that

$$\frac{dx^*(b^*, z^*)}{dK} = \frac{\partial x^*(b^*, z^*)}{\partial K} + \frac{\partial x^*(b^*, z^*)}{\partial z}\frac{\partial z^*}{\partial K} + \frac{\partial x^*(b^*, z^*)}{\partial b}\frac{\partial b^*}{\partial K} > 0.$$

The set-up cost, K, decreases the entrepreneurship probability because $1 - F(x^*)$ is decreasing in x^*.

costs of new firms are likely to vary across industries. This helps explain variations across industries of the proportion of inventors transferring technology versus becoming entrepreneurs (see Jensen and Thursby, 2001, and Zucker, Darby, and Torero, 2002).

The discussion thus far has not considered R&D by the incumbent firm. Suppose that the incumbent firm can conduct R&D to reduce its costs c_1 prior to the start of the strategic game, and suppose that the independent inventor then improves on the incumbent's technology, $c_1 > c_2$. It can be shown that the net return from own-use of tacit knowledge is increasing in the incumbent's initial cost,

$$\frac{\partial \Gamma(b, c_2)}{\partial c_1} = \frac{\partial \pi^E(c_2)}{\partial c_1} - \frac{\partial \pi^M(b, c_2)}{\partial c_1} > 0.$$

This is because the entrepreneur's profit $\pi^E(c_2)$ is increasing in the incumbent's initial cost when the independent inventor makes a non-drastic invention and otherwise does not depend on the incumbent's initial cost. Also, the return from technology transfer, $\pi^M(b, c_2)$, is increasing in the incumbent's initial cost. It follows that incumbent R&D to lower costs c_1 reduces the net return from own-use of tacit knowledge by the independent inventor and raises the critical value of the R&D shock,

$$\frac{\partial x^*(b, z)}{\partial c_1} = -\frac{\partial \Gamma(b, c_2)}{\partial c_1} \frac{1}{\Gamma_c(b, c_2) t_x(z, x^*)} < 0.$$

Incumbent R&D to lower costs c_1 thus reduces the likelihood of entrepreneurship for given investment levels by increasing the critical value, x^*. Incumbent R&D to lower costs c_1 would increase the R&D investment of an inventor anticipating entrepreneurship because $\frac{\partial^2 E\pi^E(c_2)}{\partial c_1 \partial z} < 0$. The effects of the lower costs c_1 on the inventor's equilibrium R&D and the incumbent firm's absorption investment are indeterminate.

7.3 The Tacit Knowledge Innovation Game with Product Differentiation

Consider the problem of tacit knowledge with product differentiation. Market demand is derived from the preferences of a representative consumer with quadratic utility,

$$U(q_1, q_2; b) = 2q_1 + 2q_2 - \frac{1}{2}(q_1)^2 - \frac{1}{2}(q_2)^2 - sq_1q_2, \tag{19}$$

where the substitution parameter s is such that $0 \leq s < 1$. The existing firm supplies good q_1 at price p_1 and the entrant supplies good q_2 at price p_2. The demand functions are $D_i(p_1, p_2)$, $i = 1, 2$. The analysis of the Bertrand-Nash equilibrium in this section draws on Zanchettin (2006).[20] Assume that the incumbent monopolist is viable with the initial technology, $c_1 < 2$, so the monopolist also is viable with the new technology.[21] We maintain all of the earlier assumptions for the monopoly case.[22]

Let $\Pi_1(c_1, c_2)$ represent the incumbent's profits after entry occurs, and let $\Pi_2(c_1, c_2)$ represent the entrant's profits. The incumbent firm and the entrepreneurial entrant engage in Bertrand-Nash price competition with differentiated products. The Bertrand-Nash equilibrium prices $p_1{}^*$ and $p_2{}^*$ solve

$$(20) \qquad \Pi_1(c_1, c_2) = \max_{p_1}(p_1 - c_1)D_1(p_1, p_2{}^*),$$

$$(21) \qquad \Pi_2(c_1, c_2) = \max_{p_2}(p_2 - c_2)D_2(p_1{}^*, p_2).$$

The equilibrium prices depend on the costs of the two firms and the product differentiation parameter, $p_1{}^*(c_1, c_2)$ and $p_2{}^*(c_1, c_2)$.

The entrepreneur's return from entering the market equals $\pi^E(c_2) = \Pi_2(c_1, c_2) - K$. The existing firm's return from adopting the technology is monopoly profits from technology transfer net of postentry profits with entry, $\pi^M(b, c_2) - \Pi_1(c_1, c_2)$. With product differentiation, the net return from the inventor's own-use of tacit knowledge through entrepreneurship equals

$$(22) \qquad \Gamma(b, c_2) = \Pi_2(c_1, c_2) - K - [\pi^M(b, c_2) - \Pi_1(c_1, c_2)].$$

Therefore, the net return from the inventor's own-use of tacit knowledge through entrepreneurship equals the difference between industry profits after entry and the existing firm's profits with technology transfer,

$$(23) \qquad \Gamma(b, c_2) = \Pi_1(c_1, c_2) + \Pi_2(c_1, c_2) - K - \pi^M(b, c_2).$$

Entrepreneurship occurs if and only if the net return to own-use is nonnegative, $\Gamma(b, c_2) \geq 0$.

The intensity of product-market competition depends positively on the substitution parameter s and on the new and existing technologies. The industry profits function, $\Pi_1(c_1, c_2) + \Pi_2(c_1, c_2)$, is continuous in the substitution parameter, s,

20 Although we focus on the quadratic utility case, the properties of the profit and price functions hold more generally. For additional discussion of the class of utility functions that yield similar properties for comparative statics analysis of a duopoly equilibrium, see Milgrom and Roberts (1990b). For differentiated duopoly with symmetric costs, see Singh and Vives (1984), and for differentiated duopoly with asymmetric costs and qualities, see Zanchettin (2006). The analysis can be extended to other differentiated product settings such as Hotelling-type (1929) price competition. The results also can be examined with Cournot quantity competition with differentiated products.

21 To derive the existing firm's monopoly profit, let $q_2 = 0$. The representative consumer's utility function implies that $U(q_1, 0) = 2q_1 - (1/2)(q_1)^2$. The consumer's demand for the incumbent's product is $D_1\,(p_1) = 2 - p_1$. The monopoly price is $p^M(c) = (2 + c)/2$, and monopoly profit equals $\Pi^M(c) = (p^M(c) - c)\, D_1\,(p^M(c)) = (2 - c)^{2/4}$.

22 Recall that $\Pi^M(0) - K > \pi^M\,(b, 0)$ and $\Pi^E(1) - K > 0$. Note that $p^M(0) < c_1$ holds because $p^M(0) = 1$. The assumption $p^M(1) > c_1$ requires $c_1 < 3/2$.

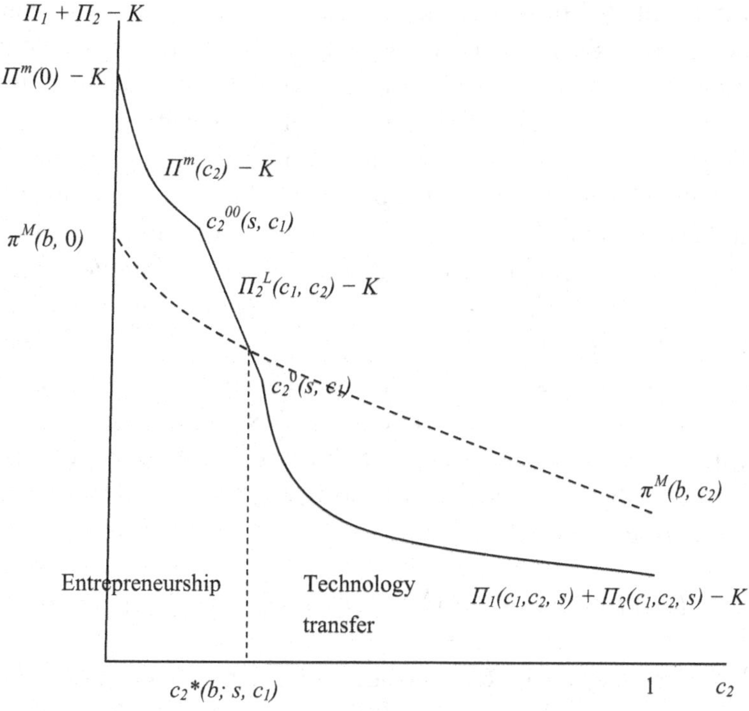

Figure 7.3. The outcome of the innovation game is entrepreneurship for low-quality inventions, high-quality inventions, $c_2 \leq c_2{}^*(c_1, b)$, and the outcome is technology transfer for lower-quality inventions, $c_2{}^*(c_1, b) < c_2$.

and is continuous and decreasing in the entrant's costs, c_2. The industry profit function has three segments corresponding to the profits of a duopoly, a limit-pricing entrant, and a monopoly-pricing entrant (see Figure 7.3). Industry profits are convex in c_2 for the duopoly, linear for the limit-pricing entrant, and convex for the monopoly-pricing entrant.

First, when the entrant's costs are not too low, $c_2 > c_2{}^0(s, c_1)$, both the entrant and the incumbent operate profitably. The entrant's cost threshold is obtained by setting $q_1 = 0$,

$$(24) \qquad c_2{}^0(s, c_1) = 2 - \frac{(2 - s^2)(2 - c_1)}{s} < c_1.$$

Second, if the entrant's costs are in an intermediate range, $c_2{}^{00}(s, c_1) < c_2 \leq c_2{}^0(s, c_1)$, the entrant drives out the incumbent firm with limit pricing and obtains profits, $\Pi_2^L(c_1, c_2) = (1/s^2)(2 - c_1)[s(2 - c_2) - (2 - c_1)]$. Third, if the entrant's costs are low, $c_2 \leq c_2{}^{00}(s, c_1)$, the entrepreneurial entrant drives out the incumbent by offering a monopoly price, $p^M(c_2) = (2 + c_2)/2$, and earns monopoly profits, $\Pi^M(c_2) = (2 - c_2)^2/4$. The lower cost threshold exists only if $c_1 + s > 2$,

$$(25) \qquad c_2{}^{00}(s, c_1) = \frac{2(c_1 + s - 2)}{s} < c_2{}^0(s, c_1).$$

This defines a *drastic invention* when products are differentiated.

With differentiated products, the marginal return to R&D is greater for an entrepreneurial firm than it is for an existing firm receiving a technology transfer under some conditions. This result is analogous to the situation with homogeneous products. If the new technology is of sufficiently high quality, $c_2 \leq c_2{}^0(s, c_1)$, the entrant displaces the existing firm either through monopoly pricing or through limit pricing. Then, the price-reducing effect of competition outweighs the demand-reducing effect of competition on output per firm so that competition increases incentives for R&D. *So, with differentiated products, an increase in R&D investment increases the net return from own-use of tacit knowledge,* $\frac{\partial \Gamma(b,c_2)}{\partial z} = \Gamma_c(b, c_2)t_z(z, x) > 0$.[23]

If the new technology is of sufficiently low quality, $c_2 > c_2{}^0(s, c_1)$, then both the entrant and the incumbent operate after entry takes place. The demand-reducing effect of entry tends to outweigh the price-reducing effect of competition on output per firm, which reduces marginal returns to cost-reducing R&D. However, if the absorption rate is low,

$$\int_0^\infty a(b, y)dG(y) < -(1/\Pi^{M\prime}(c_2))\partial(\Pi_1(c_1, c_2) + \Pi_2(c_1, c_2))/\partial c_2,$$

then, as before, an increase in R&D investment increases the net return from own-use of tacit knowledge. When both firms can operate profitably after entry, an improvement in the new technology – that is, a lower c_2 – increases the entrant's profit but decreases the postentry profit of the incumbent firm. Increasing the incumbent's profit raises the net benefit from technology adoption and correspondingly reduces the net return to own-use of tacit knowledge, which is the sum of industry profits net of the profits from technology adoption. In this case, postentry competition provides a disincentive to R&D. However, this is offset because of imperfect transmission of tacit knowledge.[24]

Vives (2008) shows that entry reduces output per firm because the demand-reducing effect of entry outweighs the price-reducing effect of competition on output per firm when all firms operate in equilibrium, thus reducing each firm's

23 By the envelope theorem, $\Pi^{L\prime}(c_2) = -D(p_2{}^L(c_1, c_2))$ and $\Pi^{M\prime}(c) = -D(p^M(c))$. Because of imperfect transmission of tacit knowledge, it follows that $c \geq c_2$, where the inequality is strict for some values of y. Therefore, $p^M(c) \geq p^M(c_2)$ so that $p^M(c_2) > p_2{}^L(c_1, c_2)$ implies that $p^M(c) > p_2{}^L(c_1, c_2)$. Because demand is downward sloping, it follows that $D(p^M(c)) < D(p_2{}^L(c_1, c_2))$ and therefore $-\Pi^{M\prime}(c) \leq -\Pi^{L\prime}(c_2)$ and strictly greater for some values of y. This implies that

$$\Gamma_c(b, c_2) \leq \Pi^{L\prime}(c_2)\left[1 - \int_0^\infty a(b, y)dG(y)\right] < 0$$

so that $t_z(z, x) < 0$ implies $\Gamma_c(b, c_2)t_z(z, x) > 0$.

24 Because $-\Pi^{M\prime}(c) \leq -\Pi^{M\prime}(c_2)$, it follows that

$$\Gamma_c(b, c_2) \leq \frac{\partial(\Pi_1(c_1, c_2) + \Pi_2(c_1, c_2))}{\partial c_2} - \Pi^{M\prime}(c_2)\int_0^\infty a(b, y)dG(y)] < 0.$$

Therefore, $\frac{\partial \Gamma(b,c_2)}{\partial z} = \Gamma_c(b, c_2)t_z(z, x) > 0$.

incentives for cost-reducing R&D. Here, competition increases incentives to innovate because the entrant has a greater output than an incumbent monopolist when the entrant displaces the incumbent,

$$z^E = \arg\max_z E\Pi_2(c_1, c_2) - K - kz \geq z^M.$$

Conversely, when both the entrant and the incumbent operate after entry, competition decreases incentives for R&D for the potential entrant in comparison with an incumbent monopolist when $-\partial\Pi_2(c_1, c_2)/\partial c_2 < -\Pi^{M\prime}(c_2)$, which implies that $z^E < z^M$. The incumbent does not conduct R&D in the present model. Investment in R&D by the incumbent would further reduce the entrant's incentives for R&D because $-\partial^2\Pi_2(c_1, c_2)/\partial c_1 \partial c_2 > 0$, so that reducing the incumbent's costs decreases the marginal returns to R&D for the entrant.

Consider now the outcome of the innovation game. We consider the situation in which industry profits with entry exceed the incumbent's profits with technology transfer, evaluating both at the lowest-quality invention. We obtain a single-crossing condition that corresponds to the situation with homogeneous products. *With differentiated products, if* $\Pi_1(c_1, 1) + \Pi_2(c_1, 1) - K \leq \pi^M(b, 1)$, *there exists a unique critical value of the R&D shock,* $x^*(b, z)$, *that is finite and nonnegative for any* b *and* z. The net return to own-use of tacit knowledge, $\Gamma(b, t(z, x^*))$, equals zero if $x^*(b, z)$ is positive and is positive if $x^*(b, z) = 0$. Entrepreneurship occurs if and only if $x \geq x^*(b, z)$.

Recall the earlier assumption that $\Pi^m(0) - K > \pi^M(b, 0)$. Then, $\Pi_1(c_1, 1) + \Pi_2(c_1, 1) - K \leq \pi^M(b, 1)$ implies that the curve representing the industry profits function, $\Pi_1(c_1, c_2) + \Pi_2(c_1, c_2) - K$, crosses the curve representing the incumbent's profit function, $\pi^M(b, c_2)$, exactly once from above at $c_2 = c_2^*(b; s, c_1)$ (see Figure 7.3). This corresponds to the situation with homogenous products, as illustrated by Figure 7.1. There is a critical value of the R&D shock, $x^* = x^*(b, z)$ that solves $t(z, x^*) = c_2^*(b; s, c_1)$. It follows that the net return to the inventor's own-use of tacit knowledge, $\Gamma(b, c_2)$, equals zero at x^*, and entrepreneurship occurs when the R&D shock is greater than or equal to x^*.

Consider now the situation in which industry profits with entry are greater than the incumbent's profits with technology transfer, evaluating both at the lowest-quality invention, $\Pi_1(c_1, 1) + \Pi_2(c_1, 1) - K > \pi^M(b, 1)$. Then, there exist two cost thresholds, such that the outcome of the innovation game is entrepreneurship for low-quality inventions, $c_2 > C_2^*(c_1, b)$, or for high-quality inventions, $c_2 \leq c_2^*(c_1, b)$, and the outcome is technology transfer for intermediate-quality inventions, $c_2^*(c_1, b) < c_2 \leq C_2^*(c_1, b)$. The two cost thresholds solve $\Gamma(b, c_2) = 0$ and are represented in Figure 7.4. The higher-cost threshold is increasing in the substitution parameter, representing less product differentiation, $\partial C_2^*(c_1, b)/\partial s \geq 0$. These cost thresholds generate two critical values for the R&D shock, $t(z, x_H^*) = c_2^*(b; s, c_1)$ and $t(z, x_L^*) = C_2^*(b; s, c_1)$, where $x_L^* < x_H^*$. Technology transfer occurs if the realization of the R&D shock is between these two values, x_L^* and x_H^*.

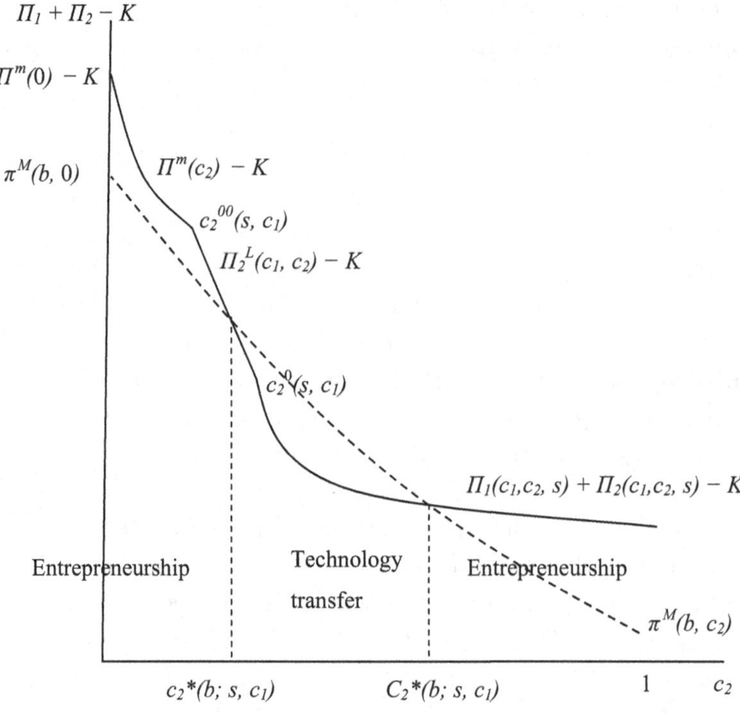

Figure 7.4. The outcome of the innovation game is entrepreneurship for low-quality inventions, $c_2 > C_2{}^*(c_1, b)$, or high-quality inventions, $c_2 \leq c_2{}^*(c_1, b)$, and the outcome is technology transfer for intermediate-quality inventions, $c_2{}^*(c_1, b) < c_2 \leq C_2{}^*(c_1, b)$.

7.4 Implications of Tacit Knowledge for Economic Models of R&D and Innovation

Tacit knowledge highlights the role of the individual inventor in R&D and innovation. Tacit knowledge provides an explanation for entrepreneurship that differs from market frictions caused by information asymmetries and imperfect IP rights.

Adverse Selection

The problem of tacit knowledge differs from asymmetric information problems in technology transfer that result from adverse selection (hidden information).[25] The tacit knowledge problem considered here does not involve any type of strategic signaling or misrepresentation of information by the inventor.[26] Tacit knowledge involves sufficiently complex know-how that may not lend itself to statistical

25 See Zeckhauser (1996), and Spulber (2011c).

26 Brocas and Carillo (2007) consider a situation in which the players are symmetrically informed but one player deliberately limits the amount of information that is gathered. The tacit information problem is related to this because the inventor and the adopter are symmetrically informed but the inventor chooses the extent of the invention.

inference. With tacit knowledge, the sender and the receiver must expend resources to transfer information, and knowledge differences tend to persist. Also, the receiver rather than the sender can affect the quality of knowledge transmitted by investing in absorptive capacity.

The problem of tacit knowledge differs from adverse selection that occurs when an economic agent with private information can "reveal" the information and often can communicate it without cost. There are intrinsic limits on the inventor's capacity to transfer know-how and the adopter's capacity to absorb it. The model of tacit knowledge presented here could be extended to include adverse selection. In addition to tacit knowledge about how to apply the invention, the inventor also may have private information about the quality of the invention, c_2. Then, the existing firm would need to provide the inventor with information rents to induce revelation of the features of the technology. Lowe (2006) considers an agency model in which the licensee's probability of success depends on the inventor's effort and an exogenous tacit knowledge parameter.

Moral Hazard

The problem of tacit knowledge also differs from asymmetric information problems that are a result of moral hazard (hidden action). The inventor's know-how places limits on the effectiveness of the inventor's efforts to transfer such knowledge, even if such efforts are observable. The model of tacit knowledge could be extended to include moral hazard by having the inventor devote effort to transferring tacit knowledge to the existing firm. Then, the net benefits of own-use of tacit knowledge would also reflect avoidance of agency costs associated with providing incentives for effort to the inventor engaged in technology transfer.

Jensen and Thursby (2001) find that more than 70 percent of university inventions are sufficiently "embryonic" that after transferring the license to a firm, the inventor must devote additional effort to improving the probability of commercial success. On the basis of this observation, Jensen and Thursby (2001) present a principal-agent model of invention with moral hazard in which the licensee's probability of commercial success depends on the inventor's effort. The contract between the existing firm and the inventor provides the agent with incentives to devote effort to improving the existing firm's success rate in applying the invention. See Macho-Stadler et al. (1996) on the role of tacit knowledge and asymmetric information in the design of licensing contracts.

Intellectual Property

The problem of tacit knowledge has implications for IP. Imperfect IP protections reinforce the effects of tacit knowledge on technology transfer. This suggests that the effects of IP protections on technology transfer decisions will differ across industries depending on systematic differences in inventors' tacit knowledge and the costs of codifying, communicating, and absorbing that knowledge. An empirical implication of the analysis is that variations in tacit knowledge across industries will affect the rate of technology transfer and the rate of entrepreneurship. Differences in technology transfer rates and entrepreneurship rates across industries can provide indications of the effects of tacit knowledge. Mansfield (1994) finds that the importance of IP rights differs across industries and suggests that this may be a result of differences in technological complexity.

The problem of tacit knowledge may increase the need for IP protections because the returns to transferring the invention must also cover the costs of codifying and communicating tacit knowledge. According to the American Inventor's Protection Act of 1999 (35 U.S.C. 112):

> The specification shall contain a written description of the invention, and of the manner and process of making and using it, in such full, clear, concise, and exact terms as to enable any person skilled in the art to which it pertains, or with which it is most nearly connected, to make and use the same, and shall set forth the best mode contemplated by the inventor of carrying out his invention.

The inherent nature of inventors' tacit knowledge may serve to limit some types of imitation and expropriation by others. The inventor can protect his IP by not codifying or communicating the knowledge to others. However, a patent need not preclude others from independently acquiring tacit knowledge.[27]

7.5 Tacit Knowledge and Entrepreneurship

The development of light-emitting diodes (LEDs) illustrates the importance of the individual inventor and tacit knowledge. Working almost alone at the Nichia Corporation in rural Japan, Shuji Nakamura developed extensive practical expertise in the manufacturing of LEDs, building his own machine and tinkering with almost every aspect of the process. Nakamura developed gallium nitride semiconductor production techniques. Because he initially had a very small budget, he made and operated his own equipment. Later, with a larger budget, he was able to purchase a metal organic chemical vapor deposition (MOCVD) reactor to grow gallium nitride crystals. He effectively rebuilt and modified the reactor to grow the high-quality crystals he needed.[28]

Carrying out his own research, development, and production of prototypes, Nakamura developed extensive tacit knowledge regarding the details of producing LEDs that would prove valuable in designing, developing, and manufacturing LEDs. Nakamura's discoveries suggest that his know-how was technically superior to that

27 http://www.uspto.gov/patents/index.jsp (accessed January 9, 2014).

28 Science Watch Interview (2000).

possessed by other companies and research laboratories that had much larger budgets and more personnel.

Nakamura was among only a few researchers at the time who worked with the semiconductor gallium nitride. After countless trials, Nakamura invented the bright blue LED that would have widespread application in lighting, DVD players, and many other products. Nakamura went on to produce a long string of discoveries, including the blue laser and the bright red LED, that eluded all other researchers. His many discoveries became known to others through patents and scientific publications, although much of his knowledge of LED manufacturing was unique, informal, intuitive, and thus highly difficult to transfer to others. Nakamura observed: "What I have managed to achieve shows that anybody with relatively little special experience in the field, no big money, and no collaborations with universities or other companies, can achieve considerable success alone when he tries a new research area without being obsessed with conventional ideas and knowledge."[29] Nakamura won the 2006 Millennium Technology Prize for his invention of blue, green, and white LEDs and the blue laser.

The problem of tacit knowledge suggests that the role of the individual inventor should be taken into account when considering both R&D and technology adoption by firms. Nakamura's tacit knowledge of LEDs and lasers was so extensive and idiosyncratic that it was likely to be difficult to transfer to others despite the high economic value of the knowledge and the many researchers who had relevant scientific and technological knowledge. The inventor develops tacit knowledge through observations of complex research processes and outcomes. The inventor's tacit knowledge is also the product of personal experiences, training, insights, creativity, and capabilities rather than organizational capital, routines, or culture. Spender (1996) emphasizes the distinction between individual psychological tacit knowledge and social collective tacit knowledge that is shared among individuals. Spender (1994) also distinguishes between individual and collective knowledge that is explicit and argues that different types of knowledge generate different economic rents. Many organizational studies have elaborated on the notion of tacit knowledge in groups (see Sandelands and Stablein, 1987; Weick and Roberts, 1993; and Nonaka and Takeuchi, 1995).

Tacit knowledge helps explain empirical observation of inventors participating in the innovation process, joining new ventures as entrepreneurs or employees. Zucker, Darby, and Brewer (1998) consider the early entrants into biotechnology and the new biotech units of existing firms. They show that the location and timing of usage of the new technology are "primarily explained by the presence at a particular time and place of scientists who are actively contributing to the basic science as represented by publications reporting genetic-sequence discoveries in academic journals."[30] Particular innovations are closely tied to the complementary

29 Nakamura et al., 2000, p. viii; see also Johnstone (2007).
30 Zucker, Darby, and Brewer (1998, p. 290).

knowledge and capabilities of individual "star scientists." Zucker, Darby, and Torero (2002, p. 630) find that for "breakthrough discoveries where scientific productivity becomes relevant to commercialization, the labor of the most productive scientists is the main resource around which firms are built or transformed."[31] Their empirical results on star scientists in biotech suggest that inventors in that industry who have tacit knowledge will tend to become entrepreneurs or work closely with firms that apply the transferred technology. Entrepreneurs bring capabilities that are complementary resources for the new firm (Alvarez and Busenitz, 2001). Ancori et al. (2000) argue that an individual's knowledge is based on his cognitive abilities (see also Nightingale, 1998, and Pozzali and Viale, 2006).

The present discussion of tacit knowledge accords with empirical observations that codification, communication, and absorption of tacit knowledge are determined endogenously. Cohen and Levinthal (1989) empirically estimate the effect of firms' R&D investment on their absorptive capacity for publicly available information. In Jensen and Thursby (2001), the licensee's probability of success depends on the inventor's effort and is assumed to be less than one so that technology transfer is necessarily imperfect. Cowan and Foray (1997) discuss codification of knowledge and absorptive capacity. Cowan and Jonard (2003) model the connection between absorptive capacity and learning difficulties and examine the extent to which knowledge is either codified or tacit. Ancori et al. (2000) distinguish between knowledge and information and explore how information is the codification of tacit knowledge. Balconi et al. (2007) emphasize that codification of knowledge is a matter of degree that depends on the information content of the codification and the extent to which other individuals can comprehend and use the information (see also Johnson et al., 2002).

Tacit Knowledge and the Inventor's Complementary Resources

During college, Bill Gross developed a new design for loudspeakers and founded GNP Loudspeakers, a play on his name and gross national product. He established GNP Development to design software for Lotus, which acquired the company and hired him as a software entrepreneur. Gross established Knowledge Adventure, which grew to be the third largest educational software publisher.[32] Internet search advertising took a major step forward in 1998 when Bill Gross' search engine GoTo introduced auctions of keywords.[33] Under GoTo's system – renamed Overture – advertisers' messages were ranked on the basis of their bids. Overture provided

31 See also Zucker and Darby (2001) for a study of Japan's star scientists in biotech, Zucker, Darby, and Armstrong (1998) on star scientists in U.S. biotech, and Zucker, Darby, and Armstrong (2002) on the economic value of the tacit knowledge of star scientists.

32 This information about Bill Gross is based on his bio as CEO of Idealab, http://www.idealab.com/about_idealab/management/bill_gross.html.

33 See http://www.searchenginehistory.com/ (accessed January 9, 2014).

its advertising system to many other search engines before Gross sold Overture to Yahoo![34] Overture obtained a patent for "[a] system and method for enabling information providers using a computer network such as the Internet to influence a position for a search listing on a search result list generated by an Internet search engine."[35] The technology is codified in the patent, and Gross is not listed as an inventor. Gross epitomizes the serial entrepreneur, having created more than fifty start-ups through his incubator Idealab founded in 1996.[36]

Serial entrepreneurship poses a puzzle that has been explained by persistent "optimistic beliefs" (Cooper et al., 1988, Landier and Thesmar, 2009) and nonpecuniary benefits of control (Moskowitz and Vissing-Jorgensen, 2002). The present analysis suggests that tacit knowledge helps explain the puzzle of the serial entrepreneur. The serial entrepreneur may be drawing on the same underlying capabilities in each new venture. These complementary capabilities also may take the form of tacit knowledge, just as the new strategy is tacit knowledge. The inventor's most important complementary resource may be his creativity. Personal attributes such as originality, imagination, inspiration, ingenuity, and scientific and technical capabilities often are difficult for others to observe and verify. These attributes are intrinsic to the individual and difficult to transfer unless the adopter employs the inventor. Entrepreneurship is a way for the inventor to benefit from his capabilities by embodying the complementary resources in a firm.

The inventor's complementary resources have limited transferability just as the inventor's discovery can be difficult to transfer to others. This helps explain why entrepreneurs are observed to bring capabilities that are complementary resources for the new firm (Alvarez and Busenitz, 2001). Capabilities often take the form of tacit knowledge that is difficult to convey to others. Biases and heuristics are commonly observed (Tversky and Kahneman, 1974) and are by no means unique to entrepreneurs. However, because entrepreneurship is a means of applying complementary resources that cannot be transmitted through contracts, the process of self-selection among innovative entrepreneurs may favor particular skills. This may explain why some argue that entrepreneurs think differently from other people – including managers – using more heuristics and informal reasoning (see, for example, Busenitz and Lau, 1996; Busenitz and Barney, 1997; Baron, 1998; and Forbes, 1999).

A number of factors explain why inventors have unique abilities that are complementary to the invention. First, having the knowledge required to create the innovation can be correlated with having the knowledge to implement the innovation. The scientific and technological knowledge needed to develop and commercialize a discovery may be closely related to the knowledge of product design and production

34 These included AllTheWeb, Altavista, AskJeeves, Hotbot, IWon, Lycos, Teoma, MSN and Yahoo! See A. Ellam (2003).

35 U.S. Patent 6,269,361 (Assignee GoTo.com, July, 31, 2001, inventors are Davis et al.).

36 Schonfeld, 2007.

processes based on the discovery. Also, the inventor's education and training may apply to developing the skills for both innovation and entrepreneurship, generating correlation between innovative and entrepreneurial capabilities. Second, the entry requirements for entrepreneurs, including the process of obtaining financing and attracting employees, will select those inventors who have the necessary entrepreneurial skills. Third, inventors who choose to become entrepreneurs have knowledge of their own skills so that self-selection by inventors may increase the likelihood that they have complementary capabilities.

Both contracting and entrepreneurship are mechanisms for converting individual knowledge to collective knowledge. If the inventor contracts with an existing firm or an entrepreneur to transfer his new strategy and complementary resources, the result will be collective knowledge involving both the inventor and the adopter. Moreover, when transferred through contracts, the innovation and complementary capabilities become collective knowledge when applied in the existing firm or in a new firm established by an entrepreneur. If the inventor chooses to become an entrepreneur, then in the process of creating a start-up and establishing a firm, the inventor's new strategy and complementary skills are shared among the members of the new organization and again make the transition from individual knowledge to collective knowledge. The managers and employees of the start-up learn, modify, and apply the innovative entrepreneur's new strategy and complementary knowledge.

Dispersion of Tacit Knowledge

Albert Einstein's observations about time were his unique knowledge when first conceived. Far from being common knowledge, Einstein's 1905 article "On the Electrodynamics of Moving Bodies" established the modern physics perspective on time and space and represented a significant departure from the classical Newtonian view.[37] His unique insights were in part the product of his education, his personal observation of patent applications for coordinated clocks at the Swiss patent office where he worked, and even the synchronized clocks at the Bern railway station across the street from the patent office. Einstein developed ideas that differed radically from the physicists of his day.[38]

Scientific and technical knowledge are not all that different from practical knowledge. When Einstein joined the Bern patent office in 1902, "clock coordination was a practical problem (trains, troops, and telegraphs) demanding workable, patentable solutions in exactly his area of greatest professional concern: precision electromechanical instrumentation."[39] As with practical knowledge, scientific and technical knowledge is widely dispersed among individuals who have unique knowledge. Scientists, mathematicians, and engineers who are actively engaged in research

37 Galison (2003, pp. 13–14).

38 Galison (2003).

39 Galison (2003, p. 325).

obtain unique knowledge about their field of study and their own discoveries that is not generally available. Only some basic types of scientific and technical information are common knowledge among experts. Discoveries begin as the knowledge of individuals. Application of scientific and technical knowledge requires investment in codification, communication, and absorption.

Much of the knowledge that inventors and entrepreneurs have is *practical* in nature rather than technical or purely scientific. Hayek points out that practical knowledge tends to be widely dispersed: "We need to remember only how much we have to learn in any occupation after we have completed our theoretical training, how big a part of our working life we spend learning particular jobs, and how valuable an asset in all walks of life is knowledge of people, of local conditions, and special circumstances."[40] The practical business knowledge of inventors and entrepreneurs also has the property of being widely dispersed.

Hayek (1945, 1991) emphasizes that governments and other institutions cannot fully observe the private knowledge of individuals. Hayek (1945, pp. 521–522) points out that almost "every individual has some advantage over all others in that he possesses unique information of which beneficial use might be made, but of which use can be made only if the decisions depending on it are left to him or are made with his active cooperation." Centralized command and control by governments necessarily faces limitations because of imperfect information. For Hayek, individuals have the best understanding of their own needs and experiences. The complexity of personal experiences and preferences suggests that individuals have tacit knowledge regarding their situation. Economic efficiency only can be achieved through market incentives and incentive mechanisms of spontaneous order such as prices rather than through centralized command and control (Hayek, 1991).

Production and Distribution of Knowledge

The concept of tacit knowledge has its origins in philosophy. Bertrand Russell (1911, p. 120) distinguishes between knowledge by acquaintance and knowledge by description and points out that "our judgment is wholly reduced to constituents with which we are acquainted." Russell (1911, p. 117) states: "The fundamental

40 Hayek (1945, p. 522) finds that "[t]o know of and put to use a machine not fully employed, or somebody's skill which could be better utilized, or to be aware of a surplus stock which can be drawn upon during an interruption of supplies, is socially quite as useful as the knowledge of better alternative techniques. And the shipper who earns his living from using otherwise empty or half-filled journeys of tramp-steamers, or the estate agent whose whole knowledge is almost exclusively one of temporary opportunities, or the *arbitrageur* who gains from local differences of commodity prices, are all performing eminently useful functions based on special knowledge of circumstances of the fleeting moment not known to others" (emphasis in original). Hayek further notes: "It is a curious fact that this sort of knowledge should today be generally regarded with a kind of contempt, and that anyone who by such knowledge gains an advantage over somebody better equipped with theoretical or technical knowledge is thought to have acted almost disreputably."

epistemological principle in the analysis of propositions containing descriptions is this: Every proposition which we can understand must be composed wholly of constituents with which we are acquainted."[41] The inventor is acquainted with the process of discovery, and some aspects of that process are the inventor's tacit knowledge. The inventor transmits the discovery to the potential adopter by describing the invention and conveying objects such as prototypes, blueprints, and formulas. The potential adopter may not be acquainted with some constituents of the discovery process and may not fully understand the invention. The concept of tacit knowledge is developed in the psychology and sociology literatures (Cowan et al., 2000). Polanyi (1962, 1967) distinguishes between tacit and explicit knowledge.[42] Sociologists Rogers (1962) and Coleman (1964) examine the imperfect diffusion of innovations.

Economic analysis of innovation builds on these foundations. Citing the sociology literature, Arrow (1969, p. 33) observes: "Different communication channels have different costs (or equivalently different capacities), where these costs include the ability of the sender to 'code' the information and the recipient to 'decode' it." Nelson and Winter (1982) introduce the concept of tacit knowledge within organizations into the theory of the firm. Machlup's (1962) landmark study recognizes that transferring knowledge is costly and tracks the increasing proportion of the labor force occupied in generating, transferring, and receiving knowledge. Machlup estimates that the economic costs of producing and distributing knowledge constitute nearly 30 percent of the U.S. economy. In contrast to Machlup's identification of costly knowledge distribution, many economic studies emphasize the costless transfer of knowledge.

Although he recognizes that communication is costly, as mentioned previously, Arrow (1962b) considers knowledge as a public good or an externality. Knowledge as a public good is non-rivalrous: the same information can be shared by an additional person without an additional cost. Knowledge as a public good is non-excludable: excluding access would be prohibitively costly so that everyone has access to the same knowledge. In other words, knowledge diffuses easily and without costs. Arrow (1962b, p. 171) argues that information is easy to steal because inventors must reveal knowledge to potential buyers, who then reproduce the knowledge "at little or no cost." As a consequence, inventors encounter difficulties in appropriating the returns from their information.

Griliches (1957, 1992) and others view knowledge as an externality or "spillover" that not only diffuses freely but also would be costly to contain (see also Cohen and Levinthal, 1989). Stiglitz (1999, p. 310) argues: "Most knowledge is a global public good" diffusing without cost not only locally but also around the

41 See also Russell (2000).

42 See also Ryle (2002) on the distinction between knowing how and knowing that. He points out that a "soldier does not become a shrewd general by knowing that there are military maxims (the strategic principles of Clausewitz) but rather from knowing how to apply them (Ryle, 2002, p. 31).

world. In contrast to these approaches, the concept of tacit knowledge recognizes constraints on the diffusion of innovation as a result of the costs of transmission.

In contrast to the view that knowledge involves spillovers or externalities, the phenomenon of tacit knowledge suggests that some types of knowledge need not be public goods. When knowledge is costly to transmit and requires significant interaction between the sender and the receiver, knowledge acquires some of the properties of private goods. For example, if an inventor must spend time explaining his discoveries to a potential user, knowledge transferred in this way is similar to a service. Although some types of explicit knowledge can have non-rivalrous usage, knowledge transmission may be rivalrous because of the resources devoted to transmitting and receiving knowledge. Costly knowledge transfer also serves to constrain access so that an inventor's tacit knowledge is excludable unless others develop it independently.

The tacit knowledge problem is related to games in which an informed party strategically conveys information to an uninformed party.[43] In models of cheap talk, the sender chooses to convey an imperfect signal by partitioning the information space and letting the receiver know only the element of the partition that contains the information (Crawford and Sobel, 1982).[44] Suppose that the information space is discrete and the quality of the information is the fineness of the partition. Then, if the receiver takes a random draw from the element of the partition that contains c_2, then the success rate β is the (contingent) likelihood the existing firm selects c_2. Crémer et al. (2007) examine the design of technical language assuming that the number of partitions of a discrete information space is given exogenously and represents the receiver's bounded rationality. The number of "words" in the language corresponds to the number of partitions, and the receiver's cost of decoding depends on the size of the elements in the partition and the probability distribution over the information space.

7.6 Tacit Knowledge and Management Strategy

Tacit knowledge affects the organization of economic institutions that transfer and apply knowledge. The choice between entrepreneurship and technology transfer contracts highlights not only the distinction between tacit and explicit knowledge

43 There is also imperfect communication in games with costly signaling (Spence, 1973). On games with information disclosure, see Grossman (1981), Jovanovic (1982b), Milgrom and Roberts (1986), Green and Stokey (2007), Brocas and Carillo (2007), and Kamenica and Gentzkow (2009). There are also games in which an individual chooses a signal as a means of commitment (Bodner and Prelec, 2003; Brocas and Carillo, 2004; Benabou and Tirole, 2004).

44 The familiar notion of "entropy" in communications channels describes the distortion of messages that result in partial transmission of information or errors in transmission. As a consequence of noisy signals, the receiver may not understand the message that is being sent. Noisy signals in technology transfer will affect the performance of the invention and diminish or eliminate the benefits of the invention to the adopter.

but also that between individual and collective knowledge. If the inventor's new strategy and complementary capabilities are tacit knowledge, they are difficult to transfer to others through contracting. This favors innovative entrepreneurship, with the inventor creating a start-up as a means of both applying his knowledge and transferring his knowledge to others. If the inventor's new strategy and complementary capabilities can be codified in the form of business plans, IP, products, and services, they can be transferred to others through contracts. Explicit knowledge being more easily transferable leads to contracting and cooperation. In contrast, tacit knowledge leads to competition and creative destruction.

Tacit Knowledge and Strategy Formulation

Inventors may express their commercial, scientific, and technological discoveries in the form of a management strategy. The inventor formulates the new strategy, which is a plan of action to achieve a goal and identification of the complementary resources that are needed. The inventor commercializes the new strategy by transferring it to others, whether to an existing firm, a prospective entrepreneur, or an intermediary in the market for innovations. Alternatively, the inventor commercializes the new strategy by becoming an entrepreneur and creating a start-up enterprise and potentially a new firm. Finally, the adopter implements the new strategy whether the adopter is an existing firm or the entrepreneurial entrant. The initial implementation of a new strategy in the market place is a Schumpeterian innovation. An innovator is the first to introduce commercial, scientific, and technological discoveries to the market.

The inventor's knowledge is the basis of the new strategy. The inventor's knowledge is likely to consist of two components: the new strategy itself and complementary knowledge that is useful for implementing the new strategy. The inventor's new strategy is the product of his discovery of market opportunities and the resources needed to realize those opportunities. The inventor's complementary knowledge includes the capabilities needed to implement the new strategy, including creating a start-up, raising financial capital, hiring personnel, forming an organization, and finding customers. The new strategy may be tacit, or it may be codified in the form of an extensive business plan, or somewhere in between. The inventor's complementary knowledge also can be tacit, or it may be codified in the form of scientific, technical, and business information. The inventor's complementary knowledge is tacit when the inventor is uniquely qualified because he understands the market opportunities or technologies that form his new strategy.

A strategy that is not fully developed is likely to be more difficult to transfer than a strategy that is deliberately designed. The inventor may not fully understand the new strategy himself; it may be little more than a hunch or a conjecture. The inventor may be improvising in response to events, generating the strategy through a process of trial and error. The strategy may be what is known as an "emergent" strategy rather than a "deliberate" strategy (Mintzberg and Waters, 1985). Even strategies that appear to be deliberate may actually be "more attributable to unconsciously acquired, culturally shaped habits of acting; a modus operandi that, though latent and invisible, nevertheless plays an active role in shaping individual choices and strategic action" (Chia and Holt, 2009, p. 23).

The inventor can more readily transfer deliberate strategies than emergent strategies. The inventor becomes an entrepreneur as a means of implementing an emergent strategy. When the strategy is driven by the inventor's beliefs, opinions, capabilities, and creative inspiration, it becomes necessary for the inventor to implement the strategy himself. The inventor can implement the basic outlines of a strategy that reflects a personal vision. The start-up enterprise is a mechanism for gathering more information, experimenting with alternative actions, and developing the new strategy. By becoming an entrepreneur, the inventor can refine the strategy in response to market feedback. The firm that emerges from the start-up process can be very different from the initial strategy.

Because of uncertain outcomes, actions that form part of a deliberately designed strategy have unanticipated consequences; the best laid plans of mice and men often go awry. In the same way, strategies that respond to immediate events without a deliberate design may turn out to bring success (Chia and Holt, 2009, p. 24). Emergent strategies have an advantage over deliberate strategies when updated for strategic responses from customers, suppliers, partners, and competitors. Business strategies that depend on incentives and decentralized interaction can outperform central planning, especially in large organizations. Uncertain outcomes affect the transferability of new strategies.

Business innovations are inherently difficult to transfer to others. By their very nature, innovations are untested and involve uncertainty. Business strategies that involve new combinations are likely to be speculative. It may be impossible to objectively determine the likelihood of success. The inventor's strategy often is founded on the inventor's beliefs about the likelihood of various outcomes and the effectiveness of the proposed strategy. Inventors may act on the basis of Bayesian personal probabilities that reflect their knowledge and experiences. An innovation that is based on the inventor's subjective beliefs about market opportunities and the application of resources is difficult to evaluate by potential adopters. An adopter must depend on the inventor's opinion and reputation, form his own judgment, or rely on the judgments of experts.

Another problem of transferability is communicating the new strategy to a potential adopter. Entrepreneurship is more likely when transferring the new strategy entails high costs of communication. The new strategy is a discovery that is known to the inventor but not to others, at least initially. To be implemented the new strategy either must be put into effect by the inventor or transferred to others. Transferring a new strategy involves many of the problems associated with transferring knowledge. The new strategy is the inventor's private information and must be communicated to the adopter. The more complex the knowledge involved, the more time and effort is required for communication between the inventor and the adopter. Communication is needed to describe the innovation and to bargain over the terms of exchange.

Innovations may be difficult to understand just as products have features that are difficult to observe. Consumers can readily discern the properties of search goods and cannot observe the properties of experience goods without actually consuming them (Nelson, 1970). In a similar way, one can distinguish between "search innovations" and "experience innovations." Firms and other adopters can readily understand the properties of search innovations although they cannot accurately evaluate the properties of experience innovations without adopting and applying them in production. Inventors may find it easier to sell search innovations than to sell experience innovations. Innovations that identify a new application for a known invention may be a search innovation. In contrast, complex business plans that involve new business techniques or new technology are likely to be experience innovations.

Tacit Knowledge and the Entrepreneur's Judgment

The innovative entrepreneur's tacit knowledge will inform his judgment of market opportunities and the capabilities needed to address those opportunities. The entrepreneur's judgment plays a central role in the classical economics literature on entrepreneurship. The inventor is likely to know more about the new strategy and its potential for success than a potential buyer who has not developed the strategy. An inventor becomes an entrepreneur when the knowledge needed to implement the new strategy requires his active cooperation.

Adam Smith (1998, p. 10) observed that many economic improvements were made by the "ingenuity... of those who are called philosophers or men of speculation, whose trade is not to do anything, but to observe everything; and who, upon that account, are often capable of combining together the powers of the most distant and dissimilar objects." Entrepreneurs gain from specialization: "In the progress of society, philosophy or speculation becomes, like every other employment, the principal or sole trade and occupation of a particular class of citizens" (Smith, 1998, p. 10).

Say (1852, I, p. 97) emphasizes that it is the entrepreneur who "judges needs and most of all the means to satisfy them, and who compares the ends with these means; also, his main quality is judgment." Say (1841, pp. 368–371) attributes only a part of the entrepreneur's profit to the presence of risk, which "limits in another way the amount of this type of services that are offered and makes them a bit more expensive." The entrepreneur's profit is a return to his "industrial abilities, that is to say his judgment, to his natural or acquired talents, to his occupation, to his spirit of order and conduct." For Say, the entrepreneur must possess the necessary combination of personal attributes: "He needs judgment, reliability, knowledge of men and things."

Knight's analysis of risk, uncertainty, and profit is entirely within the context of the entrepreneur: uncertainty is "the fact of ignorance and necessity of acting upon opinion rather than knowledge."[45] Knight (1971, p. 285) states that "true profit, therefore, depends on an absolute uncertainty in the estimation of the value of judgment." The entrepreneur receives profit in return for his private knowledge of the quality of his own judgment. The size of entrepreneurial profits varies inversely with their "optimism." The entrepreneur's profit is a return to the quality of his judgment.[46]

The inventor competes with other independent inventors and with existing firms that are potential adopters. With competing innovations, the problems of transferring knowledge are compounded. How does the inventor distinguish his innovation from those of competitors? How does the potential adopter determine which is the best innovation? When innovations are emergent and competing inventors have critical tacit knowledge, it is more difficult to establish a market for innovations. Competition may be the best way of sorting through the new strategies, which requires inventors to become entrepreneurs as a means of demonstrating the effectiveness of their new strategies.

7.7 Conclusion

The problem of tacit knowledge helps explain creative destruction. Inventors' tacit knowledge can be complementary to their commercial, scientific, and technological inventions. The inventor becomes an entrepreneur when there are net benefits from own-use of discoveries. The value of embodying the inventors' discoveries in new firms reflects the returns to entrepreneurs' tacit knowledge, as well as their judgment, capabilities, and creative efforts. In contrast, inventors who transfer their technology in the market for discoveries rely on existing firms or specialized entrepreneurs to apply their inventions.

The problem of tacit knowledge affects whether technological change occurs by transforming existing economic institutions or by establishing new ones. When there is tacit knowledge, inventors with higher-quality discoveries vertically integrate the development of a discovery with entrepreneurship, and inventors with lower-quality discoveries transfer their inventions to existing firms. The market for inventions involves greater complexity than licensing and other IP transfers. Economic efficiency may require inventors' own-use of tacit knowledge through innovative entrepreneurship.

45 Knight (1971, p. 268).

46 Casson's (1982, p. 23) definition builds on these earlier approaches: "an entrepreneur is someone who specializes in taking judgmental decisions about the coordination of scare resources." Casson (1982, 2003) characterizes judgment in terms of contemporary decision theory, referring as well to the entrepreneur's skills in delegation and organizational management.

8

Creative Destruction

Asymmetric Information

Asymmetric information in the market for inventions can make entrepreneurship more likely to occur. Contracting between an inventor and an existing firm to transfer an invention is thus subject to problems arising from information asymmetries. Even if an invention is codified and easily communicated, the inventor is likely to know much more about its features than potential adopters. When features of inventions are not perfectly observable, there may be adverse selection in the market for inventions. The inventor may choose to become an entrepreneur and establish a firm to implement the invention as a means of overcoming adverse selection problems. This chapter considers incentives for technology transfer and entrepreneurship when inventors have private information about their invention.[1]

For Arrow (1962b, p. 150) invention is the production of information, and rents fall when "information becomes a commodity." He observes that "[a]n entrepreneur will automatically acquire a knowledge of demand and production conditions in his field which is available to others only with special effort." He further points out that the transmission of knowledge is imperfect because of costly communication and errors in judgment.

Zeckhauser (1996) argues that markets form institutions to address problems in transferring technological information (TI): "Webs of relationships, formal and informal, involving universities, start-up firms, corporate giants, and venture capitalists play a major role in facilitating the production and spread of TI."[2] To address asymmetric information problems, inventors and adopters form long-term

1 Generally, both the inventor and potential adopter may have private information. The potential adopter is better able to evaluate the market value of the invention than the inventor. The potential adopter may have better information about how to implement the invention and may know more than the inventor about the availability of complementary resources. The inventor may not know the potential adopter's willingness to pay for the invention. As a consequence, negotiations between inventors and potential adopters can break down or fail to occur even when technology transfers would be efficient under full information.

2 Zeckhauser (1996, p. 12743).

contracts, partnerships, and joint ventures, which further raise the costs of knowledge transfers.[3]

Inventors address asymmetric information problems in the market for inventions by bundling knowledge with technology transfers. As Zeckhauser (1996, p. 12745) points out: "A superior video compression algorithm may be placed into an applications program specialized for the information provider. A fledgling biotech firm sells its expertise to the pharmaceutical company as a formulated product. And venture capitalists package their special expertise and connections along with a capital investment." The difficulties of transferring information often require bundling knowledge with costly patenting and other legal protections for IP, which results in delays and legal costs.[4] The many forms of bundling knowledge increase transaction costs in the market for inventions.

Entrepreneurship can be understood as another form of bundling: the inventor's knowledge is bundled with the establishment of a new firm. The invention is embodied in the new firm and used to generate new products, production processes, and transaction methods. This avoids transaction costs in the market for inventions that may be a result of asymmetric information about the features of inventions.

Information asymmetries between the inventor and the potential adopter have a number of important implications. Market "architectures" may differ in their ability to evaluate new technologies. Markets with many potential adopters may be better at evaluating new technologies than markets in which there are a few large firms with centralized decision making. Markets that are subject to incumbent inertia because of centralized decision making may give inventors greater incentives to become innovative entrepreneurs.

Experts and intermediaries in the market for inventions can help address adverse selection problems. Inventors can become innovative entrepreneurs when adverse selection problems reduce returns from technology transfers, effectively becoming expert adopters of technology. Under asymmetric information about the quality of inventions, incumbent firms' willingness to pay for inventions will be based on their expected quality. This attracts inventors with incremental inventions rather than those with major inventions, as in the classic "lemons" problem. Also, the inventor may have private information about the development costs of an invention. Inventors with less risky projects may be more likely to transfer their technologies to existing firms and inventors with riskier projects may be more likely to become innovative entrepreneurs.

Inventors can alleviate asymmetric information problems through costly signaling that indicates the features of inventions to potential adopters. When signaling is sufficiently costly, innovative entrepreneurship provides an alternative to technology transfer. Contracts between inventors and potential adopters can provide

3 See Zeckhauser (1996).

4 See Zeckhauser (1996). Arora et al. (2001b, p. 119) consider the bundling of knowledge with "codified technology" protected by IP.

information rents to inventors to induce them to reveal additional information about their inventions. Inventors have incentives to become innovative entrepreneurs when establishing a new firm is more efficient than contracting under asymmetric information.

The chapter examines the effects of asymmetric information on the outcome of the strategic innovation game. The chapter is organized as follows. Section 8.1 considers how the architecture of existing firms affects whether the innovation game results in technology transfer or entrepreneurship. Section 8.2 examines how adverse selection in the market for inventions affects entrepreneurship. Section 8.3 considers risky development and adverse selection in the market for inventions and its implications for the innovative entrepreneur. Section 8.4 introduces costly signaling by inventors in the market for inventions. Section 8.5 discusses an agency model of technology transfer with adverse selection and compares technology transfer with innovative entrepreneurship.

8.1 Market Architectures and the Innovative Entrepreneur

An existing firm may not be able to evaluate accurately the quality of technologies in the market for inventions. As a consequence, inventors may have better information about the quality of their inventions than the existing firm. This section considers the strategic innovation game when the organizational structure of existing firms affects their ability to evaluate the quality of inventions.

In practice, existing firms may evaluate inventions inaccurately for a number of reasons. Imperfect incentives and rent seeking within large firms may bias technology adoption decisions. Entrenched interests in the firm may resist technology changes that would displace existing business activities, even if such changes were profitable. Bureaucratic decision processes in large firms can be time-consuming and inflexible and can generate inefficient outcomes. Managers of existing firms may be reluctant to adopt inventions from outside the organization – the familiar "not invented here" objection. Bureaucratic impediments to commercialization of economically desirable inventions are referred to by Acs et al. (2004) and Audretsch et al. (2006) as "knowledge filters."

Asymmetric information problems can arise when potential adopters compete to purchase or license inventions.[5] Because of differences in their evaluations of new technology, potential adopters can face the problem of the winner's curse. This can occur when the inventor has a better estimate of the value of the invention than does the adopter (Zeckhauser, 1996, p. 12745). The winner's curse also can occur when there are multiple potential adopters who bid for the invention. Potential adopters face the problem of a common value because they are trying to estimate the value of the underlying invention. This differs from the situation in which buyers have

5 Auctions for new technologies are beyond the scope of this chapter.

independent values for a commodity. When there is a common value, the winning bid conveys information because it is the upper bound of the bids of all of the adopters. The winning bidder has the highest estimate of the value of the invention. More generally, adopters' estimates are statistically interdependent, reflecting different information about the possible value of the invention. Adopters lower their bids because of their concerns about overpaying for the invention. The inventor can raise the expected price in an auction by providing independent expert evaluations of the invention.[6] The need for independent testing and evaluation raises the costs of the market for inventions. Higher costs in the market for inventions make contracting less attractive and increase the likelihood of entrepreneurship.

The organizational structure of existing firms is a critical determinant of their ability to judge the inventor's discovery. Sah and Stiglitz (1986) contrast two types of market architectures, referring to a centralized market with a large firm as a *hierarchy* and referring to a market with multiple firms making independent decisions as a *polyarchy*. In the firm organized as a hierarchy, decision makers at higher levels of the organization review decisions made by those at lower levels of the organization. In contrast, in a decentralized market, individual firms make decisions independently. Existing firms may reject some projects that should be accepted, yielding Type-I errors. Existing firms may accept some projects that should be rejected, yielding Type-II errors. A market organized as a polyarchy chooses to approve a greater proportion of projects than the hierarchy (Sah and Stiglitz, 1986).

Consider how the organizational structure of existing firms affects the market for inventions. Hierarchies and polyarchies have different abilities to judge the quality of inventions. Because polyarchies tend to accept more inventions than hierarchies, inventors will transfer their technologies to polyarchies more than to hierarchies. Conversely, hierarchies will generate more entrepreneurship by rejecting more inventions. We consider these two extreme cases for purposes of illustration although an organization that combines both hierarchical and competitive approval processes may perform better than either of these decision processes taken separately.

An inventor and an existing firm play the strategic innovation game as in the preceding chapters. If the inventor and the existing firm choose to cooperate, the inventor transfers the technology to the existing firm in return for a royalty. If the inventor and the existing firm choose to compete, the inventor becomes an innovative entrepreneur and establishes a firm that enters the market using the new technology. The product offered by the existing firm and that offered by the new entrant are identical.

To highlight the effects of market architecture on the market for inventions, suppose that there are no technology transfer costs or adjustment costs for an incumbent that adopts the invention. Suppose that there are costs $K > 0$ of establishing a new firm. The new firm competes with the existing firm to enter the

6 See Milgrom (1979) and Milgrom and Weber (1982).

market, thus possibly dissipating rents from innovation. Because products are homogeneous, the new firm necessarily displaces the existing firm. Because there are costs of establishing a firm, and because competition can dissipate rents, the inventor and the existing firm would always prefer technology transfer to competition. Therefore, under full information, the innovation game always would result in technology transfer.

Market demand for the final product, $D(p)$, is a twice continuously differentiable and decreasing function of the final product price, p. The profit of a monopoly firm with price p and costs c equals $\Pi(p, c) = (p - c)D(p)$. As before, suppose that the profit function is concave in price. The profit-maximizing monopoly price, $p^M(c)$, is unique and increasing in cost c, and initial profits equal $\Pi^M(c) = \Pi(p^M(c), c)$.

The existing firm's initial technology is given by unit cost $c_1 > 1$. The inventor's discovery is represented by unit cost c, where c is some value in the unit interval. The initial price before the innovation equals the monopoly price as a function of the initial unit cost, $p_1 = p^M(c_1)$. Assume that the invention is drastic, so that entry of the new firm displaces the existing firm, $p^M(c) < c_1$. An inventor who becomes an entrepreneur earns $\Pi^M(c) - K$.

Suppose that an inventor has market power and can extract rents from the existing firm with a first-and-final offer. Then, because competition would displace the incumbent, the inventor would earn a royalty equal to the incumbent firm's monopoly profits using the new technology, $\Pi^M(c)$. Technology transfer allows the inventor to avoid the costs of establishing a firm.

Consider in contrast, the outcome of the innovation game with asymmetric information. An existing firm must evaluate the quality of the inventor's discovery. An existing firm's evaluation process is subject to risk, which reduces the inventor's expected returns from technology transfer. The inventor must commit to pursuing technology transfer or entrepreneurship before knowing the outcome of the existing firm's evaluation process.

Define a screening function, $b(c)$, as the probability that a decision maker employed by the incumbent firm approves adoption of the invention. The screening function can represent the absorptive capacity of the firm.[7] A perfect screening function would approve good inventions by setting $b(c) = 1$ for $c < c_1$ and would reject bad inventions by setting $b(c) = 0$ for $c \geq c_1$. Because all inventions are drastic, it would be efficient for the incumbent firm to approve any inventions offered the inventor. Then, a perfect screening function would always equal 1. Suppose instead that the screening function is imperfect, although it can distinguish between inventions by ranking them on the basis of quality. Let $b(c)$ be strictly decreasing in c, with $b(0) = 1$ and $\frac{1}{2} < b(c) < 1$ for all $0 < c < c_1$.

7 In a more general setting, the firm could invest in improving its evaluation procedures for new technologies.

The market is organized as a *hierarchy* if it has one existing firm with λ organizational levels. For the hierarchy to approve the invention, a decision maker at a lower level of the firm must first approve the invention, then a decision maker at a higher level of the firm must also approve the invention, and so on. The likelihood of a hierarchy with λ levels approving the invention is $(b(c))^{\lambda}$. The market is organized as a *polyarchy* if the existing firm has λ decision makers, any of whom can approve the invention. The likelihood of at least one firm approving the invention is equal to 1 minus the probability that all firms will reject the discovery, $1 - (1 - b(c))^{\lambda}$.

The hierarchy is less likely to approve the invention than the polyarchy. To see why, first let $\lambda = 2$. When the screening function is imperfect – that is, $0 < b < 1$ – it is easy to verify that

$$b^2 < 1 - (1 - b)^2.$$

So, the two-level hierarchy is less likely to approve an invention than the two-member polyarchy. Because b is such that $0 < b < 1$, for $\lambda > 2$,

$$b^{\lambda} + (1 - b)^{\lambda} < b^2 + (1 - b)^2 < 1.$$

This immediately implies that

$$b^{\lambda} < 1 - (1 - b)^{\lambda},$$

so that the λ-level hierarchy is less likely to approve inventions than the λ-member polyarchy. The hierarchy is more likely to reject inventions that should be accepted, and therefore the existing firm commits more Type-I errors, which is the only relevant type of error in the present setting. The polyarchy is more likely to accept inventions that should be rejected, and therefore would commit more Type-II errors if such errors were possible.

As the quality of the invention decreases – that is, as c increases – the gap between the approval rate of the polyarchy and that of hierarchy widens. Because $b(c) > ½$, it follows that

$$\frac{d}{dc}[1 - (1 - b(c))^{\lambda} - (b(c))^{\lambda}] = b'(c)\lambda[(1 - b(c))^{\lambda-1} - (b(c))^{\lambda-1}] > 0.$$

The increasing gap with lower-quality inventions has implications for the effects of the number of decision makers on the outcome with the two forms of market organization.

The architecture of existing firms affects the inventor's expected returns from technology transfer. An inventor who submits an invention c to an existing firm organized as an λ-level hierarchy has an expected return equal to $(b(c))^{\lambda}\Pi^M(c)$. The inventor who submits an invention c to a polyarchy with λ decision makers has an expected return equal to $[1 - (1 - b(c))^{\lambda}]\Pi^M(c)$. Because of the greater likelihood that the proposal is accepted, the expected return is greater when the market is organized as a polyarchy than when it is organized as a hierarchy.

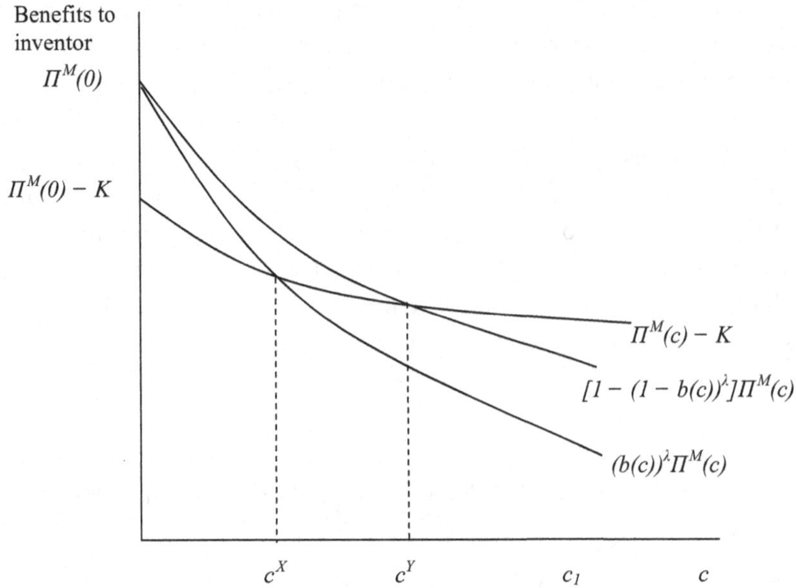

Figure 8.1. The quality of the marginal entrepreneur's discovery is greater when the existing firm is a hierarchy, c^X, than when it is a polyarchy, c^Y.

Figure 8.1 shows the outcome of the innovation game with both types of market organization. The hierarchy curve, $(b(c))^{\lambda}\Pi^M(c)$, lies everywhere below the polyarchy curve, $[1-(1-b(c))^{\lambda}]\Pi^M(c)$. Both curves are monotonically decreasing in c because both the screening function $b(c)$ and the profit function $\Pi^M(c)$ are monotonically decreasing. The gap between the curves widens as c increases.

Compare the returns to technology transfer with the returns to establishing a firm, $\Pi^M(c) - K$. The slope of the returns to establishing a firm is greater than the slope of the expected returns to transferring the technology to existing firms because for positive c, the likelihood of technology transfer is less than 1 with either type of market organization. Because $b(0) = 1$, the expected returns to technology transfer with either type of market organization equal profits $\Pi^M(c)$ when $c = 0$ and exceed the returns to entrepreneurship $\Pi^M(c) - K$.

Inventors with minor inventions become entrepreneurs, and inventors with major inventors transfer technology to an existing firm. Let c^X be the critical invention for the market organized as a hierarchy,

$$(1) \qquad (b(c^X))^{\lambda}\Pi^M(c^X) = \Pi^M(c^X) - K.$$

Also, let c^Y be the critical invention for the market organized as a polyarchy,

$$(2) \qquad [1-(1-b(c^Y))^{\lambda}]\Pi^M(cY) = \Pi^M(c^Y) - K.$$

The critical quality of the marginal entrepreneur's discovery is greater when the existing firm is a hierarchy, c^X, than when it is a polyarchy, c^Y,

$$c^X < c^Y.$$

The set of inventors who transfer technology when the existing market is a hierarchy or a polyarchy consists of those with major inventions, $[0, c^X]$ and $[0, c^Y]$. These critical values are represented in Figure 8.1.

Suppose that the inventor's discovery is a random draw from a probability distribution on the unit interval. Then, the organizational structure of the existing firm determines the likelihood of technology transfer and innovative entrepreneurship. The likelihood that inventors transfer their technology to existing firms is smaller when the market is a hierarchy than when the market is a polyarchy, $\Pr\{c \leq c^X\} < \Pr\{c \leq c^Y\}$. The hierarchical firm rejects more inventions than does a polyarchy. The greater likelihood that the invention is rejected with a hierarchy generates more entrepreneurship than does a polyarchy. This has the following implication: *innovative entrepreneurship is more likely when the existing firm is a hierarchy than when the industry is organized as a polyarchy.*

This has two interesting implications. *First, the greater the number of decision makers, λ, the greater is the performance gap between the hierarchy and the polyarchy.* The hierarchy accepts fewer inventions as the number of levels, λ, increases, and the polyarchy accepts more inventions as the number of members, λ, increases. In the limit, almost all inventors become entrepreneurs if faced with a hierarchical firm with large λ. Almost all inventors sell their invention to an existing firm if faced with a polyarchy with many decision makers, λ. When the existing firm is a hierarchy, bureaucratic decision making can prevent the acceptance of inventions. The hierarchical firm accepts fewer inventions relative to a market with many firms, each of whom independently evaluates the invention. The architecture of the market for inventions is thus an important determinant of entrepreneurship.

Second, the greater the set-up cost of establishing a firm, K, the greater is the performance gap between the hierarchy and the polyarchy. A higher set-up cost shifts down the curve representing the returns to innovative entrepreneurship. This increases the critical values of the invention for the market organized as a hierarchy and the market organized as a polyarchy. Because the gap between the two curves widens as the critical values of inventions increase, the gap between the two critical values also increases. When the existing firm is a hierarchy, bureaucratic decision making can prevent the acceptance of inventions. The hierarchical firm accepts fewer inventions relative to a firm with many decision makers, each of whom independently evaluates the invention. Market architectures, thus, are an important determinant of innovative entrepreneurship.

8.2 Adverse Selection in the Market for Inventions and the Innovative Entrepreneur

Asymmetric information in the market for inventions affects the inventor's decision. The inventor is more likely to become an innovative entrepreneur as a means of overcoming the effects of incomplete information. The inventor knows the quality of his discovery, but existing firms may not know the quality of the discovery. As a consequence, the inventor can realize returns to private information by becoming an entrepreneur and embodying the technology in a new firm.

Adverse selection in the market for inventions is thus a determinant of entrepreneurship. The effects of asymmetric information in the market for inventions are closely related to Akerlof's (1970) market for used cars, in which low-quality used cars are known as "lemons." Suppose there are only two types of inventions: low-quality inventions and high-quality inventions. Existing firms, which are the potential buyers, cannot observe the quality of an inventor's discovery. An inventor knows the quality of his discovery. Suppose that final products are homogeneous and that all inventions are drastic, so that the quality of the invention can be represented by final profits that would be earned by an existing firm or by a new firm that implemented the discovery. Let π_L and π_H be the value of the invention to an existing firm. An existing firm can only observe the quality of the invention by purchasing it. Each inventor can contract with at most one existing firm.

Consider a population of inventors with the total number of inventors normalized to 1. A proportion of inventors, α, has a high-quality invention, π_H. The rest of the inventors, with proportion $(1 - \alpha)$, have a low-quality invention, π_L. Let the proportion of inventors with high-quality inventions be such that $0 < \alpha < 1$. Suppose that an inventor's inventions can be sold to at most one existing firm. Because the quality of an invention is unobservable, existing firms have a willingness to pay equal to the expected value of a discovery,

$$E\pi = (1 - \alpha)\pi_L + \alpha\pi_H. \tag{3}$$

The inventor can profit from his discovery by establishing a firm and incurring set-up costs $K > 0$. Suppose that either type of firm is viable, $\pi_H > \pi_L > K$, and suppose also that the inventor can afford the cost of establishing a firm.

The existing firm's cost of adopting the new technology is normalized to zero. This means that it is less costly to transfer the inventor's invention to an existing firm than to establish a new firm that embodies the invention. This implies that transferring the technology to an existing firm is more efficient than establishing a new firm. The assumption that technology transfer is more efficient serves to emphasize the effects of asymmetric information on the inventor's decision.

The problem of adverse selection does not prevent the formation of a market for inventions if the inventor's expected returns from technology transfer exceed the returns to entrepreneurship for an inventor with a high-quality discovery,

$$E\pi \geq \pi_H - K.$$

When the proportion of high-quality inventions is large, adverse selection generates less market inefficiency. The expected value of a disembodied invention is greater than or equal to the value of establishing a firm. Then, both types of inventors can sell their inventions to existing firms. All innovation takes place through the market for inventions, and no new firms are established.

Adverse selection can prevent the formation of a market for inventions if the expected value of a disembodied invention is less than the return to establishing a firm,

$$E\pi < \pi_H - K.$$

Then, bad inventions drive good ones out of the market. Those inventors with high-quality inventions strictly prefer to establish a firm. Those with high-quality inventions self-select by becoming entrepreneurs. Because inventors with high-quality inventions become entrepreneurs, only those with low-quality inventions enter the market. Because it is costly to establish a firm, existing firms will be able to purchase low-quality inventions. Existing firms are able to accurately infer the quality of an invention because only low-quality inventions are offered for sale in disembodied form. Entrepreneurship occurs if the proportion of good inventions is low. The critical value of the proportion of good inventions is given by $E\pi = \pi_H - K$ and equation (3),

$$\alpha^* = 1 - \frac{K}{\pi_H - \pi_L}. \tag{4}$$

Entrepreneurship occurs when the proportion of good inventions is less than the critical level, $\alpha < \alpha^*$.

The critical proportion of good discoveries, α^*, is increasing in the difference between high-quality and low-quality discoveries. *This implies that a greater gap between high-quality and low-quality discoveries increases innovative entrepreneurship.* The critical proportion of good discoveries is decreasing in the costs of establishing a firm, K, so that as expected, greater set-up costs reduce entrepreneurship.

One way to address asymmetric information in the market for inventions is through licensing contracts. The inventor can make the existing firm's royalty payment contingent on the quality of the discovery. The inventor can license the technology with a contingent royalty contract on the basis of the returns obtained by using the invention. With a contingent contract, the existing firm pays the inventor on the basis of the firm's performance.

Suppose that it is feasible to offer the inventor a contingent royalty. The royalty function gives the existing firm the profits from the discovery minus a lump-sum, J, where $0 \leq J \leq K$,

$$R(\pi) = \pi - J. \tag{5}$$

The lump-sum J transfers rents to the existing firm and reflects the relative bargaining power of the inventor and the existing firm. Given the contingent royalty, the inventor prefers to sell the technology rather than to establish the new firm. The outcome is efficient because it is less costly to transfer the technology than to establish a new firm.

It may not be feasible to write a complete contingent contract because of transaction costs of bargaining and of monitoring such contracts. Another possibility is a constant royalty per unit of returns for the existing firm. The existing firm pays the licensing royalty only after applying the inventor's discovery. The existing firm offers a per-unit royalty r and pays $r\pi_H$ for a high-quality discovery and pays $r\pi_L$ for a low-quality discovery. The profit-maximizing firm has two options. The existing firm can pay a high royalty that can attract both types of inventors. The existing firm can pay a low royalty that only attracts inventors with low-quality inventions. The lowest royalty that will attract inventors with both types of discoveries makes the high-quality inventor indifferent between selling the discovery and starting a firm,

$$r_H\pi_H = \pi_H - K.$$

This will attract inventors with both types of inventions because for the low-quality discovery,

$$r_H\pi_L > \pi_L - K.$$

Alternatively, the lowest royalty that attracts only the inventor with a low-quality discovery equals

$$r_L\pi_L = \pi_L - K.$$

The existing firm earns an expected return from offering the low royalty equal to

$$\Pi_L = (1-\alpha)(1-r_L)\pi_L = (1-\alpha)K. \tag{6}$$

The existing firm earns an expected profit from offering the high royalty equal to

$$\Pi_H = (1-r_H)E\pi = K\frac{E\pi}{\pi_H}. \tag{7}$$

The existing firm offers the high royalty if $\Pi_H \geq \Pi_L$, which is equivalent to

$$E\pi \geq (1-\alpha)\pi_H.$$

This occurs with a high proportion of good-quality discoveries, $\alpha \geq \alpha^{**}$, where the critical value equals

$$\alpha^{**} = \frac{\pi_H - \pi_L}{2\pi_H - \pi_L}. \tag{8}$$

In this situation, the existing firm offers high royalties, and entrepreneurship does not occur.

Entrepreneurship occurs when $\alpha < \alpha^{**}$. Then, *inventors with high-quality inventions establish firms, and inventors with low-quality inventions license their inventions.* Therefore, when the proportion of inventors who have high-quality inventions is less than the critical value α^{**}, entrepreneurship takes place. With licensing, the critical value of α does not depend on the cost of establishing a firm. The critical value depends only on the relative quality of the two types of inventions.

Increasing the gap between the high-quality and low-quality inventions increases the critical value, α^{**}, and thus increases innovative entrepreneurship.

8.3 Risky Development, Adverse Selection, and the Innovative Entrepreneur

Development risks and asymmetric information can affect an inventor's commercialization decisions. Suppose that developing an invention based on a particular research discovery involves a risk of failure. After making a research discovery, an inventor must choose between letting others develop the discovery or developing the research discovery himself. If the inventor chooses to sell the discovery, it will be developed into an invention by an existing firm. If the inventor chooses to develop the discovery himself, the inventor becomes an entrepreneur and creates a start-up to develop the discovery into an invention. If the development of the discovery is successful, the entrepreneur can establish a firm and obtain the resulting rewards. If the development of the discovery is not successful, the entrepreneur will not receive any rewards.

The inventor's commercialization decision also depends on the quality of the research discovery. Suppose that the quality of the inventor's discovery, θ, is his private information. Asymmetric information about the quality of the discovery will affect the sale of the discovery to an existing firm. As a consequence, asymmetric information about the discovery will affect the inventor's choice between selling the discovery and becoming an entrepreneur.

Consider the effects of risk and asymmetric information on the strategic innovation game played by an existing firm and an inventor. Suppose that the existing firm has market power and makes the inventor a first-and-final offer of a lump-sum royalty, R. The population of entrepreneurs has discoveries that are uniformly distributed on the unit interval.

The quality of the discovery affects the returns to an invention that develops the discovery. Developing a discovery of type θ results in a profit π, which is uniformly distributed on the interval $[A - \theta, A + \theta]$, where A is a positive parameter. The expected value of the profit from the invention is A, and the variance of the profit from the invention is $\text{var}(\pi) = \theta^2/3$. The probability density of π is $1/(2\theta)$. Let K be the costs of establishing a firm and assume that $A + K < 1$. Assume that expected profit is greater than the cost of establishing a firm, $A > K$, which implies that $A + \theta > K$ for all discoveries, θ.

If the inventor chooses to become an entrepreneur, he observes π costlessly. Then, the entrepreneur successfully establishes a firm if $\pi \geq K$ and earns $\pi - K$. If $\pi < K$, development is not successful and the entrepreneur receives no rewards. The ability to observe π before paying the cost of establishing the firm allows the entrepreneur to obtain the benefits of a successful development of the discovery. As a result, the entrepreneur benefits from greater variance of profits. The greater the value of θ, the higher is the quality of the discovery for the entrepreneur. The expected benefit of the entrepreneur is positive if the upper bound on profits, $A + \theta$, is greater than the cost of establishing the firm.

The value of the discovery θ to the entrepreneur equals

$$(9) \qquad U(\theta) = \int_K^{A+\theta} \frac{\pi - K}{2\theta} d\pi = \frac{(A + \theta - K)^2}{4\theta}.$$

The marginal value of a discovery is positive,

$$(10) \qquad U'(\theta) = \frac{1}{4}\left[1 - \frac{(A - K)^2}{\theta^2}\right] > 0.$$

Note that $A + \theta > K$ implies that $\theta^2 > (A - K)^2$. The entrepreneur is made better off by having a more risky discovery. The value of the discovery is convex in the quality of the discovery, θ,

$$(11) \qquad U''(\theta) = \frac{(A - K)^2}{2\theta^3} > 0.$$

The entrepreneur benefits from risk by having the real option to decide whether or not to invest in establishing the firm. The entrepreneur invests in establishing the firm if the anticipated profit exceeds the cost of setting up the firm. This helps explain the traditional emphasis on the entrepreneur benefiting from risk. The entrepreneur does not bear risk in the same manner as an investor, except to the extent that the entrepreneur supplies his own funds. Instead, the entrepreneur experiences the risks associated with the development of his discovery. This makes the entrepreneur prefer more risk.

Stiglitz and Weiss (1981) employ a similar information structure to study the effects of adverse selection on bank credit. They find that debt makes the borrower favor risk. The observation that the entrepreneur prefers more risk is similar. Like a borrower, the entrepreneur benefits from the upside of the development process by having the option to establish a firm.

If the inventor foregoes the option of entrepreneurship, he can commercialize his discovery by selling it to an existing firm at a lump-sum royalty, R. The inventor sells the discovery to the existing firm only if the royalty is greater than or equal to the benefit from becoming an entrepreneur, $R \geq U(\theta)$. Recall that the entrepreneur's benefit function is increasing in the variance parameter, θ, so that there is a critical value θ^* defined by

$$(12) \qquad U(\theta^*) = R.$$

Inventors with low-variance parameter values, θ in $[0, \theta^*]$, sell their discoveries to the existing firm. Inventors with high-variance parameter values, θ in $(\theta^*, 1]$, become entrepreneurs and establish firms.

The existing firm is risk neutral and is unaffected by the variance in the development process. The existing firm chooses the royalty on the basis of the trade-off between the cost of paying more to the inventor and the benefit of a greater likelihood of obtaining the discovery. The existing firm's profit equals $(A - R)\theta^*(R)$. The profit-maximizing royalty solves

$$(A - R)\frac{d\theta^*(R)}{dR} - \theta^*(R) = 0. \tag{13}$$

Substituting for $d\theta^*(R)/dR = 1/U'(\theta^*)$ and solving for θ^* gives

$$\theta^* = A + K. \tag{14}$$

Then, the royalty offered by the existing firm equals

$$R^* = \frac{A^2}{A + K}. \tag{15}$$

The royalty offered by the existing firm is increasing in the expected value of the invention and decreasing in the costs of establishing a new firm.

Entrepreneurship has long been associated with taking risks. This may be in part a result of adverse selection among inventors. *Inventors with less risky projects are able to transfer their technologies to existing firms, and inventors with more risky projects choose to become innovative entrepreneurs.* The number of innovative entrepreneurs is the number of inventors with projects above the variance cutoff, θ^*,

$$n^* = 1 - \theta^* = 1 - A - K. \tag{16}$$

The number of entrepreneurs is decreasing in the expected value of the invention and decreasing in the costs of establishing a firm.

8.4 Signaling in the Market for Inventions and the Innovative Entrepreneur

The inventor may face transaction costs associated with explaining his invention to the existing firm. The discovery may be unobservable and difficult to illustrate. It may be necessary for the inventor to invest in a costly signal that is observable to the existing firm. If the costs of signaling are relatively low, the inventor can convey the necessary information to the existing firm and transfer the technology. *If the costs of signaling are relatively high, the inventor will choose to become an innovative entrepreneur and establish a firm that embodies the new technology.*

The basic issues can be illustrated by adapting Spence's (1974) signaling model in which the inventor invests in a costly signal that provides an indication of the quality of the technology. Macho-Stadler and Pérez-Castrillo (1991, 2001) present a related model with asymmetric information in which the inventor chooses among contracts on the basis of per-unit royalties to signal that the invention has a higher-quality level. Gallini and Wright (1990) also consider a model in which a licensor signals the technology type by offering an output-based royalty contract.

Suppose that there are two types of inventors in the population: those with low-quality inventions, π_L, and those with high-quality inventions, π_H. The inventor's discovery is his private information and is unobservable to the existing firm. The inventor can provide a signal s to the existing firm. The signal can be a costly business plan, technology demonstration, or product prototype. The cost of the signal is s/π, which is increasing in the signal and decreasing in the quality of the discovery.[8] The existing firm offers the inventor a royalty payment that equals the expected value of the invention given the signal,

$$R(s) = E[\pi \mid s].$$

Under some conditions, the market equilibrium with signaling is separating. This depends on the restriction placed on out-of-equilibrium beliefs.[9] At a separating equilibrium, inventors with different inventions choose different signals, s_L and s_H. The existing firm offers different royalties on the basis of the signals, R_L and R_H. For an equilibrium to be separating, the outcomes must involve choices that are incentive compatible for the inventors. The inventor with the low-quality invention reveals his invention in equilibrium and receives a royalty equal to the value of his invention, $R_L = \pi_L$. The inventor with the low-quality invention will not invest in producing a signal, so that $s_L = 0$. The inventor with the low-quality invention must prefer the outcome to choosing the same signal as the inventor with the high-quality invention,

$$\pi_L \geq \pi_H - \frac{s_H}{\pi_L}.$$

For the inventor with the high-quality invention to prefer investing in a signal, incentive compatibility requires that

$$\pi_H - \frac{s_H}{\pi_H} \geq \pi_L.$$

Combining these two inequalities gives bounds on the value of the signal of a high-quality invention,

$$\pi_L(\pi_H - \pi_L) \leq s_H \leq \pi_H(\pi_H - \pi_L).$$

This range defines a continuum of separating equilibria.

8 See Macho-Stadler and Pérez-Castrillo (1991, 2001) for a related model with asymmetric information in which the inventor chooses among contracts on the basis of per-unit royalties to signal that the invention has a higher-quality level. Gallini and Wright (1990) also consider a model in which a licensor signals the technology type by offering an output-based royalty contract.

9 See Banks and Sobel (1987) for the D2 criterion refinement and applications by Banks (1992) and Besanko and Spulber (1992).

Consider the equilibrium at which the inventor chooses the least costly signal. The inventor with the low-quality invention chooses $s_L = 0$, and the inventor with the high-quality invention chooses the signal

$$s_H = \pi_L(\pi_H - \pi_L).$$

The cost of signaling determines the outcome of the commercialization decisions of inventors. The inventor with the low-quality invention faces no signaling costs. Therefore, rather than pay the costs of establishing a firm, the inventor with the low-quality invention prefers to sell his invention to the existing firm.

The inventor with the high-quality invention chooses to signal the quality of the invention and sell to the existing firm if the costs of establishing a firm are greater than or equal to the costs of signaling,

$$K \geq \frac{s_H}{\pi_H} = \pi_L - \frac{(\pi_L)^2}{\pi_H}.$$

Otherwise, when the set-up costs of the new firm are less than the costs of signaling, $K < \pi_L - (\pi_L)^2/\pi_H$, signaling is not worthwhile. *Therefore, when signaling is costly relative to the costs of establishing a firm, an inventor with a high-quality invention becomes an innovative entrepreneur.*

8.5 Agency with Adverse Selection and the Innovative Entrepreneur

Consider the strategic innovation game with an inventor who has private information about a basic research discovery. The inventor must invest effort to apply the discovery and develop an invention. Technology transfer involves agency costs because the inventor contracts with the existing firm to develop the invention. The inventor who chooses to become an innovative entrepreneur avoids incurring agency costs although he must incur the costs of establishing the firm and competing with the existing firm. This section examines how adverse selection in technology transfer contracts affects entrepreneurship.[10] The inventor faces "countervailing incentives" due to the effects of invention costs and opportunity costs.

The strategic innovation game involves *countervailing incentives* (see Lewis and Sappington, 1989, and Maggi and Rodriguez-Clare, 1995). A better discovery increases the returns to technology transfer by reducing the costs of developing an

10 The inventor who contracts with the existing firm to develop an invention may have unobservable effort, leading to moral hazard problems in technology transfer. Jensen and Thursby (2001) present a moral hazard agency model of technology transfer and consider the implications of the agency contract for the inventor's development efforts and the design of a two-part royalty schedule. Poblete and Spulber (2013) show that the optimal agency contract for delegated R&D with moral hazard takes the form of an option.

invention. A better discovery also increases the returns to innovative entrepreneurship, again by reducing the costs of developing an invention. The returns to innovative entrepreneurship are the opportunity costs of technology transfer. Therefore, a better discovery reduces the costs of developing an invention for technology transfer while reducing the opportunity costs of technology transfer.

Let θ be the quality of the basic research discovery. The inventor invests effort a to develop an invention of quality Π, which represents the returns to a firm from adopting the invention. The production function describing the development process is

$$\Pi = \Pi(\theta, a), \tag{17}$$

which is increasing in the quality of the discovery and in the inventor's development effort. The potential adopter does not know the inventor's discovery, so that the discovery is the inventor's unobservable "type." Discoveries are distributed on the unit interval with cumulative distribution function $F(\theta)$ and probability density function $f(\theta)$. Basic research can be viewed as a random draw from the distribution $F(\theta)$.

Invert the production function to obtain the cost of development effort needed to achieve an invention of quality Π with discovery of type θ,

$$a = C(\Pi, \theta). \tag{18}$$

Assume that the discovery and the inventor's development effort are complements, $\Pi_{\theta a}(\theta, a) > 0$, and that the production technology is concave in effort and the discovery, $\Pi_{aa}(\theta, a) < 0$, $\Pi_{\theta\theta}(\theta, a) < 0$. This implies that the Spence-Mirrlees single-crossing condition holds,

$$-C_{\theta\Pi}(\Pi, \theta) = \frac{1}{\Pi_a(\theta, a)} \frac{\partial}{\partial a} \frac{\Pi_\theta(\theta, a)}{\Pi_a(\theta, a)} > 0.$$

This is equivalent to assuming that the discovery, θ, is a normal input in the production of the invention.[11]

The inventor who chooses to become an innovative entrepreneur incurs set-up costs, K, to establish a firm. Suppose that the invention makes the new firm sufficiently efficient for it to displace the existing firm. Alternatively, the invention involves a new product that is sufficiently desired by consumers for the new firm to displace the existing firm. Then, the inventor chooses the quality of the invention, Π, to maximize net returns to entrepreneurship, $U^E = \Pi - C(\Pi, \theta) - K$. The inventor who becomes an entrepreneur, therefore, chooses the quality level $\Pi^*(\theta)$ that solves the first-order condition,

$$1 = C_\Pi(\Pi^*, \theta). \tag{19}$$

11 Assume also that $\Pi_{aa}(\theta, a)\Pi_{\theta\theta}(\theta, a) - \Pi_{\theta a}(\theta, a)\Pi_{a\theta}(\theta, a) > 0$ so that $\Pi(\theta, a)$ is strictly concave.

The innovative entrepreneur with a discovery of type θ obtains a net benefit of

$$U^E(\theta) = \Pi^*(\theta) - C(\Pi^*(\theta), \theta) - K. \tag{20}$$

By the envelope theorem, the innovative entrepreneur's marginal benefit is increasing in the quality of the discovery and equals

$$U^{E\prime}(\theta) = -C_\theta(\Pi^*(\theta), \theta). \tag{21}$$

Assume that the firm's set-up costs are sufficiently low for entrepreneurship to be feasible for any discovery, $U^E(0) \geq 0$ for all θ.

From the entrepreneur's first-order condition (19), the optimal quality of the invention is increasing in the quality of the discovery,

$$\Pi^{*\prime}(\theta) = -\frac{C_{\Pi\theta}(\Pi^*(\theta), \theta)}{C_{\Pi\Pi}(\Pi^*(\theta), \theta)} > 0. \tag{22}$$

The innovative entrepreneur's net benefit $U^E(\theta)$ is strictly concave in the discovery, $U^{E\prime\prime}(\theta) < 0$.[12]

Consider now the technology transfer contract between the inventor and the existing firm. The inventor provides effort a and the discovery θ to develop an invention of quality Π. The two parties form an agency contract with the existing firm as the principal and the inventor as the agent. Because the discovery is the inventor's private information, the arrangement between the existing firm and the inventor is subject to the problem of adverse selection. The discovery, θ, is the inventor's unobservable type. Applying the revelation principle, without loss of generality, the agency contract can be expressed as a direct revelation mechanism in which the adopting firm makes a transfer $t(\theta)$ to the inventor and receives the returns from the developed invention, $\pi(\theta)$. The inventor reports the type of discovery θ to the adopting firm and receives the payment $t(\theta)$.

The returns from innovative entrepreneurship, $U^E(\theta)$, are the inventor's opportunity costs of technology transfer. The inventor's net benefit from technology transfer equals the payment net of the costs of invention and the opportunity costs of technology transfer,

$$u(\theta) = t(\theta) - C(\pi(\theta), \theta) - U^E(\theta). \tag{23}$$

The discovery, θ, affects the inventor's benefits in two opposing ways, generating the problem of "countervailing incentives." The inventor's costs, $C(\Pi, \theta)$, are

12 The effect of the discovery on the innovative entrepreneur's marginal benefit equals

$$U^{E\prime\prime}(\theta) = -C_{\theta\theta}(\Pi^*(\theta), \theta) + \frac{C_{\Pi\theta}(\Pi^*(\theta), \theta) C_{\theta\Pi}(\Pi^*(\theta), \theta)}{C_{\Pi\Pi}(\Pi^*(\theta), \theta)}.$$

Note that given our assumptions, $C_{\Pi\Pi}(\Pi^*(\theta), \theta) > 0$, $C_{\theta\theta}(\Pi^*(\theta), \theta) > 0$, and $C_{\theta\Pi}(\Pi^*(\theta), \theta) = C_{\Pi\theta}(\Pi^*(\theta), \theta) < 0$. Also, note that $U^{E\prime\prime}(\theta) = [\Pi_{aa}(\theta, a)\Pi_{\theta\theta}(\theta, a) - \Pi_{\theta a}(\theta, a)\Pi_{a\theta}(\theta, a)]\Pi_a(\theta, a)/\Pi_{aa}(\theta, a) < 0$.

decreasing in the discovery for any invention, Π, and the inventor's opportunity costs of technology transfer are increasing in the discovery. In the agency relationship with the existing firm, the inventor has an incentive to understate the discovery to indicate high costs of invention and an incentive to overstate the discovery to indicate high opportunity costs of technology transfer.

The principal's realized net benefit is $\pi(\theta) - t(\theta)$. The optimal contract maximizes the principal's expected net benefit,

$$V(\pi, t) = \int_0^1 [\pi(\theta) - t(\theta)] f(\theta) d\theta, \tag{24}$$

subject to the agent's individual rationality (IR) or participation constraint,

$$u(\theta) \geq 0,$$

and the agent's incentive compatibility (IC) constraint,

$$t(\theta) - C(\pi(\theta), \theta) \geq t(\theta') - C(\pi(\theta'), \theta),$$

for all reported discoveries θ, θ' in $[0, 1]$, where θ is the inventor's actual discovery. The necessary and sufficient conditions for IC to hold are that the outcome is increasing in the discovery, $\pi'(\theta) \geq 0$, and the inventor's marginal net benefit is given by

$$u'(\theta) = -C_\theta(\pi(\theta), \theta) - U^{E\prime}(\theta). \tag{25}$$

These conditions follow from standard arguments.[13] These necessary and sufficient conditions replace the IC condition in the principal's problem. A better discovery increases returns for innovative entrepreneurs and thus increases the opportunity costs of technology transfer. Consideration of the inventor's marginal net benefit in equation (25) shows that the discovery has two effects: an invention-cost effect and an opportunity-cost effect.

The inventor's net benefit from technology transfer can be increasing, constant, or decreasing in the quality of the discovery. If the invention-cost effect dominates the opportunity-cost effect, the inventor's net benefit is increasing in the quality of the discovery, which is the standard adverse selection incentive effect. The inventor has an incentive to understate the quality of the underlying invention so as to be compensated more for the costs of discovery. This outcome is reversed by "countervailing incentives": the opportunity-cost effect dominates the invention-cost effect. Then, the inventor's net benefit from technology transfer is decreasing in the quality of the discovery. The "countervailing incentive" effect of innovative entrepreneurship offsets the standard effect of the discovery on the costs of invention. The inventor has an incentive to overstate the quality of the discovery so as

13 See Mirrlees (1971), Laffont (1989), Lewis and Sappington (1989), and Maggi and Rodriguez-Clare (1995). The form of the inventor's marginal benefit holds if and only if local incentive compatibility holds, $t'(\theta) = C_\Pi(\pi(\theta), \theta)\pi'(\theta)$.

to be compensated for greater opportunity costs of technology transfer. The inventor's net benefit from technology transfer is convex in the quality of the discovery, $u''(\theta) \geq 0$.[14]

The optimal agency contract is such that the "countervailing incentives" of the invention-cost effect exactly offset the incentives of the opportunity-cost effect. This implies that the optimal agency contract induces the first-best agency effort, $\pi^*(\theta) = \Pi^*(\theta)$. The principal transfers to the agent all revenues net of the fixed costs of setting up a firm,

$$t^*(\theta) = C(\pi^*(\theta), \theta) + U^E(\theta) = \Pi^*(\theta) - K. \quad (26)$$

The principal obtains benefits equal to the fixed costs of setting up a firm, $V = K$. The principal essentially sells the project to the inventor for a lump-sum payment equal to K. This implies that even with adverse selection, technology transfer always occurs with an optimal agency contract. The contract satisfies the agent's IC constraint,

$$\Pi^*(\theta) - K - C(\Pi^*(\theta), \theta) \geq \Pi^*(\theta') - K - C(\Pi^*(\theta'), \theta),$$

for all θ, θ' in $[0, 1]$.[15] The contract also satisfies the agent's IR constraint,

$$u(\theta) = t(\theta) - C(\Pi^*(\theta), \theta) - U^E(\theta) = 0,$$

for all θ in $[0, 1]$.

To see why the optimal contract attains the first-best outcome, suppose instead that the invention-cost effect dominates the opportunity-cost effect, $-C_\theta(\pi^*(\theta), \theta) - U^{E\prime}(\theta) > 0$, so that the inventor's net benefit from technology transfer is increasing in the discovery. Then, by standard arguments, adverse selection implies that the inventor shirks under the technology transfer contract. Shirking would imply that the quality of the invention is lower with technology transfer than with entrepreneurship for any given discovery, $\theta, \pi^*(\theta) \leq \Pi^*(\theta)$. Shirking by an inventor with a technology transfer contract lowers the marginal effect of the discovery on the costs of invention below that with innovative entrepreneurship,

$$-C_\theta(\pi^*(\theta), \theta) \leq -C_\theta(\Pi^*(\theta), \theta) = U^{E\prime}(\theta) = 0.$$

This is a contradiction so the invention-cost effect does not dominate the opportunity-cost effect.

Suppose now that the opportunity-cost effect dominates the incentive-cost effect, $-C_\theta(\pi^*(\theta), \theta) - U^{E\prime}(\theta) < 0$, so that the inventor's net benefit from technology transfer is decreasing in the discovery. Then, the optimal contract induces

14 Recall that the innovative entrepreneur's net benefit is strictly concave in the discovery, $U^{E\prime\prime}(\theta) < 0$. Incentive compatibility implies that the outcome is increasing in the discovery, $\pi'(\theta) \geq 0$. Also, $C_{\theta\Pi}(\pi(\theta), \theta) < 0$ and $C_{\theta\theta}(\pi(\theta), \theta) < 0$, so that for $u'(\theta) \neq 0$, it follows that $u''(\theta) = -C_{\theta\Pi}(\pi(\theta), \theta)\pi'(\theta) - C_{\theta\theta}(\pi(\theta), \theta) - U^{E\prime\prime}(\theta) > 0$.

15 By the envelope theorem, the marginal benefit from the discovery is zero – that is, $u'(\theta) = -C_\theta(\pi^*(\theta), \theta) - U^{E\prime}(\theta) = 0$.

the inventor to supply effort greater than or equal to the first best, $\pi^*(\theta) \geq \Pi^*(\theta)$. This raises the marginal effect of the discovery on the costs of invention above that with innovative entrepreneurship,

$$-C_\theta(\pi^*(\theta), \theta) \geq -C_\theta(\Pi^*(\theta), \theta) = U^{E\prime}(\theta) = 0.$$

This is again a contradiction, so it follows that the opportunity-cost effect does not dominate the incentive-cost effect. Therefore, the invention-cost effect and the opportunity-cost effect cancel each other, and the optimal contract is the one that induces the first-best inventive effort.

This result depends on the inventor's development process being the same whether the inventor is transferring the technology to the existing firm or the inventor becomes an entrepreneur. Consider instead a situation in which countervailing incentives do not perfectly offset the agent's incentives. Suppose that the costs of establishing a new firm also depend on the quality of the underlying discovery, $K(\theta)$. Suppose that a better discovery lowers the costs of establishing a new firm, $K'(\theta) < 0$, and suppose also that these set-up costs are convex in the discovery, $K''(\theta) > 0$. The innovative entrepreneur's net benefit $U^E(\theta)$ is still increasing and strictly concave in the discovery, $U^{E\prime}(\theta)$ and $U^{E\prime\prime}(\theta) < 0$.

The innovative entrepreneur does not experience countervailing incentives because a better discovery lowers both the costs of establishing the firm and the costs of developing the new product. However, the inventor contracting for technology transfer does experience countervailing incentives. The beneficial effect of the discovery on the costs of establishing the firm increases the inventor's opportunity costs of contracting with the existing firm.

Because a better invention reduces the costs of establishing a firm, the opportunity-cost effect of the invention must dominate the invention-cost effect. By arguments given previously, this rules out the situation in which the inventor's net benefit is increasing in the discovery, $-C_\theta(\pi^*(\theta), \theta) + C_\theta(\Pi^*(\theta), \theta) + K'(\theta) > 0$. Therefore, the inventor does not shirk under the technology transfer contract. Shirking by inventor with a technology transfer contract would lower the marginal effect of the discovery on the costs of invention below that with innovative entrepreneurship. Shirking would imply that the quality of the invention is lower with technology transfer than with entrepreneurship for any given discovery, θ, $\pi^*(\theta) \leq \Pi^*(\theta)$, which is a contradiction.

However, now the opportunity-cost effect can dominate the incentive-cost effect, $-C_\theta(\pi^*(\theta), \theta) + C_\theta(\Pi^*(\theta), \theta) + K'(\theta) < 0$. *The optimal contract induces the inventor to supply inventive effort that is greater than or equal to the first best,* $\pi^*(\theta) \geq \Pi^*(\theta)$. This raises the marginal effect of the discovery on the costs of invention above that with innovative entrepreneurship. Then, an increase in the quality of the discovery reduces the inventor's net benefit from technology transfer, $u'(\theta) < 0$.

Because the opportunity-cost effect of the discovery outweighs the investment-cost effect, the inventor has an incentive to *overstate* the quality of the discovery. In this situation, the principal has an incentive to increase the slope of the agent's

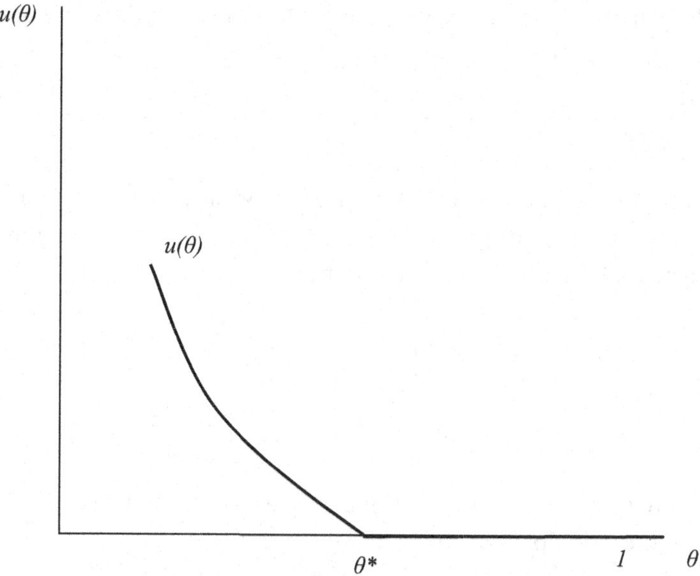

Figure 8.2. The inventor's net benefits with the technology transfer agency contract.

net benefit, $u(\theta)$.[16] The inventor's net benefit from technology transfer is strictly convex in θ, so that the IR rationality constraint holds with equality at exactly one value of the discovery, $u(\theta^*) = 0$.[17] The inventor's net benefits are shown in Figure 8.2.[18] Inventors with lower-quality discoveries have positive net benefits from technology transfer. *This implies that inventors with high-quality discoveries, $\theta \in (\theta^*, 1)$, choose to become innovative entrepreneurs, and inventors with low-quality discoveries, $\theta \in [0, \theta^*]$, transfer their technologies.*

The inventor's participation constraint is binding for lower-type agents. The principal's problem therefore can be written as

$$\max_{\pi, t} \int_0^1 [\pi(\theta) - t(\theta)] f(\theta) d\theta,$$

subject to

$$u(\theta^*) \geq 0,$$
$$u'(\theta) = -C_\theta(\pi(\theta), \theta) - U^{E\prime}(\theta),$$
$$\pi'(\theta) \geq 0.$$

16 See Lewis and Sappington (1989) and Maggi and Rodriguez-Clare (1995).

17 See Lewis and Sappington (1989) and Maggi and Rodriguez-Clare (1995).

18 The main difference between our analysis and those of Lewis and Sappington (1989) and Maggi and Rodriguez-Clare (1995) is that our analysis explicitly derives the agent's opportunity cost from the innovative entrepreneur's problem. Lewis and Sappington (1989) find that all types earn information rents if they participate in the contract, although intermediate types could also be inactive and not participate in the contract. In our setting, the higher types pursue their outside opportunity of innovative entrepreneurship.

The inventor's net benefit can be rewritten using the inventor's IC condition and IR condition, $u(\theta^*) = 0$,

$$u(\theta) = \int_{\theta}^{\theta^*} [C_\theta(\pi(\theta), \theta) + U^{E\prime}(\theta)]d\theta. \tag{27}$$

This indicates the information rents for an inventor of type $\theta \leq \theta^*$. Using the form of the inventor's net benefit, $t(\theta) = u(\theta) + C(\pi(\theta), \theta) + U^E(\theta)$, and integrating by parts, the principal's net benefit can be written as

$$V(\pi, t) = \int_0^1 \left\{ \pi(\theta) - C(\pi(\theta), \theta) - U^E(\theta) - [C_\theta(\pi(\theta), \theta) + U^{E\prime}(\theta)]\frac{F(\theta)}{f(\theta)} \right\} f(\theta)d\theta. \tag{28}$$

Let $\pi^*(\theta)$ and $t^*(\theta)$ denote the optimal revelation mechanism. The first-order condition for the principal's problem is

$$C_\Pi(\pi^*(\theta), \theta) + C_{\theta\Pi}(\pi^*(\theta), \theta)\frac{F(\theta)}{f(\theta)} = 1. \tag{29}$$

Adverse selection has the standard implication that the inventor does not supply the optimal level of effort to the development process. Equation (29) implies that the marginal cost of increasing the quality of the invention is less than 1, $C_\Pi(\pi^*(\theta), \theta) < 1$. Therefore, for any discovery θ less than θ^*, the inventor chooses to devote more effort to development than the optimal level, so that the quality of the developed invention is above the optimum, $\pi^*(\theta) > \Pi^*(\theta)$.

The principal's transfer payment to the agent can be expressed as a royalty contract, $t^*(\theta) = R(\pi^*(\theta))$. Then, the slope of the contract equals $t^{*\prime}(\theta) = R'(\pi^*(\theta))\pi^{*\prime}(\theta)$. Applying the agent's local incentive compatibility condition and the first-order condition from the principal's problem implies

$$R'(\pi^*(\theta)) = \frac{t^{*\prime}(\theta)}{\pi^{*\prime}(\theta)} = C_\pi(\pi^*(\theta), \theta) = 1 + C_{\theta\pi}(\pi^*(\theta), \theta)\frac{1 - F(\theta)}{f(\theta)}. \tag{30}$$

Cost complementarity of the discovery and the quality of the invention, $C_{\pi\theta}(\pi^*(\theta), \theta) < 0$, implies that the marginal royalty is less than 1. The inventor and the existing firm divide the marginal returns from the development process.

The previous discussion assumes that the development process for the new invention is identical with technology transfer and innovative entrepreneurship. However, it is possible that the development process with technology transfer may be more efficient than that of a start-up, because the existing firm has complementary assets that enhance product development. The existing firm's complementary assets include market knowledge, skilled personnel, laboratory facilities, and related technology. Conversely, the existing firm's development process may be less efficient than that of a start-up if the existing firm has bureaucratic inertia that raises the costs of product development. Also, the inventor who becomes an innovative entrepreneur may have tacit knowledge that is costly to transfer to the existing firm, as discussed in the preceding chapter. Then, the production function describing the development process would differ for the existing firm and the start-up. This would affect the outcome of the strategic innovation game between the inventor and the existing firm.

8.6 Conclusion

Information asymmetries in the market for inventions affect whether the strategic innovation game results in competition or cooperation. Entrepreneurship requires competing with existing firms and other entrepreneurs and potentially displacing them with a better technology. Technology transfer requires cooperating with existing firms who will purchase or license the new technology. When efficient bargaining between inventors and existing firms is feasible, entrepreneurship occurs if and only if it is socially efficient. However, when asymmetric information introduces bargaining inefficiencies, inventors have greater incentives to become innovative entrepreneurs.

Adverse selection can prevent the formation of a market for inventions when the expected value of an invention is less than the return to establishing a firm that applies the invention. When uncertainty in the development process creates risk, entrepreneurship provides a way to address development decisions. When signaling the value of inventors' discoveries is costly, entrepreneurship provides a more efficient way to use the inventors' information. When contracting for technology transfer involves agency costs for inventors, entrepreneurship provides a means for improving incentives to develop inventions. Innovative entrepreneurship increases the overall efficiency of innovation by addressing information asymmetries in the market for inventions.

9

The Wealth of Nations

International Trade and Investment

How do innovative entrepreneurs affect international trade and economic prosperity? Realizing gains from trade requires countries to adjust their consumption and production profiles. Some of these adjustments may be achieved through restructuring the activities of existing firms. However, the adjustments needed to realize gains from trade generally will require new firms and often entirely new industries. Innovative entrepreneurs are thus essential to developing the wealth of nations.

The growth of international trade has indeed sparked entrepreneurship in many countries. To better understand this phenomenon, I extend the general equilibrium model of entrepreneurship (Kihlstrom and Laffont, 1979; Lucas, 1978) to examine international trade with heterogeneous technologies (Melitz, 2003; Chaney, 2008).[1] I find that opening economies to international trade does not change extensive margins in comparison with closed economies and does not equalize factor prices, so that efficiency differences and wage differences persist in equilibrium. I then show that entrepreneurs engage in FDI to transfer technology from the country with the lower labor-technology ratio to the country with the higher labor-technology ratio. The main result is that the combination of FDI and international trade equalizes both wages and extensive margins and generates benefits from trade.

The model predicts the direction and volume of international trade and FDI; countries with relatively greater endowments of labor as compared to technology attract FDI and have international trade surpluses and deficits in FDI earnings.

1 The model in the chapter extends the occupational choice model from a Walrasian setting to one with price-setting firms that sell differentiated products and engage in monopolistic competition. Additionally, the present model applies the occupational choice model to consideration of international investment and examines how FDI affects occupational choice in each country. Kihlstrom and Laffont (1979) present an occupation choice model in which establishing firms is risky in comparison to working for others at a fixed wage. In a general equilibrium setting, they show that consumers who choose to become entrepreneurs are those who are the least risk averse. Lucas (1978) examines how the size distribution of business firms may be based on an underlying distribution of managerial talent across individuals. These models are in a neoclassical setting with a Walrasian auctioneer and price-taking firms that offer homogeneous products.

Based on differences in relative endowments of labor and technology, the model helps explain why the United States or the European Union (EU) have trade deficits while obtaining net earnings surpluses on foreign investment (Bureau of Economic Analysis, 2010). In contrast, countries such as China, with relatively larger labor-technology ratios, tend to have trade surpluses with these trading partners.

The discussion in this chapter examines how the immobility of labor and innovative technology generates differences in countries' extensive and intensive margins of technology utilization. Because potential innovators establish new firms, countries' extensive and intensive margins depend on their relative labor-technology endowments. International trade alone is not sufficient to change countries' extensive margins in comparison with the closed economies so that factor price differences and differences in technology utilization persist, even in the absence of trade frictions. However, the combination of international trade and entrepreneurial FDI, which transfers innovators' discoveries, equalizes extensive margins and harmonizes intensive margins of technology utilization across countries.

More countries are generating entrepreneurs who establish firms, and many newly established firms are engaging in international activities at their founding. These important developments raise fundamental questions about the connections between entrepreneurship, international trade, and FDI. Introducing entrepreneurs in an international trade model addresses both diffusion of entrepreneurship and interdependence between entrepreneurship and international trade. The main feature of the model is that it combines occupational choice models of entrepreneurship with industrial organizational models of international trade. Countries differ in their relative endowments of both labor and technology. Also, technology is heterogeneous across potential entrepreneurs as a result of differences in innovation and human capital. These technological heterogeneities both across countries and across potential entrepreneurs affect patterns of international trade, FDI, and entrepreneurship across countries.

The discussion in this chapter explores the connections between FDI, international trade, and entrepreneurship. The chapter is organized as follows. Section 9.1 introduces the basic entrepreneurship model for a closed economy. Section 9.2 extends the entrepreneurship model by considering international trade between two countries. Section 9.3 considers the entrepreneurship model when there is both FDI and international trade in goods. Section 9.4 considers empirical implications and extensions of the basic model.

9.1 Entrepreneurship in the Closed Economy

Countries differ in terms of their initial endowments of labor and potential entrepreneurs. The model features international trade with endogenous entrepreneurship and shows how the establishment of firms by entrepreneurs creates gains from trade. Individuals in each country choose whether to become workers or entrepreneurs on the basis of their technology endowment that represents individual differences in human capital, knowledge, and inventions.

Entrepreneurs commercialize their technologies by establishing firms as long as they obtain profits greater than their opportunity cost, which is given by the returns to labor. The model represents entrepreneurial innovation and capabilities by assuming that potential entrepreneurs are endowed with different production technologies. Also, the model represents entrepreneurial creativity by assuming that every new firm produces a unique product. Once established, firms engage in monopolistic price competition. The entrepreneur's technology endowment, capabilities, and creativity are embodied in the new firm. Entrepreneurs introduce innovations in the domestic economy that increase product variety and productive efficiency and yield gains from international trade. Entrepreneurship generates gains from trade because new firms introduce technological innovations that improve productive efficiency and new products that alter patterns of trade and yield benefits from product variety. Domestic entrepreneurs, by increasing productivity and introducing new products, potentially create gains from international trade.

Entrepreneurs introduce innovations abroad through FDI, technology transfer, and procurement contracts that yield benefits in addition to those obtained through international trade. The main insight of the analysis is that entrepreneurship improves economic efficiency and increases total benefits by harmonizing technologies across countries. The discussion defines entrepreneurial FDI as international technology transfer embodied in new firms along with foreign expenditures on fixed and operating costs and repatriation of profits. Ideas being more mobile than labor, there is a need to connect innovations with human capital across national borders. Countries having greater endowments of technology than labor benefit from exchange with countries that have greater endowments of labor than technology. International trade in final products and intermediate goods may not be sufficient to obtain all of the gains from trade that result from differences in technology.

Entrepreneurs create value in the international economy by making new combinations that connect innovations with production in different countries. Entrepreneurs provide a mode of technology transfer by establishing firms that embody technological innovations. New firms can transfer technology abroad while taking advantage of labor in the host country by locating production facilities abroad, outsourcing production offshore, licensing technology to foreign subcontractors, and offering international franchise contracts. Entrepreneurs bridge differences in technology and factors of production through FDI and contracts. The discussion shows how entrepreneurs connect innovations and human capital in the international economy.

The countries have different national endowments of technology and human capital, which can be represented without loss of generality as the same number of potential entrepreneurs and different labor forces. Without trade, the country with the higher population has a greater extensive margin of technology so that the marginal entrepreneur has a less efficient technology than in the country with a lower population. Entrepreneurship therefore endogenously generates technology differences between the two countries. International trade generates greater product variety for each of the countries as in industrial organization models of trade. However, the analysis shows that international trade is not sufficient to eliminate endogenous technology differences because of the immobility of labor and the effects of occupational choice by entrepreneurs.

The main result of the analysis is that entrepreneurial FDI in addition to international trade transfers technology across countries and harmonizes productivity. Entrepreneurial FDI increases the extensive margin of technological efficiency in the source country and reduces the extensive margin of technological efficiency in the host country. Therefore, entrepreneurial FDI results in factor price equalization taking advantage of international differences in the labor force and innovative technology. Entrepreneurial FDI transfers technology internationally that is embodied in the form of new firms. By employing workers in the host country and competing with entrepreneurs there, entrepreneurial FDI improves international productive efficiency.

This section specifies the basic model and examines the market equilibrium in the closed economy. There are two countries designated by $r = 1, 2$. The total population of consumers in each country r has measure, $H_r + G_r$, consisting of a group of workers with measure H_r and a group of potential innovative entrepreneurs with measure G_r. Each potential innovative entrepreneur chooses whether to become an entrepreneur and establish a firm or to become a worker and enter the labor force. Each potential entrepreneur has new technological knowledge that can be used to establish a firm. The group of potential innovative entrepreneurs G_r represents a country's technology endowments. Therefore, each country has different endowments of labor and innovative technologies.

Each worker and potential entrepreneur has a unit endowment of labor. Labor earns a wage w_r, which is determined endogenously. Labor is a numéraire good in a closed economy so the wage can be normalized when there is no international trade. In the open economy, however, wages are interdependent and differ across countries. An innovator can choose to establish a firm, which uses one unit of labor, or to become a worker. Labor is assumed to be an immobile factor of production. We consider the economic equilibrium when firms and technologies also are immobile. Then we compare this outcome with that in which firms and technologies are mobile through entrepreneurial FDI. To focus on the key drivers of the model, it is assumed that there are no costs of trade and no fixed costs of FDI. The effects of introducing these costs are examined in Section 9.4.

Potential entrepreneurs have access to heterogeneous technologies. Each potential entrepreneur has a technology parameter θ that takes values on the unit interval $[0, 1]$. The technology parameter θ has the cumulative distribution function $F(\theta)$ with continuous density function $f(\theta)$. The technology parameter represents the potential entrepreneur's innovation, which includes his capabilities, discoveries, inventions, product features, manufacturing processes, transaction methods, organizational designs, and business plans. If a potential entrepreneur establishes a firm, it then embodies his production technology θ. Let A_r designate the set of innovators in country r who choose to become entrepreneurs. Then, the effective labor force in country r equals

$$(1) \qquad N_r = H_r + G_r(1 - F(A_r)),$$

for $r = 1, 2$. The critical difference between the two countries is the *labor-technology ratio*, which is the ratio of the number of workers to the number of potential entrepreneurs, $L_r = H_r / G_r$. The labor-technology ratio represents the relative endowments of the two countries. The two countries are identical in all respects except that country 2 has a greater labor-technology ratio than country 1, $L_2 > L_1$.

Differences in entrepreneurs' profits reflect rents to their diverse technologies. Entrepreneurs establish firms that employ workers, produce differentiated products, and engage in monopolistic price competition. Once established each firm produces a distinct product. To produce q_j units of good j, requires $a + \theta q_j$ units of labor, where a is fixed costs and θ is marginal cost. Letting p_j denote the price of good j, firm j's profit equals

$$(2) \qquad \Pi_j(p_j, \theta) = (p_j - w_r\theta)q_j - w_r a.$$

Potential entrepreneurs choose between becoming workers and becoming innovative entrepreneurs. A consumer who works for a firm earns income $I = w_r$. A consumer who chooses to become an entrepreneur invests his endowment of labor to establish a firm. The entrepreneur's labor costs of establishing a firm represents the effort required to commercialize the technology, design the organization, and gather factors of production. Having established a firm, the entrepreneur becomes an owner and has income equal to the firm's profits, $I = \pi$. A potential entrepreneur in country r chooses to establish a firm if and only if the firm earns profit greater than or equal to labor income, $\pi \geq w_r$.

Each consumer has a utility function with the CES form,

$$(3) \qquad u(x) = \left[\int_0^m x_j^{(s-1)/s} dj\right]^{s/(s-1)},$$

where x_j is consumption of good j. The preference parameter is greater than 1, $s > 1$, which is necessary and sufficient for products to be substitutes in demand. The consumer's problem is to maximize utility subject to the budget constraint, $\max_x u(x)$ subject to $\int_0^m p_j x_j dj \leq I$. The consumer's problem yields the level of consumption of each good j, $x_j = I(p_j^{-s} / P^{s-1})$, where P is an index of prices given by $P = [\int_0^m (1/p_i)^{s-1} di]^{1/(s-1)}$.

Each consumer's benefit depends on prices, income, and the number of goods, $u(p, I) = IP$. A worker's benefit is $u(p, I) = P$, and an entrepreneur's benefit is $u(p, \Pi) = \Pi(p, \theta)P$. The entrepreneur becomes an owner after establishing the firm. By the form of the owner's benefit function, the profit-maximizing price maximizes the owner's utility. This result extends the neoclassical Fisher Separation Theorem to a setting in which firms engage in monopolistic competition and set prices. Each owner takes the equilibrium prices of other firms as given. The derivative of the price index with respect to any price is zero because there is a continuum of goods. Therefore, the owner of the firm chooses the profit-maximizing price as an equilibrium best response to other prices (Spulber, 2009a).

The own-price elasticity of demand for each good j for any consumer is equal to the elasticity of substitution s because the derivative of the price index with respect to any price is zero when there is a continuum of goods. The elasticity of substitution is also the elasticity of aggregate demand. Profit maximization implies that the markup above marginal cost equals price divided by demand elasticity, $p_j - w_r\theta = p_j/s$. Each firm and the good that it produces can be designated by its home country and the technology parameter θ. Market equilibrium prices vary across firms,

$$p_r^*(\theta) = s w_r \theta/(s-1). \tag{4}$$

Because firms offer different prices depending on their marginal costs, the amounts of the goods that are demanded from each firm also will vary. Let $q_r^0(\theta)$ denote the total consumption in country r of a good produced by a type θ firm. The profit of a firm of type θ from selling in country r can be written as

$$\pi_r^0(\theta) = [w_r\theta/(s-1)]q_r^0(\theta) - w_r a. \tag{5}$$

At the competitive equilibrium with differentiated products, it can be shown that potential entrepreneurs with the most efficient technologies choose to establish firms, whereas those with less efficient technologies choose to become workers. The critical technology yields profits equal to what the entrepreneur could earn as a worker,

$$\pi_r^0(\theta_r^0) - w_r = 0. \tag{6}$$

The indifference conditions for the marginal entrepreneur differ from entry conditions because they depend on occupational choice decisions by potential entrepreneurs. The marginal entrepreneur's indifference conditions determine the equilibrium extensive margins in each country, θ_1^0 and θ_2^0.

In equilibrium, consumers with marginal costs in the interval $A_r = [0, \theta_r^0]$ will choose to become entrepreneurs, whereas consumers with marginal costs in the interval $[\theta_r^0, 1]$ will choose to become workers. Each firm produces a unique product so that the number of goods consumed in each country equals the number of potential innovators who choose to be entrepreneurs, $m_r^0 = G_r F(\theta_r^0)$, $r = 1$. The supply of labor equals the labor force plus potential entrepreneurs that choose to become workers, $N_r = H_r + G_r(1 - F(\theta_r^0))$. The marginal entrepreneur determines the extensive margin of technology utilization. The marginal cost of the marginal entrepreneur is the highest marginal cost across operating firms. Hollander (1991) points out that Ricardo understood the role of demand in determining the extensive margin of land cultivation, with farmers seeking additional land of lower quality. The supply of labor and demand for goods as determined by income and the substitution parameter endogenously determine the extensive margin of technology utilization. Increases in the supply of labor and the demand for goods in each country motivate entrepreneurs to apply lower-quality technologies.

Summing individual consumer demands gives aggregate demand for each good θ in country r,

$$q_r^0(\theta) = \left(\frac{sw_r\theta}{s-1}\right)^{-s}\left(\frac{I_r}{P(\theta_r^0)^{s-1}}\right). \tag{7}$$

The price index in each country is a function of the wage and the extensive margin,

$$P_r(\theta_r^0) = \frac{s-1}{sw_r}\left(G_r\int_0^{\theta_r^0} z^{1-s}dF(z)\right)^{1/(s-1)}. \tag{8}$$

The price index, $P_r(\theta)$, is increasing in the critical value of the cost parameter, θ.

Total income in each country is the sum of the income of workers and the profits of entrepreneurs,

$$I_r = w_r\left[H_r + G_r(1 - F(\theta_r^0)\right] + G_r\int_0^{\theta_r^0}\pi_r(z)dF(z). \tag{9}$$

Consumers' budget constraints are binding so that income equals expenditures, $I_r = G_r\int_0^{\theta_r^0} p_r(z)q_r(z)dF(z)$. Substituting for profits in the total income equation, where $\pi_r(\theta) = (p_r(\theta) - w_r\theta)\,q_r(\theta) - w_r a$, and applying the consumers' budget constraints implies that the demand for labor and the supply of labor are equal in each country,

$$aG_rF(\theta_r^0) + G_r\int_0^{\theta_r^0} zq_r^0(z)dF(z) = H_r + G_r(1 - F(\theta_r^0)). \tag{10}$$

The wage cancels on both sides of the marginal entrepreneur's indifference condition (6) using the profit function in equation (5) and the output function in equation (7).

The equilibrium in the closed economies can be characterized using the marginal entrepreneurs' indifference conditions and consumer demands. The equilibrium output of the marginal entrepreneur in country r is obtained from the marginal entrepreneur's indifference condition (6) by noting the form of profits in equation (5), $q_r^0(\theta_r^0) = (a+1)(s-1)/\theta_r^0$, $r = 1, 2$. Each country's income can be written as a function of the wage and the extensive margin using the form of profits in equation (5) and the labor market equilibrium condition (10),

$$I_r(\theta_r^0) = \frac{sw_r}{s-1}\left\{H_r + G_r\left[1 - (a+1)F(\theta_r^0)\right]\right\}. \tag{11}$$

Substituting for income and using the labor market condition (10) in the aggregate demand for each good θ in country r in equation (7) gives the equilibrium output of a type-θ firm in country r, $q_r^0(\theta) = (a+1)(s-1)\theta^{-s}(\theta_r^0)^{s-1}$, $r = 1, 2$.

The equilibrium extensive margin in each country, $\theta_r^0 = \psi(L_r, a, s)$, is the unique solution to the following condition,

$$(12) \qquad (a+1)(sw_r)^s\left(\frac{\theta_r^0}{s-1}\right)^{s-1}\left(P_r(\theta_r^0)\right)^{s-1} = I_r(\theta_r^0).$$

To obtain this condition, substitute from the equilibrium output of a type-θ firm in country r into the labor market equilibrium.

Assume that L_r, a, and s are such that the extensive margin is an interior solution, $0 < \theta_r^0 < 1$. To understand this assumption, suppose for example that the distribution of technologies is uniform on the unit interval. Then, the extensive margin in country r equals

$$\theta_r^0 = \frac{(L_r+1)(2-s)}{a+1}.$$

The assumption requires that $s < 2$. Also, the assumption requires that $(a+1)/(L_r+1) > 2-s$. This inequality holds if $a > L_r$.

The extensive margin in each country, $\theta_r{}^0$, is unique because the income function $I_r(\theta)$ is decreasing in θ and the price index function $P_r(\theta)$ is increasing in θ, so the left-hand side of (12) is increasing in θ. The equilibrium extensive margin, $\theta_r^0 = \psi(L_r, a, s)$, does not depend on the wage because the wage cancels on both sides of (12).[2] Because the wage does not determine the critical cost value of the marginal entrepreneur, labor is the numéraire good in the closed economy. This generally does not hold with international trade as will be seen in the next section. Differences in fixed costs and in preference for variety in the two countries will generate differences in market outcomes in the two countries. The extensive margin and entrepreneurship are decreasing in fixed costs, $\partial\theta_r^0/\partial a < 0$, and in the substitution parameter, $\partial\theta_r^0/\partial s < 0$. Product variety, $m_r^0 = G_r F(\theta_r^0)$, is decreasing in fixed costs and in the substitution parameter and increasing in the number of workers, $\partial m_r^0/\partial H_r > 0$.

The equilibrium condition, $\theta_r^0 = \psi(L_r, a, s)$, implies that the country with the larger labor-technology ratio has a greater extensive margin, $\theta_2^0 > \theta_1^0$. The greater labor-technology ratio in country 2 stimulates demand and increases the returns to entrepreneurship in comparison to country 1, leading to higher production costs at the extensive margin.[3] The marginal entrepreneur has greater costs in

2 Equation (12) simplifies to $(a+1)(s-1)(\theta_r^0)^{s-1}\int_0^{\theta_r^0} z^{1-s}dF(z) = L_r + 1 - (a+1)F(\theta_r^0)$.

3 From equation (12), note that $\frac{\partial\theta_r^0}{\partial L_r} = \frac{1}{(a+1)[sf(\theta_r^0)+(s-1)^2(\theta_r^0)^{s-2}\int_0^{\theta_r^0} z^{1-s}dF(z)]}$.

the country with the larger labor-technology ratio. This means that the country with the larger labor-technology ratio has more entrepreneurs so that firms are less efficient at the margin. Ricardo found that a greater population led to usage of inferior land, whereas in the present model, a greater population and equal technology endowments lead to usage of inferior technology. Because technology differences result from population differences, these induce endogenous differences in the extensive margin of technology.

The outputs of inframarginal firms represent the intensive margin of technology. Output and profit are greater in the larger population country, so that the country with a larger labor-technology ratio has a greater *intensive* margin, $q_1^0(\theta) < q_2^0(\theta)$, and greater total output, where $Q_r^0 = \int_0^{\theta_r^0} q_r^0(z)dF(z)$. The output of each firm is increasing in the extensive margin, $\theta_r{}^0$, and does not depend directly on the labor-technology ratio so that total output also is increasing in the labor-technology ratio, $q_1^0(\theta) < q_2^0(\theta)$ and $Q_1^0 < Q_2^0$. Each firm earns profit $\pi_r^0(\theta) = (a+1)\theta^{1-s}(\theta_r^0)^{s-1} - a$, and total profit equals $\Pi_r^0 = (a+1)(\theta_r^0)^{s-1} \int_0^{\theta_r^0} z^{1-s}dF(z) - aF(\theta_r^0)$. Each firm's profit and total profit are increasing in the labor-technology ratio, $\pi_1^0(\theta) < \pi_2^0(\theta)$ and $\Pi_1^0 < \Pi_2^0$. With normalized wages, income in each country is an increasing function of the labor endowment and the technology endowment.

To evaluate the efficiency of the market equilibrium, consider the total benefits of consumers in country r,

$$(13) \quad U_r(\theta_r^0) = I_r(\theta_r^0)P(\theta_r^0) = (G_r)^{s/(s-1)}\left[L_r + 1 - F(\theta_r^0) - aF(\theta_r^0)\right] \times \left(\int_0^{\theta_r^0} z^{1-s}dF(z)\right)^{1/(s-1)}, \quad r = 1, 2.$$

The equilibrium in the closed economy results in an efficient amount of entrepreneurship given that firms engage in monopolistic competition. Without an outside good, relative markups for each good are equal. The extensive margin of technology utilization is efficient in each of the closed economies. Maximizing $U(\theta)$ over θ in equation (13) gives the first-order condition, $U_r'(\theta_r^0) = 0$, that corresponds exactly to the market equilibrium condition (12). It can be shown that $U_r'(\theta) > (<)\, 0$ as $\theta < (>)\, \theta_r^0$. Therefore, the market equilibrium extensive margin, $\theta_r = \theta_r^0$, maximizes total benefits in country r.

The market equilibrium extensive margin therefore is optimal in the closed economy. Although entrepreneurship is efficient in the closed economy, the differences in the extensive margin indicate that there are potential gains from trade. Because the extensive margin of technology is greater in the country with the larger labor-technology ratio, $\theta_2^0 > \theta_1^0$, there is an international inefficiency. The marginal costs of production are greater in country 2 than in country 1 at the extensive margin. In the next sections, we explore how international trade and FDI affect this type of international inefficiency.

9.2 Entrepreneurship with International Trade

Consider entrepreneurship in each country when the two countries trade differentiated goods. For ease of presentation, suppose that there are no costs of trade. It can be shown that all the results in this section hold with iceberg trade costs. Each firm produces a differentiated good so that the total number of products is the sum of products produced in each country. A type-θ firm in one country produces a different good from a type-θ firm in the other country. Let $q_{rr}(\theta)$ denote consumption of type-θ domestically produced goods in country r, and let $q_{ri}(\theta)$ denote consumption in country i of type-θ goods produced in country r and imported by country i, where $r \neq i$, $r, i = 1, 2$. The output of a type-θ firm producing in country r includes domestic and international sales, $Q_r(\theta) = q_{rr}(\theta) + q_{ri}(\theta))$, $r \neq i$, $r, i = 1, 2$. Product variety in each country is the sum of all products, $m_1 + m_2 = G_1 F(\theta_1) + G_2 F(\theta_2)$. A type-$\theta$ firm in country r produces for domestic sales and for export. Firms engage in pricing to market, where p_{rr} is the domestic price and p_{ri} is the export price, $r \neq i$, so that profits are

$$(14) \qquad \Pi_r(p_{rr}, p_{ri}, \theta) = (p_{rr} - w_r\theta)q_{rr}(p_{rr}) + (p_{ri} - w_r\theta)q_{ri}(p_{ri}) - w_r a, \quad r \neq i, r, i = 1, 2.$$

Each country's labor market clears if and only if trade is in balance. To see why this is so, observe that international trade is balanced when consumption of imports is equal across the two countries,

$$(15) \qquad G_1 \int_0^{\theta_2} p_{12}(z)q_{12}(z)dF(z) = G_2 \int_0^{\theta_1} p_{21}(z)q_{21}(z)dF(z).$$

Total income in each country is the sum of the income of workers and the profits of entrepreneurs,

$$(16) \qquad \begin{aligned} I_r = {} & G_r \int_0^{\theta_r} p_{rr}(z)q_{rr}(z)dF(z) \\ & + G_r \int_0^{\theta_i} p_{ri}(z)q_{ri}(z)dF(z) - w_r a G_r F(\theta_r) \\ & - G_r w_r \int_0^{\theta_r} zQ_r(z)dF(z) + w_r(L_r + 1 - F(\theta_r)), \end{aligned}$$

where $r \neq i$, r, $i = 1, 2$. Consumer budget constraints in each country reflect expenditures on domestically produced goods and imports,

$$(17) \qquad I_r = G_r \int_0^{\theta_r} p_{rr}(z)q_{rr}(z)dF(z) + G_i \int_0^{\theta_i} p_{ir}(z)q_{ir}(z)dF(z).$$

Combining (15)–(17) shows that the balance of trade occurs if and only if the labor market is in equilibrium in each country,

$$(18) \qquad aF(\theta_r) + \int_0^{\theta_r} zQ_r(z)dF(z) = L_r + 1 - F(\theta_r), \quad r = 1, 2.$$

A firm in country r offers the same price domestically and abroad because its production costs and demand elasticities are the same, $p_{rr}(\theta) = p_{ri}(\theta) = sw_r\theta/(s-1)$, $r \neq i$, $r, i = 1, 2$.[4] Substituting for domestic and export prices, a type-θ firm that produces in country r earns profit that can be expressed on the basis of output, $\pi_r(\theta) = [w_r\theta/(s-1)]\,Q_r(\theta) - w_r a$, $r = 1, 2$. The marginal entrepreneur' profit equal the wage in each country, $\pi_r(\theta_r) - w_r = 0$, $r = 1, 2$. The marginal entrepreneurs' indifference conditions in the two countries determine the extensive margin in each country, θ_r, $r = 1, 2$. The wage cancels on both sides of the indifference condition, which determines the marginal firm's total output, $Q_r(\theta_r) = (a+1)(s-1)/\theta_r$. The price indices are the same in the two countries,

$$(19) \qquad P(\theta_1, \theta_2) = \frac{s-1}{s}\left\{(w_1)^{1-s} G_1 \int_0^{\theta_1} z^{1-s} dF(z) + (w_2)^{1-s} G_2 \int_0^{\theta_2} z^{1-s} dF(z)\right\}^{1/(s-1)}.$$

Consumption of a domestically produced good equals $q_{rr}(\theta) = I_r p_{rr}(\theta)^{-s}/P^{s-1}$. Consumption of a good exported from country r to country i equals $q_{ri}(\theta) = I_i p_{ri}(\theta)^{-s}/P^{s-1}$, $r \neq i$, $r, i = 1, 2$. Summing individual consumer demands in the two countries, a type-θ firm that produces in country r has output

$$(20) \qquad Q_r(\theta) = \left(\frac{sw_r\theta}{s-1}\right)^{-s}\left(\frac{I_1 + I_2}{P^{s-1}}\right).$$

Each country's income can be written as before, $I_r(\theta_r) = w_r[s/(s-1)][L_r + 1 - (a+1)F(\theta_r)]$, $r = 1, 2$.

International trade does not change the equilibrium level of entrepreneurship in either country as compared to autarky. The differences between countries are induced by differences in population for comparable technology endowments. Let $\theta_1{}^T$ and $\theta_2{}^T$ denote the equilibrium extensive margins with international trade. *With international trade, the extensive margins, the levels of entrepreneurship, output per firm, and profits are the same as in the closed economies,* $\theta_r^T = \theta_r^0$, $r = 1, 2$.

To show that there is inertia in extensive margins with international trade, substituting for the marginal firm's output $Q_r(\theta_r) = (a+1)(s-1)/\theta_r$ gives two

4 Prices changed by a firm domestically and abroad will differ in the presence of iceberg trade costs, but the results still hold with price differences.

equations that together determine the extensive margins in the two countries,

$$(21)\qquad (a+1) = \left(\frac{\theta_r}{s-1}\right)^{1-s} (w_r s)^{-s} \left(\frac{I_1 + I_2}{p^{s-1}}\right), \quad r \neq i, r, \quad i = 1, 2.$$

Combining equations (20) and (21) gives output as a function of unit costs and the marginal entrepreneur's critical costs,

$$(22)\qquad Q_r(\theta) = (a+1)(s-1)(\theta_r)^{s-1}\theta^{-s}.$$

Substitute for output in the labor market equilibrium condition, $aF(\theta_r) + \int_0^{\theta_r} zQ_r(z)dF(z) = L_r + 1 - F(\theta_r)$. This results in equation (12), which implies that $\theta_r^T = \theta_r^0$, $r = 1, 2$.

The extensive margin of technology utilization is greater in the country with the higher labor-technology ratio, $\theta_2^T > \theta_1^T$. The intensive margin is greater in the country with the higher labor-technology ratio, $Q_2(\theta) > Q_1(\theta)$, for all θ less than or equal to θ_2 and total output is greater in the country with the higher labor-technology ratio, $Q_2 > Q_1$. This is because the greater extensive margin in country 2, $\theta_2^T > \theta_1^T$, and equation (22) imply that $Q_2(\theta) > Q_1(\theta)$ and also because total output equals $Q_r = \int_0^{\theta_r^T} Q_r(z)dF(z)$, it follows that $Q_2 > Q_1$.

The country with the larger number of workers has more entrepreneurs and produces more products. This is because the number of products produced in each country is the same as under autarky, and if H_r is greater than H_i, it follows that $m_r > m_i$, $r \neq i$, $r, i = 1, 2$.

International trade increases product variety in each country without changing production levels because $m_1 = m_1^0$ and $m_2 = m_2^0$, and consumers in each country consume both of the products, $m_1^0 + m_2^0 > \max\{m_2^0, m_1^0\}$. In comparison with autarky, international trade with entrepreneurship generates greater variety and makes everyone in each country better off so that each country obtains gains from trade.

International trade is Pareto dominant over autarky. The number of entrepreneurs does not change under international trade so that each individual has the same occupation as under autarky. Each worker is strictly better off as a result of greater product variety, and the wage cancels,

$$U_r^W(\theta_1, \theta_2) = w_r P(\theta_1, \theta_2) > \left\{G_r \int_0^{\theta_r} [(s-1)/(sz)]^{s-1} dF(z)\right\}^{1/(s-1)}$$
$$= U(\theta_r^0), \quad r = 1, 2.$$

Each entrepreneur has net benefits equal to $U_r(\theta_1, \theta_2) = \pi_r(\theta) P(\theta_1, \theta_2)$. So, each entrepreneur is made strictly better off because of greater product variety, and the wage cancels,

$$U_r^E(\theta_1, \theta_2) = [(w_r\theta)(a+1)(s-1)(\theta_r)^{s-1}\theta^{-s} - w_r a] P(\theta_1, \theta_2)$$
$$> \pi_r^0(\theta) P_r(\theta_r^0), \quad r = 1, 2.$$

Market equilibrium wages in the two countries are linked by international trade in goods.[5] This affects relative wages in the two countries as well as relative profits. *With international trade, the country with the higher labor-technology ratio has lower wages,* $w_1 > w_2$, *and firms have greater profits for any given technology,* $\pi_1(\theta) < \pi_2(\theta)$ *for all* θ. *Also, the market equilibrium wages maximize total benefits* $U(\theta_1, \theta_2) = (I_1(\theta_1) + I_2(\theta_2))\, P(\theta_1, \theta_2)$. These results hold because the marginal entrepreneurs' indifference conditions determine relative wages, so that from equation (21), $(\theta_1^T)^{1-s}(w_1)^{-s} = (\theta_2^T)^{1-s}(w_2)^{-s}$. Therefore, $\theta_2{}^{\mathrm{T}} > \theta_1{}^{\mathrm{T}}$ implies that $w_1 > w_2$. Profits for any given technology equal

$$\pi_r(\theta) = \left(\frac{s w_r \theta}{s-1}\right)^{-s} \left(\frac{I_1 + I_2}{P^{s-1}}\right) - w_r a, \quad r = 1, 2. \tag{23}$$

Profits are decreasing in wages for any given ratio of total income to the price index. Because the country with the higher labor-technology ratio has lower wages, $w_1 > w_2$, the country with the higher labor-technology ratio has higher profits for any given technology, $\pi_1(\theta) < \pi_2(\theta)$ for all θ. Normalize wages in country 2, so that $w_2 = 1$. Given $\theta_1{}^T$ and $\theta_2{}^T$, total benefits $U(\theta_1{}^{\mathrm{T}}, \theta_2{}^{\mathrm{T}}) = (I_1(\theta_1{}^{\mathrm{T}}) + I_2(\theta_2{}^{\mathrm{T}}))\, P(\theta_1{}^{\mathrm{T}}, \theta_2{}^{\mathrm{T}})$ are maximized when w_1 solves $(\theta_1{}^T)^{1-s}(w_1)^{-s} = (\theta_2{}^T)^{1-s}(w_2)^{-s}$.

9.3 Entrepreneurship with International Trade and FDI

We now consider the market equilibrium with international trade when entrepreneurs can engage in FDI by establishing firms in another country. It bears emphasis that, in the present model, firms that engage in FDI only produce in the foreign country and then sell their goods *both* in the host country and through exports to the other country. This means that FDI is not a mechanism for avoiding the costs of trade. Instead, FDI is a mechanism for entrepreneurs to take advantage of differences in wages, effectively taking into account differences in labor supplies and technological differences at the extensive margin. FDI serves to bring technology to another country. Without FDI, international trade does not affect the extensive margins in the two countries in comparison with autarky, as shown in the previous section. The persistence of different extensive margins across countries suggests that there are potential returns to entrepreneurial FDI. These returns could be obtained by those entrepreneurs who establish firms abroad.

Entrepreneurs who establish firms in a foreign country incur production costs in the host country. Those entrepreneurs repatriate their earnings and purchase consumption goods in their home country. The firms that they establish abroad

5 The connection between wages and labor endowments is complex in the presence of costs of trade, but the result that the country with the higher labor-technology ratio has lower wages holds generally.

through FDI sell their products to consumers in both countries. Entrepreneurs engage in FDI by investing their labor to establish the firm that operates facilities abroad. The entrepreneur's effort required to establish the firm is the measure of FDI in the current model. Additionally, the entrepreneurs who engage in FDI transfer their technology abroad because the firm operates with their unit cost θ, and these entrepreneurs incur fixed costs, a, abroad.

The present model of FDI is consistent with several additional interpretations. Entrepreneurial FDI can be implemented through different modes of entry that may not require investment. Entrepreneurial FDI corresponds to outsourcing production abroad in which the new firm transfers the technology θ to a supplier or partner in the host country that provides the product at cost, $\theta q + a$. The firm in country 1 outsources production in country 2 and sells domestically in country 2 and imports the goods for sale in country 1. Also, entrepreneurial FDI corresponds to technology licensing such that the entrepreneur transfers the technology θ abroad in return for a contingent royalty equal to the profits obtained by employing the technology. The foreign licensee sells in country 2 and exports to country 1. Finally, entrepreneurial FDI can be viewed as franchising in which the entrepreneur in country 1 sells a franchise to operate in country 2 in return for royalties equal to the firm's operating profits.

At the international market equilibrium with FDI, each entrepreneur has an incentive to invest in the country with the largest profits. A type-θ entrepreneur in either country has profits

$$\Pi^*(\theta) = \max\{\pi_1^*(\theta), \pi_2^*(\theta)\}. \tag{24}$$

The profit of a firm operating in country r is given by equation (24). Because profit $\Pi^*(\theta)$ is downward sloping, active entrepreneurs in country r are such that $0 \leq \theta \leq \theta_r^*$, where the marginal entrepreneur in each country is given by

$$\Pi^*(\theta_r^*) = w_r, \quad r = 1, 2. \tag{25}$$

Equilibrium FDI decisions can be represented by functions $\beta_r{}^*(\theta)$ that denote the equilibrium proportion of active type-θ entrepreneurs from country r who operate in country 1. So, $(1 - \beta_r{}^*(\theta))$ denotes those active entrepreneurs who operate in country 2, $r = 1, 2$. Then, for active entrepreneurs, $\beta_1{}^*(\theta) = \beta_2{}^*(\theta) = 1$ if $\pi_1{}^*(\theta) > \pi_2{}^*(\theta)$, and $\beta_1{}^*(\theta) = \beta_2{}^*(\theta) = 0$ if $\pi_1{}^*(\theta) < \pi_2{}^*(\theta)$. Also, if $\pi_1{}^*(\theta) = \pi_2{}^*(\theta)$, then $\beta_1{}^*(\theta)$ and $\beta_2{}^*(\theta)$ take values in $[0, 1]$. We restrict attention to symmetric equilibria, so that $\beta_1{}^*(\theta) = \beta_2{}^*(\theta)$ when type-θ entrepreneurs are active in both countries.

Entrepreneurship in each country depends critically on the wage. The international market equilibrium has the following property. Because profit $\Pi^*(\theta)$ is downward sloping, the type of the marginal entrepreneur in country 1 is greater than, equal to, or less than the type of the marginal entrepreneur in country 2 as the wage in country 1 is less than, equal to, or greater than the wage in country 2.

Income in each country, r, equals wage income and entrepreneurs' profits,

$$I_r = w_r[H_r + G_r(1 - F(\theta_r^*))] + G_r \int_0^{\theta_r^*} \beta_r^*(z)\pi_1(z)dF(z) + G_r \int_0^{\theta_r^*} (1 - \beta_r^*(z))\pi_2(z)dF(z), \tag{26}$$

where $r = 1, 2$. The labor market equilibrium conditions are as follows:

$$\sum_{r=1}^{2} G_r \int_0^{\theta_r^*} \beta_r^*(z)(zQ_1^*(z) + a)dF(z) = H_1 + G_1(1 - F(\theta_1^*)), \tag{27}$$

$$\sum_{r=1}^{2} G_r \int_0^{\theta_r^*} (1 - \beta_r^*(z))(zQ_2^*(z) + a)dF(z) = H_2 + G_2(1 - F(\theta_2^*)). \tag{28}$$

Because of FDI, international trade need not be balanced. Trade imbalances can be offset by net transfers equal to differences in the profits earned abroad by entrepreneurs from each country. Country 2's *net trade* is the difference between country 2's exports and country 2's imports,

$$\Delta = \sum_{r=1}^{2} G_r \int_0^{\theta_r^*} (1 - \beta_r^*(z))\, p_{21}(z)q_{21}^*(z)dF(z) - \sum_{r=1}^{2} G_r \int_0^{\theta_r^*} \beta_r^*(z)\, p_{12}(z)q_{12}^*(z)dF(z). \tag{29}$$

Country 2's exports are $q_{21}(\theta) = I_1\, p_{21}(\theta)^{-s}/P^{s-1}$. and country 2's imports are $q_{12}(\theta) = I_2\, p_{12}(\theta)^{-s}/P^{s-1}$. Country 2's *net transfers* are equal to the profits earned in country 2 by country 1's entrepreneurs minus the profits earned in country 1 by country 2's entrepreneurs,

$$T = G_1 \int_0^{\theta_1^*} (1 - \beta_1^*(z))\pi_2(z)dF(z) - G_2 \int_0^{\theta_2^*} \beta_2^*(z)\pi_1(z)dF(z). \tag{30}$$

The negative of the net transfer term for country 2, $-T$, corresponds to the current account component referred to as *net income from FDI* (Bureau of Economic Analysis, 2010). Country 2's current account is in balance when country 2's net trade equals country 2's net transfers, $\Delta = T$.

Country 2's current account is in balance, $\Delta = T$, if and only if labor markets clear in each country. Sum the consumers' budget constraints in each country,

$$I_1 = \sum_{r=1}^{2} G_r \int_0^{\theta_r^*} \beta_r^*(z)\, p_{11}(z)q_{11}^*(z)dF(z) + \sum_{r=1}^{2} G_r \int_0^{\theta_r^*} (1 - \beta_r^*(z))\, p_{21}(z)q_{21}^*(z)dF(z), \tag{31}$$

$$I_2 = \sum_{r=1}^{2} G_r \int_0^{\theta_r^*} \beta_r^*(z)\, p_{12}(z)q_{12}^*(z)dF(z) + \sum_{r=1}^{2} G_r \int_0^{\theta_r^*} (1 - \beta_r^*(z))\, p_{22}(z)q_{22}^*(z)dF(z). \tag{32}$$

Substitute for income in the consumer budget equations (31) and (32) using the country income equations (26). Then, combine these two conditions with the current account balance condition, $\Delta = T$, and equations (29) and (30). This gives the labor market equilibrium conditions (27) and (28). It is therefore equivalent to define the equilibrium in terms of the current account balance condition, $\Delta = T$, or the labor market equilibrium conditions.

International trade is not sufficient to equalize factor prices because entrepreneurs are needed to establish firms in each country, as shown in the previous section. The combination of international trade and FDI eliminates the international disparity in the costs of the marginal entrepreneur, which equalizes factor prices. Opening economies to FDI in addition to international trade improves aggregate productive efficiency. Entrepreneurs have an incentive to invest in the higher profit country. At the market equilibrium with FDI, it cannot be the case that one country's profits are greater than the other country's profits for all cost levels. If this were so, entrepreneurs would shift their FDI to the high-profit country, thereby increasing wages and reducing profits in the host country while reducing wages and increasing profits in the low-profit country. This implies that the profit levels, as a function of costs, must be equal for at least one cost level.[6]

At the market equilibrium with international trade and FDI without costs of trade, wages are equalized, $w_1{}^* = w_2{}^* = 1$, profits are equalized, $\pi_1{}^*(\theta) = \pi_2{}^*(\theta)$, the extensive margins are equalized, $\theta_1{}^* = \theta_2{}^* = \theta^*$, and the intensive margins are equalized, $Q_1{}^*(\theta) = Q_2{}^*(\theta) = Q^*(\theta)$. From equation (23), equality of profits at any one cost level implies equal wages. Outputs equal $Q_r(\theta) = \left(\frac{sw_r\theta}{s-1}\right)^{-s}\left(\frac{I_1+I_2}{P^{s-1}}\right)$, so that wage equalization results in equal outputs for type-θ firms operating in either country. The equality of wages and of profits implies that the marginal entrepreneurs' unit costs are equal in the two countries, so that profits and outputs also are equalized across the two countries.

FDI and international trade equalize factor prices so the extensive margin for the two countries is harmonized and determined by $\pi^*(\theta^*) = 1$. Output has the form $Q^*(\theta) = (a+1)(s-1)(\theta^*)^{s-1}\theta^{-s}$. Profits can be written as $\pi^*(\theta) = [\theta/(s-1)]Q^*(\theta) - a$, so that profits equal $\pi^*(\theta) = (a+1)(\theta^*)^{s-1}\theta^{1-s} - a$. Prices are equal in each country, $p_{11}(\theta) = p_{22}(\theta) = p_{12}(\theta) = p_{21}(\theta) = s\theta/(s-1)$. The price indices are equal in the absence of trade costs and are given by

$$P^*(\theta^*) = \frac{s-1}{s}\left[(G_1 + G_2)\int_0^{\theta^*} z^{1-s}\,dF(z)\right]^{1/(s-1)}. \tag{33}$$

6 Profit can be expressed on the basis of output as given by equation (23), $\pi_r(\theta) = [w_r\theta/(s-1)]Q_r(\theta) - w_r a$, $r = 1, 2$. From equation (19) and the envelope theorem, the effect of production costs on a firm's profit equals the wage times the output, $\pi_r{}^{*\prime}(\theta) = -w_r Q_r(\theta)$, $r = 1, 2$. Profit is decreasing and convex in costs because output is decreasing is costs, $\pi_r{}^{*\prime\prime}(\theta) = -w_r Q_r'(\theta) > 0$. The ratio of marginal profits remains constant, $\frac{\pi_1^{*\prime}(\theta)}{\pi_2^{*\prime}(\theta)} = \left(\frac{w_1}{w_2}\right)^{1-s}$. This implies that profits intersect at most once over the range of costs, unless they are equal everywhere.

The total income function is

$$(34) \qquad I^*(\theta^*) = \frac{s}{s-1}\{H_1 + H_2 + (G_1 + G_2)[1 - (a+1)F(\theta^*)]\}.$$

Now, compare the market equilibrium extensive margin with international trade and FDI with the extensive margins in the open economies without FDI and in the closed economics. *At the market equilibrium with international trade and FDI, the extensive margin, θ^*, solves the equilibrium condition that would apply to a closed economy with the aggregate labor-technology ratio, $\theta^* = \psi(\frac{H_1+H_2}{G_1+G_2}, a, s)$. The extensive margin at the market equilibrium with FDI is located between the extensive margins of the open economies without FDI or in comparison to the closed economies, $\theta_1{}^T < \theta^* < \theta_2{}^T$. FDI increases the output of each type of firm in the lower labor-technology ratio country and decreases the output of each type of firm in the higher labor-technology ratio country in comparison to the open economies without FDI and in comparison to the closed economies,* $Q_1(\theta) < Q^*(\theta) < Q_2(\theta)$. Add the labor market equilibrium conditions (27) and (28) and substitute for output $Q^*(\theta) = (a+1)(s-1)(\theta^*)^{s-1}\theta^{-s}$ to obtain an expression similar to equation (12),

$$(35) \qquad (a+1)(s)^s \left(\frac{\theta^*}{s-1}\right)^{s-1} (P^*(\theta^*))^{s-1} = I^*(\theta^*).$$

The extensive margin $\theta^* = \psi(\frac{H_1+H_2}{G_1+G_2}, a, s)$ solves (35). The aggregate labor-technology ratio is a weighted average of the ratios of the two countries,

$$(36) \qquad \frac{H_1 + H_2}{G_1 + G_2} = \frac{G_1}{G_1 + G_2}L_1 + \frac{G_2}{G_1 + G_2}L_2,$$

so that $\theta_1{}^T < \theta^* < \theta_2{}^T$. This in turn implies that $Q_1(\theta) < Q^*(\theta) < Q_2(\theta)$. Equalization of the extensive margins across the two countries reflects integration of the two economies. The market equilibrium with international trade and FDI corresponds to a closed economy with the weighted average of the labor-technology ratio of the two countries.

The market equilibrium with international trade and FDI has the following properties. At the market equilibrium with international trade and FDI, the extensive market is increasing in either country's labor force, decreasing in fixed costs, a, and in the substitution parameter, s. $d\theta^*/dH_1 > 0$, $d\theta^*/dH_2 > 0$, $d\theta^*/da < 0$ and $d\theta^*/ds < 0$. Each firm's output and total output in each country are increasing in labor force of either country, $dQ^*(\theta)/dH_1 > 0$, $dQ^*(\theta)/dH_2 > 0$ and $dQ^*/dH_1 > 0$, $dQ^*/dH_2 > 0$. Each firm's profit and total profit are increasing labor force of either country, $d\pi^*(\theta)/dH_1 > 0$, $d\pi^*(\theta)/dH_2 > 0$ and $d\Pi^*/dH_1 > 0$, $d\Pi^*/dH_2 > 0$.

Entrepreneurship and product variety equal $m^* = (G_1 + G_2)F(\theta^*)$. So, product variety is increasing the labor force of either country, $dm^*/dH_1 > 0$, $dm^*/dH_2 > 0$, decreasing in the substitution parameter, $dm^*/ds < 0$, and decreasing in fixed costs, $dm^*/da < 0$. The extensive margin with international trade and FDI is increasing in the labor force. The movement of entrepreneurs from country 1 to country 2 equalizes the costs of the marginal entrepreneur in both countries and eliminates the inefficiency that results from different production costs at the margin. The movement of entrepreneurs from country 1 to country 2 increases the critical cost parameter for entrepreneurs in country 1, but only a fraction of those entrepreneurs supply goods in country 1. Conversely in country 2, the critical cost parameter is lower, but there are both domestic and foreign entrepreneurs.

With international trade and FDI, the extensive margin is greater than that of the smaller closed economy but less than that of the larger closed economy. However, because total product variety increases, international trade and FDI increase entrepreneurship and product variety relative to either of the closed economies. *At the market equilibrium with international trade and FDI, entrepreneurship and product variety increase relative to either of the closed economies,* $m^* > m_1{}^0$ and $m^* > m_2{}^0$.[7] With international trade and FDI, total entrepreneurship and product variety, $m^* = (G_1 + G_2)F(\theta^*)$, may be greater than, equal to, or less than total entrepreneurship in the economies with international trade, which equals the total of entrepreneurship in the closed economies, $G_1 F(\theta_1{}^0) + G_2 F(\theta_2{}^0)$.

There are multiple equilibrium allocations of FDI between the two countries. It is useful to characterize the equilibrium in which each type of entrepreneur is equally likely to engage in FDI. In this situation, the proportion of all entrepreneurs who invest in country 1 is a constant, β^*. FDI from country 2 to country 1 equals $\beta^* G_2 F(\theta^*)$, and FDI from country 1 to country 2 equals $G_1(1 - \beta^*)F(\theta^*)$. Country 2's net transfers abroad equal the earnings of country 1's entrepreneurs who operate in country 2 minus the earnings of country 2's entrepreneurs, who operate in country 1,

$$T = [G_1(1 - \beta^*) - G_2\beta^*] \int_0^{\theta^*} \pi^*(z)dF(z). \tag{37}$$

At the market equilibrium with international trade and FDI without costs of trade, the country with the larger labor-technology ratio (country 2) has a trade surplus, $\Delta = T > 0$, and positive net FDI inflows (and country 1 has negative net FDI inflows). To obtain this result, notice that the labor market conditions give the proportion of entrepreneurs in country 2 who invest in country 1,

$$\beta^* = \frac{H_1 + G_1(1 - F(\theta^*))}{H_1 + H_2 + (G_1 + G_2)(1 - F(\theta^*))}, \tag{38}$$

7 Because $\theta_1^0 < \theta^*$, it is apparent that $G_1 F(\theta_1^0) < (G_1 + G_2) F(\theta^*)$. Define the decreasing function $J_r(\theta)$ as follows, $J_r(\theta) = \frac{H_r + G_r}{a+1} + G_r(s-1)\theta^{s-1} \int_0^\theta z^{1-s} dF(z)$, $r = 1, 2$.

Then, we can write equation (35) as $(G_1 + G_2)F(\theta^*) = J_1(\theta^*) + J_2(\theta^*)$. Also, from equation (12), we have $G_r F(\theta_r{}^0) = J_r(\theta_r{}^0)$, $r = 1, 2$. Let $\theta_r{}'$ solve $G_r F(\theta_r{}') = J_1(\theta_r{}') + J_2(\theta_r{}')$. Note that $F(\theta)$ is increasing in θ, and $J_r(\theta)$ is decreasing in θ, $G_r F(\theta) < (G_1 + G_2)F(\theta)$ and $J_r(\theta) < J_1(\theta) + J_2(\theta)$. Therefore, $m_r{}^0 = G_r F(\theta_r{}^0) < G_r F(\theta_r{}') < (G_1 + G_2)F(\theta^*) = m^*$.

so that $0 < \beta^* < 1$. Substituting for β^* in (37) implies

$$[G_1(1-\beta^*) - G_2\beta^*] = \frac{G_1 G_2 (L_2 - L_1)}{H_1 + H_2 + (G_1 + G_2)(1 - F(\theta^*))} > 0.$$

So, $\Delta = T > 0$.

Country 2's trade surplus reflects profits repatriated by country 1's entrepreneurs who invest in country 2 and country 2's entrepreneurs who invest in country 1. This helps explain how labor and technology endowments affect the pattern of international trade and FDI. Country 2's trade surplus is a result of its larger population, which leads to more FDI by entrepreneurs from country 1 than by entrepreneurs from country 2. To place this result in context, consider China and the United States. China has a greater labor force but a relatively lower technology endowment in comparison to the United States. The model correctly predicts that China has a trade surplus and positive transfers in its relationship with the United States.

The combination of international trade and FDI increases total benefits in comparison to the market equilibrium with international trade but without FDI. FDI increases total output in the lower labor-technology ratio country and decreases total output of each type of firm in the higher labor-technology ratio country in comparison to the open economies without FDI and in comparison to the closed economies, $Q_1 < Q^* < Q_2$. *The market equilibrium with international trade and FDI increases total benefits in comparison to international trade without FDI.* To obtain this result, notice that total benefits with international trade and FDI equal $U^*(\theta^*) = I^*(\theta^*)P^*(\theta^*)$. With international trade and without FDI, total benefits equal $U(\theta_1, \theta_2) = (I_1(\theta_1) + I_2(\theta_2))P(\theta_1, \theta_2)$. Maximizing total benefits $U(\theta_1, \theta_2)$ for fixed wages implies that the optimal extensive margins satisfy the market equilibrium wages condition, $(\theta_1)^{1-s}(w_1)^{-s} = (\theta_2)^{1-s}(w_2)^{-s}$. Normalize the wage in country 2, $w_2 = 1$, and note that the equilibrium extensive margins that maximize $U(\theta_1, \theta_2)$ depend on the wage in country 1, w_1. Then, it can be shown that

$$\left.\frac{dU(\theta_1, \theta_2)}{dw_1}\right|_{w_1=1} = P^*(\theta^*)\frac{s}{s-1}\frac{G_1 G_2}{G_1 + G_2}(L_1 - L_2) < 0.$$

Therefore, maximizing $U(\theta_1, \theta_2)$ with respect to w_1 subject to $w_1 \geq 1$ implies that the constraint is binding, so that $w_1 = 1$ and $\theta_1 = \theta_2 = \theta^*$. Therefore, $U^*(\theta^*) > U(\theta_1{}^T, \theta_2{}^T)$.

By equalizing factor prices and extensive margins, FDI increases total benefits for the two countries that engage in international trade. The aggregate benefits of technology transfer outweigh the effects of changing the extensive margin of technology utilization. FDI increases total benefits by affecting productive efficiency and product variety. FDI increases total income multiplied by the price index, so that total benefits are increased by some combination of income effects and price index effects. Although FDI increases total benefits, adding FDI to international trade has distributional implications. FDI need not increase both incomes and product variety. Workers in country 1 have lower wages at the equilibrium with FDI in comparison with trade only, but they may benefit if product variety increases. Also, workers in country 2 can benefit from FDI if product variety increases. Some potential entrepreneurs in country 1 benefit from FDI because there are more entrepreneurs with FDI in comparison with trade only. Conversely, some potential entrepreneurs in country 2 are workers with FDI who would be entrepreneurs with trade only because FDI reduces the extensive margin. The general distributive effects are related to Helpman's (1984) observation that the distribution of income becomes more equitable the greater is the volume of trade. Total benefits rise with FDI in the present setting so that both countries can be made better off by FDI, or some losses in country 2 are offset by greater gains in country 1.

9.4 Extensions and Empirical Implications

The model has several key differences with the international trade literature. First, the literature assumes that wages are identical across countries (see the heterogeneous technology models of Melitz, 2003, Chaney, 2008, and the references therein). In contrast, the present model allows wages to be endogenous and to differ across countries. The analysis shows that wage differences persist in the presence of international trade with or without trade frictions and with international trade and FDI when there are trade frictions. Second, instead of the standard free-entry-of-firms assumption in monopolistic competition models (Melitz, 2003; Chaney, 2008), the present model examines how occupational choices of prospective entrepreneurs determine the equilibrium number of firms in each country.[8] In the present analysis, the marginal entrepreneur earns profit equal to his opportunity costs as a worker, which determines the equilibrium market structure. Third, instead of the standard approach in which costs of trade drive FDI, the present model examines how differences in labor forces and technology endowments determine FDI. These three features of the model generate empirical implications that show the connection between entrepreneurship, technology, investment, and international trade.

Empirical Implications

The main empirical implications of the model depend on the effects of opening the closed economies to trade and to FDI. Opening closed economies to international

8 The oligopoly model of Dixit and Stiglitz (1977) and Lancaster (1980) and its application by Krugman (1979) to international trade assume identical marginal costs. Krugman (1979) and Helpman (1981) show that international trade increases product variety without sacrificing economies of scale. These types of models generally assume free entry of firms, without consideration of entrepreneurship.

trade without also opening to FDI generates the standard benefits of product variety but does not affect the extensive margins of technology utilization. This is because each country has the same technological endowments, and technology utilization is determined by the occupational choices of entrepreneurs. In contrast, opening economies to FDI and trade does change the extensive and intensive margins of technology utilization, increasing the extensive margin in the country with the lower labor force and reducing it in the country with the higher labor force. This implies that opening trade and FDI between the United States and China should result in a narrowing of the extensive margins, with the United States becoming less efficient at the margin and China becoming more efficient at the margin. The analysis also suggests that entrepreneurship and technology transfer will be reflected in variations in product trade imbalances and net transfers of income on foreign investment.

The analysis helps explain productivity differences between countries on the basis of countries' population differences and endowments of individuals who have access to new technologies. These cross-country differences persist as a result of restrictions on FDI that may limit technology transfers by international entrepreneurs. The productivity differences across countries are consistent with Lucas (1988, 1990) who considers the implications for economic development resulting from the trade-off between investment in physical capital and in human capital. Hall and Jones (1999) find significant productivity differences between countries that they attribute to differences in technology. Evenson and Westphal (1995) suggest that tacit knowledge can help explain cross-country productivity differences. This is consistent with the present analysis because entrepreneurs have different capabilities and the model shows that entrepreneurial FDI helps transfer tacit knowledge from north to south. Acemoglu and Zilibotti (2001) point out that there are large productivity differences across countries even when they have access to the same set of technologies, particularly when the technologies used by the south are imported from the north. They find that technologies developed by the north may require highly skilled labor that may not be available in the south, so that a technology-skill mismatch helps explain lower productivity in the south. The present analysis differs from Acemoglu and Zilibotti (2001) because it does not differentiate between labor skills in the two countries and does not relate the appropriate skills to technology. Chaney (2008) finds that with costs of trade, the extensive margin and the intensive margin are affected in opposite directions by the elasticity of substitution and shows that, although many of the empirical predictions of the Krugman model still hold, introducing heterogeneity of firms weakens the effects of the elasticity of substitution on the impact of trade barriers. However, Chaney's analysis depends on international trade without consideration of FDI effects.

FDI is motivated by profit differences between the two countries that result from different relative endowments of labor and technology. Helpman et al. (2004) find that firms invest abroad to avoid trade costs with more productive firms engaging in foreign trade and FDI (see also Eaton et al., 2004; Melitz, 2003; and Ramondo and Rodríguez-Clare, 2009). Instead of restricting FDI through investment costs, the present model allow all types of active entrepreneurs to engage in FDI, without limiting FDI to only the most productive ones. I show that FDI is a way of matching entrepreneurs and new technologies with labor forces in other countries. The result obtained here, that firms with productivity differences invest abroad to match with supplies of labor, is related to the discussions in Helpman (1984) and Burstein and Monge-Naranjo (2009) although their approaches are not based on occupational choice and entrepreneurship. The analysis of FDI presented here generates some novel empirical implications about the interaction between innovation and the size of the labor force.

Countries have different regulatory environments that affect openness to FDI. These include the costs of doing business in the country and rules directly governing FDI such as domestic ownership requirements. The model suggests that cross-country variations in FDI should affect entrepreneurial activity from both domestic and foreign entrepreneurs. Countries that are more open to FDI will have extensive margins of technology utilization that are more harmonized with other open economies than are countries that are more closed to FDI. This effect must be tempered by consideration of other factors that affect entrepreneurship identified in the present model, in particular the effects of labor endowments and technology endowments.

Opening the economies to international trade need not narrow wage differences because the extensive margins are determined by technological endowments and occupation choices of entrepreneurs. However, opening to FDI does narrow wage differences. This suggests that in practice, investment flows should be associated with factor price equalization. In addition, the model predicts trade and investment imbalances. With trade and FDI between the United States and China, the model predicts that the United States would run a trade deficit and have a foreign investment income surplus. A similar prediction would apply to the United States and India, all other things equal. However, India imposes greater restrictions on FDI than China, suggesting that U.S. trade with India more closely resembles the trade-only equilibrium, and U.S. trade with China resembles the trade and FDI equilibrium. This suggests that international interactions between the United States and China trade should narrow their differences in extensive margins more than interactions between the United States and India.

Many Countries

The analysis generalizes readily to allow many countries. Let n be the number of countries. Then, with international trade and without FDI, the marginal entrepreneur will remain the same as in the closed economies. However, with both international trade and FDI, extensive margins will be harmonized across all of the countries. The marginal entrepreneurs' costs depends on the average labor endowment, $H = (1/n)\sum_{r=1}^{n} H_r$, divided by the average technology endowment, $G = (1/n)\sum_{r=1}^{n} G_r$, so we obtain

$$\theta^* = \psi\left(\frac{H}{G}, a, s\right).$$

This means that increasing the average labor force in a trading bloc increases the extensive margin when there is both FDI and international trade.

Adding India or China to a trade bloc increases the extensive margin, whereas adding Canada or Sweden reduces the extensive margin. The effect of adding countries to a trade bloc is exactly the same as in the two-country model with the initial trade bloc and the additional country representing two economies. The resulting marginal technology is between that of the trade bloc and that of the additional country. With international trade and FDI, the total number of products equals $m^* = nF(\theta^*)$. Adding a country with a larger-than-average labor force increases product variety. Increasing the average labor force increases the extensive margin of technology utilization. The results of the analysis suggest that trade blocs with different rules governing both trade and FDI will have substantially different patterns of wages and productive efficiency.

Differences in the Costs of Doing Business

The costs of doing business, including the effects of a country's legal and regulatory climate, are important determinants of entrepreneurship. Suppose that country 1 has greater costs of doing business than country 2. This can be represented as differences in the fixed costs of establishing a firm, $a_1 > a_2$, which implies that $\theta_1 < \theta_2$. The effects of a greater population and higher costs of doing business are offsetting. Smaller, emerging market countries with high costs of doing business may still experience high extensive margins, leading to inefficiencies. Larger, emerging market countries with very high costs of doing business can have small extensive margins, but this implies that entrepreneurship and product variety are low.

Differences in the costs of doing business across countries affect entrepreneurship in a manner that is similar to population differences. Increasing the costs of doing business reduces the number of entrepreneurs as well as product variety, as noted previously. A country with a higher cost of doing business will tend to have less entrepreneurship than a country with a lower cost of doing business. In the present model, differences in the costs of doing business drive a wedge between costs of the marginal entrepreneurs in the two countries, so that the marginal entrepreneur is more efficient in the country with a relatively higher cost of doing business. A combination of international trade and FDI causes a shift in entrepreneurs toward the economy with a relatively lower cost of doing business. Lowering the costs of doing business stimulates domestic entrepreneurship.

Differences in Preferences for Variety

Cross-country variations in customer preferences for variety affect wages and extensive margins under autarky and with international trade. The number of entrepreneurs is decreasing in the substitution parameter, s. The substitution parameter indicates a preference for variety and determines consumers' elasticity of demand for each good. Differences in the preference for variety across countries cause a wedge between the efficiencies of marginal entrepreneurs, so that $s_1 > s_2$ implies that $\theta_1 < \theta_2$. The marginal entrepreneur will be more efficient in a country with a greater value of the substitution parameter – that is, in a country with less preference for variety. Variations in customer preferences for variety help explain the effects of FDI on entrepreneurship and economic performance. The combination of international trade and FDI causes a shift in entrepreneurs toward the economy with a relatively lower substitution parameter.

Technological Change

The present model shows that FDI generates technology transfer by being embodied in the new firm established abroad. International trade in disembodied technology increases the quality of innovation and generates additional gains from trade. Spulber (2008c, 2010b) shows that increasing the extent of the market through international trade in technology improves the quality of innovation by widening the pool of inventions and applying the best invention in multiple countries. In Spulber (2008c), I present a general equilibrium model of international trade with technology transfers to consumers who can enhance their human capital. Goods are provided by firms that engage in monopolistic competition and employ consumers as workers. The model shows that technology transfer yields gains from trade. Spulber (2010b) considers a strategic model of international technology transfer with duopoly firms that compete internationally. The present model differs from these models by focusing on innovation by entrepreneurs who apply technology rather than considering how inventors develop technology and sell the technology internationally.

The present analysis also helps explain international licensing patterns. Instead of FDI, start-ups may choose to transfer their technology abroad through licensing. Technology licensing provides another mode of entry so that entrepreneurs can license their production technology to host countries where labor and technology endowments differ from those of their home country. Arora et al. (2001a, 2001b) provide evidence for international technology markets and consider the effects of firm size on incentives to license technology. Arora et al. (2001b) observe that the chemical industry in developed economies created "specialized engineering firms" that focused on the design and engineering of chemical processes. These firms provided technology and supporting services to firms in developing countries (Arora and Gambardella, 1998). In the international context, Anand and Khanna (2000) find licensing agreements in chemicals, electronics, and computers. Tilton (1971) and Grindley and Teece (1997) examine licensing in the international diffusion of semiconductors and electronics.

The analysis suggests that differences in per capita technology endowments across countries result in licensing to transfer technology from high per capita technology countries to low technology per capita countries. Thus, international variations in per capita technology endowments help explain the pattern of disembodied technology transfers. This is consistent with observed patterns of technology flows particularly from developed economies to less developed economies, taking into account the size of the labor force (see, for example, OECD, 2008a, 2008b).

Van Stel et al. (2005) find that entrepreneurship can have negative effects on growth in less developed countries and positive effects on growth in developed countries. They hypothesize that different country effects may be a result of entrepreneurs in less developed countries having lower endowments of human capital than those in developed economies. This corresponds to the different technologies of individual entrepreneurs in our model. In the present model, different technology endowments relative to the labor force endowments suggest that there will be differences in extensive margins in economies that are closed to FDI, even though they are open to trade. This helps explain the observed differences in growth impacts of entrepreneurship. Van Stel et al. (2005) further suggest that developing economies can benefit from FDI by multinational corporations (MNCs), which will stimulate domestic entrepreneurship.

9.5 Conclusion

There are important interactions between entrepreneurship, international trade, and FDI. At the extensive margin of technology utilization, potential entrepreneurs are indifferent between entrepreneurship and entering the labor market. Entrepreneurs' endowments of technology and human capital and their occupational choices affect technological change and economic development in their home countries. In addition, entrepreneurial decisions regarding investment and the location of production can affect trade flows and countries' net earnings from foreign investment.

Without entrepreneurial FDI, wages and extensive margins show persistent differences across countries as countries open to trade. Even a combination of FDI and international trade is not sufficient to overcome this inertia when trade frictions are present. This helps explain observed differences in wages and productive efficiency across countries even when there is trade and FDI. However, without trade frictions, international trade and entrepreneurial FDI equalize factor prices and harmonize technology utilization across countries. Firms in the two countries with the same marginal costs produce the same level of output. Entrepreneurial FDI also increases total benefits for countries by increasing the extensive margin in countries with relatively lower labor to technology endowment ratios and, conversely, by decreasing the extensive margin in countries with relatively higher labor to technology endowment ratios.

Entrepreneurial FDI not only impacts economic development but also helps explain international trade imbalances and imbalances in countries' receipts from foreign investment. Countries' international trade and FDI are affected by their relative labor versus technology endowments. In practice, technological endowments are endogenously determined through R&D. The present analysis takes the underlying stock of technological knowledge as given and focuses on innovation by entrepreneurs who embodied technology in new firms. Entrepreneurs transfer technology embodied in new firms through FDI and partnerships, which gives countries access to new technologies. This provides another channel of technology transfer that supplements international trade in technology embodied in advanced products and capital equipment as well as trade in disembodied inventions. Additional insights may be gained by introducing endogenous R&D into the international entrepreneurship model; see Spulber (2008c, 2010b) on invention and international trade. The combination of international trade and entrepreneurial FDI may provide incentives for invention that improve the quality of innovation and yield additional gains from trade.

10

Conclusion

The innovative entrepreneur contributes to the dynamism of capitalist economies. From the industrial revolution to the scientific revolution to the business revolution, innovation is critical for economic growth and development. Innovative entrepreneurs establish firms that introduce many commercial, scientific, and technological inventions to the market place. In this way, the individual initiative of innovative entrepreneurs helps drive economic innovation.

Public policies that affect innovative entrepreneurs can significantly impact economic growth and development. Public policies aimed at stimulating economic growth and development tend to have a macroeconomic focus, using such instruments as fiscal and monetary policy. Microeconomic policies aimed at economic growth and development often target firms and industries through regulations, subsidies, and tax incentives. However, growth-oriented microeconomic policies should take into account the critical role of individuals who are potential innovative entrepreneurs. The most successful policies will be those that remove barriers to individual initiative and creativity.

10.1 Entrepreneurial Motivation

Entrepreneurs create start-ups and establish firms to accumulate assets in the context of their life-cycle consumption and saving decisions. Individuals choose to become entrepreneurs in comparison to alternative occupations and investment opportunities. Creative individuals choose innovative entrepreneurship when own-use of inventions generates greater returns than technology transfers to incumbent firms. Innovative entrepreneurs choose to implement discoveries when they provide greater returns than replicative entrepreneurship.

Entrepreneurs maximize their life-cycle utility of consumption. During the start-up phase, entrepreneurs' consumption and savings decisions are interdependent with their business decisions. Because of imperfect financial separation, entrepreneurs' preferences, wealth, age, and other personal characteristics affect their business decisions. This suggests that public policies seeking to promote economic growth and development should not deter individuals from becoming innovative entrepreneurs.

Individual Initiative

Individual initiative is essential for economic growth and development. The innovative entrepreneur applies *entrepreneurial leverage*; by establishing an innovative firm the entrepreneur can affect an entire industry. The creativity of the individual is magnified because a new firm can contribute significantly to economic growth and development. Just one innovative entrepreneur can establish a firm that enriches tens of thousands of investors, hires hundreds of thousands of employees, and improves the lives of millions of customers. Just one innovative entrepreneur can inspire others to create new industries and new markets that generate employment and prosperity.

The theory of the innovative entrepreneur helps explain the dynamism and success of capitalist economies.[1] Economic dynamism requires new firms, new products, new manufacturing processes, and new transaction methods. Economic dynamism also requires institutional change in the form of new industries, new organizations, and new markets. Entrepreneurs generate economic dynamism in a number of ways.

First, innovative entrepreneurs establish *new firms* that are the first to embody commercial, scientific, and technological inventions. Innovative entrepreneurs combine IP, human capital, and financial capital to create start-ups and establish new firms. In developed economies, firms that embody inventions provide a mechanism for introducing technological change in the economy. Entrepreneurs make the necessary investments to absorb inventions and to develop market applications of new technology.

Second, clusters of entrepreneurs establish *new industries* when green field investment is required. In developed economies, entrepreneurs establish new industries at the world's technological frontier, creating the automobile, computer, biotech, and many other industries. In developing economies, entrepreneurs create entirely new industries that may be within the world's technological frontier, establishing such traditional industries as retail, wholesale, banking, insurance, and manufacturing.

Third, by establishing firms, innovative entrepreneurs create *new types of markets and organizations.* Firms such as eBay create and operate thousands of auction markets that intermediate between buyers and sellers. Retail and wholesale firms

1 The sociologist Richard Swedberg (2002) discusses the "puzzle" of dynamic capitalism; see also Geoffrey Ingham (2003, 2008). See also Swedberg (2002) for comparisons of Max Weber and Schumpeter. In explaining economic dynamism, economists and sociologists tend to emphasize the importance of a specific factor such as inventions, entrepreneurial efforts, or financing.

create and operate market places for their customers and suppliers. Manufacturing firms create internal allocation mechanisms within their organizations. Merchants' associations create trade fairs and business networks. Brokers' associations create financial markets. In addition to creating markets, new firms create organizations, with divisions, hierarchies, incentives, training, and management.

Fourth, by establishing firms, entrepreneurs contribute to the development of *complementary political, social, and legal institutions.* The firms established by entrepreneurs join the larger set of social institutions that include law, government, language, norms, and customs.[2] By creating wealth, entrepreneurs increase demand for education, health care, housing, transportation, and financial services, thus further transforming society. By generating tax revenue, new firms provide support for the development of governments and legal systems. By establishing manufacturing, retail, and wholesale distribution, new firms provide the demand that supports public infrastructure expenditures. The growth of private business often fosters the development of public institutions such as commercial law and regulation that are needed to accommodate transactions. Economic dynamism stimulated by innovative entrepreneurs often transforms political, social, and legal institutions.

Before the firm is established, the innovative entrepreneur's consumption and savings decisions are financially interdependent with the start-up's business decisions. When the firm is established, the foundational shift occurs, and the period of entrepreneurship ends with the entrepreneur becoming an owner of the firm. Then, the conditions of the Fisher Separation Theorem are satisfied, and there is financial separation between the individual and the new firm. The imperfect financial separation of the entrepreneur and the start-up has a number of critical public policy implications.

Public Policy Implications

Each dollar of public spending, whether financed through taxation or debt, comes at the cost of a dollar of private spending. Even redistributive expenditures that are simply transfers require taxation of productive activities. The Keynesian prescription of increased government spending during recessions displaces private consumption and investment. Any evaluation of the multiplier effects of public expenditures, if any such effects exist, must adjust for the negative effects of reducing private expenditures.

2 Douglass North (1990, p. 3) offers the following definition: "Institutions are the rules of the game in a society or, more formally, are the humanly devised constraints that shape human interaction." Acemoglu and Robinson (2008) and Aghion and Howitt (2009) examine institutions in economic growth and development. Glaeser et al. (2004) highlight the importance of human capital in contrast to political and legal institutions, suggesting that growth improves political and legal institutions (see also Djankov et al., 2003, 2008, and Przeworski, 2004).

John Maynard Keynes (1936), in the *General Theory of Employment, Interest and Money*, frequently mentions entrepreneurs and their role as employers. For Keynes an entrepreneur is simply a capitalist and the word *innovation* is entirely absent from *General Theory*. Keynes (1936, p. 61) observes, however, that the marginal efficiency of capital is influenced by expectations of changes in the cost of production, including not only labor costs but also the effects of "inventions and new technique." As Schumpeter (1946, p. 512) observes, Keynes's framework is decidedly short run, spanning a few years at most, so that capitalist evolution "issues into a stationary state that constantly threatens to break down."

The question is whether economic growth is increased or reduced by greater public spending. Robert Barro observes: "There are two ways to view Keynesian stimulus through transfer programs. It's either a divine miracle – where one gets back more than one puts in – or else it's the macroeconomic equivalent of blood-letting. Obviously, I lean toward the latter position, but I am still hoping for more empirical evidence."[3] In addition to transfers, public spending also includes some expenditures that are likely to be less productive than corresponding private sector activities, including the operation of public enterprises such as the postal service (Sidak and Spulber, 1996).

The corresponding reductions in private spending reduce economic growth by diminishing private consumption and investment. In particular, the loss of *private multiplier effects* from innovative entrepreneurship may be substantial. Consider, for example, the relatively small expenditures initially made by the innovative entrepreneurs who founded Walmart, Microsoft, Apple, Google, or Facebook in comparison to the astronomical market values of these companies. Of course, many entrepreneurs are unsuccessful, but the overall returns to innovative entrepreneurship are positive for the economy.

Innovative entrepreneurs generate disproportionate benefits for the overall economy through entrepreneurial leverage. The effects of public policies on individuals are magnified by that leverage. Public policies that facilitate entrepreneurship have very low costs but potentially deliver large economic benefits by stimulating economic growth and development. Conversely, seemingly minor public policies that needlessly hinder entrepreneurship can have severe economic consequences, reducing growth and economic development.

Innovative entrepreneurship requires a supply of individuals who aspire to become entrepreneurs and who have the necessary capabilities and human capital. Public policies that remove tax and regulatory barriers to entrepreneurship by individuals have macroeconomic effects because of entrepreneurial leverage. The result can be substantial investment and innovation at relatively low public costs. Conversely, high marginal tax rates and regulatory barriers to establishing

3 Robert J. Barro, "Keynesian Economics vs. Regular Economics," *Wall Street Journal*, August 24, 2011, http://www.hoover.org/news/daily-report/90486.

new firms that discourage individual initiative will negatively impact innovative entrepreneurship.

Hayek (2002, p. 19) emphasizes the universality of entrepreneurship: "Having seen what I have of the world, it appears to me that the proportion of people who are prepared to try out new possibilities that promise to improve their situation – as long as others do not prevent them from doing so – is more or less the same everywhere." Hayek draws an important lesson for public policy:

> It seems to me that the much-lamented lack of entrepreneurial spirit in many young countries is not an unchangeable attribute of individuals, but the consequence of limitations placed on individuals by the prevailing point of view. For precisely this reason, the effect would be fatal if, in such countries, the collective will of the majority were to control the efforts of individuals, rather than that public power limits itself to protecting the individual from the pressure of society – and only the institution of private property, and all the liberal institutions of the rule of law associated with it, can bring about the latter.

Innovative entrepreneurship requires not only individual initiative but also the freedom to exercise it.

Social customs also affect innovative entrepreneurship because of the importance of attitudes toward individual achievement and business success (McClosky, 2006). General business knowledge within the population is critical, as evidenced by difficulties faced by China, Russia, and Eastern European countries in implementing market capitalism after varying periods of communism. The quality of education affects entrepreneurship through training in commercial, scientific, and technological subjects. This helps explain the observation by Glaeser et al. (2004) that accumulation of human capital and productive capital may be more essential for growth than are public institutions.

There must be preconditions such that potential entrepreneurs make the necessary occupational, commercialization, and investment choices. Because of interdependence effects, the preferences and endowments of individuals in the economy affect the potential supply of entrepreneurs. Rates of time preference, attitudes toward risk taking, the trade-off between labor and leisure, and enjoyment of independent endeavors affect the choices of potential entrepreneurs. Using estate and income tax data, Holtz-Eakin et al. (1994a, 1994b) show that the size of an inheritance affects the likelihood of an individual becoming an entrepreneur, which demonstrates that income and wealth matter.

Public policies that affect the motivation of individual entrepreneurs include income taxes, capital gains taxes, estate taxes, and bankruptcy rules. Personal income taxes affect the decisions of innovative entrepreneurs because of the imperfect financial separation between the entrepreneur and the start-up. Increases in tax rates may affect the number of individuals who choose to become entrepreneurs. Lundstrom and Stevenson (2005, p. 44) argue that public policy makers should consider the "pre-start, the start-up and post start-up phases of the entrepreneurial process" with the policy objective of "encouraging more people in the population to consider entrepreneurship as an option, to move into the nascent stage of taking the steps to get started and then to proceed into the infancy and early stages of a business."

Public policies that penalize business success will tend to discourage entrepreneurship generally and innovative entrepreneurship in particular. Because innovative entrepreneurship can involve greater risks and costs than replicative entrepreneurship, public policies that discourage risk taking are likely to reduce innovation. Tax rates can affect the proportion of entrepreneurs who choose innovative over replicative entrepreneurship. Success is uncertain and rare; tax rates that reduce the returns to successful entrepreneurship diminish expected returns to entrepreneurship.

Innovative entrepreneurship involves the risk of failure. Accordingly, bankruptcy rules can affect not only the settlement of business bankruptcies when they occur but also the decisions of individuals whether or not to go into business. In a sample of fifteen countries in Europe and North America, Armour and Cumming (2008) find that bankruptcy law affects self-employment rates when controlling for GDP growth. Ayotte (2007) suggests that bankruptcy rules should take into account the value of a fresh start for entrepreneurs. Berkovitch et al. (1997) model the effects of bankruptcy law on financing for entrepreneurs.

The life-cycle theory of entrepreneurship has additional macroeconomic implications. Life-cycle models of consumption predict aggregate patterns of saving in the economy on the basis of the age distribution of the population. Population growth and income growth increase the rate of aggregate asset accumulation. Because entrepreneurship is a form of asset accumulation, the life-cycle theory of entrepreneurship suggests that a growing population could increase the amount of entrepreneurship in the population as younger individuals create start-ups as a means of asset accumulation.

10.2 Innovative Advantage

The innovative entrepreneur has an innovative advantage when existing firms face innovative inertia. The individual initiative of innovative entrepreneurs embodies commercial, scientific, and technological inventions in new firms. The new firms established by innovative entrepreneurs form new industries and generate new markets. The competitive reactions of incumbent firms and imitation by replicative entrepreneurs multiply the force of innovative entrepreneurs, further diffusing commercial, scientific, and technological inventions. This suggests avoiding public policies that block individual initiative.

Capital investment, population expansion, and commercial, scientific, and technological discoveries are not sufficient to drive economic growth. There must be a mechanism for bringing discoveries to the market place. When existing firms delay technology adoption or reject new technologies because of the replacement effect and other rigidities, innovative entrepreneurs can enter the market and embody the technology in new firms. Innovative incumbents face adjustment costs of restructuring their businesses. Incumbents also experience innovative inertia because of limited management attention to new businesses, management misperceptions of competitive threats and opportunities, organizational rent seeking, and bureaucratic routines. This helps explain why innovative entrepreneurs and creative destruction are essential for economic growth and development.

Innovative entrants make economic contributions despite the costs and risks of creative destruction. Innovative entrants must overcome entry barriers, credit constraints, and resistance to economic change. Innovative entrants also must address the presumed advantage of incumbents that benefit from ownership of complementary assets (Teece, 1986, 2006). Innovative entrants compete with the capabilities and organizational capital of incumbent firms. Thompson (2012) questions whether existing firms benefit from organizational learning as output increases, which suggests that learning need not confer first-mover advantages.

Creative destruction depends on innovative entry. The turnover of firms in itself does not explain technological change and economic growth because new capacity can be added by replicative entrepreneurs and expansion of incumbent competitors. Firms exit the market for many reasons: their rivals gain competitive advantages, their customers' tastes change, they encounter financial losses and legal difficulties, they provide poor service, they are badly managed, and they experience changes in taxes and regulations that affect their profitability. Also, the failure of firms need not cause the retirement of productive capacity because entrants can purchase and employ the productive capacity of existing firms.

Public policies designed to promote innovation thus should reduce or remove regulatory barriers to new entry. For example, regulations that exempt incumbents through "grandfather" provisions generate barriers to entry that discourage entrepreneurship. Public policies that subsidize incumbents also generate barriers to entry, often discouraging the very innovation the subsidies are designed to support. Legal and regulatory costs of establishing and expanding firms also deter entrepreneurs. By reducing barriers to entry and exit of new firms, public policies allow entrepreneurs to establish new industries and to challenge incumbent firms in existing industries. Policies that protect existing firms from entry diminish incentives to innovate for both incumbents and entrants.

Dynamic economies can experience periods of GDP expansion and contraction resulting from innovative entry and creative destruction. In responding to contractions with expansionary fiscal and monetary policies, public policy makers should avoid dampening competition. Creative destruction is essential for improvements in economic efficiency and recovery from economic downturns. Public policies that facilitate the creation of start-ups and the establishment of new firms are important for generating economic growth. Governments hamper creative destruction when they pick particular companies and technologies to be the technology winners, providing tax preferences, subsidies, or regulatory assistance. Governments also hamper creative destruction by attempting to assist losers in the contest between incumbent firms and entrepreneurial entrants. Helping inefficient incumbents may simply delay their inevitable exit.

Industrial policies that mitigate the effects of creative destruction are subject to a fundamental inconsistency. Entrepreneurial creativity offers the benefits of improved technology that necessarily are accompanied by destruction of obsolete technology. Government policies should not block entry to protect incumbent firms because doing so preserves outdated technologies, products, and business methods; nor should governments "help" entrepreneurs through subsidies or special treatment. Governments are inept at picking technology winners, so that favoring any particular entrepreneur will bias market experiments.

Understanding innovation requires extensive commercial, scientific, and technological knowledge. Government agencies cannot expect to replicate or improve on the diffuse knowledge of the vast private sector. The benefits of new technologies and the returns to commercial development are uncertain. Public policy makers lack the necessary information about the preferences of consumers, the objectives of firms, the ideas of inventors, and the insights of innovative entrepreneurs.

10.3 Competitive Pressures

Competitive pressures increase incentives for invention and innovation. Innovative entrepreneurs face competition from existing firms, informal institutions of exchange, replicative entrepreneurs, and other innovative entrepreneurs. Entrepreneurial competition yields market experiments that generate information about the relative performance of innovations. Competition between entrepreneurs and a monopoly incumbent with multiple projects generates more innovative projects than would an incumbent firm without competition. Competition among innovative entrepreneurs generates more innovative projects than an incumbent monopoly with multiple projects. Competition among innovative entrepreneurs through market entry increases the expected quality of the best innovation. Competition among innovative entrepreneurs also limits the returns to the winning entrepreneur, increases cost-reducing investment, and reduces prices.

Competitive Pressures and Public Policy

Public policies consistent with economic growth and development should not erect barriers to entry or favor incumbent firms. Innovative entrants compete with incumbent firms to introduce new products, manufacturing processes, and transaction methods. Competition from innovative entrepreneurs can increase existing firms' incentives to innovate. In sectors that are close to the technology frontier, Aghion et al. (2009) find that competitive threats from innovative entrepreneurs encourage innovation by incumbents seeking to diminish the effects of creative destruction. Conversely, threats from innovative entrepreneurs in sectors farther from the frontier can discourage innovation by incumbents because entry dissipates rents from R&D.

Innovative entrepreneurs in many countries face a wide array of entry and operating costs imposed by government regulations. These costs often favor larger incumbent firms in contrast to entrants and smaller incumbents because larger firms may have economies of scale in compliance. The World Bank's (2012, p. 3) *Doing Business* report identifies costs of doing business that affect ten areas in the life cycle of a business: "starting a business, dealing with construction permits, getting electricity, registering property, getting credit, protecting investors, paying taxes, trading across borders, enforcing contracts and resolving insolvency." These indicators of the costs of doing business are evaluated in terms of property rights and investor productions and the costs and efficiency of regulator processes.[4]

The World Bank (2012, p. 3) points out: "Policy makers worldwide recognize the role that entrepreneurs play in creating economic opportunities for themselves and for others, and often take measures to improve the investment climate and boost productivity growth." The World Bank (2012, p. 1) observes:

> a faster pace of regulatory reform is good news for entrepreneurs in developing economies. Starting a business is a leap of faith under any circumstances. For the poor, starting a business or finding a job is an important way out of poverty. In most parts of the world small and medium-size businesses are often the main job creators. Yet entrepreneurs in developing economies tend to encounter greater obstacles than their counterparts in high-income economies.

Ardagna and Lusardi (2010) find that government regulation tends to reduce entrepreneurial benefits from social networks, business skills, and work status.[5]

Antitrust policy that supports competition affects incentives for invention and innovation. Antitrust policy should consider not only demand-side competition among producers who use inventions but also supply-side competition among inventors. Greater entry of inventors improves the expected best technology and reduces rents to the winning inventor. Competing inventors include university researchers, research laboratories, and new and existing firms that supply embodied and disembodied technology. Independent inventors also compete against the internal R&D of firms that vertically integrate invention and production, so that

4 The World Bank (2012) compares indicators of regulatory and legal transaction costs for 183 countries as they apply to SMEs.

5 Ardagna and Lusardi (2010) consider the effects of regulatory constraints on entrepreneurship for thirty-seven developed and developing economies using the Global Entrepreneurship Monitor (GEM) data set. They examine both potential entrepreneurs and owners and managers of new firms. Barseghyan (2008) considers the effects of entry costs on country differences in output and productivity. See Acs et al. (2008) for a comparison of the GEM and the World Bank *Doing Business* data.

the market for inventions should include both sales of inventions and internally supplied R&D.

The Department of Justice and the Federal Trade Commission recognize the importance of competition among owners of IP. The Antitrust Guidelines for Licensing of Intellectual Property (U.S. Department of Justice, 1995, p. 2) regard IP as "essentially comparable to any other form of property" for the purposes of antitrust analysis. The guidelines further state: "The Agencies do not presume that intellectual property creates market power in the antitrust context." Finally, the guidelines "recognize that intellectual property licensing allows firms to combine complementary factors of production and is generally procompetitive."

The benefits of innovation resulting from Schumpeterian or "dynamic" competition are reflected in discussions of antitrust policy. The focus of antitrust policy is often on product market innovation (Katz and Shelanski, 2005; Sidak and Teece, 2009).[6] The importance of the market for inventions suggests that antitrust policy also should take into account competition among inventors (Spulber, 2013b).

The benefits of competition among independent inventors may temper policy concerns about the effects of downstream product market concentration on innovation. Ziedonis (2004) points out that firms may choose to combine internal R&D with external purchases of inventions (make-and-buy) when there are duplicative inventions and simultaneous use of those inventions by producers, thus improving their post-invention bargaining position and reducing legal conflicts. Ziedonis (2004) finds evidence that with more fragmented technology markets, firms will patent more aggressively, which can raise their costs of invention.

Public policies that reduce the earnings of successful inventors include antitrust enforcement targeting IP owners, compulsory licensing, and mandated disclosure of inventions. Antitrust policies and regulations that seek to reduce the returns from successful innovation may reduce incentives to invent.[7] Reductions in the number of inventors can lower the expected quality of inventions and diminish innovation. Public policies that reduce IP protections for commercial discoveries such as business method inventions are likely to negatively impact innovative entrepreneurship. Commercial discoveries also are important for innovation based on implementing scientific and technological discoveries, which often require new business models. Innovative entrepreneurship depends critically on the supply of commercial discoveries.

6 Gilbert and Sunshine (1995) consider antitrust policy toward mergers of vertically integrated producers who conduct R&D for their own use. Focusing on internal R&D, Gilbert and Sunshine (1995, p. 594) define an innovation market for the purpose of antitrust policy as "a set of activities and a geographical area in which a hypothetical monopolist would impose at least a small but significant and nontransitory reduction in R&D effort." Gilbert and Sunshine (1995, p. 570) argue that "delineating innovation markets can be a valuable instrument for evaluating the effects of merger-induced structural changes on the incentives for research and development and the resulting pace of industrial innovation."

7 See Spulber (2008a, 2014).

Competitive Pressures and Economic Development

Entrepreneurs in developing economics face competitive pressures from traditional and informal organizations. Developing countries often have a large traditional sector and a fledgling modern sector (Lewis, 1954). The traditional sector includes non-firm institutions such as barter, handicrafts, subsistence agriculture, casual labor, money lending, farmers' markets, and cooperatives. Traditional and informal institutions include small family enterprises, buyers' cooperatives, workers' cooperatives, farmers' cooperatives, basic partnerships, and clubs. Developing countries are often plagued by missing markets for capital, labor, and goods and services. Individuals transact directly with each other through search, negotiation, barter, spot transactions, and informal contracts.

Innovative entrepreneurs in developing economics establish firms in the modern sector that compete with these traditional and informal institutions. New firms help create markets for capital, labor, and goods and services. Modern retail stores compete with outdoor markets and mom-and-pop vendors in the informal sector. Entrepreneurs establish financial institutions that compete with informal insurance and financial transactions (Jain, 1999). For example, microfinance offered by entrepreneurial entrants competes with traditional credit arrangements (Yunus, 2003; Armendáriz and Morduch, 2010). Credit rating agencies compete with informal reputation building and credit systems. Social networking sites, such as Facebook, compete with traditional social networks.

The contributions of innovative entrepreneurs to economic development have not been fully appreciated despite Schumpeter's early insights. Naudé (2010, p. 1) observes:

> The fields of development economics and entrepreneurship both developed very rapidly over the past 50 years as sub-disciplines within the respected fields of economics and management, but they did so in relative isolation, with the entrepreneurship field being more concerned with the process of entrepreneurship and the development economics field being more concerned with the global and country-level determinants of economic performance.

As a result, public policy debates on economic development have tended to focus on the design of public institutions such as legal systems, government agencies, and infrastructure.

Private institutions such as firms and markets are essential for economic development. Newly established firms create markets and organizations that replace informal transaction arrangements. As Hayek (1960, 1991) emphasized, such institutions provide private spontaneous ordering through incentives and coordination. Because individuals have better information about their situation, private ordering by firms and markets provides far more efficient coordination than government regulations and centralized command and control. Entrepreneurs induce structural change in the economy through development of private institutions.

Firms organize practically all economic activity outside of government: innovating, pricing, contracting, raising financial capital, producing, marketing products, and employing resources, labor, and capital goods. Firms manage every sector of the economy, including manufacturing, services, retail, wholesale, transportation, construction, energy, and communications. Entrepreneurial entry establishes firms that displace less efficient institutions in the informal sector, creating wealth, increasing production, and generating economic growth.

Firms improve economic efficiency by serving as intermediaries and creating market mechanisms. Firms centralize exchange by creating networks, matching buyers and sellers, posting prices, and disseminating information about goods and services. Innovative entrepreneurs establish the suppliers, distributors, and partners of other new firms.

Firms such as corporations offer financial separation from the consumption objectives of its owners in the sense of the Fisher Separation Theorem. This further distinguishes firms in the formal sector from traditional organizations such as consumer cooperatives, worker cooperatives, and basic partnerships. The organizations created by firms in the formal sector offer transaction efficiencies through relational contracts, delegation of authority, incentives for performance, and formal monitoring and communication systems.[8]

Entrepreneurial competition with informal and traditional organizations solves an important coordination problem. Schumpeter stresses that entrepreneurial innovation requires access to credit. However, where does credit come from in a developing economy? The answer to this puzzle is that most credit comes from banks, which are themselves a type of firm. Entrepreneurs establish the firms that operate the economy's financial system, including banks, brokerages, insurers, and mutual funds. These financial institutions in turn provide funding for entrepreneurial start-ups and existing firms. Entrepreneurial innovation in the financial sector is therefore a critical element of economic growth and development.

10.4 Creative Destruction

Creative destruction is an efficient form of innovation when frictions in the market for inventions generate benefits from entry of new firms and displacement of existing firms. Frictions in the market for inventions can result in creative destruction even if incumbent firms can implement inventions more efficiently than start-ups. Innovative entrepreneurs then increase economic growth and development through own-use of inventions.

Various transaction costs in the market for inventions can give inventors an own-use advantage over existing firms. The market for inventions is subject to costs of search, bargaining, and contracting. It may be difficult to transfer complex

8 See Spulber (1996a, 1996b, 1998, 1999, 2002a, 2002b, 2003, 2009a).

multidimensional inventions, so that inventors have an incentive to make "new combinations" through own-use of their inventions. When inventors have tacit knowledge, own-use of the inventions can offer advantages over the complementary assets of existing firms. Audretsch et al. (2006) point out that entrepreneurial start-ups must invest to develop the capacity to absorb new technology that is generated externally.[9] Asymmetric information inherent in markets for new technologies also can provide incentives for inventors to become innovative entrepreneurs.

Because of the critical role of inventions, public policies toward IP are likely to impact innovative entrepreneurship. Weak IP protections provide incentives for inventors to become innovative entrepreneurs as a means of reducing imitation or expropriation that could result from efforts to license inventions to start-ups and existing firms. However, strong IP protections help innovative entrepreneurs generate returns from new products, obtain licensing revenues, and raise finance capital (Graham et al., 2009). IP protections generate greater disclosure and foster commercialization by giving inventors more confidence in arranging technology transfer contracts.

Public policies that protect IP (patents, trademarks, copyrights) are important for employment and economic growth. The U.S. Department of Commerce et al. (2012) finds that "[d]irect employment in the subset of most IP-intensive industries . . . amounted to 27.1 million jobs in 2010, while indirect activities associated with these industries provided an additional 12.9 million jobs throughout the economy in 2010, for a total of 40.0 million jobs, or 27.7 percent of all jobs in the economy."[10] The report states:

> Innovation protected by IP rights is key to creating new jobs and growing exports. Innovation has a positive pervasive effect on the entire economy, and its benefits flow both upstream and downstream to every sector of the U.S. economy. Intellectual property is not just the final product of workers and companies – every job in some way, produces, supplies, consumes, or relies on innovation, creativity, and commercial distinctiveness. Protecting our ideas and IP promotes innovative, open, and competitive markets, and helps ensure that the U.S. private sector remains America's innovation engine.[11]

According to the report, "IP-intensive industries accounted for about $5.06 trillion in value added, or 34.8 percent of U.S. gross domestic product (GDP), in 2010."[12]

9 Audretsch et al. (2006) emphasize that firms and research organizations expend resources to develop additions to the stock of knowledge; see also Audretsch (1995a). The resulting knowledge does not diffuse automatically but instead requires active efforts of entrepreneurs to translate them into commercial opportunities. See also Audretsch and Thurik (2000, 2001) on the innovative contributions of entrepreneurial firms in developed economies.

10 U.S. Department of Commerce et al. (2012, p. 5). The report identifies 75 industries as IP-intensive from among a total of 313 industries.

11 U.S. Department of Commerce et al. (2012, p. i).

12 U.S. Department of Commerce et al. (2012, p. vii).

Also, the report observes: "Growth in copyright-intensive industries (2.4 percent), patent-intensive industries (2.3 percent), and trademark-intensive industries (1.1 percent) all outpaced gains in non-IP-intensive industries."[13]

Competition and appropriability of IP are complements in promoting innovation. This suggests that competition policy and IP policies are complementary. Weak IP protections will diminish participation in markets for inventions and will tend to increase the extent of vertical integration of R&D and production. With vertical integration, competition among producers will tend to reduce incentives to innovate. In contrast, IP protections for inventors not only will provide greater incentives to invent but also will support the development of markets for invention. When there are markets for inventions, greater competition among independent inventors and greater competition among producers will tend to increase incentives for invention and innovation (Spulber, 2013a, 2013b).

10.5 The Wealth of Nations

Innovative entrepreneurs provide important gains from trade that contribute to the wealth of nations. The increasing diffusion of entrepreneurship across countries and the internationalization of new ventures suggest that the process of creative destruction is expanding internationally. Adapting to world markets requires countries to change their mix of products and manufacturing activities. If incumbent firms are subject to innovative inertia, a country cannot benefit fully from participating in international markets. Innovative entrepreneurs increase a country's ability to benefit from international trade.

Innovative entrepreneurs help realize opportunities generated by access to international markets. Innovative entrepreneurs establish new firms that provide the mix of products, manufacturing activities, and transaction methods needed for international markets. New firms carry out imports and exports needed to achieve gains from trade. Innovative entrepreneurs make investments in productive capacity and engage in FDI and international technology transfers to help countries achieve gains from trade. In economies making a transition from socialism to capitalism, entrepreneurs establish new firms to replace or privatize government enterprises.

Innovative entrepreneurs contribute to the wealth of nations by establishing firms that introduce inventions to domestic and international markets. For example, world trade in Information and Communications Technology (ICT) exceeds $4 trillion per year.[14] ICT trade has grown rapidly, increasing at a rate of more than 10 percent per year from 1996 to 2008, tripling world trade in this category.[15] The U.S. Commerce Department finds that "[m]erchandise exports of IP-intensive

13 U.S. Department of Commerce (2012, p. vii).

14 This level of trade in ICT was reached in 2008; see Anderson and Mohs (2010).

15 Anderson and Mohs (2010).

industries totaled $775 billion in 2010, accounting for 60.7 percent of total U.S. merchandise exports."[16] Innovative entrepreneurs establish firms that participate in international IP-intensive industries.

In developing economies, the traditional and informal sector may be isolated from international trade. Achieving gains from trade requires innovative entrepreneurs to establish firms in the modern sector that can engage in international trade. Innovative entrepreneurs establish firms that make green field investments and form new industries in the modern sector. Innovative entrepreneurs in the modern sector export goods and services and import advanced technologies and transaction methods.

Innovative entrepreneurs in developing countries benefit from lower labor costs that enable them to manufacture and export goods and services. Innovative entrepreneurs in developing countries also form new firms that import technology and develop the modern sector. This helps explain the significant increase in entrepreneurship observed in China, India, and other countries when they open their economies to international trade. Khanna (2008) argues that the opening of India and China to international trade has generated opportunities for "billions" of potential entrepreneurs in those countries.

Typically, wages are higher in the modern sector than in the traditional sector. Various market frictions slow wage equalization within the economy including information differences, education and training disparities, transportation costs, and housing barriers. The modern sector tends be urban and the traditional sector tends be rural. The modern sector has greater economic development, higher incomes, and better infrastructure, which tend to foster innovative entrepreneurship. Replicative entrepreneurship occurs in both the modern and the traditional sector. Loayza (1996) argues that when governments impose taxes and regulations that they cannot enforce, some firms leave the formal sector, and activities move to the informal sector. Gries and Naudé (2010) present a two-sector development model suggesting that innovative entrepreneurship in the modern sector drives structural change in both sectors.

In both developed and developing economies, new and young ventures can globalize through many different methods: FDI, exports, outsourcing, contracts, and technology licensing. Reductions in the costs of trade and improvements in regulatory barriers to trade have increased the internationalization of new ventures. Many countries have entrepreneurial firms with an international orientation (Bosman and Levie, 2009). There is evidence that some entrepreneurs establish firms that engage in international trade at their founding.[17] For example, the Chinese

16 Department of Commerce (2012, p. viiii). Although there is limited data on foreign trade of IP-intensive service-providing industries, the Commerce Department reports that "exports of IP-intensive service-providing industries accounted for approximately 19 percent of total U.S. private services exports in 2007."

17 See Zahra and George (2002), Oviatt and McDougall (2005), George et al. (2005), Zahra (2005), Rialp et al. (2005), Coeurderoy and Murray (2008), and the references therein.

business matchmaking website Alibaba.com went international from its inception and in a few years served more than 40 million registered business users from more than 240 countries.[18] Many of Alibaba.com's users were newly established SMEs that themselves went international by engaging in either outsourcing abroad or production for foreign outsourcers (Davison and Ou, 2008).

10.6 Conclusion

Innovative entrepreneurs drive economic development by transforming economic institutions. In developed economies, their individual initiative and creativity challenge existing firms and form new industries. In emerging economies, entrepreneurs shape the formal sector, establish firms, create markets for goods, services, labor, and finance, and build basic industries.

Innovative entrepreneurship and economic growth are thus mutually reinforcing. Economic growth and development offer opportunities for entrepreneurs by increasing consumer demand, generating finance capital, and promoting institutional change. In turn, innovative entrepreneurs foster economic growth and development by boosting employment, creating wealth, and driving technological change.

18 Company overview, http://news.alibaba.com/specials/aboutalibaba/aligroup/index.html (accessed December 23, 2013).

Bibliography

Abernathy, W. J., and J. M. Utterback, 1978, "Patterns of Industrial Innovation," *Technology Review*, 80, June/July, pp. 40–47.

Acemoglu, D., 1999, "Changes in Unemployment and Wage Inequality: An Alternative Theory and Some Evidence," *American Economic Review*, 89, 5, pp. 1259–1278.

Acemoglu, D., 2002, "Technical Change, Inequality and the Labor Market," *Journal of Economic Literature*, 40, 1, pp. 7–72.

Acemoglu, D., 2008, "Innovation by Incumbents and Entrants," MIT Economics Working Paper.

Acemoglu, D., and J. Linn, 2004, "Market Size in Innovation: Theory and Evidence from the Pharmaceutical Industry," *Quarterly Journal of Economics*, 119, 3, pp. 1049–1090.

Acemoglu, D., and J. Robinson, 2008, "The Role of Institutions in Growth and Development," Working Paper No. 10, International Bank for Reconstruction and Development, The World Bank, Washington, DC.

Acemoglu, D., and F. Zilibotti, 2001, "Productivity Differences," *Quarterly Journal of Economics*, 116, 2, May, pp. 563–606.

Acs, Z. J., and D. B. Audretsch, 1987, "Innovation, Market Structure, and Firm Size," *The Review of Economics and Statistics*, 69, 4, November, pp. 567–574.

Acs, Z. J., and D. B. Audretsch, 1988, "Innovation in Large and Small Firms: An Empirical Analysis," *American Economic Review*, 78, 4, September, pp. 678–690.

Acs, Z. J., and D. B. Audretsch, 2003a, "Innovation and Technological Change," in Z. J. Acs and D. B. Audretsch, eds., *The International Handbook of Entrepreneurship*, Dordrecht: Kluwer, pp. 55–79.

Acs, Z. J., and D. B. Audretsch, 2003b, *The International Handbook of Entrepreneurship*, Dordrecht: Kluwer.

Acs, Z. J., and D. B. Audretsch, 2003c, "Introduction," in Z. J. Acs and D. B. Audretsch, eds., *The International Handbook of Entrepreneurship*, Dordrecht: Kluwer, pp. 3–20.

Acs, Z. J., D. B. Audretsch, P. Braunerhjelm, and B. Carlsson, 2004, "The Missing Link: The Knowledge Filter and Entrepreneurship in Economic Growth," CEPR Working Paper No. 4358.

Acs, Z., S. Desai, and L. Klapper, 2008, "What Does 'Entrepreneurship' Data Really Show? A Comparison of the Global Entrepreneurship Monitor and World Bank Group Datasets," World Bank Policy Research Working Paper no. 4667, Washington, DC.

Adachi, T., 2008, "A Life-Cycle Model of Entrepreneurial Choice: Understanding Entry into and Exit from Self-Employment," Working Paper, Tokyo Institute of Technology, October.

Aggarwal, R., and S. Dahiya, 2006, "Demutualization and Public Offerings of Financial Exchanges," *Journal of Applied Corporate Finance*, 18, 3, Summer, pp. 96–106.

Aghion, P., N. Bloom, R. Blundell, R. Griffith, and P. Howitt, 2005, "Competition and Innovation: An Inverted U Relationship," *Quarterly Journal of Economics*, 120, 2, pp. 701–728.

Aghion, P., R. Blundell, R. Griffith, P. Howitt, and S. Prantl, 2009, "The Effects of Entry on Incumbent Innovation and Productivity," *Review of Economics and Statistics*, 91 (1), February, pp. 20–32.

Aghion, P., M. Dewatripont, and P. Rey, 1994, "Renegotiation Design with Unverifiable Information," *Econometrica*, 62, pp. 257–282.

Aghion, P., C. Harris, P. Howitt, and J. Vickers, 2001, "Competition, Imitation and Growth with Step-by-Step Innovation," *Review of Economic Studies*, 68, 3, July, pp. 467–492.

Aghion, P., and P. Howitt, 1992, "A Model of Growth through Creative Destruction," *Econometrica*, 60, 2, March, pp. 323–351.

Aghion, P., and P. Howitt, 1998, *Endogenous Growth Theory*, Cambridge, MA: MIT Press.

Aghion, P., and P. Howitt, 2009, *The Economics of Growth*, Cambridge, MA: MIT Press.

Akerlof, G. A., 1970, "The Market for 'Lemons': Quality Uncertainty and the Market Mechanism," *Quarterly Journal of Economics*, 84, pp. 488–500.

Alchian, A. A., 2007, "Property Rights," *The Concise Encyclopedia of Economics*, 2nd ed., http://www.econlib.org/library/Enc/PropertyRights.html, accessed June 15, 2010.

Alchian, A. A., and H. Demsetz, 1972, "Production, Information Costs, and Economic Organization," *The American Economic Review*, 62, 5, December, pp. 777–795.

Allen, D. W., and D. Lueck, 2002, The Nature of the Farm: Contracts, Risk, and Organization in Agriculture, Cambridge, MA: MIT Press.

Allen, J. A., 1967, *Scientific Innovation and Industrial Prosperity*, Amsterdam: Elsevier.

Allison, J. R., and S. D. Hunter, 2006, "On the Feasibility of Improving Patent Quality One Technology at a Time: The Case of Business Methods," *Berkeley Technology Law Journal*, 21, 2, pp. 729–794.

Allison, J. R., and E. H. Tiller, 2003, "The Business Method Patent Myth," *Berkeley Technology Law Journal*, 18, 4, pp. 987–1084.

Alpern, S., and D. J. Snower, 1988, "High-Low Search in Product and Labor Markets," *American Economic Review*, Papers and Proceedings of the One-Hundredth Annual Meeting of the American Economic Association, 78, 2, May, pp. 356–362.

Alvarez, S. A., and L. W. Busenitz, 2001, "The Entrepreneurship of Resource-Based Theory," *Journal of Management*, 27, pp. 755–775.

Amato, J., and H. S. Shin, 2006, "Imperfect Common Knowledge and the Information Value of Prices," *Economic Theory*, 27, 1, pp. 213–241.

Anand, B., and T. Khanna, 2000, "The Structure of Licensing Contracts," *Journal of Industrial Economics*, 48, 1, March, pp. 103–135.

Ancori, B., A. Bureth, and P. Cohendet, 2000, "The Economics of Knowledge: The Debate about Codified and Tacit Knowledge," *Industrial and Corporate Change*, 9, 2, pp. 255–287.

Anderson, M., and J. Mohs, 2011, "The Information Technology Agreement: An Assessment of World Trade in Information Technology Products," *Journal of International Commerce and Economics*, 3, 1, May, pp. 109–156.

Anderson, R. C. and D. M. Reeb, 2003, "Founding-Family Ownership and Firm Performance: Evidence from the S&P 500," *Journal of Finance*, 58, 3, June, pp. 1301–1328.

Andrews, K. R., 1971, *The Concept of Corporate Strategy*, Homewood, IL: Irwin.

Angelmar, R., 1985, "Market Structure and Research Intensity in High-Technological-Opportunity Industries," *Journal of Industrial Economics*, 34, 1, September, pp. 69–79.

Anton, J. J., and D. A. Yao, 1994, "Expropriation and Inventions: Appropriable Rents in the Absence of Property Rights," *American Economic Review*, 84, 1, pp. 190–209.

Anton, J. J., and D. A. Yao, 1995, "Starts-Ups, Spin-Offs, and Internal Projects," *Journal of Law, Economics, & Organization*, 11, October, pp. 362–378.

Anton, J. J., and D. A. Yao, 2002, "The Sale of Ideas: Strategic Disclosure, Property Rights, and Contracting," *Review of Economic Studies*, 69, 3, pp. 513–531S.

Anton, J. J., and D. A. Yao, 2003, "Patents, Invalidity, and the Strategic Transmission of Enabling Information," *Journal of Economics & Management Strategy*, 12, Summer, pp. 151–178.

Anton, J. J., and D. A. Yao, 2004, "Little Patents and Big Secrets: Managing Intellectual Property," *Rand Journal of Economics*, 35, Spring, pp. 1–22.

Aoki, M., 1986, *The Co-operative Game Theory of the Firm*, New York: Clarendon Press.

Arabsheibani, G. D., D. de Meza, R. J. Maloney, and B. Pearson, 2000, "And a Vision Appeared unto Them of a Great Profit: Evidence of Self-Deception among the Self-employed," *Economic Letters*, 67, 1, pp. 35–41.

Ardagna, S., and A. Lusardi, 2010, "Explaining International Differences in Entrepreneurship: The Role of Individual Characteristics and Regulatory Constraints," in Josh Lerner and Antoinette Schoar, eds., *International Differences in Entrepreneurship*, National Bureau of Economic Research, Chicago: University of Chicago Press, pp. 17–62.

Armendáriz, B., and J. Morduch, 2010, *The Economics of Microfinance*, 2nd edition, Cambridge, MA: MIT Press.

Armour, J., and D. Cumming, 2008, "Bankruptcy Law and Entrepreneurship," *American Law and Economics Review*, 10 (2), pp. 303–350.

Arora, A., 1995, "Licensing Tacit Knowledge: Intellectual Property Rights and the Market for Know-How," *Economics of Innovation and New Technology*, 4, 1, pp. 41–60.

Arora, A., 1996, "Contracting for Tacit Knowledge: The Provision of Technical Services in Technology Licensing Contracts," *Journal of Development Economics*, 50, 2, pp. 233–256.

Arora, A., 1997, "Appropriating Rents from Innovation: Patents, Licensing and Market Structure in the Chemical Industry," *Research Policy*, 27, pp. 391–403.

Arora, A., A. Fosfuri, and A. Gambardella, 2001a, "Markets for Technology and Their Implications for Corporate Strategy," *Industrial and Corporate Change*, 10, 2, pp. 419–451.

Arora, A., A. Fosfuri, and A. Gambardella, 2001b, *Markets for Technology: The Economics of Innovation and Corporate Strategy*, Cambridge, MA: MIT Press.

Arora, A., A. Fosfuri, and A. Gambardella, 2001c, "Specialized Technology Suppliers, International Spillovers and Investment: Evidence from the Chemical Industry," *Journal of Development Economics*, 65, pp. 31–54.

Arora, A., and A. Gambardella, 1994, "The Changing Technology of Technological Change: General and Abstract Knowledge and the Division of Innovative Labour," *Research Policy*, 23, 5, September, pp. 523–532.

Arora, A., and A. Gambardella, 1998, "Evolution of Industry Structure in the Chemical Industry," in A. Arora, R. Landau, and N. Rosenberg, eds., *Chemicals and Long-Term Economic Growth*, New York: Wiley, pp. 379–414.

Arora, A., and A. Gambardella, 2010, "Ideas for Rent: An Overview of Market for Technology," *Industrial and Corporate Change*, 19, 3, pp. 775–803.

Arora, A., and R. P. Merges, 2004, "Specialized Supply Firms, Property Rights and Firm Boundaries," *Industrial and Corporate Change*, 13, pp. 451–475.

Arrow, K. J., 1962a, "The Economic Implications of Learning by Doing," *Review of Economic Studies*, 29, 3, June, pp. 155–173.

Arrow, K. J., 1962b, "Economic Welfare and the Allocation of Resources for Invention," in National Bureau of Economic Research, *The Rate and Direction of Inventive Activity*, Princeton, NJ: Princeton University Press, pp. 609–626.

Arrow, K. J., 1969, "Classificatory Notes on the Production and Transmission of Technological Knowledge," *American Economic Review*, Papers and Proceedings, 59, 2, May, pp. 29–35.

Arrow, K. J., 1974, *The Limits of Organization*, New York: Norton.

Arrow, K. J., and F. H. Hahn, 1971, *General Competitive Analysis*, San Francisco: Holden-Day.

Artle, R., and P. Varaiya, 1978, "Life Cycle Consumption and Homeownership," *Journal of Economic Theory*, 18, pp. 38–58.

Åstebro, T., and I. Bernhardt, 2003, "Start-up Financing, Owner Characteristics, and Survival," *Journal of Economics and Business*, 55, 4, pp. 303–319.

Åstebro, T., and I. Bernhardt, 2004, "The Winner's Curse of Human Capital," *Small Business Economics*, 24, 1, pp. 63–78.

Astrachan, J. H., and M. C. Shanker, 2003, "Family Businesses' Contribution to the U.S. Economy: A Closer look," *Family Business Review*, 16, 3, pp. 211–219.

Atrostic, B. K., P. Boegh-Nielsen, K. Motohashi, and S. Nguyen, 2004, "IT, Productivity and Growth in Enterprises: New Results from International Micro Data," in OECD, *The Economic Impact of ICT – Measurement, Evidence and Implications*, Paris: OECD, pp. 279–300.

Atrostic, B. K., J. Gates, and R. Jarmin, 2000, "Measuring the Electronic Economy: Current Status and Next Steps," Center for Economic Studies, U.S. Bureau of the Census, Working Paper No. CES-WP-00–10.

Attanasio, O., and M. Browning, 1995, "Consumption over the Life Cycle and over the Business Cycle," *American Economic Review*, 85, pp. 1118–1137.

Audretsch, D. B., 1991, "New Firm Survival and the Technological Regime," *Review of Economics and Statistics*, 73, pp. 441–450.

Audretsch, D. B., 1995a, *Innovation and Industry Evolution*, Cambridge, MA: MIT Press.

Audretsch, D. B., 1995b, "Innovation, Growth and Survival: The Post-Entry Performance of Firms," *International Journal of Industrial Organization*, 13, 4, December, pp. 441–457.

Audretsch, D. B., 2001, "The Role of Small Firms in U.S. Biotechnology Clusters," *Small Business Economics*, 17, pp. 3–15.

Audretsch, D. B., and M. Keilbach, 2004, "Entrepreneurship Capital and Economic Performance," *Regional Studies*, 38, 8, November, pp. 949–959.

Audretsch, D. B., M. C. Keilbach, and E. E. Lehmann, 2006, *Entrepreneurship and Economic Growth*, Oxford: Oxford University Press.

Audretsch, D. B., and A. R. Thurik, 2000, "Capitalism and Democracy in the 21st Century: From the Managed to the Entrepreneurial Economy," *Journal of Evolutionary Economics*, 10, 1, pp. 17–34.

Audretsch, D. B., and A. R. Thurik, 2001, "What's New about the New Economy? From the Managed to the Entrepreneurial Economy," *Industrial and Corporate Change*, 10, 1, pp. 267–315.

Autor, D. H., L. F. Katz, and M. S. Kearney, 2008, "Trends in U.S. Wage Inequality: Revising the Revisionists," *Review of Economics and Statistics*, 90, 2, pp. 300–323.

Autor, D. H., F. Levy, and R. J. Murnane, 2003, "The Skill Content of Recent Technological Change: An Empirical Exploration," *Quarterly Journal of Economics*, 118, 4, pp. 1279–1333.

Ayers, I., 2005, *Optional Law: The Structure of Legal Entitlements*, Chicago: University of Chicago Press.

Ayotte, K., 2007, "Bankruptcy and Entrepreneurship: The Value of a Fresh Start," *Journal of Law, Economics and Organization*, 23, 1, pp. 161–185.

Ayres, I., and P. Klemperer, 1999, "Limiting Patentees' Market Power without Reducing Innovation Incentives: The Perverse Benefits of Uncertainty and Non-Injunctive Remedies," *Michigan Law Review*, 97, pp. 985–1033.

Bagwell, K., G. Ramey, and D. F. Spulber, 1997, "Dynamic Retail Price and Investment Competition," *Rand Journal of Economics*, 28, Summer, pp. 207–227.

Baker, J. B., and T. F. Bresnahan, 2006, "Economic Evidence in Antitrust: Defining Markets and Measuring Market Power," Stanford Law School, Working Paper No. 328.

Balconi, M., A. Pozzali, and R. Viale, 2007, "The 'Codification Debate' Revisited: A Conceptual Framework to Analyze the Role of Tacit Knowledge in Economics," *Industrial and Corporate Change*, 16, 5, October, pp. 823–849.

Banks, J. S., 1992, "Monopoly Pricing and Regulatory Oversight," *Journal of Economics & Management Strategy*, 1, Spring, pp. 203–233.

Banks, J. S., and J. Sobel, 1987, "Equilibrium Selection in Signaling Games," *Econometrica*, 55, 3, May, pp. 647–661.

Baptista, R., 1999, "The Diffusion of Process Innovations: A Selective Review," *International Journal of the Economics of Business*, 6, 1, pp. 107–129.

Baron, R., 1998, "Cognitive Mechanisms in Entrepreneurship: Why and When Entrepreneurs Think Differently than Other People," *Journal of Business Venturing*, 13, pp. 275–294.

Barseghyan, L., 2008, "Entry Costs and Cross-Country Differences in Productivity and Output," *Journal of Economic Growth*, 13, 2, pp. 145–167.

Bartelsman, E. J., and M. E. Doms, 2000, "Understanding Productivity: Lessons from Longitudinal Microdata," *Journal of Economic Literature*, 38, 3, pp. 569–594.

Barzel, Y., 1968, "Optimal Timing of Innovations," *Review of Economics & Statistics*, 50, 3, August, pp. 348–355.

Barzel, Y., 1987, "The Entrepreneur's Reward for Self-Policing," *Economic Inquiry*, 25, January, pp. 103–116.

Baumol, W. J., 1968, "Entrepreneurship in Economic Theory," *American Economic Review*, Papers and Proceedings, 58, 2, May, pp. 64–71.

Baumol, W. J., 1986, "Productivity Growth, Convergence, and Welfare: What the Long-Run Data Show," *American Economic Review*, 76, 5, pp. 1072–1085.

Baumol, W. J., 1993, *Entrepreneurship, Management, and the Structure of Payoffs*, Cambridge, MA: MIT Press.

Baumol, W. J., 2002, *The Free-Market Innovation Machine: Analyzing the Growth Miracle of Capitalism*, Princeton, NJ: Princeton University Press.

Baumol, W. J., 2006, "Return of the Invisible Men: The Microeconomic Value Theory of Inventors and Entrepreneurs," Special Session on Entrepreneurship, Innovation and Growth I: Theoretical Approach, American Economic Association Meetings, https://www.aeaweb.org/assa/2006/0107_1015_0301.pdf (downloaded December 16, 2013).

Baumol, W. J., 2010, *The Microtheory of Innovative Entrepreneurship*, Princeton, NJ: Princeton University Press.

Baumol, W. J., R. E. Litan, and C. J. Schramm, 2007, *Good Capitalism, Bad Capitalism, and the Economics of Growth and Prosperity*, New Haven, CT: Yale University Press.

Baye, M. R., and H. C. Hoppe, 2003, "The Strategic Equivalence of Rent-Seeking, Innovation, and Patent-Race Games," *Games and Economic Behavior*, 44, pp. 217–226.

Baye, M. R., D. Kovenock, and C. G. de Vries, 1994, "The Solution to the Tullock Rent-Seeking Game When R > 2: Mixed-Strategy Equilibria and Mean Dissipation Rates," *Public Choice*, 81, pp. 363–380.

Baye, M. R., D. Kovenock, and C. G. de Vries, 1996, "The All-Pay Auction with Complete Information," *Economic Theory*, 8, pp. 291–305.

Bayh, B., J. P. Allen, and H. W. Bremer, 2009, "Universities, Inventors, and the Bayh-Dole Act," *Life Sciences Law & Industry Report*, 3, 24, December 18, pp. 1–5.

Bayus, B. L., and R. Agarwal, 2007, "The Role of Pre-Entry Experience, Entry Timing, and Product Technology Strategies in Explaining Firm Survival," *Management Science*, 53, December, pp. 1887–1902.

Bebchuk, L. A., J. M. Fried, and D. I. Walker, 2002, "Managerial Power and Rent Extraction in the Design of Executive Compensation," *University of Chicago Law Review*, 69, pp. 751–846.

Becker, G. S., 1975, *Human Capital: A Theoretical and Empirical Analysis with Special Reference to Education*, 2nd ed., New York: National Bureau of Economic Research.

Becker, G. S., and K. M. Murphy, 1995, "The Division of Labor, Coordination Costs, and Knowledge," in R. Febero and P. S. Schwartz, eds., *The Essence of Becker*, Stanford: Hoover Institution Press, pp. 608–632.

Benabou, R., and J. Tirole, 2004, "Willpower and Personal Rules," *Journal of Political Economy*, 112, 4, pp. 848–885.

Benhabib, J., and A. Rustichini, 1991, "Vintage Capital, Investment, and Growth," *Journal of Economic Theory*, 55, 2, December, pp. 323–339.

Ben-Porath, Y., 1980, "The F-connection: Families, Friends, and Firms in the Organization of Exchange," *Population and Development Review*, 6, March, pp. 1–30.

Berkovitch, E., R. Israel, and J. F. Zender, 1997, "Optimal Bankruptcy Law and Firm-Specific Investments," *European Economic Review*, 41, 3–5, April, pp. 487–497.

Berle, A. A., and G. C. Means, 1932 [1967], *The Modern Corporation and Private Property*, New York: Harcourt, Brace & World.

Besanko, D., and D. F. Spulber, 1992, "Sequential Equilibrium Investment by Regulated Firms," *Rand Journal of Economics*, 23, Summer, pp. 153–170.

Besen, S. M., and L. J. Raskind, 1991, "An Introduction to the Law and Economics of Intellectual Property," *Journal of Economic Perspectives*, 5, 1, Winter, pp. 3–27.

Bessen, J., and R. M. Hunt, 2007, "An Empirical Look at Software Patents," *Journal of Economics & Management Strategy*, 16, Spring, pp. 157–189.

Bessen, J., and M. J. Meurer, 2008, *Patent Failure: How Judges, Bureaucrats and Lawyers put Innovations at Risk*, Princeton, NJ: Princeton University Press.

Bester, H., and E. Petrakis, 1993, "The Incentives for Cost Reduction in a Differentiated Industry," *International Journal of Industrial Organization*, 11, pp. 519–534.

Bhidé, A., 1994, "How Entrepreneurs Craft Strategies that Work," *Harvard Business Review*, 72, pp. 150–161.

Bhidé, A., 1999, *The Origin and Evolution of New Businesses*, Oxford: Oxford University Press.

Bitler, M. P., T. J. Moskowitz, and A. Vissing-Jørgensen, 2005, "Testing Agency Theory with Entrepreneur Effort and Wealth," *Journal of Finance*, 60, 2, pp. 539–576.

Blair, M. M., 1995, *Ownership and Control: Rethinking Corporate Governance for the Twenty-First Century*, Washington, DC: Brookings Institution.

Blair, M. M., 2003, "Locking in Capital: What Corporate Law Achieved for Business Organizers in the Nineteenth Century," *UCLA Law Review*, 51, pp. 387–455.

Blair, M. M., 2004, "The Neglected Benefits of the Corporate Form: Entity Status and the Separation of Asset Ownership from Control," in A. Grandori, ed., *Corporate Governance and Firm Organization: Microfoundations and Structural Forms*, Oxford: Oxford University Press, pp. 45–66.

Blair, R. D., and F. Lafontaine, 2005, *The Economics of Franchising*, Cambridge: Cambridge University Press.

Blanchflower, D. G., and A. J. Oswald, 1998, "What Makes an Entrepreneur?," *Journal of Labor Economics*, 16, January, pp. 26–60.

Blaug, M., 1962, *Economic Theory in Retrospect*, Cambridge: Cambridge University Press.

Blonigen, B. A., and C. T. Taylor, 2000, "R&D Activity and Acquisitions in High Technology Industries: Evidence from the US Electronics Industry," *Journal of Industrial Economics*, 48, pp. 47–70.

Blundell, R., R. Griffith, and J. Van Reenen, 1999, "Market Share, Market Value and Innovation in a Panel of British Manufacturing Firms," *Review of Economic Studies*, 66, pp. 529–554.

Bodner, R., and D. Prelec, 2003, "Self-Signaling and Diagnostic Utility in Everyday Decision Making," in I. Brocas and J. D. Carrillo, eds., *The Psychology of Economic Decisions*, Oxford: Oxford University Press, pp. 105–123.

Bolton, P., and M. Dewatripont, 2004, *Contract Theory*, Cambridge, MA: MIT Press.

Bonaccorsi, A., and P. Giuri, 2000, "When Shakeout Doesn't Occur: The Evolution of the Turboprop Engine Industry," *Research Policy*, 29, pp. 847–870.

Borensztein, E., J. De Gregorio, and J.-W. Lee, 1998, "How Does Foreign Direct Investment Affect Economic Growth?," *Journal of International Economics*, 45, pp. 115–135.

Bork, R. H., 1993, *The Antitrust Paradox*, New York: Free Press.

Boroush, M., 2008, "New Estimates of National Research and Development Expenditures Show 5.8% Growth in 2007," NSF 08–317, National Science Foundation, Washington, DC, August.

Bosma, N., and J. Levie, 2010, *Global Entrepreneurship Monitor 2009 Executive Report*, Babson College, Babson Park, MD: Global Entrepreneurship Research Association.

Bosworth, B. P., and J. E. Triplett, 2007a, "The Early 21st Century U.S. Productivity Expansion is *Still* in Services," *International Productivity Monitor*, 14, pp. 3–19.

Bosworth, B. P., and J. E. Triplett, 2007b, "Services Productivity in the United States: Griliches' Services Volume Revisited," in E. R. Berndt and C. M. Hulten, eds., *Hard-to-Measure Goods and Services: Essays in Memory of Zvi Griliches*, Chicago: University of Chicago Press, pp. 413–448.

Bourgeois, L. J., III, 1985, "Strategic Goals, Perceived Uncertainty, and Economic Performance in Volatile Environments," *Academy of Management Journal*, 28, 3, September, pp. 548–573.

Box, S., 2009, "OECD Work on Innovation – A Stocktaking of Existing Work," Science and Technology Policy Working Paper 2009/2, Organization for Economic Cooperation and Development, Paris, February.

Bresnahan, T., S. Greenstein, and R. Henderson, 2011, "Schumpeterian Competition and Diseconomies of Scope; Illustrations from the Histories of Microsoft and IBM," in J. Lerner and S. Stern, eds., *The Rate and Direction of Inventive Activity Revisited*, Cambridge, MA: National Bureau of Economic Research, pp. 203–276.

Bresnahan, T. F., and D. M. G. Raff, 1991, "Intra-Industry Heterogeneity and the Great Depression: The American Motor Vehicles Industry, 1929–1935," *Journal of Economic History*, 51, June, pp. 317–331.

Bris, A., I. Welch, and N. Zhu, 2006, "The Costs of Bankruptcy: Chapter 7 Liquidation versus Chapter 11 Reorganization," *Journal of Finance*, 61, 3, June, pp. 1253–1303.

Brocas, I., and J. D. Carillo, 2004, "Entrepreneurial Boldness and Excessive Investment," *Journal of Economics & Management Strategy*, 13, pp. 321–350.

Brocas, I., and J. D. Carillo, 2007, "Influence through Ignorance," *Rand Journal of Economics*, 38, 4, Winter, pp. 931–947.

Brouwer, E., and A. Kleinknecht, 1996, "Firm Size, Small Business Presence and Sales of Innovative Products: A Micro-Econometric Analysis," *Small Business Economics*, 8, 3, pp. 189–201.

Brouwer, M. T., 1991, *Schumpeterian Puzzles, Technological Competition and Economic Evolution*, Ann Arbor: University of Michigan Press, Harvester Wheatsheaf.

Brouwer, M. T., 2002, "Weber, Schumpeter and Knight on Entrepreneurship and Economic Development," *Journal of Evolutionary Economics*, 12, pp. 83–105.

Brown, W. O., Jr., 2001, "Faculty Participation in University Governance and the Effects on University Performance," *Journal of Economic Behavior and Organization*, 44, pp. 129–143.

Browning, M., and T. F. Crossley, 2001, "The Life-Cycle Model of Consumption and Saving," *Journal of Economic Perspectives*, 15, 3, Summer, pp. 3–22.

Brumfiel, G., 2010, "Andre Geim: in Praise of Graphene," *Nature*, October 7, doi:10.1038/news.2010.525, http://www.nature.com/news/2010/101007/full/news.2010.525.html (accessed December 23, 2013).

Brush, C. G., 1995, *International Entrepreneurship: The Effects of Firm Age on Motives of Internationalization*, New York: Garland.

Brynjolfsson, E., and L. M. Hitt, 2000, "Beyond Computation: Information Technology, Organizational Transformation and Business Performance," *Journal of Economic Perspectives*, 14, 4, pp. 23–48.

Budd, C., C. Harris, and J. Vickers, 1993, "A Model of the Evolution of Duopoly: Does the Asymmetry between Firms Tend to Increase or Decrease?," *Review of Economic Studies*, 60, pp. 543–574.

Buera, F. J., 2009, "A Dynamic Model of Entrepreneurship with Borrowing Constraints," *Annals of Finance*, 5, pp. 443–464.

Buiter, W. H., 1988, "Death, Birth, Productivity Growth and Debt Neutrality," *Economic Journal*, 98, pp. 279–293.

Bullard, J., and J. Feigenbaum, 2007, "A Leisurely Reading of the Life-Cycle Consumption Data," *Journal of Monetary Economics*, 54, 8, November, pp. 2305–2320.

Bureau of Economic Analysis, U.S. Department of Commerce, 2010, "U.S. International Transactions: First Quarter 2010," news release, June 17.

Burk, D. L., and M. A. Lemley, 2009, *Patent Crisis and How the Courts Can Solve It*, Chicago: University of Chicago Press.

Burstein, A. T., and A. Monge-Naranjo, 2009, "Foreign Know-How, Firm Control, and the Income of Developing Countries," *Quarterly Journal of Economics*, 124, 1, February, pp. 149–195.

Busenitz, L., and J. Barney, 1997, "Differences between Entrepreneurs and Managers in Large Organizations: Biases and Heuristics in Strategic Decision-Making," *Journal of Business Venturing*, 12, pp. 9–30.

Busenitz, L., and C. Lau, 1996, "A Cross-Cultural Cognitive Model of New Venture Creation," *Entrepreneurship Theory and Practice*, 20, 4, pp. 25–39.

Cabral, L. M. B., 2003, "R&D Competition When Firms Choose Variance," *Journal of Economics & Management Strategy*, 12, 1, Spring, pp. 139–150.

Cabral, L. M. B., and M. H. Riordan, 1994, "The Learning Curve, Market Dominance, and Predatory Pricing," *Econometrica*, 62, pp. 1115–1140.

Calabresi, G., and A. D. Melamed, 1972, "Property Rules, Liability Rules, and Inalienability: One View of the Cathedral," *Harvard Law Review*, 85, pp. 1089–1128.

Campanale, C., 2009, "Private Equity Returns in a Model of Entrepreneurial Choice with Learning," Working Paper, University of Alicante, March.

Campbell, J. Y., 2006, "Household Finance," *Journal of Finance*, 61, 4, August, pp. 1553–1604.

Cantillon, R., 1755 [2010], *An Essay on Economic Theory*, An English translation of Richard Cantillon's *Essai sur la nature du commerce en général*, C. Saucier, trans, M. Thornton, ed., Auburn, AL: Ludwig von Mises Institute. http://library.mises.org/books/Richard%20Cantillon/An%20Essay%20on%20Economic%20Theory.pdf.

Carlsson, B., Z. J. Acs, D. B. Audretsch and P. Braunerhjelm, 2009, "Knowledge Creation, Entrepreneurship, and Economic Growth: a Historical Review," *Industrial and Corporate Change*, 18, 6, pp. 1193–1229.

Carlsson, B., and A.-C. Fridh, 2002, "Technology Transfer in United States Universities: A Survey and Statistical Analysis," *Journal of Evolutionary Economics*, 12, 1–2, pp. 199–232.

Carroll, C., 1994, "How Does Future Income Affect Current Consumption?," *Quarterly Journal of Economics*, 109, pp. 111–148.

Casadesus-Masanell, R., and J. E. Ricart, 2010, "From Strategy to Business Model and onto Tactics," *Long Range Planning*, 43, 2–3, pp. 195–215.

Casadesus-Masanell, R., and F. Zhu, 2013, "Business Model Innovation and Competitive Imitation: The Case of Sponsor-Based Business Models," *Strategic Management Journal*, 34, 4, April, pp. 464–482.

Cass, D., 1965, "Optimum Growth in an Aggregative Model of Capital Accumulation," *Review of Economic Studies*, 32, July, pp. 233–240.

Cassiman, B., and R. Veugelers, 2002, "R&D Cooperation and Spillovers: Some Empirical Evidence from Belgium," *American Economic Review*, 92, pp. 1169–1184.

Cassiman, B., and R. Veugelers, 2006, "In Search of Complementarity in Innovation Strategy: Internal R&D and External Knowledge Acquisition," *Management Science*, 52, 1, pp. 68–82.

Casson, M., 1982, *The Entrepreneur: An Economic Theory*, Totowa, NJ: Barnes & Noble Books.

Casson, M., 1987, *The Firm and the Market*, Cambridge, MA: MIT Press.

Casson, M., 1997, *Information and Organization: A New Perspective on the Theory of the Firm*, New York: Clarendon Press.

Casson, M., 2003, *The Entrepreneur; An Economic Theory*, 2nd ed., Cheltenham, UK: Edward Elgar.

Caulfield, T., R. M. Cook-Deegan, F. S. Kieff, and J. P. Walsh, 2006, "Evidence and Anecdotes: An Analysis of Human Gene Patenting Controversies," *Nature Biotechnology*, 24, 9, pp. 1091–1094.

Ceccagnoli, M., S. J. H. Graham, M. J. Higgins, and J. Lee, 2010, "Productivity and the Role of Complementary Assets in Firms' Demand for Technology Innovation," *Industrial and Corporate Change*, 19, 3, pp. 839–869.

Chandler, A. D., 1977, *The Visible Hand: The Managerial Revolution in American Business*, Cambridge, MA: Harvard University Press.

Chandler, A. D., 1990, *Scale and Scope: The Dynamics of Industrial Capitalism*, Cambridge, MA: Harvard University Press.

Chaney, T., 2008, "Distorted Gravity: The Intensive and Extensive Margins of International Trade," *American Economic Review*, 98, 4, pp. 1707–1721.

Che, Y.-K., and I. Gale, 2003, "Optimal Design of Research Contests," *American Economic Review*, 93, pp. 646–671.

Chemla, G., 2003, "Downstream Competition, Foreclosure, and Vertical Integration," *Journal of Economics & Management Strategy*, 12, 3, Summer, pp. 261–289.

Chen, Y., and M. Schwartz, 2009, "Product Innovation Incentives: Monopoly vs. Competition," Working Paper, University of Colorado, Boulder, May.

Chia, R. C. H., and R. Holt, 2009, *Strategy without Design: The Silent Efficacy of Indirect Action*, Cambridge: Cambridge University Press.

Chiappetta, V., 2000–2001, "Defining the Proper Scope of Internet Patents: If We Don't Know Where We Want to Go, We're Unlikely to Get There," *Michigan Telecommunications & Technology Review*, 7, pp. 289–361.

Chiappetta, V., 2004, "TRIP-ping Over Business Method Patents," *Vanderbilt Journal of Transnational Law*, 37, pp. 181–202.

Chowdhury, A., and G. Mavrotas, 2006, "FDI, and Growth: What Causes What?," *World Economy*, 29, 1, January, pp. 9–19.

Christensen, C. M., 1997, *The Innovator's Dilemma: When New Technologies Cause Great Firms to Fail*, Boston: Harvard Business School Press.

Chung, T.-Y., 1991, "Incomplete Contracts, Specific Investments, and Risk Sharing," *Review of Economic Studies*, 58, pp. 1031–1042.

Clark, J. B., 1894, "Insurance and Profits," *Quarterly Journal of Economics*, 7, pp. 40–54.

Clausen, T., M. Pohjola, K. Sappraserty, and B. Verspagenz, 2012, "Innovation Strategies as a Source of Persistent Innovation," *Industrial and Corporate Change*, 21, 3, pp. 553–585.

Clayton, T., C. Criscuolo, P. Goodridge, and K. Waldron, 2004, "Enterprise E-Commerce: Measurement and Impact," in OECD, *The Economic Impact of ICT – Measurement, Evidence and Implications*, Paris: OECD, pp. 241–260.

Clemens, C., 2008, "Imperfect Competition and Growth with Entrepreneurial Risk," *German Economic Review*, 9, pp. 180–206.

Clemens, C., and M. Heinemann, 2006, "On the Effects of Redistribution on Growth and Entrepreneurial Risk–Taking," *Journal of Economics*, 88, 2, pp. 131–158.

Clower, R., and A. Leijonhufvud, 1975, "The Coordination of Economic Activities: A Keynesian Perspective," *American Economic Review*, 65, pp. 182–188.

Coase, R. H., 1937, "The Nature of the Firm," *Economica*, 4, 16, pp. 386–405.

Coase, R. H., 1960, "The Problem of Social Cost," *Journal of Law and Economics*, 3, pp. 1–44.

Coase, R. H., 1988, "The Nature of the Firm: Origin, Meaning, Influence," *Journal of Law, Economics & Organization*, 4, 1, pp. 3–47. (Reprinted 1991, in O. E. Williamson and

S. G. Winter, eds., *The Nature of the Firm: Origin, Meaning, Influence*, Oxford: Oxford University Press, pp. 34–74.)

Coase, R. H., 1994a, *Essays on Economics and Economists*, Chicago: University of Chicago Press.

Coase, R. H., 1994b, "The Institutional Structure of Production," the 1991 Alfred Nobel Memorial Prize Lection in Economic Sciences, in R. H. Coase, *Essays on Economics and Economists*, Chicago: University of Chicago Press, pp. 3–14.

Cocco, J. F., F. J. Gomes, and P. J. Maenhout, 2005, "Consumption and Portfolio Choice over the Life Cycle," *Review of Financial Studies*, 18, 2, pp. 491–533.

Coeurderoy, R., and G. Murray, 2008, "Regulatory Environments and the Location Decision: Evidence from the Early Foreign Market Entries of New-Technology-Based Firms," *Journal of International Business Studies*, 39, pp. 670–687.

Cohen, J. E., and M. A. Lemley, 2001, "Patent Scope and Innovation in the Software Industry," *California Law Review*, 89, 1, pp. 1–57.

Cohen, W. M., 2010, "Fifty Years of Empirical Studies of Innovative Activity and Performance, in B. H. Hall and N. Rosenberg, eds., *Handbook of the Economics of Innovation*, Vol. 1, Chapter 4, Amsterdam: Elsevier, pp. 129–213.

Cohen, W. M., and R. Levin, 1989, "Empirical Studies of Innovation and Market Structure," in R. Schmalensee and R. Willig, eds., *The Handbook of Industrial Organization*, Vol. I, Amsterdam: North-Holland, pp. 1059–1107.

Cohen, W. M., and D. A. Levinthal, 1989, "Innovation and Learning: The Two Faces of R & D," *Economic Journal*, 99, 397, September, pp. 569–596.

Cohen, W. M., and D. A. Levinthal, 1990, "Absorptive Capacity: A New Perspective on Learning and Motivation," *Administrative Science Quarterly*, 35, 1, March, pp. 128–152.

Coleman, J. S., 1964, *Introduction to Mathematical Sociology*, New York: Free Press.

Collins, H. M., 1974, "The TEA Set: Tacit Knowledge and Scientific Networks," *Science Studies*, 4, 2, April, pp. 165–185.

Comanor, W. S., 1965, "Research and Technical Change in the Pharmaceutical Industry," *Review of Economics and Statistics*, 47, 2, May, pp. 182–190.

Comanor, W. S., 1967, "Market Structure, Product Differentiation and Industrial Research," *Quarterly Journal of Economics*, 81, 4, November, pp. 639–657.

Commons, J. R., 1931, "Institutional Economics," *American Economic Review*, 21, pp. 648–657.

Cooper, A., C. Woo, and W. Dunkelberg, 1988, "Entrepreneurs' Perceived Chances for Success," *Journal of Business Venturing*, 3, pp. 97–108.

Cooper, R. W., and J. C. Haltiwanger, 2006, "On the Nature of Capital Adjustment Costs," *Review of Economic Studies*, 73, 3, July, pp. 611–633.

Cowan, R., P. David, and D. Foray, 2000, "The Explicit Economics of Codification and Tacitness," *Industrial and Corporate Change*, 9, pp. 211–253.

Cowan, R., and D. Foray, 1997, "Quandaries in the Economics of Dual Technologies and Spillovers from Military to Civilian Research and Development," *Research Policy*, 24, pp. 851–868.

Cowan, R., and N. Jonard, 2003, "The Dynamics of Collective Invention," *Journal of Economic Behavior & Organization*, 52, pp. 513–532.

Craswell, R., and M. R. Fratrik, 1985–1986, "Predatory Pricing Theory Applied: The Case of Supermarkets vs. Warehouse Stores," *Case Western Reserve Law Review*, 36, pp. 49–87.

Crawford, V. P., and J. Sobel, 1982, "Strategic Information Transmission," *Econometrica*, 50, 6, November, pp. 1431–1451.

Creane, A., 1996, "An Informational Externality in a Competitive Market," *International Journal of Industrial Organization*, 14, 3, May, pp. 331–344.

Crémer, J., L. Garicano, and A. Prat, 2007, "Language and the Theory of the Firm," *Quarterly Journal of Economics*, 122, 1, February, pp. 373–407.

Cugno, F., and E. Ottoz, 2006, "Trade Secret vs. Broad Patent: The Role of Licensing," *Review of Law and Economics*, 2, 2, pp. 209–221.

Cyert, R. M., and J. G. March, 1963, *A Behavioral Theory of the Firm*, Englewood Cliffs, NJ: Prentice Hall.

Danaher, P. J., I. W. Wilson, and R. A. Davis, 2003, "A Comparison of Online and Offline Consumer Brand Loyalty," *Marketing Science*, 22, 4, Autumn, pp. 461–476.

Dasgupta, P., and J. Stiglitz, 1980a, "Industrial Structure and the Nature of Innovative Activity," *Economic Journal*, 90, June, pp. 266–293.

Dasgupta, P., and J. Stiglitz, 1980b, "Uncertainty, Industrial Structure, and the Speed of R&D," *Bell Journal of Economics*, 11, Spring, pp. 1–28.

Davison, R. M., and C. X. Ou, 2008, "Guanxi, Knowledge and Online Intermediaries in China," *Chinese Management Studies*, 2, 4, pp. 281–302.

Deardorff, A. V., 1992, "Welfare Effects of Global Patent Protection," *Economica*, 59, February, pp. 35–51.

Deaton, A., 1991, "Saving and Liquidity Constraints," *Econometrica*, 59, 5, September, pp. 1221–1248.

Deaton, A., 2005, "Franco Modigliani and the Life Cycle Theory of Consumption," Working Paper, Princeton University, March.

De Backer, K., V. Lopez-Bassols, and C. Martinez, 2008, "Open Innovation in a Global Perspective – What Do Existing Data Tell Us?," SRI Working Paper 2008/4 Statistical Analysis of Science, Technology and Industry, OECD Directorate for Science, Technology and Industry.

Deily, M. E., 1991, "Exit Strategies and Plant-Closing Decisions: The Case of Steel," *Rand Journal of Economics*, 22, Summer, pp. 250–263.

de Meza, D., and C. Southey, 1996, "The Borrower's Curse: Optimism, Finance, and Entrepreneurship," *Economic Journal*, 106, pp. 375–386.

Demsetz, H., 1968, "The Cost of Contracting," *Quarterly Journal of Economics*, 87, February, pp. 33–53.

Demsetz, H., 1983, "The Structure of Ownership and the Theory of the Firm," *Journal of Law and Economics*, 26, pp. 375–390.

Demsetz, H., 1991, "The Theory of the Firm Revisited," in O. E. Williamson and S. G. Winter, eds., *The Nature of the Firm*, Oxford: Oxford University Press, pp. 159–178.

Demsetz, H., and K. Lehn, 1985, "The Structure of Corporate Ownership: Causes and Consequences," *Journal of Political Economy*, 93, pp. 1155–1177.

Denicolò, V., and L. A. Franzoni, 2004, "The Contract Theory of Patents," *International Review of Law and Economics*, 23, pp. 365–380.

Dessein, W., 2002, "Authority and Communication in Organizations," *Review of Economic Studies*, 69, 4, October, pp. 811–838.

Dessein, W., and T. Santos, 2006, "Adaptive Organizations," *Journal of Political Economy*, 114, 5, pp. 956–995.

Deutsch, C. H., 1995, "For Law Firms, the Shakeout in the Business World Has Finally Hit," *New York Times*, February 17, p. B13.

Devlin, A., and N. Sukhatme, 2009, "Self-Realizing Inventions and the Utilitarian Foundation of Patent Law," *William & Mary Law Review*, 51, pp. 897–955.

Dewatripont, M., 2006, "Presidential Address Costly Communication and Incentives," *Journal of the European Economic Association*, Papers and Proceedings of the Twentieth Annual Congress of the European Economic Association, 4, 2/3, April–May, pp. 253–268.

Díaz-Giménez, J., V. Quadrini, and J. V. Ríos-Rull, 1997, "Dimensions of Inequality: Facts on the U.S. Distributions of Earnings, Income, and Wealth," *Federal Reserve Bank of Minneapolis Quarterly Review*, 21, 2, pp. 3–21.

Dixit, A. K., 1980, "The Role of Investment in Entry-Deterrence," *Economic Journal*, 90, pp. 95–106.

Dixit, A. K., and J. E. Stiglitz, 1977, "Monopolistic Competition and Optimum Product Diversity," *American Economic Review*, 67, June, pp. 297–308.

Djankov, S., T. Ganser, C. McLiesh, R. Ramalho, and A. Shleifer, 2008, "The Effect of Corporate Taxes on Investment and Entrepreneurship," NBER Working Paper No. 13756, January.

Djankov, S., E. Glaeser, R. La Porta, F. Lopez-de-Silanes, and A. Shleifer, 2003, "The New Comparative Economics," *Journal of Comparative Economics*, 31, 4, December, pp. 595–619.

Domar, E. D., 1946, "Capital Expansion, Rate of Growth, and Employment," *Econometrica*, 14, 2, April, pp. 137–147.

Domar, E. D., 1957, *Essays in the Theory of Economic Growth*, Oxford: Oxford University Press.

Dow, G., 2003, *Governing the Firm: Workers' Control in Theory and Practice*, New York: Cambridge University Press.

Dratler, J., Jr., 2003, "Does Lord Darcy Yet Live? The Case against Software and Business-Method Patents," *Santa Clara Law Review*, 43, pp. 823–899.

Dratler, J., Jr., 2005, "Alice in Wonderland Meets the U.S. Patent System," *Akron Law Review*, 38, pp. 299–336.

Dreyfuss, R. C., 2000, "Are Business Method Patents Bad for Business?," *Santa Clara Computer & High Technology Law Journal*, 16, 2, pp. 263–280.

Dunlop, J. T., and J. W. Rivkin, 1997, "Introduction," in S. A. Brown, *Revolution at the Checkout Counter: The Explosion of the Bar Code*, Cambridge, MA: Harvard University Press, pp. 5–9.

Dunn, T., and D. Holtz-Eakin, 2000, "Financial Capital, Human Capital, and the Transition to Self Employment: Evidence from Inter-generational Links," *Journal of Labor Economics*, 18, 2, pp. 282–305.

Durham, A. L., 1999, "'Useful Arts' in the Information Age," *BYU Law Review*, 4, pp. 1419–1528.

Easterbrook, F. H., and D. R. Fischel, 1989, "The Corporate Contract," *Columbia Law Review*, 89, pp. 1416–1448.

Easterbrook, F. H., and D. R. Fischel, 1991, *The Economic Structure of Corporate Law*, Cambridge, MA: Harvard University Press.

Eaton, J., and S. Kortum, 1996, "Trade in Ideas: Patenting and Productivity in the OECD," *Journal of International Economics*, 40, pp. 251–278.

Eaton, J., and S. Kortum, 1999, "International Technology Diffusion: Theory and Measurement," *International Economic Review*, 40, pp. 537–570.

Eaton, J., and S. Kortum, 2001, "Technology, Trade, and Growth: A Unified Framework," *European Economic Review*, Papers and Proceedings, 45, pp. 742–755.

Eaton, J., and S. Kortum, 2002, "Technology, Geography and Trade," *Econometrica*, 70, 5, September, pp. 1741–1779.

Eaton, J., S. Kortum, and F. Kramarz, 2004, "Dissecting Trade: Firms, Industries, and Export Destinations," *American Economic Review*, Papers and Proceedings, 94, 2, May, pp. 150–154.

Edgeworth, F. Y., 1881, *Mathematical Psychics, An Essay on the Application of Mathematics to the Moral Sciences*, London: C. Kegan Paul & Co. (Reprinted 1967, New York: Augustus M. Kelley Publishers.)

Edlin, A. S., and S. Reichelstein, 1996, "Holdups, Standard Breach Remedies and Optimal Investment," *American Economic Review*, 86, pp. 478–501.

Efficient Frontier, 2009, "U.S. Search Engine Performance Report: Q4 2008," January, White Paper.

Eisner, R., and R. H. Strotz, 1963, "Determinants of Business Investment," in *Commission on Money and Credit, Impacts of Monetary Policy*, Englewood Cliffs, NJ: Prentice-Hall, pp. 60–138.

Ekelund, R. B., Jr., R. F. Hébert, R. D. Tollison, G. M. Anderson, and A. B. Davidson, 1996, *Sacred Trust: The Medieval Church as an Economic Firm*, Oxford: Oxford University Press.

Ellam, A., 2003, "Overture and Google: Internet Pay-Per-Click (PPC) Advertising Auctions," Case Study CS-03–022, London Business School, March.

Ellis, H. S., and W. Fellner, 1943, "External Economies and Diseconomies," *American Economic Review*, 33, 3, September, pp. 493–511.

Epstein, R. A., 1997, "A Clear View of the Cathedral: The Dominance of Property Rules," *Yale Law Journal*, 106, pp. 2091–2120.

Epstein, R. J., and P. Malherbe, 2011, "Reasonable Royalty Patent Infringement Damages After *Uniloc*," *AIPLA Quarterly Journal*, 39, 1, Winter, pp. 3–33.

Erutku, C., and Y. Richelle, 2007, "Optimal Licensing Contracts and the Value of a Patent," *Journal of Economics & Management Strategy*, 16, 2, Summer, pp. 407–436.

Evans, D. S., and B. Jovanovic, 1989, "An Estimated Model of Entrepreneurial Choice under Liquidity Constraints," *Journal of Political Economy*, 97, 4, August, pp. 808–827.

Evans, D. S., and L. S. Leighton, 1989, "Some Empirical Aspects of Entrepreneurship," *American Economic Review*, 79, June, pp. 519–535.

Evans, G. H., Jr., 1944, "A Theory of Entrepreneurship," *Journal of Economic History*, 2, December, Supplement: The Tasks of Economic History, pp. 142–146.

Evans, G. H., Jr., 1949, "The Entrepreneur and Economic Theory: A Historical and Analytical Approach," *American Economic Review*, Papers and Proceedings, 39, 3, May, pp. 336–348.

Evenson, R. E., and L. E. Westphal, 1995, "Technological Change and Technology Strategy," in J. Behrman and T. N. Srinivansan, eds., *Handbook of Development Economics*, Vol. III, Amsterdam: North-Holland, pp. 2209–2299.

Fagerberg, J., 1994, "Technology and International Differences in Growth Rates," *Journal of Economic Literature*, 32, 3, September, pp. 1147–1175.

Fairlie, R., 1999, "The Absence of African-American Owned Business: An Analysis of the Dynamics of Self-employment," *Journal of Labor Economics*, 17, 1, pp. 80–108.

Farrell, J., and M. Rabin, 1996, "Cheap Talk," *Journal of Economic Perspectives*, 10, 3, Summer, pp. 103–118.

Fauli-Oller, R., and J. Sandonis, 2002, "Welfare Reducing Licensing," *Journal of Games and Economic Behavior*, 41, pp. 192–205.

Fein, A. J., 1998, "Understanding Evolutionary Processes in Non-Manufacturing Industries: Empirical Insights from the Shakeout in Pharmaceutical Wholesaling," *Journal of Evolutionary Economics*, 8, pp. 231–270.

Feinstein, C. H., 1998, "Pessimism Perpetuated: Real Wages and the Standard of Living in Britain during and after the Industrial Revolution," *Journal of Economic History*, 58, 3, pp. 625–658.

Feldman, M. P., 1996, "R&D Spillovers and the Geography of Innovation and Production," *American Economic Review*, 86, 3, June, pp. 630–640.

Ferrier, G. D., and C. A. Knox Lovell, 1990, "Measuring Cost Efficiency in Banking: Econometric and Linear Programming Evidence," *Journal of Econometrics*, 46, pp. 229–245.

Fischel, D. R., 1982, "The Corporate Governance Movement," *Vanderbilt Law Review*, 35, pp. 1259–1292.

Fisher, F. M., and P. Temin, 1973, "Returns to Scale in Research and Development: What Does the Schumpeterian Hypothesis Imply?," *Journal of Political Economy*, 81, 1, January-February, pp. 56–70.

Fisher, I., 1906, *The Nature of Capital and Income*, New York: The Macmillan Company.

Fisher, I., 1907, *Rate of Interest: Its Nature, Determination and Relation to Economic Phenomena*, New York: The Macmillan Company.

Fisher, I., 1930, *The Theory of Interest: As Determined by Impatience to Spend Income and Opportunity to Invest It*, New York: The Macmillan Company.

Fisher, I., 1933, "The Debt-Deflation Theory of Great Depressions," *Econometrica*, 1, October, pp. 337–357.

Flaherty, T. M., 1980, "Industry Structure and Cost-Reducing Investment," *Econometrica*, 48, pp. 1187–1209.

Forbes, D. P., 1999, "Cognitive Approaches to New Venture Creation," *International Journal of Management Review*, 1, pp. 415–439.

Fuchs, V. R., 1968, *The Service Economy*, Cambridge, MA: National Bureau of Economic Research.

Furman, J. L., and M. MacGarvie, 2009, "Academic Collaboration and Organizational Innovation: The Development of Research Capabilities in the US Pharmaceutical Industry, 1927–1946," *Industrial and Corporate Change*, 18, 5, pp. 929–961.

Galambos, L., and J. L. Sturchio, 1998, "Pharmaceutical Firms and the Transition to Biotechnology: A Study in Strategic Innovation," *Business History Review*, 72, 2, Summer, pp. 250–278.

Gallini, N. T., 1992, "Patent Policy and Costly Imitation," *Rand Journal of Economics*, 23, pp. 52–63.

Gallini, N. T., 2002, "The Economics of Patents: Lessons from Recent U.S. Patent Reform," *Journal of Economic Perspectives*, 16, 2, Spring, pp. 131–154.

Gallini, N. T. and S. Scotchmer, 2002, "Intellectual Property: When Is It the Best Incentive System?," *Innovation Policy and the Economy*, 2, pp. 51–77.

Gallini, N. T. and B. D. Wright, 1990, "Technology Transfer under Asymmetric Information," *Rand Journal of Economics*, 21, 1, Spring, pp. 147–160.

Galison, P., 2003, *Einstein's Clocks, Poincaré's Maps: Empires of Time*, New York: Norton.

Ganguly, C., and I. Ray, 2008, "On Mediated Equilibria of Cheap-Talk Games," Working Paper 05–08, University of Birmingham, May.

Gans, J. S., D. H. Hsu, and S. Stern, 2002, "When Does Start-Up Innovation Spur the Gale of Creative Destruction?," *Rand Journal of Economics*, 33, Winter, pp. 571–586.

Gans, J. S., and S. Stern, 2000, "Incumbency and R&D Incentives: Licensing the Gale of Creative Destruction," *Journal of Economics & Management Strategy*, 9, 4, pp. 485–511.

Gans, J. S., and S. Stern, 2003, "The Product Market and the Market for 'Ideas': Commercialization Strategies for Technology Entrepreneurs," *Research Policy*, 32, 2, pp. 333–350.

Garcia, R., and R. Calantone, 2002, "A Critical Look at Technological Innovation Typology and Innovativeness Terminology: A Literature Review," *Journal of Product Innovation Management*, 19, pp. 110–132.

Gentry, W. M., and G. R. Hubbard, 2000, "Tax Policy and Entrepreneurial Entry," *American Economic Review*, Papers and Proceedings, 90, 2, May, pp. 283–287.

Gentry, W. M., and G. R. Hubbard, 2001, "Entrepreneurship and Household Saving," NBER Working Paper No. 7894.

Gentry, W. M., and G. R. Hubbard, 2004, "Entrepreneurship and Household Saving," *Advances in Economic Analysis & Policy*, 4, 1, August, DOI: 10.2202/1538-0637.1053.

George, G., J. Wiklund, and S. Zahra, 2005, "Ownership and Internationalization of Small Firms," *Journal of Management*, 31, 2, April, pp. 210–233.

Geroski, P. A., 1995, "What Do We Know about Entry?," *International Journal of Industrial Organization*, 13, pp. 421–440.

Gertler, M. S., 2003, "Tacit Knowledge and the Economic Geography of Context, or the Undefinable Tacitness of Being (There)," *Journal of Economic Geography*, 3, 1, pp. 75–99.

Ghemawat, P., and B. Nalebuff, 1985, "Exit," *Rand Journal of Economics*, 16, pp. 184–194.

Giarratana, M. S., 2004, "The Birth of a New Industry: Entry by Start-ups and the Drivers of Firm Growth: The Case of Encryption Software," *Research Policy*, 33, 5, pp. 787–806.

Gilbert, R., 2006, "Looking for Mr. Schumpeter: Where Are We in the Competition-Innovation Debate?," *NBER Innovation Policy and the Economy*, 6, pp. 159–215.

Gilbert, R. J., and D. M. G. Newbery, 1982, "Preemptive Patenting and the Persistence of Monopoly," *American Economic Review*, 72, 3, June, pp. 514–526.

Gilbert, R. J., and S. C. Sunshine, 1995, "Incorporating Dynamic Efficiency Concerns in Merger Analysis: The Use of Innovation Markets," *Antitrust Law Journal*, 63, pp. 569–601.

Gilligan, T. W., M. L. Smirlock, and W. Marshall, 1984, "Scale and Scope Economies in the Multi-Product Banking Firm," *Journal of Monetary Economics*, 13, pp. 393–405.

Glaeser, E. L., and W. R. Kerr, 2009, "Local Industrial Conditions and Entrepreneurship: How Much of the Spatial Distribution Can We Explain?," *Journal of Economics & Management Strategy*, 18, 3, Fall, pp. 626–663.

Glaeser, E. L., R. La Porta, F. Lopez-de-Silanes, and A. Shleifer, 2004, "Do Institutions Cause Growth?," *Journal of Economic Growth*, 9, 3, pp. 271–303.

Goldin, C., and L. F. Katz, 1998, "The Origins of Technology-Skill Complementarity," *Quarterly Journal of Economics*, 113, 3, pp. 693–732.

Goldstein, P., 1992, "Copyright," *Law & Contemporary Problems*, 55, Spring, pp. 79–91.

Gompers, P. A., A. Kovner, J. Lerner, and D. S. Scharfstein, 2008, "Performance Persistence in Entrepreneurship," Finance, Entrepreneurial Management Working Paper No. 09–028, September.

Gourinchas, P.-O., and J. A. Parker, 2002, "Consumption over the Life-Cycle," *Econometrica*, 70, 1, pp. 47–89.

Grabowski, H., and D. Mueller, 1970, "Industrial Organization: The Role and Contribution of Econometrics," *American Economic Review*, 60, 2, May, pp. 100–104.

Graham, S. J. H., R. P. Merges, P. Samuelson, and T. Sichelman, 2009, "High Technology Entrepreneurs and the Patent System: Results of the 2008 Berkeley Patent Survey," *Berkeley Technology Law Journal*, 24, 4, Fall, pp. 1255–1328.

Green, J. R., and N. L. Stokey, 2007, "A Two-Person Game of Information Transmission," *Journal of Economic Theory*, 135, 1, pp. 90–104.

Greenstein, S., and G. Ramey, 1998, "Market Structure, Innovation and Vertical Product Differentiation," *International Journal of Industrial Organization*, 16, 3, May, pp. 285–311.

Greif, A., 1989, "Reputation and Coalitions in Medieval Trade: Evidence on the Maghribi Traders," *Journal of Economic History*, 49, pp. 857–882.

Greif, A., 1993, "Contract Enforceability and Economic Institutions in Early Trade: The Maghribi Traders' Coalition," *American Economic Review*, 83, pp. 525–548.

Gries, T., and W. Naudé, 2010, "Entrepreneurship and Structural Economic Transformation," *Small Business Economics*, 34, pp. 13–29.

Griliches, Z., 1957, "Hybrid Corn: An Exploration in the Economics of Technological Change," *Econometrica*, 25, 4, October, pp. 501–522.

Griliches, Z., 1969, "Capital-Skill Complementarity," *Review of Economics and Statistics*, 51, 4, pp. 465–468.

Griliches, Z., 1979, "Issues in Assessing the Contribution of Research and Development to Productivity Growth," *Bell Journal of Economics*, 10, Spring, pp. 92–116.

Griliches, Z., 1992, "The Search for R&D Spillovers," *Scandinavian Journal of Economics*, 94, Supplement, Proceedings of a Symposium on Productivity Concepts and Measurement Problems: Welfare, Quality and Productivity in the Service Industries, pp. S29–S47.

Grindley, P. C., and D. J. Teece, 1997, "Managing Intellectual Capital: Licensing and Cross-Licensing in Semiconductors and Electronics," *California Management Review*, 39, Winter, pp. 8–41.

Gromb, D., and D. Scharfstein, 2005, "Entrepreneurship in Equilibrium," Working Paper, London Business School, London, March.

Gros, D., 2006, "Foreign Investment in the US (II): Being Taken to the Cleaners?," CEPS Working Document No. 243, Brussels, Belgium: Centre for European Policy Studies, April.

Grossman, G. M., 1984, "International Trade, Foreign Investment, and the Formation of the Entrepreneurial Class," *American Economic Review*, 74, 4, pp. 605–614.

Grossman, G. M., and E. Helpman, 1990, "Comparative Advantage and Long-Run Growth," *American Economic Review*, 80, September, pp. 796–815.

Grossman, G. M., and E. Helpman, 1991a, *Innovation and Growth in the Global Economy*, Cambridge, MA: MIT Press.

Grossman, G. M., and E. Helpman, 1991b, "Quality Ladders in the Theory of Growth," *Review of Economic Studies*, 58, 1, January, pp. 43–61.

Grossman, S. J., 1981, "The Informational Role of Warranties and Private Disclosure about Product Quality," *Journal of Law and Economics*, 24, 3, pp. 461–483.

Grossman, S. J., and O. D. Hart, 1986, "The Costs and Benefits of Ownership: A Theory of Vertical and Lateral Integration," *Journal of Political Economy*, 94, August, pp. 691–719.

Grout, P. A., 1984, "Investment and Wages in the Absence of Binding Contracts: A Nash Bargaining Approach," *Econometrica*, 52, March, pp. 449–460.

Guo, J., I. H. Lam, I. Lei, X. Guan, P. H. Iong, and M. C. Ieong, 2006, "Alibaba International: Building a Global Electronic Marketplace," *e-Business Engineering, ICEBE '06, IEEE International Conference*, October, pp. 545–548.

Gurnick, D., and S. Vieux, 1999, "Case History of the American Business Franchise," *Oklahoma City University Law Review*, 24, pp. 37–65.

Hahn, F. H., and R. C. O. Matthews, 1964, "The Theory of Economic Growth: A Survey," *Economic Journal*, 74, December, pp. 779–891.

Hall, B. H., 2009, "Business and Financial Method Patents, Innovation, and Policy," *Scottish Journal of Political Economy*, 56, s1, pp. 443–473.

Hall, B. H., G. Thoma, and S. Torrisi, 2009, "Financial Patenting in Europe," *European Management Review*, 6, 1, pp. 45–63.

Hall, B. H., and R. H. Ziedonis, 2001, "The Patent Paradox Revisited: An Empirical Study of Patenting in the U.S. Semi-conductor Industry, 1979–1995," *Rand Journal of Economics*, 32, 1, pp. 101–128.

Hall, R., and C. I. Jones, 1999, "Why Do Some Countries Produce So Much More Output per Worker than Others?," *Quarterly Journal of Economics*, 114, pp. 83–116.

Hamberg, D., 1964, "Size of Firm, Oligopoly, and Research: The Evidence," *Canadian Journal of Economics and Political Science*, 30, 1, February, pp. 62–75.

Hamilton, B. H., 2000, "Does Entrepreneurship Pay? An Empirical Analysis of the Returns to Employment," *Journal of Political Economy*, 108, 3, pp. 604–631.

Hamilton Consultants, Inc., J. Deighton, and J. Quelch, 2009, "Economic Value of the Advertising-Supported Internet Ecosystem," Cambridge, MA: The Interactive Advertising Bureau, http://www.iab.net/media/file/Economic-Value-Report.pdf (accessed December 23, 2013).

Hansmann, H., 1980, "The Role of Nonprofit Enterprise," *Yale Law Journal*, 89, 5, April, pp. 835–901.

Hansmann, H., 1981, "The Rationale for Exempting Nonprofit Organizations from Corporate Income Taxation," *Yale Law Journal*, 91, 1, November, pp. 54–100.

Harrigan, K. R., 1980, *Strategies for Declining Businesses*, Lexington, MA: D.C. Heath.

Harris, L., 2003, *Trading and Exchanges: Market Microstructure for Practitioners*, New York: Oxford University Press.

Harrod, R. F., 1939, "An Essay in Dynamic Theory," *Economic Journal*, 49, March, pp. 14–33.

Hart, O., and B. Holmström, 1986, "The Theory of Contracts," in T. F. Bewley, ed., *Advances in Economic Theory Fifth World Congress*, Cambridge: Cambridge University Press, pp. 71–155.

Hart, O., and J. Moore, 1988, "Incomplete Contracts and Renegotiation," *Econometrica*, 56, July, pp. 755–785.

Hart, O., and J. Moore, 1990, "Property Rights and the Nature of the Firm," *Journal of Political Economy*, 98, 6, December, pp. 1119–1158.

Hart, R., P. Holmes, and J. Reid, 2000, "The Economic Impact of Patentability of Computer Programs, Report to the European Commission," OECD.

Hartog, J., J. Van der Sluis, and M. Van Praag, 2007, "Returns to Intelligence: Entrepreneurs versus Employees," University of Amsterdam Working Paper, Amsterdam, Netherlands.

Hartwell, R. M., 1967, "Editor's Introduction," in R. M. Hartwell, ed., *The Causes of the Industrial Revolution in England*, London: Methuen & Co., pp. 1–30.

Hawley, F. B., 1893, "The Risk Theory of Profit," *Quarterly Journal of Economics*, 7, July, pp. 459–479.

Hawley, F. B., 1901, "Final Objections to the Risk Theory of Profit: A Reply," *Quarterly Journal of Economics*, 15, August, pp. 603–620.

Hawley, F. B., 1907, *Enterprise and the Productive Process*, New York: G. P. Putnam's Sons.

Hayek, F. A., 1945, "The Use of Knowledge in Society," *American Economic Review*, 35, 4, September, pp. 519–530.

Hayek, F. A., 1960, *The Constitution of Liberty*, Chicago: Chicago University Press.

Hayek, F. A., 1973, *Law, Legislation and Liberty, Volume 1: Rules and Order*, Chicago, IL: University of Chicago Press.

Hayek, F. A., 1977, "The Creative Powers of a Free Civilization," in F. Morley, ed., *Essays on Individuality*, Indianapolis, IN: The Liberty Fund.

Hayek, F. A., 1991, "Spontaneous ('Grown') Order and Organized ('Made') Order," in G. Thompson, J. Francis, R. Levacic, and J. Mitchell, eds., *Market, Hierarchies & Networks: The Coordination of Social Life*, London: Sage Publications, pp. 293–301.

Hayek, F. A., 2002, "Competition as a Discovery Procedure," M. S. Snow, trans., *The Quarterly Journal of Austrian Economics*, 5, 3, Fall, pp. 9–23.

Heald, P. J., 2005, "A Transaction Costs Theory of Patent Law," *Ohio State Law Journal*, 66, 3, pp. 473–509.

Heaton, J., and D. Lucas, 2000, "Portfolio Choice and Asset Prices: The Importance of Entrepreneurial Risk," *Journal of Finance*, 55, 3, pp. 1163–1198.

Heckman, J., 1974, "Life Cycle Consumption and Labor Supply: An Explanation of the Relationship Between Income and Consumption over the Life Cycle," *American Economic Review*, 64, pp. 188–194.

Heidrun, C., and E. Ozdenoren, 2005, "Intermediation in Innovation," *International Journal of Industrial Organization*, 23, pp. 483–503.

Hellmann, T., 2005, "When Do Employees Become Entrepreneurs?," Working Paper, University of British Columbia, April.

Hellmann, T., 2007, "Entrepreneurs and the Process of Obtaining Resources," *Journal of Economics & Management Strategy*, 16, 1, Spring, pp. 81–109.

Hellmann, T., and M. Puri, 2000, "The Interaction Between Product Market and Financing Strategy: The Role of Venture Capital," *Review of Financial Studies*, 13, Winter, pp. 959–984.

Helpman, E., 1981, "International Trade in the Presence of Product Differentiation, Economies of Scale and Monopolistic Competition: A Chamberlin–Heckscher–Ohlin Approach," *Journal of International Economics*, 11, pp. 305–340.

Helpman, E., 1984, "A Simple Theory of International Trade with Multinational Corporations," *Journal of Political Economy*, 92, pp. 451–471.

Helpman, E., M. J. Melitz, and S. R. Yeaple, 2004, "Export versus FDI with Heterogeneous Firms," *American Economic Review*, 94, 1, March, pp. 300–316.

Henderson, M. T., 2009, "The Story of Dodge v. Ford Motor Company: Everything Old is New Again," in J. M. Ramseyer, ed., *Corporate Law Stories*, New York: Foundation Press, pp. 37–75.

Henderson, R., 1993, "Underinvestment and Incompetence as Responses to Radical Innovation – Evidence from the Photolithographic Alignment Equipment Industry," *Rand Journal of Economics*, 24, 2, pp. 248–270.

Henderson, R., and K. Clark, 1990, "Architectural Innovation: The Reconfiguration of Existing Product Technologies and the Failure of Established Firms," *Administrative Science Quarterly*, 35, pp. 9–30.

Hernandez-Murillo, R., and G. Llobet, 2006, "Patent Licensing Revisited: Heterogeneous Firms and Product Differentiation," *International Journal of Industrial Organization*, 24, 1, pp. 149–175.

Hicks, A. R., 2008, "Controlling a Ray Bundle with a Free-Form Reflector," *Optics Letters*, 33, 15, August, pp. 1672–1674.

Hollander, S., 1991, "On the Endogeneity of the Margin and Related Issues in Ricardian Economics," *Journal of the History of Economic Thought*, 13, 2, pp. 159–174.

Holmes T. J., and J. A. Schmitz, Jr., 1990, "A Theory of Entrepreneurship and Its Application to the Study of Business Transfers," *Journal of Political Economy*, 98, 2 April, pp. 265–294.

Holmes T. J., and J. A. Schmitz, Jr., 1995, "On the Turnover of Business Firms and Business Managers," *Journal of Political Economy*, 103, 5, October, pp. 1005–1038.

Holmes T. J., and J. A. Schmitz, Jr., 1996, "Managerial Tenure, Business Age, and Small Business Turnover," *Journal of Labor Economics*, 14, 1, January, pp. 79–99.

Holmström, B., and J. Roberts, 1998, "The Boundaries of the Firm Revisited," *Journal of Economic Perspectives*, 12, 4, Fall, pp. 73–94.

Holtz-Eakin, D., 2000, "Public Policy toward Entrepreneurship," *Small Business Economics*, 15, 4, December, pp. 283–291.

Holtz-Eakin, D., D. Joulfaian, and H. S. Rosen, 1994a, "Entrepreneurial Decisions and Liquidity Constraints," *Rand Journal of Economics*, 25, Summer, pp. 334–347.

Holtz-Eakin, D., D. Joulfaian, and H. S. Rosen, 1994b, "Sticking It Out: Entrepreneurial Survival and Liquidity Constraints," *Journal of Political Economy*, 102, February, pp. 53–75.

Hopenhayn, H., 1992, "Entry, Exit, and Firm Dynamics in Long Run Equilibrium," *Econometrica*, 60, pp. 1127–1150.

Hopenhayn, H., 1993, "The Shakeout," University of Pompeu Fabra, Working Paper No. 33.

Hopkins, E., 1982, "Working Hours and Conditions during the Industrial Revolution: A Re-Appraisal," *Economic History Review*, 35, 1, pp. 52–66.

Hoppe, H. C., 2002, "The Timing of New Technology Adoption: Theoretical Models and Empirical Evidence," *The Manchester School*, 70, 1, January, pp. 56–76.

Horstmann, I., G. M. MacDonald, and A. Slivinski, 1985, "Patent as Information Transfer Mechanisms: To Patent or (Maybe) Not To Patent," *Journal of Political Economy*, 93, pp. 837–858.

Horvath, M., F. Schivardi, and M. Woywode, 2001, "On Industry Life-Cycles: Delay, Entry, and Shakeout in Beer Brewing," *International Journal of Industrial Organization*, 19, July, pp. 1023–1052.

Hotelling, H., 1929, "Stability in Competition," *Economic Journal*, 39, 153, March, pp. 41–57.

Hounshell, D. A., 1985, *From the American System to Mass Production, 1800–1932: The Development of Manufacturing Technology in the United States*, Baltimore, MD: Johns Hopkins University Press.

Hu, Q., X. Wu, C. K. Wang, 2004, "Lessons from Alibaba.com: Government's Role in Electronic Contracting," *info*, 6, 5, pp. 298–307.

Hubbard, R. G., and A. Kashyap, 1992, "Internal Net Worth and the Investment Process: An Application to U.S. Agriculture," *Journal of Political Economy*, 100, June, pp. 506–534.

Hubbard, R. G., J. Skinner, and S. Zeldes, 1994, "Precautionary Savings and Social Insurance," *Journal of Political Economy*, 103, pp. 360–399.

Huckman, R. S., 2003, "The Utilization of Competing Technologies within the Firm: Evidence from Cardiac Procedures," *Management Science*, 49, 5, May, pp. 599–617.

Hunt, R. M., 2010, "Business Method Patents and U.S. Financial Services," *Contemporary Economic Policy*, 28, 3, July, pp. 322–352.

Hurst, E., and A. Lusardi, 2004, "Liquidity Constraints, Wealth Accumulation and Entrepreneurship," *Journal of Political Economy*, 112, 2, pp. 319–347.

Ingham, G., 2003, "Schumpeter and Weber on the Institutions of Capitalism: Solving Swedberg's 'Puzzle'," *Journal of Classical Sociology*, 3, 3, pp. 297–309.

Ingham, G., 2008, *Capitalism*, Cambridge: Polity Press.

Jackson, T., 1997, *Inside Intel: Andy Grove and the Rise of the World's Most Powerful Chip Company*, New York: Dutton.

Jackson, T. H., and A. T. Kronman, 1979, "Secured Financing and Priorities Among Creditors," *Yale Law Journal*, 88, pp. 1143–1182.

Jaffe, A. B., and J. Lerner, 2006, "Innovation and Its Discontents," *Capitalism and Society*, 1, 3, pp. 1–36, http://www.degruyter.com/view/j/cas.2006.1.3/issue-files/cas.2006.1.issue-3.xml (accessed December 23, 2013).

Jain, S., 1999, "Symbiosis vs. Crowding-out: the Interaction of Formal and Informal Credit Markets in Developing Countries," *Journal of Development Economics*, 59, pp. 419–444.

Jensen, M., and W. Meckling, 1976, "Theory of the Firm: Managerial Behavior, Agency Costs and Ownership Structure," *Journal of Financial Economics*, 3, pp. 305–360.

Jensen, R., 1983, "Innovation, Adoption and Diffusion When There Are Competing Innovations," *Journal of Economic Theory*, 29, pp. 161–171.

Jensen, R., J. G. Thursby, and M. Thursby, 2001, "Objectives, Characteristics and Outcomes of University Licensing: A Survey of Major U.S. Universities," *Journal of Technology Transfer*, 26, pp. 59–72.

Jensen, R., J. G. Thursby, and M. Thursby, 2003, "The Disclosure and Licensing of University Inventions: The Best We Can Do With the S**t We Get To Work With," *International Journal of Industrial Organization*, 21, pp. 1271–1300.

Jensen, R., and M. Thursby, 2001, "Proofs and Prototypes for Sale: The Licensing of University Inventions," *American Economic Review*, 91, pp. 240–259.

Jewkes, J., D. Sawers, and R. Stillerman, 1958, *The Sources of Invention*, New York: St. Martin's Press.

Johansen, L., 1959, "Substitution versus Fixed Production Coefficients in the Theory of Economic Growth: A Synthesis," *Econometrica*, 27, 2, April, pp. 157–176.

Johansson, D., 2004, "Economics without Entrepreneurship or Institutions: A Vocabulary Analysis of Graduate Textbooks," *Econ Journal Watch*, Atlas Economic Research Foundation, 1, 3, December, pp. 515–538, http://econjwatch.org/articles/economics-without-entrepreneurship-or-institutions-a-vocabulary-analysis-of-graduate-textbooks (accessed December 23, 2013).

Johnson, B., E. Lorenz, and B.-A. Lundvall, 2002, "Why All This Fuss About Codified and Tacit Knowledge?," *Industrial and Corporate Change*, 11, pp. 245–262.

Johnstone, B., 2007, *Brilliant!: Shuji Nakamura and the Revolution in Lighting Technology*, New York: Prometheus Books.

Jorda, K. F., 2007, "Trade Secrets and Trade-Secret Licensing," in A. Krattiger, R. T. Mahoney, L. Nelson, et al., eds., *Intellectual Property Management in Health and Agricultural Innovation: A Handbook of Best Practices*, Davis, CA: PIPRA, pp. 1043–1057.

Jovanovic, B., 1982a, "Selection and the Evolution of Industry," *Econometrica*, 50, pp. 649–670.

Jovanovic, B., 1982b, "Truthful Disclosure of Information," *Bell Journal of Economics*, 13, 1, pp. 36–44.

Jovanovic, B., and G. M. MacDonald, 1994, "The Life Cycle of a Competitive Industry," *Journal of Political Economy*, 102, April, pp. 322–347.

Kaldor, N., and J. A. Mirrlees, 1962, "A New Model of Economic Growth," *Review of Economic Studies*, 29, 3, June, pp. 174–192.

Kalnins, A., and F. Lafontaine, 2004, "Multi-Unit Ownership in Franchising: Evidence from the Fast-food Industry in Texas," *RAND Journal of Economics*, 35, pp. 747–761.

Kamenica, E., and M. Gentzkow, 2009, "Bayesian Persuasion," Working Paper, University of Chicago.

Kamien, M. I., and N. L. Schwartz, 1976, "On the Degree of Rivalry for Maximum Innovative Activity," *Quarterly Journal of Economics*, 90, 2, May, pp. 245–260.

Kanbur, S. M. R., 1982, "Entrepreneurial Risk Taking, Inequality, and Public Policy: An Application of Inequality Decomposition Analysis to the General Equilibrium Effects of Progressive Taxation," *Journal of Political Economy*, 90, February, pp. 1–21.

Kaplan, S., B. A. Sensoy, and P. Strömberg, 2005, "What are Firms? Evolution from Birth to Public Companies," Center for Economic Policy Research, Discussion Paper No. 5224, September.

Karlson, S. H., 1986, "Adoption of Competing Inventions by United States Steel Producers," *Review of Economics and Statistics*, 68, 3, August, pp. 415–422.

Kato, A., 2007, "Chronology of Lithography Milestones Version 0.9," May, http://www.lithoguru.com/scientist/litho_history/Kato_Litho_History.pdf, accessed August 31, 2010.

Katz, M. L., and C. Shapiro, 1986, "How to License Intangible Property," *Quarterly Journal of Economics*, 101, 3, August, pp. 567–590.

Katz, M. L., and C. Shapiro, 1987, "R&D Rivalry with Licensing or Imitation," *American Economic Review*, 77, pp. 402–420.

Katz, M. L., and H. A. Shelanski, 2005, "'Schumpeterian' Competition and Antitrust Policy in High-Tech Markets," *Competition*, 14, pp. 47–67.

Keller, W., and S. R. Yeaple, 2005, "Multinational Enterprises, International Trade, and Productivity Growth: Firm-Level Evidence from the United States," Deutsche Bundesbank Discussion Paper Series 1: Economic Studies No 07/2005.

Kennedy, C., and A. P. Thirlwall, 1972, "Surveys in Applied Economics: Technical Progress," *Economic Journal*, 82, 325, March, pp. 11–72.

Kerr, W. R., and R. Nanda, 2009, "Democratizing Entry: Banking Deregulations, Financing Constraints, and Entrepreneurship," *Journal of Financial Economics*, 94, 1, October, pp. 124–149.

Kerr, W. R., and R. Nanda, 2010, "Banking Deregulations, Financing Constraints and Firm Entry Size," *Journal of the European Economic Association*, 8, 2–3, April–May, pp. 582–593.

Kerr, W. R., and R. Nanda, 2011, "Financing Constraints and Entrepreneurship," in D. Audretsch, O. Falck, S. Heblich, and A. Lederer, eds., *Handbook of Research on Innovation and Entrepreneurship*, Cheltenham, UK: Edward Elgar Publishing.

Kesan, J. P., 2002, "Carrots and Sticks to Create a Better Patent System," *Berkeley Technology Law Journal*, 17, 2, Spring, pp. 763–797.

Kesan, J. P., and M. Banik, 2000, "Patents as Incomplete Contracts: Aligning Incentives for R&D Investment with Incentives to Disclose Prior Art," *Washington University Journal of Law and Policy*, 2, pp. 23–54.

Keynes, J. M., 1936, *The General Theory of Employment Interest and Money*, McMillan: London. (Reprinted, 1962, New York: Harcourt, Brace.)

Khanna, T., 2008, *Billions of Entrepreneurs: How China and India Are Reshaping Their Futures – and Yours*, Cambridge, MA: Harvard Business School Press.

Khanna, T., and J. Singh, 2002, "What Drives Innovation by Foreign Multinationals?," Harvard Business School, Working Paper, July.

Kieff, F. S., 2001, "Property Rights and Property Rules for Commercializing Inventions," *Minnesota Law Review*, 85, pp. 697–754.

Kieff, F. S., 2003, "The Case for Registering Patents and the Law and Economics of Present Patent-Obtaining Rules," *Boston College Law Review*, 45, 1, pp. 55–123.

Kieff, F. S., 2006, "Coordination, Property, and Intellectual Property: An Unconventional Approach to Anticompetitive Effects and Downstream Access," *Emory Law Journal*, 56, 2, pp. 327–438.

Kieff, F. S., 2007, "On Coordinating Transactions in Intellectual Property: A Response to Smith's Delineating Entitlements in Information," *Yale Law Journal Pocket Part*, 117, pp. 101–109.

Kieff, F. S., 2009, "The Case for Preferring Patent-Validity Litigation over Second-Window Review and Gold-Plated Patents: When One Size Doesn't Fit All, How Could Two Do the Trick?," *University of Pennsylvania Law Review*, 157, pp. 1937–1963.

Kienle, H., D. German, S. Tilley, and H. A. Muller, 2004, "Intellectual Property Aspects of Web Publishing," *ACM Special Interest Group for Design of Communication, Proceedings of the 22nd Annual International Conference on Design of Communication: The Engineering of Quality Documentation*, New York, NY: Association for Computing Machinery, pp. 136–144.

Kihlstrom, R. E., and J.-J. Laffont, 1979, "A General Equilibrium Entrepreneurial Theory of Firm Formation Based on Risk Aversion," *Journal of Political Economy*, 87, August, pp. 719–748.

Kihlstrom, R. E., and J.-J. Laffont, 1982, "A Competitive Entrepreneurial Model of a Stock Market," in J. J. McCall, ed., *The Economics of Information and Uncertainty*, NBER Conference Report No. 32, Chicago: University of Chicago Press.

Kim, D. D., B. M. Lindberg, and J. M. Monaldo, 2009, "Annual Industry Accounts: Advance Statistics on GDP by Industry for 2008," *Survey of Current Business*, 89, 5, pp. 22–37.

Kimes, B. R., and H. A. Clark, 1996, *Standard Catalog of American Cars 1805 to 1942*, 3rd ed., Iola, WI: Krause Publications.

Kindleberger, C. P., 1996, *Manias, Panics, and Crashes: A History of Financial Crises*, New York: Wiley.

King, C., 2000, "Abort, Retry, Fail: Protection for Software-Related Inventions in the Wake of State Street Bank & Trust Co. v. Signature Financial Group, Inc.," *Cornell Law Review*, 85, 4, pp. 1118–1180.

King, R. G., and R. Levine, 1993, "Finance, Entrepreneurship, and Growth: Theory and Evidence," *Journal of Monetary Economics*, 32, pp. 513–542.

King, S., and G. Timmins, 2001, *Making Sense of the Industrial Revolution: English Economy and Society, 1700–1850*, Manchester: Manchester University Press.

King, S. R., 1998, "Staying in Vogue," *New York Times*, November 4, p. C1.

Kinneckell, A. B., 2000, "Wealth Measurement in the Survey of Consumer Finances: Methodology and Directions for Future Research," Working Paper, Federal Reserve Board of Governors, Federal Reserve Board, Washington, DC.

Kirzner, I. M., 1973, *Competition and Entrepreneurship*, Chicago: University of Chicago Press.

Kirzner, I. M., 1979, *Perception, Opportunity, and Profit, Studies in the Theory of Entrepreneurship*, Chicago: University of Chicago Press.

Kirzner, I. M., 1997, "Entrepreneurial Discovery and the Competitive Market Process: An Austrian Approach," *Journal of Economic Literature*, 35, March, pp. 60–85.

Kitch, E. W., 1977, "The Nature and Function of the Patent System," *Journal of Law and Economics*, 20, 2, October, pp. 265–290.

Kitch, E. W., 2000, "Elementary and Persistent Errors in the Economic Analysis of Intellectual Property," *Vanderbilt Law Review*, 53, pp. 1727–1741.

Klapper, L., R. Amit, and M. F. Guillen, 2010, "Entrepreneurship and Firm Formation Across Countries," in J. Lerner and A. Shoar, eds., *NBER Volume on International Differences in Entrepreneurship*, Chicago: University of Chicago Press.

Klein, B. H., 1977, *Dynamic Economics*, Cambridge, MA: Harvard University Press.

Klein, B., R. G. Crawford, and A. A. Alchian, 1978, "Vertical Integration, Appropriable Rents, and the Competitive Contracting Process," *Journal of Law and Economics*, 21, October, pp. 297–326.

Klemperer, P., 1995, "Competition When Consumers Have Switching Costs: An Overview with Applications to Industrial Organization, Macroeconomics, and International Trade," *Review of Economic Studies*, 62, 4, October, pp. 515–539.

Klette, T. J., and S. Kortum, 2004, "Innovating Firms and Aggregate Innovation," *Journal of Political Economy*, 112, 5, pp. 986–1018.

Kline, S. J., and N. Rosenberg, 1986, "An Overview of Innovation," in R. Landau and N. Rosenberg, eds., *The Positive Sum Strategy: Harnessing Technology for Economic Growth*, Washington, DC: National Academy Press, pp. 275–306.

Knight, F. H., 1921, *Risk, Uncertainty and Profit*, Houghton, Mifflin. (Reprinted Chicago: University of Chicago Press, 1971).

Knight, F. H., 1924, "Some Fallacies in the Interpretation of Social Cost," *Quarterly Journal of Economics*, 38, August, pp. 582–606.

Kohn, M., and J. T. Scott, 1982, "Scale Economics in Research and Development: The Schumpeterian Hypothesis," *Journal of Industrial Economics*, 30, 3, pp. 239–249.

Koolman, G., 1971, "Say's Conception of the Role of the Entrepreneur," *Economica*, New Series, 38, 151, August, pp. 269–286.

Koopmans, T. C., 1965, "On the Concept of Optimal Economic Growth," in *The Econometric Approach to Development Planning*, Amsterdam: North-Holland.

Kovacic, W. E., and C. Shapiro, 2000, "Antitrust Policy: A Century of Economic and Legal Thinking," *Journal of Economic Perspectives*, 14, pp. 43–60.

Krishna, K., 1993, "Auctions with Endogenous Valuations: The Persistence of Monopoly Revisited," *American Economic Review*, 83, 1, March, pp. 147–160.

Krishna, V., 2002, *Auction Theory*, San Diego: Academic Press.

Krishna, V., and J. Morgan, 2004, "The Art of Conversation: Eliciting Information from Experts Through Multi-stage Communication," *Journal of Economic Theory*, 117, pp. 147–179.

Krugman, P. R., 1979, "Increasing Returns, Monopolistic Competition, and International Trade," *Journal of International Economics*, 9, November, pp. 469–479.

Kuemmerle, W., 1999, "The Drivers of Foreign Direct Investment into Research and Development: An Empirical Investigation," *Journal of International Business Studies*, 30, 1, pp. 1–24.

Laffont, J.-J., 1989, *Economics of Uncertainty and Information*, Cambridge, MA: MIT Press.

Lafontaine, F., 2009, "The Evolution of Franchising and Franchise Contracts: Evidence from the United States," *Entrepreneurial Business Law Journal*, 3, pp. 381–434.

Lafontaine, F., and K. L. Shaw, 1999, "The Dynamics of Franchise Contracting: Evidence from Panel Data," *Journal of Political Economy*, 107, pp. 1041–1080.

Lafontaine, F., and K. L. Shaw, 2005, "Targeting Managerial Control: Evidence from Franchising," *RAND Journal of Economics*, 36, pp. 131–150.

Lamoreaux, N. R., and K. L. Sokoloff, 2002, "Intermediaries in the U.S. Market for Technology, 1870–1920," NBER Working Paper No. 9017.

Lancaster, K., 1980, "Intra-Industry Trade under Perfect Monopolistic Competition," *Journal of International Economics*, 10, pp. 151–175.

Landes, D. S., 1969, The Unbound Prometheus: Technological Change and Industrial Development in Western Europe from 1750 to the Present, Cambridge: Cambridge University Press.

Landes, D. S., 1998, *The Wealth and Poverty of Nations: Why Some Are So Rich and Some So Poor*, New York: Norton.

Landes, W. M., and R. A. Posner, 2003, *The Economic Structure of Intellectual Property Law*, Cambridge, MA: Harvard University Press.

Landier, A., and D. Thesmar, 2005, "Financial Contracting with Optimistic Entrepreneurs: Theory and Evidence," Working Paper, NYU.

Landier, A., and D. Thesmar, 2009, "Financial Contracting with Optimistic Entrepreneurs," *Review of Financial Studies*, 22, 1, pp. 117–150.

Laudon, K. C., and C. G. Traver, 2010, *E-Commerce: Business, Technology, Society*, 6th ed., Boston: Prentice Hall.

Laursen, K., M. I. Leone, and S. Torrisiy, 2010, "Technological Exploration Through Licensing: New Insights from the Licensee's Point of View," *Industrial and Corporate Change*, 19, 3, pp. 871–897, doi:10.1093/icc/dtq034.

Lazear, E. P., 2004, "Balanced Skills and Entrepreneurship," *American Economic Review*, Papers and Proceedings, 94, 2, May, pp. 208–211.

Lazear, E. P., 2005, "Entrepreneurship," *Journal of Labor Economics*, 23, 4, pp. 649–680.

Lee, T., and L. L. Wilde, 1980, "Market Structure and Innovation: A Reformulation," *Quarterly Journal of Economics*, March, 94, pp. 429–436.

Leibenstein, H., 1968, "Entrepreneurship and Development," *American Economic Review*, May, 58, 2, pp. 72–83.

Lemley, M. A., 2001, "Rational Ignorance at the Patent Office," *Northwestern University Law Review*, 95, pp. 1495–1532.

Lemley, M. A., and D. L. Burk, 2003, "Policy Levers in Patent Law," *Virginia Law Review*, 89, 7, pp. 1575–1696.

Lemley, M. A., and L. Lessig, 2001, "The End of End-to-End: Preserving the Architecture of the Internet in the Broadband Era," *UCLA Law Review*, 48, 4, April, pp. 925–972.

Lerner, J., 2006, "The New New Financial Thing: The Origins of Financial Innovations," *Journal of Financial Economics*, 79, 2, pp. 223–255.

Lerner, J., 2009, *Boulevard of Broken Dreams: Why Public Efforts to Boost Entrepreneurship and Venture Capital Have Failed – and What to Do About It*, Princeton, NJ: Princeton University Press.

Lerner, J., and R. Merges, 1998, "The Control of Strategic Alliances: An Empirical Analysis of the Biotechnology Industry," *Journal of Industrial Economics*, 46, pp. 125–156.

Lessig, L., 2001, *The Future of Ideas: The Fate of the Commons in a Connected World*, New York: Vintage.

Levie, J., and E. Autio, 2008, "A Theoretical Grounding and Test of the GEM Model," *Small Business Economics*, 31, 3, pp. 235–263.

Levin, R. C., W. M. Cohen, and D. C. Mowery, 1985, "R&D Appropriability, Opportunity, and Market Structure: New Evidence on Some Schumpeterian Hypotheses," *American Economic Review*, 75, 2, May, pp. 20–24.

Levitt, T., 1960, "Marketing Myopia," *Harvard Business Review*, 38, July–August, pp. 24–47.

Levy, F., and R. J. Murnane, 1996, "With What Skills Are Computers a Complement?," *American Economic Review, Papers and Proceedings*, 86, 2, pp. 258–262.

Lewis, T., and D. E. M. Sappington, 1989, "Countervailing Incentives in Agency Problems," *Journal of Economic Theory*, 49, pp. 294–313.

Lewis, W. A., 1954, "Economic Development with Unlimited Supplies of Labour," *The Manchester School*, 22, 2, pp. 139–191.

Lieberman, M. B., 1990, "Exit from Declining Industries: 'Shakeout' or 'Stakeout'?," *Rand Journal of Economics*, 21, Winter, pp. 538–554.

Liebowitz, S. J., and S. E. Margolis, 1994, "Network Externality: An Uncommon Tragedy," *Journal of Economic Perspectives*, 8, pp. 133–150.

Liebowitz, S. J., and S. E. Margolis, 2002, "Network Effects," in M. E. Cave, S. K. Majumdar, and I. Vogelsang, eds., *Handbook of Telecommunications Economics*, Vol. 1, Amsterdam: Elsevier Science B.V.

Lin, L., X. Geng, and A. B. Whinston, 2005, "A Sender-Receiver Framework for Knowledge Transfer," *MIS Quarterly*, 29, 2, June, pp. 197–219.

Lindberg, B. M., and J. M. Monaldo, 2008, "Annual Industry Accounts: Advance Statistics on GDP by Industry for 2007," *Survey of Current Business*, 88, 5, pp. 38–50, Washington, DC: Bureau of Economic Analysis.

Lindert, P. H., and J. G. Williamson, 1983, "English Workers' Living Standards during the Industrial Revolution: A New Look," *Economic History Review*, 36, 1, pp. 1–25.

Link, A. N., 1980, "Firm Size and Efficient Entrepreneurial Activity: A Reformulation of the Schumpeter Hypothesis," *Journal of Political Economy*, 88, 4, August, pp. 771–782.

Litt, M. D., H. Tennen, G. Affleck, and S. Klock, 1992, "Coping and Cognitive Factors in Adaptation to In Vitro Fertilization Failure," *Journal of Behavioral Medicine*, 15, pp. 171–187.

Livingston, J., 2007, *Founders at Work: Stories of Startups Early Days*, Berkeley, CA: Apress.

Loayza, N. V., 1996, "The Economics of the Informal Sector: A Simple Model and Some Empirical Evidence from Latin America," *Carnegie-Rochester Conference Series on Public Policy*, 45, pp. 129–162.

López, R. E., 1984, "Estimating Labor Supply and Production Decisions of Self-Employed Producers," *European Economic Review*, 24, pp. 61–82.

López, R. E., 1986, "A Structural Non-Recursive Model of the Farm-Household," in I. J. Singh, L. Squire, and J. Strauss, eds., *Agricultural Household Models: Extensions and Applications*, Baltimore, MD: Johns Hopkins University Press, pp. 306–325.

Lowe, R. A., 2006, "Who Develops a University Invention? The Impact of Tacit Knowledge and Licensing Policies," *Journal of Technology Transfer*, 31, pp. 415–429.

Lowe, R. A., and A. Ziedonis, 2006, "Overoptimism and the Performance of Entrepreneurial Firms," *Management Science*, 52, 2, pp. 173–186.

Lu, J. W., and P. W. Beamish, 2001, "The Internationalization and Performance of SMEs," *Strategic Management Journal*, 22, 6/7, June–July, pp. 565–586.

Lucas, R. E., Jr., 1973, "Some International Evidence on Output-Inflation Tradeoffs," *American Economic Review*, 63, 3, pp. 326–334.

Lucas, R. E., Jr., 1978, "On the Size Distribution of Business Firms," *Bell Journal of Economics*, 9, Autumn, pp. 508–523.

Lucas, R. E., Jr., 1988, "On the Mechanics of Economic Development," *Journal of Monetary Economics*, 22, pp. 3–42.

Lucas, R. E., Jr., 1990, "Why Doesn't Capital Flow from Rich to Poor Countries?," *American Economic Review*, Papers and Proceedings, 80, 2, May, pp. 92–96.

Lucking-Reiley, D., and D. F. Spulber, 2001, "Business-to-Business Electronic Commerce," *Journal of Economic Perspectives*, 15, Winter, pp. 55–68.

Lundstrom, A., and L. A. Stevenson, 2005, *Entrepreneurship Policy: Theory and Practice*, Springer.

MacAvoy, P. W., and I. M. Millstein, 2003, *The Recurrent Crisis in Corporate Governance*, New York: Palgrave Macmillan.

MacDonald, G. M., 1988, "The Economics of Rising Stars," *American Economic Review*, 78, March, pp. 155–166.

Mach, T. L., and J. D. Wolken, 2006, "Financial Services Used by Small Businesses: Evidence from the 2003 Survey of Small Business Finances," *Federal Reserve Bulletin*, October, pp. A167–A195.

Machlup, F., 1962, *The Production and Distribution of Knowledge in the United States*, Princeton, NJ: Princeton University Press.

Machlup, F., and M. Taber, 1960, "Bilateral Monopoly, Successive Monopoly, and Vertical Integration," *Economica*, New Series, 27, 106, May, pp. 101–119.

Macho-Stadler, I., and J. D. Pérez-Castrillo, 1991, "Contrats de Licences et Asymétrie d'Information," *Annales d'Economie et de Statistique*, 24, October–December, pp. 189–208.

Macho-Stadler, I., X. Martínez-Giralt, and J. D. Pérez-Castrillo, 1996, "The Role of Information in Licensing Contract Design," *Research Policy*, 25, 1, January, pp. 43–57.

Macho-Stadler, I., and J. D. Pérez-Castrillo, 2001, *An Introduction to the Economics of Information: Incentives and Contracts*, Oxford: Oxford University Press.

MacLeod, B., and J. Malcomson, 1993, "Investments, Hold-up, and the Form of Market Contracts," *American Economic Review*, 83, pp. 811–837.

Macneil, I. R., 1974, "The Many Futures of Contracts," *Southern California Law Review*, 47, pp. 691–816.

Macneil, I. R., 1978, *Contracts: Exchange Transactions and Relations; Cases and Materials*, Mineola, NY: Foundation Press.

Macneil, I. R., 1980, *The New Social Contract: An Inquiry into Modern Contractual Relations*, New Haven, CT: Yale University Press.

Maggi, G., and A. Rodriguez-Clare, 1995, "On Countervailing Incentives," *Journal of Economic Theory*, 66, pp. 238–263.

Malerba, F., 2007, "Innovation and the Dynamics and Evolution of Industries: Progress and Challenges," *International Journal of Industrial Organization*, 25, pp. 675–699.

Malerba, F., and L. Orsenigo, 1997, "The Dynamics and Evolution of Industries," *Industrial and Corporate Change*, 6, pp. 51–87.

Malerba, F., and L. Orsenigo, 2002, "Innovation and Market Structure in the Dynamics of the Pharmaceutical Industry: Towards a History Friendly Model," *Industrial and Corporate Change*, 11, 4, pp. 667–703.

Maney, K., 1995, *Megamedia Shakeout: The Inside Story of the Leaders and the Losers in the Exploding Communications Industry*, New York: Wiley.

Mankiw, N. G., and R. Reis, 2002, "Sticky Information versus Sticky Prices: A Proposal to Replace the New Keynesian Phillips Curve," *Quarterly Journal of Economics*, 117, 4, pp. 1295–1328.

Manne, H. G., 1965, "Mergers and the Market for Corporate Control," *Journal of Political Economy*, 73, 2, April, pp. 110–120.

Manne, H. G., 1966, *Insider Trading and the Stock Market*, New York: Free Press.

Manne, H. G., 1967, "Our Two Corporation Systems: Law & Economics," *University of Virginia Law Review*, 53, March, pp. 259–284.

Mansfield, E., 1962, "Entry, Gibrat's Law, Innovation, and the Growth of Firms," *American Economic Review*, 52, pp. 1025–1051.

Mansfield, E., 1964, "Industrial Research and Development Expenditures: Determinants, Prospects, and Relation of Size of Firm and Inventive Output," *Journal of Political Economy*, 72, 4, August, pp. 319–340.

Mansfield, E., 1994, "Intellectual Property Protection, Foreign Direct Investment, and Technology Transfer," International Finance Corporation, Discussion Paper 19, Washington, DC.

March, J. G., and H. A. Simon, 1958, *Organizations*, New York: John Wiley.

Mariger, R. P., 1987, "A Life-Cycle Consumption Model with Liquidity Constraints: Theory and Empirical Results," *Econometrica*, 55, 3, May, pp. 533–557.

Marin, P. L., and G. Siotis, 2001, "Innovation and Market Structure: An Empirical Evaluation of the 'Bounds Approach' in the Chemical Industry," *Journal of Industrial Economics*, 55, pp. 93–111.

Markham, J., 1965, "Market Structure, Business Conduct and Innovation," *American Economic Review*, 55, 1/2, March, pp. 323–332.

Marschak, J., and R. Radner, 1972, *Economic Theory of Teams*, New Haven, CT: Yale University Press.

Martin, A., 2008, "Endogenous Credit Cycles," Universitat Pompeu Fabra, Working Paper, August.

Martin, S., 1993, "Endogenous Firm Efficiency in a Cournot Principal-Agent Model," *Journal of Economic Theory*, 59, 2, April, pp. 445–450.

Marx, K., 1867 [1992], *Capital: Volume 1: A Critique of Political Economy*, New York: Penguin Classics.

Marx, T. G., 1985, "The Development of the Franchise Distribution System in the U.S. Automobile Industry," *Business History Review*, 59, 3, Autumn, pp. 465–474.

Maskin, E., and J. Riley, 1984, "Optimal Auctions with Risk Averse Buyers," *Econometrica*, 52, pp. 1473–1518.

Masten, S., 2006, "Authority and Commitment: Why Universities, Like Legislatures, Are Not Organized as Firms," *Journal of Economics & Management Strategy*, 15, 3, Fall, pp. 648–684.

McClellan, S. T., 1984, *The Coming Computer Industry Shakeout: Winners, Losers, and Survivors*, New York: Wiley.

McCloskey, D. N., 2006, *The Bourgeois Virtues: Ethics for an Age of Commerce*, Chicago: University of Chicago Press.

McCormick, R. E., and R. Meiners, 1989, "University Governance: A Property Rights Perspective," *Journal of Law and Economics*, 31, pp. 423–442.

McCraw, T. K., 2007, *Prophet of Innovation: Joseph Schumpeter and Creative Destruction*, Cambridge, MA: Belknap Press of Harvard University Press.

McDonough, J. F., 2006, "The Myth of the Patent Troll: An Alternative View of the Function of Patent Dealers in an Idea Economy," *Emory Law Journal*, 56, pp. 189–228.

Meh, C. A., 2005, "Entrepreneurship, Wealth Inequality and Taxation," *Review of Economic Dynamics*, 8, 3, pp. 688–719.

Melitz, M. J., 2003, "The Impact of Trade on Intra-Industry Reallocations and Aggregate Industry Productivity," *Econometrica*, 71, 6, November, pp. 1695–1725.

Merges, R. P., 1994, "Of Property Rules, Coase, and Intellectual Property," *Columbia Law Review*, 94, pp. 2655–2673.

Merges, R. P., 1999, "As Many as 6 Impossible Patents Before Breakfast: Property Rights for Business Concepts and Patent System Reform," *Berkeley Technology Law Journal*, 14, 2, pp. 577–615.

Merrill, T. W., and H. E. Smith, 2001a, "The Property/Contract Interface," *Columbia Law Review*, 101, pp. 773–852.

Merrill, T. W., and H. E. Smith, 2001b, "What Happened to Property in Law and Economics?," *Yale Law Journal*, 111, pp. 357–398.

Merton, R. C., 1992, "Financial Innovation and Economic Performance," *Journal of Applied Corporate Finance*, 4, pp. 12–22.

Meurer, M. J., 2002, "Business Method Patents and Patent Floods," *Washington University Journal of Law & Policy*, 8, pp. 309–339.

Michael, S. C., 2003, "First Mover Advantage through Franchising," *Journal of Business Venturing*, 18, pp. 61–80.

Microsoft Corporation, "Taking Business Web Sites to the Next Level," http://msdn.microsoft.com/en-us/library/ms953581.aspx, Accessed March 6, 2014.

Microsoft Corporation, 1997, "Microsoft Internet Commerce Strategy: A Foundation for Doing Business on the Internet," http://msdn.microsoft.com/en-us/library/ms953599.aspx, Accessed March 6, 2014.

Milgrom, P. R., 1979, "A Convergence Theorem for Competitive Bidding with Differential Information," *Econometrica*, 47, pp. 679–688.

Milgrom, P. R., and J. Roberts, 1986, "Relying on the Information of Interested Parties," *Rand Journal of Economics*, 17, 1, pp. 18–32.

Milgrom, P. R., and J. Roberts, 1990a, "The Economics of Modern Manufacturing: Technology, Strategy and Organization," *American Economic Review*, 80, pp. 511–528.

Milgrom, P. R., and J. Roberts, 1990b, "Rationalizability, Learning, and Equilibrium in Games with Strategic Complementarities," *Econometrica*, 58, 6, November, pp. 1255–1277.

Milgrom, P. R., and J. Roberts, 1994, "Comparing Equilibria," *American Economic Review*, 84, 3, June, pp. 441–459.

Milgrom, P. R., and R. J. Weber, 1982, "A Theory of Auctions and Competitive Bidding," *Econometrica*, 50, 5, September, pp. 1089–1122.

Miller, M. H., 1986, "Financial Innovation: The Last Twenty Years and the Next," *Journal of Financial and Quantitative Analysis*, 21, pp. 459–471.

Mintzberg, H., and J. A. Waters, 1985, "Of Strategies, Deliberate and Emergent," *Strategic Management Journal*, 6, 3, pp. 257–272.

Mirrlees, J. A., 1971, "An Exploration in the Theory of Optimum Income Taxation." *Review of Economic Studies*, 38, pp. 175–208.

Mises, L., 1949 [1998], *Human Action: A Treatise on Economics*, Auburn, AL: Ludwig von Mises Institute.

Modigliani, F., 1976, "Life-Cycle, Individual Thrift, and the Wealth of Nations," *American Economic Review*, 76, 3, pp. 297–313.

Modigliani, F., 1998, "The Role of Intergenerational Transfers and Life-Cycle Saving in the Accumulation of Wealth," *Journal of Economic Perspectives*, 2, 2, pp. 15–20.

Modigliani, F., and R. H. Brumberg, 1954, "Utility Analysis and the Consumption Function: An Interpretation of Cross-Section Data," in K. K. Kurihara, ed., *Post-Keynesian Economics*, New Brunswick, NJ: Rutgers University Press, pp. 388–436.

Modiglinai, F., and R. H. Brumberg, 1990, "Utility Analysis and Aggregate Consumption Functions: An Attempt at Integration," in A. Abel, ed., *The Collected Papers of Franco Modigliani: Volume 2, The Life Cycle Hypothesis of Saving*, Cambridge, MA: MIT Press, pp. 128–197.

Mondragón-Vélez, C., 2009, "The Probability of Transition to Entrepreneurship Revisited: Wealth, Education, and Age," *Annals of Finance Special Issue on Entrepreneurship*, 5, pp. 421–441.

Mondragón-Vélez, C., 2010, "The Transition to Entrepreneurship: Human Capital, Wealth and the Role of Liquidity Constraints," Working Paper, International Finance Corporation, World Bank.

Moriwaki, L., 1996, "Shakeout Brewing," *Seattle Times*, November 3.

Morris, S., and H. S. Shin, 2002, "The Social Value of Public Information," *American Economic Review*, 92, 5, pp. 1521–1534.

Morris, S., and H. S. Shin, 2006, "Information Diffusion in Macroeconomics, Inertia of Forward-Looking Expectations," *American Economic Review*, Papers and Proceedings, 96, 2, May, pp. 152–157.

Morrison, S. A., and C. Winston, 1995, *The Evolution of the Airline Industry*, Washington, DC: Brookings Institution.

Moskowitz, T. J., and A. Vissing-Jorgensen, 2002, "The Returns to Entrepreneurial Investment: A Private Equity Premium Puzzle?," *American Economic Review*, 92, 4, pp. 745–778.

Mowery, D. C., 1983, "The Relationship between Intrafirm and Contractual Forms of Industrial Research in American Manufacturing, 1900–1940," *Explorations in Economic History*, 20, October, pp. 351–374.

Mowery, D. C., 1990, "The Development of Industrial Research in US Manufacturing," *American Economic Review*, 80, 2, pp. 345–349.

Mowery, D. C., 1995, "The Boundaries of the U.S. firm in R&D," in N. R. Lamoreaux and D. M. G. Raff, eds., *Coordination and Information: Historical Perspectives on the Organization of Enterprise*, Chicago: University of Chicago Press, pp. 147–176.

Mowery, D. C., and N. Rosenberg, 1991, *Technology and the Pursuit of Economic Growth*, Cambridge: Cambridge University Press.

Muto, S., 1993, "On Licensing Policies in Bertrand Competition," *Journal of Games and Economic Behavior*, 5, pp. 257–267.

Myers, S. C., 1984, "The Capital Structure Puzzle," *Journal of Finance*, Papers and Proceedings, American Finance Association, San Francisco, 39, 3, July, pp. 575–592.

Myers, S. C., 1999, "Financial Architecture," *European Financial Management*, 5, 2, pp. 133–141.

Myers, S. C., 2000, "Outside Equity," *Journal of Finance*, 55, 3, June, pp. 1005–1037.

Myers, S. C., and N. S. Majluf, 1984, "Corporate Financing and Investment Decisions When Firms Have Information That Investors Do Not Have," *Journal of Financial Economics*, 13, 2, June, pp. 187–221.

Myerson, R., 1981, "Optimal Auction Design," *Mathematics of Operations Research*, 6, pp. 58–73.

Nakamura, S., S. J. Pearton, and G. Fasol, 2000, *The Blue Laser Diode: The Complete Story*, Berlin: Springer Verlag.

Naudé, W., 2010, "Entrepreneurship, Developing Countries, and Development Economics: New Approaches and Insights," *Small Business Economics*, 34, pp. 1–12.

Nelson, P., 1970, "Information and Consumer Behavior," *Journal of Political Economy*, 78, 2, pp. 311–329.

Nelson, R. R., 1961, "Uncertainty, Learning, and the Economics of Parallel Research and Development Efforts," *Review of Economics and Statistics*, 43, pp. 351–364.

Nelson, R. R., 1964, "Aggregate Production Functions and Medium-Range Growth Projections," *American Economic Review*, 54, 5, September, pp. 575–606.

Nelson, R. R., and S. G. Winter, 1977, "In Search of Useful Theory of Innovation," *Research Policy*, 6, 1, pp. 36–76.

Nelson, R. R., and S. G. Winter, 1982, *An Evolutionary Theory of Economic Change*, Cambridge, MA: Harvard University Press.

Nickell, S., 1996, "Competition and Corporate Performance," *Journal of Political Economy*, 104, pp. 724–746.

Nightingale, P., 1998, "A Cognitive Model of Innovation," *Research Policy*, 27, 7, November, pp. 689–709.

Nonaka, I., and H. Takeuchi, 1995, *The Knowledge-creating Company: How Japanese Companies Create the Dynamics of Innovation*, New York: Oxford University Press.

North, D., 1990, *Institutions, Institutional Change and Economic Performance*, Cambridge: Cambridge University Press.

O'Donoghue, T., S. Scotchmer, and J.-F. Thisse, 1998, "Patent Breadth, Patent Life, and the Pace of Technological Progress," *Journal of Economics & Management Strategy*, 7, 1, pp. 1–32.

OECD (Organization for Economic Cooperation and Development), 2002, *Frascati Manual: Proposed Standard Practice for Surveys on Research and Experimental Development*, Paris: OECD Publishing.

OECD (Organization for Economic Cooperation and Development), 2008a, *Compendium of Patent Statistics*, Paris: OECD Publishing.

OECD (Organization for Economic Cooperation and Development), 2008b, *The Internationalization of Business R&D: Evidence, Impacts and Implications*, June, Paris: OECD Publishing.

OECD (Organization for Economic Cooperation and Development), 2008c, *Open Innovation in Global Networks*, October, Paris: OECD Publishing.

OECD (Organization for Economic Cooperation and Development), 2008d, *Science, Technology, and Industry Outlook*, Paris: OECD Publishing.

Olsen, S., 2004, "Google, Yahoo Bury the Legal Hatchet," *CNET News*, August 9, 2004, http://news.cnet.com/Google,-Yahoo-bury-the-legal-hatchet/2100-1024_3-5302421.html (accessed December 23, 2013).

Orsenigo, L., 1991, *The Emergence of Biotechnology: Institutions and Markets in Industrial Innovation*, London: Pinter.

O'Shea, R., T. Allen, A. Chevalier, and F. Roche, 2005, "Entrepreneurial Orientation, Technology Transfer and Spinoff Performance of U.S. Universities," *Research Policy*, 34, 7, pp. 994–1009.

Oviatt, B. M., and P. P. McDougall, 2005, "Toward a Theory of International New Ventures," *Journal of International Business Studies*, 36, 1, January, pp. 29–41.

Oxford English Dictionary, 1989, Oxford: Oxford University Press, 2nd ed., http://www.oed.com/.

Page, W. H., 1989, "The Chicago School and the Evolution of Antitrust: Characterization, Antitrust Injury, and Evidentiary Sufficiency," *Virginia Law Review*, 75, pp. 1221–1308.

Pareja, S., 2008, "Sales Gone Wild: Will the FTC's Business Opportunity Rule Put an End to Pyramid Marketing Schemes," *McGeorge Law Review*, 39, pp. 83–130.

Parker, S. C., 2009, *The Economics of Entrepreneurship*, Cambridge: Cambridge University Press.

Patrick, A., 2009, "Patent Eligibility and Computer-Related Processes: A Critique of in re Bilski and the Machine-or-Transformation Test," *Virginia Journal of Law and Technology*, 14, 3, pp. 181–211.

Pellegrino, G., M. Pivaa, and M. Vivarelli, 2012, "Young Firms and Innovation: A Microeconometric Analysis," *Structural Change and Economic Dynamics*, 23, 4, pp. 329–340.

Penrose, E. T., 1959, *The Theory of the Growth of the Firm*, Oxford: Basil Blackwell.

Perez-Gonzalez, F., 2006, "Inherited Control and Firm Performance," *American Economic Review*, 96, 5, December, pp. 1559–1588.

Peterson, B. S., and J. Glab, 1994, *Rapid Descent: Deregulation and the Shakeout in the Airlines*, New York: Simon and Schuster.

Phelps, E. S., 1966, "Models of Technical Progress and the Golden Rule of Research," *Review of Economic Studies*, 33, 2, April, pp. 133–145.

Phelps, E. S., 1970, "Introduction," in E. S. Phelps et al., eds., *Microeconomic Foundations of Employment and Inflation Theory*, New York: W. W. Norton & Company, pp. 1–23.

Pigou, A. C., 1912, *Wealth and Welfare*, London: Macmillan Company.

Pigou, A. C., 1924, "Comment," *Economic Journal*, 34, p. 31.

Pigou, A. C., 1932, *The Economics of Welfare*, 4th edition, London: Macmillan.

Pilat, D., 2004, "The ICT Productivity Paradox: Insights from Micro Data," *OECD Economic Studies*, 1, pp. 37–64.

Pisano, G. P., 1990, "The R&D Boundaries of the Firm: An Empirical Analysis," *Administrative Science Quarterly*, 35, 1, March, Special Issue: Technology, Organizations, and Innovation, pp. 153–176.

Plehn-Dujowich, J. M., 2009, "The Impact of Innovation and Information Risk on Endogenous Growth," Temple University, Working Paper.

Poblete, J., and D. F. Spulber, 2007, "Entrepreneurs, Partnerships, and Corporations: Incentives, Investment and the Financial Structure of the Firm," Northwestern University Working Paper.

Poblete, J., and D. F. Spulber, 2012, "The Form of Incentive Contracts: Agency with Moral Hazard, Limited Liability, and Risk Neutrality," *Rand Journal of Economics*, 43, 2, Summer, pp. 215–234.

Poblete, J., and D. F. Spulber, 2013, "Managing Innovation: Optimal Agency Contracts for Delegated R&D," Northwestern University Working Paper.

Polanyi, K., 1944 [2001], *The Great Transformation: The Political and Economic Origins of Our Time*, Boston: Beacon Press.

Polanyi, M., 1962, *Personal Knowledge: Towards a Post-Critical Philosophy*, Chicago: University of Chicago Press.

Polanyi, M., 1967, *The Tacit Dimension*, Garden City, NY: Anchor Books.

Pollack, M., 2002, "The Multiple Unconstitutionality of Business Method Patents," *Rutgers Computer & Technology Law Journal*, 28, 1, pp. 61–96.

Posner, R. A., 1979, "The Chicago School of Antitrust," *University of Pennsylvania Law Review*, 127, pp. 925–948.

Posner, R. A., 2005, "The Summers Controversy and University Governance," The Becker-Posner Blog, February 27, http://www.becker-posner-blog.com/2005/02/the-summers-controversy-and-university-governance.html, accessed May 16, 2011.

Pound, A., 1934, The Turning Wheel; The Story of General Motors through Twenty-Five Years, 1908–1933, Garden City, NY: Doubleday, Doran & Company, Inc.

Pozen, D. E., 2008, "We Are All Entrepreneurs Now," *Wake Forest Law Review*, 43, pp. 283–340.

Pozzali, A., and R. Viale, 2007, "Cognition, Types of 'Tacit Knowledge' and Technology Transfer," in R. Topol and B. Walliser, eds., *Cognitive Economics: New Trends*, Amsterdam: Elsevier, pp. 205–224.

Prevezer, M., 1997, "The Dynamics of Industrial Clustering in Biotechnology," *Small Business Economics*, 9, 3, pp. 255–271.

Przeworski, A., 2004, "The Last Instance: Are Institutions the Primary Cause of Economic Development?," *European Journal of Sociology*, 45, 2, pp. 165–188.

Puri, M., and D. T. Robinson, 2007, "Optimism and Economic Choice," *Journal of Financial Economics*, 86, 1, October, pp. 71–99.

Puri, M., and D. T. Robinson, 2013, "The Economic Psychology of Entrepreneurship and Family Business," *Journal of Economics & Management Strategy*, 22, 2, Summer, pp. 423–444.

Quadrini, V., 1999, "The Importance of Entrepreneurship for Wealth Concentration and Mobility," *Review of Income and Wealth*, 45, pp. 1–19.

Quadrini, V., 2000, "Entrepreneurship, Saving and Social Mobility," *Review of Economic Dynamics*, 3, pp. 1–40.

Qiu, L., 1997, "On the Dynamic Efficiency of Bertrand and Cournot Equilibria," *Journal of Economic Theory*, 75, pp. 213–229.

Quinn, E. R., 2002, "The Proliferation of Electronic Commerce Patents: Don't Blame the PTO," *Rutgers Computer & Technology Law Journal*, 28, 1, pp. 121–154.

Rai, A. K., 2000, "Addressing the Patent Gold Rush: The Role of Deference to PTO Patent Denials," *Washington University Journal of Law and Policy*, 2, pp. 199–227.

Ramondo, N., and A. Rodríguez-Clare, 2009, "Trade, Multinational Production, and the Gains from Openness," NBER Working Paper No. 15604, Cambridge, MA: National Bureau of Economic Research, December.

Rapport, M., 2009, *1848: Year of Revolution*, New York: Basic Books.

Rasmusen, E., 1988, "Entry for Buyout," *Journal of Industrial Economics*, 36, 3, March, pp. 281–299.

Ravetz, J., 1971, *Scientific Knowledge and Its Social Problems*, Oxford: Oxford University Press.

Reinganum, J. F., 1981, "Dynamic Games of Innovation," *Journal of Economic Theory*, 25, pp. 1–41.

Reinganum, J. F., 1982, "A Dynamic Game of R and D: Patent Protection and Competitive Behavior," *Econometrica*, 50, pp. 671–688.

Reinganum, J. F., 1989, "The Timing of Innovation: Research, Development, and Diffusion," in R. Schmalensee and R. D. Willig, eds., *Handbook of Industrial Organization*, Vol. 1, New York: Elsevier Science Publishers, pp. 849–908.

Reynolds, P. D., 1997a, "New and Small Firms in Expanding Markets," *Small Business Economics*, 9, 1, pp. 79–84.

Reynolds, P. D., 1997b, "Who Starts New Firms? Preliminary Explorations of Firms-in-Gestation," *Small Business Economics*, 9, 5, October, pp. 449–462.

Reynolds, P. D., 2000, "National Panel Study of U. S. Business Startups: Background and Methodology," *Databases for the Study of Entrepreneurship*, 4, pp. 153–227.

Reynolds, P. D., N. M. Carter, W. B. Gartner, and P. G. Greene, 2004, "The Prevalence of Nascent Entrepreneurs in the United States: Evidence from the Panel Study of Entrepreneurial Dynamics, Small Business Economics," 23, 4, November, pp. 263–284.

Reynolds, R. L., 1952, "Origins of Modern Business Enterprise: Medieval Italy," *Journal of Economic History*, 12, pp. 350–365.

Reynolds, S. S., 1988, "Plant Closings and Exit Behavior in Declining Industries," *Economica*, 55, pp. 493–503.

Rialp, A., J. Rialp, and G. A. Knight, 2005, "The Phenomenon of Early Internationalizing Firms: What Do We Know After a Decade (1993–2003) of Scientific Enquiry?," *International Business Review*, 14, 2, pp. 147–166.

Ribstein, L. E., 2009a, "Partnership Governance of Large Firms," *University of Chicago Law Review*, 76, pp. 289–310.

Ribstein, L. E., 2009b, *The Rise of the Uncorporation*, Oxford: Oxford University Press.

Ribstein, L. E., 2009c, "The Uncorporation and Corporate Indeterminacy," *University of Illinois Law Review*, 2009, pp. 131–166.

Rich, B. R., and L. Janos, 1994, *Skunk Works: A Personal Memoir of My Years at Lockheed*, Boston: Little Brown.

Richards, H., 1999, *Life and Worklife Expectancies*, Tucson, AZ: Lawyers & Judges Publishing Company.

Rivera-Batiz, L., and P. Romer, 1991, "Economic Integration and Endogenous Growth," *Quarterly Journal of Economics*, 106, 2, pp. 531–555.

Rivette, K. G., and D. Kline, 2000, *Rembrandts in the Attic: Unlocking the Hidden Value of Patents*, Cambridge, MA: Harvard Business School Press.

Rogers, E., 1962, *Diffusion of Innovations*, New York: Free Press.

Rogerson, W. P., 1992, "Contractual Solutions to the Hold-Up Problem," *Review of Economic Studies*, 59, 4, October, pp. 777–793.

Romer, P. M., 1986, "Increasing Returns and Long-run Growth," *Journal of Political Economy*, 94, 5, October, pp. 1002–1037.

Romer, P. M., 1990, "Endogenous Technological Change," *Journal of Political Economy*, 98, 5, October, Part 2: The Problem of Development: A Conference of the Institute for the Study of Free Enterprise Systems, pp. S71–S102.

Ropera, S., J. Dub, and J. H. Loveb, 2008, "Modelling the Innovation Value Chain," *Research Policy*, 37, pp. 961–977.

Rosen, S., 1981, "The Economics of Superstars," *American Economic Review*, 71, December, pp. 845–858.

Rosenberg, J. B., 1976, "Research and Market Share: A Reappraisal of the Schumpeter Hypothesis," *Journal of Industrial Economics*, 25, 2, December, pp. 101–112.

Rosenberg, N., 1963, "Technological Change in the Machine Tool Industry, 1840–1910," *Journal of Economic History*, 23, 4, pp. 414–443.

Rosenberg, N., 1972a, "Factors Affecting the Diffusion of Technology," *Explorations in Economic History*, 10, 1, pp. 3–33.

Rosenberg, N., 1972b, *Technology and American Economic Growth*, New York: Harper & Row.

Rosenberg, N., 1992, "Economic Experiments," *Industrial and Corporate Change*, 1, pp. 181–203.

Rostocker, M., 1983, "PTC Research Report: A Survey of Corporate Licensing," *IDEA – Journal of Law and Technology*, 24, pp. 59–92.

Royal Swedish Academy of Sciences, 2010, *Scientific Background on the Nobel Prize in Physics 2010: Graphene*, Stockholm, Sweden, October 5.

Ruback, R. S., and M. C. Jensen, 1983, "The Market for Corporate Control: The Scientific Evidence," *Journal of Financial Economics*, 11, pp. 5–50.

Rubinstein, A., 1982, "Perfect Equilibrium in a Bargaining Model," *Econometrica*, 50, 1, January, pp. 97–109.

Russell, B., 1911, "Knowledge by Acquaintance and Knowledge by Description," *Proceedings of the Aristotelian Society, New Series*, 11, 1910–1911, pp. 108–128.

Russell, B., 2000, *Theory of Knowledge: The 1913 Manuscript*, in The Collected Papers of Bertrand Russell, Vol. 7, New York: Routledge.

Ryle, G., 1949 [2002], *The Concept of Mind*, Chicago: University of Chicago Press.

Sah, R. K., and J. E. Stiglitz, 1986, "The Architecture of Economic Systems: Hierarchies and Polyarchies," *American Economic Review*, 76, 4, September, pp. 716–727.

Salant, S. W., 1984, "Preemptive Patenting and the Persistence of Monopoly: Comment," *American Economic Review*, 74, pp. 247–250.

Samphantharak, K., and R. M. Townsend, 2010, Households as Corporate Firms: An Analysis of Household Finance Using Integrated Household Surveys and Corporate Financial Accounting, Cambridge: Cambridge University Press.

Samuelson, P. A., 1954a, "The Pure Theory of Public Expenditure," *Review of Economics and Statistics*, 36, pp. 387–389.

Samuelson, P. A., 1954b, "The Transfer Problem and Transport Costs, II: Analysis of Effects of Trade Impediments," *Economic Journal*, 64, June, pp. 264–289.

Sandelands, L. E., and R. E. Stablein, 1987, "The Concept of Organization Mind," *Research in the Sociology of Organizations*, 5, pp. 135–161.

Sarada, 2013, "The Unobserved Returns from Entrepreneurship," Working paper, Duke University.

Say, J.-B., 1841, *Traité d'Économie Politique*, 6th ed. (Reprinted 1982, Geneva: Slatkine.)

Say, J.-B., 1852, *Cours Complet d'Économie Politique: Pratique*, Vols. I and II, 3rd ed., Paris: Guillaumin et Ce.

SBA (United States Small Business Administration, Office of Advocacy), 2001, *Small Business Economic Indicators: 2000*, Washington, DC: SBA.

SBA (United States Small Business Administration, Office of Advocacy), 2009, *The Small Business Economy: A Report to the President*, Washington, DC: United States Government Printing Office.

Scarpetta, S., P. Hemmings, T. Tressel, and J. Woo, 2002, "The Role of Policy and Institutions for Productivity and Firm Dynamics: Evidence From Micro and Industry Data," Organization for Economic Cooperation and Development, Working Paper No. 320.

Scheier, M. F., and C. S. Carver, 1985, "Optimism, Coping and Health: Assessment and Implications of Generalized Outcome Expectancies," *Health Psychology*, 4, pp. 219–247.

Scheier, M. F., C. S. Carver, and M. W. Bridges, 1994, "Distinguishing Optimism from Neuroticism (and Trait Anxiety, Self-Mastery, and Self-Esteem): A Re-Evaluation of the Life Orientation Test," *Journal of Personality and Social Psychology*, 67, pp. 1063–1078.

Scherer, F. M., 1965a, "Size of Firm, Oligopoly, and Research: A Comment," *Canadian Journal of Economics and Political Science*, 31, 2, May, pp. 256–266.

Scherer, F. M., 1965b, "Firm Size, Market Structure, Opportunity, and the Output of Patented Inventions," *American Economic Review*, 55, 5, December, pp. 1097–1125.

Schiesel, S., 1997, "Web Publishers Start to Feel Lack of Advertising, an On-line Shakeout Has Affected Mainstream Media and Start-Ups," *New York Times*, March 25, p. C1.

Schlicher, J. W., 2000, "Measuring Patent Damages by the Market Value of Inventions – The Grain Processing, Rite-Hite, and Aro Rules," *Journal of the Patent and Trademark Office Society*, 82, pp. 503–535.

Schmidt, K. M., 1997, "Managerial Incentives and Product Market Competition," *Review of Economic Studies*, 64, 2, April, pp. 191–214.

Schmookler, J., 1959, "Bigness, Fewness, and Research," *Journal of Political Economy*, 67, 6, December, pp. 628–632.

Schmookler, J., 1962, "Economic Sources of Inventive Activity," *Journal of Economic History*, 22, pp. 1–20.

Schmookler, J., 1966, *Invention and Economic Growth*, Cambridge, MA: Harvard University Press.

Schneider, P. H., 2005, "International Trade, Economic Growth and Intellectual Property Rights: A Panel Data Study of Developed and Developing Countries," *Journal of Development Economics*, 78, pp. 529–547.

Schonfeld, E., 2007, "The Startup King's New Gig," *Business 2.0 Magazine*, September 26, http://money.cnn.com/2007/09/25/news/companies/Startupking.biz2/index.htm?postversion=2007092614, accessed April 9, 2009.

Schramm, C. J., 2006a, "Entrepreneurial Capitalism and the End of Bureaucracy: Reforming the Mutual Dialog of Risk Aversion," presented at the American Economic Association meetings, Boston, MA.

Schramm, C. J., 2006b, *The Entrepreneurial Imperative: How American's Economic Miracle Will Reshape the World (and Change Your Life)*, New York: HarperCollins.

Schramm, C. J., 2006c, "Law Outside the Market: The Social Utility of the Private Foundation," *Harvard Journal of Law and Public Policy*, 30, pp. 355–415.

Schramm, C. J., R. Litan, and D. Stangler, 2009, "New Business, Not Small Business, Is What Creates Jobs," *Wall Street Journal*, November 6, http://online.wsj.com/article/SB10001424052748704013004574517303668357682.html, accessed January 4, 2010.

Schultz, T. W., 1975, "The Value of the Ability to Deal with Disequilibria," *Journal of Economic Literature*, 13, 3, pp. 827–846.

Schumpeter, J. A., 1912, *Theorie der Wirtschaftlichen Entwicklung*, Leipzig: Verlag von Duncker & Humbolt.

Schumpeter, J. A., 1934 [1997], *The Theory of Economic Development*, New Brunswick, NJ: Transaction Publishers.

Schumpeter, J. A., 1939, *Business Cycles: A Theoretical, Historical, and Statistical Analysis of the Capitalist Process*, Vol. 1 and 2, New York: McGraw-Hill.

Schumpeter, J. A., 1942 [1975], *Capitalism, Socialism and Democracy*, New York: Harper & Row.

Schumpeter, J. A., 1946, "John Maynard Keynes 1883–1946," *American Economic Review*, 36, 4, September, pp. 495–518.

Schumpeter, J. A., 1947, *Capitalism, Socialism and Democracy*, 2nd ed., London: Allen and Unwin.

Schweikart, L., and L. P. Doti, 2010, *American Entrepreneur: The Fascinating Stories of the People Who Defined Business in the United States*, New York: Amacom.

Science Watch Interview, 2000, "Nichia 's Shuji Nakamura: Dream of the Blue Laser Diode," *Science Watch*, 11, 1, January/February, http://engphys.mcmaster.ca/undergraduate/outlines/4e03/Nichia%20's%20Shuji%20Nakamura%20Dream%20of%20the%20Blue%20Laser%20Diode.htm (accessed December 23, 2013).

Scotchmer, S., 1991, "Standing on the Shoulders of Giants: Cumulative Research and the Patent Law," *Journal of Economic Perspectives*, 5, 1, Winter, pp. 29–41.

Scott Morton, F. M., 1999, "Entry Decisions in the Generic Drug Industry," *Rand Journal of Economics*, 30, 3, Fall, pp. 421–440.

Scott Morton, F. M., 2002, "Horizontal Integration between Brand and Generic Firms in the Pharmaceutical Industry," *Journal of Economics & Management Strategy*, 11, 1, Spring, pp. 135–168.

Sealey, C. W., Jr., and J. T. Lindley, 1977, "Inputs, Outputs, and a Theory of Production and Cost at Depository Financial Institutions," *Journal of Finance*, 32, pp. 1251–1266.

Search Engine History, http://www.searchenginehistory.com/ (accessed December 23, 2013).

Segal, I., and M. D. Whinston, 2007, "Antitrust in Innovative Industries," *American Economic Review*, 97, 5, December, pp. 1703–1730.

Seltzer, L. H., 1928, *A Financial History of the American Automobile Industry; A Study of the Ways in Which the Leading American Producers of Automobiles Have Met Their Capital Requirements*, Boston: Houghton Mifflin.

Shaffer, S., 1997, "Network Diseconomies and Optimal Structure," Working Paper No. 97–19, Federal Reserve Bank of Philadelphia, July.

Shaked, A., and J. Sutton, 1982, "Relaxing Price Competition through Product Differentiation," *Review of Economic Studies*, 49, 1, pp. 3–14.

Shaked, M., and J. G. Shanthikumar, 2007, *Stochastic Orders*, New York: Springer.

Shan, W., 1990, "An Empirical Analysis of Organizational Strategies by Entrepreneurial High-Technology Firms," *Strategic Management Journal*, 11, 2, February, pp. 129–139.

Shane, G., and G. Ramey, 1998, "Market Structure, Innovation and Vertical Product Differentiation," *International Journal of Industrial Organization*, 16, 3, May, pp. 285–311.

Shane, S., 2001, "Technological Opportunities and New Firm Creation," *Management Science*, 47, February, pp. 205–220.

Shane, S., 2003, *A General Theory of Entrepreneurship: The Individual-Opportunity Nexus*, Cheltenham, UK: Edward Elgar.

Shelanski, H. A., 2000, "Competition and Deployment of New Technology in U.S. Telecommunications," *University of Chicago Legal Forum*, 2000: Antitrust in the Information Age, pp. 85–118.

Shell, K., 1967, "A Model of Inventive Activity and Capital Accumulation," in K. Shell, ed., *Essays on the Theory of Optimal Growth*, Cambridge, MA: MIT Press, pp. 67–85.

Shleifer, A., and R. Vishny, 1989, "Management Entrenchment: The Case of Manager-Specific Investments," *Journal of Financial Economics*, 25, pp. 123–139.

Shleifer, A., and R. Vishny, 1997, "A Survey of Corporate Governance," *Journal of Finance*, 52, pp. 737–783.

Siegel, D., D. Waldman, and A. Link, 2000, "Assessing the Impact of Organizational Practices on the Productivity of University Technology Transfer Offices: An Exploratory Study," NBER Working Paper 7256.

Sidak, J. G., and D. F. Spulber, 1996, *Protecting Competition from the Postal Monopoly*, Washington, DC: American Enterprise Institute.

Sidak, J. G., and D. Teece, 2009, "Dynamic Competition in Antitrust Law," *Journal of Competition Law & Economics* 5: 581–631.

Sikander, J., and V. Sarma, 2010, "A Prescriptive Architecture for Electronic Commerce and Digital Marketing," Microsoft Corporation White Paper, http://www.microsoft.com/commerceserver/en/us/white-papers.aspx, accessed July 17, 2010.

Silk, A. J., and E. R. Berndt, 1994, "Costs, Institutional Mobility Barriers, and Market Structure: Advertising Agencies as Multiproduct Firms," *Journal of Economics & Management Strategy*, 3, 3, Fall, pp. 437–480.

Simcoe, T. S., S. J. Graham, and M. P. Feldman, 2009, "Competing on Standards? Entrepreneurship, Intellectual Property and Platform Technologies," *Journal of Economics & Management Strategy*, 18, 3, Fall, pp. 775–816.

Simon, H. A., 1945, *Administrative Behavior*, 3rd ed., New York: Free Press.

Simon, H. A., 1955, "A Behavioral Model of Rational Choice," *Quarterly Journal of Economics*, 69, pp. 99–118.

Simon, H. A., 1972, "Theories of Bounded Rationality," in C. B. McGuire and R. Radner, eds., *Decisions and Organizations*, Amsterdam: North Holland, pp. 161–176.

Sims, C. A., 2003, "Implications of Rational Inattention," *Journal of Monetary Economics*, 50, 3, pp. 665–690.

Singh, N., and X. Vives, 1984, "Price and Quantity Competition in a Differentiated Duopoly," *Rand Journal of Economics*, 15, pp. 546–554.
Smith, A., 1776 [1998], *An Inquiry into the Nature and Causes of the Wealth of Nations*, Washington, DC: Regnery Publishing.
Smith, H. E., 2003, "The Language of Property: Form, Context, and Audience," *Stanford Law Review*, 55, pp. 1105–1191.
Smith, H. E., 2007, "Intellectual Property as Property: Delineating Entitlements in Information," *Yale Law Journal*, 116, pp. 1742–1822.
Sobel, R., and D. B. Sicilia, 1986, *The Entrepreneurs: An American Adventure*, Boston: Houghton Mifflin.
Sokoloff, K. L., 1988, "Inventive Activity in Early Industrial America: Evidence from Patent Records, 1790–1846," *Journal of Economic History*, 48, 4, pp. 813–850.
Solow, R. M., 1956, "A Contribution to the Theory of Economic Growth," *Quarterly Journal of Economics*, 70, 1, February, pp. 65–94.
Solow, R. M., 1957, "Technical Change and the Aggregate Production Function," *Review of Economics and Statistics*, 39, 3, August, pp. 312–320.
Solow, R. M., 1960, "Investment and Technical Progress," in K. J. Arrow, S. Karlin, and P. Suppes, eds., *Mathematical Methods in the Social Sciences*, Stanford: Stanford University Press, pp. 89–104.
Solow, R. M., 1962, "Technical Progress, Capital Formation, and Economic Growth," *American Economic Review*, Papers and Proceedings, 52, 2, May, pp. 76–86.
Solow, R. M., 1970, *Growth Theory: An Exposition*, Oxford: Clarendon Press.
Sowell, T., 2009, *Intellectuals and Society*, New York: Basic Books.
Spence, A. M., 1973, "Job Market Signaling," *Quarterly Journal of Economics*, 87, 3, pp. 355–374.
Spence, A. M., 1974, *Market Signaling*, Cambridge, MA: Harvard University Press.
Spence, A. M., 1977, "Entry, Investment and Oligopolistic Pricing," *Bell Journal of Economics*, 8, Autumn, pp. 534–544.
Spence, A. M., 1984, "Cost Reduction, Competition, and Industry Performance," *Econometrica*, 52, pp. 101–121.
Spender, J. C., 1994, "Organizational Knowledge, Collective Practice and Penrose Rents," *International Business Review*, 3, pp. 353–367.
Spender, J. C., 1996, "Making Knowledge the Basis of a Dynamic Theory of the Firm," *Strategic Management Journal*, 17, pp. 45–62.
Spulber, D. F., 1977, "Research, Development and Technological Change in a Growing Economy," Center for Mathematical Studies, Northwestern University, Discussion Paper No. 282, June.
Spulber, D. F., 1980, "Research and Development of a Backstop Energy Technology in a Growing Economy," *Energy Economics*, 2, 4, October, pp. 199–207.
Spulber, D. F., 1981, "Capacity, Output, and Sequential Entry," *American Economic Review*, 71, pp. 503–514.
Spulber, D. F., 1989, *Regulation and Markets*, Cambridge, MA: MIT Press.
Spulber, D. F., 1995, "Bertrand Competition When Rivals' Costs Are Unknown," *Journal of Industrial Economics*, 43, pp. 1–11.
Spulber, D. F., 1996a, "Market Making by Price Setting Firms," *Review of Economic Studies*, 63, pp. 559–580.
Spulber, D. F., 1996b, "Market Microstructure and Intermediation," *Journal of Economic Perspectives*, 10, Summer, pp. 135–152.

Spulber, D. F., 1998, *The Market Makers: How Leading Companies Create and Win Markets*, New York: McGraw Hill/ Business Week Books.

Spulber, D. F., 1999, *Market Microstructure: Intermediaries and the Theory of the Firm*, New York: Cambridge University Press.

Spulber, D. F., 2002a, "Market Microstructure and Incentives to Invest," *Journal of Political Economy*, 110, April, pp. 352–381.

Spulber, D. F., 2002b, "Transaction Innovation and the Role of the Firm," in M. R. Baye, ed., *The Economics of the Internet and E-commerce, Advances in Applied Micro-Economics*, Vol. 11, Oxford: Elsevier Science, pp. 159–190.

Spulber, D. F., 2003, "The Intermediation Theory of the Firm: Integrating Economic and Management Approaches to Strategy," *Managerial and Decision Economics*, 24, pp. 253–266.

Spulber, D. F., 2006, "Firms and Networks in Two-Sided Markets," in T. Hendershott, ed., *The Handbook of Economics and Information Systems*, Vol. 1, Amsterdam: Elsevier, pp. 137–200.

Spulber, D. F., 2008a, "Competition Policy and the Incentive to Innovate: The Dynamic Effects of Microsoft v. Commission," *Yale Journal on Regulation*, 25, 2, Summer, pp. 247–301.

Spulber, D. F., 2008b, "Consumer Coordination in the Small and in the Large: Implications for Antitrust in Markets with Network Effects," *Journal of Competition Law and Economics*, 4, 2, pp. 207–262.

Spulber, D. F., 2008c, "Innovation and International Trade in Technology," *Journal of Economic Theory*, 138, January, pp. 1–20.

Spulber, D. F., 2008d, "Unlocking Technology: Innovation and Antitrust," *Journal of Competition Law and Economics*, 4, 4, December, pp. 915–966.

Spulber, D. F., 2009a, *The Theory of the Firm: Microeconomics with Endogenous Entrepreneurs, Firms, Markets, and Organizations*, Cambridge: Cambridge University Press.

Spulber, D. F., 2009b, "Discovering the Role of the Firm: The Separation Criterion and Corporate Law," *Berkeley Business Law Journal*, 6, 2, Spring, pp. 298–347.

Spulber, D. F., 2010a, "Competition among Entrepreneurs," *Industrial and Corporate Change*, 19, 1, February, pp. 25–50.

Spulber, D. F., 2010b, "The Quality of Innovation and the Extent of the Market," *Journal of International Economics*, 80, 2, pp. 260–270.

Spulber, D. F., 2011a, "The Role of the Entrepreneur in Economic Growth," in Robert Litan, ed., *Handbook of Law, Innovation, and Growth*, Northampton, MA: Edward Elgar, pp. 11–44.

Spulber, D. F., 2011b, "Should Business Method Inventions Be Patentable?," *Journal of Legal Analysis*, 3, 1, Spring, pp. 265–340.

Spulber, D. F., 2011c, "The Innovator's Decision: Entrepreneurship versus Technology Transfer," in David Audretsch, O. Falck, Stephan Heblich, and Adam Lederer, eds., *Handbook of Research on Innovation and Entrepreneurship*, Northampton, MA: Edward Elgar, pp. 315–336.

Spulber, D. F., 2011d, "Intellectual Property and the Theory of the Firm," in F. S. Kieff and T. Paredes, eds., *Perspectives on Commercializing Innovation*, Cambridge: Cambridge University Press, pp. 9–46.

Spulber, D. F., 2012a, "Tacit Knowledge and Innovative Entrepreneurship," *International Journal of Industrial Organization*, 30, 6, November, pp. 641–653.

Spulber, D. F., 2012b, "How Entrepreneurs Affect the Rate and Direction of Inventive Activity," in Josh Lerner and Scott Stern, eds., *The Rate and Direction of Inventive Activity Revisited*, National Bureau of Economic Research Conference, Chicago: University of Chicago Press, pp. 277–315.

Spulber, D. F., 2013a, "Competing Inventors and the Incentive to Invent," *Industrial and Corporate Change*, 22, 1, pp. 33–72.

Spulber, D. F., 2013b, "How Do Competitive Pressures Affect Incentives to Innovate When There Is a Market for Inventions?," *Journal of Political Economy*, 121, 6, pp. 1007–1054.

Spulber, D. F., and R. A. Becker, 1983, "Regulatory Lag and Deregulation with Imperfectly Adjustable Capital," *Journal of Economic Dynamics & Control*, 6, pp. 137–151.

Stangler, D., 2010, *High-Growth Firms and the Future of the American Economy*, Kansas City, MO: Ewing Marion Kauffman Foundation.

Stangler, D., and P. Kedrosky, 2010a, *Exploring Firm Formation: Why Is the Number of New Firms Constant?*, Kansas City, MO: Ewing Marion Kauffman Foundation.

Stangler, D., and P. Kedrosky, 2010b, *Neutralism and Entrepreneurship: The Structural Dynamics of Startups, Young Firms, and Job Creation*, Kansas City, MO: Ewing Marion Kauffman Foundation.

Steil, B., 2002, "Changes in the Ownership and Governance of Securities Exchanges: Causes and Consequences," in R. Herring and R. E. Litan, eds., *Brookings-Wharton Papers on Financial Services: 2002*, Washington, DC: Brookings Institution Press, pp. 61–91.

Stein, J. C., 1989, "Efficient Capital Markets, Inefficient Firms: A Model of Myopic Corporate Behavior," *Quarterly Journal of Economics*, 104, 4, November, pp. 655–669.

Stern, S., 1995, "Incentives and Focus in University and Industrial Research: The Case of Synthetic Insulin," in N. Rosenberg and A. Gelijns, eds., *Sources of Medical Technology: Universities and Industry*, Washington, DC: National Academy Press, pp. 157–187.

Stiglitz J. E., 1999, "Knowledge as a Global Public Good," in I. Kaul, I. Grunberg, and M. A. Stern, eds., *Global Public Goods: International Cooperation in the 21st Century*, New York: Oxford University Press, pp. 308–325.

Stiglitz, J. E., and A. Weiss, 1981, "Credit Rationing in Markets with Imperfect Information," *American Economic Review*, 71, June, pp. 393–410.

Stinchcombe, A. L., 1990, *Information and Organization*, Berkeley, CA: University of California Press.

Stoll, H. R., 2002, "Comment and Discussion," in R. Herring and R. E. Litan, eds., *Brookings-Wharton Papers on Financial Services: 2002*, Washington, DC: Brookings Institution Press, pp. 83–90.

Stoneman, P., and O. Toivanen, 1997, "The Diffusion of Multiple Technologies: An Empirical Study," *Economics of Innovation and New Technology*, 5, 1, pp. 1–17.

Suarez, F. F., and J. M. Utterback, 1995, "Dominant Designs and the Survival of Firms," *Strategic Management Journal*, 16, September, pp. 415–430.

Sutton, J., 1996, "Schumpeter Lecture: Technology and Market Structure," *European Economic Review*, 40, pp. 511–530.

Sutton, J., 1998, *Technology and Market Structure: Theory and History*, Cambridge, MA: MIT Press.

Swedberg, R., 2002, "The Economic Sociology of Capitalism: Weber and Schumpeter," *Journal of Classical Sociology*, 2, 3, pp. 227–255.

Taylor, C. R., 1995, "Digging for Golden Carrots: An Analysis of Research Tournaments," *American Economic Review*, 85, September, pp. 872–890.

Taylor, C., and Z. Silberston, 1973, *The Economic Impact of the Patent System*, Cambridge: Cambridge University Press.

Taylor, M. S., 1994, "Trips, Trade and Growth," *International Economic Review*, 35, May, pp. 361–381.

Tedeshi, B., 2000, "E-Commerce Report," *New York Times*, May 1, p. C10.

Teece, D. J., 1986, "Profiting from Technological Innovation: Implications for Integration, Collaboration, Licensing, and Public Policy," *Research Policy*, 15, 6, pp. 285–305.

Teece, D. J., 1988, "Technological Change and the Nature of the Firm," in G. Dosi, C. Freeman, R. Nelson, and L. Soete, eds., *Technical Change and Economic Theory*, London: Frances Pinter, pp. 256–281.

Teece, D. J., 2006, "Reflections on 'Profiting from Innovation,'" *Research Policy*, 35, pp. 1131–1146.

Teece, D. J., 2010, "Business Models, Business Strategy and Innovation," *Long Range Planning*, 43, 2–3, pp. 172–194.

Temple, J., 2010, "Google Instant Predicts What Users Are Searching For," *San Francisco Chronicle*, September 8.

Thomas, J. R., 1999, "The Patenting of the Liberal Professions," *Boston College Law Review*, 40, 5, pp. 1139–1186.

Thompson, P., 2001, "The Microeconomics of an R&D-Based Model of Endogenous Growth," *Journal of Economic Growth*, 6, December, pp. 263–283.

Thompson, P., 2012, "The Relationship between Unit Cost and Cumulative Quantity and the Evidence for Organizational Learning-by-Doing," *Journal of Economic Perspectives*, 26, 3, Summer, pp. 203–224.

Thurik, A. R., M. A. Carree, A. van Stel, and D. B. Audretsch, 2008, "Does Self-Employment Reduce Unemployment?," *Journal of Business Venturing*, 23, pp. 673–686.

Tilton, J. E., 1971, *International Diffusion of Technology: The Case of Semiconductors*, Washington, DC: Brookings Institution.

Tobin, J., 1967, "Life Cycle Savings and Balanced Growth," in W. Fellner et al., eds., *Ten Economic Studies in the Tradition of Irving Fisher*, New York: Wiley.

Tobin, J., 1972, "Wealth, Liquidity, and the Propensity to Consume," in E. Strumpel, J. Morgan, and E. Zahn, eds., *Human Behavior in Economic Affairs, Essays in Honor of George S. Katona*, New York: Elsevier Science.

Topkis, D. M., 1978, "Minimizing a Submodular Function on a Lattice," *Operations Research*, 26, March-April, pp. 305–321.

Topkis, D. M., 1998, *Supermodularity and Complementarity*, Princeton, NJ: Princeton University Press.

Torrisi, S., 1998, *Industrial Organisation and Innovation: An International Study of the Software Industry*, Cheltenham, UK: Edward Elgar Publishing.

Triplett, J. E., and B. P. Bosworth, 2004, *Services Productivity in the United States: New Sources of Economic Growth*, Washington, DC: Brookings Institution Press.

Triplett, J. E., and B. P. Bosworth, 2006, "'Baumol's Disease' Has Been Cured: IT and Multifactor Productivity in U.S. Services Industries," in D. W. Jansen, ed., *The New Economy and Beyond: Past, Present, and Future*, Cheltenham, UK: Edgar Elgar, pp. 34–71.

Tufano, P., 2003, "Financial Innovation," in G. Constantinides, M. Harris, and R. Stulz, eds., *Handbook of the Economics of Finance*, Vol. 1A, Amsterdam: North-Holland, pp. 307–336.

Tversky, A., and D. Kahneman, 1974, "Judgment under Uncertainty: Heuristics and Biases," *Science*, 185, September 27, pp. 1124–1131.

Tybout, J. R., 2000, "Manufacturing Firms in Developing Countries: How Well Do They Do, and Why?," *Journal of Economic Literature*, 38, 1, March, pp. 11–44.

UNCTAD (United Nations Conference on Trade and Development), 2009, *World Investment Report 2009: Transnational Corporations, Agricultural Production and Development*, Geneva: United Nations Conference on Trade and Development.

United States Census Bureau, 2006, *Annual Survey of Manufactures, Statistics for Industry Groups and Industries: 2005*, Washington, DC: U.S. Government Printing Office.

United States Department of Commerce, 1994, *U.S. Industrial Outlook 1994*, Washington, DC: U.S. Government Printing Office.

United States Department of Commerce, Economics and Statistics Administration and the United States Patent and Trademark Office, 2012, *Intellectual Property and the U.S. Economy: Industries in Focus*, March, Washington, DC: Department of Commerce.

United States Department of Justice, Computer Crime & Intellectual Property Section, 2013, *Prosecuting Intellectual Property Crimes*, 4th ed., September, Washington, DC: Office of Legal Education, Executive Office for United States Attorneys, http://www.justice.gov/criminal/cybercrime/docs/prosecuting_ip_crimes_manual_2013.pdf (accessed December 23, 2013).

United States Department of Justice (and Federal Trade Commission), 1995, *Antitrust Guidelines for the Licensing of Intellectual Property*, §§ 2.0, 2.2 (1995), reprinted in 4 Trade Reg. Rep. (CCH) ¶ 13,132, at 20, pp. 734–735.

United States Patent and Trademark Office, "Patent Full-Text Databases," http://patft.uspto.gov/ (accessed December 23, 2013).

United States Patent and Trademark Office, "Patent Technology Monitoring Team, Patenting in Technology Classes," 2009, http://www.uspto.gov/web/offices/ac/ido/oeip/taf/tecasg/705_tor.htm (accessed July 12, 2010).

United States Patent and Trademark Office, 2009, "Data Processing: Financial, Business Practice, Management, or Cost/Price Determination," USPTO Patent Class 705, Section II, 705–1–705–3.

United States Patent and Trademark Office, 2010a, "Automated Financial or Management Data Processing Methods," USPTO White Paper, http://www.uspto.gov/web/menu/busmethp/index.html#origins, accessed June 3, 2010.

United States Patent and Trademark Office, 2010b, "Patent Counts by Class by Year," Washington, DC, http://www.uspto.gov/web/offices/ac/ido/oeip/taf/cbcby.pdf (accessed June 3, 2010).

Utterback, J. M., and W. Abernathy, 1975, "A Dynamic Model of Process and Product Innovation," *Omega*, 33, pp. 639–656.

Utterback, J. M., and F. F. Suarez, 1993, "Innovation, Competition, and Industry Structure," *Research Policy*, 22, 1, pp. 1–21.

Uzawa, H., 1965, "Optimum Technical Change in an Aggregative Model of Economic Growth," *International Economic Review*, 6, 1, January, pp. 18–31.

Van der Sluis, J., M. Van Praag, and A. Van Witteloostuijn, 2006, "Why Are the Returns to Education Higher for Entrepreneurs than for Employees?," University of Amsterdam Working Paper, Amsterdam, Netherlands.

Van der Sluis, J., M. Van Praag, and W. Vijverberg, 2008, "Education and Entrepreneurship Selection and Performance: A Review of the Empirical Literature," *Journal of Economic Surveys*, 22, 5, pp. 795–841.

Van Gelderen, M., R. Thurik, and N. Bosma, 2005, "Success and Risk Factors in the Pre-Startup Phase," *Small Business Economics*, 24, pp. 365–380.

Van Praag, C. M., and P. H. Versloot, 2007, "What is the Value of Entrepreneurship? A Review of Recent Research," *Small Business Economics*, 29, pp. 351–382.

Van Stel, A., M. Carree, and R. Thurik, 2005, "The Effect of Entrepreneurial Activity on National Economic Growth," *Small Business Economics*, 24, pp. 311–321.

Van Zanden, J. L., 1993, *The Rise and Decline of Holland's Economy: Merchant Capitalism and the Labour Market*, Manchester: Manchester University Press.

Vereshchagina, G., and H. Hopenhayn, 2009, "Risk Taking by Entrepreneurs," *American Economic Review*, 99, 5, December, pp. 1808–1830.

Veugelers, R., and B. Cassiman, 1999, "Make and Buy in Innovation Strategies: Evidence from Belgian Manufacturing Firms," *Research Policy*, 28, pp. 63–80.

Veyne, P., 1987, *The Roman Empire*, Cambridge, MA: Harvard University Press.

Vickrey, W., 1962, "Auctions and Bidding Games," in *Recent Advances in Game Theory*, (Conference Proceedings), Princeton, NJ: Princeton University Press, pp. 15–27.

Villard, H., 1958, "Competition, Oligopoly and Research," *Journal of Political Economy*, 66, 6, December, pp. 483–497.

Vives, X., 2008, "Innovation and Competitive Pressure," *Journal of Industrial Economics*, 56, 3, September, pp. 419–469.

Vohora, A., M. Wright, and A. Lockett, 2004, "Critical Junctures in the Development of University High-Tech Spinout Companies," *Research Policy*, 33, pp. 147–175.

Wagner, S., 2008, "Business Method Patents in Europe and Their Strategic Use – Evidence from Franking Device Manufacturers," *Economics of Innovation and New Technology*, 17, 3, pp. 173–194.

Wallison, P. J., and C. W. Calomiris, 2008, "The Last Trillion-Dollar Commitment: The Destruction of Fannie Mae and Freddie Mac," *Financial Services Outlook, AEI Online*, September 30, http://www.aei.org/article/economics/monetary-policy/the-last-trillion-dollar-commitment/ (accessed December 23, 2013).

Weber, M., 1968, *Economy and Society*, G. Roth and C. Wittich, eds., New York: Bedminster Press.

Weick, K. E., and K. H. Roberts, 1993, "Collective Mind in Organizations: Heedful Interrelating on Flight Decks," *Administrative Science Quarterly*, 38, pp. 357–381.

Weinstein, N., 1980, "Unrealistic Optimism about Future Life Events," *Journal of Personality and Social Psychology*, 39, 5, pp. 806–820.

Wennekers, A. R. M., and A. R. Thurik, 1999, "Linking Entrepreneurship and Economic Growth," *Small Business Economics*, 13, pp. 27–55.

Weyl, G. E., and M. Fabinger, 2012, "Pass-Through as an Economic Tool: Principles of Incidence Under Imperfect Competition," *Journal of Political Economy*, 121, 3, June, pp. 528–583.

Williamson, O. E., 1975, *Markets and Hierarchies*, New York: Free Press.

Williamson, O. E., 1985, *The Economic Institutions of Capitalism*, New York: Free Press.

Winkler, R. L., 1968, "The Consensus of Subjective Probability Distributions," *Management Science*, 15, 2, Application Series, October, pp. B61–B75.

Winter, S. G., 1984, "Schumpeterian Competition in Alternative Technological Regimes," *Journal of Economic Behavior & Organization*, 5, 3–4, September–December, pp. 287–320.

World Bank and International Finance Corporation, 2012, *Doing Business 2012: Doing Business in a More Transparent World*, Washington, DC: World Bank.

Worley, J. S., 1961, "Industrial Research and the New Competition," *Journal of Political Economy*, 69, 2, April, pp. 183–186.

Yaari, M. E., 1964. "On the Consumer's Lifetime Allocation Process," *International Economic Review*, 5, pp. 304–317.

Yaari, M. E., 1965, "Uncertain Lifetime, Life Insurance, and the Theory of the Consumer," *Review of Economic Studies*, 32, pp. 137–150.

Yao, R., and H. Zhang, 2005, "Optimal Consumption and Portfolio Choices with Risky Housing and Borrowing Constraints," *Review of Financial Studies*, 18, 1, pp. 197–239.

Yoo, C. S., 2002, "Vertical Integration and Media Regulation in the New Economy," *Yale Journal on Regulation*, 19, pp. 171–300.

Yoo, C. S., 2004, "Copyright and Product Differentiation," *New York University Law Review*, 79, April, pp. 212–280.

Yunus, M., 2003, *Banker to the Poor: Micro-Lending and the Battle Against World Poverty*, New York: Public Affairs.

Yuskavage, R. E., 1994, "Gross Product by Industry, 1991–92," *Survey of Current Business*, 74, 10, pp. 30–34.

Zahra, S. A., 2005, "Theory of International New Ventures: A Decade of Research," *Journal of International Business Studies*, 36, 1, January, pp. 20–28.

Zahra, S. A., and G. George, 2002, "International Entrepreneurship: The Current Status of the Field and Future Research Agenda," in M. Hitt, D. Ireland, D. Sexton and M. Camp, eds., *Strategic Entrepreneurship: Creating an Integrated Mindset*, Strategic Management Series, Oxford: Blackwell Publishers, pp. 255–288.

Zahra, S. A., R. D. Ireland, and M. A. Hitt, 2000, "International Expansion by New Venture Firms: International Diversity, Mode of Market Entry, Technological Learning, and Performance," *Academy of Management Journal*, 43, 5, October, pp. 925–950.

Zanchettin, P., 2006, "Differentiated Duopoly with Asymmetric Costs," *Journal of Economics & Management Strategy*, 15, 4, Winter, pp. 999–1015.

Zeckhauser, R., 1996, "The Challenge of Contracting for Technological Information," *Proceedings of the National Academy of Sciences*, 93, November, pp. 12743–12748.

Zeira, J., 1987, "Investment as a Process of Search," *Journal of Political Economy*, 95, 1, February, pp. 204–210.

Zeira, J., 1994, "Informational Cycles," *Review of Economic Studies*, 61, pp. 31–44.

Ziedonis, R. H., 2004, "Don't Fence Me in: Fragmented Markets for Technology and the Patent Acquisition Strategies of Firms," *Management Science*, 50, 6, June, pp. 804–820.

Zucker, L., and M. Darby, 2001, "Capturing Technological Opportunity via Japan's Star Scientists: Evidence from Japanese Firms' Biotech Patents and Products," *Journal of Technology Transfer*, 26, 1–2, January, pp. 37–58.

Zucker, L., M. Darby, and J. Armstrong, 1998, "Geographically Localized Knowledge: Spillovers or Markets?," *Economic Inquiry*, 36, pp. 65–86.

Zucker, L., M. Darby, and J. Armstrong, 2002, "Commercializing Knowledge: University Science, Knowledge Capture, and Firm Performance in Biotechnology," *Management Science*, 48, 1, pp. 138–153.

Zucker, L., M. Darby, and M. B. Brewer, 1998, "Intellectual Human Capital and the Birth of U.S. Biotechnology Enterprises," *American Economic Review*, 88, 1, March, pp. 290–306.

Zucker, L., M. Darby, and M. Torero, 2002, "Labor Mobility from Academe to Commerce," *Journal of Labor Economics*, 20, 3, pp. 629–660.

Index

Printed in the United States
By Bookmasters